Natural Language Processing and Machine Learning for Developers

LICENSE, DISCLAIMER OF LIABILITY, AND LIMITED WARRANTY

By purchasing or using this book and its companion files (the "Work"), you agree that this license grants permission to use the contents contained herein, but does not give you the right of ownership to any of the textual content in the book or ownership to any of the information, files, or products contained in it. *This license does not permit uploading of the Work onto the Internet or on a network (of any kind) without the written consent of the Publisher.* Duplication or dissemination of any text, code, simulations, images, etc. contained herein is limited to and subject to licensing terms for the respective products, and permission must be obtained from the Publisher or the owner of the content, etc., in order to reproduce or network any portion of the textual material (in any media) that is contained in the Work.

Mercury Learning and Information ("MLI" or "the Publisher") and anyone involved in the creation, writing, production, accompanying algorithms, code, or computer programs ("the software"), and any accompanying Web site or software of the Work, cannot and do not warrant the performance or results that might be obtained by using the contents of the Work. The author, developers, and the Publisher have used their best efforts to insure the accuracy and functionality of the textual material and/or programs contained in this package; we, however, make no warranty of any kind, express or implied, regarding the performance of these contents or programs. The Work is sold "as is" without warranty (except for defective materials used in manufacturing the book or due to faulty workmanship).

The author, developers, and the publisher of any accompanying content, and anyone involved in the composition, production, and manufacturing of this work will not be liable for damages of any kind arising out of the use of (or the inability to use) the algorithms, source code, computer programs, or textual material contained in this publication. This includes, but is not limited to, loss of revenue or profit, or other incidental, physical, or consequential damages arising out of the use of this Work.

The sole remedy in the event of a claim of any kind is expressly limited to replacement of the book and only at the discretion of the Publisher. The use of "implied warranty" and certain "exclusions" vary from state to state, and might not apply to the purchaser of this product.

Companion files also available for downloading from the publisher by writing to info@merclearning.com.

Natural Language Processing and Machine Learning for Developers

Oswald Campesato

Mercury Learning and Information
Dulles, Virginia
Boston, Massachusetts
New Delhi

Copyright ©2021 by MERCURY LEARNING AND INFORMATION LLC. All rights reserved.

This publication, portions of it, or any accompanying software may not be reproduced in any way, stored in a retrieval system of any type, or transmitted by any means, media, electronic display or mechanical display, including, but not limited to, photocopy, recording, Internet postings, or scanning, without prior permission in writing from the publisher.

Publisher: David Pallai
MERCURY LEARNING AND INFORMATION
22841 Quicksilver Drive
Dulles, VA 20166
info@merclearning.com
www.merclearning.com
1-800-232-0223

O. Campesato. *Natural Language Processing and Machine Learning for Developers.*
ISBN: 978-1-68392-618-4

The publisher recognizes and respects all marks used by companies, manufacturers, and developers as a means to distinguish their products. All brand names and product names mentioned in this book are trademarks or service marks of their respective companies. Any omission or misuse (of any kind) of service marks or trademarks, etc. is not an attempt to infringe on the property of others.

Library of Congress Control Number: 2021936681

212223321   Printed on acid-free paper in the United States of America.

Our titles are available for adoption, license, or bulk purchase by institutions, corporations, etc.
For additional information, please contact the Customer Service Dept. at 800-232-0223(toll free).

All of our titles are available in digital format at *academiccourseware.com* and other digital vendors. The sole obligation of MERCURY LEARNING AND INFORMATION to the purchaser is to replace the book, based on defective materials or faulty workmanship, but not based on the operation or functionality of the product.

*I'd like to dedicate this book to my parents–
may this bring joy and happiness into their lives.*

Contents

Preface	xxvii
Chapter 1 Introduction to NumPy	**1**
What is NumPy?	2
Useful NumPy Features	2
What are NumPy Arrays?	2
Working with Loops	4
Appending Elements to Arrays (1)	4
Appending Elements to Arrays (2)	5
Multiply Lists and Arrays	6
Doubling the Elements in a List	6
Lists and Exponents	7
Arrays and Exponents	7
Math Operations and Arrays	8
Working with "-1" Subranges with Vectors	9
Working with "-1" Subranges with Arrays	9
Other Useful NumPy Methods	10
Arrays and Vector Operations	10
NumPy and Dot Products (1)	11
NumPy and Dot Products (2)	12
NumPy and the "Norm" of Vectors	13
NumPy and Other Operations	14
NumPy and the `reshape()` Method	14

Calculating the Mean and Standard Deviation 16
    Trimmed Mean and Weighted Mean 16
    Code Sample with Mean and Standard Deviation 17
Working with Lines in the Plane (Optional) 18
Plotting a Line with NumPy and Matplotlib 21
Plotting a Quadratic with NumPy and Matplotlib 22
What is Linear Regression? 23
    What is Multivariate Analysis? 24
    What about Nonlinear Datasets? 24
The MSE Formula 25
    Other Error Types 25
    Nonlinear Least Squares 26
Calculating the MSE Manually 26
Find the Best-Fitting Line with NumPy 28
Calculating MSE by Successive Approximation (1) 29
Calculating MSE by Successive Approximation (2) 32
What is Jax? 34
Google Colaboratory 34
    Uploading CSV Files in Google Colaboratory 35
Summary 36

Chapter 2   Introduction to Pandas 37

What is Pandas? 37
    Pandas Options and Settings 38
    Pandas Data Frames 39
    Data Frames and Data Cleaning Tasks 39
    Alternatives to Pandas 40
A Pandas Data Frame with NumPy Example 40
Describing a Pandas Data Frame 42
Pandas Boolean Data Frames 44
    Transposing a Pandas Data Frame 45
Pandas Data Frames and Random Numbers 46
Reading CSV Files in Pandas 48
The `loc()` and `iloc()` Methods in Pandas 49
Converting Categorical Data to Numeric Data 49
Matching and Splitting Strings in Pandas 53
Converting Strings to Dates in Pandas 55
Merging and Splitting Columns in Pandas 56
Combining Pandas `Data frames` 58
Data Manipulation with Pandas Data Frames (1) 59
Data Manipulation with Pandas Data Frames (2) 60
Data Manipulation with Pandas Data Frames (3) 61
Pandas Data Frames and CSV Files 62

Managing Columns in Data Frames	65
Switching Columns	65
Appending Columns	66
Deleting Columns	67
Inserting Columns	67
Scaling Numeric Columns	68
Managing Rows in Pandas	70
Selecting a Range of Rows in Pandas	70
Finding Duplicate Rows in Pandas	71
Inserting New Rows in Pandas	74
Handling Missing Data in Pandas	75
Multiple Types of Missing Values	77
Test for Numeric Values in a Column	78
Replacing NaN Values in Pandas	79
Sorting Data Frames in Pandas	80
Working with `groupby()` in Pandas	82
Working with `apply()` and `mapapply()` in Pandas	84
Handling Outliers in Pandas	87
Pandas Data Frames and Scatterplots	89
Pandas Data Frames and Simple Statistics	90
Aggregate Operations in Pandas Data Frames	92
Aggregate Operations with the titanic.csv Dataset	93
Save Data Frames as CSV Files and Zip Files	95
Pandas Data Frames and Excel Spreadsheets	96
Working with JSON-based Data	97
Python Dictionary and JSON	98
Python, Pandas, and JSON	98
Pandas and Regular Expressions (Optional)	100
Useful One-Line Commands in Pandas	104
What is Method Chaining?	105
Pandas and Method Chaining	106
Pandas Profiling	106
What is Texthero?	107
Summary	108

Chapter 3   NLP Concepts (I)   109

The Origin of Languages	110
Language Fluency	112
Major Language Groups	113
Peak Usage of Some Languages	115
Languages and Regional Accents	115
Languages and Slang	116
Languages and Dialects	117

The Complexity of Natural Languages	118
Word Order in Sentences	119
What about Verbs?	120
Auxiliary Verbs	121
What are Case Endings?	122
Languages and Gender	124
Singular and Plural Forms of Nouns	124
Changes in Spelling of Words	125
Japanese Grammar	125
Japanese Postpositions (Particles)	125
Ambiguity in Japanese Sentences	128
Japanese Nominalization	129
Google Translate and Japanese	130
Japanese and Korean	131
Vowel-Optional Languages and Word Direction	131
Mutating Consonant Spelling	131
Expressing Negative Opinions	132
Phonetic Languages	133
Phonemes and Morphemes	134
English Words of Greek and Latin Origin	135
Multiple Ways to Pronounce Consonants	135
The Letter "j" in Various Languages	135
"Hard" versus "Soft" Consonant Sounds	136
"Ess," "zee," and "sh" Sounds	137
Three Consecutive Consonants	138
Diphthongs and Triphthongs in English	138
Semi-Vowels in English	139
Challenging English Sounds	139
English in Canada, UK, Australia, and the United States	140
English Pronouns and Prepositions	141
What is NLP?	142
The Evolution of NLP	143
A Wide-Angle View of NLP	144
NLP Applications and Use Cases	145
NLU and NLG	146
What is Text Classification?	147
Information Extraction and Retrieval	148
Word Sense Disambiguation	149
NLP Techniques in ML	149
NLP Steps for Training a Model	150
Text Normalization and Tokenization	151
Word Tokenization in Japanese	152
Text Tokenization with Unix Commands	153

Handling Stop Words	154
What is Stemming?	155
Singular versus Plural Word Endings	155
Common Stemmers	155
Stemmers and Word Prefixes	156
Over Stemming and Under Stemming	157
What is Lemmatization?	157
Stemming/Lemmatization Caveats	158
Limitations of Stemming and Lemmatization	158
Working with Text: POS	158
POS Tagging	158
POS Tagging Techniques	159
Working with Text: NER	159
Abbreviations and Acronyms	160
NER Techniques	161
What is Topic Modeling?	161
Keyword Extraction, Sentiment Analysis, and Text Summarization	162
Summary	163

Chapter 4 NLP Concepts (II) 165

What is Word Relevance?	166
What is Text Similarity?	166
Sentence Similarity	167
Sentence Encoders	167
Working with Documents	168
Document Classification	168
Document Similarity (doc2vec)	168
Techniques for Text Similarity	169
Similarity Queries	170
What is Text Encoding?	170
Text Encoding Techniques	171
Document Vectorization	171
One-Hot Encoding (OHE)	172
Index-Based Encoding	174
Additional Encoders	174
The BoW Algorithm	175
What are n-grams?	176
Calculating Probabilities with N-grams	178
Calculating tf, idf, and tf-idf	179
What is Term Frequency (TF)?	180
What is Inverse Document Frequency (IDF)?	181
What is tf-idf?	181

Limitations of tf-idf	183
Pointwise Mutual Information (PMI)	184
The Context of Words in a Document	184
What is Semantic Context?	184
Textual Entailment	185
Discrete, Distributed, and Contextual Word Representations	185
What is Cosine Similarity?	186
Text Vectorization (aka Word Embeddings)	188
Overview of Word Embeddings and Algorithms	189
Word Embeddings	190
Word Embedding Algorithms	190
What is Word2vec?	191
The Intuition for Word2vec	193
The Word2vec Architecture	193
Limitations of Word2vec	194
The CBoW Architecture	194
What are Skip-grams?	195
Skip-gram Example	196
The Skip-gram Architecture	196
Neural Network Reduction	198
What is GloVe?	199
Working with GloVe	200
What is FastText?	200
Comparison of Word Embeddings	201
What is Topic Modeling?	202
Topic Modeling Algorithms	202
LDA and Topic Modeling	203
Text Classification versus Topic Modeling	204
Language Models and NLP	204
How to Create a Language Model	205
Vector Space Models	205
Term-Document Matrix	207
Tradeoffs of the VSM	207
NLP and Text Mining	208
Text Extraction Preprocessing and N-Grams	208
Relation Extraction and Information Extraction	208
What is a BLEU Score?	209
ROUGE Score: An Alternative to BLEU	210
Summary	210

Chapter 5   Algorithms and Toolkits (I)   211

Cleaning Data with Regular Expressions	212
Handling Contracted Words	216

Python Code Samples of BoW	219
One-Hot Encoding Examples	222
Sklearn and Word Embedding Examples	224
What is BeautifulSoup?	231
Web Scraping with Pure Regular Expressions	234
What is Scrapy?	237
What is SpaCy?	238
SpaCy and Stop Words	238
SpaCy and Tokenization	239
SpaCy and Lemmatization	241
SpaCy and NER	242
SpaCy Pipelines	243
SpaCy and Word Vectors	244
The scispaCy Library (Optional)	247
Summary	247

Chapter 6 Algorithms and Toolkits (II) — 249

What is NLTK?	249
NLTK and BoW	250
NLTK and Stemmers	251
NLTK and Lemmatization	254
NLTK and Stop Words	256
What is Wordnet?	258
Synonyms and Antonyms	260
NLTK, lxml, and XPath	261
NLTK and n-grams	263
NLTK and POS (1)	264
NLTK and POS (2)	268
NLTK and Tokenizers	270
NLTK and Context-Free Grammars (Optional)	271
What is Gensim?	273
Gensim and tf-idf Example	274
Saving a Word2vec Model in Genism	275
An Example of Topic Modeling	276
A Brief Comparison of Popular Python-Based NLP Libraries	278
Miscellaneous Libraries	279
Summary	282

Chapter 7 Introduction to Machine Learning — 283

What is Machine Learning?	284
Learning Style of Machine Learning Algorithms	285
Types of Machine Learning Algorithms	286
Machine Learning Tasks	290

Preparing a Dataset and Training a Model	292
Feature Engineering, Selection, and Extraction	293
Feature Engineering	294
Feature Selection	294
Feature Extraction	296
Model Selection	296
Working with Datasets	296
Training Data versus Test Data	297
What is Cross-Validation?	297
Overfitting versus Underfitting	298
What is Regularization?	299
ML and Feature Scaling	299
Data Normalization Techniques	300
Metrics in Machine Learning	301
R-Squared and its Limitations	301
Confusion Matrix	302
Precision, Recall, and Specificity	303
The ROC Curve and AUC	304
Metrics for Model Evaluation and Selection	305
What is Linear Regression?	305
Linear Regression versus Curve-Fitting	306
When are Solutions Exact Values?	307
What is Multivariate Analysis?	307
Other Types of Regression	308
Working with Lines in the Plane (Optional)	309
Scatter Plots with NumPy and Matplotlib (1)	311
Why the "Perturbation Technique" is Useful	313
Scatter Plots with NumPy and Matplotlib (2)	313
A Quadratic Scatterplot with NumPy and Matplotlib	314
The Mean Squared Error (MSE) Formula	316
A List of Error Types	316
Nonlinear Least Squares	317
Calculating the MSE Manually	317
Approximating Linear Data with `np.linspace()`	319
What are Ensemble Methods?	319
Four Types of Ensemble Methods	321
Bagging	321
Boosting	321
Stacked Models and Blending Models	322
What is Bootstrapping?	323
Common Boosting Algorithms	323
Hyperparameter Optimization	325
Grid Search	325

Randomized Search	325
Bayesian Optimization	326
AutoML, AutoML-Zero, and AutoNLP	326
Miscellaneous Topics	327
What is Causality?	327
What is Explainability?	327
What is Interpretability?	328
Summary	328

Chapter 8 Classifiers in Machine Learning — 329

What is Classification?	330
What are Classifiers?	330
Common Classifiers	331
Binary versus Multiclass Classification	332
Multilabel Classification	332
What are Linear Classifiers?	333
What is kNN?	333
How to Handle a Tie in kNN	333
SMOTE and kNN	334
kNN for Data Imputation	334
What are Decision Trees?	335
Trade-offs with Decision Trees	336
Decision Tree Algorithms	337
Decision Tree Code Samples	337
Decision Trees, Gini Impurity, and Entropy	341
What are Random Forests?	344
What are Support Vector Machines?	345
Trade-offs of SVMs	345
What is a Bayesian Classifier?	346
Types of Naïve Bayes Classifiers	347
Training Classifiers	347
Evaluating Classifiers	349
Trade-offs for ML Algorithms	350
What are Activation Functions?	352
Why Do we Need Activation Functions?	353
How Do Activation Functions Work?	353
Common Activation Functions	354
Activation Functions in Python	356
Keras Activation Functions	356
The ReLU and ELU Activation Functions	357
The Advantages and Disadvantages of ReLU	357
ELU	358

Sigmoid, Softmax, and Hardmax Similarities — 358
   Softmax — 358
   Softplus — 359
   Tanh — 359
Sigmoid, Softmax, and HardMax Differences — 359
Hyperparameters for Neural Networks — 360
   The Loss Function Hyperparameter — 360
   The Optimizer Hyperparameter — 360
   The Learning Rate Hyperparameter — 361
   The Dropout Rate Hyperparameter — 361
   What is Backward Error Propagation? — 361
What is Logistic Regression? — 362
   Setting a Threshold Value — 363
   Logistic Regression: Important Assumptions — 363
   Linearly Separable Data — 364
Keras, Logistic Regression, and Iris Dataset — 364
Sklearn and Linear Regression — 367
SciPy and Linear Regression — 369
Keras and Linear Regression — 371
Summary — 374

Chapter 9 NLP Applications — 375

What is Text Summarization? — 376
   Extractive Text Summarization — 376
   Abstractive Text Summarization — 377
Text Summarization with gensim and SpaCy — 377
What are Recommender Systems? — 381
   Movie Recommender Systems — 382
   Factoring the Rating Matrix R — 383
Content-Based Recommendation Systems — 384
   Analyzing only the Description of the Content — 384
   Building User Profiles and Item Profiles — 384
Collaborative Filtering Algorithm — 385
   User–User Collaborative Filtering — 385
   Item–Item Collaborative Filtering — 385
   Recommender System with Surprise — 386
Recommender Systems and Reinforcement Learning (Optional) — 386
   Basic Reinforcement Learning in Five Minutes — 386
   What is RecSim? — 389
What is Sentiment Analysis? — 390
   Useful Tools for Sentiment Analysis — 392
   Aspect-Based Sentiment Analysis — 392
   Deep Learning and Sentiment Analysis — 393

Sentiment Analysis with Naïve Bayes	393
Sentiment Analysis in NLTK and VADER	398
Sentiment Analysis with Textblob	400
Sentiment Analysis with Flair	403
Detecting Spam	405
Logistic Regression and Sentiment Analysis	405
Working with COVID-19	408
What are Chatbots?	410
Open Domain Chatbots	411
Chatbot Types	411
Logic Flow of Chatbots	411
Chatbot Abuses	412
Useful Links	412
Summary	414

Chapter 10   NLP and TF2/Keras   415

Term-Document Matrix	416
Text Classification Algorithms in Machine Learning	416
A Keras-Based Tokenizer	417
TF2 and Tokenization	419
TF2 and Encoding	421
A Keras-Based Word Embedding	423
An Example of BoW with TF2	426
The 20newsgroup Dataset	427
Text Classification with the kNN Algorithm	428
Text Classification with a Decision Tree Algorithm	433
Text Classification with a Random Forest Algorithm	437
Text Classification with the SVC Algorithm	440
Text Classification with the Naïve Bayes Algorithm	443
Text Classification with the kMeans Algorithm	446
TF2/Keras and Word Tokenization	451
TF2/Keras and Word Encodings	453
Text Summarization with TF2/Keras and Reuters Dataset	455
Summary	458

Chapter 11   Transformer, BERT, and GPT   459

What is Attention?	460
Types of Word Embeddings	460
Types of Attention and Algorithms	461
An Overview of the Transformer Architecture	462
The Transformers Library from HuggingFace	463
Transformer and NER Tasks	464

Transformer and QnA Tasks	465
Transformer and Sentiment Analysis Tasks	465
Transformer and Mask Filling Tasks	466
What is T5?	467
What is BERT?	468
BERT Features	468
How is BERT Trained?	468
How BERT Differs from Earlier NLP Techniques	469
The Inner Workings of BERT	469
What is MLM?	469
What is NSP?	470
Special Tokens	470
BERT Encoding: Sequence of Steps	472
Subword Tokenization	474
Sentence Similarity in BERT	476
Word Context in BERT	476
Generating BERT Tokens (1)	478
Generating BERT Tokens (2)	479
The BERT Family	481
Surpassing Human Accuracy: deBERTa	483
What is Google Smith?	483
Introduction to GPT	483
Installing the Transformers Package	484
Working with GPT-2	484
What is GPT-3?	492
What is the Goal?	493
GPT-3 Task Strengths and Mistakes	494
GPT-3 Architecture	494
GPT versus BERT	494
Zero-Shot, One-Shot, and Few Shot Learners	495
GPT Task Performance	495
The Switch Transformer: One Trillion Parameters	496
Looking Ahead	496
Summary	497

Appendix A Data and Statistics — 499

What are Datasets?	500
Data Preprocessing	501
Data Types	502
Preparing Datasets	503
Continuous versus Discrete Data	504
"Binning" Continuous Data	504
Scaling Numeric Data via Normalization	505

Scaling Numeric Data via Standardization	507
What to Look for in Categorical Data	508
Mapping Categorical Data to Numeric Values	508
Working with Dates	510
Working with Currency	511
Missing Data, Anomalies, and Outliers	511
Anomalies and Outliers	512
Outlier Detection	513
Missing Data: MCAR, MAR, and MNAR	514
What is Data Drift?	514
What is Imbalanced Classification?	515
Undersampling and Oversampling	515
Limitations of Resampling	517
What is SMOTE?	517
SMOTE Extensions	518
Analyzing Classifiers	518
What is LIME?	518
What is ANOVA?	519
What is a Probability?	519
Calculating the Expected Value	521
Random Variables	522
Discrete versus Continuous Random Variables	522
Well-Known Probability Distributions	523
Fundamental Concepts in Statistics	523
The Mean	523
The Median	524
The Mode	524
The Variance and Standard Deviation	525
Population, Sample, and Population Variance	525
Chebyshev's Inequality	526
What is a p-Value?	526
The Moments of a Function (Optional)	526
Skewness	527
Kurtosis	527
Data and Statistics	528
The Central Limit Theorem	529
Correlation versus Causation	529
Statistical Inferences	530
The Bias-Variance Trade-off	530
Types of Bias in Data	531
Gini Impurity, Entropy, and Perplexity	532
What is Gini Impurity?	533
What is Entropy?	534

Calculating Gini Impurity and Entropy Values	534
Multidimensional Gini Index	535
What is Perplexity?	535
Cross-Entropy and KL Divergence	536
What is Cross Entropy?	536
What is KL Divergence?	537
What's their Purpose?	537
Covariance and Correlation Matrices	538
Covariance Matrix	538
Covariance Matrix: An Example	539
Correlation Matrix	540
Eigenvalues and Eigenvectors	540
Calculating Eigenvectors: A Simple Example	540
Gauss Jordan Elimination (Optional)	541
Principal Component Analysis (PCA)	542
The New Matrix of Eigenvectors	544
Dimensionality Reduction	545
Dimensionality Reduction Techniques	546
The Curse of Dimensionality	547
What are Manifolds (Optional)?	547
Singular Value Decomposition (SVD)	548
Locally Linear Embedding (LLE)	549
UMAP	549
t-SNE ("tee-snee")	550
PHATE	550
Linear Versus Nonlinear Reduction Techniques	551
Types of Distance Metrics	552
Other Well-Known Distance Metrics	554
Pearson Correlation Coefficient	554
Jaccard Index (or Similarity)	555
Local Sensitivity Hashing (Optional)	555
What is Sklearn?	556
Sklearn, Pandas, and the IRIS Dataset	558
Sklearn and Outlier Detection	560
What is Bayesian Inference?	562
Bayes Theorem	562
Some Bayesian Terminology	563
What is MAP?	563
Why Use Bayes Theorem?	563
What are Vector Spaces?	564
Summary	565

Appendix B Introduction to Python   567

Tools for Python   567
   easy_install and pip   568
   virtualenv   568
   IPython   568
Python Installation   569
Setting the PATH Environment Variable (Windows Only)   570
Launching Python on Your Machine   570
   The Python Interactive Interpreter   570
Python Identifiers   571
Lines, Indentation, and Multilines   572
Quotation and Comments in Python   573
Saving Your Code in a Module   574
Some Standard Modules in Python   575
The help() and dir() Functions   575
Compile Time and Runtime Code Checking   577
Simple Data Types in Python   577
Working with Numbers   578
   Working with Other Bases   579
   The chr() Function   579
   The round() Function in Python   580
   Formatting Numbers in Python   580
Working with Fractions   581
Unicode and UTF-8   582
Working with Unicode   582
Working with Strings   583
   Comparing Strings   584
   Formatting Strings in Python   585
Uninitialized Variables and the Value None in Python   585
Slicing and Splicing Strings   586
   Testing for Digits and Alphabetic Characters   586
Search and Replace a String in Other Strings   587
Remove Leading and Trailing Characters   588
Printing Text without NewLine Characters   589
Text Alignment   590
Working with Dates   591
   Converting Strings to Dates   592
Exception Handling in Python   592
Handling User Input   594
Python and Emojis (Optional)   596
Command-Line Arguments   597
Summary   598

Appendix C Introduction to Regular Expressions — 599

What are Regular Expressions? — 600
Metacharacters in Python — 600
Character Sets in Python — 603
    Working with "^" and "\" — 603
Character Classes in Python — 604
Matching Character Classes with the `re` Module — 605
Using the `re.match()` Method — 605
Options for the `re.match()` Method — 609
Matching Character Classes with the `re.search()` Method — 609
Matching Character Classes with the `findAll()` Method — 610
    Finding Capitalized Words in a String — 611
Additional Matching Function for Regular Expressions — 612
Grouping with Character Classes in Regular Expressions — 613
Using Character Classes in Regular Expressions — 614
    Matching Strings with Multiple Consecutive Digits — 614
    Reversing Words in Strings — 615
Modifying Text Strings with the `re` Module — 616
Splitting Text Strings with the `re.split()` Method — 616
Splitting Text Strings Using Digits and Delimiters — 617
Substituting Text Strings with the `re.sub()` Method — 617
Matching the Beginning and the End of Text Strings — 618
Compilation Flags — 620
Compound Regular Expressions — 620
Counting Character Types in a String — 621
Regular Expressions and Grouping — 622
Simple String Matches — 622
Additional Topics for Regular Expressions — 623
Summary — 624
Exercises — 624

Appendix D Introduction to Keras — 625

What is Keras? — 625
    Working with Keras Namespaces in TF 2 — 626
    Working with the tf.keras.layers Namespace — 627
    Working with the tf.keras.activations Namespace — 628
    Working with the keras.tf.datasets Namespace — 628
    Working with the tf.keras.experimental Namespace — 629
    Working with Other tf.keras Namespaces — 629
    TF 2 Keras versus "Standalone" Keras — 630
Creating a Keras-Based Model — 630
Keras and Linear Regression — 633

Keras, MLPs, and MNIST	635
Keras, CNNs, and cifar10	637
Resizing Images in Keras	639
Keras and Early Stopping (1)	641
Keras and Early Stopping (2)	642
Keras and Metrics	645
Saving and Restoring Keras Models	646
Summary	649

Appendix E Introduction to TensorFlow 2 **651**

What is TF 2?	652
TF 2 Use Cases	654
TF 2 Architecture: The Short Version	654
TF 2 Installation	655
TF 2 and the Python REPL	655
Other TF 2-Based Toolkits	656
TF 2 Eager Execution	657
TF 2 Tensors, Data Types, and Primitive Types	657
TF 2 Data Types	658
TF 2 Primitive Types	658
Constants in TF 2	659
Variables in TF 2	660
The `tf.rank()` API	661
The `tf.shape()` API	662
Variables in TF 2 (Revisited)	664
TF 2 Variables versus Tensors	665
What is `@tf.function` in TF 2?	665
How Does `@tf.function` Work?	666
A Caveat about `@tf.function` in TF 2	666
The `tf.print()` Function and Standard Error	668
Working with `@tf.function` in TF 2	668
An Example without `@tf.function`	668
An Example with `@tf.function`	669
Overloading Functions with `@tf.function`	670
What is AutoGraph in TF 2?	671
Arithmetic Operations in TF 2	671
Caveats for Arithmetic Operations in TF 2	672
TF 2 and Built-In Functions	673
Calculating Trigonometric Values in TF 2	674
Calculating Exponential Values in TF 2	675
Working with Strings in TF 2	676
Working with Tensors and Operations in TF 2	677

Second-Order Tensors in TF 2 (1)	679
Second-Order Tensors in TF 2 (2)	679
Multiplying Two Second-Order Tensors in TF	680
Convert Python Arrays to TF Tensors	681
Conflicting Types in TF 2	681
Differentiation and `tf.GradientTape` in TF 2	682
Examples of `tf.GradientTape`	683
Using Nested Loops with `tf.GradientTape`	684
Other Tensors with `tf.GradientTape`	685
A Persistent Gradient Tape	686
What is Trax?	687
Google Colaboratory	688
Other Cloud Platforms	689
GCP SDK	690
TF2 and `tf.data.Dataset`	690
The TF 2 `tf.data.Dataset`	691
Creating a Pipeline	691
A Simple TF 2 `tf.data.Dataset`	694
What are Lambda Expressions?	694
Working with Generators in TF 2	695
Summary	697

Appendix F   Data Visualization   699

What is Data Visualization?	700
Types of Data Visualization	701
What is `Matplotlib`?	701
Horizontal Lines in `Matplotlib`	702
Slanted Lines in `Matplotlib`	703
Parallel Slanted Lines in `Matplotlib`	704
A Grid of Points in `Matplotlib`	705
A Dotted Grid in `Matplotlib`	706
Lines in a Grid in `Matplotlib`	707
A Colored Grid in `Matplotlib`	708
A Colored Square in an Unlabeled Grid in `Matplotlib`	709
Randomized Data Points in `Matplotlib`	710
A Histogram in `Matplotlib`	712
A Set of Line Segments in `Matplotlib`	712
Plotting Multiple Lines in `Matplotlib`	713
Trigonometric Functions in `Matplotlib`	714
Display IQ Scores in `Matplotlib`	715
Plot a Best-Fitting Line in `Matplotlib`	716
Introduction to Sklearn (scikit-learn)	717

The Digits Dataset in `Sklearn`	718
The Iris Dataset in `Sklearn`	721
Sklearn, Pandas, and the Iris Dataset	723
The Iris Dataset in Sklearn (Optional)	725
The `faces` Dataset in `Sklearn` (Optional)	728
Working with `Seaborn`	729
Features of Seaborn	730
`Seaborn` Built-in Datasets	731
The Iris Dataset in `Seaborn`	731
The Titanic Dataset in `Seaborn`	732
Extracting Data from the Titanic Dataset in `Seaborn` (1)	733
Extracting Data from the Titanic Dataset in `Seaborn` (2)	736
Visualizing a Pandas Dataset in `Seaborn`	738
Data Visualization in Pandas	740
Summary	741

Index   **743**

Preface

What Is the Primary Value Proposition for This Book?

This book contains a fast-paced introduction to as much relevant information about NLP and machine learning as possible that can be reasonably included in a book of this size. Some chapters contain topics that are discussed in great detail (such as the first half of Chapter 3), and other chapters contain advanced statistical concepts that you can safely omit during your first pass through this book. The book casts a wide net to help developers who have a range of technical backgrounds, which is the rationale for the inclusion of numerous topics. Regardless of your background, please keep in mind the following point: *you will not become an expert in machine learning or NLP by reading this book, and be prepared to read some of the content in this book multiple times.*

However, you will be exposed to *many* NLP and machine learning topics, and many topics are presented in a cursory manner for two reasons. First, it's important that you be exposed to these concepts. In some cases, you will find topics that might pique your interest, and motivate you to learn more about them through self-study; in other cases, you will probably be satisfied with a brief introduction.

Second, a full treatment of all the topics that are covered in this book would probably triple the size of this book, and few people are interested in reading 1,000-page technical books. Subsequently, the book provides a broad view of the NLP and machine learning landscape, based on the belief that this approach will be more beneficial for readers who are already experienced developers, but need to learn about NLP and machine learning.

The Target Audience

The book is intended primarily for people who have a solid background as software developers. Specifically, it is for developers who are accustomed to searching online for more detailed information about technical topics. If you are a beginner, there are other books that are more suitable for you, and you can find them by performing an online search.

The book is also intended to reach an international audience of readers with highly diverse backgrounds in various age groups. While many readers know how to read English, their native spoken language is not English (which could be their second, third, or even fourth language). Consequently, this book uses standard English rather than colloquial expressions that might be confusing to those readers. As you know, many people learn by different types of imitation, which includes reading, writing, or hearing new material. This book takes these points into consideration in order to provide a comfortable and meaningful learning experience for the intended readers.

Why Such a Massive Number of Topics in This Book?

As mentioned in the response to the previous question, this book is intended for developers who want to learn NLP concepts and machine learning. Since this encompasses people with vastly different technical backgrounds, there are readers who "don't know what they don't know" regarding NLP. Therefore, it exposes people to a plethora of NLP-related concepts, after which they can decide which topics to select for greater study. Consequently, this book does *not* have a "zero-to-hero" approach, nor is it necessary to master all the topics that are discussed in the chapters and the appendices; rather, they are a go-to source of information to help you decide where you want to invest your time and effort.

As you might already know, learning often takes place through an iterative and repetitive approach whereby the cumulative exposure leads to a greater level of comfort and understanding of technical concepts. For some readers, this will be the first step in their journey toward mastering NLP and machine learning.

Please read the document `ChapterOutline.doc` that provides the rationale for each chapter, as well as the sequence in which you can read the chapters in this book.

How Is the Book Organized and What Will I Learn?

Most of this book is organized as paired chapters: the first two chapters contain introductory material for `NumPy` and `Pandas`, followed by a pair of chapters that contain `NLP` concepts, and then another pair of chapters that contain `Python` code samples that illustrate the `NLP` concepts.

The next pair of chapters introduce machine learning concepts and algorithms (such as Decision Trees, Random Forests, and SVMs), followed by chapter nine that explores sentiment analysis, recommender systems, COVID-19 analysis, spam detection, and a short discussion regarding chatbots. The tenth chapter contains examples of performing NLP tasks using TF2 and Keras, and the eleventh chapter presents the Transformer architecture, BERT-based models, and the GPT family of models, all of which have been developed during the past three years and to varying degrees they are considered SOTA ("state of the art").

The appendices contain introductory material (including Python code samples) for various topics, including Python 3, Regular Expressions, Keras, TF2, Matplotlib and Seaborn. The Appendix A (which is the most extensive in terms of page count) contains myriad topics, such as working with datasets that contain different types of data, handling missing data, statistical concepts, how to handle imbalanced features (SMOTE), how to analyze classifiers, variance and correlation matrices, dimensionality reduction (including SVD and t-SNE), and a section that discusses Gini impurity, entropy, and KL-divergence.

Why Is There Minimal Coverage of Deep Learning?

This book is for developers who are looking for an introduction to NLP, along with an introduction to machine learning. If you peruse the table of contents, you will see that this book covers a vast assortment of topics, and weighs in around 600 pages. Books have a "tipping point" in terms of page count, beyond which few people have the time to read 1000-page books on technical topics, especially when the field is undergoing continual innovation.

With the preceding points in mind, the inclusion of an extensive section pertaining to deep learning is beyond the scope of an introductory book, and better suited in a book called "Deep Learning and NLP" (or some other similar title).

Why Are the Code Samples Primarily in Python?

Most of the code samples are short (usually less than one page and sometimes less than half a page), and if need be, you can easily and quickly copy/paste the code into a new Jupyter notebook.

The machine learning code samples that perform more time-consuming computations are available as Python scripts as well as Jupyter notebooks. For the Python code samples that reference a CSV file, you do not need any additional code in the corresponding Jupyter notebook to access the CSV file. Moreover, the code samples execute quickly, so you won't need to avail yourself of the free GPU that is provided in Google Colaboratory.

If you do decide to use Google Colaboratory, you can easily copy/paste the Python code into a notebook, and also use the upload feature to upload existing Jupyter notebooks. Keep in mind the following point: if the Python code references a CSV file, make sure that you include the appropriate code snippet (as explained in Chapter 1) to access the CSV file in the corresponding Jupyter notebook in Google Colaboratory.

How Much Keras Knowledge Is Needed for This Book?

Some exposure to `Keras` is helpful, and you can read Appendix D if Keras is new to you. In addition, one of the appendices provides an introduction to TensorFlow 2. Please keep in mind that Keras is well-integrated into TensorFlow 2 (in the `tf.keras` namespace), and it provides a layer of abstraction over "pure" TensorFlow that will enable you to develop prototypes more quickly.

Do I Need to Learn the Theory Portions of This Book?

Once again, the answer depends on the extent to which you plan to become involved in NLP and machine learning. In addition to creating a model, you will use various algorithms to see which ones provide the level of accuracy (or some other metric) that you need for your project. If you fall short, the theoretical aspects of machine learning can help you perform a "forensic" analysis of your model and your data, and ideally assist in determining how to improve your model.

How Were the Code Samples Created?

The code samples in this book were created and tested using Python 3 and Keras that's built into TensorFlow 2 on a MacBook Pro with OS X 10.12.6 (macOS Sierra). Regarding their content: the code samples are derived primarily from the author for his Deep Learning and `Keras` graduate course. In some cases, there are code samples that incorporate short sections of code from discussions in online forums. The key point to remember is that the code samples follow the "Four Cs": they must be Clear, Concise, Complete, and Correct to the extent that it's possible to do so, given the size of this book.

Getting the Most from This Book

Some programmers learn well from prose, others learn well from sample code (and lots of it), which means that there's no single style that can be used for everyone.

Moreover, some programmers want to run the code first, see what it does, and then return to the code to delve into the details (and others use the opposite approach).

Consequently, there are various types of code samples in this book: some are short, some are long, and other code samples "build" from earlier code samples.

What Do I Need to Know for This Book?

Current knowledge of Python 3.x is the most helpful skill. Knowledge of other programming languages (such as Java) can also be helpful because of the exposure to programming concepts and constructs. The less technical knowledge that you have, the more diligence will be required in order to understand the various topics that are covered.

If you want to be sure that you can grasp the material in this book, glance through some of the code samples to get an idea of how much is familiar to you and how much is new for you.

Doesn't the Companion Disc Obviate the Need for This Book?

The companion files contain all the code samples to save you time and effort from the error-prone process of manually typing code into a text file. In addition, there are situations in which you might not have easy access to these files. Furthermore, the code samples in the book provide explanations that are not available on the companion files.

The companion files are available for downloading by writing to the publisher at info@merclearning.com.

Does This Book Contain Production-Level Code Samples?

The primary purpose of the code samples is to show you Python-based libraries for solving a variety of NLP-related tasks in conjunction with machine learning. Clarity has higher priority than writing more compact code that is more difficult to understand (and possibly more prone to bugs). If you decide to use any of the code in a production Website, you ought to subject that code to the same rigorous analysis as the other parts of your code base.

What Are the Non-Technical Prerequisites for This Book?

Although the answer to this question is more difficult to quantify, it's especially important to have a strong desire to learn about machine learning, along with the motivation and discipline to read and understand the code samples.

Even simple machine language APIs can be a challenge the first time you encounter them, so be prepared to read the code samples several times.

How Do I Set Up a Command Shell?

If you are a Mac user, there are three ways to do so. The first method is to use `Finder` to navigate to `Applications > Utilities` and then double click on the `Utilities` application. Next, if you already have a command shell available, you can launch a new command shell by typing the following command:

```
open /Applications/Utilities/Terminal.app
```

A second method for Mac users is to open a new command shell on a MacBook from a command shell that is already visible simply by clicking `command+n` in that command shell, and your Mac will launch another command shell.

If you are a PC user, you can install Cygwin (open source *https://cygwin.com/*) that simulates bash commands, or use another toolkit such as MKS (a commercial product). Please read the online documentation that describes the download and installation process. Note that custom aliases are not automatically set if they are defined in a file other than the main start-up file (such as .bash_login).

Companion Files

All the code samples and figures in this book may be obtained by writing to the publisher at *info@merclearning.com*.

Other Books by the Author

This book contains several appendices that are portions from the following books that are also published by Mercury Learning and Information:

1. Python Pocket Primer:
   9781938549854

2. Regular Expressions Pocket Primer:
   9781683922278

3. Data Cleaning Pocket Primer
   9781683922179

What Are the "Next Steps" After Finishing This Book?

The answer to this question varies widely, mainly because the answer depends heavily on your objectives. If you are interested primarily in NLP, then you can learn more advanced concepts, such as attention, transformers, and the BERT-related models.

If you are primarily interested in machine learning, there are some subfields of machine learning, such as deep learning and reinforcement learning (and deep reinforcement learning) that might appeal to you. Fortunately, there are many resources available, and you can perform an Internet search for those resources. One other point: the aspects of machine learning for you to learn depend on who you are: the needs of a machine learning engineer, data scientist, manager, student, or software developer are all different.

Oswald Campesato
April 2021

CHAPTER 1

INTRODUCTION TO NUMPY

This chapter provides a quick introduction to the `Python NumPy` package that provides very useful functionality, not only for `Python` scripts, but also for `Python`-based scripts with `TensorFlow`. This chapter contains `NumPy` code samples with loops, arrays, and lists. You will also learn about dot products, the `reshape()` method (very useful!), how to plot with `Matplotlib` (discussed in Appendix F), and examples of linear regression.

The first part of this chapter briefly introduces `NumPy` and some of its useful features. The second part contains examples of working arrays in `NumPy`, and contrasts some of the APIs for lists with the same APIs for arrays. In addition, you will see how easy it is to compute the exponent-related values (square, cube, and so forth) of elements in an array.

The second part of the chapter introduces subranges, which are very useful (and frequently used) for extracting portions of datasets in machine learning tasks. In particular, you will see code samples that handle negative (-1) subranges for vectors as well as for arrays, because they are interpreted one way for vectors and a different way for arrays.

The third part of this chapter delves into other `NumPy` methods, including the `reshape()` method, which is extremely useful (and very common) when working with images files: some `TensorFlow` APIs require converting a 2D array of `(R,G,B)` values into a corresponding one-dimensional vector.

The fourth part of this chapter delves into linear regression, the mean squared error (MSE), and how to calculate MSE with the `NumPy linspace()` API.

What is NumPy?

`NumPy` is a `Python` module that provides many convenience methods and also better performance. `NumPy` provides a core library for scientific computing in `Python`, with performant multidimensional arrays and good vectorized math functions, along with support for linear algebra and random numbers.

`NumPy` is modeled after `MatLab`, with support for lists, arrays, and so forth. `NumPy` is easier to use than `MatLab`, and it's very common in `TensorFlow` 2.x code as well as `Python` code. Moreover, Chapter 2 contains code samples that combine `NumPy` with `Pandas`.

Useful NumPy Features

The `NumPy` package provides the `ndarray` object that encapsulates multidimensional arrays of homogeneous data types. Many `ndarray` operations are performed in compiled code in order to improve performance.

`NumPy` arrays have the following properties:

- They have a fixed size
- Elements have the same data type
- Elements have the same size (except for objects)
- Modifying an array involves creating a new array

Now that you have a general idea about `NumPy`, let's delve into some examples that illustrate how to work with `NumPy` arrays, which is the topic of the next section.

What are NumPy Arrays?

An array is a set of consecutive memory locations used to store data. Each item in the array is called an element. The number of elements in an array is called the dimension of the array. A typical array declaration is shown here:

```
arr1 = np.array([1,2,3,4,5])
```

The preceding code snippet declares `arr1` as an array of five elements, which you can access via `arr1[0]` through `arr1[4]`. Notice that the first element has an index value of 0, the second element has an index value of 1, and so forth. Thus, if you declare an array of 100 elements, then the 100th element has index value of 99.

> **NOTE** *The first position in a `NumPy` array has index 0.*

`NumPy` treats arrays as vectors and mathematical operations are performed on an element-by-element basis. Remember the following difference: "doubling" an array multiplies each element by 2, whereas "doubling" a list appends a list to itself.

Listing 1.1 displays the contents of `nparray1.py` that illustrates some operations on a `NumPy` array.

LISTING 1.1: nparray1.py

```
import numpy as np

list1 = [1,2,3,4,5]
print(list1)

arr1  = np.array([1,2,3,4,5])
print(arr1)

list2 = [(1,2,3),(4,5,6)]
print(list2)

arr2  = np.array([(1,2,3),(4,5,6)])
print(arr2)
```

Listing 1.1 defines the variables `list1` and `list2` (which are `Python` lists), as well as the variables `arr1` and `arr2` (which are `NumPy` arrays), and prints their values. The output from launching Listing 1.1 is here:

```
[1, 2, 3, 4, 5]
[1 2 3 4 5]
[(1, 2, 3), (4, 5, 6)]
[[1 2 3]
 [4 5 6]]
```

As you can see, `Python` lists and `NumPy` arrays are very easy to define, and now we're ready to look at some loop operations for lists and arrays.

Working with Loops

Listing 1.2 displays the contents of loop1.py that illustrates how to iterate through the elements of a NumPy array and a Python list.

LISTING 1.2: loop1.py

```
import numpy as np

list = [1,2,3]
arr1 = np.array([1,2,3])

for e in list:
 print(e)

for e in arr1:
 print(e)
```

Listing 1.2 initializes the variable list, which is a Python list, and also the variable arr1, which is a NumPy array. The next portion of Listing 1.2 contains two loops, each of which iterates through the elements in list and arr1. As you can see, the syntax is identical in both loops. The output from launching Listing 1.2 is here:

```
1
2
3
1
2
3
```

Appending Elements to Arrays (1)

Listing 1.3 displays the contents of append1.py that illustrates how to append elements to a NumPy array and a Python list.

LISTING 1.3: append1.py

```
import numpy as np

arr1 = np.array([1,2,3])

# these do not work:
#arr1.append(4)
#arr1 = arr1 + [5]

arr1 = np.append(arr1,4)
arr1 = np.append(arr1,[5])
```

```
for e in arr1:
 print(e)

arr2 = arr1 + arr1

for e in arr2:
 print(e)
```

Listing 1.3 initializes the variable `list`, which is a Python list, and also the variable `arr1`, which is a NumPy array. The output from launching Listing 1.3 is here:

```
1
2
3
4
5
2
4
6
8
10
```

Appending Elements to Arrays (2)

Listing 1.4 displays the contents of append2.py that illustrates another example of appending elements to a NumPy array and a Python list.

LISTING 1.4: append2.py

```
import numpy as np

arr1 = np.array([1,2,3])
arr1 = np.append(arr1,4)

for e in arr1:
 print(e)

arr2 = arr1 + arr1

for e in arr2:
 print(e)
```

Listing 1.4 initializes the variable `arr1`, which is a NumPy array. Notice that NumPy arrays do not have an "append" method: this method is available through NumPy itself. Once again, note that one difference between Python lists and NumPy arrays: the "+" operator concatenates Python lists, whereas this operator doubles the elements in a `NumPy` array. The output from launching Listing 1.4 is here:

```
4
2
4
6
```

Multiply Lists and Arrays

Listing 1.5 displays the contents of `multiply1.py` that illustrates how to multiply elements in a `Python` list and a `NumPy` array.

LISTING 1.5: multiply1.py

```
import numpy as np

list1 = [1,2,3]
arr1  = np.array([1,2,3])

print('list:   ',list1)
print('arr1:   ',arr1)
print('2*list:',2*list)
print('2*arr1:',2*arr1)
```

Listing 1.5 contains a `Python` list called `list` and a `NumPy` array called `arr1`. The `print()` statements display the contents of `list` and `arr1` as well as the result of doubling `list1` and `arr1`. Recall that "doubling" a `Python` list is different from doubling a `NumPy` array, which you can see in the output from launching Listing 1.5:

```
('list:   ', [1, 2, 3])
('arr1:   ', array([1, 2, 3]))
('2*list:', [1, 2, 3, 1, 2, 3])
('2*arr1:', array([2, 4, 6]))
```

Doubling the Elements in a List

Listing 1.6 displays the contents of `double_list1.py` that illustrates one way to double the elements in a `Python` list.

LISTING 1.6: double_list1.py

```
import numpy as np

list1 = [1,2,3]
list2 = []
```

```
for e in list1:
  list2.append(2*e)

print('list1:',list1)
print('list2:',list2)
```

Listing 1.6 contains a `Python` list called `list1` and an empty `Python` list called `list2`. The next code snippet iterates through the elements of `list1` and appends them to the variable `list2`. The pair of `print()` statements display the contents of `list1` and `list2` to show you that they are the same. The output from launching Listing 1.6 is here:

```
('list: ', [1, 2, 3])
('list2:', [2, 4, 6])
```

Lists and Exponents

Listing 1.7 displays the contents of `exponent_list1.py` that illustrates how to compute exponents of the elements in a `Python` list.

LISTING 1.7: exponent_list1.py

```
import numpy as np

list1 = [1,2,3]
list2 = []

for e in list1:
  list2.append(e*e) # e*e = squared

print('list1:',list1)
print('list2:',list2)
```

Listing 1.7 contains a `Python` list called `list1` and an empty `NumPy` list called `list2`. The next code snippet iterates through the elements of `list1` and appends the square of each element to the variable `list2`. The pair of `print()` statements display the contents of `list1` and `list2`. The output from launching Listing 1.7 is here:

```
('list1:', [1, 2, 3])
('list2:', [1, 4, 9])
```

Arrays and Exponents

Listing 1.8 displays the contents of `exponent_array1.py` that illustrates how to compute exponents of the elements in a `NumPy` array.

LISTING 1.8: exponent_array1.py

```
import numpy as np

arr1 = np.array([1,2,3])
arr2 = arr1**2
arr3 = arr1**3

print('arr1:',arr1)
print('arr2:',arr2)
print('arr3:',arr3)
```

Listing 1.8 contains a NumPy array called `arr1` followed by two NumPy arrays called `arr2` and `arr3`. Notice the compact manner in which the NumPy `arr2` is initialized with the square of the elements in in `arr1`, followed by the initialization of the NumPy array `arr3` with the cube of the elements in `arr1`. The three `print()` statements display the contents of `arr1`, `arr2`, and `arr3`. The output from launching Listing 1.8 is here:

```
('arr1:', array([1, 2, 3]))
('arr2:', array([1, 4, 9]))
('arr3:', array([ 1,  8, 27]))
```

Math Operations and Arrays

Listing 1.9 displays the contents of `mathops_array1.py` that illustrates how to compute exponents of the elements in a NumPy array.

LISTING 1.9: mathops_array1.py

```
import numpy as np

arr1 = np.array([1,2,3])
sqrt = np.sqrt(arr1)
log1 = np.log(arr1)
exp1 = np.exp(arr1)

print('sqrt:',sqrt)
print('log1:',log1)
print('exp1:',exp1)
```

Listing 1.9 contains a NumPy array called `arr1` followed by three NumPy arrays called `sqrt`, `log1`, and `exp1` that are initialized with the square root, the logarithm, and the exponential value of the elements in `arr1`, respectively. The three `print()` statements display the contents of `sqrt`, `log1`, and `exp1`. The output from launching Listing 1.9 is here:

```
('sqrt:', array([1.        , 1.41421356, 1.73205081]))
('log1:', array([0.        , 0.69314718, 1.09861229]))
('exp1:', array([2.71828183, 7.3890561 , 20.08553692]))
```

Working with "-1" Subranges with Vectors

Listing 1.10 displays the contents of `npsubarray2.py` that illustrates how to use "-1" for ranges of elements in a NumPy array.

LISTING 1.10: npsubarray2.py

```
import numpy as np

# -1 => "all except the last element in …" (row or col)

arr1  = np.array([1,2,3,4,5])
print('arr1:',arr1)
print('arr1[0:-1]:',arr1[0:-1])
print('arr1[1:-1]:',arr1[1:-1])
print('arr1[::-1]:', arr1[::-1]) # reverse!
```

Listing 1.10 contains a NumPy array called `arr1` followed by four `print` statements, each of which displays a different subrange of values in `arr1`. The output from launching Listing 1.10 is here:

```
('arr1:',       array([1, 2, 3, 4, 5]))
('arr1[0:-1]:', array([1, 2, 3, 4]))
('arr1[1:-1]:', array([2, 3, 4]))
('arr1[::-1]:', array([5, 4, 3, 2, 1]))
```

Working with "-1" Subranges with Arrays

Listing 1.11 displays the contents of `np2darray2.py` that illustrates how to select different ranges of elements in a two-dimensional NumPy array.

LISTING 1.11: np2darray2.py

```
import numpy as np

# -1 => "the last element in …" (row or col)

arr1  = np.array([(1,2,3),(4,5,6),(7,8,9),(10,11,12)])
print('arr1:',       arr1)
print('arr1[-1,:]:', arr1[-1,:])
print('arr1[:,-1]:', arr1[:,-1])
print('arr1[-1:,-1]:',arr1[-1:,-1])
```

Listing 1.11 contains a NumPy array called `arr1` followed by four `print` statements, each of which displays a different subrange of values in `arr1`. The output from launching Listing 1.11 is here:

```
(arr1:', array([[1,  2,  3],
                [4,  5,  6],
                [7,  8,  9],
                [10, 11, 12]]))
(arr1[-1,:]]', array([10, 11, 12]))
(arr1[:,-1]:', array([3,  6,  9, 12]))
(arr1[-1:,-1]]', array([12]))
```

Other Useful NumPy Methods

In addition to the NumPy methods that you saw in the code samples prior to this section, the following (often intuitively named) NumPy methods are also very useful.

The method np.zeros() initializes an array with 0 values.

The method np.ones() initializes an array with 1 values.

The method np.empty()initializes an array with 0 values.

The method np.arange() provides a range of numbers:

The method np.shape() displays the shape of an object:

The method np.reshape() <= very useful!

The method np.linspace() <= useful in regression

The method np.mean() computes the mean of a set of numbers:

The method np.std() computes the standard deviation of a set of numbers:

Although the np.zeros() and np.empty() both initialize a 2D array with 0, np.zeros() requires less execution time. You could also use np.full(size, 0), but this method is the slowest of the three methods.

The reshape() method and the linspace() method are very useful for changing the dimensions of an array and generating a list of numeric values, respectively. The reshape() method appears in TensorFlow code, and the linspace() method is useful for generating a set of numbers in linear regression (discussed in Chapter 8). The mean() and std() methods are useful for calculating the mean and the standard deviation of a set of numbers. For example, you can use these two methods in order to resize the values in a Gaussian distribution so that their mean is 0 and the standard deviation is 1. This process is called standardizing a Gaussian distribution.

Arrays and Vector Operations

Listing 1.12 displays the contents of array_vector.py that illustrates how to perform vector-based operations on the elements in a NumPy array.

LISTING 1.12: array_vector.py

```
import numpy as np

a = np.array([[1,2], [3, 4]])
b = np.array([[5,6], [7,8]])

print('a:         ', a)
print('b:         ', b)
print('a + b:     ', a+b)
print('a - b:     ', a-b)
print('a * b:     ', a*b)
print('a / b:     ', a/b)
print('b / a:     ', b/a)
   print('a.dot(b):',a.dot(b))
```

Listing 1.12 contains two NumPy arrays called a and b followed by eight print statements, each of which displays the result of invoking various arithmetic operations on the NumPy arrays a and b. The output from launching Listing 1.12 is here:

```
('a    :     ', array([[1, 2], [3, 4]]))
('b    :     ', array([[5, 6], [7, 8]]))
('a + b:     ', array([[ 6,  8], [10, 12]]))
('a - b:     ', array([[-4, -4], [-4, -4]]))
('a * b:     ', array([[ 5, 12], [21, 32]]))
('a / b:     ', array([[0, 0], [0, 0]]))
('b / a:     ', array([[5, 3], [2, 2]]))
('a.dot(b):', array([[19, 22], [43, 50]]))
```

NumPy and Dot Products (1)

Listing 1.13 displays the contents of dotproduct1.py that illustrates how to perform the dot product on the elements in a NumPy array.

LISTING 1.13: dotproduct1.py

```
import numpy as np

a = np.array([1,2])
b = np.array([2,3])

dot2 = 0
for e,f in zip(a,b):
 dot2 += e*f

print('a:   ',a)
print('b:   ',b)
print('a*b: ',a*b)
print('dot1:',a.dot(b))
print('dot2:',dot2)
```

Listing 1.13 contains two NumPy arrays called a and b followed by a simple loop that computes the dot product of a and b. The next section contains five print statements that display the contents of a and b, their inner product that's calculated in three different ways. The output from launching Listing 1.13 is here:

```
('a:     ', array([1, 2]))
('b:     ', array([2, 3]))
('a*b:   ', array([2, 6]))
('dot1:', 8)
('dot2:', 8)
```

NumPy and Dot Products (2)

NumPy arrays support a "dot" method for calculating the inner product of an array of numbers, which uses the same formula that you use for calculating the inner product of a pair of vectors. Listing 1.14 displays the contents of dotproduct2.py that illustrates how to calculate the dot product of two NumPy arrays.

LISTING 1.14: dotproduct2.py

```
import numpy as np

a = np.array([1,2])
b = np.array([2,3])

print('a:              ',a)
print('b:              ',b)
print('a.dot(b):       ',a.dot(b))
print('b.dot(a):       ',b.dot(a))
print('np.dot(a,b):',np.dot(a,b))
print('np.dot(b,a):',np.dot(b,a))
```

Listing 1.14 contains two NumPy arrays called a and b followed by six print statements that display the contents of a and b, and also their inner product that's calculated in three different ways. The output from launching Listing 1.14 is here:

```
('a:           ', array([1, 2]))
('b:           ', array([2, 3]))
('a.dot(b):    ', 8)
('b.dot(a):    ', 8)
('np.dot(a,b):', 8)
('np.dot(b,a):', 8)
```

NumPy and the "Norm" of Vectors

The norm of a vector (or an array of numbers) is the length of a vector, which is the square root of the dot product of a vector with itself. NumPy also provides the sum() and square() functions that you can use to calculate the norm of a vector.

Listing 1.15 displays the contents of array_norm.py that illustrates how to calculate the magnitude (norm) of a NumPy array of numbers.

LISTING 1.15: array_norm.py

```
import numpy as np
a       = np.array([2,3])
asquare = np.square(a)
asqsum  = np.sum(np.square(a))
anorm1  = np.sqrt(np.sum(a*a))
anorm2  = np.sqrt(np.sum(np.square(a)))
anorm3  = np.linalg.norm(a)

print('a:      ',a)
print('asquare:',asquare)
print('asqsum: ',asqsum)
print('anorm1: ',anorm1)
print('anorm2: ',anorm2)
print('anorm3: ',anorm3)
```

Listing 1.15 contains an initial NumPy array called a, followed by the NumPy array asquare and the numeric values asqsum, anorm1, anorm2, and anorm3. The NumPy array asquare contains the square of the elements in the NumPy array a, and the numeric value asqsum contains the sum of the elements in the NumPy array asquare.

Next, the numeric value anorm1 equals the square root of the sum of the square of the elements in a. The numeric value anorm2 is the same as anorm1, computed in a slightly different fashion. Finally, the numeric value anorm3 is equal to anorm2, but as you can see, anorm3 is calculated via a single NumPy method, whereas anorm2 requires a succession of NumPy methods.

The last portion of Listing 1.15 consists of six print statements, each of which displays the computed values. The output from launching Listing 1.15 is here:

```
('a:      ', array([2, 3]))
('asquare:', array([4, 9]))
('asqsum: ', 13)
('anorm1: ', 3.605551275463989)
('anorm2: ', 3.605551275463989)
('anorm3: ', 3.605551275463989)
```

NumPy and Other Operations

`NumPy` provides the "*" operator to multiply the components of two vectors to produce a third vector whose components are the products of the corresponding components of the initial pair of vectors. This operation is called a Hadamard product. If you then add the components of the third vector, the sum is equal to the inner product of the initial pair of vectors.

Listing 1.16 displays the contents of `otherops.py` that illustrates how to perform other operations on a `NumPy` array.

LISTING 1.16: otherops.py

```
import numpy as np

a = np.array([1,2])
b = np.array([3,4])

print('a:           ',a)
print('b:           ',b)
print('a*b:         ',a*b)
print('np.sum(a*b): ',np.sum(a*b))
print('(a*b.sum()): ',(a*b).sum())
```

Listing 1.16 contains two `NumPy` arrays called a and b, followed five `print` statements that display the contents of a and b, their Hadamard product, and also their inner product that's calculated in two different ways. The output from launching Listing 1.16 is here:

```
('a:           ', array([1, 2]))
('b:           ', array([3, 4]))
('a*b:         ', array([3, 8]))
('np.sum(a*b): ', 11)
('(a*b.sum()): ', 11)
```

NumPy and the `reshape()` Method

`NumPy` arrays support the `reshape()` method that enables you to restructure the dimensions of an array of numbers. In general, if a `NumPy` array contains m elements, where m is a positive integer, then that array can be restructured as an m1 x m2 `NumPy` array, provided that m1 and m2 are positive integers such that m1*m2 = m.

Listing 1.17 displays the contents of `numpy_reshape.py` that illustrates how to use the `reshape()` method on a `NumPy` array.

LISTING 1.17: numpy_reshape.py

```
import numpy as np

x = np.array([[2, 3], [4, 5], [6, 7]])
print(x.shape) # (3, 2)

x = x.reshape((2, 3))
print(x.shape) # (2, 3)
print('x1:',x)

x = x.reshape((-1))
print(x.shape) # (6,)
print('x2:',x)

x = x.reshape((6, -1))
print(x.shape) # (6, 1)
print('x3:',x)

x = x.reshape((-1, 6))
print(x.shape) # (1, 6)
print('x4:',x)
```

Listing 1.17 contains a 3x2 NumPy array called x, followed by a set of invocations of the `reshape()` method that reshape the dimensions of x. The first invocation of the `reshape()` method changes the shape of x from 3x2 to 2x3. The second invocation changes the shape of x from 2x3 to 6x1. The third invocation changes the shape of x from 1x6 to 6x1. The final invocation changes the shape of x from 6x1 to 1x6 again.

Each invocation of the `reshape()` method is followed by a `print()` statement so that you can see the effect of the invocation. The output from launching Listing 1.17 is here:

```
(3, 2)
(2, 3)
('x1:', array([[2, 3, 4],
     [5, 6, 7]]))
(6,)
('x2:', array([2, 3, 4, 5, 6, 7]))
(6, 1)
('x3:', array([[,
       [3],
       [4],
       [5],
       [6],
       [7]]))
   (1, 6)
```

Calculating the Mean and Standard Deviation

If you need to review these concepts from statistics (and perhaps also the mean, median, and mode as well), please read the appropriate section in Appendix A.

`NumPy` provides various built-in functions that perform statistical calculations, such as the following list of methods:

```
np.linspace() <= useful for regression
np.mean()
np.std()
```

The `np.linspace()` method generates a set of equally spaced numbers between a lower bound and an upper bound. The `np.mean()` and `np.std()` methods calculate the mean and standard deviation, respectively, of a set of numbers. Listing 1.18 displays the contents of `sample_mean_std.py` that illustrates how to calculate statistical values from a `NumPy` array.

LISTING 1.18: sample_mean_std.py

```
import numpy as np

x2 = np.arange(8)
print 'mean = ',x2.mean()
print 'std  = ',x2.std()

x3 = (x2 - x2.mean())/x2.std()
print 'x3 mean = ',x3.mean()
print 'x3 std  = ',x3.std()
```

Listing 1.18 contains a `NumPy` array x2 that consists of the first eight integers. Next, the `mean()` and `std()` that are "associated" with x2 are invoked in order to calculate the mean and standard deviation, respectively, of the elements of x2. The output from launching Listing 1.18 is here:

```
('a:          ', array([1, 2]))
('b:          ', array([3, 4]))
```

Trimmed Mean and Weighted Mean

In addition to the arithmetic mean, there are variants that are known as weighted mean and a trimmed mean (also called a truncated mean).

A trimmed mean is known as a robust estimate (i.e., a metric that is not sensitive to outliers). As a simple example of a trimmed mean, suppose that you have five scores for the evaluation of a product: simply drop the highest and lowest scores and then compute the average of the remaining three scores. If you have multiple sets of five scores, repeat the preceding process and then compute the average of the set of trimmed mean values.

A weighted mean is useful when sample data represents different groups in a dataset. Assigning a larger weight to groups that are under-represented yields a weighted mean that more accurate represents the various groups in the dataset. However, keep in mind that outliers can affect the mean as well as the weighted mean.

The weighted mean is the same as the expected value. In case you are unfamiliar with the notion of an expected value, suppose that the set `P = {p1,p2,...,pn}` is a probability distribution, which means that the numeric values in the set `P` must be nonnegative and have a sum equal to 1. In addition, suppose that `V = {v1,v2,...,vn}` is a set of numeric scores that are assigned to n features of a product `M`. The values in the set `V` are probably positive integers in some range (e.g., between 1 and 10).

Then the expected value `E(M)` for that product is computed as follows:

`E(M) = p1*v1 + p2*v2 + ... + pn*vn`

The preceding formula is the same formula for calculating the weighted mean of a set of numbers.

Code Sample with Mean and Standard Deviation

The code sample in this section extends the code sample in the previous section with additional statistical values, and the code can be used for any data distribution. Keep in mind that the code sample uses random numbers simply for the purposes of illustration: after you have launched the code sample, replace those numbers with values from a CSV file or some other dataset containing meaningful values.

Moreover, this section does not provide details regarding the meaning of quartiles, but you can learn about quartiles here:

https://en.wikipedia.org/wiki/Quartile

Listing 1.19 displays the contents of `stat_values.py` that illustrates how to display various statistical values from a NumPy array of random numbers.

LISTING 1.19: *stat_values.py*

```
import numpy as np

from numpy import percentile
from numpy.random import rand
```

```
# generate data sample
data = np.random.rand(1000)

# calculate quartiles, min, and max
quartiles = percentile(data, [25, 50, 75])
data_min, data_max = data.min(), data.max()

# print summary information
print('Minimum:  %.3f' % data_min)
print('Q1 value: %.3f' % quartiles[0])
print('Median:   %.3f' % quartiles)
print('Mean Val: %.3f' % data.mean())
print('Std Dev:  %.3f' % data.std())
print('Q3 value: %.3f' % quartiles)
print('Maximum:  %.3f' % data_max)
```

The data sample (shown in bold) in Listing 1.19 is from a uniform distribution between 0 and 1. The NumPy `percentile()` function calculates a linear interpolation between observations, which is needed to calculate the median on a sample with an even number of values. As you can surmise, the NumPy functions `min()` and `max()` calculate the smallest and largest values in the data sample. The output from launching Listing 1.19 is here:

```
Minimum:   0.000
Q1 value:  0.237
Median:    0.500
Mean Val:  0.495
Std Dev:   0.295
Q3 value:  0.747
Maximum:   0.999
```

As a prelude, Appendix F contains more detailed information about `matplotlib` in order to plot various charts and graphs. However, the Python code samples in the next several sections contain some rudimentary APIs from `matplotlib`. The code samples start with simple examples of line segments, followed by an introduction to linear regression.

Working with Lines in the Plane (Optional)

This section contains a short review of lines in the Euclidean plane, so you can skip this section if you are comfortable with this topic. A minor point that's often overlooked is that lines in the Euclidean plane have infinite length. If you select two distinct points of a line, then all the points between those two selected points is a line segment. A ray is a "half infinite" line: when you select one point as an endpoint, then all the points on one side of the line constitutes a ray.

For example, the points in the plane whose y-coordinate is 0 is a line and also the x-axis, whereas the points between (0,0) and (1,0) on the x-axis form a line segment. In addition, the points on the x-axis that are to the right of (0,0) form a ray, and the points on the x-axis that are to the left of (0,0) also form a ray.

For simplicity this book uses the terms "line" and "line segment" interchangeably. Just in case you're a bit fuzzy on the details, here is the equation of any (non-vertical) line in the Euclidean plane:

```
y = m*x + b
```

The value of m is the slope of the line and the value of b is the y-intercept (i.e., the point (0,b) where the nonvertical line intersects the y-axis). Alternatively, the following form for a line in the plane is a more general equation that also includes vertical lines:

```
a*x + b*y + c = 0
```

However, we won't be working with vertical lines, so we'll stick with the first formula. Figure 1.1 displays three horizontal lines whose equations (from top to bottom) are y = 3, y = 0, and y = -3, respectively.

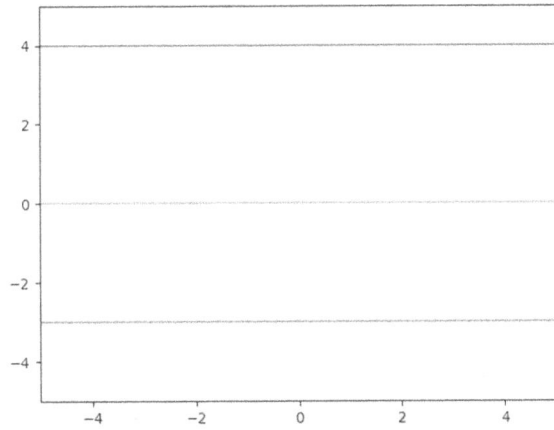

Figure 1.1. A Graph of Three Horizontal Line Segments.

Figure 1.2 displays two slanted lines whose equations are y = x and y = −x, respectively.

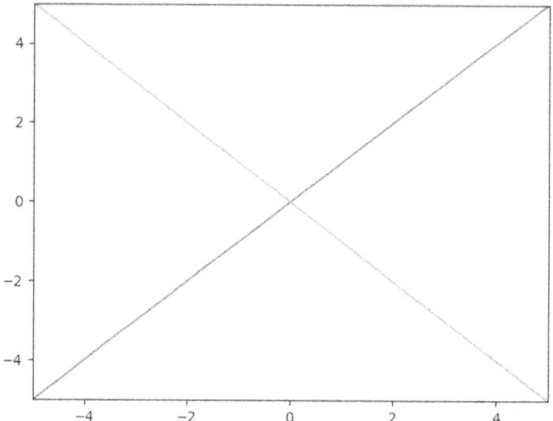

Figure 1.2. A Graph of Two Diagonal Line Segments.

Figure 1.3 displays two slanted parallel lines whose equations are y = 2*x and y = 2*x+3, respectively.

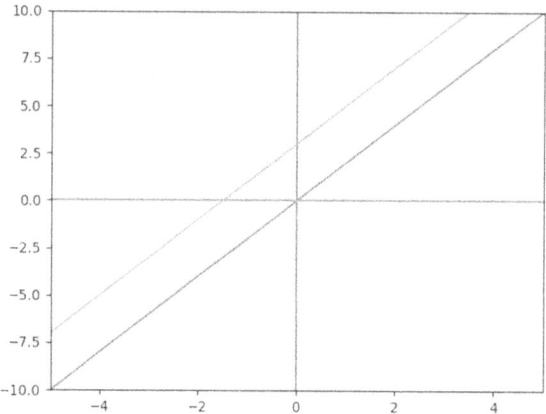

Figure 1.3. A Graph of Two Slanted Parallel Line Segments.

Figure 1.4 displays a piece-wise linear graph consisting of connected line segments.

Now that you have seen some basic examples of lines in the Euclidean plane, let's look at some code samples that use NumPy and Matplotlib to display scatter plots of points in the plane.

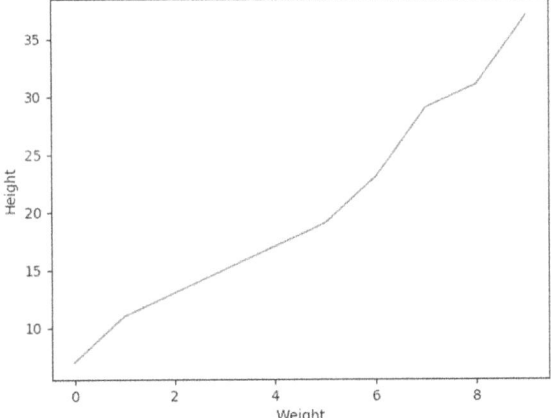

Figure 1.4. A PieceWise Linear Graph of Line Segments.

Plotting a Line with NumPy and Matplotlib

Listing 1.20 displays the contents of `np_plot.py` that illustrates how to plot multiple points on a line in the plane.

LISTING 1.20: np_plot.py

```
import numpy as np
import matplotlib.pyplot as plt
x = np.random.randn(15,1)
y = 2.5*x + 5 + 0.2*np.random.randn(15,1)

plt.scatter(x,y)
plt.show()
```

Listing 1.20 starts with two `import` statements, followed by the initialization of x as a set of random values via the `NumPy randn()` API. Next, y is assigned a range of values that consist of two parts: a linear equation with input values from the x values, which is combined with a randomization factor. Figure 1.5 displays the output generated by the code in Listing 1.20.

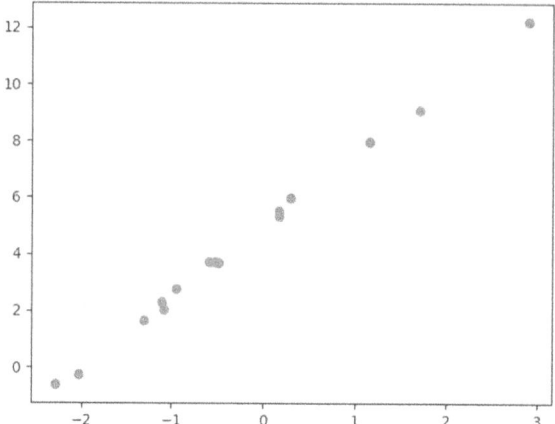

Figure 1.5. A Dataset with Potential Linear Regression.

Plotting a Quadratic with NumPy and Matplotlib

Listing 1.21 displays the contents of np_plot_quadratic.py that illustrates how to plot a quadratic function in the plane.

LISTING 1.21: *np_plot_quadratic.py*

```
import numpy as np
import matplotlib.pyplot as plt

x = np.linspace(-5,5,num=100)[:,None]
y = -0.5 + 2.2*x +0.3*x**3+ 2*np.random.randn(100,1)

plt.plot(x,y)
plt.show()
```

Listing 1.21 starts with two `import` statements, followed by the initialization of `x` as a range of values via the `NumPy linspace()` API. Next, `y` is assigned a range of values that fit a quadratic equation, which are based on the values for the variable `x`. Figure 1.6 displays the output generated by the code in Listing 1.21.

Now that you have seen an assortment of line graphs and scatterplots, let's delve into linear regression, which is the topic of the next section.

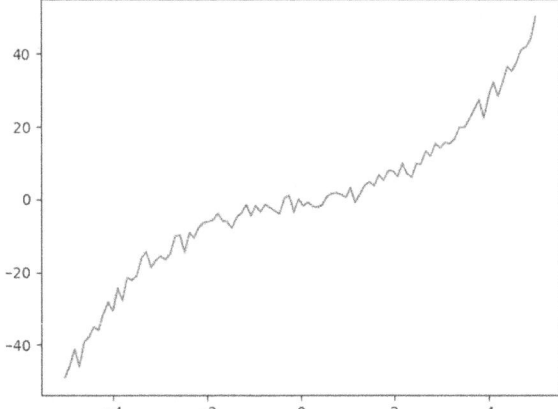

Figure 1.6. A Dataset with Potential Linear Regression.

What is Linear Regression?

Linear regression finds the equation of the best-fitting hyperplane that approximates a dataset, where a hyperplane has degree one less than the dimensionality of the dataset. In particular, if the dataset is in the Euclidean plane, the hyperplane is simply a line; if the dataset is in 3D the hyperplane is a plane.

Linear regression is suitable when the points in a dataset are distributed in such a way that they can reasonably be approximated by a hyperplane. If not, then you can try to fit other types of surfaces to the points in the dataset.

Keep in mind two other details. First, the best-fitting hyperplane does not necessarily intersect all (or even most of) the points in the dataset. In fact, the best-fitting hyperplane might not intersect any points in the dataset. The purpose of a best-fitting hyperplane is to approximate the points in dataset as closely as possible. Second, linear regression is not the same as curve fitting, which attempts to find a polynomial that passes through a set of points.

Some details about curve fitting: given n points in the plane (no two of which have the same x value), there is a polynomial of degree less than or equal to n-1 that passes through those points. Thus, a line (which has degree one) will pass through any pair of non-vertical points in the plane. For any triple of points in the plane, there is a quadratic equation or a line that passes through those points.

In some cases a lower degree polynomial is available. For instance, consider the set of 100 points of the form (x, x): The x value equals the y value, and the line y = x (a polynomial of degree one) passes through all of those points.

However, keep in mind that the extent to which a line "represents" a set of points in the plane depends on how closely those points can be approximated by a line.

What is Multivariate Analysis?

Multivariate analysis generalizes the equation of a line in the Euclidean plane, and it has the following form:

```
y = w1*x1 + w2*x2 + . . . + wn*xn + b
```

As you can see, the preceding equation contains a linear combination of the variables `x1`, `x2`, ..., `xn`. In this book, we will usually work with datasets that involve lines in the Euclidean plane.

What about Nonlinear Datasets?

Simple linear regression finds the best-fitting line that approximates a dataset, but what happens if the dataset does not fit a line in the plane? This is an excellent question! In such a scenario, we look for other curves to approximate the dataset, such a quadratic, cubic, or higher-degree polynomials. However, these alternatives involve trade-offs, as we'll discuss later.

Another possibility is to use a continuous piece-wise linear function, which is a function that comprises a set of line segments, where adjacent line segments are connected. If one or more pairs of adjacent line segments are not connected, then it's a piece-wise linear function (i.e., the function is discontinuous). In either case, line segments have degree one, which involves lower computational complexity than higher order polynomials.

Thus, given a set of points in the plane, try to find the "best fitting" line that approximates those points, after addressing the following questions:

1. How do we know that a line "fits" the data?

2. What if a different type of curve is a better fit?

3. What does "best fit" mean?

One way to check if a line fits the data well is through a simple visual check: display the data in a graph and if the data conforms to the shape of a line reasonably well, then a line might be a good fit. However, this is a subjective decision, and a sample dataset that does not fit a line is displayed in Figure 1.7.

Figure 1.7 displays a dataset containing four points that do not fit a line.

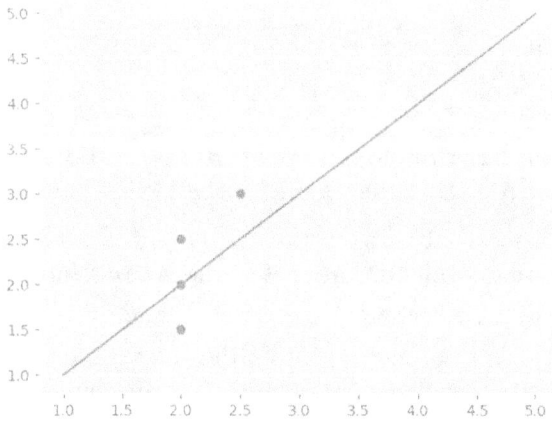

Figure 1.7. A Nonlinear Dataset.

However, if a line does not appear to be a good fit for the data, then perhaps a quadratic or cubic (or even higher degree) polynomial has the potential of being a better fit. Let's defer the nonlinear scenario and let's make the assumption that a line would be a good fit for the data. There is a well-known technique for finding the "best fitting" line for such a dataset, and it's called mean squared error (MSE).

The MSE Formula

Figure 1.8 displays the formula for the MSE. Translated into English: the MSE is the average of the sum of the squares of the difference between an actual y value and the predicted y value, where the latter is the y value that each datapoint would have if that datapoint were actually on the best-fitting line.

Figure 1.8 displays the formula for MSE (Mean Squared Error) for calculating the best-fitting line for a set of points in the plane.

$$\text{MSE} = \frac{1}{n} \sum_{i=1}^{n} (Y_i - \check{Y}_i)^2$$

Figure 1.8. The MSE Formula.

Other Error Types

Although we will only discuss MSE for linear regression in this book, there are other types of formulas that you can use for linear regression, some of which are listed here:

- MSE

- RMSE
- RMSPROP
- MAE

The MSE is the basis for the preceding error types. For example, root mean squared error (RMSE) is the square root of MSE.

However, mean absolute error (MAE) is the average of the sum of the absolute value of the differences of the y terms (not the square of the differences of the y terms).

The RMSProp optimizer utilizes the magnitude of recent gradients to normalize the gradients. Maintain a moving average over the RMS gradients, and then divide that term by the current gradient.

Although it's easier to compute the derivative of MSE (because it's a differentiable function), it's also true that MSE is more susceptible to outliers, more so than MAE. The reason is simple: a squared term can be significantly larger than adding the absolute value of a term. For example, if a difference term is 10, then the squared term 100 is added to MSE, whereas only 10 is added to MAE. Similarly, if a difference term is −20, then the squared term 400 is added to MSE, whereas only 20 (which is the absolute value of −20) is added to MAE.

Nonlinear Least Squares

When predicting housing prices, where the dataset contains a wide range of values, techniques such as linear regression or random forests can cause the model to overfit (discussed in Chapter 7), which means that the model does not generalize well to other datasets.

In this scenario, you can try an error metric such as relative error that reduces the importance of fitting the samples with the largest values. This technique is called non-linear least squares, which may use a log-based transformation of labels and predicted values.

Calculating the MSE Manually

Let's look at two simple graphs, each of which contains a line that approximates a set of points in a scatter plot. Notice that the line segment is the same for both sets of points, but the datasets are slightly different. We will manually calculate the MSE for both datasets and determine which value of MSE is smaller.

Figure 1.9 displays a set of points and a line that is a potential candidate for best-fitting line for the data.

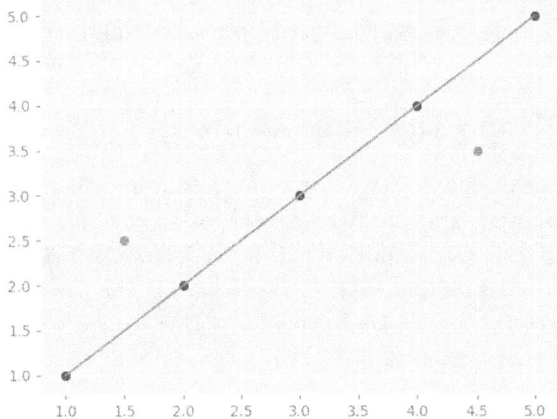

Figure 1.9. A Line Graph that Approximates Points of a Scatter Plot.

The MSE for the line in Figure 1.9 is computed as follows:

```
MSE = [(-2)*(-2) + 2*2]/7 = 8/7
```

Look at Figure 1.10 that also displays a set of points and a line that is a potential candidate for best-fitting line for the data.

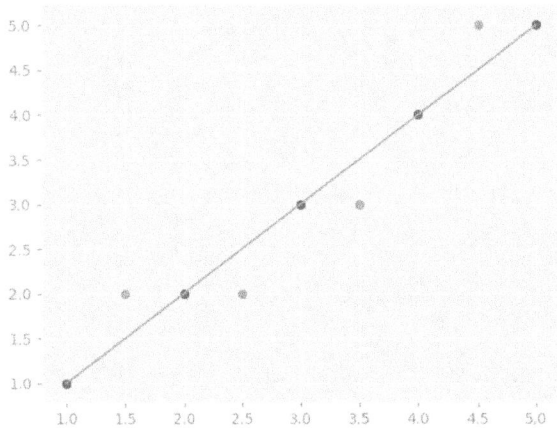

Figure 1.10. A Line Graph that Approximates Points of a Scatter Plot.

The MSE for the line in Figure 1.10 is computed as follows:

```
MSE = [1*1 + (-1)*(-1) + (-1)*(-1) + 1*1]/7 = 4/7
```

Thus, the line in Figure 1.10 has a smaller MSE than the line in Figure 1.9, which might have surprised you (or did you guess correctly?)

In these two figures we calculated the MSE easily and quickly, but in general it's significantly more tedious. For instance, if we plot 10 points in the Euclidean plane that do not closely fit a line, with individual terms that involve non-integer values, we would probably need a calculator. A better solution involves NumPy functions, as discussed in the next section.

Find the Best-Fitting Line with NumPy

Earlier in this chapter you saw examples of lines in the plane, including horizontal, slanted, and parallel lines. Most of those lines have a positive slope and a non-zero value for their y-intercept. Although there are scatterplots of datapoints in the plane where the best-fitting line has a negative slope, the examples in this book involve scatterplots whose best-fitting line has a positive slope.

Listing 1.22 displays the contents of plot_best_fit2.py that illustrates how to determine the bestfitting line for a set of points in the Euclidean plane. The solution is based on so-called "closed form" formulas that are available from Statistics.

LISTING 1.22: plot_best_fit2.py

```
import numpy as np

xs = np.array([1,2,3,4,5], dtype=np.float64)
ys = np.array([1,2,3,4,5], dtype=np.float64)

def best_fit_slope(xs,ys):
 m = (((np.mean(xs)*np.mean(ys))-np.mean(xs*ys)) /
      ((np.mean(xs)**2) - np.mean(xs**2)))
 b = np.mean(ys) - m * np.mean(xs)

 return m, b

m,b = best_fit_slope(xs,ys)
print('m:',m,'b:',b)
```

Listing 1.22 starts with two NumPy arrays xs and ys that are initialized with the first five positive integers. The Python function best_fit_slope() calculate the optimal values of m (the slope) and b (the y-intercept) of a set of numbers. The output from Listing 1.22 is here:

```
m: 1.0 b: 0.0
```

Notice that the NumPy arrays xs and ys are identical, which means that these points lie on the line y=x whose slope is 1. By simple extrapolation, the point (0,0) is also a point on the same line. Hence, the y-intercept of this line must equal 0.

Figure 1.11 displays another line segment that approximates a scatter plot consisting of a larger number of points.

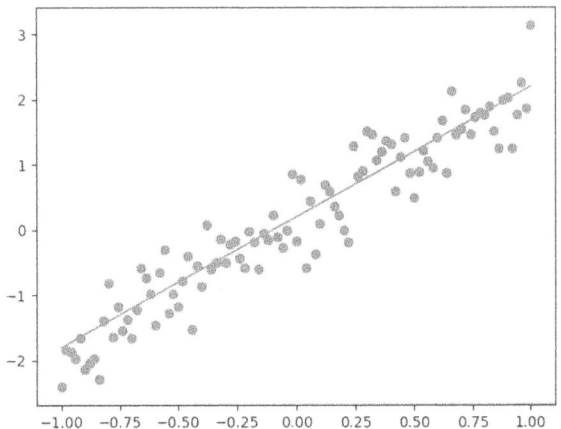

Figure 1.11. A Line Graph that Approximates a Generalized Scatter Plot.

If you are really interested, you can search online to find the derivation for the values of m and b. In this chapter we're going to skip the derivation, and proceed with examples of calculating the MSE. The first example involves calculating the MSE manually, followed by an example that uses NumPy formulas to perform the calculations.

Calculating MSE by Successive Approximation (1)

This section contains a code sample that uses a simple technique for successively determining better approximations for the slope and y-intercept of a best-fitting line. Recall that an approximation of a derivative is the ratio of "delta y" divided by "delta x." The delta values calculate the difference of the y values and the difference of the x values, respectively, of two nearby points (x1,y1) and (x2,y2) on a function. Hence, the delta-based approximation ratio is (y2-y1)/(x2-x1).

The technique in this section involves a simplified approximation for the delta values: we assume that the denominators are equal to 1. As a result, we need only calculate the numerators of the "delta" values: in this code sample, those numerators are the variables dw and db.

Listing 1.23 displays the contents of plain_linreg1.py that illustrates how to compute the MSE with simulated data.

LISTING 1.23: plain_linreg1.py

```
import numpy as np
import matplotlib.pyplot as plt

X = [0,0.12,0.25,0.27,0.38,0.42,0.44,0.55,0.92,1.0]
Y = [0,0.15,0.54,0.51,0.34,0.1, 0.19,0.53,1.0,0.58]

losses = []

#Step 1: Parameter initialization
W = 0.45 # the initial slope
b = 0.75 # the initial y-intercept

for i in range(1, 100):
 #Step 2: Calculate Loss
 Y_pred = np.multiply(W, X) + b
 loss_error = 0.5 * (Y_pred - Y)**2
 loss = np.sum(loss_error)/10

 #Step 3: Calculate dw and db
 db = np.sum((Y_pred - Y))
 dw = np.dot((Y_pred - Y), X)
 losses.append(loss)

 #Step 4: Update parameters:
 W = W - 0.01*dw
 b = b - 0.01*db

 if i%10 == 0:
   print("Loss at", i,"iteration = ", loss)

#Step 5: Repeat via a for loop with 1000 iterations

#Plot loss versus # of iterations
print("W = ", W,"& b = ",  b)
plt.plot(losses)
plt.ylabel('loss')
plt.xlabel('iterations (per tens)')
plt.show()
```

Listing 1.23 defines the variables X and Y that are simple arrays of numbers (this is our dataset). Next, the losses array is initialized as an empty array, and we will append successive loss approximations to this array. The variables W and b correspond to the slope and y-intercept, and they are initialized with the values 0.45 and 0.75, respectively (feel free to experiment with these values).

The next portion of Listing 1.23 is a for loop that executes 100 times. During each iteration, the variables Y_pred, loss_error, and loss are computed, and they correspond to the predicted value, the error, and the loss, respectively. (Remember: we are performing linear regression). The value of loss (which is the error for the current iteration) is then appended to the losses array.

Next, the variables dw and db are calculated: these correspond to "delta w" and "delta b" that we'll use to update the values of W and b, respectively. The code is reproduced here:

```
#Step 4: Update parameters:
W = W - 0.01*dw
b = b - 0.01*db
```

Notice that dw and db are both multiplied by the value 0.01, which is the value of our "learning rate" (you can experiment with this value as well).

The next code snippet displays the current loss, which is performed every tenth iteration through the loop. When the loop finishes execution, the values of W and b are displayed, and a plot is displayed that shows the loss values on the vertical axis and the loop iterations on the horizontal axis. The output from Listing 1.23 is here:

```
Loss at 10 iteration =   0.04114630674619491
Loss at 20 iteration =   0.026706242729839395
Loss at 30 iteration =   0.024738889446900423
Loss at 40 iteration =   0.023850565034634254
Loss at 50 iteration =   0.0231499048706651
Loss at 60 iteration =   0.02255361434242207
Loss at 70 iteration =   0.0220425055291673
Loss at 80 iteration =   0.021604128492245713
Loss at 90 iteration =   0.021228111750568435
W =  0.47256473531193927 & b =  0.19578262688662174
```

Figure 1.12 displays the plot of loss-versus-iterations for Listing 1.23.

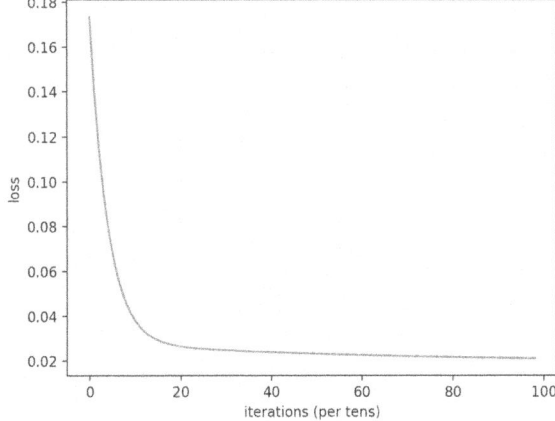

Figure 1.12. A Plot of Loss-versus-Iterations.

Calculating MSE by Successive Approximation (2)

In the previous section, you saw how to calculate "delta" approximations in order to determine the equation of a best-fitting line for a set of points in a 2D plane. The example in this section generalizes the code in the previous section by adding an outer loop that represents the number of epochs. The number of epochs specifies the number of times that an inner loop is executed.

Listing 1.24 displays the contents of `plain_linreg2.py` that illustrates how to compute the MSE with simulated data.

LISTING 1.24: *plain_linreg2.py*

```
import numpy as np
import matplotlib.pyplot as plt

# %matplotlib inline
X = [0,0.12,0.25,0.27,0.38,0.42,0.44,0.55,0.92,1.0]
Y = [0,0.15,0.54,0.51, 0.34,0.1,0.19,0.53,1.0,0.58]

#uncomment to see a plot of X versus Y values
#plt.plot(X,Y)
#plt.show()

losses = []
#Step 1: Parameter initialization
W = 0.45
b = 0.75

epochs = 100
lr = 0.001

for j in range(1, epochs):
 for i in range(1, 100):
   #Step 2: Calculate Loss
   Y_pred = np.multiply(W, X) + b
   Loss_error = 0.5 * (Y_pred - Y)**2
   loss = np.sum(Loss_error)/10

   #Step 3: Calculate dW and db
   db = np.sum((Y_pred - Y))
   dw = np.dot((Y_pred - Y), X)
   losses.append(loss)

   #Step 4: Update parameters:
   W = W - lr*dw
   b = b - lr*db

   if i%50 == 0:
     print("Loss at epoch", j,"= ", loss)
```

```
#Plot loss versus # of iterations
print("W = ", W,"& b = ",  b)
plt.plot(losses)
plt.ylabel('loss')
plt.xlabel('iterations (per tens)')
plt.show()
```

Compare the new contents of Listing 1.24 (shown in bold) with the contents of Listing 1.23: the changes are minimal, and the main difference is to execute the inner loop 100 times for each iteration of the outer loop, which also executes 100 times. The output from Listing 1.24 is here:

```
('Loss at epoch', 1, '= ', 0.07161762489862147)
('Loss at epoch', 2, '= ', 0.030073922512586938)
('Loss at epoch', 3, '= ', 0.025415528992988472)
('Loss at epoch', 4, '= ', 0.024227826373677794)
('Loss at epoch', 5, '= ', 0.02346241967071181)
('Loss at epoch', 6, '= ', 0.022827707922883803)
('Loss at epoch', 7, '= ', 0.022284262669854064)
('Loss at epoch', 8, '= ', 0.02181735173716673)
('Loss at epoch', 9, '= ', 0.021416050179776294)
('Loss at epoch', 10, '= ', 0.02107112540934384)
// details omitted for brevity
('Loss at epoch', 90, '= ', 0.018960749188638278)
('Loss at epoch', 91, '= ', 0.01896074755776306)
('Loss at epoch', 92, '= ', 0.018960746155994725)
('Loss at epoch', 93, '= ', 0.018960744951148113)
('Loss at epoch', 94, '= ', 0.018960743915559485)
('Loss at epoch', 95, '= ', 0.018960743025451313)
('Loss at epoch', 96, '= ', 0.018960742260386375)
('Loss at epoch', 97, '= ', 0.018960741602798474)
('Loss at epoch', 98, '= ', 0.018960741037589136)
('Loss at epoch', 99, '= ', 0.018960740551780944)
('W = ', 0.6764145874436108, '& b = ', 0.09976839618922698)
```

Figure 1.13 displays the plot of loss-versus-iterations for Listing 1.24.

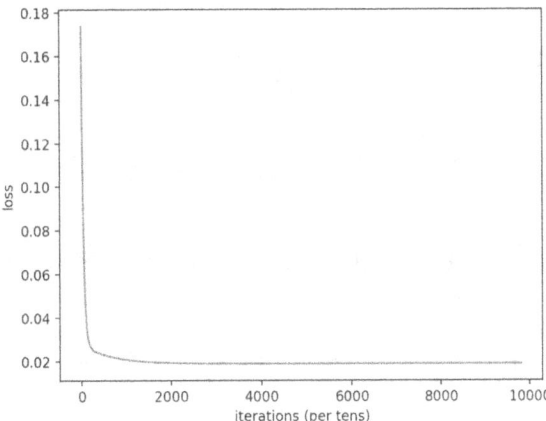

Figure 1.13. A Plot of Loss-versus-Iterations.

Notice that Figure 1.13 has 10,000 iterations on the horizontal axis, whereas Figure 1.12 has only 100 iterations on the horizontal axis.

What is Jax?

`Jax` is an open source package that uses more modern techniques to speed up `NumPy` and `Python` computations on CPUs, GPUS, and TPUs, which is probably why `Jax` has been called "`NumPy` on steroids". The `Jax` documentation is here:

https://jax.readthedocs.io/en/latest/developer.html

You can build `Jax` in two steps from its source code (with or without `CUDA`) as described in the preceding link, or you can install `Jax` on your machine via `pip3`, as shown here:

```
pip3 install jaxlib
```

`Jax` is also the default for `Trax` (see Appendix E), and you can also set `Jax` in Google Colaboratory.

In case you're interested, `tf.experimental.numpy` implements `NumPy` on TensorFlow, as described here:

https://www.tensorflow.org/api_docs/python/tf/experimental/numpy

Google Colaboratory

Depending on the hardware, GPU-based TF 2 code can be 10 times faster than CPU-based TF 2 code. However, the price of a good GPU can be a significant factor. Although NVIDIA provides GPUs, those consumer-based GPUs are not optimized for multi-GPU support (which is supported by TF 2).

Fortunately Google Colaboratory is an affordable alternative that provides free GPU support, and also runs as a `Jupyter` notebook environment. In addition, Google Colaboratory executes your code in the cloud and involves zero configuration, and it's available here:

https://colab.research.google.com/notebooks/welcome.ipynb

The preceding `Jupyter` notebook is suitable for training simple models and testing ideas quickly. Google Colaboratory makes it easy to upload local files, install software in `Jupyter` notebooks, and even connect Google Colaboratory to a `Jupyter` runtime on your local machine.

Some of the supported features of Colaboratory include TF 2 execution with GPUs, visualization using Matplotlib, and the ability to save a copy of your Google Colaboratory notebook to Github by using `File > Save a copy to GitHub`.

Moreover, you can load any Jupyter notebook on GitHub by just adding the path to the URL `colab.research.google.com/github/` (see the Colaboratory website for details).

Google Colaboratory has support for other technologies such as HTML and SVG, enabling you to render SVG-based graphics in notebooks that are in Google Colaboratory. In case you're interested, you can launch Tensorboard inside a Google Colaboratory notebook with the following command (replace the specified directory with your own location):

```
%tensorboard --logdir /logs/images
```

Keep in mind the following details about Google Colaboratory. First, whenever you connect to a server in Google Colaboratory, you start what's known as a session. You can execute the code in a session with a CPU (the default), a GPU, or a TPU, and you can execute your code without any time limit for your session. However, if you select the GPU option for your session, only the first 12 hours of GPU execution time are free. Any additional GPU time during that same session incurs a small charge (see the website for those details).

The other point to keep in mind is that any software that you install in a Jupyter notebook during a given session will not be saved when you exit that session. For example, the following code snippet installs `TFLearn` in a Jupyter notebook:

```
!pip install tflearn
```

When you exit the current session and at some point later you start a new session, you need to install `TFLearn` again, as well as any other software (such as Github repositories) that you also installed in any previous session.

Incidentally, you can also run TF 2 code and TensorBoard in Google Colaboratory, with support for CPUs, GPUs, and TPU. Navigate to this link for more information:

https://colab.research.google.com

Uploading CSV Files in Google Colaboratory

Listing 1.25 displays the contents `upload_csv_file.ipynb` that illustrates how to upload a CSV file in a Google Colaboratory notebook.

LISTING 1.25: *upload_csv_file.ipynb*

```
import pandas as pd

from google.colab import files
uploaded = files.upload()
df = pd.read_csv("weather_data.csv")
print("dataframe df:")
df
```

Listing 1.25 uploads the CSV file `weather_data.csv` whose contents are not shown here because they are not important for this example. The code shown in bold is the Colaboratory-specific code that is required to upload the CSV file. When you launch this code, you will see a small button labeled "Browse," which you must click and then select the CSV file that is listed in the code snippet. After doing so, the rest of the code is executed and you will see the contents of the CSV file displayed in your browser session.

Summary

This chapter introduced you to the `NumPy` package for `Python`. You learned how to write `Python` scripts containing loops, arrays, and lists. You also saw how to work with dot products, the `reshape()` method, plotting with `Matplotlib` (discussed in more detail in Appendix F), and examples of linear regression.

Then you learned how to work with subranges of arrays, and also negative subranges of vectors and arrays, both of which are very useful for extracting portions of datasets in machine learning tasks. You also saw various other `NumPy` operations, such as the `reshape()` method that is extremely useful (and very common) when working with images files.

Next, you learned how to use `NumPy` for linear regression, the mean squared error (MSE), and how to calculate MSE with the `NumPy linspace()` method. Finally, you learned about Google Colaboratory, which provides CPU, GPU, and TPU support for the execution of Jupyter notebooks in the cloud.

CHAPTER 2

INTRODUCTION TO PANDAS

This chapter introduces you to `Pandas` and provides various code samples that illustrate some of its useful features. As you will see, the purpose of each section is self-explanatory, and they have a succinct style that focuses on the code samples. If you are familiar with these topics, feel free to skim through the material and peruse the code samples, just in case they contain some new information.

The first part of this chapter contains a brief introduction to `Pandas` and some of its useful features. This section contains code samples that illustrate some features of data frames and a brief discussion of series, which are two of the main features of `Pandas`.

The second part of this chapter discusses various types of data frames that you can create, such as numeric and Boolean data frames. In addition, you will see examples of creating data frames with `NumPy` functions and random numbers. You will also see examples of converting between `Python` dictionaries and `JSON`-based data, and also how to create a `Pandas` data frame from `JSON`-based data.

What is Pandas?

`Pandas` is a `Python` package that is compatible with other `Python` packages, such as `NumPy`, `Matplotlib`, and so forth. Install `Pandas` by opening a command shell and invoking this command for `Python` 3.x:

```
pip3 install pandas
```

In many ways the semantics of the APIs in the `Pandas` library are similar to a spreadsheet, along with support for `xsl`, `xml`, `html`, `csv` file types. `Pandas` provides a data type called a `DataFrame` with extremely powerful functionality, which is discussed in the next section.

`Pandas` data frames support a variety of input types, such as `ndarrays`, lists, `dicts`, or `Series`.

`Pandas` also provides another data type called `Pandas Series` that provides another mechanism for managing data. In addition to performing an online for more details regarding `Series`, the following article contains a good introduction:

https://towardsdatascience.com/20-examples-to-master-pandas-series-bc4c68200324

Pandas Options and Settings

You can change default values of environment variables in `Pandas`, an example of which is shown here:

```
import pandas as pd
display_settings = {
   'max_columns': 8,
   'expand_frame_repr': True,  # Wrap to multiple pages
   'max_rows': 20,
   'precision': 3,
   'show_dimensions': True
}

for op, value in display_settings.items():
pd.set_option("display.{}".format(op), value)
```

Include the preceding code block in your own code if you want `Pandas` to display a maximum of 20 rows and 8 columns, and floating point numbers displayed with 3 decimal places. Set `expand_frame_rep` to True if you want the output to "wrap around" to multiple pages. The preceding `for` loop iterates through `display_settings` and sets the options equal to their corresponding values.

In addition, the following code snippet displays all `Pandas` options and their current values in your code:

```
print(pd.describe_option())
```

There are various other operations that you can perform with options and their values (such as the `pd.reset()` method for resetting values), as described in the `Pandas` user guide:

https://pandas.pydata.org/pandas-docs/stable/user_guide/options.html

Pandas Data Frames

In simplified terms, a `Pandas` data frame is a two-dimensional data structure, and it's convenient to think of the data structure in terms of rows and columns. Data frames can be labeled (rows as well as columns), and the columns can contain different data types. The source of the dataset for a `Pandas` data frame can be a data file, a database table, a web service, and so forth. `Pandas` data frame features include:

- Data Frame Methods
- Data Frame Statistics
- Grouping, Pivoting, and Reshaping
- Handle Missing Data
- Join Data Frames

The `Pandas` code samples in this chapter show you almost all the features in the preceding list.

Data Frames and Data Cleaning Tasks

The specific tasks that you need to perform depend on the structure and contents of a dataset. In general you will perform a workflow with the following steps, not necessarily always in this order (and some might be optional). All of the following steps can be performed with a `Pandas` data frame:

- Read data into a data frame
- Display top of data frame
- Display column data types
- Display nonmissing values
- Replace NA with a value
- Iterate through the columns
- Statistics for each column
- Find Missing Values
- Total missing values
- Percentage of missing values
- Sort table values

- Print summary information
- Columns with > 50% missing
- Rename columns

This chapter contains sections that illustrate how to perform many of the steps in the preceding list.

Alternatives to Pandas

Before delving into `Pandas` code samples, there are alternatives to `Pandas` that offer very useful features, some of which are in the following list:

- PySpark (for large datasets)
- Dask (for distributed processing)
- Modin (faster performance)
- Datatable (R data.table for Python)

The inclusion of these alternatives is not intended to diminish `Pandas`: indeed, you might not need any of the functionality in the preceding list. However, you might need such functionality in the future, so it's worthwhile for you to know about these alternatives now (and there may be even more powerful alternatives at some point in the future).

A Pandas Data Frame with NumPy Example

Listing 2.1 displays the contents of `pandas_df.py` that illustrates how to define several `Pandas` data frames and display their contents.

LISTING 2.1: pandas_df.py

```
import pandas as pd
import numpy as np

myvector1 = np.array([1,2,3,4,5])
print("myvector1:")
print(myvector1)
print()

mydf1 = pd.DataFrame(myvector1)
print("mydf1:")
print(mydf1)
print()
```

```
myvector2 = np.array([i for i in range(1,6)])
print("myvector2:")
print(myvector2)
print()

mydf2 = pd.DataFrame(myvector2)
print("mydf2:")
print(mydf2)
print()

myarray = np.array([[10,30,20], [50,40,60],[1000,2000,3000]])
print("myarray:")
print(myarray)
print()

mydf3 = pd.DataFrame(myarray)
print("mydf3:")
print(mydf3)
print()
```

Listing 2.1 starts with standard `import` statements for `Pandas` and `NumPy`, followed by the definition of two one-dimensional `NumPy` arrays and a two-dimensional `NumPy` array. The `NumPy` syntax ought to be familiar to you from the examples in Chapter 1. Each `NumPy` variable is followed by a corresponding `Pandas` data frame `mydf1`, `mydf2`, and `mydf3`. Now launch the code in Listing 2.1 and you will see the following output, and you can compare the `NumPy` arrays with the `Pandas` data frames:

```
myvector1:
[1 2 3 4 5]

mydf1:
   0
0  1
1  2
2  3
3  4
4  5

myvector2:
[1 2 3 4 5]

mydf2:
   0
0  1
1  2
2  3
3  4
4  5
```

```
myarray:
[[   10   30   20]
 [   50   40   60]
 [1000 2000 3000]]

mydf3:
      0     1     2
0    10    30    20
1    50    40    60
2  1000  2000  3000
```

By contrast, the following code block illustrates how to define a `Pandas Series`:

```
names = pd.Series(['SF', 'San Jose', 'Sacramento'])
sizes = pd.Series([852469, 1015785, 485199])
df = pd.DataFrame({ 'Cities': names, 'Size': sizes })
print(df)
```

Create a `Python` file with the preceding code (along with the required `import` statement) and when you launch that code you will see the following output:

```
   City name     sizes
0         SF    852469
1   San Jose   1015785
2  Sacramento   485199
```

Describing a Pandas Data Frame

Listing 2.2 displays the contents of pandas_df_describe.py that illustrates how to define a `Pandas Data frame` that contains a 3×3 NumPy array of integer values, where the rows and columns of the data frame are labeled. Various other aspects of the data frame are also displayed.

LISTING 2.2: pandas_df_describe.py

```
import numpy as np
import pandas as pd

myarray = np.array([[10,30,20], [50,40,60],[1000,2000,3000]])

rownames = ['apples', 'oranges', 'beer']
colnames = ['January', 'February', 'March']

mydf = pd.DataFrame(myarray, index=rownames, columns=colnames)
print("contents of df:")
print(mydf)
print()
```

```
print("contents of January:")
print(mydf['January'])
print()

print("Number of Rows:")
print(mydf.shape[0])
print()

print("Number of Columns:")
print(mydf.shape)
print()

print("Number of Rows and Columns:")
print(mydf.shape)
print()

print("Column Names:")
print(mydf.columns)
print()

print("Column types:")
print(mydf.dtypes)
print()

print("Description:")
print(mydf.describe())
print()
```

Listing 2.2 starts with two standard `import` statements followed by the variable `myarray`, which is a 3×3 NumPy array of numbers. The variables `rownames` and `colnames` provide names for the rows and columns, respectively, of the Pandas data frame `mydf`, which is initialized as a Pandas data frame with the specified datasource (i.e., `myarray`).

The first portion of the output below requires a single `print` statement (which simply displays the contents of `mydf`). The second portion of the output is generated by invoking the `describe()` method that is available for any Pandas data frame. The `describe()` method is very useful: you will see various statistical quantities, such as the mean, standard deviation minimum, and maximum performed by columns (not rows), along with values for the 25th, 50th, and 75th percentiles. The output of Listing 2.2 is here:

```
contents of df:
         January  February  March
apples        10        30     20
oranges       50        40     60
beer        1000      2000   3000

contents of January:
apples        10
```

```
oranges          50
beer           1000
Name: January, dtype: int64
```

```
Number of Rows:
3

Number of Columns:
3

Number of Rows and Columns:
(3, 3)

Column Names:
Index(['January', 'February', 'March'], dtype='object')

Column types:
January    int64
February   int64
March      int64
dtype: object

Description:
           January      February         March
count     3.000000      3.000000      3.000000
mean    353.333333    690.000000   1026.666667
std     560.386771   1134.504297   1709.073823
min      10.000000     30.000000     20.000000
25%      30.000000     35.000000     40.000000
50%      50.000000     40.000000     60.000000
75%     525.000000   1020.000000   1530.000000
max    1000.000000   2000.000000   3000.000000
```

Pandas Boolean Data Frames

Pandas supports Boolean operations on Data frames, such as the logical OR, the logical AND, and the logical negation of a pair of Data frames. Listing 2.3 displays the contents of pandas_boolean_df.py that illustrates how to define a Pandas data frame whose rows and columns are Boolean values.

LISTING 2.3: pandas_boolean_df.py

```
import pandas as pd

df1 = pd.DataFrame({'a': [1, 0, 1], 'b': [0, 1, 1] },
dtype=bool)
df2 = pd.DataFrame({'a': [0, 1, 1], 'b': [1, 1, 0] },
dtype=bool)

print("df1 & df2:")
print(df1 & df2)
```

```
print("df1 | df2:")
print(df1 | df2)

print("df1 ^ df2:")
print(df1 ^ df2)
```

Listing 2.3 initializes the Data frames df1 and df2, and then computes df1 & df2, df1 | df2, df1 ^ df2, which represent the logical AND, the logical OR, and the logical negation, respectively, of df1 and df2. The output from launching the code in Listing 2.3 is here:

```
df1 & df2:
       a      b
0  False  False
1  False   True
2   True  False
df1 | df2:
       a      b
0   True   True
1   True   True
2   True   True
df1 ^ df2:
       a      b
0   True   True
1   True  False
2  False   True
```

Transposing a Pandas Data Frame

The T attribute (as well as the transpose function) enables you to generate the transpose of a Pandas data frame, similar to a NumPy ndarray. The transpose operation switches rows to columns and columns to rows. For example, the following code snippet defines a Pandas data frame df1 and then displays the transpose of df1:

```
df1 = pd.DataFrame({'a': [1, 0, 1], 'b': [0, 1, 1] },
dtype=int)

print("df1.T:")
print(df1.T)
```

The output is here:

```
df1.T:
   0  1  2
a  1  0  1
b  0  1  1
```

The following code snippet defines Pandas data frames df1 and df2 and then displays their sum:

```
df1 = pd.DataFrame({'a' : [1, 0, 1], 'b' : [0, 1, 1] }, dtype=int)
df2 = pd.DataFrame({'a' : [3, 3, 3], 'b' : [5, 5, 5] }, dtype=int)

print("df1 + df2:")
print(df1 + df2)
```

The output is here:

```
df1 + df2:
   a  b
0  4  5
1  3  6
2  4  6
```

Pandas Data Frames and Random Numbers

Listing 2.4 displays the contents of pandas_random_df.py that illustrates how to create a Pandas data frame with random numbers.

LISTING 2.4: *pandas_random_df.py*

```
import pandas as pd
import numpy as np

df = pd.DataFrame(np.random.randint(1, 5, size=(5, 2)),
columns=['a','b'])
df = df.append(df.agg(['sum', 'mean']))

print("Contents of data frame:")
print(df)
```

Listing 2.4 defines the Pandas data frame df that consists of 5 rows and 2 columns of random integers between 1 and 5. Notice that the columns of df are labeled "a" and "b." In addition, the next code snippet appends two rows consisting of the sum and the mean of the numbers in both columns. The output of Listing 2.4 is here:

```
        a     b
0     1.0   2.0
1     1.0   1.0
2     4.0   3.0
3     3.0   1.0
4     1.0   2.0
sum  10.0   9.0
mean  2.0   1.8
```

Listing 2.5 displays the contents of pandas_combine_df.py that illustrates how to combine Pandas data frames.

LISTING 2.5: pandas_combine_df.py

```
import pandas as pd
import numpy as np

df = pd.DataFrame({'foo1' : np.random.randn(5),
                   'foo2' : np.random.randn(5)})

print("contents of df:")
print(df)

print("contents of foo1:")
print(df.foo1)

print("contents of foo2:")
print(df.foo2)
```

Listing 2.5 defines the Pandas data frame df that consists of 5 rows and 2 columns (labeled "foo1" and "foo2") of random real numbers between 0 and 5. The next portion of Listing 2.5 displays the contents of df and foo1. The output of Listing 2.5 is here:

```
contents of df:
       foo1      foo2
0   0.274680  _0.848669
1  _0.399771  ⁻0.814679
2   0.454443  ⁻0.363392
3   0.473753   0.550849
4  _0.211783  _0.015014
contents of foo1:
0     0.256773
1     1.204322
2     1.040515
3    _0.518414
4    ⁻0.634141
Name: foo1, dtype: float64
contents of foo2:
0    _2.506550
1    ⁻0.896516
2    ⁻0.222923
3     0.934574
4     0.527033
Name: foo2, dtype: float64
```

Reading CSV Files in Pandas

Pandas provides the `read_csv()` method for reading the contents of CSV files. For example, Listing 2.6 displays the contents of `sometext.txt` that contains labeled data (spam or ham), and Listing 2.7 displays the contents of `read_csv_file.py` that illustrates how to read the contents of a CSV file.

LISTING 2.6: sometext.csv

```
type    text
ham     Available only for today
ham     I'm joking with you
spam    Free entry in 2 a wkly comp
ham     U dun say so early hor
ham     I don't think he goes to usf
spam    FreeMsg Hey there
ham     my brother is not sick
ham     As per your request Melle
spam    WINNER!! As a valued customer
```

LISTING 2.7: read_csv_file.py

```
import pandas as pd
import numpy as np

df = pd.read_csv('sometext.csv', delimiter='\t')

print("=> First five rows:")
print(df.head(5))
```

Listing 2.7 reads the contents of `sometext.csv`, whose columns are separated by a tab ("\t") delimiter. Launch the code in Listing 2.7 and you will see the following output:

```
=> First five rows:
   type                         text
0   ham     Available only for today
1   ham          I'm joking with you
2  spam  Free entry in 2 a wkly comp
3   ham       U dun say so early hor
4   ham I don't think he goes to usf
```

The default value for the `head()` method is 5, but you can display the first n rows of a data frame `df` with the code snippet `df.head(n)`.

You can also use the `sep` parameter specifies a different separator, and the `names` parameter specifies the column names in the data that you want to read, an example of which is here:

```
df2 = pd.read_csv("data.csv",sep="|",
          names=["Name","Surname","Height","Weight"])
```

Pandas also provides the `read_table()` method for reading the contents of CSV files, which uses the same syntax as the `read_csv()` method.

The `loc()` and `iloc()` Methods in Pandas

If you want to display the contents of a record in a data frame, specify the index of the row in the Pandas `loc()` method. For example, the following code snippet displays the data by feature name in a Data frame df:

```
df.loc[feature_name]
```

Select the first row of the "height" column in a Data frame:

```
df.loc([0], ['height'])
```

However, the following code snippet uses the `iloc()` function to display the first 8 records of the name column with this code snippet:

```
df.iloc[0:8]['name']
```

Converting Categorical Data to Numeric Data

One common task in machine learning involves converting a feature containing character data into a feature that contains numeric data. Listing 2.8 displays the contents of cat2numeric.py that illustrates how to replace a text field with a corresponding numeric field.

LISTING 2.8: *cat2numeric.py*

```
import pandas as pd
import numpy as np

df = pd.read_csv('sometext.csv', delimiter='\t')

print("=> First five rows (before):")
print(df.head(5))
print("------------------------")
print()

# map ham/spam to 0/1 values:
df['type'] = df['type'].map( {'ham':0 , 'spam':1} )

print("=> First five rows (after):")
print(df.head(5))
print("------------------------")
```

Listing 2.8 initializes the data frame `df` with the contents of the CSV file `sometext.csv`, and then displays the contents of the first five rows by invoking `df.head(5)`, which is also the default number of rows to display.

The next code snippet in Listing 2.8 invokes the `map()` method to replace occurrences of `ham` with 0 and replace occurrences of `spam` with 1 in the column labeled `type`, as shown here:

```
df['type'] = df['type'].map( {'ham':0 , 'spam':1} )
```

The last portion of Listing 2.8 invokes the `head()` method again to display the first five rows of the dataset after having renamed the contents of the column type. Launch the code in Listing 2.8 and you will see the following output:

```
=> First five rows (before):
   type                         text
0  ham       Available only for today
1  ham            I'm joking with you
2  spam  Free entry in 2 a wkly comp
3  ham         U dun say so early hor
4  ham   I don't think he goes to usf
------------------------

=> First five rows (after):
   type                         text
0     0     Available only for today
1     0          I'm joking with you
2     1  Free entry in 2 a wkly comp
3     0       U dun say so early hor
4     0  I don't think he goes to usf
------------------------
```

As another example, Listing 2.9 displays the contents of `shirts.csv` and Listing 2.10 displays the contents of `shirts.py` that illustrates four techniques for converting categorical data to numeric data.

LISTING 2.9: *shirts.csv*

```
type,ssize
shirt,xxlarge
shirt,xxlarge
shirt,xlarge
shirt,xlarge
shirt,xlarge
shirt,large
shirt,medium
shirt,small
shirt,small
```

```
shirt,xsmall
shirt,xsmall
shirt,xsmall
```

LISTING 2.10: shirts.py

```
import pandas as pd

shirts = pd.read_csv("shirts.csv")
print("shirts before:")
print(shirts)
print()

# TECHNIQUE #1:
#shirts.loc[shirts['ssize']=='xxlarge','size'] = 4
#shirts.loc[shirts['ssize']=='xlarge', 'size'] = 4
#shirts.loc[shirts['ssize']=='large',  'size'] = 3
#shirts.loc[shirts['ssize']=='medium', 'size'] = 2
#shirts.loc[shirts['ssize']=='small',  'size'] = 1
#shirts.loc[shirts['ssize']=='xsmall', 'size'] = 1

# TECHNIQUE #2:
#shirts['ssize'].replace('xxlarge', 4, inplace=True)
#shirts['ssize'].replace('xlarge',  4, inplace=True)
#shirts['ssize'].replace('large',   3, inplace=True)
#shirts['ssize'].replace('medium',  2, inplace=True)
#shirts['ssize'].replace('small',   1, inplace=True)
#shirts['ssize'].replace('xsmall',  1, inplace=True)

# TECHNIQUE #3:
#shirts['ssize'] = shirts['ssize'].apply({'xxlarge':4,
'xlarge':4, 'large':3, 'medium':2, 'small':1, 'xsmall':1}.get)

# TECHNIQUE #4:
shirts['ssize'] = shirts['ssize'].replace(regex='xlarge',
value=4)
shirts['ssize'] = shirts['ssize'].replace(regex='large',
value=3)
shirts['ssize'] = shirts['ssize'].replace(regex='medium',
value=2)
shirts['ssize'] = shirts['ssize'].replace(regex='small',
value=1)

print("shirts after:")
print(shirts)
```

Listing 2.10 starts with a code block of six statements that uses direct comparison with strings to make numeric replacements. For example, the following code snippet replaces all occurrences of the string xxlarge with the value 4:

```
shirts.loc[shirts['ssize']=='xxlarge','size'] = 4
```

The second code block consists of six statements that use the `replace()` method to perform the same updates, an example of which is shown here:

```
shirts['ssize'].replace('xxlarge', 4, inplace=True)
```

The third code block consists of a single statement that use the `apply()` method to perform the same updates, as shown here:

```
shirts['ssize'] = shirts['ssize'].apply({'xxlarge':4,
'xlarge':4, 'large':3, 'medium':2, 'small':1, 'xsmall':1}.get)
```

The fourth code block consists of four statements that use regular expressions to perform the same updates, an example of which is shown here:

```
shirts['ssize'] = shirts['ssize'].replace(regex='xlarge',
                                          value=4)
```

Since the preceding code snippet matches `xxlarge` as well as `xlarge`, we only need four statements instead of six statements. If you are unfamiliar with regular expressions, you can read Appendix C. Now launch the code in Listing 2.10 and you will see the following output:

```
shirts before
     type     size
0    shirt    xxlarge
1    shirt    xxlarge
2    shirt    xlarge
3    shirt    xlarge
4    shirt    xlarge
5    shirt    large
6    shirt    medium
7    shirt    small
8    shirt    small
9    shirt    xsmall
10   shirt    xsmall
11   shirt    xsmall

shirts after:
     type   size
0    shirt    4
1    shirt    4
2    shirt    4
3    shirt    4
4    shirt    4
5    shirt    3
6    shirt    2
7    shirt    1
8    shirt    1
9    shirt    1
10   shirt    1
11   shirt    1
```

Matching and Splitting Strings in Pandas

Listing 2.11 displays the contents of shirts_str.py that illustrates how to match a column value with an initial string and also how to split a column value based on a letter.

LISTING 2.11: shirts_str.py

```
import pandas as pd

shirts = pd.read_csv("shirts.csv")
print("shirts:")
print(shirts)
print()

print("shirts starting with xl:")
print(shirts[shirts.ssize.str.startswith('xl')])
print()

print("Exclude 'xlarge' shirts:")
print(shirts[shirts['ssize'] != 'xlarge'])
print()

print("first three letters:")
shirts['sub1'] = shirts['ssize'].str[:3]
print(shirts)
print()

print("split ssize on letter 'a':")
shirts['sub2'] = shirts['ssize'].str.split('a')
print(shirts)
print()

print("Rows 3 through 5 and column 2:")
print(shirts.iloc[2:5, 2])
print()
```

Listing 2.11 initializes the data frame df with the contents of the CSV file shirts.csv, and then displays the contents of df. The next code snippet in Listing 2.11 uses the startswith() method to match the shirt types that start with the letters xl, followed by a code snippet that displays the shorts whose size does not equal the string xlarge.

The next code snippet uses the construct str[:3] to display the first three letters of the shirt types, followed by a code snippet that uses the split() method to split the shirt types based on the letter "a."

The final code snippet invokes iloc[2:5,2] to display the contents of rows 3 through 5 inclusive, and only the second column. The output of

Listing 2.11 is here:
```
shirts:
     type    ssize
0    shirt   xxlarge
1    shirt   xxlarge
2    shirt   xlarge
3    shirt   xlarge
4    shirt   xlarge
5    shirt    large
6    shirt   medium
7    shirt    small
8    shirt    small
9    shirt   xsmall
10   shirt   xsmall
11   shirt   xsmall

shirts starting with xl:
     type   ssize
2    shirt  xlarge
3    shirt  xlarge
4    shirt  xlarge

Exclude 'xlarge' shirts:
     type    ssize
0    shirt   xxlarge
1    shirt   xxlarge
5    shirt    large
6    shirt   medium
7    shirt    small
8    shirt    small
9    shirt   xsmall
10   shirt   xsmall
11   shirt   xsmall

first three letters:
     type    ssize  sub1
0    shirt   xxlarge  xxl
1    shirt   xxlarge  xxl
2    shirt   xlarge   xla
3    shirt   xlarge   xla
4    shirt   xlarge   xla
5    shirt    large   lar
6    shirt   medium   med
7    shirt    small   sma
8    shirt    small   sma
9    shirt   xsmall   xsm
10   shirt   xsmall   xsm
11   shirt   xsmall   xsm

split ssize on letter 'a':
     type    ssize  sub1      sub2
0    shirt   xxlarge  xxl   [xxl, rge]
```

```
1     shirt    xxlarge    xxl    [xxl, rge]
2     shirt     xlarge    xla     [xl, rge]
3     shirt     xlarge    xla     [xl, rge]
4     shirt     xlarge    xla     [xl, rge]
5     shirt      large    lar      [l, rge]
6     shirt     medium    med      [medium]
7     shirt      small    sma      [sm, ll]
8     shirt      small    sma      [sm, ll]
9     shirt     xsmall    xsm     [xsm, ll]
10    shirt     xsmall    xsm     [xsm, ll]
11    shirt     xsmall    xsm     [xsm, ll]

Rows 3 through 5 and column 2:
2    xlarge
3    xlarge
4    xlarge
Name: ssize, dtype: object
```

Converting Strings to Dates in Pandas

Listing 2.12 displays the contents of string2date.py that illustrates how to convert strings to date formats.

LISTING 2.12: string2date.py

```
import pandas as pd

bdates1 = {'strdates':  ['20210413','20210813','20211225'],
           'people': ['Sally','Steve','Sarah']
          }

df1 = pd.DataFrame(bdates1, columns = ['strdates','people'])
df1['dates'] = pd.to_datetime(df1['strdates'],
format='%Y%m%d')
print("=> Contents of data frame df1:")
print(df1)
print()
print(df1.dtypes)
print()

bdates2 = {'strdates':  ['13Apr2021','08Aug2021','25Dec2021'],
           'people': ['Sally','Steve','Sarah']
          }

df2 = pd.DataFrame(bdates2, columns = ['strdates','people'])
df2['dates'] = pd.to_datetime(df2['strdates'],
format='%d%b%Y')
print("=> Contents of data frame df2:")
print(df2)
print()
```

```
print(df2.dtypes)
print()
```

Listing 2.12 initializes the data frame `df1` with the contents of `bdates1`, and then converts the `strdates` column to dates using the `'%Y%m%d'` format. The next portion of Listing 2.12 initializes the data frame `df2` with the contents of `bdates2`, and then converts the `strdates` column to dates using the `'%d%b%Y'` format. Now launch the code in Listing 2.12 and you will see the following output:

```
=> Contents of data frame df1:
   strdates people       dates
0  20210413  Sally  2021-04-13
1  20210813  Steve  2021-08-13
2  20211225  Sarah  2021-12-25

strdates            object
people              object
dates       datetime64[ns]
dtype: object

=> Contents of data frame df2:
   strdates people       dates
0  13Apr2021  Sally  2021-04-13
1  08Aug2021  Steve  2021-08-08
2  25Dec2021  Sarah  2021-12-25

strdates            object
people              object
dates       datetime64[ns]
dtype: object
```

Merging and Splitting Columns in Pandas

Listing 2.13 displays the contents of `employees.csv` and Listing 2.14 displays the contents of `emp_merge_split.py` that illustrates how to merge columns and split columns of a CSV file.

LISTING 2.13: *employees.csv*

```
name,year,month
Jane-Smith,2015,Aug
Dave-Smith,2020,Jan
Jane-Jones,2018,Dec
Jane-Stone,2017,Feb
Dave-Stone,2014,Apr
Mark-Aster,,Oct
Jane-Jones,NaN,Jun
```

LISTING 2.14: emp_merge_split.py

```
import pandas as pd

emps = pd.read_csv("employees.csv")
print("emps:")
print(emps)
print()

emps['year']  = emps['year'].astype(str)
emps['month'] = emps['month'].astype(str)

# separate column for first name and for last name:
emps['fname'],emps['lname'] = emps['name'].str.split("-",1).str

# concatenate year and month with a "#" symbol:
emps['hdate1'] = emps['year'].astype(str)+"#"+emps['month'].
astype(str)

# concatenate year and month with a "-" symbol:
emps['hdate2'] = emps[['year','month']].agg('-'.join, axis=1)

print(emps)
print()
```

Listing 2.14 initializes the data frame df with the contents of the CSV file employees.csv, and then displays the contents of df. The next pair of code snippets invoke the astype() method to convert the contents of the year and month columns to strings.

The next code snippet in Listing 2.14 uses the split() method to split the name column into the columns fname and lname that contain the first name and last name, respectively, of each employee's name:

```
emps['fname'],emps['lname'] = emps['name'].str.
split("-",1).str
```

The next code snippet concatenates the contents of the year and month string with a "#" character to create a new column called hdate1, as shown here:

```
emps['hdate1'] = emps['year'].
astype(str)+"#"+emps['month'].astype(str)
```

The final code snippet concatenates the contents of the year and month string with a "-" to create a new column called hdate2, as shown here:

```
emps['hdate2'] = emps[['year','month']].agg('-'.join, axis=1)
Now launch the code in Listing 2.14 and you will see the
following output:
```

```
emps:
           name     year  month
0    Jane-Smith   2015.0    Aug
1    Dave-Smith   2020.0    Jan
2    Jane-Jones   2018.0    Dec
3    Jane-Stone   2017.0    Feb
4    Dave-Stone   2014.0    Apr
5    Mark-Aster      NaN    Oct
6    Jane-Jones      NaN    Jun

           name     year  month  fname  lname      hdate1      hdate2
0    Jane-Smith   2015.0    Aug   Jane  Smith  2015.0#Aug  2015.0-Aug
1    Dave-Smith   2020.0    Jan   Dave  Smith  2020.0#Jan  2020.0-Jan
2    Jane-Jones   2018.0    Dec   Jane  Jones  2018.0#Dec  2018.0-Dec
3    Jane-Stone   2017.0    Feb   Jane  Stone  2017.0#Feb  2017.0-Feb
4    Dave-Stone   2014.0    Apr   Dave  Stone  2014.0#Apr  2014.0-Apr
5    Mark-Aster      nan    Oct   Mark  Aster     nan#Oct     nan-Oct
6    Jane-Jones      nan    Jun   Jane  Jones     nan#Jun     nan-Jun
```

One other detail regarding the following commented out code snippet:

```
#emps['fname'],emps['lname'] = emps['name'].str.split("-",1).str
```

The following deprecation message is displayed if you uncomment the preceding code snippet:

```
#FutureWarning: Columnar iteration over characters
#will be deprecated in future releases.
```

Combining Pandas `Data frames`

`Pandas` supports the `concat()` method in `Pandas` in order to concatenate `Data frames`. Listing 2.15 displays the contents of `concat_frames.py` that illustrates how to combine two `Pandas Data frames`.

LISTING 2.15: concat_frames.py

```
import pandas as pd

can_weather = pd.DataFrame({
   "city": ["Vancouver","Toronto","Montreal"],
   "temperature": [72,65,50],
   "humidity": [40, 20, 25]
})

us_weather = pd.DataFrame({
   "city": ["SF","Chicago","LA"],
   "temperature": [60,40,85],
   "humidity": [30, 15, 55]
})
```

```
df = pd.concat([can_weather, us_weather])
print(df)
```

The first line in Listing 2.15 is an `import` statement, followed by the definition of the `Pandas` data frames `can_weather` and `us_weather` that contain weather-related information for cities in Canada and the United States, respectively. The `Pandas` data frame `df` is the vertical concatenation of `can_weather` and `us_weather`. The output from Listing 2.15 is here:

```
0    Vancouver        40              72
1      Toronto        20              65
2     Montreal        25              50
0           SF        30              60
1      Chicago        15              40
2           LA        55              85
```

Data Manipulation with Pandas Data Frames (1)

As a simple example, suppose that we have a two-person company that keeps track of income and expenses on a quarterly basis, and we want to calculate the profit/loss for each quarter, and also the overall profit/loss.

Listing 2.16 displays the contents of `pandas_quarterly_df1.py` that illustrates how to define a `Pandas` data frame consisting of income-related values.

LISTING 2.16: pandas_quarterly_df1.py

```
import pandas as pd

summary = {
   'Quarter': ['Q1', 'Q2', 'Q3', 'Q4'],
   'Cost':    [23500, 34000, 57000, 32000],
   'Revenue': [40000, 40000, 40000, 40000]
}

df = pd.DataFrame(summary)

print("Entire Dataset:\n",df)
print("Quarter:\n",df.Quarter)
print("Cost:\n",df.Cost)
print("Revenue:\n",df.Revenue)
```

Listing 2.16 defines the variable `summary` that contains hard-coded quarterly information about cost and revenue for our two-person company. In general these hard-coded values would be replaced by data from another source (such as a CSV file), so think of this code sample as a simple way to illustrate some of the functionality that is available in `Pandas` data frames.

The variable `df` is a `Pandas Data frame` based on the data in the `summary` variable. The three `print` statements display the quarters, the cost per quarter, and the revenue per quarter. The output from Listing 2.16 is here:

```
Entire Dataset:
    Cost Quarter  Revenue
0  23500      Q1    40000
1  34000      Q2    60000
2  57000      Q3    50000
3  32000      Q4    30000

Quarter:
0    Q1
1    Q2
2    Q3
3    Q4
Name: Quarter, dtype: object

Cost:
0    23500
1    34000
2    57000
3    32000
Name: Cost, dtype: int64

Revenue:
0    40000
1    60000
2    50000
3    30000
Name: Revenue, dtype: int64
```

Data Manipulation with Pandas Data Frames (2)

In this section, let's suppose that we have a two-person company that keeps track of income and expenses on a quarterly basis, and we want to calculate the profit/loss for each quarter, and also the overall profit/loss.

Listing 2.17 displays the contents of `pandas_quarterly_df2.py` that illustrates how to define a `Pandas` data frame consisting of income-related values.

LISTING 2.17: pandas_quarterly_df2.py

```
import pandas as pd

summary = {
    'Quarter': ['Q1', 'Q2', 'Q3', 'Q4'],
```

```
   'Cost':    [-23500, -34000, -57000, -32000],
   'Revenue': [40000, 40000, 40000, 40000]
}

df = pd.DataFrame(summary)
print("First Dataset:\n",df)

df['Total'] = df.sum(axis=1)
print("Second Dataset:\n",df)
```

Listing 2.17 defines the variable `summary` that contains quarterly information about cost and revenue for our two-person company. The variable `df` is a `Pandas` data frame based on the data in the `summary` variable. The three `print()` statements display the quarters, the cost per quarter, and the revenue per quarter. The output from Listing 2.17 is here:

```
First Dataset:
    Cost  Quarter  Revenue
0 -23500       Q1    40000
1 -34000       Q2    60000
2 -57000       Q3    50000
3 -32000       Q4    30000
Second Dataset:
    Cost  Quarter  Revenue  Total
0 -23500       Q1    40000  16500
1 -34000       Q2    60000  26000
2 -57000       Q3    50000  -7000
3 -32000       Q4    30000  -2000
```

Data Manipulation with Pandas Data Frames (3)

Let's start with the same assumption as the previous section: we have a two-person company that keeps track of income and expenses on a quarterly basis, and we want to calculate the profit/loss for each quarter, and also the overall profit/loss. In addition, we want to compute column totals and row totals.

Listing 2.18 displays the contents of `pandas_quarterly_df3.py` that illustrates how to define a `Pandas` data frame consisting of income-related values.

LISTING 2.18: pandas_quarterly_df3.py

```
import pandas as pd

summary = {
   'Quarter': ['Q1', 'Q2', 'Q3', 'Q4'],
   'Cost':    [_23500, _34000, _57000, _32000],
```

```
    'Revenue': [40000, 40000, 40000, 40000]
}

df = pd.DataFrame(summary)
print("First Dataset:\n",df)

df['Total'] = df.sum(axis=1)
df.loc['Sum'] = df.sum()
print("Second Dataset:\n",df)

# or df.loc['avg'] / 3
#df.loc['avg'] = df[:3].mean()
#print("Third Dataset:\n",df)
```

Listing 2.18 defines the variable `summary` that contains quarterly information about cost and revenue for our two-person company. The variable `df` is a `Pandas` data frame based on the data in the `summary` variable. The three `print()` statements display the quarters, the cost per quarter, and the revenue per quarter. The output from Listing 2.18 is here:

```
First Dataset:
     Cost    Quarter  Revenue
0  -23500       Q1     40000
1  -34000       Q2     60000
2  -57000       Q3     50000
3  -32000       Q4     30000

Second Dataset:
       Cost    Quarter  Revenue  Total
0    -23500       Q1     40000  16500
1    -34000       Q2     60000  26000
2    -57000       Q3     50000  -7000
3    -32000       Q4     30000  -2000
Sum -146500   Q1Q2Q3Q4  180000  33500
```

Pandas Data Frames and CSV Files

The code samples in several earlier sections contain hard-coded data inside the Python scripts. However, it's also very common to read data from a CSV file. You can use the Python `csv.reader()` function, the `NumPy` `loadtxt()` function, or the `Pandas` function `read_csv()` function (shown in this section) to read the contents of CSV files.

Listing 2.19 displays the contents of `weather_data.py` that illustrates how to read a CSV file, initialize a `Pandas` data frame with the contents of that CSV file, and display various subsets of the data in the `Pandas` data frames.

LISTING 2.19: weather_data.py

```
import pandas as pd

df = pd.read_csv("weather_data.csv")

print(df)
print(df.shape)   # rows, columns
print(df.head())  # df.head(3)
print(df.tail())
print(df[1:3])
print(df.columns)
print(type(df['day']))
print(df[['day','temperature']])
print(df['temperature'].max())
```

Listing 2.19 invokes the `Pandas read_csv()` function to read the contents of the CSV file `weather_data.csv`, followed by a set of `Python print()` statements that display various portions of the CSV file. The output from Listing 2.19 is here:

```
day,temperature,windspeed,event
7/1/2018,42,16,Rain
7/2/2018,45,3,Sunny
7/3/2018,78,12,Snow
7/4/2018,74,9,Snow
7/5/2018,42,24,Rain
7/6/2018,51,32,Sunny
```

In some situations you might need to apply `Boolean` conditional logic to "filter out" some rows of data, based on a condition that's applied to a column value.

Listing 2.20 displays the contents of the CSV file `people.csv` and Listing 2.21 displays the contents of `people_pandas.py` that illustrates how to define a `Pandas` data frame that reads the CSV file and manipulates the data.

LISTING 2.20: people.csv

```
fname,lname,age,gender,country
john,smith,30,m,usa
jane,smith,31,f,france
jack,jones,32,m,france
dave,stone,33,m,italy
sara,stein,34,f,germany
eddy,bower,35,m,spain
```

LISTING 2.21: people_pandas.py

```
import pandas as pd

df = pd.read_csv('people.csv')
df.info()
print('fname:')
print(df['fname'])
print('_____')
print('age over 33:')
print(df['age'] > 33)
print('_____')
print('age over 33:')
myfilter = df['age'] > 33
print(df[myfilter])
```

Listing 2.21 populate the `Pandas` data frame `df` with the contents of the CSV file `people.csv`. The next portion of Listing 2.21 displays the structure of `df`, followed by the first names of all the people.

Next, Listing 2.21 displays a tabular list of six rows containing either True or False depending on whether a person is over 33 or at most 33, respectively. The final portion of Listing 2.21 displays a tabular list of two rows containing all the details of the people who are over 33. The output from Listing 2.21 is here:

```
myfilter = df['age'] > 33
<class 'pandas.core.frame.Data frame'>
RangeIndex: 6 entries, 0 to 5
Data columns (total 5 columns):
fname      6 non_null object
lname      6 non_null object
age        6 non_null int64
gender     6 non_null object
country    6 non_null object
dtypes: int64(1), object(4)
memory usage: 320.0+ bytes

fname:
0     john
1     jane
2     jack
3     dave
4     sara
5     eddy
Name: fname, dtype: object
_____
age over 33:
0     False
1     False
2     False
```

```
3    False
4    True
5    True
Name: age, dtype: bool
```

```
age over 33:
  fname  lname  age gender country
4  sara  stein   34      f  france
5  eddy  bower   35      m  france
```

Managing Columns in Data Frames

This section contains various subsections with short code blocks that illustrate how to perform column-based operations on a data frame, which resemble the operations on a `Python` dictionary.

For example, the following code snippet illustrates how to define a `Pandas` data frame whose data values are from a `Python` dictionary:

```
df = pd.DataFrame.from_dict(dict([('A',[1,2,3]),
('B',[4,5,6])]),
             orient='index', columns=['one', 'two', 'three'])
print(df)
```

The output from the preceding code snippet is here:

```
   one  two  three
A    1    2      3
B    4    5      6
```

Switching Columns

The following code snippet defines a `Pandas` data frame and then switches the order of the columns:

```
df = pd.DataFrame.from_dict(dict([('A',[1,2,3]),
('B',[4,5,6])]),
             orient='index', columns=['one', 'two', 'three'])

print("initial data frame:")
print(df)
print()

switched = ['three','one','two']
df=df.reindex(columns=switched)
print("switched columns:")
print(df)
print()
```

The output from the preceding code block is here:
```
initial data frame:
   one  two  three
A   1    2     3
B   4    5     6

switched columns:
   three  one  two
A    3     1    2
B    6     4    5
```

Appending Columns

The following code snippet computes the product of two columns and appends the result as a new column to the contents of the data frame `df`:

```
df['four'] = df['one'] * df['two']
print(df)
```

The output from the preceding code block is here:

```
   one  two  three  four
A   1    2     3     2
B   4    5     6    20
```

The following operation squares the contents of a column in the data frame `df`:

```
df['three'] = df['two'] * df['two']
print(df)
```

The output from the preceding code block is here (notice the numbers shown in bold):

```
   one  two  three  four
A   1    2     4     2
B   4    5    25    20
```

The following operation appends a new column called `flag` that contains True or False, based on whether or not the numeric value in the "one" column is greater than 2:

```
import numpy as np
rand = np.random.randn(2)
df.insert(1, 'random', rand)
print(df)
```

The output from the preceding code block is here:

```
   one   random   two  three  four  flag
A   1  -1.703111   2     4     2   False
B   4   1.139189   5    25    20   True
```

Deleting Columns

Columns can be deleted, as shown in the following code snippet that deletes the "two" column:

```
del df['two']
print(df)
```

The output from the preceding code block is here:

```
   one    random  three  four   flag
A  1     -0.460401    4     2  False
B  4      1.211468   25    20   True
```

Columns can be removed, as shown in the following code snippet that deletes the "three" column:

```
three = df.pop('three')
print(df)
```

```
   one    random  four   flag
A  1     -0.544829    2  False
B  4      0.581476   20   True
```

Inserting Columns

Keep in mind that when inserting a scalar value, it will be propagated to fill the column:

```
df['foo'] = 'bar'
print(df)
```

The output from the preceding code snippet is here:

```
   one    random  four   flag  foo
A  1     -0.187331    2  False  bar
B  4     -0.169672   20   True  bar
```

When inserting a Series that does not have the same index as the data frame, it will be "conformed" to the index of the Data frame:

```
df['one_trunc'] = df['one'][:1]
print(df)
```

The output from the preceding code snippet is here:

```
   one    random  four   flag  foo  one_trunc
A  1      0.616572    2  False  bar        1.0
B  4     -0.802656   20   True  bar        NaN
```

You can insert raw ndarrays but their length must match the length of the index of the data frame.

The following operation inserts a column of random numbers in index position 1 (which is the second column) in the data frame `df`:

```
import numpy as np
rand = np.random.randn(2)
df.insert(1, 'random', rand)
print(df)
```

The output from the preceding code block is here:

```
   one    random  two  three  four
A    1 -1.703111    2      4     2
B    4  1.139189    5     25    20
```

Scaling Numeric Columns

`Pandas` makes it easy to scale the values in numeric columns. As you will see in the code sample in this section, the value in every numeric column of the first row is assigned the value of 1, and the remaining column values are scaled accordingly. Note that values are scaled on a column-by-column basis, which is to say, the columns are treated independently of each other.

Listing 2.22 displays the contents of `numbers.csv` and Listing 2.23 displays the contents of `scale_columns.py` that illustrates how to scale the values in numeric columns.

LISTING 2.22: numbers.csv

```
qtr1,qtr2,qtr3,qtr4
100,330,445,8000
200,530,145,3000
2000,1530,4145,5200
900,100,280,2000
```

LISTING 2.23: scale_columns.py

```
import pandas as pd

filename="numbers.csv"

# read CSV file and display its contents:
df = pd.read_table(filename,delimiter=',')
print("=> contents of df:")
print(df)
print()

print("=> df.iloc[0]:")
print(df.iloc[0])
print()

df2 = df # save the data frame
```

```
# df/df.iloc[0] scales the columns:
df = df/df.iloc[0]
print("=> contents of df:")
print(df)
print()

# df2/df2['qtr1'].iloc[0] scales column qtr1:
df2['qtr1'] = df2['qtr1']/(df2['qtr1']).iloc[0]
print("=> contents of df2:")
print(df2)
print()
```

Listing 2.23 initializes the variable df as a Pandas data frame with the contents of the CSV file numbers.csv. Next, a print() statement displays the contents of df, followed by the contents of the column whose index is 0.

Next, the data frame df2 is initialized as a copy of df, followed by a division operation in df whereby the elements of every row are divided by their counterparts in df.iloc[0]. The final code block in Listing 2.23 updates the first column of df2 (which is a copy of the original contents of df) by an operation that effectively involves division by 100. Now launch the code in Listing 2.23 and you will see the following output:

```
=> contents of df:
   qtr1  qtr2  qtr3  qtr4
0   100   330   445  8000
1   200   530   145  3000
2  2000  1530  4145  5200
3   900   100   280  2000

=> df.iloc[0]:
qtr1     100
qtr2     330
qtr3     445
qtr4    8000
Name: 0, dtype: int64

=> contents of df:
   qtr1      qtr2      qtr3   qtr4
0   1.0  1.000000  1.000000  1.000
1   2.0  1.606061  0.325843  0.375
2  20.0  4.636364  9.314607  0.650
3   9.0  0.303030  0.629213  0.250

=> contents of df2:
   qtr1  qtr2  qtr3  qtr4
0   1.0   330   445  8000
1   2.0   530   145  3000
2  20.0  1530  4145  5200
3   9.0   100   280  2000
```

Keep in mind that the preceding code will result in an error if the CSV file contains any nonnumeric columns. However, in the latter case, you can specify the list of numeric columns whose values are to be scaled, an example of which is shown in the final code block in Listing 2.23.

Managing Rows in Pandas

`Pandas` supports various row-related operations, such as finding duplicate rows, selecting a range of rows, deleting rows, and inserting new rows. The following subsections contain code sample that illustrate how to perform these operations.

Selecting a Range of Rows in Pandas

Listing 2.24 displays the contents of `duplicates.csv` and Listing 2.25 displays the contents of `row_range.py` that illustrates how to select a range of rows in a `Pandas` data frame.

LISTING 2.24: duplicates.csv

```
fname,lname,level,dept,state
Jane,Smith,Senior,Sales,California
Dave,Smith,Senior,Devel,California
Jane,Jones,Year1,Mrktg,Illinois
Jane,Jones,Year1,Mrktg,Illinois
Jane,Stone,Senior,Mrktg,Arizona
Dave,Stone,Year2,Devel,Arizona
Mark,Aster,Year3,BizDev,Florida
Jane,Jones,Year1,Mrktg,Illinois
```

LISTING 2.25: row_range.py

```
import pandas as pd

df = pd.read_csv("duplicates.csv")

print("=> contents of CSV file:")
print(df)
print()

print("=> Rows 4 through 7 (loc):")
print(df.loc[4:7,:])
print()

print("=> Rows 4 through 6 (iloc):")
print(df.iloc[4:7,:])
print()
```

Listing 2.25 initializes the data frame df with the contents of the CSV file duplicates.csv, and then displays the contents of df. The next portion of Listing 2.25 displays the contents of rows 4 through 7, followed by the contents of rows 4 through 6. Now launch the code in Listing 2.25 and you will see the following output:

```
=> contents of CSV file:
  fname  lname  level   dept       state
0 Jane   Smith  Senior  Sales    California
1 Dave   Smith  Senior  Devel    California
2 Jane   Jones  Year1   Mrktg      Illinois
3 Jane   Jones  Year1   Mrktg      Illinois
4 Jane   Stone  Senior  Mrktg       Arizona
5 Dave   Stone  Year2   Devel       Arizona
6 Mark   Aster  Year3   BizDev      Florida
7 Jane   Jones  Year1   Mrktg      Illinois

=> Rows 4 through 7 (loc):
  fname  lname  level   dept      state
4 Jane   Stone  Senior  Mrktg    Arizona
5 Dave   Stone  Year2   Devel    Arizona
6 Mark   Aster  Year3   BizDev   Florida
7 Jane   Jones  Year1   Mrktg    Illinois

=> Rows 4 through 6 (iloc):
  fname  lname  level   dept      state
4 Jane   Stone  Senior  Mrktg    Arizona
5 Dave   Stone  Year2   Devel    Arizona
6 Mark   Aster  Year3   BizDev   Florida
```

Finding Duplicate Rows in Pandas

Listing 2.26 displays the contents of duplicates.py that illustrates how to find duplicate rows in a Pandas data frame.

LISTING 2.26: duplicates.py

```
import pandas as pd

df = pd.read_csv("duplicates.csv")
print("Contents of data frame:")
print(df)
print()

print("Duplicate rows:")
#df2 = df.duplicated(subset=None)
df2 = df.duplicated(subset=None, keep='first')
print(df2)
print()
```

```
print("Duplicate first names:")
df3 = df[df.duplicated(['fname'])]
print(df3)
print()

print("Duplicate first name and level:")
df3 = df[df.duplicated(['fname','level'])]
print(df3)
print()
```

Listing 2.26 initializes the data frame `df` with the contents of the CSV file `duplicates.csv`, and then displays the contents of `df`. The next portion of Listing 2.26 displays the duplicate rows by invoking the `duplicated()` method, whereas the next portion of Listing 2.26 displays only the first name `fname` of the duplicate rows.

The final portion of Listing 2.26 displays the first name `fname` as well as the level of the duplicate rows. Launch the code in Listing 2.26 and you will see the following output:

```
Contents of data frame:
  fname  lname   level   dept      state
0  Jane  Smith  Senior   Sales  California
1  Dave  Smith  Senior   Devel  California
2  Jane  Jones   Year1   Mrktg    Illinois
3  Jane  Jones   Year1   Mrktg    Illinois
4  Jane  Stone  Senior   Mrktg     Arizona
5  Dave  Stone   Year2   Devel     Arizona
6  Mark  Aster   Year3  BizDev     Florida
7  Jane  Jones   Year1   Mrktg    Illinois

Duplicate rows:
0    False
1    False
2    False
3     True
4    False
5    False
6    False
7     True
dtype: bool

Duplicate first names:
  fname  lname   level   dept     state
2  Jane  Jones   Year1  Mrktg  Illinois
3  Jane  Jones   Year1  Mrktg  Illinois
4  Jane  Stone  Senior  Mrktg   Arizona
5  Dave  Stone   Year2  Devel   Arizona
7  Jane  Jones   Year1  Mrktg  Illinois
```

```
Duplicate first name and level:
  fname  lname  level   dept    state
3 Jane   Jones  Year1   Mrktg   Illinois
4 Jane   Stone  Senior  Mrktg   Arizona
7 Jane   Jones  Year1   Mrktg   Illinois
```

Listing 2.27 displays the contents of drop_duplicates.py that illustrates how to remove duplicate rows in a Pandas data frame.

LISTING 2.27: drop_duplicates.py

```
import pandas as pd

df = pd.read_csv("duplicates.csv")
print("Contents of data frame:")
print(df)
print()

print("=> number of duplicate rows:", df.duplicated().sum())
print()

print("=> row number(s) of duplicate rows:")
print(np.where(df.duplicated() == True)[0])
print()

fname_filtered = df.drop_duplicates(['fname'])
print("Drop duplicate first names:")
print(fname_filtered)
print()

fname_lname_filtered = df.drop_duplicates(['fname','lname'])
print("Drop duplicate first and last names:")
print(fname_lname_filtered)
print()
```

Listing 2.27 initializes the data frame df with the contents of the CSV file duplicates.csv, and then displays the contents of df. The next portion of Listing 2.27 deletes the rows that have duplicate fname values, followed by a code block that drops rows with duplicate fname and lname values. Launch the code in Listing 2.27 and you will see the following output:

```
Contents of data frame:
  fname  lname   level   dept     state
0 Jane   Smith   Senior  Sales    California
1 Dave   Smith   Senior  Devel    California
2 Jane   Jones   Year1   Mrktg    Illinois
3 Jane   Jones   Year1   Mrktg    Illinois
4 Jane   Stone   Senior  Mrktg    Arizona
5 Dave   Stone   Year2   Devel    Arizona
6 Mark   Aster   Year3   BizDev   Florida
7 Jane   Jones   Year1   Mrktg    Illinois
```

```
=> number of duplicate rows: 2

=> row number(s) of duplicate rows:
[3 7]


Drop duplicate first names:
  fname  lname   level    dept       state
0  Jane  Smith  Senior   Sales  California
1  Dave  Smith  Senior   Devel  California
6  Mark  Aster   Year3  BizDev     Florida

Drop duplicate first and last names:
  fname  lname   level    dept       state
0  Jane  Smith  Senior   Sales  California
1  Dave  Smith  Senior   Devel  California
2  Jane  Jones   Year1   Mrktg    Illinois
4  Jane  Stone  Senior   Mrktg     Arizona
5  Dave  Stone   Year2   Devel     Arizona
6  Mark  Aster   Year3  BizDev     Florida
```

Inserting New Rows in Pandas

Listing 2.28 displays the contents of `emp_ages.csv` and Listing 2.29 displays the contents of `insert_row.py` that illustrates how to insert a new row in a `Pandas` data frame.

LISTING 2.28: emp_ages.csv

```
fname,lname,age
Jane,Smith,32
Dave,Smith,10
Jane,Jones,65
Jane,Jones,65
Jane,Stone,25
Dave,Stone,45
Mark,Aster,53
Jane,Jones,58
```

LISTING 2.29: insert_row.py

```python
import pandas as pd

filename="emp_ages.csv"
df = pd.read_table(filename,delimiter=',')

new_row = pd.DataFrame({'fname':'New','lname':'Person','age':7
77},index=[0])
df = pd.concat([new_row, df]).reset_index(drop = True)

print("insert new first row in df:")
```

```
print(df.head(3))
print()
```

Listing 2.29 contains an `import` statement and then initializes the variable `df` with the contents of the CSV file `emp_ages.csv`. The next code snippet defines the variable `new_row` whose contents are compatible with the structure of `df`, and then appends the contents of `new_row` to the Pandas data frame `df`. Now launch the code in Listing 2.29 and you will see the following output:

```
    fname   lname  age
0   New     Person 777
1   Jane    Smith   32
2   Dave    Smith   10
```

Handling Missing Data in Pandas

Listing 2.30 displays the contents of `employees2.csv` and Listing 2.31 displays the contents of `dup_missing.py` that illustrates how to find duplicate rows and missing values in a `Pandas` data frame.

LISTING 2.30: employees2.csv

```
name,year,month
Jane-Smith,2015,Aug
Jane-Smith,2015,Aug
Dave-Smith,2020,
Dave-Stone,,Apr
Jane-Jones,2018,Dec
Jane-Stone,2017,Feb
Jane-Stone,2017,Feb
Mark-Aster,,Oct
Jane-Jones,NaN,Jun
```

LISTING 2.31: missing_values.py

```
import pandas as pd
import matplotlib.pyplot as plt
import numpy as np
import seaborn as sns

# the meaning of two strings:
#NA:  Not Available (Pandas)
#NaN: Not a Number (Pandas)
#NB:  NumPy uses np.nan() to check for NaN values

df = pd.read_csv("employees2.csv")

print("=> contents of CSV file:")
```

```
print(df)
print()

print("=> any NULL values per column?")
print(df.isnull().any())
print()

print("=> count of NAN/MISSING values in each column:")
print(df.isnull().sum())
print()

print("=> count of NAN/MISSING values in each column:")
print(pd.isna(df).sum())
print()

print("=> count of NAN/MISSING values in each column
(sorted):")
print(df.isnull().sum().sort_values(ascending=False))
print()

nan_null = df.isnull().sum().sum()
miss_values = df.isnull().any().sum()

print("=> count of NaN/MISSING values:",nan_null)
print("=> count of MISSING values:",miss_values)
print("=> count of NaN values:",nan_null-miss_values)
```

Listing 2.31 initializes the data frame `df` with the contents of the CSV file `employees2.csv`, and then displays the contents of `df`. The next portion of Listing 2.31 displays the number of null values that appear in any row or column. The next portion of Listing 2.31 displays the fields and the names of the fields that have null values, which are the `year` and `month` columns of the CSV file.

The next two code blocks of Listing 2.31 display the number of `NaN` values in the data frame using the method `df.isnull().sum()` and `pd.isna(df).sum()`, respectively (the result is the same).

The final portion of Listing 2.21 initializes the variables `nan_null` and `miss_values` that are 4 and 2, respectively, and then displays their values as well as the differences of their values. Now launch the code in Listing 2.31 and you will see the following output:

```
=> contents of CSV file:
         name     year  month
0   Jane-Smith  2015.0    Aug
1   Jane-Smith  2015.0    Aug
2   Dave-Smith  2020.0    NaN
3   Dave-Stone     NaN    Apr
4   Jane-Jones  2018.0    Dec
5   Jane-Stone  2017.0    Feb
```

```
6    Jane-Stone   2017.0   Feb
7    Mark-Aster      NaN   Oct
8    Jane-Jones      NaN   Jun
```

```
=> any NULL values per column?
name     False
year      True
month     True
dtype: bool

=> count of NAN/MISSING values in each column:
name     0
year     3
month    1
dtype: int64

=> count of NAN/MISSING values in each column:
name     0
year     3
month    1
dtype: int64

=> count of NAN/MISSING values in each column (sorted):
year     3
month    1
name     0
dtype: int64

=> count of NaN/MISSING values: 4
=> count of MISSING values: 2
=> count of NaN values: 2
```

Multiple Types of Missing Values

Listing 2.32 displays the contents of `employees3.csv` that contains multiple types of missing values, and Listing 2.33 displays the contents of the Python file `missing_multiple_types.py` that illustrates how to specify multiple missing value types when reading `employees3.csv` into a Pandas data frame.

LISTING 2.32: *employees3.csv*

```
name,year,month
Jane-Smith,2015,Aug
Dave-Smith,2020,NaN
Dave-Stone,?,Apr
Jane-Jones,2018,Dec
Jane-Stone,2017,Feb
Jane-Stone,2017,Feb
Mark-Aster,na,Oct
Jane-Jones,!,Jun
```

LISTING 2.33: missing_multiple_types.py

```
import pandas as pd

missing_values = ["na", "?", "!", "NaN"]
df = pd.read_csv("employees3.csv", na_values = missing_ values)

print("=> contents of CSV file:")
print(df)
print()
```

Listing 2.33 is almost the same as previous examples. The only difference is shown in the pair of code snippets (shown in bold) that illustrates how to specify multiple missing value types.

Test for Numeric Values in a Column

Listing 2.34 displays the contents of `test_for_numeric.py` that illustrates how to check if a value in a row is numeric.

Listing 2.34: test_for_numeric.py
```
import pandas as pd
import numpy as np

missing_values = ["na", "?", "!", "NaN"]
df = pd.read_csv("employees3.csv", na_values = missing_values)

print("=> contents of CSV file:")
print(df)
print()

count = 0
for row in df['year']:
 try:
   int(row)
   df.loc[count," "] = np.nan
 except ValueError:
   count += 1

print("non-numeric count:",count)
```

Now launch the code in Listing 2.34 and you will see the following output:

```
=> contents of CSV file:
        name      year  month
0  Jane-Smith   2015.0   Aug
1  Jane-Smith   2015.0   Aug
2  Dave-Smith   2020.0   NaN
3  Dave-Stone      NaN   Apr
4  Jane-Jones   2018.0   Dec
5  Jane-Stone   2017.0   Feb
6  Jane-Stone   2017.0   Feb
```

```
7  Mark-Aster    NaN   Oct
8  Jane-Jones    NaN   Jun

non-numeric count: 3
```

Replacing NaN Values in Pandas

Listing 2.35 displays the contents of `missing_fill_drop.py` that illustrates how to replace missing values in a Pandas data frame.

LISTING 2.35: missing_fill_drop.py

```
import pandas as pd

df = pd.read_csv("employees2.csv")

print("=> contents of CSV file:")
print(df)
print()

print("Check for NANs:")
print(pd.isna(df))
print()

print("Drop missing data:")
df2 = df.dropna(axis=0, how='any')
print(df2)
print()

print("Replace missing data:")
print(df.fillna(7777))
print()
```

Listing 2.35 initializes the data frame `df` with the contents of the CSV file `employees2.csv`, and then displays the contents of `df`. The next portion of Listing 2.35 checks for `NaN` values and displays a tabular result in which each cell is either False or True depending on whether the respective entry is `NaN` or not `NaN`, respectively.

The next code snippet initializes the data frame `df2` with the contents of `df`, and then drops all rows in `df2` that contain a `NaN` value. The final code snippet in Listing 2.35 replaces all occurrences of `NaN` with the value 7777 (there is nothing special about this value: it's simply for the purpose of demonstration).

Now launch the code in Listing 2.35 and you will see the following output:

```
=> contents of CSV file:
       name       year   month
0  Jane-Smith    2015.0   Aug
```

```
1  Jane-Smith  2015.0  Aug
2  Dave-Smith  2020.0  NaN
3  Dave-Stone     NaN  Apr
4  Jane-Jones  2018.0  Dec
5  Jane-Stone  2017.0  Feb
6  Jane-Stone  2017.0  Feb
7  Mark-Aster     NaN  Oct
8  Jane-Jones     NaN  Jun

=> Check for NANs:
   name   year   month
0  False  False  False
1  False  False  False
2  False  False  True
3  False  True   False
4  False  False  False
5  False  False  False
6  False  False  False
7  False  True   False
8  False  True   False

=> Drop missing data:
        name     year  month
0  Jane-Smith  2015.0  Aug
1  Jane-Smith  2015.0  Aug
4  Jane-Jones  2018.0  Dec
5  Jane-Stone  2017.0  Feb
6  Jane-Stone  2017.0  Feb

=> Replace missing data:
        name     year  month
0  Jane-Smith  2015.0  Aug
1  Jane-Smith  2015.0  Aug
2  Dave-Smith  2020.0  7777
3  Dave-Stone  7777.0  Apr
4  Jane-Jones  2018.0  Dec
5  Jane-Stone  2017.0  Feb
6  Jane-Stone  2017.0  Feb
7  Mark-Aster  7777.0  Oct
8  Jane-Jones  7777.0  Jun
```

Sorting Data Frames in Pandas

Listing 2.36 displays the contents of `sort_df.py` that illustrates how to sort the rows in a `Pandas` data frame.

LISTING 2.36: sort_df.py

```
import pandas as pd
```

Introduction to Pandas • 81

```
df = pd.read_csv("duplicates.csv")
print("Contents of data frame:")
print(df)
print()

df.sort_values(by=['fname'], inplace=True)
print("Sorted (ascending) by first name:")
print(df)
print()

df.sort_values(by=['fname'], inplace=True,ascending=False)
print("Sorted (descending) by first name:")
print(df)
print()

df.sort_values(by=['fname','lname'], inplace=True)
print("Sorted (ascending) by first name and last name:")
print(df)
print()
```

Listing 2.36 initializes the data frame `df` with the contents of the CSV file `duplicates.csv`, and then displays the contents of `df`. The next portion of Listing 2.36 displays the rows in ascending order based on the first name, and the next code block displays the rows in descending order based on the first name.

The final code block in Listing 2.36 displays the rows in ascending order based on the first name as well as the last name. Launch the code in Listing 2.36 and you will see the following output:

```
Contents of data frame:
   fname  lname  level   dept      state
0   Jane  Smith  Senior  Sales  California
1   Dave  Smith  Senior  Devel  California
2   Jane  Jones  Year1   Mrktg    Illinois
3   Jane  Jones  Year1   Mrktg    Illinois
4   Jane  Stone  Senior  Mrktg     Arizona
5   Dave  Stone  Year2   Devel     Arizona
6   Mark  Aster  Year3   BizDev    Florida
7   Jane  Jones  Year1   Mrktg    Illinois

Sorted (ascending) by first name:
   fname  lname  level   dept      state
1   Dave  Smith  Senior  Devel  California
5   Dave  Stone  Year2   Devel     Arizona
0   Jane  Smith  Senior  Sales  California
2   Jane  Jones  Year1   Mrktg    Illinois
3   Jane  Jones  Year1   Mrktg    Illinois
4   Jane  Stone  Senior  Mrktg     Arizona
7   Jane  Jones  Year1   Mrktg    Illinois
6   Mark  Aster  Year3   BizDev    Florida
```

```
Sorted (descending) by first name:
  fname  lname   level   dept      state
6  Mark  Aster   Year3   BizDev    Florida
0  Jane  Smith   Senior  Sales     California
2  Jane  Jones   Year1   Mrktg     Illinois
3  Jane  Jones   Year1   Mrktg     Illinois
4  Jane  Stone   Senior  Mrktg     Arizona
7  Jane  Jones   Year1   Mrktg     Illinois
1  Dave  Smith   Senior  Devel     California
5  Dave  Stone   Year2   Devel     Arizona

Sorted (ascending) by first name and last name:
  fname  lname   level   dept      state
1  Dave  Smith   Senior  Devel     California
5  Dave  Stone   Year2   Devel     Arizona
2  Jane  Jones   Year1   Mrktg     Illinois
3  Jane  Jones   Year1   Mrktg     Illinois
7  Jane  Jones   Year1   Mrktg     Illinois
0  Jane  Smith   Senior  Sales     California
4  Jane  Stone   Senior  Mrktg     Arizona
6  Mark  Aster   Year3   BizDev    Florida
```

Working with groupby() in Pandas

Listing 2.37 displays the contents of groupby1.py that illustrates how to invoke the Pandas groupby() method in order to compute subtotals of feature values.

LISTING 2.37: groupby1.py

```
import pandas as pd

# colors and weights of balls:
data = {'color':['red','blue','blue','red','blue'],
        'weight':[40,50,20,30,90]}
df1 = pd.DataFrame(data)
print("df1:")
print(df1)
print()
print(df1.groupby('color').mean())
print()

red_filter = df1['color']=='red'
print(df1[red_filter])
print()
blue_filter = df1['color']=='blue'
print(df1[blue_filter])
print()

red_avg = df1[red_filter]['weight'].mean()
```

```
blue_avg = df1[blue_filter]['weight'].mean()
print("red_avg,blue_avg:")
print(red_avg,blue_avg)
print()

df2 = pd.DataFrame({'color':['blue','red'],'weight':[red_
avg,blue_avg]})
print("df2:")
print(df2)
print()
```

Listing 2.37 defines the variable data containing color and weight values, and then initializes the data frame df with the contents of the variable data. The next two code blocks define red_filter and blue_filter that match the rows whose colors are red and blue, respectively, and then prints the matching rows.

The next portion of Listing 2.37 defines the two filters red_avg and blue_avg that calculate the average weight of the red value and the blue values, respectively. The last code block in Listing 2.37 defines the data frame df2 with a color color and a weight column, where the latter contains the average weight of the red values and the blue values. Launch the code in Listing 2.37 and you will see the following output:

```
initial data frame:
df1:
  color  weight
0   red      40
1  blue      50
2  blue      20
3   red      30
4  blue      90

       weight
color
blue   53.333333
red    35.000000

  color  weight
0   red      40
3   red      30

  color  weight
1  blue      50
2  blue      20
4  blue      90

red_avg,blue_avg:
35.0 53.333333333333336
```

```
df2:
  color     weight
0  blue   35.000000
1   red   53.333333
```

Working with `apply()` and `mapapply()` in Pandas

Earlier in this chapter you saw an example of the `Pandas apply()` method for modifying the categorical values of a feature in the CSV file `shirts.csv`. This section contains more examples of the `apply()` method.

Listing 2.38 displays the contents of `apply1.py` that illustrates how to invoke the `Pandas apply()` method in order to compute the cube of a column of numbers.

LISTING 2.38: *apply1.py*

```
import pandas as pd

df = pd.DataFrame({'X1': [1,2,3], 'X2': [10,20,30]})

def cube(x):
  return x * x * x

df1 = df.apply(cube)
# same result:
# df1 = df.apply(lambda x: x * x * x)

print("initial data frame:")
print(df)
print("cubed values:")
print(df1)
```

Listing 2.38 initializes the data frame `df` with columns `X1` and `X2`, where the values for `X2` are 10 times the corresponding values in `X1`. Next, the `Python` function `cube()` returns the cube of its argument. Listing 2.38 then defines the variable `df1` by invoking the `apply()` function, which specifies the user-defined `Python` function `cube()`, and then prints the values of `df` as well as `df1`. Launch the code in Listing 2.38 and you will see the following output:

```
initial data frame:
   X1  X2
0   1  10
1   2  20
2   3  30
cubed values:
   X1    X2
0   1  1000
```

```
1   8    8000
2   27   27000
```

Apply a function to a `Data frame` that multiplies all values in the "height" column of the data frame by 3:

```
df["height"].apply(lambda height: 3 * height)
```

OR:

```
def multiply(x):
    return x * 3
df["height"].apply(multiply)
```

Listing 2.39 displays the contents of `apply2.py` that illustrates how to invoke the Pandas `apply()` method in order to compute the sum of a set of values.

LISTING 2.39: apply2.py

```
import pandas as pd
import numpy as np

df = pd.DataFrame({'X1': [10,20,30], 'X2': [50,60,70]})

df1 = df.apply(np.sum, axis=0)
df2 = df.apply(np.sum, axis=1)

print("initial data frame:")
print(df)
print("add values (axis=0):")
print(df1)
print("add values (axis=1):")
print(df2)
```

Listing 2.39 is a variation of Listing 2.38: the variables `df1` and `df2` contain the column-wise sum and the row-wise sum, respectively, of the data frame `df`. Launch the code in Listing 2.39 and you will see the following output:

```
     X1   X2
0    10   50
1    20   60
2    30   70

add values (axis=0):
X1     60
X2    180
dtype: int64

add values (axis=1):
0     60
1     80
2    100
dtype: int64
```

Listing 2.40 displays the contents of mapapply1.py that illustrates how to invoke the Pandas mapapply() method in order to compute the square of a column of numbers.

LISTING 2.40: mapapply1.py

```
import pandas as pd
import math

df = pd.DataFrame({'X1': [1,2,3], 'X2': [10,20,30]})
df1 = df.applymap(math.sqrt)

print("initial data frame:")
print(df)
print("square root values:")
print(df1)
```

Listing 2.40 is yet another variant of Listing 2.38: in this case, the variable df1 is defined by invoking the mapapply() function on the variable df, which in turn references (but does not execute) the math.sqrt() function.

Next, a print() statement displays the contents of df, followed by a print() statement that displays the contents of df1. It is at this point that the built-in math.sqrt() function is invoked in order to calculate the square root of the numeric values in df. Launch the code in Listing 2.40 and you will see the following output:

```
initial data frame:
   X1  X2
0   1  10
1   2  20
2   3  30

square root values:
         X1        X2
0  1.000000  3.162278
1  1.414214  4.472136
2  1.732051  5.477226
```

Listing 2.41 displays the contents of mapapply2.py that illustrates how to invoke the Pandas applymap() method in order to convert strings to lowercase and uppercase.

LISTING 2.41: mapapply2.py

```
import pandas as pd

df = pd.DataFrame({'fname': ['Jane'], 'lname': ['Smith']},
                  {'fname': ['Dave'], 'lname': ['Jones']})
```

```
df1 = df.applymap(str.lower)
df2 = df.applymap(str.upper)

print("initial data frame:")
print(df)
print()
print("lowercase:")
print(df1)
print()
print("uppercase:")
print(df2)
print()
```

Listing 2.41 initializes the variable df with two first and last name pairs, and then defines the variables df1 and df2 by invoking the applymap() method to the strings in the data frame df. The data frame df1 converts its input values to lowercase, whereas the data frame df2 converts its input values to uppercase. Launch the code in Listing 2.41 and you will see the following output:

```
initial data frame:
       fname   lname
fname  Jane    Smith
lname  Jane    Smith

lowercase:
       fname   lname
fname  jane    smith
lname  jane    smith

uppercase:
       fname   lname
fname  JANE    SMITH
lname  JANE    SMITH
```

Handling Outliers in Pandas

If you are unfamiliar with outliers and anomalies, please read the sections in the appendix that discusses these two concepts because this section uses Pandas to find outliers in a dataset. The key idea involves finding the "z score" of the values in the dataset, which involves calculating the mean sigma and standard deviation std, and then mapping each value x in the dataset to the value (x-sigma)/std.

Next, you specify a value of z (such as 3) and find the rows whose z score is greater than 3. These are the rows that contain values that are considered outliers. Note that a suitable value for the z score is your decision (not some other external factor).

Listing 2.42 displays the contents of outliers_zscores.py that illustrates how to find rows of a dataset whose z-score greater than (or less than) a specified value.

LISTING 2.42: outliers_zscores.py

```
import numpy as np
import pandas as pd
from scipy import stats
from sklearn import datasets

df = datasets.load_iris()
columns = df.feature_names
iris_df = pd.DataFrame(df.data)
iris_df.columns = columns

print("=> iris_df.shape:",iris_df.shape)
print(iris_df.head())
print()

z = np.abs(stats.zscore(iris_df))
print("z scores for iris:")
print("z.shape:",z.shape)

upper = 2.5
lower = 0.01
print("=> upper outliers:")
print(z[np.where(z > upper)])
print()

outliers = iris_df[z < lower]
print("=> lower outliers:")
print(outliers)
print()
```

Listing 2.42 initializes the variable df with the contents of the built-in Iris dataset (see the appropriate appendix for an introduction to Sklearn). Next, the variable columns is initialized with the column names, and the data frame iris_df is initialized from the contents of df.data that contains the actual data for the Iris dataset. In addition, iris_df.columns is initialized with the contents of the variable columns.

The next portion of Listing 2.42 displays the shape of the data frame iris_df, followed by the zscore of the iris_df data frame, which is computed by subtracting the mean and then dividing by the standard deviation (performed for each row).

The last two portions of Listing 2.42 display the outliers (if any) whose `zscore` is outside the interval [0.01, 2.5]. Launch the code in Listing 2.42 and you will see the following output:

```
=> iris_df.shape: (150, 4)
  sepal length (cm)  sepal width (cm)  petal length (cm)  petal width
(cm)
0                5.1               3.5                1.4          0.2
1                4.9               3.0                1.4          0.2
2                4.7               3.2                1.3          0.2
3                4.6               3.1                1.5          0.2
4                5.0               3.6                1.4          0.2

z scores for iris:
z.shape: (150, 4)

=> upper outliers:
[3.09077525 2.63038172]

=> lower outliers:
  sepal length (cm)  sepal width (cm)  petal length (cm)  petal width
(cm)
73               6.1               2.8                4.7          1.2
82               5.8               2.7                3.9          1.2
90               5.5               2.6                4.4          1.2
92               5.8               2.6                4.0          1.2
95               5.7               3.0                4.2          1.2
```

Pandas Data Frames and Scatterplots

Listing 2.43 displays the contents of `pandas_scatter_df.py` that illustrates how to generate a scatterplot from a `Pandas` data frame.

LISTING 2.43: pandas_scatter_df.py

```
import numpy as np
import pandas as pd
import matplotlib.pyplot as plt
from pandas import read_csv
from pandas.plotting import scatter_matrix

myarray = np.array([[10,30,20], [50,40,60],[1000,2000,3000]])

rownames = ['apples', 'oranges', 'beer']
colnames = ['January', 'February', 'March']

mydf = pd.DataFrame(myarray, index=rownames, columns=colnames)

print(mydf)
print(mydf.describe())
```

```
scatter_matrix(mydf)
plt.show()
```

Listing 2.43 starts with various `import` statements, followed by the definition of the NumPy array `myarray`. Next, the variables `myarray` and `colnames` are initialized with values for the rows and columns, respectively. The next portion of Listing 2.43 initializes the Pandas data frame `mydf` so that the rows and columns are labeled in the output, as shown here:

```
         January  February  March
apples        10        30     20
oranges       50        40     60
beer        1000      2000   3000

            January     February        March
count      3.000000     3.000000     3.000000
mean     353.333333   690.000000  1026.666667
std      560.386771  1134.504297  1709.073823
min       10.000000    30.000000    20.000000
25%       30.000000    35.000000    40.000000
50%       50.000000    40.000000    60.000000
75%      525.000000  1020.000000  1530.000000
max     1000.000000  2000.000000  3000.0000000
```

Pandas Data Frames and Simple Statistics

Listing 2.44 displays a portion of the CSV file `housing.csv` and Listing 2.45 displays the contents of `housing_stats.py` that illustrates how to gather basic statistics from `housing.csv` in a Pandas data frame.

LISTING 2.44: housing.csv

```
price,bedrooms,bathrooms,sqft_living
221900,3,1,1180
538000,3,2.25,2570
180000,2,1,770
604000,4,3,1960
510000,3,2,1680
// details omitted for brevity
785000,4,2.5,2290
450000,3,1.75,1250
228000,3,1,1190
345000,5,2.5,3150
600000,3,1.75,1410
```

LISTING 2.45: housing_stats.py

```
import pandas as pd

df = pd.read_csv("housing.csv")
```

```
minimum_bdrms = df["bedrooms"].min()
median_bdrms  = df["bedrooms"].median()
maximum_bdrms = df["bedrooms"].max()

print("minimum # of bedrooms:",minimum_bdrms)
print("median  # of bedrooms:",median_bdrms)
print("maximum # of bedrooms:",maximum_bdrms)
print("")

print("median values:",df.median().values)
print("")

prices = df["price"]
print("first 5 prices:")
print(prices.head())
print("")

median_price = df["price"].median()
print("median price:",median_price)
print("")

corr_matrix = df.corr()
print("correlation matrix:")
print(corr_matrix["price"].sort_values(ascending=False))
```

Listing 2.45 initializes the `Pandas` data frame `df` with the contents of the CSV file `housing.csv`. The next three variables are initialized with the minimum, median, and maximum number of bedrooms, respectively, and then these values are displayed.

The next portion of Listing 2.45 initializes the variable `prices` with the contents of the `prices` column of the `Pandas` data frame `df`. Next, the first five rows are printed via the `prices.head()` statement, followed by the median value of the prices.

The final portion of Listing 2.45 initializes the variable `corr_matrix` with the contents of the correlation matrix for the `Pandas` data frame `df`, and then displays its contents. The output from Listing 2.45 is here:

```
minimum # of bedrooms: 2
median  # of bedrooms: 3.0
maximum # of bedrooms: 5

median values: [4.5900e+05 3.0000e+00 1.7500e+00 1.7125e+03]

first 5 prices:
0    221900
1    538000
2    180000
3    604000
4    510000
```

```
Name: price, dtype: int64

median price: 459000.0

correlation matrix:
price          1.000000
sqft_living    0.620634
bathrooms      0.440047
bedrooms       0.379300
Name: price, dtype: float64
```

Aggregate Operations in Pandas Data Frames

The `agg()` function is an alias for aggregate, which performs aggregate (multiple) operations on columns (the `Pandas` documentations states "use the alias").

Listing 2.46 displays the contents of `aggregate1.py` that illustrates how to perform aggregate operations with the data in a `Pandas` data frame.

LISTING 2.46: aggregate1.py

```
import pandas as pd

df = pd.DataFrame([[4, 2, 3, 1],
                   [8, 1, 5, -4],
                   [6, 9, 8, -8]],
                   columns=['X1', 'X2', 'X3', 'X4'])

print("=> data frame:")
print(df)
print()

print("=> Aggregate sum and min over the rows:")
print(df.agg(['sum', 'min', 'max']))
print()

print("=> Aggregate mean over the columns:")
print(df.agg("mean", axis="columns"))
print()
```

Listing 2.46 initializes the data frame df with the contents of a 3×4 array of numeric values, and then displays the contents of df. The next code snippet invokes the `agg()` method in order to append the methods `sum()`, `min()`, and `max()` to df. The result is a new 3×4 array of values where the rows contain the sum, minimum, and maximum of the values in each column of df. The final code snippet displays a row of data that contains the mean of each column of df. Now launch the code in Listing 2.46 and the output is here:

```
=> data frame:
   X1  X2  X3  X4
0   4   2   3   1
1   8   1   5  -4
2   6   9   8  -8

=> Aggregate sum and min over the rows:
     X1  X2  X3  X4
sum  18  12  16 -11
min   4   1   3  -8
max   8   9   8   1

=> Aggregate mean over the columns:
0    2.50
1    2.50
2    3.75
dtype: float64
```

Aggregate Operations with the titanic.csv Dataset

Listing 2.47 displays the contents of aggregate2.py that illustrates how to perform aggregate operations with columns in the CSV file titanic.csv.

LISTING 2.47: aggregate2.py

```
import pandas as pd

#Loading titanic.csv in Seaborn:
#df = sns.load_dataset('titanic')
df = pd.read_csv("titanic.csv")

# convert floating point values to integers:
df['survived'] = df['survived'].astype(int)

# specify column and aggregate functions:
aggregates1 = {'embark_town': ['count', 'nunique', 'size']}

# group by 'deck' value and apply aggregate functions:
result = df.groupby(['deck']).agg(aggregates1)
print("=> Grouped by deck:")
print(result)
print()

# some details regarding count() and nunique():
# count() excludes NaN values whereas size() includes them
# nunique() excludes NaN values in the unique counts

# group by 'age' value and apply aggregate functions:
result2 = df.groupby(['age']).agg(aggregates1)
print("=> Grouped by age (before):")
```

```
print(result2)
print()

# some "age" values are missing (so drop them):
df = df.dropna()

# convert floating point values to integers:
df['age'] = df['age'].astype(int)

# group by 'age' value and apply aggregate functions:
result3 = df.groupby(['age']).agg(aggregates1)
print("=> Grouped by age (after):")
print(result3)
print()
```

Listing 2.47 initializes the data frame `df` with the contents of the CSV file `titanic.csv`. The next code snippet converts floating point values to integer, followed by defining the variable `aggregates1` that specifies the functions `count()`, `nunique()`, and `size()` that will be invoked on the `embark_town` field.

The next code snippet initializes the variable `result` after invoking the `groupby()` method on the `deck` field, followed by invoking the `agg()` method.

The next code block performs the same computation to initialize the variable `result2`, except that the `groupby()` function is invoked on the `age` field instead of the `embark_town` field. Notice the comment section regarding the `count()` and `nunique()` functions: let's drop the rows with missing values via `df.dropna()` and investigate how that affects the calculations.

After dropping the rows with missing values, the final code block initializes the variable `result3` in exactly the same way that `result2` was initialized. Now launch the code in Listing 2.47 and the output is shown here:

```
=> Grouped by deck:
     embark_town
           count nunique size
deck
A            15       2   15
B            45       2   47
C            59       3   59
D            33       2   33
E            32       3   32
F            13       3   13
G             4       1    4
```

```
=> Grouped by age (before):
       age
       count nunique size
age
0.42    1       1       1
0.67    1       1       1
0.75    2       1       2
0.83    2       1       2
0.92    1       1       1
...    ...     ...     ...
70.00   2       1       2
70.50   1       1       1
71.00   2       1       2
74.00   1       1       1
80.00   1       1       1

[88 rows x 3 columns]

=> Grouped by age (after):
      age
      count nunique size
age
0      1       1       1
1      1       1       1
2      3       1       3
3      1       1       1
4      3       1       3
6      1       1       1
11     1       1       1
14     1       1       1
15     1       1       1
// details omitted for brevity
60     2       1       2
61     2       1       2
62     1       1       1
63     1       1       1
64     1       1       1
65     2       1       2
70     1       1       1
71     1       1       1
80     1       1       1
```

Save Data Frames as CSV Files and Zip Files

Listing 2.48 displays the contents of save2csv.py that illustrates how to save a Pandas data frame as a CSV file and also as a zip file that contains both the CSV file and the contents of the data frame.

LISTING 2.48: *save2csv.py*

```
import pandas as pd
```

```
df = pd.DataFrame({'fname':'Jane','lname':'Smith','age':25},
                  {'fname':'Dave','lname':'Jones','age':35},
                  {'fname':'Sara','lname':'Stone','age':45})

# save data frame to CSV file:
print("Saving data to save.csv:")
print(df.to_csv("save.csv",index=False))

# save data frame as CSV file in a zip file:
compression_opts = dict(method='zip',archive_name='save2.csv')
df.to_csv('save2.zip', index=False, compression=compression_
opts)
```

Listing 2.48 defines the `Pandas` data frame `df` that contains three rows of data, with values for the first name, last name, and age of three people. The next code snippet invokes the `to_csv()` method in order to save the contents of `df` to the CSV file `save2.csv`. The final code snippet also invokes the `to_csv()` method, this time in order to save the contents of `save2.csv` in the zip file `save2.zip`. Now launch the code in Listing 2.48, after which you will see two new files in the directory where you launched this Python script:

```
save.csv
save2.zip
```

Pandas Data Frames and Excel Spreadsheets

Listing 2.49 displays the contents of `write_people_xlsx.py` that illustrates how to read data from a CSV file and then create an Excel spreadsheet with that data.

LISTING 2.49: write_people_xlsx.py

```
import pandas as pd

df1 = pd.read_csv("people.csv")
df1.to_excel("people.xlsx")

#optionally specify the sheet name:
#df1.to_excel("people.xlsx", sheet_name='Sheet_name_1')
```

Listing 2.49 contains the usual `import` statement, after which the variable `df1` is initialized with the contents of the CSV file `people.csv`. The final code snippet then creates the Excel spreadsheet `people.xlsx` with the contents of the data frame `df1`, which contains the contents of the CSV file `people.csv`.

Now launch `write_people_xlsx.py` from the command line and then open the newly created Excel spreadsheet `people.xlsx` to confirm its contents.

Listing 2.50 displays the contents of `read_people_xslx.py` that illustrates how to read data from an Excel spreadsheet and create a `Pandas` data frame with that data.

LISTING 2.50: *read_people_xslx.py*

```
import pandas as pd

df = pd.read_excel("people.xlsx")
print("Contents of Excel spreadsheet:")
print(df)
```

Listing 2.50 is straightforward: the `Pandas` data frame `df` is initialized with the contents of the spreadsheet `people.xlsx` (whose contents are the same as `people.csv`) via the `Pandas` function `read_excel()`. The output from Listing 2.48 is here:

```
df1:
   Unnamed: 0 fname  lname  age gender  country
0           0  john  smith   30      m      usa
1           1  jane  smith   31      f   france
2           2  jack  jones   32      m   france
3           3  dave  stone   33      m    italy
4           4  sara  stein   34      f  germany
5           5  eddy  bower   35      m    spain
```

Working with JSON-based Data

A JSON object consists of data represented as colon-separated name/value pairs and data objects are separated by commas. An object is specified inside curly braces {}, and an array of objects is indicated by square brackets []. Note that character-valued data elements are inside quotes "" (no quotes for numeric data).

Here is a simple example of a JSON object:

```
{ "fname":"Jane", "lname":"Smith", "age":33, "city":"SF" }
```

Here is a simple example of an array of JSON objects:

```
[
{ "fname":"Jane", "lname":"Smith", "age":33, "city":"SF" },
{ "fname":"John", "lname":"Jones", "age":34, "city":"LA" },
{ "fname":"Dave", "lname":"Stone", "age":35, "city":"NY" },
]
```

Python Dictionary and JSON

The Python `json` library enables you to work with JSON-based data in `Python`.

Listing 2.51 displays the contents of `dict2json.py` that illustrates how to convert a `Python` dictionary to a JSON string.

LISTING 2.51: *dict2json.py*

```
import json

dict1 = {}
dict1["fname"] = "Jane"
dict1["lname"] = "Smith"
dict1["age"]   = 33
dict1["city"]  = "SF"

print("Python dictionary to JSON data:")
print("dict1:",dict1)
json1 = json.dumps(dict1, ensure_ascii=False)
print("json1:",json1)
print("")

# convert JSON string to Python dictionary:
json2 = '{"fname":"Dave", "lname":"Stone", "age":35, "city":"NY"}'
dict2 = json.loads(json2)
print("JSON data to Python dictionary:")
print("json2:",json2)
print("dict2:",dict2)
```

Listing 2.51 invokes the `json.dumps()` function to perform the conversion from a `Python` dictionary to a JSON string. Launch the code in Listing 2.51 and you will see the following output:

```
Python dictionary to JSON data:
dict1: {'fname': 'Jane', 'lname': 'Smith', 'age': 33, 'city':
     'SF'}
json1: {"fname": "Jane", "lname": "Smith", "age": 33, "city":
     "SF"}

JSON data to Python dictionary:
json2: {"fname":"Dave", "lname":"Stone", "age":35, "city":"NY"}
dict2: {'fname': 'Dave', 'lname': 'Stone', 'age': 35, 'city':
     'NY'}
```

Python, Pandas, and JSON

Listing 2.52 displays the contents of `pd_python_json.py` that illustrates how to convert a `Python` dictionary to a `Pandas` data frame and then convert the data frame to a JSON string.

LISTING 2.52: pd_python_json.py

```
import json
import pandas as pd

dict1 = {}
dict1["fname"] = "Jane"
dict1["lname"] = "Smith"
dict1["age"]   = 33
dict1["city"]  = "SF"

df1 = pd.DataFrame.from_dict(dict1, orient='index')
print("Pandas df1:")
print(df1)
print()

json1 = json.dumps(dict1, ensure_ascii=False)
print("Serialized to JSON1:")
print(json1)
print()

print("Data frame to JSON2:")
json2 = df1.to_json(orient='split')
print(json2)
```

Listing 2.52 initializes a Python dictionary dict1 with multiple attributes for a user (first name, last name, and so forth). Next, the data frame df1 is created from the Python dictionary dict2json.py, and its contents are displayed.

The next portion of Listing 2.52 initializes the variable json1 by serializing the contents of dict2json.py, and its contents are displayed. The last code block in Listing 2.52 initializes the variable json2 to the result of converting the data frame df1 to a JSON string. Launch the code in Listing 2.52 and you will see the following output:

```
dict1: {'fname': 'Jane', 'lname': 'Smith', 'age': 33, 'city': 'SF'}
Pandas df1:
           0
fname   Jane
lname   Smith
age     33
city    SF

Serialized to JSON1:
{"fname": "Jane", "lname": "Smith", "age": 33, "city": "SF"}

Data frame to JSON2:
{"columns":[0],"index":["fname","lname","age","city"],"data":
[["Jane"],["Smith"],[33],["SF"]]}
json1: {"fname": "Jane", "lname": "Smith", "age": 33, "city": "SF"}
```

Pandas and Regular Expressions (Optional)

This section is marked "optional" because the code snippets require an understanding of regular expressions. If this topic does not interest you, feel free to skip this section with no loss of continuity. Alternatively, you can read Appendix C (if necessary) regarding regular expressions and then you can return to this portion of the chapter.

Listing 2.53 displays the contents `pandas_regexs.py` that illustrates how to extract data from a `Pandas` data frame using regular expressions.

LISTING 2.53: pandas_regexs.py

```
import pandas as pd

schedule = ["Monday: Prepare lunch at 12:30pm for VIPs",
            "Tuesday: Yoga class from 10:00am to 11:00am",
            "Wednesday: PTA meeting at library at 3pm",
            "Thursday: Happy hour at 5:45 at Julie's house.",
            "Friday: Prepare pizza dough for lunch at 12:30pm.",
            "Saturday: Early shopping for the week at 8:30am.",
            "Sunday: Neighborhood bbq block party at 2:00pm."]

# create a Pandas data frame:
df = pd.DataFrame(schedule, columns = ['dow_of_week'])

# convert to lowercase:
df = df.applymap(lambda s:s.lower() if type(s) == str else s)
print("df:")
print(df)
print()

# character count for each string in df['dow_of_week']:
print("string lengths:")
print(df['dow_of_week'].str.len())
print()

# the number of tokens for each string in df['dow_of_week']
print("number of tokens in each string in df['dow_of_week']:")
print(df['dow_of_week'].str.split().str.len())
print()

# the number of occurrences of digits:
print("number of digits:")
print(df['dow_of_week'].str.count(r'\d'))
print()

# display all occurrences of digits:
print("show all digits:")
```

```
print(df['dow_of_week'].str.findall(r'\d'))
print()

# display hour and minute values:
print("display (hour, minute) pairs:")
print(df['dow_of_week'].str.findall(r'(\d?\d):(\d\d)'))
print()

# create new columns from hour:minute value:
print("hour and minute columns:")
print(df['dow_of_week'].str.extract(r'(\d?\d):(\d\d)'))
print()
```

Listing 2.53 initializes the variable `schedule` with a set of strings, each of which specifies a daily to-do item for an entire week. The format for each to-do item is of the form `day:task`, where `day` is a day of the week and `task` is a string that specifies what needs to be done on that particular day.

Next, the data frame `df1` is initialized with the contents of schedule, followed by an example of defining a lambda expression that converts string-based values to lower case, as shown here:

```
df = df.applymap(lambda s:s.lower() if type(s) == str else s)
```

The preceding code snippet is useful because you do not need to specify individual columns of a data frame: the code ignores any nonstring values (such as integers and floating point values).

The next pair of code blocks involve various operations using the methods `applymap()`, `split()`, and `len()` that you have seen in previous examples. The next code block displays the number of digits in each to-do item by means of the regular expression in the following code snippet:

```
print(df['dow_of_week'].str.count(r'\d'))
```

The next code block displays the actual digits (instead of the number of digits) in each to-do item by means of the regular expression in the following code snippet:

```
print(df['dow_of_week'].str.findall(r'\d'))
```

The final code block displays the strings of the form `hour:minutes` by means of the regular expression in the following code snippet:

```
print(df['dow_of_week'].str.findall(r'(\d?\d):(\d\d)'))
```

As mentioned in the beginning of this section, you can learn more about regular expressions by reading Appendix C of this book. Launch the code in Listing 2.53 and you will see the following output:

```
=> df:
                                                    dow_of_week
```

```
0         monday: prepare lunch at 12:30pm for vips
1         tuesday: yoga class from 10:00am to 11:00am
2         wednesday: pta meeting at library at 3pm
3         thursday: happy hour at 5:45 at julie's house.
4         friday: prepare pizza dough for lunch at 12:30pm.
5         saturday: early shopping for the week at 8:30am.
6         sunday: neighborhood bbq block party at 2:00pm.

=> string lengths:
0    41
1    43
2    40
3    46
4    49
5    48
6    47
Name: dow_of_week, dtype: int64

=> number of tokens in each string in df['dow_of_week']:
0    7
1    7
2    7
3    8
4    8
5    8
6    7
Name: dow_of_week, dtype: int64

=> number of digits:
0    4
1    8
2    1
3    3
4    4
5    3
6    3
Name: dow_of_week, dtype: int64

=> show all digits:
0              [1, 2, 3, 0]
1    [1, 0, 0, 0, 1, 1, 0, 0]
2                       [3]
3                 [5, 4, 5]
4              [1, 2, 3, 0]
5                 [8, 3, 0]
6                 [2, 0, 0]
Name: dow_of_week, dtype: object

=> display (hour, minute) pairs:
0              [(12, 30)]
1    [(10, 00), (11, 00)]
2                      []
```

```
3                    [(5, 45)]
4                    [(12, 30)]
5                    [(8, 30)]
6                    [(2, 00)]
Name: dow_of_week, dtype: object

=> hour and minute columns:
      0    1
0    12   30
1    10   00
2   NaN  NaN
3     5   45
4    12   30
5     8   30
6     2   00
```

Listing 2.54 displays the contents of the CSV file `email.csv` and Listing 2.55 displays the contents `check_email.py` that illustrates how to process email addresses in a Pandas data frame using regular expressions.

LISTING 2.54: email.csv

```
fname,lname,email

Jane,Smith,jasmith@aol.com
Dave,Smith,dasmith@acme.com
Jane,Jones,jajones@yahoo.com
Jane,Stone,jastone@gmail.com
Dave,Stone,dastone@yahoo.com
Mark,Aster,mcaster@gmail.com
```

LISTING 2.55: check_email.py

```python
import re
import pandas as pd

df = pd.read_csv("email.csv")

print("=> contents of email.csv:")
print(df)
print()

#check for the occurrence of "gmail":
print("=> email containing gmail:")
print(df["email"].str.contains("gmail"))
print()

print("=> email id, email type, and domain:")
# pattern splits email address into three components:
```

```
pattern = "([A-Z0-9._%+-]+)@([A-Z0-9.-]+)\.([A-Z]{2,4})"
print(df["email"].str.findall(pattern, flags=re.IGNORECASE))
```

Listing 2.55 contains two `import` statements followed by the initialization of the data frame `df` with the contents of the CSV file `email.csv`. Next, the contents of `df` are displayed, followed by a `print()` statement that displays True or False depending on whether or not the `email` address in each row of `df` contains the string `gmail`.

The final code block in Listing 2.55 initializes the variable `pattern` as a regular expression that splits `email` addresses into their three components. Now launch the code in Listing 2.55 and you will see the following output:

```
=> contents of email.csv:
   fname   lname              email
0  Jane    Smith      jasmith@aol.com
1  Dave    Smith      dasmith@acme.com
2  Jane    Jones      jajones@yahoo.com
3  Jane    Stone      jastone@gmail.com
4  Dave    Stone      dastone@yahoo.com
5  Mark    Aster      mcaster@gmail.com

=> email containing gmail:
0      False
1      False
2      False
3       True
4      False
5       True
Name: email, dtype: bool

=> email id, email type, and domain:
0       [(jasmith, aol, com)]
1       [(dasmith, acme, com)]
2       [(jajones, yahoo, com)]
3       [(jastone, gmail, com)]
4       [(dastone, yahoo, com)]
5       [(mcaster, gmail, com)]
Name: email, dtype: object
```

Useful One-Line Commands in Pandas

This section contains an eclectic mix of one-line commands in `Pandas` (some of which you have already seen in this chapter) that are useful to know:

Drop a feature in a data frame:
```
df.drop('feature_variable_name', axis=1)
```

Convert object type to float in a `Data frame`:
`pd.to_numeric(df["feature_name"], errors='coerce')`

Convert data in a `Pandas` data frame to `NumPy` array:
`df.as_matrix()`

Rename the fourth column of the data frame as "height":
`df.rename(columns = {df.columns[3]:'height'}, inplace=True)`

Get the unique entries of the column "first" in a data frame:
`df["first"].unique()`

Display the number of different values in the first column:
`df["first"].nunique()`

Create a data frame with columns 'first" and "last" from an existing `Data frame`:
`new_df = df[["name", "size"]]`

Sort the data in a data frame:
`df.sort_values(ascending = False)`

Filter the data column named "size" to display only values equal to 7:
`df[df["size"] == 7]`

Display at most 1000 characters in each cell:
`pd.set_option('max_colwidth', 1000)`

Display at most 20 data frame rows:
`pd.set_option('max_rows', 20)`

Display at most 1000 columns:
`pd.set_option('max_columns', 1000)`

Display a random set of n rows:
`df.sample(n)`

What is Method Chaining?

Method chaining refers to combining method invocations without intermediate code. Method chaining is available in many languages, including Java, Scala, and JavaScript. Code that uses method chaining tends to be more compact, more performant, and easier to understand. Yet debugging such code can be more difficult, especially in long method chains.

As a general rule, start by invoking a sequence of methods, and after ensuring that the code is correct, construct method chains with at most five or six methods. However, if a method inside a method chain also invokes other functions, then you can split the chain into two parts in order to increase readability. Since there is no "best" way to determine the number of methods in a method chain, experiment with method chains of different sizes (and differing complexity) until you determine a style that works best for you.

Pandas and Method Chaining

Recently `Pandas` improved its support for method chaining, which includes the methods `assign()`, `pivot_table()`, and `query()`. Moreover, the `pipe()` method supports method chaining that contains user-defined methods. The following code snippet illustrate show to use method chaining in order to invoke several `Pandas` methods:

```
import pandas as pd
pd.read_csv('data.csv')
  .fillna(...)
  .query('...')
  .assign(...)
  .pivot_table(...)
  .rename(...)
```

Consult the online documentation for more details regarding method chaining in `Pandas`.

Pandas Profiling

Pandas profiling is an extremely useful `Python` library that performs an analysis on a dataset, which can be exported as a JSON-based file or an HTML Web page. Launch the following command in a command shell in order to install `Pandas Profiling`:

```
pip3 install pandas_profiling
```

Listing 2.56 displays a very small portion of the CSV file `titanic.csv` that is analyzed in Listing 2.57.

LISTING 2.56: *titanic.csv*

```
PassengerId,Survived,Pclass,Name,Sex,Age,SibSp,Parch,Ticket,Fa
re,Cabin,Embarked
1,0,3,"Braund, Mr. Owen Harris",male,22,1,0,A/5 21171,7.25,,S
2,1,1,"Cumings, Mrs. John Bradley (Florence Briggs
Thayer)",female,38,1,0,PC 17599,71.2833,C85,C
```

```
3,1,3,"Heikkinen, Miss. Laina",female,26,0,0,STON/O2.
3101282,7.925,,S
4,1,1,"Futrelle, Mrs. Jacques Heath (Lily May Peel)",female,35
,1,0,113803,53.1,C123,S
[details omitted for brevity]
```

Listing 2.57 displays the contents of `profile_titanic.py` that illustrates how to invoke `Pandas` profiling to generate an HTML Web page that contains an analysis of the `titanic.csv` dataset.

LISTING 2.57: profile_titanic.py

```
import pandas as pd
import numpy as np
from pandas_profiling import ProfileReport

df = pd.read_csv("titanic.csv")

#generate the report:
profile = ProfileReport(df, title='Pandas Profiling Report',
explorative=True)
profile.to_file("profile_titanic.html")
```

Listing 2.57 contains several `import` statements, followed by the initialization of the variable `df` as a `Pandas` data frame that contains the contents of the CSV file `titanic.csv`. The next code snippet initializes the variable `profile` as an instance of the `ProfileReport` class, followed by an invocation of the `to_file()` method that generates an HTML file with the contents of the CSV file `titanic.csv`.

Now launch the code in Listing 2.57, after which you will see the HTML Web page `profile_titanic.html` whose contents you can view in a Web browser.

What is Texthero?

Texthero is a `Python`-based open-source toolkit that functions as a layer of abstraction over `Pandas`, and its home page is here:

https://texthero.org/

Texthero leverages Gensim, NLTK, SpaCy and Sklearn (all of which are discussed in later chapters). Moreover, `texthero` supports the following (topics that are explained in subsequent chapters):

- NER and topic modeling
- TF-IDF, term frequency, and word embeddings

- DBSCAN, Hierarchical, k-Means, and Meanshift algorithms
- Various types of text visualization

Open a command shell and install `texthero` with the following command:

```
pip3 install texthero
```

Texthero supports various other algorithms, such as LDA and LSI, as well as the dimensionality reduction algorithms PCA and t-SNE. Navigate to the following link for documentation and other information about `texthero`:

https://texthero.org/docs/getting-started

Summary

This chapter introduced you to `Pandas` for creating labeled data frames and displaying metadata of `Pandas` data frames. Then you learned how to create `Pandas` data frames from various sources of data, such as random numbers and hard-coded data values.

You also learned how to read Excel spreadsheets and perform numeric calculations on that data, such as the minimum, mean, and maximum values in numeric columns. Then you saw how to create `Pandas` data frames from data stored in CSV files.

You also received a brief introduction to `JSON`, along with an example of converting a `Python` dictionary to `JSON`-based data (and vice versa). Finally, you learned about `texthero`, which is an open-source `Python`-based toolkit that is a layer of abstraction over `Pandas`.

CHAPTER 3

NLP Concepts (I)

This chapter is the first chapter that contains NLP-related material, starting with a high-level introduction to some major language groups and also substantive grammatical differences among languages. Then you will learn some basic concepts in NLP, such as text normalization, the concepts of stop words, stemming, and lemmatization (the dictionary form of words), POS (parts of speech) tagging, and NER (named entity recognition). As you will soon see, this chapter is lengthy, with a highly eclectic mix of topics. In case you haven't already done so, now would be a good time to read the preface that provides more information regarding the purpose of this book.

This chapter focuses on NLP concepts, and while some NLP algorithms are mentioned in this chapter, the relevant code samples are provided Chapter 5 and Chapter 6. Depending on your NLP background, you might decide to read the sections in a nonsequential fashion. If your goal is to proceed quickly to code samples, you can skip some sections in this chapter, and later you can return to read those omitted sections.

The first part of the chapter provides an abbreviated tour of several languages that belong to major human language groups, illustrating some of the facets of human languages that can make NLP a truly challenging endeavor. However, please keep in mind that this section contains many details that will *appeal primarily to language aficionados*. This section contains grammatical details that differentiate various languages from each other that highlight the complexity of generating native-level syntax as well as native-level pronunciation. Depending on your level of interest, feel free to read the portions of this section that interest you and then proceed to the next section of this chapter.

Also keep in mind that the discussion regarding regional accents and slang contain anecdotal observations based on the experiences of the author: there is no scientifically rigorous basis or any studies to support those observations, which means that they are not necessarily true in a general case. However, you might find some of the sections somewhat interesting (and in some cases, they might be similar to your own experiences).

Indeed, various subsections reflect the author's experiences in multilingual environments while living and working in various countries: in particular, this includes Italian, Spanish, French, and Japanese, as well as language dialects (the Venetian dialect and Venezuelan criollo), the challenges facing nonnative-English speakers, and also the fascinating Japanese language.

The second part of the chapter introduces you to NLP and a brief history of the major stages of NLP. You will also learn about NLP applications, NLP use cases, NLU, and NLG. Then you will learn about word sense disambiguation. This section only provides a very brief description of these topics, some of which can fill entire books and full-length courses.

The third part of this chapter discusses various NLP techniques and the major steps in an NLP-related process. You will also learn about standard NLP-related tasks, such as text normalization, tokenization, stemming, lemmatization, and the removal of stop words. As you will see, some of these tasks (e.g., tokenization) involve implicit assumptions that are not true for all languages.

The final section introduces Named Entity Recognition (NER) and topic modeling, which pertains to finding the main topic(s) in a text document.

Last, please keep in mind that the first portion of this chapter contrasts some grammatical aspects of languages from an informal perspective; if you are interested in a formal linguistic analysis, you can find such details through an online search.

The Origin of Languages

Someone once remarked that "the origin of language is an enigma," which is viscerally appealing because it has at least a kernel of truth. Although there are multiple theories that attempt to explain how and why languages developed, none of them has attained universal consensus. Nevertheless, there is no doubt that humans have far surpassed all other species in terms of language development.

There is also the question of how the vocabulary of a language is formed, which can be the confluence of multiple factors, as well as meaning in a language. According to Ludwig Wittgenstein (1953), who was an influential philosopher in many other fields, language derives its meaning from use.

One theory about the evolution of language in humans asserts that the need for communication between humans makes language a necessity. Another explanation is that language is influenced by the task creating complex tools, because the latter requires a precise sequence of steps, and ultimately spurred the development of languages.

Without delving into their details, the following list contains some theories that have been proposed regarding language development. Keep in mind that they vary in terms of their support in the academic community:

- Strong minimalist thesis
- The FlintKnapper
- The Sapir-Whorf hypothesis
- Universal grammar (Noam Chomsky)

The strong minimalist thesis (SRT) asserts that language is based on something called hierarchical syntactic structure.

The FlintKnapper asserts that the ability to create complex tools involved an intricate sequence of steps, which in turn necessitated communication between people.

In simplified terms, the Sapir–Whorf hypothesis (also called the linguistic relativity hypothesis, which is a slightly weaker form) posits that the language we speak influences how we think. Consider how our physical environment can influence our spoken language: Eskimos have several words to describe snow, whereas people in some parts of the Middle East have never seen a snow storm.

Universal grammar is a genetic-based theory by Noam Chomsky in which he asserts that all humans have an innate capacity to learn languages (provided that they are raised in a reasonably normal environment). This innate capacity is not bound to a grammar or vocabulary of any human language, and diverges from earlier "tabula rasa" (blank slate) theories regarding the human mind at birth. While Chomsky's theory has appealing aspects, there are critic of UG, which you can read here if you are interested in the details:

https://en.wikipedia.org/wiki/Universal_grammar

Indeed, despite the grammatical diversity of human languages and the rich set of sounds that are possible in human languages, consider the following fact: a healthy newborn infant from one country can be placed in any other country and learn to speak the common language of that country, regardless of the genetic makeup of the infant.

Hence, humans have a universal capacity to learn languages, and seem to have an innate ability to learn multiple languages. This capacity to learn languages separates us from animals because the latter are unable to create a language that is close to the complexity of human languages. Noam Chomsky explains that this capability exists in humans because of a broader skill: humans have a recursive-like capacity to mentally combine objects in order to create new objects.

If the origin of languages is a topic that appeals to you, there are many resources available through an Internet search that provide a myriad of detailed explanations from which you can select the theories that seem most plausible to you.

Language Fluency

As mentioned in the previous section, human infants are capable of producing the sounds of any language, given enough opportunity to imitate those sounds. Alas, they tend to lose some of that capacity as they become older, which might explain why some adults speak another language with an accent (of course, there are plenty of exceptions).

Interestingly, babies respond favorably to the sound of vowel-rich parentese, and yet a study in 2018 suggests that babies prefer the sound of other babies instead of their mother:

https://eurekalert.org/pub_releases/2018-05/asoa-ftm042618.php

https://getpocket.com/explore/item/babies-prefer-the-sounds-of-other-babies-to-the-cooing-of-their-parents

Be that as it may, there are two interesting cases in which people can acquire native-level speech capability. The first case is intuitive: people who have been raised in a bilingual (or multilingual) environment tend to have a greater capacity for learning how to speak other languages with native level (or near native level) speech. Second, people who speak phonetic languages have an advantage when they study another phonetic language, especially one that is in their language group, because they already know how to pronounce the majority of vowel sounds.

However, there are consonants that occur in a limited number of languages whose pronunciation can be a challenge for practically every nonnative speaker. For example, letters that have a guttural sound (Dutch, German, and Arabic), the glottal stop (most noticeable in Arabic), and the letter "ain" in Arabic are generally more challenging to pronounce for native speakers of romance languages and some Asian languages (although there are exceptions, of course).

To some extent, the nonphonetic nature of the English language might explain why some monolingual native-English speakers might struggle with learning to speak other languages with native-level speech. Perhaps the closest language to English (in terms of cadence) is Dutch, and people from Holland can often speak native-level English. This tends to be true of Swedes and Danes as well, whose languages are Germanic, but not necessarily true of Germans, who can speak perfect grammatical English but sometimes still speak with a discernible German accent.

Perhaps somewhat ironically, sometimes accents can impart a sort of cachet, such as speaking with a British or Australian accent in the United States. Indeed, a French accent can also add a certain *je-ne-sais-quoi* to a speaker in various parts of the United States.

Major Language Groups

There are more than 140 language families, and the six largest language families (based on language count) are listed here:

- Niger-Congo
- Austronesian
- Trans-New Guinea
- Sino-Tibetan
- Indo-European
- Afro-Asiatic

English belongs to the Indo-European group, Mandarin belongs to the Sino-Tibetan, and Arabic belongs to the Afro-Asiatic group. According to Wikipedia, Indo-European languages comprise almost 600 languages, including most of the languages in Europe, the northern Indian subcontinent, and the Iranian plateau. Almost half the world speaks an Indo-European language as a native language, which is greater than any of the language groups listed in the introduction of this section. Indo-European has several major language subgroups, which are Germanic, Slavic, and Romance languages. The preceding information is from the following Wikipedia link:

https://en.wikipedia.org/wiki/List_of_language_families

As of 2019, the top four languages that are spoken in the world, which counts the number of people who are native speakers or secondary speakers, are as follows:

English	:	1.268 billion
Mandarin	:	1.120 billion
Hindi	:	637.3 million
Spanish	:	537.9 million
French	:	276.6 million

The preceding information is from the following Wikipedia link:

https://en.wikipedia.org/wiki/List_of_languages_by_total_number_of_speakers

Many factors can influence the expansion of a given language into multiple countries, such as commerce, economic factors, technological influence, and even warfare can result in the introduction of foreign words into another language. Somewhat intuitively, countries with a common border influence each other's language, sometimes resulting in new hybrid languages. For example, Catalan is a hybrid of Spanish and French and Provencal is a hybrid of French and Italian (both of which have delicious cuisine) that are spoken by people who live close to the border of the respective adjacent countries. Other examples include the influence of Farsi on Urdu (spoken in Pakistan) and the influence of French on Vietnamese and the presence of French words in some Arab countries.

Surprisingly, sometimes languages from geographically distant countries share linguistic features. For example, the Finno-Ugric (or Finno-Ugrian) language group comprises Hungarian, Finnish, and Estonian because they are related, despite their geographic distance from each other. Nevertheless, a plausible explanation may well exist; the other explanation for their commonality is due to random events (which seems unlikely).

Peak Usage of Some Languages

As you might have surmised, different languages have been in an influential position during the past 2,000 years. If you trace the popularity and influence of Indo-European languages, you will find periods of time with varying degrees of influence involving multiple languages, including Hebrew, Greek, Latin, Arabic, French, and English.

Latin is an Indo-European language (apparently derived from the Etruscan and Greek alphabets), and during the 1st century AD, Latin became a mainstream language. In addition, romance languages are derived from Latin. Today, Latin is considered a dead language in the sense that it's not actively spoken on a daily basis by large numbers of people. The same is true of Sanskrit, which is a very old language from India.

During the Roman Empire, Latin and Greek were the official languages for administrative as well as military activities. In addition, Latin was an important language for diplomacy among countries for many centuries after the fall of the Roman Empire.

You might be surprised to know that Arabic was the lingua franca throughout the Mediterranean during the 10th and 11th centuries AD. As another example, French was spoken in many parts of Europe during the 18th century, including the Russian aristocracy.

Today, English appears to be in its ascendancy in terms of the number of native English speakers as well as the number of people who speak English as a second (or third or fourth) language. Although Mandarin is a widely spoken Asian language, English is the lingua franca for commerce as well as technology: virtually every computer language is based on English.

Languages and Regional Accents

Accents, slang, and dialects have some common features, but there can be some significant differences. Accents involve modifying the standard pronunciation of words, which can vary significantly in different parts of the same country.

One interesting phenomenon pertains to the southern region of some countries (in the northern hemisphere), which tend to have a more "relaxed" pronunciation compared to the northern region of that country. For example, some people in the southeastern United States speak with a so-called "drawl," whereas newscasters will often speak with a midwestern pronunciation, which is considered a neutral pronunciation. The same is true of people in Tokyo, who often speak Japanese with a "flat" pronunciation (which is also true of Japanese newscasters on NHK), versus people from the Kansai region (Kyoto, Kobe, and Osaka) of Japan, who vary the tone and emphasis of Japanese words.

Regional accents can also involve modifying the meaning of words in ways that are specific to the region in question. For example, Texans will say "I'm fixing to graduate this year" whereas people from other parts of the United States would say "going" instead of "fixing." In France, Parisians are unlikely to say *Il faut fatiguer la salade* ("it's necessary to toss the salad"), whereas this sentence is much more commonplace in southern France. (The English word "fatigue" is derived from the French verb "fatiguer.")

Languages and Slang

The existence of slang words is interesting and perhaps inevitable: they seem to flourish in every human language. Sometimes slang words are used for obfuscation so that only members of an "in group" understand the modified meaning of those words. Slang words can also be a combination of existing words, new words (but not officially recognized), and short-hand expressions. Slang can also invert the meaning of words ("bad" instead of "good"), which can be specific to an age group, minority, or region. In addition, slang can also assign an entirely unrelated meaning to a standard word (e.g., the slang terms "that's dope," "that's sick," and "the bomb").

Slang words can also be specific to an age group in order to prevent communication with members of different age groups. For example, Japanese teens can communicate with each other by reversing the order of the syllables in a word, which renders those "words" incomprehensible to adults. The inversion of syllables is far more complex than "pig Latin" in which the first letter of a word is shifted to the end of the word, followed by the syllable "ay." For example, "East Bay" (an actual location in the Bay Area in Silicon Valley) is humorously called "beast" in pig Latin.

Teenagers also use acronyms (perhaps as another form of slang) when sending text messages to each other. For example, the acronym "aos" means "adult over shoulder." The acronym "bos" has several different meanings, including "brother over shoulder" and "boyfriend over shoulder."

The slang terms that you use with your peers invariably simplifies communication with others in your in-group, sometimes accompanied by specialized interpretations to words (such as reversing their meaning). A simple example is the word zanahoria, which is the Spanish word for carrot. In colloquial speech in Venezuela, calling someone a zanahoria means that that person is very conservative and as "straight" as a carrot.

Slang enables people to be creative and also playfully break the rules of language. Both slang and colloquial speech simplify formal language and rarely (if ever) introduce greater complexity in alternate speech rules.

Perhaps that's the reason that slang and colloquial speech cannot be controlled or regulated by anyone (or by any language committee): like water, they are fluid and easily change in unpredictable directions.

One more observation: while slang can be viewed as a creative by-product of standard speech, there is a reverse effect that can occur in certain situations. For example, you have probably noticed how influential subgenres are eventually absorbed (perhaps only partially) into mainstream culture: witness how commercials eventually incorporated a "softened" form of rap music and its rhythm in commercials for personal products. Indeed, there's a certain irony in hearing "Stairway to Heaven" as elevator music.

Another interesting concept is a "meme" (which includes Internet memes) in popular culture, which refers to something with humorous content. While slang words are often used to exclude people, a meme often attempts to communicate a particular sentiment. One such meme is "Ok Boomer," which some people view as a derogatory remark that's sometimes expressed in a snarky manner, and much less often interpreted as a humorous term. Although language dialects can also involve regional accents and slang, they also have more distinct characteristics, as discussed in the next section.

Languages and Dialects

Dialects often replace standard words with substantively different words that have the same meaning as their standard counterpart. In fact, dialects often include words that do not even exist in the language that they are based on. However, dialects also tend to have a consistent set of grammatical rules for conjugating verbs.

For example, despite having a population of under 60 million people, Italian has multiple distinct dialects, some of which are pair-wise incomprehensible to people from different regions of Italy. For instance here are some words in the Venetian dialect (word spellings are approximate and some accent marks have been omitted), along with their counterpart in standard Italian, followed by their translation into English:

```
"bragghe" means "pantaloni"  ("pants"))
"ciappa"  means "ha preso"   ("he/she got")
```

```
"coppa"    means "ammazza"   ("kills")
"ghe xe"   means "c'e"       ("there is")
"schei"    means "soldi"     ("money")
"toxhi"    means "bambini"   ("children")
```

As you can see, the spelling of the preceding words in the Venetian dialect bear no resemblance to their counterparts in standard Italian.

Dialects can also have significant differences, even in cities that are relatively close to each other. For example, Milan and Vicenza are two cities in northern Italy, with Milan located to the west of Vicenza, and slightly more than 100 kilometers (60 miles) apart. Maniago is a town in northeastern Italy (and well known for its production of steel blades that are in knives), located roughly 50 kilometers (32 miles) northwest of Vicenza. However, Milanese and the Venetian dialect are much closer to each other than to Friuliano, which is the dialect spoken in Maniago. In fact, Maniago is close to the border of Yugoslavia, and the influence of the latter is visible in the names of towns and highway signs that are near Maniago.

Given the differences in the dialects of Italian, how can people communicate? In large cities such as Milan, which comprise people from many parts of Italy, the only way that everyone can communicate with each other is to speak standard Italian.

The Complexity of Natural Languages

This section contains many subsections, and to give you some context, consider the scenario in which two people are having a conversation in which they do not speak a common language. In addition to human translators, there are software applications to perform the translation task. However, in the latter case, translating a sentence to a different language in such a way that it sounds like a native speaker involves many, many details. This section highlights some aspects of the translation process between different languages, and especially between languages that are in different language groups.

Natural languages involve a set of grammar rules of varying degrees of complexity, along with language specific features. For example, English, romance languages, and some Asian languages have a subject/verb/object pattern for many sentences.

By contrast, Japanese and Korean have a subject/object/verb pattern (German has SVOV for compound verbs), along with declension of adjectives and nouns (in German and Slavic languages) or postpositions (in

Japanese) that serve as "markers" for the grammatical function of nouns in sentences. As a result, it's possible to change the order of the words in sentences in German, Japanese, and Slavic languages and still maintain exactly the same meaning of those sentences.

Another interesting fact: although most languages are written in a left-to-right manner, some are written in a right-to-left fashion (including Hebrew and Arabic) or a top-to-bottom fashion (Japanese does both). If that doesn't impress you, consider the fact that some languages (including Hebrew and Arabic) also treat vowels as optional: native speakers of these languages have the advantage of having learned their vocabulary since childhood, so they recognize the meaning of words without vowels.

Word Order in Sentences

As mentioned previously, German and Slavic languages allow for a rearrangement of the words in sentences because those languages support *declension*, which involves modifying the endings of articles and adjectives in accordance with the grammatical function of those words in a sentence (such as subject, direct object, indirect object, and so forth). Those word endings are loosely comparable to prepositions in English, and sometimes they have the same spelling for different grammatical functions. For example, in German the article *den* precedes a masculine noun that is a direct object and also a plural noun that is an indirect object: ambiguity can occur if the singular masculine noun has the same spelling in its plural form.

Alternatively, since English is word order dependent, ambiguity can still arise in sentences, which we have learned to parse correctly without any conscious effort.

Groucho Marx often incorporated ambiguous sentences in his dialogues, such as the following paraphrased examples:

```
"This morning I shot an elephant in my pajamas. How he got
into my pajamas I have no idea."
"In America a woman gives birth to a child every fifteen minutes.
Somebody needs to find that woman and stop her."
```

Now consider the following pair of sentences involving a boy, a mountain, and a telescope:

```
I saw the boy on the mountain with the telescope.
I saw the boy with the telescope on the mountain.
```

Everyone understands that both English sentences as having the same meaning; however, arriving at the same interpretation is less obvious from the standpoint of a purely NLP task. Why does this ambiguity in the preceding example not arise in Russian? The reason is simple: the preposition *with* is associated with the instrumental case in Russian, whereas *on* is not the instrumental case, and therefore the nouns have suffixes that indicate the distinction.

What about Verbs?

Verbs exist in every written language, and they undergo conjugation that reflects their tense and mood in a sentence. Such languages have an overlapping set of verb tenses, but there are differences. For instance, Portuguese has a future perfect subjunctive, as does Spanish (but it's almost never used in spoken form), whereas these verb forms do not exist in English. English verb tenses (in the indicative mood) can include:

present
present perfect
present progressive
present perfect progressive
preterite (simple past)
past perfect
past progressive
past perfect progressive
future tense
future perfect
future progressive
future perfect progressive (does not exist in Italian)

Here are some examples of English sentences that illustrate (most of) the preceding verb forms:

I read a book.
I have read a book.
I am reading a book.
I have been reading a book.
I read a book.
I have read a book.
I had been reading a book.
I will read a book.
I will have read a book.
I will be reading a book.
At 6 p.m. I will have been reading a book for 3 hours.

Verb moods can be indicative (as listed in the preceding list), subjunctive (discussed soon), and conditional ("I would go but I have work to do"). In English, subjunctive verb forms can include the present subjunctive ("I insist that he do the task"), the past subjunctive ("If I were you"), and the pluperfect subjunctive ("Had I but known …"). Interestingly, Portuguese also provides a future perfect subjunctive verb form; Spanish also has this verb form but it's never used in conversation.

Perhaps some native English speakers do not know that there are modern languages, such as Mandarin, that have only one verb tense: they rely on other words in a sentence (such as time adverbs or aspect particles) to convey the time frame. Such languages would express the present, the past, and the future in a form that is comparable to the following:

"I read a book now"
"I read a book yesterday"
"I read a book tomorrow"

Auxiliary Verbs

Languages such as Italian and French use the verbs "to be" and "to have" as auxiliary verbs. In particular, Italian uses the verb "essere" and French uses the verb "etre" (note that an accent mark is missing here) as an auxiliary verb with intransitive (no direct object) verbs of motion. By contrast, English always uses the verb "to have" in sentences that contain compound verb forms.

Here are some examples of sentences that contain auxiliary verbs in English, French, and Italian:

"I have gone to school."
«*Je suis allé à l'école.*»
"Sono andato a scuola."

French compound verbs for motion use "etre," Italian uses "stare" and "essere," but English always uses "to have." Hence, the following sentences are *incorrect* because the French sentence has the verb *avoir* and the Italian sentence has the verb *avere* as the auxiliary verb:

"J'ai allé à l'école."
"Ho andato a scuola."

One other detail: French and Italian tend to use the "present perfect" (which involves an auxiliary verb) in conversations, whereas English, Portuguese, and Spanish tend to use the simple past (also called the "preterite" which does not involve an auxiliary verb):

Spanish:

Fui a la escuela ("I went to school")
He ido a la escuela("I have gone to school")

Portuguese:

Eu fui a escola ("I went to school")
Eu he ido para a escola ("I have gone to school")

Spanish and Portuguese have an additional interesting feature: they have two verbs "estar" and "ser" that are related "to be" yet have different connotations. The verb "estar" refers to a temporary or transient state, such as "Estoy aqui" (I am here) or "Estoy cansado" (I am tired), whereas the verb "ser" refers to a (perceived) longer term state, such as "Soy rico" (I am rich) or "Soy viejo" (I am old).

In Portuguese, the corresponding sentences are "Estou aqui" (I am here), "Estou cansado" (I am tired), "Sou rico" (I am rich), and "Sou velho" (I am old). The word "rico" is singular masculine: rica and ricos are for singular feminine and plural (male and female), respectively.

By the way, verbs sometimes undergo changes in pronunciation and sentence undergo "contractions" in casual conversation. Here are examples of three sentences that mean "I do not know" in French, and only the first sentence is grammatically correct:

"Je ne sais pas."
"Je sais pas."
"Sheh pas." (similar to English "I dunno.")

What are Case Endings?

A case ending is a suffix of a word that indicates the grammatical function of a word in a sentence. English has no case endings (except in rare cases) and is also word-order dependent, which means that the following pair of sentences have the opposite meaning:

The man sees the dog
The dog sees the man

The first sentence can be written in two ways in German (notice the definite articles den and der), both of which have the same meaning:

Der Mann sieht **den** Hund
Den Hund sieht der Mann

The German article *den* (above) indicates a direct object, which means that the previous pair of sentences have the same meaning in German.

German has case endings for articles and adjectives. For example, "ein," "diese," and "gut" mean "a," "the," and "good," respectively, in German. When these words are used in the dative (indirect object) case, they become "einem," "diesem," and "gutem," respectively, for a masculine noun. Here's a summary of case endings for German:

```
    Masc Fem Neut Plural
Nom der  die das  die
Gen des  der des  der
Dat dem  der dem  den
Acc den  die das  die
```

Notice that the indirect object particle *dem* in German has the counterpart *him* in English, and the word *ihr* in German is the counterpart to the word *her* in English. Thus the syntax and worder order in the following German sentence is similar to its English counterpart:

```
Ich gebe ihm das Buch (I give him the book)
Ich gebe ihr das Buch (I give her the book)
```

The preceding sentence has a subject/verb/object structure because the verb is a simple verb. If you use a compound verb involving an auxiliary verb, then the structure of the sentence is subject/object/verb. For example, the following German sentence means "I have given him a book":

Ich **habe** *ihm* das Buch **gegeben** (**I have given** *him* the book)

Returning to the topic of case endings: the following languages also have case endings (in increasing order with respect to the number of cases in each language):

Arabic (3)
German (4)
Greek (5)
Russian (6)
Lithuanian (7)
Latin (15)
Finnish (21 (but no gender)

By contrast, English, romance languages, and Asian languages (Cantonese, Mandarin, Japanese, and Korean) do not have case endings. The meaning of sentences in English and romance languages is typically word-order dependent. However, Korean and Japanese both have postpositions that indicate the grammatical function of the nouns in a sentence, so it's possible to reorder sentences in both of these languages and still retain the same meaning of the original sentence. Context is often important, especially in Japanese sentences that are ambiguous in terms of the number of people (or objects) that are referenced.

Languages and Gender

Romance languages have a masculine and feminine form for nouns and are preceded by definite articles that reflect the gender and number of nouns (more later). Although Romanian is a romance language, it has masculine, feminine, and also has a neuter form for nouns. When you consider the fact that romance languages are derived from Latin, which has a masculine, feminine, and neuter form for nouns, perhaps Romanian is the only romance language that retained the neuter form for nouns.

Germanic languages and Slavic languages also have three genders, and the endings of adjectives and definite/indefinite articles that precede them are modified (see the section regarding case endings). By contrast, English, Finnish, Japanese, and Korean do not have gender forms for nouns.

Singular and Plural Forms of Nouns

All the languages in the preceding section that have two or more genders also have singular and plural forms for nouns. Here are examples of sentences in Italian about buying one or more books:

"Ho comperato il libro."   [I bought the book.]
"L'ho comperat**o**."   [I bought it (ex: a book).]
"L'ho comperat**a**."   [I bought it (ex: a car).]
"Ho comperato i libri."   [I bought the books.]
"Gli ho comperati."   [I bought them (the books).]

Notice the use of "il" for the singular case and "i" for the plural case, as well as "L'ho" and "gli ho" for the direct object referring to one versus multiple books, respectively. In addition, the second sentence changes the verb from *comperato* to *comperata* to *comperati*, because its form must agree in gender and number when there is a preceding direct object. Hence, the English sentence "I bought them" when referring to a feminine plural noun is written as follows in Italian:

"Le ho comperate."

Once again, Finnish, Japanese, and Korean do not have a plural form for nouns, which avoids having to learn rules for forming the plural of nouns. However, most of these languages involve other grammatical challenges for nonnative speakers.

Changes in Spelling of Words

Another example involves different spellings for the same word: center/centre, favor/favour, color/colour, and so forth. These variations in spelling appear in different English speaking countries (United States, Canada, UK, and Australia). Yet another example is a "false cognate" in which a word in one language has an entirely different meaning in another language. A simple example is the German word "gift," which translates as "poison" in English.

Japanese Grammar

The Foreign Service Institute (FSI) ranks various languages from the perspective of an English speaker, and provides an estimate of the number of hours that are required to achieve a general level of proficiency. The FSI does note that "some language speakers or experts may disagree with the ranking."

Level 5 is the most difficult, and consists of Arabic, Cantonese, Japanese, Korean, and Mandarin. Language that are "usually more difficult" for native English speakers include Japanese and seven other languages, as shown here:

https://effectivelanguagelearning.com/language-guide/language-difficulty/

This section contains several subsections that describe grammatical features, some of which are unique to Japanese and also pose interesting challenges for NLP.

Japanese Postpositions (Particles)

Instead of prepositions, Japanese uses "post positions" (which can occur multiple times in a sentence). Here are some common Japanese postpositions that are written in Romanji:

Ka (a marker for a question)
Wa (the "topic" of a sentence)
Ga (the subject of a sentence)
O (direct object)
To (can mean "for" and "and")
Ni (physical motion toward something)
E (toward something)

The particle "ka" at the end of a sentence in Japanese indicates a question. A simple example of "ka" is the Romanji sentence "Nan desu ka", which means "what is it?"

An example of "wa" is the following sentence: "Watashi **wa** Nihon jin desu," which means "As for me, I'm Japanese." By contrast, the sentence "Watashi **ga** Nihon jin desu," which means "It is I (not somebody else) who is Japanese."

As you can see, Japanese makes a distinction between the topic of a sentence (with "wa") versus the subject of a sentence (with "ga"). A Japanese sentence can contain both particles "wa" and "ga," with the following twist: if a negative fact is expressed about the noun that precedes "ga," then "ga" is replaced with "wa" *and* the main verb is written in the negative form. For example, the Romanji sentence "I still have not studied Kanji" is translated into Hiragana as follows:

Watashi **wa** kanji **wa** mada benkyou shite imasen.

わたし わ かんじ わ まだ べんきょ して いません

However, Google Translate generates the following humorous translation for the preceding Romanji sentence:

```
I'm a toilet I haven't done it yet
```

By contrast, if you enter the sentence "I have studied Kanji", Google Translate generates the following:

漢字を勉強しました

Kanji o benkyō shimashita

As you can see, the preceding Romanji sentence omits "Watashi wa" and treats the noun "Kanji" as the direct object of the verb "studied."

Yet another use of "ga" is to express "but," as in the sentence "Today, I will work, but tomorrow I will play tennis," where the Japanese sentence consists of Kanji, Hiragana, and Katakana (for the word tennis) and does not contain spaces between words, whereas the Romanji translation includes spaces for your convenience:

今日は勉強しますが明日はテニスをします

Kyō wa benkyō shimasu ga ashita wa tenisu o shimasu

As you can see from the preceding examples, there are multiple rules regarding the various combinations of "wa" and "ga" in the same sentence.

An example of a direct object is illustrated in the sentence "Watashi wa terebi **o** miru", which means "I watch television" because "o" follows "terebi" (and the latter is derived from "television").

The sentence "Tomodachi **to** isshyo ni ikimashita" means "I went with my friend" (and other translations are possible as well).

Japanese sentences can contain a combination of Hiragana, Katakana (just for foreign words), and Kanji. For example, the following sentence in Romanji means "He loves drinking beer":

Kare wa biru o nomu no ga daisuki desu.

Although the Japanese verb "nomu" means "to drink," the preceding sentence contains "nomu no ga," which is called "nominalizing a verb" (discussed later).

The preceding sentence written using a combination of Hiragana, Katakana, and Kanji is here (and it's obviously much more complex than Romanji):

彼はビールを飲むのが大好きです

If you use Google Translate, the following sentence is generated, which is almost identical to the preceding sentence (the only difference is the direct object particle):

彼わビルお飲むのが大好きです

Consecutive postpositions in Japanese are also possible. For example, the sentence "Nihon e iku **toki ni wa**, sushi o tabemasu" means "when (whenever) [I] go to Japan, I eat sushi," and also contains three consecutive post positions. The pronoun "I" is in square brackets because the speaker might be one or more different people.

However, multiple consecutive postpositions adhere to rules (i.e., not all combinations are possible), which creates more complexity for nonnative-Japanese speakers. If a Japanese sentence in Hiragana is written without spaces, ambiguity can arise regarding whether to interpret a syllable as a postposition or as part of a word. To illustrate this detail, consider the interesting Japanese sentence "The artist drew a picture," whose translation is clear when it's written as follows::

Gaka ga e o kaita

As you already know, the particles "ga" and "o" are postpositions; the word "e" is a postposition as well, but in this case it's a homonym for the word "picture." This is an example whereby two words with different Kanji have the same pronunciation (and the same is true for Mandarin and Cantonese).

Now consider what happens when the preceding Romanji sentence is written without any spaces:

Gakagaeokaita

The preceding sentence might appear to have six consecutive postpositions: ga, ka, ga, e, o, and ka. As you can see, knowledge of Japanese vocabulary is necessary in order to parse the preceding sentence correctly. Incidentally, the preceding Romanji sentence can also be written as shown here, with no change in meaning, because the postpositions are "markers" for the grammatical function of the nouns in the sentence:

E o gaka ga kaita

In case you are interested, the following link contains an extensive list of Japanese sentences with postpositions:

https://en.wikipedia.org/wiki/Japanese_particles

Ambiguity in Japanese Sentences

Since Japanese does not pluralize nouns, the same word is used for singular as well as plural, which requires contextual information in order to determine the exact meaning of a Japanese sentence. As a simple illustration, which is discussed in more detail later in this chapter under the topic of tokenization, here is a Japanese sentence written in Romanji, followed by Hiragana and Kanji (the second and third sentences are from Google Translate):

```
Watashi wa tomodachi ni hon o agemashita
```

わたし わ ともだち に ほん お あげました

友達に本をあげた

The preceding sentence can mean any of the following, and the correct interpretation depends on the context of a conversation:

- I gave a book to a friend
- I gave a book to friends
- I gave books to a friend
- I gave books to friends

Moreover, the context for the words *friend* and *friends* in the Japanese sentence is also ambiguous: they do not indicate whose friends (mine, yours, his, hers, and so forth). In fact, the following Japanese sentence is also grammatically correct and ambiguous:

```
Tomodachi ni hon o agemashita
```

The preceding sentence does not specify who gave a book (or books) to a friend (or friends), but its context will be clear during a conversation. Incidentally, Japanese people often omit the subject pronoun (unless the sentence becomes ambiguous), so it's more common to see the second sentence (i.e., without "Watashi wa") instead of the first Romanji sentence.

Contrast the earlier Japanese sentence with its counterpart in the romance languages Italian, Spanish, French, Portuguese, and finally in German (some accent marks are missing for some words):

```
Italian:    Ho dato un libro a mio amico
Spanish:    [Yo] Le di un libro a mi amigo
Portuguese: Eu dei um livro para meu amigo
French:     J'ai donne un livre au mon ami
German:     Ich habe ein Buch dem Freund gegeben
```

Notice that the Italian and French sentences use a compound verb whose two parts are consecutive (adjacent), whereas German uses a compound verb in which the second part (the past participle) is at the end of the sentence. However, the Spanish and Portuguese sentences use the simple past (the "preterite") form of the verb "to give."

Japanese Nominalization

Nominalizers convert verbs (or even entire sentences) into a noun. Nominalizers resemble a "that" clause in English, and they are useful when speaking about an action as a noun. Japanese has two nominalizers: "no" and "koto ga."

The nominalizer の (no) is required with verbs of perception, such as 見る (to see) and 聞く (to listen). For example, the following sentence means "I love listening to music," written in Romanji in the first sentence, followed by a second sentence that contains a mixture of Kanji and Hiragana:

```
Watashi wa ongaku o kiku no ga daisuki desu
```
私わ音楽おきくのが大好きです

The next three sentences all mean "He loves reading a newspaper," written in Romanji and then Hiragana and Kanji:

```
Kare wa shimbun o yomu no ga daisuki desu
```
かれは新聞を読みのがだいすきです
彼わ　しmぶんお読むのが大好きです

The "koto ga" nominalizer, which is the other Japanese nominalizer, is used sentences of the form "have you ever . . ." For example, the following sentence means "Have you (ever) been in Japan":

Nihon ni ita koto ga dekimasu ka

にほんにいたことがですか

Google Translate and Japanese

Google Translate provides a wonderful service, yet sometimes its translations from Japanese to English are incorrect. This point is not intended as a criticism of Google Translate; on the contrary, it's an indication of the complexity of the translation process, even for simple Japanese sentences.

For example, the following sentence means "I love reading a newspaper" but is incorrectly translated in Google Translate as "I love reading":

彼わしmぶんお読むのが大好きです

Note that the letter m in the preceding sentence is due to a limitation of the keyboard in translating ASCII letters to Japanese. As another example, the following (almost identical) sentence is incorrectly translated in Google Translate as "I love to read him" *because of the white space that precedes "yomu" (読む)*:

彼わしmぶんお 読むのが大好きです

If you enter the following sentence in Hiragana in Google Translate, the correct Romanji is generated:

ゆきがほんお読みました

Yuki ga hon o yomimashita

The preceding sentence means "Yuki read the book"; however, Google Translate provides this incorrect English translation:

I just read Yuki

As another example, the following sentence in Hiragana is translated correctly in Google Translate:

すしが ゆきに 食べられた

Sushi ga yuki ni taberareta

Sushi was eaten by Yuki

Notice how the particle (postposition) "ni" in the preceding sentence is translated as "by" when it's used in the context of the passive voice in English.

Japanese and Korean

As you learned earlier in this chapter, both Japanese and Korean have postpositions, some of which are similar. There appears to be some degree of comingling among Korean and Japanese, both of which have been influenced by Chinese. The following link contains some interesting details (i.e., a mixture of speculation, conjectures, and some facts) regarding the common aspects of Japanese and Korean:

https://linguistics.stackexchange.com/questions/41/are-the-japanese-and-korean-subject-particles-known-to-be-related-in-any-way-in

Vowel-Optional Languages and Word Direction

Some languages treat vowels as optional in written form, which includes the right-to-left languages Hebrew and Arabic. Native speakers of these languages know the correct vowels to insert in written text so that they can read newspapers and articles correctly. Interestingly, Arabic provides a letter called *sukun*, which looks like a small circle placed between two consecutive consonants to indicate that a vowel is *not* required between the consonants.

As mentioned earlier, most languages are written in a left-to-right fashion. By contrast, Japanese Kanji is written from top-to-bottom, and then in a right-to-left fashion. Moreover, letters in Arabic words can be vertically "stacked" as they are written in a right-to-left manner.

Arabic also has the concept of a "cluster" of three consonants that pertain to related concepts. For example, the sequence of three consonants k-t-b can be "filled in" with different vowels, and all of those combinations are related to the verb "read."

Mutating Consonant Spelling

Most languages with alphabets have a single form for each letter in their respective alphabet. However, a letter in Arabic can be written in two, three, or four different ways, depending on its location in a word or sentence. Specifically, the initial, medial, stand-alone, or terminal positions of a letter determine the manner in which the letter is written. For example, the stand-alone Arabic letters k, t, and b are shown here (from left to right):

ك ت ب

In fact, the Arabic word "kitab" (book) is the three preceding Arabic letters (i.e., no vowels are written).

ك ت ب

In Farsi the word "kitab" is translated in Google Translate as follows (which includes the short vowel "i"):

کِتاب

In Urdu the word "kitab" is translated in Google Translate as follows (which includes the long vowel "y" that is pronounced "ee" as in "meek"):

کیتاب

As another example, the following letter is the standalone Arabic letter "s":

سین

However, the Arabic letters that spell "seen" are as follows:

ن ي س

As you can see, only the right-most portion of the letter "s" is displayed in the preceding text, followed by the long vowel "y," and then the letter "n."

Another example is the Arabic word for "lemon," as shown below:

ليمون

The preceding Arabic word consists of the letters (from right to left) l, long y, m, u, and n (in left to right order). However, the letter m in stand-alone position looks like the following:

م

A complete list of the Arabic alphabet and many additional nuances and details is here:

https://en.wikipedia.org/wiki/Arabic_alphabet

Expressing Negative Opinions

In addition to the plethora of grammar rules in Japanese, there is another aspect in Japanese culture: how to decide which sentence to use when there is more than one way to express a negative opinion.

For example, the following English sentences are essentially the same in meaning:

```
I do not think he will go to Tokyo.
I think he will not go to Tokyo.
```

However, Japanese people view "I do not think" in the first sentence as expressing a personal belief that is stronger than "I think" in the second sentence. In general, it's better to avoid personal opinions when it's possible to do so, and therefore Japanese people will favor the second sentence over the first sentence.

The preceding example illustrates a subtle cultural detail that is not encoded in grammar rules, which can pose a challenge for NLP to generate a translation that is 100% correct from the perspective of a native Japanese speaker.

Now that you have a high-level view of various languages, let's briefly look at the other end of the linguistic spectrum, which is the topic of the next section.

Phonetic Languages

Many Indo-European languages and most Asian languages are phonetic, which facilitates the task of learning to pronounce words in an unrelated language. For example, Japanese and Italian are both phonetic, and a native Italian speaker can easily learn to pronounce Japanese words correctly (learning the vocabulary and grammar are far more complex).

By way of comparison, a native-English speaker knows that every word in the following list has the same vowel sound, and can also pronounce these words with ease: {I, eye, sigh, why, guy, fly, buy, tie}. However, try explaining to a non-English speaker why all the words in the preceding set have the same vowel sound. By contrast, the following set of Italian words have the same pronunciation for the vowel "o" because no other vowel has the same sound: {forno, bocca, giorno, dio, guasto, sporco, andiamo, and vediamo}.

Vowels in phonetic languages have one pronunciation, regardless of their location in a word. Consonants *usually* have a single pronunciation, although there are situations in which an adjacent consonant can change the pronunciation of its preceding consonant. For example, in Italian the letter "h" can *modify* the pronunciation of the consonant that appears immediately prior to the letter "h," such as "c'e" and "che," "ge" and "ghe" in Italian words (discussed later).

Thus, the letter "h" can modify the pronunciation of a preceding consonant, whereas in English the combination of "gh" can be silent (which never happens in Italian), such as the words "bough" or "bought," which have entirely different meanings even though they differ by a single consonant.

Many languages have words that contain double consonants, and in phonetic languages double consonants maintain the same pronunciation while doubling the amount of time to pronounce the two consonants. For example, the double consonant in the Italian words "vacca" and "nanna" merely lengthen the pronunciation of the letter "c" or the letter "n," and sometimes change the meaning of the word (such as "nanna" versus "nana").

Note that Spanish has very few double consonants (the Spanish word for "vaca" is the same as the Italian word "vacca").

By contrast, English words with double consonants sometimes change the pronunciation of the second consonant, such as the English words "accent," "accident," and "flaccid" (which has two different acceptable pronunciations). By contrast, the consecutive occurrences of the letter k in "bookkeeper" do not change their pronunciation (and are twice as long as a single k).

Although the Romance languages Italian, Spanish, and Portuguese (in Portugal) are phonetic, the pronunciation of French words is an exception, even though French is also a Romance language. Some French words have a distinctly nasal pronunciation, and other French words comprise multiple consecutive vowels. For example, the word "oiseau" (French for "bird") is pronounced "wa-ZOE," which is far different from the spelling of the word. French is also unusual because of the number of words that contain three consecutive vowels. Romance languages are derived from Latin, which includes French, despite the fact that the latter is a nonphonetic language. Interestingly, many words in Brazilian Portuguese can be pronounced in multiple ways (and not always phonetically).

English is particularly interesting because it's assuredly not a phonetic language, and yet it's ranked first in terms of the number of people who speak English. Although there are many nonnative-English speakers who can speak English fluently (and grammatically correct), it's sometimes more challenging for nonnative-English speaking adults to speak English without an accent.

However, when Dutch speakers speak their native language, they have a similar cadence as English. This detail is plausible, because Dutch is a Germanic language, which in turn had a significant influence on old English, just as Latin and Greek have had a significant influence on English.

Although English pronunciation can be a challenge for some people, it pales in comparison to Gaelic, whose pronunciation rules are as complex as they are remarkable. The number of people who speak Gaelic appears to be slowly decreasing, even in Ireland, and perhaps the language is slowly disappearing (to my Irish friends I will simply say, `Éirinn go Brách`.)

Phonemes and Morphemes

In linguistics, a *phoneme* is the smallest unit of speech in a language. Although standard English contains 26 letters, there are 44 phonemes in

English. For example, the word "bat" consists of the three phonemes "b," "a," and "t." Phonemes exclude diphthongs and triphthongs that consist of two phonemes and three phonemes, respectively.

Alternatively, a *morpheme* is the smallest meaningful unit of a language. A morpheme carries meaning, whereas a phoneme does not (the latter is a sound unit). Morphemes (and words) are combinations of phonemes, and they can be prefixes, syllables, or prefixes of words. For example, "disappeared" consists of the three morphemes "dis." "appear," and "ed."

English Words of Greek and Latin Origin

There are many interesting words in English whose roots are in Greek. Words with the suffix "ology," which means "study of," are of Greek origin. Examples include biology ("bios" = "life"), anthropology ("anthros" = "man"), anthropomorphism ("morphism" = "to change") to ascribe human characteristics to inanimate objects or nonhumans (such as pets).

If you love languages, then you are a linguaphile, and if you love words, then you are a logophile, which are derived from the Greek words lingua, philia, and logos that mean language, love, and words, respectively.

The English word "telephone" is derived from the Greek words "telos" (far away) and "phonos" (to speak), whose combination means "to speak far away" (which is a suitable combination for the word telephone).

Multiple Ways to Pronounce Consonants

The pronunciation of letters such as "c" and "g" in Italian words depends on the vowel that follows these letters. In German, when the letters "b," "d," and "g" appear at the end of a word, they are pronounced "p," "t," and "k," respectively. The following subsections illustrate the changes in the pronunciation of the consonants in words in various languages. (Be prepared for a lengthy read!)

The Letter "j" in Various Languages

The letter "j" in English words sounds like the letter "j" in "John", and the letter "g" can sound like the letters "g" in "go", "j" in "just", and "j" in "je suis", such as the letter "g" in the English word "mirage" (which is a word borrowed from French). The latter pronunciation of the letter "j" also occurs in Portuguese, Russian, and in parts of Argentina that is close to the border with Brazil. However, the more common pronunciation of "j" in Spanish is similar to "ch" in the German word "achtung." As an added twist, some Spanish speakers pronounce the word "yo" that sounds similar to "Joe."

In addition, the double "l" in "calle" is pronounced like "KA-yeh" in Spanish-speaking countries, with the exception of Argentina (perhaps because it's near Brazil), where the Spanish word "calle" sounds like "KA-jeh" (pronounced like the "j" in "je suis").

However, the "j" sound (as in "mirage") does not exist in standard Spanish that is spoken in other regions, nor does this sound exist in Italian. In fact, the letter "j" is not part of the original Italian alphabet. In Italian the correct pronunciation of the combination "ga," "go," and "gu" sounds like the letter "g" in the English word "gap." whereas "ge," "gi," and "gio" sound like the letter "j" in "John." Thus, the correct pronunciation of the Italian word "parmigiano" sounds like "par-meh-JA-no," like "jacket", and "JA" and "no" have short vowel sounds.

"Hard" versus "Soft" Consonant Sounds

For example, Italian words containing the letter "c" or "g" are immediately followed by the letter "h," the pronunciation is modified when the vowel that immediately follows the letter "h" is either "e" or "I."

Specifically, the combinations "ci" and "c'e" are pronounced like "ch" in "cheek" and "check." respectively, whereas the combinations "chi" and "che" are pronounced like "k" in "keep" and "kettle," respectively. Hence, the word "cecci" (chickpeas) is pronounced with two consecutive "ch" sounds as in "check." or "CHE-chee." The same pattern applies to "gi" and "ge" versus "ghi" and "ghe."

The preceding paragraph brings us to the proper noun Giorgio (George), which is sometimes pronounced as four distinct syllables ("gee-OR-gee-OH") by nonnative-Italian speakers, in an earnest attempt at making the correct pronunciation. Despite all of the preceding rules, Italians pronounce Giorgio as two syllables "JYOR-jo" (which admittedly is not entirely phonetic).

In addition, some German consonants also undergo changes in pronunciation: words that end in the letters "b." "d," or "g" are pronounced as "p." "t." and "k." respectively. Hence, "ab" (a prefix), "tod" (death), and "berg" (mountain) are pronounced as "ap," "tot," and "berk." Thus, Bergman is translated as "mountain man."

Another interesting grammatical scenario involves pairs of voiceless and voiced consonants, which is discussed in the next section.

"Ess," "zee," and "sh" Sounds

Some languages have pronunciation rules involving consecutive consonants that do not exist in English. For example, the letter "s" can be voiceless (as in "seed") or a voiced consonant that sounds like "z" (as in "boys"). In Italian, the letter "s" can also be a voiceless or a voiced consonant. The consonant "n" in English and Italian is a voiced consonant.

In addition, Italian also has a grammatical rule that a voiceless consonant that is immediately followed by a voiced consonant must be "converted" to a voiced consonant as well. Consequently, some Italians pronounce the English word "snow" as "znow," and "slice" is pronounced as "zlice."

However, the letter "z" in the initial position of Italian words (such as "zio" or "zia") is pronounced like "ds" in the word "ads." Moreover, an "s" between two vowels is pronounced as a voiced "s," whereas a double "z" is pronounced as a voiceless "s," which means that "pizza" is *not* pronounced "PEET-suh." By the way, in Spanish the letter "z" is always pronounced as a voiceless "s." and a voiced counterpart of the letter "z" does not exist in Spanish.

The pair of consonants "st" and "sp" are pronounced with a voiced "s," as in "street" or "spa." However, in Naples the letter "s" in the pair "sp" sounds like "sh" as in "sheep." Hence, Neapolitans say "SHpaghetti" instead of "spaghetti." Coincidentally, the pair of consonants "st" and "sp" in Arabic words rarely (never?) have an intermediate consonant, which is indicated by the letter sukun.

By the way, Spanish also undergoes some changes when the article "la" precedes a feminine noun with initial letter "a." For example, "agua" is feminine, but instead of "la agua," the correct sequence in Spanish is "el agua."

In Venezuela many people speak "criollo," whose pronunciation differs from spoken Spanish in the other South American countries. One significant difference in criollo involves the silent letter "s" at the end of a word. To be more precise, the letter "s" in terminal position is pronounced like the letter "h" in the word "hot."

For example, the sentence *El eta alla en la equina con do uiqui* in criollo is equivalent to the Spanish sentence "El esta alla en la esquina con dos uisquis" (accent marks have been omitted). Also keep in mind that Spanish refers to someone from Spain, whereas "Castellano" is the language that is spoken by people in Hispanic countries.

Three Consecutive Consonants

English has various word that contain three consecutive consonants, such as "street," "straight," "spray," and so forth. However, some languages avoid the occurrence of three consecutive consonants in a word, sometimes by changing the preceding article ("a" or "the") that precedes such a word.

For example, Italian uses "la" for feminine ("la casa") and "il" for masculine ("il libro"), and "lo" for masculine words that start with two consecutive consonants. Thus, "lo sport" is used instead of "il sport," and "lo stile" instead of "il stile," thereby avoiding the three consecutive consonants "lsp" and "lst."

In addition, "lo zucchero" and "lo zio" are correct, even though the sequence "il zucccero" involves a two-consonant sequence "lz." However, the initial rule still stands, because an initial "z" in Italian words is pronounced like "ds" in the English word "ads," which in turn sound like "dz" in English. Thus, "lo zucchero" is correct because it avoids three consecutive consonants "ldz" resulting from "il zucccero," and similarly for "lo zio," "lo zain," and so forth (clever, n'est-ce pas?).

Arabic also avoids three consecutive consonants. However, since vowels are optional and frequently omitted in written Arabic, fluent readers can silently insert vowels between consecutive consonants. In some cases of consecutive consonants there is no intermediate vowel, which readers will know due to the presence of the "sukun" symbol, which is a small open circle that appears between the pair of consecutive consonants.

Diphthongs and Triphthongs in English

Instead of "pure" vowels, English words typically contain diphthongs (and also some triphthongs) that are combinations of phonetic vowels. Here are some examples of English vowels and their phonetic counterparts:

```
"a" is phonetic "e" + "i"       (when it sounds like "pay")
"i" is phonetic "a" + "i"       (when it sounds like "eye")
"o" is phonetic "o" + "u"       (when it sounds like "foe")
"u" is phonetic "i" + "u"       (when it sounds like "you")
"y" is phonetic "y" + "a" + "i" (when it sounds like "why")
```

Thus, the English vowels a, o, and u are diphthongs, and the English letter y is actually a triphthong. The lone exception is the letter "e", which is a phonetic "i" when it rhymes with "pea."

Semi-Vowels in English

In addition to vowels, English also has consonants that can sometimes function as semi-vowels, such as the letter "m" in "prism," the letter "l" in "castle," and the letter "r" in "centre." There are other languages with consonants that can function as semi-vowels. One humorous (and challenging) example is the following Czech sentence that contains the semi-vowel "r" and no vowels ("Stick finger through throat"):

```
Strč prst skrz krk
```

Challenging English Sounds

Some sounds in English are difficult for nonnative-English speakers, generally for people whose native language is phonetic. For example, the combination "or" and "er" is simple when they are pronounced like "or" in the word "for" and "er" in "feral." However, the "er" sound in the following words can be more challenging for nonnative-English speakers:

world
hurt
her
earnest ("ear" + "nest"?)
girth

Notice how different combinations the verb-plus-consonant in the preceding words, and yet all of them have the same "er" sound.

Other difficult combinations are "th" in words such as "three", which is approximated as "tree" with a "trilled r" sound, and "third" is pronounced as "turd," and also with a "trilled r" sound. The sound of "th" in the word "then" can also be difficult, and it's sometimes approximated as "den."

As an aside, during a late evening talk show, Charlize Theron once explained that her last name is pronounced like "tron," with a strong trilled "r" sound, instead of "thur-ON," whereas the former pronunciation makes more sense to people who speak phonetic languages.

Silent letters can be especially challenging for nonnative-English speakers. People who speak phonetic languages will sometimes say "PLUM-ber" instead of "plummer." Sometimes the reverse happens: they pronounce a letter that is actually silent, such as the letter "h": they will say "HON-est" instead of "ON-est." Another fun set of English words and the variations in their pronunciation: *but* versus *put* versus *putrid* versus *purple*; low versus plow, and row (a boat) versus row (an argument). Now try explaining the logic behind the pronunciation of the following words containing "ou" that sounds like "ow," "oh," "uh," "oo," "er," and "yoo" to a non-English speaker:

```
plough
bough
rough
through
furlough
fur
eunuch
```

Another combination that is challenging (and sometimes for native-English speakers as well) is the combination of "th" and "z" sound in a word such as "youths." Sometimes you will hear "youths" pronounced as "yoots," depending on the speaker's location in the United States.

English in Canada, UK, Australia, and the United States

There are some relatively minor differences in the spelling of words in English spoken in the United States versus other English-speaking countries. One such difference is replacing "ou" with "o," as in color, favor, and neighbor instead of colour, favour, and neighbor. Another difference involves replacing "ll" or "pp" with a single "l" or "p," such as traveled and worshiped instead of travelled and worshipped.

Other simple changes: tire instead of tyre (UK), trunk instead of boot (UK), aluminum instead of aluminium, and eraser instead of rubber. Changes in pronunciation include "PRY-vacy" instead of "PRIV-acy" and "a-LOO-minum" instead of "a-loo-MIN-ium."

Perhaps the most important point to keep in mind is that the main purpose of speech is communication between people, regardless of the grammatical errors or accents of the speaker. Now that you have an understanding of the many nuances of human languages, you have a greater understanding of the various challenges and nuances facing NLP.

Perhaps the most important point to keep in mind is that the main purpose of speech is communication between people, regardless of the grammatical errors or accents of the speaker. Now that you have an understanding of the many nuances of human languages, you now have a greater understanding of the various challenges and nuances facing NLP.

English Pronouns and Prepositions

If you have struggled with the correct combination of pronouns and prepositions in English, there is a simple rule to remember: a subject pronoun in English (I, he, she, and so forth) can *never* follow a preposition (such as to, for, between, and so forth).

The following table displays subject pronouns, direct object pronouns, and indirect object pronouns in English:

Subject	Direct	Indirect
I	me	me
you	you	you
he/she/it	him/her/it	him/her/it
we	us	us
you	you	you
they	them	them

Based on the contents of the preceding table, which of the following fragments is correct:

1. "you and I disagree"

2. "between you and I"

3. "between you and me"

4. "between you and him"

5. "between we and him"

6. "between us and him"

7. "between we and they"

8. "him and I went to the store"

[Correct answers: 1, 3, 4, and 6]

If you replace the word "between" with the word "for" or "to" (or any other English preposition) in the preceding list, *the list of correct answers is the same*. In case you are interested, a list of English prepositions is available here:

https://www.englishclub.com/grammar/prepositions-list.htm

This concludes the whirlwind tour of languages, and by now you are probably saturated with the bewildering variety of grammatical rules, word order, declensions, gender, plural forms, and pronunciation rules. Keep in mind that there are thousands of human languages, most of which have not even been touched in this introduction. The next section starts with an introduction to NLP, followed by various NLP-related concepts.

What is NLP?

NLP is an important branch of AI that pertains to processing human languages with machines. In fact, you are surrounded by NLP through voice assistants, search engines, and machine translation services whose purpose is to simplify your tasks and aspects of your daily life.

NLP faces a variety of challenges, such as determining the context of words and their multiple meanings in different sentences in a document or corpus. Other challenging tasks include identifying emotions (such as irony and sarcasm), statements with multiple meanings, and sentences with contradictory statements.

With regard to language translation, Facebook has created an impressive model called the M2M model, which was trained on more than 2,000 languages and provides translation between any pair of 100 languages.

In high-level terms, there are three main approaches to solving NLP tasks: rule-based (oldest), traditional machine learning, and neural networks (most recent).

Rule-based approaches, which can utilize regular expressions, work well on various NLP tasks.

Traditional machine learning for NLP tasks (which includes various types of classifiers) involves training a model on a training set and then making inferences on a test set of data. This approach is still useful for handling NLP tasks such as sequence labeling.

By contrast, neural networks take *word embeddings* (vector-based representations of words) as input and are then trained using backward error propagation. Examples of neural network architectures include CNNs, RNNs, and LSTMs. Moreover, there has been significant research in combining deep learning with NLP, which has resulted in state of the art (SOTA) results.

In particular, the transformer architecture (which relies on the concept of attention) has eclipsed earlier neural network architectures. In fact, the transformer architecture is the basis for BERT, which is a pretrained NLP model with 1.5 billion parameters, along with numerous other pretrained models that are based (directly or indirectly) on BERT. Chapter 11 introduces the transformer architecture and BERT-related models.

Regardless of the methodology, NLP algorithms involve samples in the form of documents or collections of documents containing text. A corpus can vary in size, and can be domain specific and/or language specific. In some cases, such as GPT-3 (discussed in Chapter 11), models are trained on a corpus of 500 gigabytes of text.

As a historical aside, the Brown University Standard Corpus of Present-Day American English, also called Brown Corpus, was created during the 1960s for linguistics. This corpus contains 500 samples of English-language text, with a total of approximately 1,000,000 words. More information about this corpus is here:

https://en.wikipedia.org/wiki/Brown_Corpus

As a concrete example of NLP, consider the task of determining the main topics in a document. While this task is straightforward for a text document consisting of a few pages, finding the main topics of a hundred documents, each of which might contain several hundred pages, is impractical to complete via a manual process (and if you "farmed out" this work to multiple people you obviously would have to pay them).

Fortunately, there is an NLP technique called topic modeling that performs the task of analyzing documents and determining the main topics in those documents. This type of document analysis can be performed in a variety of situations that involve large amounts of text. Keep in mind that NLP can help you analyze documents that contain structured data as well as unstructured data (or a combination of both types of data).

The Evolution of NLP

NLP has undergone many changes since the mid-20th century, the earliest of which might seem primitive when you compare them with modern NLP. Several major stages of NLP are listed below, starting from 1950 up until 2020 or so, that highlight the techniques that were commonly used in NLP.

1950s-1980s: rule-based systems
1990s-2000s: corpus-based statistics
2000s-2014: machine learning
2014-2020: deep learning

Early NLP (1950s–1990s) spans several decades and primarily focused on rule-based systems, which means that they used a lot of conditional logic.

When you consider the structure of a sentence in English, it's often of the form subject-verb-object. However, a sentence can have one or more subordinate clauses, each of which can involve multiple nouns, prepositions, adjectives, and adverbs.

Even more complex is maintaining a reference between two sentences, such as the following:

```
Yesterday was a hot day and many people were uncomfortable. I
wonder what that means for the coming days."
```

Although you can infer the meaning of the word "that" in the second sentence, the correct interpretation is difficult using rule-based methods (but not with modern NLP methods). This era of NLP also performed various statistical analyses of sentences to predict which words were more likely to follow a given word.

The next phase of NLP (1990s–2000s) shifted away from a rule-based analysis toward a primarily statistical analysis of collections of documents. The third phase involved machine learning for NLP, which embraced algorithms such as decision trees and Markov chains. Once again, an important task involved predicting the next word in a sequence of words.

The most recent phase of NLP is the past decade and the combination of neural networks with NLP. In fact, 2012 was a significant turning point involving convolutional neural networks (CNNs) that achieved a breakthrough in terms of accurate image classification. Researchers then learned how use CNNs in order to analyze audio waves and perform NLP tasks.

The use of CNNs for NLP then evolved into the use of recurrent neural networks (RNNs) and long short term memory (LSTMs), which are two architectures that belong to deep learning, for even better accuracy. These architectures have been superseded by the Transformer architecture (also considered a part of deep learning) that was developed by Google toward the end of 2017. Transformer-based architectures (there are many of them) have achieved state-of-the-art performance that surpass all the previous attempts in the NLP arena.

A Wide-Angle View of NLP

This section contains aspects of NLP, as well as many NLP applications and use cases, which are summarized in this list:

- NLP applications
- NLP use cases

- NLU (natural language understanding)
- NLG (natural language generation)
- text summarization
- text classification

The following subsections provide additional information for each topic in the preceding list.

NLP Applications and Use Cases

There are many useful and well-known applications that rely on NLP, some of which are listed here:

Chatbots
Search (text and audio)
Advertisement
Automated translation
Sentiment analysis
Document classification
Speech recognition
Customer support

In particular, chatbots are receiving a great deal of attention because of their increasing ability to perform tasks that previously required human interaction.

Sentiment analysis is a subset of text summarization that attempts to determine the attitude or emotional reaction of a speaker toward a particular topic (or in general). Possible sentiments are positive, neutral, and negative, which are typically represented by the numbers 1, 0, and -1, respectively.

Document classification is a generalization of sentiment analysis and typically involves more than three possible flags per article:

https://towardsdatascience.com/natural-language-processing-pipeline-decoded-f97a4da5dbb7

In addition to the preceding list of sample applications, there are many use cases for NLP, some of which are listed here:

- Question answering
- Filter email messages
- Detect fake news

- Improve clinical documentation
- Automatic text summarization
- Sentiment analysis and semantics
- Machine translation and generation
- Personalized marketing

Some of the use cases in the preceding list (such as sentiment analysis) are discussed in later chapters.

NLU and NLG

NLU is an acronym for natural language understanding and although you might not see numerous books about this topic, it's a very significant subset of NLP. In very high-level terms, NLU attempts to understand human language in determining the context of a text string or document. NLU addresses various NLP tasks, such as sentiment analysis and topic classification. Another extremely important NLU task is called *relation extraction*, which is the task of extracting semantic relations that may exist in a text string. Moreover, the sources of input text can be from chatbots, documents, blog posts, and so forth.

As a simple example, consider this block of text and notice the different meanings of the pronouns "he" and "them":

```
"John lived in France and he attended an International school.
Mary lived in Germany and she also attended an International
school. Dave lived in London and met both of them in Paris.
One of these days, when he has some free time, they will meet
up again. Steve met all of them on New Year's Eve."
```

Although the preceding paragraph is easy for humans to understand, it poses some challenges for NLU, such as determining the correct answers to the following questions:

1. Who does the first occurrence of "he" refer to?

2. Who does the second occurrence of "he" refer to? Is it ambiguous?

3. Who does the first occurrence of "them" refer to?

4. Who does the second occurrence of "them" refer to? Is it ambiguous?

As you undoubtedly know, one of the challenges of human language involves the correct interpretation of words that are used ambiguously in a sentence, and such ambiguity can be classified into several types. For example, *lexical ambiguity* occurs when a word has multiple meanings, which can change the meaning of a sentence that contains that word. One approach to handling this type of ambiguity involves POS (Parts Of Speech) techniques, which is illustrated in the chapter with NLTK content.

Another type of ambiguity is *syntactical ambiguity* is also called grammatically ambiguity, which occurs when a *sequence* of words (instead of a single word) has multiple meanings.

Yet another type of ambiguity is *referential ambiguity* that can occur when a noun in one location is referenced elsewhere via a pronoun, and the reference is not completely clear.

Another very important subset of NLP is natural language generation (NLG), which is the process of producing meaningful phrases and sentences in the form of natural language from some internal representation. One impressive example of NLG is the ability of GPT-3 (discussed in Chapter 11) to generate meaningful responses to a wide variety of questions.`

NLP can be used to analyze speech (not discussed in this book), words, and the structure of sentences. As such, we need to become acquainted with text classification, which is the topic of the next section.

What is Text Classification?

Text classification is a supervised approach for determining the category or class of a text-based corpus, which can be in the form of a blog post, the contents of a book, the contents of a Web page, and so forth. The possible classes are known in advance, and they do not change; the classes are often (but not always) mutually exclusive.

Text classification involves examining text to determine the nature of its content, such as:

- topic labeling (the major topics of a document)
- the sentiment of the text (positive or negative)
- the human language of the text
- categorizing products on websites
- whether or not it's spam

However, most text-based data is unstructured, which complicates the task of analyzing text-based documents. From a business perspective, machine learning text classification algorithms are valuable when they structure and analyze text in a cost-effective manner, thereby expediting business processes and decision-making processes.

As you can probably surmise, text classification is important for customer service, which can involve routing customer requests based on the (human) language of the text, determining if it's a request for assistance (products or services), detecting issues with products, and so forth.

Note that some older text classification algorithms are based on bag of words (BoW) that only determines word frequency in documents. The BoW algorithm is explained in Chapter 5, along with code samples for BoW in Chapter 6.

One more thing: text summarization is related to text classification, and it's described in Chapter 9 in the section that discusses recommender system.

Information Extraction and Retrieval

The purpose of information extraction is to automatically extract structured information from one or more sources, which could contain unstructured data in documents. For example, an article might provide details of an IPO of a successful start-up, or the acquisition of a larger company by an even larger company. Information extraction would involve generating a summary sentence from the contents of the article. In a larger context, information extraction is related to topic modeling (i.e., finding the main topics in a document) that is discussed toward the end of this chapter.

Information extraction also requires information retrieval, where the latter involves methods for indexing and classifying large documents. Information extraction involves various subtasks, such as identifying named entities (i.e., nouns for people, places, and companies), automatically populating a template with information from an article, or extracting data from tables in a document.

As a simple example, suppose that a program regularly scrapes (retrieves) the contents of HTML pages to summarize their contents. One of the first tasks that must be performed is data cleaning, which in this case involves removing HTML tags, removing punctuation, converting text to lower case, and then splitting sentences into tokens (words). Fortunately, the BeautifulSoup Python library can easily perform each of the preceding tasks.

Another area of great interest in NLP is the proliferation of chatbots, which interact with users to provide information (directions, hours of operation, and so forth) or perform specific tasks (make reservations, book hotels, car rentals, and so forth).

Word Sense Disambiguation

Up until several years ago, word sense disambiguation was an elusively difficult task because words can be overloaded (i.e., possess multiple meanings). A well-known NYT article describes one humorous misinterpretation in machine learning. The following sentence was translated into Russian and then translated from Russian into English:

```
The spirit is willing, but the flesh is weak
```

The result of the second translation is here:

```
the vodka is good, but the meat is rotten
```

Here is the link to the NYT article:

https://www.nytimes.com/1983/04/28/business/technology-the-computer-as-translator.html

As another simple example of an overloaded word, consider the following four sentences:

You can bank on that result.
You can take that to the bank.
You see that river bank?
Bank the car to the left.

In the preceding four sentences, the word "bank" has four meanings. The task of determining the meaning of a word requires some type of content. The dismal state of word sense disambiguation resulted in a precipitous drop in enthusiasm vis-a-vis machine learning. However, the situation has dramatically improved during the past several years. For example, in 2018 Microsoft developed a system for translating from Chinese to English whose accuracy was comparable to humans.

NLP Techniques in ML

Earlier you briefly learned about NLU (Natural Language Understanding) and NLG (Natural Language Generation). The purpose of NLU is to "understand" a section of text, and then use NLG to generate a suitable response (or find a suitable response from a repository). This type of task is related to question answering and knowledge extraction.

Since there are many types of NLP tasks, there are also many NLP techniques that have been developed, some of which are listed here:

text embeddings
text summarization
text classification
sentence segmentation
POS (part-of-speech tagging)
NER (Named entity recognition)
word sense disambiguation
text categorization
topic modeling
text similarity
syntax and parsing
language modeling
dialogs
probabilistic parsing
clustering

Most of the items in the preceding list are discussed in Chapter 4; in some cases, there are associated Python code samples in Chapter 5 and Chapter 6.

NLP Steps for Training a Model

Although the specific set of text-related tasks depends on the specific task that you're trying to complete, the following set of steps is common:

[1] convert words to lowercase
[1] noise removal
[2] normalization
[3] text enrichment
[3] stop word removal
[3] stemming
[3] lemmatization

The number in brackets in the preceding bullet list indicates the type of task. Specifically, the values [1], [2], and [3] indicate "must do," "should do," and "task dependent," respectively.

Text Normalization and Tokenization

Text normalization involves several tasks, such as the removal of unwanted hash tags, emojis, URLs, special characters such as "&," "!," "$," and so forth. However, you might need to make decisions regarding some punctuation marks.

First, what about the period (".") punctuation mark? If you retain every period (".") in a dataset, consider whether or not to treat this character as a token during the tokenization step. However, if you remove every period (".") from a dataset, this will also remove every ellipsis (three consecutive periods), and also the period from the strings "Mr.," "U.S.A.," "P.O.," and so forth. If the dataset is small, perform a visual inspection of the dataset. If the dataset is very large, try inspecting several smaller and randomly selected subsets of the original dataset.

Second, although you might think it's a good idea to remove question marks ("?"), the opposite is true: in general, question marks enable you to identify questions (as opposed to statements) in a corpus.

Third, you also need to determine whether or not to remove numbers, which can convey quantity when they are separate tokens ("1,000 barrels of oil") or they can be data entry errors when they are embedded in alphabetic strings. For example, it's probably okay to remove the 99 from the string "large99 oranges," but what about the 99 in "99large oranges"?

Another standard normalization task involves converting all words to lowercase ("case folding"). Chinese characters do not have uppercase text, so converting text to lowercase is unnecessary. Keep in mind that text normalization is entirely unrelated to normalizing database tables in an RDBMS, or normalizing (scaling) numeric data in machine learning tasks. The task of converting categorical (character) data into a numeric counterpart.

Although "case folding" is a straightforward task, this step can be problematic. For instance, accents are optional for uppercase French words, and after case folding some words do require an accent. A simple example is the French word peche, which means fish or peach with one accent mark, and sin with a different accent mark. The Italian counterparts are pesce, pesca, and peccato, respectively, and there is no issue regarding accents marks. Incidentally, the plural of pesce is pesci (so Joe Pesci is Joe Fish or Joe Fishes, depending on whether you are referring to one type of fish or multiple types of fish). To a lesser extent, converting English words from uppercase to lowercase can cause issues: is the word "stone" from the noun "stone" or from the surname "Stone"?

After normalizing a dataset, tokenization involves "splitting" a sentence, paragraph, or document into its individual words (tokens). The complexity of this task can vary significantly between languages, depending on the nature of the alphabet of a specific language. In particular, tokenization is straightforward for Indo-European languages because those languages use a space character to separate words.

However, although tokenization can be straightforward when working with regular text, the process can be more challenging when working with biomedical data that contains acronyms and a higher frequency use of punctuation. One NLP technique for handling acronyms is named entity recognition (NER), which is discussed later in this chapter.

Word Tokenization in Japanese

Unlike most languages, the use of a space character in Japanese text is optional. Another complicating factor is the existence of multiple alphabets in Japanese, and sentences often contain a mixture of these alphabets. Specifically, Japanese supports Romanji (essentially the English alphabet), Hiragana, Katakana (used exclusively for words imported to Japanese from other languages), and Kanji characters.

As a simple example, navigate to Google translate in your browser and enter the following sentence, which means "I gave a book to my friend" in English:

```
watashiwatomodachinihonoagemashita
```

The translation (which is almost correct) is the following text in Hiragana:

わたしはこれだけのほげあげました

Now enter the same sentence, but with spaces between each word, as shown here:

```
watashi wa tomodachi ni hon o agemashita
```
Now Google translate produces the following correct translation in Hiragana:

私はともだちに本をあげました

The preceding sentence starts with the Kanji character 私 that is the correct translation for "watashi."

Mandarin and Cantonese are two more languages that involves complicated tokenization. Both of these languages are tonal, and they use pictographs instead of an alphabets. Mandarin provides Pinyin, which is the romanization of the sounds in Mandarin, along with 4 digits to indicate the specific tone for each syllable (the neutral sound does not have a tone). Mandarin has 6 tones, of which 4 are commonly used, whereas Cantonese has 9 tones (but does not have a counterpart to Pinyin).

As a simple example, the following sentences are in Mandarin and in Pinyin, respectively, and their translation into English is "How many children do you have":

你有几个孩子
```
Nǐ yǒu jǐ gè háizi
Ni3 you3 ji3ge4 hai2zi (digits instead of tone marks)
```

The second and third sentences in the preceding group are both Pinyin. The third sentence contains the numbers 2, 3, and 4 that correspond to the second, third, and fourth tones, respectively, in Mandarin. The third sentence is used in situations where the tonal characters are not supported (such as older browsers). Navigate to Google Translate and type the following words for the source language:

```
ni you jige haizi
```

Select Mandarin for the target language and you will see the following translation:

```
how many kids do you have
```

The preceding translation is quite impressive, when you consider that the tones were omitted, which can significantly change the meaning of words. If you are skeptical, look at the translation of the string "ma" when it's written with the first tone, then the second tone, and again with the third tone and the fourth tone: the meanings of these our words are entirely unrelated.

Tokenization can be performed via regular expressions (which are discussed in Appendix C) and rule-based tokenization. However, rule-based tokenizers are not well-equipped to handle rare words or compound words that are very common in German. In Chapter 4, you will see code samples involving the `NLTK` tokenizer and the `SpaCy` tokenizer for tokening one or more English sentences.

Text Tokenization with Unix Commands

Text tokenization can be performed not only in `Python` but also from the Unix command line. For example, consider the text file words.txt whose contents are shown here:

```
lemmatization: removing word endings edit distance: measure the
distance between two words based on the number of changes needed
```

based on the inner product of 2 vectors a metric for determining word similarity

The following command illustrates how to tokenize the preceding paragraph using several Unix commands that are connected via the Unix pipe ("|") symbol:

```
tr -sc 'A-Za-z' '\n' < words.txt | sort | uniq
```

The output from the preceding command is shown below:

1 a
2 based
1 between
1 changes
1 determining
2 distance
1 edit
1 endings
1 for
1 inner
1 lemmatization
. . . .

As you can see, the preceding output is an alphabetical listing of the tokens of the contents of the text file `words.txt`, along with the frequency of each token.

Handling Stop Words

Stop words are words that are considered unimportant in a sentence. Although the omission of such words would result in grammatically incorrect sentences, in some cases the meaning of such sentences might still be recognizable.

In English, stop words include the words "a," "an," and "the," along with common words and prepositions ("inside," "outside," and so forth). Stop words are usually filtered from search queries because they would return a vast amount of unnecessary information. As you will see later, `Python` libraries such as `NLTK` provide a list of built-in stop words, and you can supplement that list of words with your own list.

Removing stop words works fine with `BoW` and `tf-idf`, both of which are discussed in the next chapter, but they can adversely models that use word context to detect semantic meaning. A more detailed explanation (and an example) is here:

https://towardsdatascience.com/why-you-should-avoid-removing-stopwords-aa7a353d2a52

Keep in mind that a universal list of stop words does not exist, and different toolkits (NLTK, gensim, and so forth) have different sets of stop words. The Sklearn library provides a list of stop words that consists of basic words ("and," "the," "her," and so forth). However, a list of stop words for the text in a marketing-related Website is probably different from such a list for a technical Website. Fortunately, Sklearn enables you to specify your own list of stop words via the hyperparameter stop_words.

Finally, the following link contains a list of stop words for an impressive number of languages:

https://github.com/Alir3z4/stop-words

What is Stemming?

This concept refers to reducing words to their root or base unit. Keep in mind that a stemmer operates on individual words without any context for those words. Stemming will "chop off" the ends of words, which means that "fast" is the stem for the words `fast`, `faster`, and `fastest`. Stemming algorithms are typically rule-based and involve conditional logic. In general, stemming is simpler than lemmatization (discussed later), and it's a special case of normalization.

Singular versus Plural Word Endings

The manner in which the plural of a word is formed varies among languages. In many cases, the letter "s" "or es" is the plural form of words in English. In some cases, English words have a singular form that ends in s/us/x (basis, abacus, and box), and a plural form with the letter "i": cactus/cacti, appendix/appendices, and so forth.

However, German can form the plural of a noun with "er" and "en," such as buch/bucher, frau/frauen, and so on.

Common Stemmers

The following list contains several commonly used stemmers in NLP:

Porter stemmer (English)
Lancaster stemmer

SnowballStemmers (more than 10 languages)
ISRIStemmer (Arabic)
RSLPSStemmer (Portuguese)

The `Porter` stemmer was developed in the 1980s, and while it's good in a research environment, it's not recommended for production. The `Snowball` stemmer is based on the `Porter2` stemming algorithm, and it's an improved version of `Porter` (about 5% better).

The `Lancaster` stemmer is a good stemming algorithm, and you can even add custom rules to the `Lancaster` stemmer in `NLTK` (but results can be odd). The other three stemmers support non-English languages.

As a simple example, the following code snippet illustrates how to define two stemmers using the `NLTK` library:

```
import nltk
from nltk.stem import PorterStemmer, SnowballStemmer
porter = PorterStemmer()
porter.stem("Corriendo")

snowball = SnowballStemmer("spanish", ignore_stopwords=True)
snowball.stem("Corriendo")
```

Notice that the second stemmer defined in the preceding code block also ignores stop words.

Stemmers and Word Prefixes

Word prefixes can pose interesting challenges. For example, the prefix "un" often means "not" (such as the word unknown) but not in the case of "university." One approach for handling this type of situation involves creating a word list and after removing a prefix, check if the remaining word is in the list: if not, then the prefix in the original word is not a negative. Among the few (only?) stemmers that provides prefix stemming in `NLTK` are Arabic stemmers:

https://github.com/nltk/nltk/blob/develop/nltk/stem/arlstem.py#L115

https://github.com/nltk/nltk/blob/develop/nltk/stem/snowball.py#L372

However, it's possible to write custom Python code to remove prefixes. First, navigate to this URL to see a list of prefixes in the English language is here:

https://dictionary.cambridge.org/grammar/british-grammar/word-formation/prefixes

https://stackoverflow.com/questions/62035756/how-to-find-the-prefix-of-a-word-for-nlp

Next, a Python code sample that implements a basic prefix finder is here:

https://stackoverflow.com/questions/52140526/python-nltk-stemmers-never-remove-prefixes

Over Stemming and Under Stemming

Over stemming occurs when too much of a word is truncated, which can result in unrelated words having the same stem. For example, consider the following sequence of words:

university, universities, universal, universe

The stem for the four preceding words is *universe*, even though these words have different meanings.

Under stemming is the opposite of over stemming: this happens when a word is insufficiently "trimmed." For example, the words `data` and `datum` both have the stem `dat`, but what about the word `date`? This simple example illustrates that it's difficult to create good stemming algorithms.

What is Lemmatization?

Lemmatization determines whether or not words have the same root, which involves the removal of inflectional endings of words. Lemmatization involves the `WordNet` database during the process of finding the root word of each word in a corpus.

Lemmatization finds the base form of a word, such as the base word *good* for the three words good, better, and best. Lemmatization determines the dictionary form of words and therefore requires knowledge of parts of speech. In general, creating a lemmatizer is more difficult than a heuristic stemmer. The `NLTK` lemmatizer is based on the `WordNet` database.

Lemmatization is also relevant for verb tenses. For instance, the words run, runs, running, and ran are variants of the verb "run." Another example of lemmatization involves irregular verbs, such as "to be" and "to have" in romance languages. Thus, the collection of verbs is, was, were, and be are all variants of the verb "be." Keep in mind that there is a trade-off: lemmatization can produce better results than stemming at the cost of being more computationally expensive.

Stemming/Lemmatization Caveats

Both techniques are designed for "recall", whereas precision tends to suffer. Results can also differ significantly in non-English languages even those that seem related to English, because the implementation details of some concepts are quite different.

Although both techniques generate the root form of inflected words, the stem might not be an actual word, whereas the lemma *is* an actual language word. In general, use stemming if you are primarily interested in higher speed, and use lemmatization if you are primarily interested in higher accuracy.

Limitations of Stemming and Lemmatization

Although stemming and lemmatization are suitable for Indo-European languages, these techniques are not as well-suited for Chinese because a Chinese character can be a combination of two other characters, all three of which can have different meanings.

For example, the character for mother is the combination of the radical for female and the radical for horse. Hence, separating the two radicals for mother via stemming and lemmatization change the meaning of the word from "mother" to "female." More detailed information regarding Chinese natural language processing is available here:

https://towardsdatascience.com/chinese-natural-language-pre-processing-an-introduction-995d16c2705f

Working with Text: POS

The acronym `POS` refers to parts of speech, which involves identifying the parts of speech for words in a sentence. The following subsections provide more details regarding `POS`, some `POS` techniques, and also `NER` (named entity recognition).

POS Tagging

Parts of Speech (POS) are the grammatical function of the words in a sentence. Consider the following simple English sentence:

```
The sun gives warmth to the Earth.
```

In the preceding example, "sun" is the subject, "gives" is the verb, "warmth" is the direct object, and Earth is the indirect object. In addition, the subject, direct object, and direct object are also nouns.

When the meaning of a word "overloaded," its function depends on the context. Here are three examples of using the word "bank" in three different contexts:

He went to the bank.
He sat on the river bank.
He can't bank on that outcome.

POS tagging refers to assigning a grammatical tag to the words in a corpus, and useful for developing lemmatizers. POS tags are used during the creation of parse trees and to define NERs (discussed in the next section). Chapter 6 contains a `Python` code sample that uses NLTK to perform POS tagging on a corpus (which is just a sentence, but you can easily extend to a document).

POS Tagging Techniques

The major POS tagging techniques (followed by brief descriptions) are listed here:

Lexical-Based Methods
Rule-Based Methods
Probabilistic Methods
Deep Learning Methods

Lexical-based methods assign POS tags based on the most frequently occurring in a given corpus. By contrast, *rule-based methods* use grammar-based rules to assign POS tags. For example, words that end in the letter "s" are the plural form (which is not always true). Note that this rule applies to English and Spanish words. Alternatively, German words that end in the letter "e" are often plural forms (but they can be the feminine form of a word as well). Italian words ending in "i" or "e" are often the plural form of words.

Probabilistic methods assign POS tags based on the probability of the occurrence of a particular tag sequence. Finally, *deep learning methods* use deep learning architectures (such as RNNs) for POS tagging.

Working with Text: NER

NER is an acronym for named entity recognition, which is known by various names, including named entity identification, entity chunking, and entity extraction. NER is a subtask of information extraction, and its purpose is to find named entities in a corpus and then classify those named entities based on predefined entity categories. As a result, NER can assist in transforming unstructured data to structured data.

In high level terms, a "named entity" is a real-world object that is assigned a name, which can be a word or a phrase that distinguishes one "item" from other items in a corpus. Moreover, there are various predefined named entity types, such as PERSON (people, including fictional), ORG (companies, agencies, institutions), and GPE (countries, cities, states). A complete list of named entity types is here:

https://spacy.io/api/annotation

Although NER is very useful, there are situations in which NER can produce incorrect results, such as:

- insufficient number of tokens
- too many tokens
- incorrectly partitioning adjacent entities
- assigning an incorrect type

Later in this book you will see Python code samples from NLP toolkits, such as NLTK, that provide support for NER.

Abbreviations and Acronyms

As a reminder, an acronym consists of the first letter of several words, such as NLP (natural language processing), whereas an abbreviation is a shortened form of a word, such as prof for professor. Depending on the domain, a corpus can contain many acronyms or abbreviations (or both).

Detection of abbreviations is a task of sentence segmentation and tokenization processes, which includes disambiguating sentence endings from punctuation attached to abbreviations. This task is domain-dependent and of varying complexity (and higher complexity for the medical field).

The following link contains information about CARD (clinical abbreviation recognition and disambiguation) that recognizes abbreviations in a corpus:

https://academic.oup.com/jamia/article/24/e1/e79/2631496

In addition, you can customize the tokenizer in spaCy (discussed later) by adding extra rules, as described here: https://spacy.io/usage/linguistic-features

Furthermore, the PUNKT system was been developed for sentence boundary detection, and it can also detect abbreviations with high accuracy.

Chunking refers to the process of extracting phrases from unstructured text. For example, instead of treating Empire State Building as three unrelated words, they are treated as a single chunk. Chapter 4 contains an example of performing a chunking operation on some text.

NER Techniques

Currently NER techniques can be classified into four general categories, as shown below:

- rule-based
- feature-based supervised learning
- unsupervised learning
- deep learning

Rule-based techniques rely on manually specified rules, which means that they do not require annotated data. Unsupervised learning techniques do not require labeled data, whereas supervised learning techniques involve feature engineering. Various supervised machine learning algorithms for NER are available, such as hidden Markov models (HMM), decision trees, maximum entropy models, support vector machines (SVM), and conditional random fields (CRF).

Finally, deep learning techniques automatically discover classification from the input data. However, deep learning techniques require a significant amount of annotated data, which might not be readily available. In addition, NER involves some complex tasks, such as detecting nested entities, multitype entities, and unknown entities.

What is Topic Modeling?

Topic modeling refers to a technique for determining topics that exist in a document or a set of documents, which is useful for providing a synopsis of articles and documents. Topic modeling involves unsupervised learning (such as clustering), so the set of possible topics are unknown. The topics are defined during the process of generating topic models. Topic modeling is generally not mutually-exclusive because the same document can have its probability distribution spread across many topics.

In addition, there are hierarchical topic modeling methods for handling topics that contain multiple topics. Moreover, topics can change over time; they may emerge, later disappear, and then reemerge as topics.

There are several algorithms available for topic modeling, some of which are in the following list:

- LDA (latent Dirichlet allocation)
- LSA (latent semantic analysis)
- Correlated topic modeling

LDA (latent Dirichlet allocation) is a well-known unsupervised algorithm for topic modeling. In high-level terms, LDA determines the word tokens in a document and extracts topics from those tokens. LDA is a nondeterministic algorithm that produces different topics each time the algorithm is invoked.

By way of analogy, LDA resembles the `kMeans` algorithm (discussed later in this book): LDA requires that you specify a value for the number of topics, just as `kMeans` requires a value for the number of clusters. Next, LDA calculates the probability that each word belongs to its assigned "topic" (cluster), and does so iteratively until the algorithm converges to a stable solution (i.e., words are no longer reassigned to different topics).

After the clustering-related task is completed, `LDA` examines each document and determines which topics to associate with that document. Keep in mind that `kMeans` and `LDA` differ in one important respect: `kMeans` has a one-to-one relationship between an "item" and a cluster, whereas `LDA` supports a one-to-many relationship whereby a document can be associated with multiple topics. The latter case makes sense: the longer the document, the greater the possibility that that document contains multiple topics. Moreover, `LDA` computes an associated probability that a document is associated with multiple topics. For example, `LDA` might determine that a document has three different topics, with probabilities 60%, 30%, and 10% for those three topics.

Keyword Extraction, Sentiment Analysis, and Text Summarization

Keyword extraction is an NLP process whereby the most significant and frequent words of a document are extracted. There are various techniques for performing keyword extraction, such as computing `tf-idf` (term frequency-inverse document frequency) values of words in a corpus (discussed in Chapter 4) and BERT models (discussed in Chapter 11). Other algorithms include TextRank, TopicRank, and KeyBERT, all of which are discussed in this article:

https://towardsdatascience.com/keyword-extraction-python-tf-idf-textrank-topicrank-yake-bert-7405d51cd839

Incidentally, NER (described in a previous section) relies on key word extraction as a step toward assigning a name to real-world objects. If you generalize even further, you can think of NER as a special case of relation extraction in NLU.

Sentiment analysis determines the sentiment of a document, which can be positive, neutral, or negative and often represented by the numbers 1, 0, and -1, respectively. Sentiment analysis is actually a subset of text summarization. Sentiment analysis can be implemented using supervised or unsupervised techniques, in a number of algorithms, including Naive Bayes, gradient boosting, and random forests.

Text summarization is just what the term implies: given a document, summarize its contents. Text summarization is a two-phase process that involves various techniques, including keyword extraction and topic modeling.

The first phase creates a summary of the most important parts of a document, followed by the creation of a second summary that represents a summary of the document.

There are various text summarization algorithms, such as *LexRank* and *TextRank*. The LexRank algorithm uses a ranking model (based on similarity of sentences) in order to categorize the sentences in a document: sentences with a higher similarity have a higher ranking.

TextRank is an extractive and unsupervised technique that determines words embeddings for the sentences in a corpus, calculates and stores sentence similarities in a similarity matrix, and then converts the matrix to a graph. A summary is based on the top-ranked sentences in the graph. Chapter 9 contains additional details regarding text summarization and sentiment analysis.

Summary

This chapter started with a high-level overview of human languages, how they might have evolved, and the major language groups. Next you learned about grammatical details that differentiate various languages from each other that highlight the complexity of generating native-level syntax as well as native-level pronunciation.

In addition, you got a brief introduction to NLP applications, NLP use cases, NLU, and NLG. Then you learn about concepts such as word sense disambiguation, text normalization, tokenization, stemming, lemmatization, and the removal of stop words. Finally, you learned about POS (parts of speech) and NER (named entity recognition) and topic modeling in NLP.

CHAPTER 4

NLP Concepts (II)

This is the second chapter that discusses NLP concepts, such as word relevance, vectorization, basic NLP algorithms, language models, and word embeddings. Please keep in mind that this chapter focuses on NLP concepts, and Chapters 4 and 5 contain Python-based code samples that illustrate many of the concepts that are discussed in this chapter as well as the previous chapter.

The first part of this chapter discusses word relevance, text similarity, and text encoding techniques. The second part of this chapter discusses text encoding techniques and the notion of word encodings. The third part of this chapter introduces you to word embeddings, which are highly useful in NLP. In addition, you will learn about vector space models, n-grams, and skip-grams.

The final section discusses word relevance and dimensionality reduction techniques, some of which are based on advanced mathematical concepts. As such, these algorithms are covered in a high-level fashion, and if you feel inspired, you can perform an Internet search to find more detailed explanations of these algorithms. If you are not interested in the more theoretical underpinnings of machine learning algorithms, you can skim through this section of the chapter and perhaps return to this material when you need to learn more about the details of dimensionality reduction algorithms.

What is Word Relevance?

If you are wondering what it means to say that a word is "relevant," there is no precise definition. The underlying idea is that the relevance of a word in a document is related (proportional) to how much information that word provides in a document ("**how much**" **is an estimated value**). Stated differently, words have higher relevance if they enable us to gain a better understanding of the contents of a document without reading the entire document.

If a word rarely occurs in a document, that would suggest that the word could have higher relevance. Contrastingly, if a word occurs frequently, then the relevance of the word is generally (but not always) lower. For example, if the word *unicorn* has a limited number of occurrences in a document, then it has higher word relevance, whereas stop words such as "a," "the," "or" have very low word relevance. Another scenario involves word relevance in multiple documents: suppose we have 100 documents, and the word *unicorn* appears frequently in a single document but not in the other 99 documents. Once again, the word *unicorn* probably has significant relevance.

Another factor in the relevance of a word is related to the number of synonyms that exist for a given word. The words "unicorn" and "death" do not have direct synonyms (although the latter does have euphemisms), which means that in some cases the words will appear more frequently in a document, and yet they still have higher word relevance than stop words.

In addition to determining the words that are relevant in a document or a corpus, we might also want to know whether or not two text strings (such as sentences or documents) are similar, which is the topic of the next section.

What is Text Similarity?

Text similarity calculates the extent to which a pair of text strings (such as documents) are similar to each other. *However, two text strings can be similar yet they can have a different meaning.*

For example, the two sentences "The man sees the dog" and "The dog sees the man" contain *identical words* (and also have the same word relevance), yet they differ in their meaning because English is word-order dependent. Replace "sees" with "bites" in the preceding pair of sentences to convey a more vivid contrast in meaning. Clearly we need to take into account the context of the words in the two sentences, and not just the set of words.

Note that German is *not* word order dependent, so the words in a sentence can be rearranged without losing the original meaning. As you learned in the previous chapter, German supports declension of articles and adjectives (discussed in Chapter 3). In the following example of two identical German sentences, notice that the word order is reversed in the second sentence (see Chapter 3 for an explanation):

```
Der Mann sieht den Hund.
Den Hund sieht der Mann.
```

One approach to handle the word order dependency aspect of languages such as English involves creating floating point vectors for words. Then we can calculate the cosine similarity of two vectors, and if the value is close to 1, we infer that the words associated with the vectors are closely related. This technique is called *word vectorization*, and it's the topic of a section later in this chapter, after the section that discusses the meaning of text encoding.

Sentence Similarity

There are various algorithms for calculating sentence similarity, such as Jaccard similarity (discussed in Appendix A), word2vec with cosine similarity (the latter is discussed in this chapter), Latent Dirichlet Analysis (LDA is discussed later in this chapter) with Jenson-Shannon distance and a universal sentence encoder.

One class of algorithms involves cosine similarity (discussed earlier in this chapter), and another class of algorithms involves deep learning architectures, such as Transformer, LSTMs (Long Short Term Memory), and VAEs (Variational Auto Encoders), where the latter two are beyond the scope of this book. You might be surprised to discover that you can even use the `kMeans` clustering algorithm in machine learning to perform sentence similarity. Yet another technique is a universal sentence encoder, as discussed in the next section.

Sentence Encoders

Pretrained sentence encoders for sentences are the counterpart of word2vec and GloVe (both are discussed later in this chapter) for words. The embeddings are useful for various tasks, including text classification. Sentence encoders can capture additional semantic information when they are trained on supervised and unsupervised data. Models that encode words in context are also called sentence embedding models.

In particular, Google created the Universal Sentence Encoder that encodes text into high dimensional vectors that can be used for various natural language tasks, and the pretrained model is available at the TensorFlow Hub (TFH):

https://tfhub.dev/google/collections/universal-sentence-encoder

One variant of this model was trained with the Transformer encoder, which has higher accuracy, and another variant was trained with deep averaging network (DAN), which has lower accuracy. In fact, there are 11 models available at the TFH that have been trained to perform different tasks.

Working with Documents

Two tasks pertaining to documents involve document classification (determining the nature of a document) and document similarity (i.e., comparing documents), both of which are discussed in the following subsections.

Document Classification

Document classification can be performed with different levels of granularity, from document-level down to subsentence level of granularity. The specific level that you choose depends on your task-specific requirements.

Document classification can be performed in several ways in machine learning. One way to do so involves well-known algorithms such as support vector machines (SVMs) and Naive Bayes.

Document Similarity (doc2vec)

There are several algorithms for determining document similarity, including Jaccard (see Appendix A), `doc2vec` (discussed in this section), and `BERT` (discussed in Chapter 11).

The `doc2vec` algorithm is an unsupervised algorithm that converts documents into a corresponding vector and then computes their cosine similarity. The `doc2vec` algorithm learns fixed-length feature embeddings from variable-length pieces of texts. Despite its name, `doc2vec` works on sentences and paragraphs as well as documents. Details about the `doc2vec` algorithm are in the original paper which is online here:

https://arxiv.org/abs/1405.4053

The choice of algorithm for document similarity depends on the criteria that are used to judge document similarity, such as:

- tag overlap
- section
- subsections
- story style
- theme

The following article evaluates several algorithms for document similarity that takes into account the items in the preceding bullet list:

https://towardsdatascience.com/the-best-document-similarity-algorithm-in-2020-a-beginners-guide-a01b9ef8cf05

In case you're interested, the following link contains an example of using the `doc2vec` algorithm:

https://medium.com/@japneet121/document- vectorization-301b06a041

Techniques for Text Similarity

In general, a set of documents with the same theme typically contain words that are common throughout those documents. In some cases, a pair of documents might contain only generic words, and yet the documents share the same theme. For example, suppose one document only discusses tigers and another document only discusses lions. Although these two documents discuss a different animal, both documents pertain to wild animals, which clearly shows that they belong to the same theme.

As you can see, there is an indirect connection between the documents that discuss tigers and lions: they are both "instances" of the higher-level (and more generic) topic called "wild animals." However, tf-idf values for these two documents will not determine that the documents are similar: doing so involves a distributed representation (such as `doc2vec`) for the word embeddings of the words in the two documents.

The following article performs a comparison of different algorithms for calculating document similarity:

https://towardsdatascience.com/the-best-document-similarity-algorithm-in-2020-a-beginners-guide-a01b9ef8cf05

The preceding article compares the accuracy of `tf-idf`, Jaccard, USE, and BERT (discussed in Chapter 11) on a set of documents to determine document similarity. Interestingly, `tf-idf` is the fastest algorithm (by far) of the four algorithms, and in some cases `tf-idf` out-performed the other three algorithms in terms of accuracy.

In Chapter 5, you will see an example of performing document similarity using the `gensim` Python library.

Similarity Queries

Suppose that we have a corpus consisting of a set of text documents. A *similarity query* determines which of those documents is the most similar to a given query. Here is a very high-level sequence of steps in the algorithm:

1. Index every document in the corpus.

2. Find the distance between the query and each document.

3. Select the documents with the lowest distance values.

The distance between a query and a document can be computed in several ways, and one of the most popular techniques is called cosine similarity that is explained in more detail later in this chapter. As a preview, the cosine similarity of two vectors is the cosine of the angle between the two vectors; when this number is close to 1 the angle between the vectors is close to 0, which in turn suggests that the words associated with the two vectors are probably close in meaning.

What is Text Encoding?

Many online articles use the terms text encoding and text vectorization interchangeably to indicate a vector of numeric values. However, this chapter distinguishes between vectors whose values are calculated by training a neural network (word vectorization) versus vectors whose values are calculated directly (text encoding).

Please keep in mind that the purpose of this distinction is assist in understanding the differences (as well as similarities) among various vectorization documents (i.e., it's not to be pedantic). Please note that this distinction is not an industry standard.

Based on the distinction between text encoding and text vectorization, the following algorithms are text encodings:

- BoW
- N-grams
- Tf-idf

The algorithms in the preceding list have a simple intuition; however, they do not capture the context of words, nor do they track the grammatical aspects (such as subject, verb, noun) of the words in a document. Note that BoW and n-grams generate word vectors that have integer values, whereas tf-idf generates floating point numbers. Moreover, these three techniques can result in sparse vectors when the vocabulary is large.

Text Encoding Techniques

There are three well-known techniques for text encoding (all of which involve integer-valued vector), as listed here:

1. Document vectorization

2. One-hot encoding

3. Based encoding

The following subsections provide a summary of each of the preceding text encoding techniques. In Chapter 5, you will see code samples that illustrate these techniques. Another technique involves word embeddings, but since this technique involves more complexity than those in the preceding bullet list, word embeddings are discussed later. (If you would prefer not to wait: word embeddings are calculated by training a shallow neural network or by means of a technique called matrix factorization.)

Document Vectorization

Document vectorization creates a dictionary of unique words in the document and each word becomes a column in the vector space. Each text becomes a vector of 0s and 1s, where 1 = the presence and 0 the absence of a word. This is called a one-hot document vectorization. Although this does not preserve word order in input text, it's easy to interpret and easy to generate as well.

As an illustration, the following technique performs document vectorization by performing the following steps:

- Determine the unique words in the corpus (let's call this M)

- count the occurrences of each unique word in each document
- for i = 1 to N (= number of documents):
-     for document i create a 1xM vector W
-         for j = 1 to M:
-             W[j] = 1 if word j is in document i

For example, suppose we have the following 3 documents (N=3):

Doc1: Steve loves deep dish Chicago pizza.
Doc2: Dave also loves Chicago pizza.
Doc3: Both like Guinness.

The list of unique words (M=11) in the preceding three documents is shown here:

{also,both,Chicago,Dave,deep,dish,Guinness,like,loves,pizza,Steve}

A text encoding for Doc1, Doc2, and Doc3 consists of 1x11 vectors containing integer values, as shown here:

Doc1: [0,0,1,0,1,1,0,0,1,1,1]
Doc2: [1,0,1,1,0,0,0,0,1,1,0]
Doc3: [0,1,0,0,0,0,1,1,0,0,0]

While document vectorization works reasonably well for a limited number of unique words, it's less efficient for a large number of unique words because the text encoding of sentences will tend to have many occurrences of 0, which is called sparse data. In this example there are 11 unique words, but consider what happens when there are several hundred unique words contained in multiple sentences: each sentence is (generally) much shorter than the list of unique words, and therefore the corresponding vector contains mostly 0s.

The preceding technique populates vectors with 0 and 1 values. However, there is a *frequency-based vectorization* that uses the frequency of each word in the document instead of just its presence or absence. This is accomplished by modifying the innermost loop in the preceding code with the following code snippet:

W[j] = # of occurrences of word j in document i

One-Hot Encoding (OHE)

An OHE is a compromise between preserving the word order in the sequence and the easy interpretability of the result. Each word in a vocabulary is represented as a vector with a single 1 and the remaining values of the vector are all 0. For example, if you have a vocabulary of 10 words, then each row in a 10×10 identity matrix is a one-hot encoding that can be associated with one of the ten words in the vocabulary. In general, each row of an n×n identity matrix can represent a categorical variable that has n distinct values. Unfortunately, this technique can result in a very sparse and very large input tensor. Chapter 5 contains a code sample that illustrates a one-hot encoding of a vocabulary.

An OHE relies on a BoW representation of the words in a vocabulary. An OHE assumes that words are independent, which means that synonyms are represented by different vectors. The size of each vector equals the number of words in the vocabulary. Thus, a vocabulary of 100 words is encoded as 100 vectors, each of which as 100 elements (99 of them are 0 and one of them is 1).

As a simple example, the sentence "I love thick pizza" can be tokenized as ["i," "love," "thick," "pizza"] and one-hot encoded as follows:

```
[1,0,0,0]
[0,1,0,0]
[0,0,1,0]
[0,0,0,1]
```

The sentence "We also love thick pizza" can be encoded as follows:

```
[0,1,1,1] = [0,1,0,0] + [0,0,1,0] + [0,0,0,1] = [0,1,1,1]
```

As you can see, the left-side vector [0,1,1,1] is the component-based sum of the three vectors that represent the one-hot encoding of the words love, thick, and pizza, respectively.

There are two points to notice about this encoding. First, the first index of this vector is 0 because this sentence contains "we" instead of "i." Second, the words "we" and "also" are not part of the vocabulary: they are called out of vocabulary (OOV) words.

One algorithm that can handle OOV words is `fastText` (developed by Facebook), which is discussed later in this chapter. Another approach involves a model that is based on bi-LSTMs (bidirectional LSTMs), as described here:

https://medium.com/@shabeelkandi/handling-out-of-vocabulary-words-in-natural-language-processing-based-on-context-4bbba16214d5

The key idea in the preceding link involves determining the most likely embedding for OOV words.

Another article regarding OOV words involves the skip-gram model that is discussed later in this chapter, but it's included here in case you are already familiar with this model (alternatively, you can wait until after we discuss the skip-gram model):

https://towardsdatascience.com/creating-word-embeddings-for-out-of-vocabulary-oov-words-such-as-singlish-3fe33083d466

Index-Based Encoding

This technique tries to address input data size reduction as well as sequence order preservation. Index-based encoding maps each word to an integer index and groups the index sequence into a collection type column. Here is the sequence of steps (in high-level terms):

- Create a dictionary of words from the corpus.
- Map words in the dictionary to indexes.
- Represent a document by replacing its words with indexes.

Although this technique supports variable-length documents, note that this technique creates an artificial (and misleading) distance between documents.

Additional Encoders

Although the previous sections discussed just three word encoders, there are *many* other encoding techniques available, some of which are in the following list:

- BaseEncoder
- BinaryEncoder
- CatBoostEncoder
- CountEncoder
- HashingEncoder
- LeaveOneOutEncoder
- MEstimateEncoder
- OrdinalEncoder
- SumEncoder
- TargetEncoder

We will not cover these word encoders, but information regarding the text encoders (along with with Python code snippets) in the preceding list is here:

https://towardsdatascience.com/beyond-one-hot-17-ways-of-transforming-categorical-features-into-numeric-features-57f54f199ea4

Now let's take a look at the `BoW` algorithm in more detail, as discussed in the next section, followed by a discussion of the `tf-idf` algorithm.

The BoW Algorithm

The `BoW` algorithm is straightforward: it's based on a dictionary of unique words that appear in a document, `BoW` generates an array with the number of occurrences in the document of each dictionary word. The advantages of `BoW` include simplicity and also an easy way to see the frequency of each word in a document. As you will see later, `BoW` is essentially an n-gram model with n=1 (n-grams are discussed later in this chapter).

However, `BoW` does not maintain any word order and no form of context, and in the case of multiple documents, `BoW` does not take into account the length of the documents.

As a simple example, suppose that we have a dictionary consisting of the words in the sentence "This is a short sentence." Then the corresponding 1x5 vector for the dictionary is (this, is, a, short, sentence). Hence, the phrase "This sentence" is encoded as the vector (1, 0, 0, 0, 1). As you can see, this (and any other) sentence is treated as a "bag of words" in which word order is lost. In general, a dictionary consists of a list of N distinct words, and any sentence consisting of words from that vocabulary is mapped to a 1xN vector of zeroes and positive integers that indicate the number of times that words appear in a sentence.

The `Sklearn` library (briefly discussed in an appendix) provides a `CountVectorizer` class that implements the `BoW` algorithm. The CountVectorizer class tokenizes the words in a corpus and generates a numeric vector that contains the word counts (frequency) of each word in the corpus. Moreover, this class can also remove stop words and examine the most popular 'N' unigrams, bigrams and trigrams. However, words inside `CountVectorizer` are assigned an index value instead of storing words as strings. Here is the set of parameters (and their default values) for the `CountVectorizer` class, which are explained in more detail in the `Sklearn` documentation page for this class:

```
class sklearn.feature_extraction.text.CountVectorizer(*,
input='content', encoding='utf-8', decode_error='strict',
strip_accents=None, lowercase=True, preprocessor=None,
tokenizer=None, stop_words=None, token_pattern='(?u)\b\w\
w+\b', ngram_range=(1, 1), analyzer='word', max_df=1.0,
min_df=1, max_features=None, vocabulary=None, binary=False,
dtype=<class 'numpy.int64'>)
```

As another example, with the corresponding code in a later chapter, suppose that we have the following set of sentences:

1. I love Chicago deep dish pizza

2. New York style pizza is also good

3. San Francisco pizza can be very good

The set of BoW word/index pairs is here:

```
{'love': 9, 'chicago': 3, 'deep': 4, 'dish': 5, 'pizza':
11, 'new': 10, 'york': 15, 'style': 13, 'is': 8, 'also': 0,
'good': 7, 'san': 12, 'francisco': 6, 'can': 2, 'be': 1,
'very': 14}
```

The BoW encoding for the initial three sentences is here:

I love Chicago deep dish pizza:

```
[[0 0 0 1 1 1 0 0 0 1 0 1 0 0 0 0]]
```

New York style pizza is also good:

```
[[1 0 0 0 0 0 0 1 1 0 1 1 0 1 0 1]]
```

San Francisco pizza can be very good:

```
[[0 1 1 0 0 0 1 1 0 0 0 1 1 0 1 0]]
```

As you have probably deduced, BoW models lose useful information, such as the semantics, structure, sequence and context around nearby words in each text document.

What are n-grams?

An n-gram is a technique for creating a vocabulary from N adjacent words together. Hence it retains some word positions. The value of N specifies the size of the group. In many cases n-grams are from a text or speech corpus when items are words, n-grams may be called shingles. One common use for n-grams is to supply them to the word2vec algorithm, which in turn calculates vectors of floating-point numbers that represent words.

In highly simplified terms, the key idea of n-grams involves determining a context word that is missing from a sequence of words. For example, suppose we have five consecutive words in which the third word is missing. This is called a "bigram" because we have two words on the left side and two words on the right side of the missing word.

There are two types of N-grams: word n-grams and character n-grams. Word N-grams include all of the following:

- 1-gram or unigram when N=1
- a bigram or a word pair when N=2
- a trigram when N=3

The preceding list also applies to character-based N-grams. In addition, the items in n-grams can be any of the following: phonemes, syllables, letters, words/base pairs according to the application. Here are examples of 2-grams and 3-grams:

Example #1: "This is a sentence" has the following 2-grams (bigrams):

(this, is), (is, a), (a, sentence)

Example #2: "This is a sentence" has the following 3-grams (trigrams):

(this, is, a), (is, a, sentence)

Example #3: "The cat sat on the mat" has the following 3-grams:

"The cat sat"
"cat sat on"
"sat on the"
"on the mat"

As yet another example, with the corresponding code deferred until a later chapter, suppose that we have the following set of sentences:

```
I love Chicago deep dish pizza
New York style pizza is also good
San Francisco pizza can be very good
```
The bigram pairs are here:

```
{'love chicago': 8, 'chicago deep': 3, 'deep dish': 4, 'dish pizza': 5, 'new york': 9, 'york style': 15, 'style pizza': 13,
```

'pizza is': 11, 'is also': 7, 'also good': 0, 'san francisco':
12, 'francisco pizza': 6, 'pizza can': 10, 'can be': 2, 'be
very': 1, 'very good': 14}

The ngram encoding for the initial three sentences is here:

```
I love Chicago deep dish pizza:
[[0 0 0 1 1 1 0 0 1 0 0 0 0 0 0]]
New York style pizza is also good:
[[1 0 0 0 0 0 0 1 0 1 0 1 0 1 0 1]]
San Francisco pizza can be very good:
[[0 1 1 0 0 0 1 0 0 0 1 0 1 0 1 0]]
```

Compare the bigram encoding of the same three sentences using a BoW encoding in an earlier section.

Calculating Probabilities with N-grams

As a simple illustration, consider the following collection of sentences, which we'll use to calculate some probabilities:

```
1) 'the mouse ate the cheese'
2) 'the horse ate the hay'
3) 'the mouse saw the horse'
4) 'the mouse scared the horse'
```

The word *mouse* appears in three sentences, and it's followed by the word *ate* (once) and the word *scared* (once). We can calculate the associated probabilities of which of *ate* and *scared* will follow the word *mouse* as follows:

```
Number of occurrences of "mouse ate" = 1
Number of occurrences of "mouse" = 3
probability of "ate" following "mouse" = 1/3
```

In a similar fashion, we have the following values pertaining to the word *scared*:

```
Number of occurrences of "mouse scared" = 1
Number of occurrences of "mouse" = 3
probability of "scared" following "mouse" = 1/3
```

As a result, if we have the sequence of words "mouse ___", we can predict that the missing word is *ate* with a probability of 1/3, and it's *scared* with a probability of 1/3.

As another illustration, consider the following modification of the previous collection of sentences, which we'll also use to calculate some probabilities:

```
1) 'the big mouse ate the cheese'
2) 'the big mouse ate the hay'
3) 'the big mouse saw the horse'
4) 'the mouse scared the horse'
```

The word *mouse* appears in four sentences, and it's followed by the word *ate* (twice), the word *saw* (once), and the word *scared* (once). We can calculate the associated probabilities of which of ate, saw, and scared will follow the word "mouse" as follows:

```
Number of occurrences of "mouse ate" = 2
Number of occurrences of "mouse" = 4
probability of "ate" following "mouse" = 2/4
```

In a similar fashion, we have the following values pertaining to the word "saw":

```
Number of occurrences of "mouse saw" = 1
Number of occurrences of "mouse" = 4
   Hence the probability of "saw" following "mouse" = 1/4
```

Finally, we have the following values pertaining to the word "scared":

```
Number of occurrences of "mouse scared" = 1
Number of occurrences of "mouse" = 4
probability of "scared" following "mouse" = 1/4
```

As a result, if we have the sequence of words "mouse ___", we can predict that the missing word is "ate" with a probability of 2/4, it's "saw" with a probability of 1/4, and it's "scared" with a probability of 1/4.

You can also calculate the probabilities of the word that follows the pair of words "big mouse ___": the probability that the third word is "ate" is 2/3 and the probability that the third word is "saw" is 1/3.

Although these examples are simple (and hardly practical), they illustrate the intuition of n-grams. When we look at n-grams for realistic sentences in a corpus that contains millions of words, the probabilities (and therefore the predictive accuracy) increase dramatically.

Now let's explore the details of tf (term frequency) and idf (inverse document frequency), after which we can look at the tf-idf algorithm in more detail.

Calculating tf, idf, and tf-idf

The following subsections discuss the numeric quantities tf, idf, and tf-idf (which equals the arithmetic product of tf and idf). As you will see, `tf-idf` provides a more accurate assessment of word relevance in a document than using just `tf` or `idf`.

The tf-idf algorithm is an improvement over BoW because tf-idf takes into account the number of occurrences of a given word in each document as well as the number of documents that contain that word. As a result, tf-idf indicates the relative importance of a specific word in a set of documents. In fact, the Sklearn package provides the class `TfidfVectorizer` that computes `tf-idf` values, as you will see later on in a code sample.

What is Term Frequency (TF)?

The *term frequency* of a word equals the number of times that a word appears in a document. If you have a set of documents, and a word that appears in several of those documents, then its term frequency can be different in different documents. For example, consider the two documents Doc1 and Doc2:

```
Doc1 = "This is a short sentence" (5 words)
Doc2 = "yet another short sentence" (4 words)
```

We can easily calculate the term frequencies for the words "is" and "short" in `Doc1` and `Doc2`, as shown here:

```
tf(is) = 1/5 for doc1
tf(is) = 0 for doc2
tf(short) = 1/5 for doc1
tf(short) = 1/4 for doc2
```

The following (albeit contrived) example shows you how to use term frequency to calculate numeric vectors associated with three documents in order to determine which pair of documents are more closely related.

Let's suppose that `doc1`, `doc2`, and `doc3` contain the words "pizza," "steak," "shrimp," and "caviar" with the following frequencies:

```
         doc1   doc2   doc3
------------------------
beer   |  10  |  50  |  20
pizza  |  30  |  50  |  30
steak  |  50  |   0  |  50
shrimp |  10  |   0  |   0
caviar |   0  |   0  |   0
------------------------
```

Now let's normalize the column vectors in the preceding table, which gives us the following table of values:

```
           doc1   doc2   doc3
-------------------------------
beer    |  .10  | .50  |  .20
pizza   |  .30  | .50  |  .30
steak   |  .50  |  0   |  .50
shrimp  |  .10  |  0   |   0
caviar  |   0   |  0   |   0
-------------------------------
```

For simplicity, let's use an asterisk ("*") to denote inner product of each pair of columns vectors, which means that we have the following values:

```
doc1*doc2 = (.10)*(.50)+(.30)*(.50)+0+0+0              = 0.20
doc1*doc3 = (.10)*(.20)+(.30)*(.30)+(.50)*(.50)+0+0    = 0.36
doc2*doc3 = (.50)*(.20)+(.30)*(.30)+0+0+0              = 0.19
```

Hence, the documents doc1 and doc3 are most closely related, followed by the pair doc1 and doc2, and then the pair doc2 and doc3.

The next section discusses inverse document frequency, followed by tf-idf, which we could use instead of the tf values to determine which pair of documents in the preceding example are most closely related.

What is Inverse Document Frequency (IDF)?

The following example illustrates how to calculate the idf value for the words in a set of documents. Given a set of N documents (ex: N = 10):

1. for each word in each document:

2. set dc = # of documents containing that word

3. set idf = log(N/dc)

Let's consider the following example with N = 2 and Doc1 and Doc2 defined as shown here:

```
Doc1 = "This is a short sentence"
Doc2 = "yet another short sentence"
```

Then the idf values for "is" and "short" for the documents Doc1 and Doc2 are shown below:

```
idf("is")    = log(2/1) = log(2)
idf("short") = log(2/2) = 0.
```

What is tf-idf?

The tf-idf value of a word in a corpus is the product of its tf value and its idf value. Keep in mind that tf-idf values are a measure of word *relevance* (not frequency). Recall that tf (term frequency) measures the number of times that words appear in a given document, so a high-frequency word indicates a topic in a document, and has a higher tf.

On the other hand, the `idf` (inverse-document frequency) of a word is inversely proportional to the log of the number of occurrences of a word in multiple documents. Thus, a word that appears in many documents makes that word less valuable, and hence lowers its `idf` value. By contrast, rare words are more relevant than popular ones, so they help to extract relevance. The `tf-idf` relevance of each word is a normalized data format also adds up to 1.

Notice that the `idf` value involves the logarithm of `N/dc`. This is because word frequencies are distributed exponentially, and the logarithm provides a better weighting of a word's overall popularity. In addition, `tf-idf` assumes a document is a "bag of words."

Note the following idf and tf-idf values:

- idf = 0 for words that appear in every document
- tfidf = 0 for words that appear in every document
- idf = log(N) for words that appear in one document

In addition, a word that appears frequently in a *single* document will have a higher `tf-idf` value. Moreover, a word that appears frequently in a document is probably part of a topic.

For example, suppose that the word `syzygy` appears in a collection of documents. The word syzygy can be a sort of differentiator because it probably appears in a low number of documents of that collection.

After the `tf-idf` values are computed for the words in the corpus, the words are sorted in decreasing order, based on their `tf-idf` value, and then the highest scoring words are selected. The number of selected words depends on you: it can be as small as 5 or as large as 100 (or even larger).

By way of comparison, `BoW` and `tf-idf` differ from word embeddings (discussed later in this chapter) in two important ways:

1. `BoW` and `tf-idf` calculate one number per word whereas word embeddings create one vector per word.
2. `BoW` and `tf-idf` work better for classifying entire documents, whereas word embeddings are useful for determining the context of words in a document.

Incidentally, you can implement a rudimentary search algorithm based on `tf-idf` scores for the words in a corpus, and make a determination based on the most relevant words (which is based on their `tf-idf` value) in a corpus.

As another example, with the corresponding code in a later chapter, suppose that we have the following set of sentences:

```
1) I love Chicago deep dish pizza
2) New York style pizza is also good
3) San Francisco pizza can be very good
```

The `tf-idf` pairs are here:

```
{'love': 5, 'chicago': 0, 'deep': 1, 'dish': 2, 'pizza': 7,
'new': 6, 'york': 10, 'style': 9, 'good': 4, 'san': 8,
'francisco': 3}
```

The tf-idf encoding for the initial three sentences is here:

```
I love Chicago deep dish pizza:
[[0.47952794 0.47952794 0.47952794 0.        0.
0.47952794 0.         0.28321692 0.        0.        0.        ]]

New York style pizza is also good:
[[0.        0.         0.         0.         0.38376993
0.        0.50461134 0.29803159 0.         0.50461134 0.50461134]]

San Francisco pizza can be very good:
[[0.        0.         0.         0.5844829  0.44451431
0. 0.        0.34520502 0.5844829  0.        0.        ]]
```

Compare the `tf-idf` encoding of the same three sentences using a `BoW` encoding and an ngram encoding in an earlier section.

Limitations of tf-idf

The `tf-idf` value is useful for calculating the word relevance of individual words, but can be less effective when trying to match a phrase in one or more documents. If you allow partial matches, then the set of matching phrases can contain phrases that are less relevant.

For example, suppose a set of documents pertains to various animals, and you want to find the documents that contain the phrase "strong beautiful racing horse." Would you accept the phrase "strong beautiful racing dog" as a match? If this phrase has the same `tf-idf` value as the original search phrase, then `tf-idf` cannot distinguish between them, and so `tf-idf` cannot reject the latter phrase in the matching set of documents.

As you will see, a better solution involves `word2vec` (or even better, an attention-based mechanism such as the transformer architecture) because `word2vec` provides word vectors that contain contextual information about words (which is not the case for `tf-idf` values). Even better is the Transformer-based architecture is discussed in the final chapter of this book.

As you know, `BoW` models lose useful information, such as the semantics, structure, sequence, and context around nearby words in each text document. A better approach involves statistical language models, as discussed later in this chapter.

Pointwise Mutual Information (PMI)

`PMI` is an alternative to `tf-idf`, which works well for both word–context matrices as well as term–document matrices. However, `PMI` is biased towards infrequent events.

A better alternative to `PMI` is a variant known as positive PMI (`PPMI`) that replaces negative `PMI` values with zero (which is conceptually similar to ReLU in machine learning). Some empirical results indicate that `PPMI` has superior performance when measuring semantic similarity with word-context matrices.

The Context of Words in a Document

There are two types of context for words: semantic context and pragmatic context, both of which are discussed in the following subsections. You will also learn about the distributional hypothesis regarding the context of words. An important point to keep in mind is that the distributional hypothesis is based on something called a heuristic, which means that it is based on an assumption that is often true. In fact, the assumption is true to that extent that its accuracy is reliable enough that it outweighs the frequency of its incorrect estimates.

In a subsequent section, you will also learn about the cosine similarity metric that is used to measure the distance between two floating point vectors that represents two words.

What is Semantic Context?

Semantic context refers to the manner in which words are related to each other. For example, if you hear a sentence that starts with "Once in a blue ___," you might infer that the missing word is "moon." Another example is "I'm feeling fine and ___," where the missing word is "dandy."

The *distributional hypothesis* asserts that words that occur in a similar context tend to have similar meanings. The *context* of a word is the words that commonly occur around that word. For example, in the sentence "the cat sat on the mat," here is the context of the word "sat":

```
("the", "cat", "on", "the", "mat")
```

The key idea is worth repeating here: words with similar contexts share meaning and their reduced vector representations will be similar.

Another interesting concept is pragmatics, which is a subfield of linguistics that studies the relationship between context and meaning. As a simple example, consider the following sentence: "He was in his prison cell talking on his new cell phone while a nurse extracted some of his blood cell samples." As you can see, the word cell has three different meanings in the previous sentence, and therefore any embedding that takes into account both semantic and pragmatic context must generate three different vectors. More information about pragmatics is here:

https://en.wikipedia.org/wiki/Pragmatics

Textual Entailment

Another interesting NLP task is called *textual entailment*, which analyzes a pair of sentences to predict whether or not the facts in the first sentence imply the facts in the second sentence. This type of analysis is important in various NLP-based applications, and actual results do vary (as you might expect). In fact, one of the techniques for training the BERT model is called NSP, which is an acronym for next sentence prediction. More details regarding NSP are in Chapter 11.

Discrete, Distributed, and Contextual Word Representations

Discrete text representations refer to techniques in which words are represented independently of each other. For example, the `tf-idf` value of each word in a corpus is based on its term frequency multiplied by the logarithm of its inverse document frequency. Thus, the `tf-idf` value of each word is unaffected by the semantics of the other words in the corpus.

Moreover, if a new document is added to a corpus, or an existing document is reduced or increased in size, then the initial `tf-idf` value will change for some of the words in the original corpus. However, the new value does not include any of the semantics of the newly added words.

By contrast, distributed text representations create representations that *are* based on multiple words: thus, the representations of words are not mutually exclusive. For example, distributed text representations include co-occurrence matrices, `word2vec`, and `GloVe`, and `fastText`. Keep in mind that `word2vec` involves a neural network to generate word vectors, whereas GloVe uses a matrix oriented technique (with SVD), which is discussed in Chapter 6. In addition, `word2vec` and `GloVe` are limited to *one* word embedding for every word, which means that a word that's used with two or more different contexts will have the same embedding for every occurrence of that word.

Finally, contextual word representations are representations that take into account all the other words in a given sentence. Hence, if a word appears in two sentences with two different meanings (i.e., context), then the word will have two different word embeddings for the two sentences. This is the fundamental idea that underlies the statement "all you need is attention." The attention mechanism is used in transformers, both of which are discussed in Chapter 11.

What is Cosine Similarity?

You are probably familiar with the Euclidean distance metric for finding the distance between a pair of points in the Euclidean plane: their distance can be calculated via the Pythagorean theorem. The Euclidean distance metric can be generalized to n-dimensions by generalizing the formula for the Pythagorean theorem from two dimensions to n-dimensions.

If we represent words as numeric vectors, then it's reasonable to ask: if two words have similar meanings, then how do we compare their vector representations? One way involves calculating the difference between the two vectors. For instance, suppose we are in two-dimensions (because this will simplify the example), and word U is a vector u with components `[u1,u2]`, and word V is a vector v with components `[v1,v2]`. Then the difference between these two vectors is `[u1-v1, u2-v2]`.

However, the difference between these vectors increases significantly if we multiply each of these vectors by a positive integer. In essence, we want to treat the vectors u and v as having the same property as u and `10*v`, which we cannot accomplish if we use the Euclidean metric.

The solution is to calculate the cosine of the *angle* between a pair of vectors, which is called the *cosine similarity* of two vectors. The *cosine* function is a trigonometric function of the angle between the two vectors. In brief, suppose that a right-angled triangle has sides of length `a` and `b`, a hypotenuse of length `c` (that's the "slanted" side), and the angle between the sides of length `a` and `c` is `theta`. Then the cosine of the angle `theta` is defined as follows:

```
cosine(theta) = a/c
```

The preceding formula applies to values of `theta` between 0 and 90 degrees (inclusive). Since `a` and `c` are positive, then `a/c > 0`, and since `a < c`, then `a/c < 1`. In addition, the definition can be extended as follows:

```
if   0 <= theta <=  90:  cosine(theta) = a/c (as defined above)
if  90 <= theta <= 180:  cosine(theta) = (-1)*cosine(180-theta)
if 180 <= theta <= 270:  cosine(theta) = (-1)*cosine(270-theta)
if 270 <= theta <= 360:  cosine(theta) = (+1)*cosine(360-theta)
```

As you can see, the cosine of `theta` is negative when `theta` is between 90 and 180, and its range of values is between 0 and -1. Since the cosine of `theta` is between 0 and 1 when `theta` is between 0 and 90, we arrive at the following result:

```
-1 <= cosine(theta) <= 1 (for 0<= theta <= 360)
```

We can generalize further for angles that are less than 0 or greater than 360: simply add (or subtract) multiples of 360 until we get an angle between 0 and 360:

```
cosine(-100) = cosine(-100+1*360) = cosine(260) =
(-1)*cosine(10)
cosine(750) = cosine(750-2*360) = cosine(30)
```

However, two vectors always form an angle that is between 0 and 180 inclusive. Since values of the cosine function are always between −1 and 1 inclusive, the cosine similarity of two vectors is also between −1 and 1 inclusive. As a reminder, the cosine of 0 degrees is 1, the cosine of 90 degrees is 0, and the cosine of 180 degrees is −1.

The intuition of cosine similarity is that "closer" vectors have a smaller angle between them, which means that the cosine of the angle is closer to 1, and so the words have similar meanings. Two vectors whose angle between them is close to 90 have a cosine similarity that is close to 0, and so the words are less related to each other. Finally, two vectors that "point" in opposite directions will have an angle of 180 degrees, and the cosine of 180 is -1, so the two words are potential antonyms.

You can get the inner product of two vectors A and B as:

```
A "dot" B = |A|*|B|*cosine(theta)
cosine(theta) = (A "dot" B) /( |A|*|B|)
```

```
Example: suppose that A = [1, 1] B = [2, 0]:
cosine(theta) = (1*2+1*0)/[sqrt(2)*2] = 1/sqrt(2)
In this case, theta is 45 degrees
```

Note that vectors are often "normalized," which means that they are scaled so that their length equals 1. Scaling a vector involves dividing a vector by its magnitude (also called the "norm"), which is calculated via the Pythagorean theorem.

```
Example #1:
If A = [1,1], then |A| = sqrt(1*1+1*1) = sqrt(2), and:
A/|A| = [1/sqrt(2), 1/sqrt(2)] (about [0.707,0.707])

Example #2:
If A = [2,0], then |A| = sqrt(2*2+0*0) = sqrt(4) = 2, and:
A/|A| = [2/2, 0/2] = [1, 0]

Example #3:
If A = [3,4], then |A| = sqrt(3*3+4*4) = sqrt(25) = 5, and:
A/|A| = [3/5, 4/5]

Example #4:
If A = [-4,3], then |A| = sqrt((-4)*(-4)+3*3) = sqrt(25) = 5,
and:
A/|A| = [-4/5, 3/5]
```

Although cosine similarity works well in many cases, it's not a perfect solution. For example, it's possible to have two sparse vectors representing two sentences with similar meaning, even if they have no words in common, they could have a cosine similarity around 0.6.

In addition to cosine similarity, there are other well-known distance metrics, some of which are discussed in Appendix A.

Text Vectorization (aka Word Embeddings)

In common parlance, *text vectorization* involves the creation of word embeddings, where each word embedding is a dense one-dimensional vector of floating point numbers. Moreover, the word embeddings are generated by a shallow neural network or MF. The good news is that there are various publicly available word embeddings available, so you don't need to be concerned about generating those vectors.

Depending on your task, you might be able to work with small vectors, such as 1x16 or 1x32 vectors. By comparison, the word embeddings in the BERT model (discussed in Chapter 11) are 1x512 vectors.

Since we can add floating point vectors that have the same number of components, we can calculate the average of two or more word vectors. Hence, it's possible to represent a document as the average vector of the words vectors in that document. However, such a vector is not necessarily meaningful with respect to the document.

You can use word embeddings to find co-occurrences. For example, "good" and "bad" both appear in a corpus and are near each other in an embedding space, despite the fact that "good" and "bad" are antonyms.

From a different perspective, it might be helpful to think of a word embedding as a projection of the index-based encoding (or a one-hot encoding) into a numerical vector to a lower-dimension space. The new space is defined by the numerical output of an embedding layer in a neural network. This results in a close mapping of words with similar role, but it does involves a higher degree of complexity.

Text vectorization is typically performed after various other tasks that are discussed in Chapter 3, such as normalization, stop word removal, lemmatization, and so forth.

As you will see later in this chapter, `word2vec` (developed in 2013) is one of the first text vectorization algorithms that produces word embeddings by training a shallow neural network (i.e., a single hidden layer), and every word is represented by a vector of floating point numbers. These vectors are *context vectors* because they contain contextual information for the associated words (the meaning of context will be explained later).

However, `word2vec` does have a significant limitation: a word in a document can only have a *single* context vector. Hence, the same context vector is used for a given word, regardless of whether or not that word has a different context in different sentences. The good news is that the Transformer architecture (discussed in Chapter 11) achieved a breakthrough by overcoming this limitation of `word2vec`. Thus, the context vector for a given word depends on the context of that word in a sentence, which means that the same word can be represented by different context vectors.

Overview of Word Embeddings and Algorithms

The section contains several subsections, starting with a description of word embeddings, followed by brief description of word embedding algorithms. Some of these algorithms, such as CBoW and skip-grams, are discussed in more detail later in this chapter. In addition to word embeddings, there is the concept of *entity embedding* that generalizes the concept of a word embedding: an entity can be a word, a sentence, or a document.

Word Embeddings

According to Wikipedia, *word embeddings* are defined as: the collective name for a set of language modeling and feature learning techniques in natural language processing (NLP) where words or phrases from the vocabulary are mapped to vectors of real numbers.

The goal is to capture as much semantic information as possible by finding a reliable word representation with real-number vectors. Techniques such as term frequencies or one-hot encodings do *not* provide any context for words in a sentence or a document. On the other hand, word embeddings *do* provide context for words, which enables you to create more powerful language models.

A word embedding is a representation of the underlying text corpus (i.e., a collection of text-based documents). Word embeddings are a context-independent embedding or representation.

Word embeddings are useful for document classification, which involves supervised learning (i.e., labeled data). You can also use word embeddings for document clustering, which involves unsupervised learning (i.e., unlabeled data).

Word embeddings reduce large one-hot word vectors into smaller vectors while simultaneously preserving some of the meaning and context of the words. One of the most popular methods for performing this reduction is called word2vec (discussed later in this chapter).

Fortunately, word embeddings are useful for analyzing text data in many languages (i.e., not just English text). Moreover, there are pretrained word embeddings available, and it's worthwhile performing an analysis at those word embeddings to see if they meet your needs. If not, then you can certainly create custom word embeddings.

Word Embedding Algorithms

There are several well-known word embedding algorithms, as shown in the following list:

- word2vec

- GloVe
- fasttext
- other lesser-known algorithms

The `word2vec` algorithm consists of two algorithms: CBoW (Continuous Bag of Words) and skip-grams. Both `word2vec` algorithms create word embeddings (i.e., vectors of floating point numbers) by training a shallow neural network that contains a single hidden layer.

The `GloVe` algorithm was developed at Stanford (more details are in Chapter 6), whereas the `fastText` algorithm is from Facebook, with more details elsewhere in this chapter. One of the most popular Python-based libraries for word embeddings is `word2vec`, which is the topic of the next section.

What is Word2vec?

A group of Google researchers developed `word2vec` in 2013, and it has become the foundation of NLP that is also incorporated in `BERT`. Word2vec provides an efficient method to represent words as vectors in a lower-dimensional space.

`Word2vec` takes text-based input and generates a vector consisting of floating points for each word in a text corpus. This task involves a neural network consisting of an input layer, a hidden layer (with no activation function), and an output layer that has the same dimension as the input layer. If you have studied deep learning, then you probably recognize this neural network as an autoencoder. If need be, you can use a dimensionality reduction technique to further reduce the dimensionality of the word vectors.

One point to keep in mind is that `word2vec` is described as an unsupervised algorithm because there is no need to label the training data. However, the shallow network that is used to generate word embeddings involves backward error propagation, which in turn requires labeled data. More accurately, `word2vec` involves self-supervision, which is a subset of supervised learning.

The material presented earlier in this chapter discussed the CBoW model (which uses n-gram) and the skip-gram model, both of which are part of `word2vec`. Later you will learn about GloVe, which is another `word2vec` model.

`Word2vec` is used for making predictions rather than counting words. In particular, `word2vec` is designed to accomplish the following:

- learn the distributed representations for words
- focus on the meaning of words
- attempt to understand meaning and semantic relationships among words
- handle unlabeled data
- works similar to deep approaches (such as RNNs)
- is computationally more efficient
- learns quickly relative to other models

Recall that the context of a word is the set of words that occur on either side of a given word. For example, consider the following sentence:

"The quick brown fox **jumped** over the lazy dog"

The context of the word "**jumped**" in the preceding sentence is shown here:

("The," "quick," "brown," "fox," "over," "the," "lazy," "dog")

In `word2vec`, words with similar contexts have similar reduced vector representations. `Word2vec` also has a skip-gram model whose goal is to predict the context words that surround a given word. For example, suppose we start with the given word "jumped": the skip-gram model would attempt to predict the context that is listed earlier in this section.

The context is derived through an iterative process that produces an embedding layer where the rows are vector representations of the words in a vocabulary.

In `word2vec`, every word in a vocabulary is represented as a vector. As a result, `word2vec` groups the vectors of similar words together in a vector space, and it detect similarities mathematically. Thus, `word2vec` creates vectors that are distributed numerical representations of word features, such as the context of individual words. In addition, `word2vec` does not require human intervention.

There are two well-known techniques that are part of `word2vec`: CBoW and skip-grams, and the latter is discussed earlier in this chapter.

The Intuition for Word2vec

An underlying assumption of word2vec is that the meaning of words can be inferred from their surrounding words. Suppose that two words have similar neighbors (meaning: the context in which it's used is about the same), then these words are probably quite similar in meaning or are at least related. For example, the words shocked, appalled and astonished are usually used in a similar context. As you saw earlier in this chapter:

"The meaning of a word can be inferred by the company it keeps."

Word2vec is well-suited for sentiment analysis based on a corpus of user-based reviews (such as movies, books, and so forth). This type of data is unstructured because there are almost no restrictions on the content of reviews (beyond a profanity rule). Other use cases for word2vec include:

- genes, code, likes, playlists, social media graphs
- other verbal or symbolic series in which patterns may be discerned

Word2vec can also be used for labeled data as well as unlabeled data. Keep in mind that algorithms which are designed to work with supervised data tend to require a large set of examples.

The Word2vec Architecture

The word2vec architecture options are skip-gram (default) or continuous bag of words. The training algorithm involves hierarchical softmax (default) or negative sampling.

Minimum word count: This helps limit the size of the vocabulary to meaningful words. Any word that does not occur at least this many times across all documents is ignored.

Reasonable values could be between 10 and 100. Suppose a set of movie titles occur 30 times: then set the minimum word count to 40, to avoid attaching too much importance to individual movie titles. Higher values also help limit run time.

The following link contains information about backward error propagation in word2vec, with details for CBoW and skip-grams:

http://www.claudiobellei.com/2018/01/06/backprop-word2vec/

Limitations of Word2vec

`Word2vec` provides only one word embedding per word. Moreover, a word embedding can only store one vector for each word. Other limitations of `word2vec` are listed below:

> difficult to train on large datasets
> fine tuning is not possible
> training models is a domain-specific task
> trained on a shallow neural network with one hidden layer

As you will see in Chapter 11, the attention-based mechanism overcomes the limitations of `word2vec`.

The CBoW Architecture

Given a set of words, the `CBoW` model architecture starts with a set of surrounding words and then attempts to predict the target word (which is the center word). The CBoW model (which is one type of `word2vec` model) involves a feed forward neural network that determines word embeddings. The neural network consists of the following:

- an input layer
- a hidden layer (no activation function)
- an output layer (softmax activation function)

In addition, the input layer and output layer have the same size. Hence, this neural network resembles an autoencoder, which (in case you don't already know) "squashes" the input values into a smaller vector to obtain a more compact representation of the input data.

Figure 4.1 displays the `CBoW` architecture and Figure 4.2 in the next section displays the skip-grams architecture, both of which are shallow neural networks.

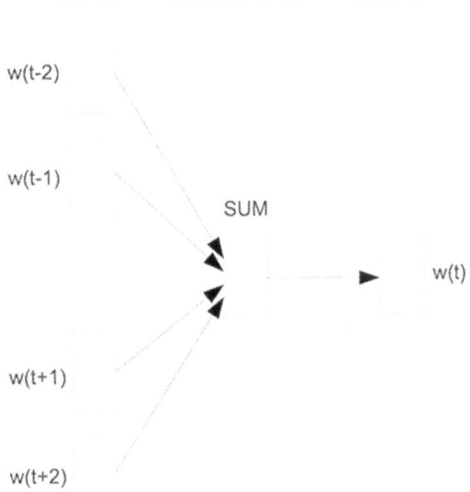

CBOW

Figure 4.1 The CBoW Architecture.

Source: "Efficient Estimation of Word Representations in Vector Space." Tomas Mikolov, Kai Chen, Greg Corrado, Jeffrey Dean. [arXiv:1301.3781v2 [cs.CL] (CC BY 4.0)]

What are Skip-grams?

As you learned in the previous section, n-grams infer a missing word from the words that appear on both sides of the word, whereas skip-grams start with the "missing" word and attempt to infer the words that are most likely to appear on both sides of that missing word. In a sense, the key idea of skip-grams is sort of like an "inversion" of n-grams.

Skip-gram models predict the surrounding context words of a target word, and they are based on a neural network architecture that is discussed later in this chapter. In a sense, the skip-gram model works in the opposite manner of the CBoW model: skip-gram attempts to predict the surrounding words of a target word instead of a missing center word.

In slightly more detailed terms, the following sequence of steps provides a high-level description of the skip-gram algorithm:

- Treat the target word and a neighboring context word as positive examples.
- Randomly sample other words in the lexicon to get negative samples.

- Use logistic regression to train a classifier to distinguish those two cases.
- Use the weights as the embeddings.

Later you will see a diagram that displays the skip-gram architecture, right after you see an example of finding skip-grams, which is discussed in the next section.

Skip-gram Example

A skip-gram is a tuple that contains words before and after a given word. The size of the type is an integer, which can be as small as 1. In particular, 1-grams, 2-grams, and 3-grams are also called unigrams, bigrams, and trigrams.

Let's consider the following sentence (taken from the previous section):

```
'the big mouse ate the cheese'
```

The set of 1-grams for "ate" is here:

```
[mouse, the]
```

The set of 2-grams is here:

```
[(ate,the), (ate,big), (ate,mouse), (ate, the), (ate,cheese)]
```

The set of 3-grams is here:

```
[(ate,the,big), (ate,big,mouse), (ate,the,cheese)]
```

The Skip-gram Architecture

Figure 4.2 displays the skip-gram architecture that is based on a shallow neural network.

In order to fully understand this architecture, you need some familiarity with basic neural networks, the softmax activation function, and the concept of backward error propagation. In essence, the skip-gram architecture (along with the n-gram architecture) is based on machine learning concepts. If need be, you can read the relevant appendix that discusses neural networks.

As you can see from Figure 4.2, the skip-gram architecture consists of the following components:

- the input layer is a single word
- a hidden layer
- an output layer (predicted context words)

Each word from the corpus is processed through the neural network, and after the model has been trained, the hidden layer contains the word

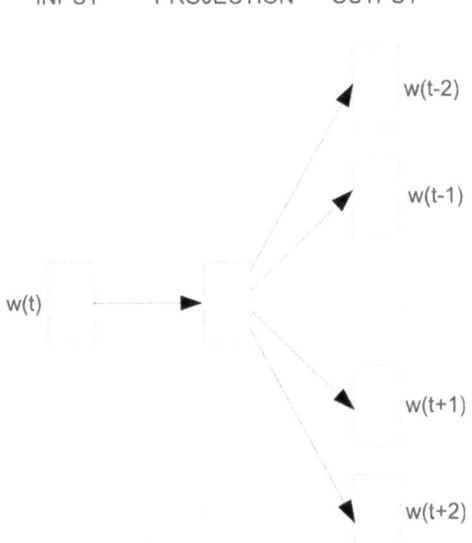

Skip-gram

Figure 4.2. The Skip-gram Architecture.

Source: "Efficient Estimation of Word Representations in Vector Space."
Tomas Mikolov, Kai Chen, Greg Corrado, Jeffrey Dean. [arXiv:1301.3781v2 [cs.CL] (CC BY 4.0)]

embeddings. The concept of skip-grams is probably less intuitive than n-grams: how can we guess at the words that surround a single word?

An interesting point: although the skip-gram model has a larger memory requirement, its word embeddings are better than those generated by an n-gram model.

Keep in mind the following details regarding the shallow network for the skip-gram model:

- There is no bias term.
- There is no activation function between the input layer and the hidden layer.
- There is a softmax activation function from the hidden layer to the output layer.
- The input layer and the output layer have the same size.

If you are familiar with convolutional neural networks (CNNs), then you already know that the softmax activation function is applied between the right-most hidden layer and the output layer because it generates a set of positive numbers whose sum equals one. Thus, that set of output numbers is a probability distribution, and the index position with the highest probability value is compared with the index of the number 1 in the one-hot encoding of the input data: if the index values are equal, then it's a match (otherwise it's not a match).

Since the input layer and the output layer have the same size, this shallow network is very similar to an autoencoder, whose purpose is to compress the one-hot encoded words of a vocabulary into a smaller representation (similar to the purpose of PCA in machine learning).

For example, suppose we have a vocabulary of 10,000 words (assume they're English words to keep things simple), and we want to find a representation for each word that consists of a 1×300 vector of floating point numbers. Then the weight matrix between the input layer and the hidden layer is a 10,000 × 300 matrix (let's call it W1), and the matrix between the hidden layer and the output layer is a 300 × 10,000 matrix. (Let's call it W2.)

The neural network is "trained," which means that the weights of the edges in the neural network are updated by a process called "backward error propagation." When the training process is completed, we discard everything except for the weight matrix W1, which consists of 10,000 rows, each of which is a word in the initial vocabulary. Each row is 300 columns wide, and this 1×300 vector of floating point numbers is the encoding for the current word.

Neural Network Reduction

There are two techniques to reduce the size of the weight matrices in the neural network that is described in the previous section:

- subsample frequent words (which decreases the number of training examples)
- modify the optimization objective via "negative sampling"

These two techniques reduce the computational complexity and also improve the quality of the results.

The intuition underlying negative sampling is to modify a small portion of the model weights, which involves finding skip-grams for a given word.

An earlier section showed you how to find the bigrams of a simple sentence, which is reproduced here:

`[(ate,the), (ate,big), (ate,mouse), (ate, the), (ate,cheese)]`

As you can see, the previous set of bigrams includes stop words, which you can remove during the cleaning process. Alternatively, there is a formula to calculate the probability of retaining a word that appears in a vocabulary. If `w1` is a word in a vocabulary and f(w1) is the frequency of the word in a document, then the probability `P(w1)` that `w1` will be retained is given here:

`P(w1) = [1 + sqrt(f(w1)*1000) * 0.001/f(w1)`

Another important Python library for generating distributed word embeddings is `GloVe`, which is the topic of the next section.

What is GloVe?

As you learned earlier in this chapter, `word2vec` algorithms are based on neural networks. By contrast, `GloVe` uses *matrix factorization* techniques from linear algebra and word-content matrices. `GloVe` creates a co-occurrence matrix for a given (local) context, and then decomposes the global matrix.

`GloVe` is similar to `word2vec`, with an important difference: Glove exploits the global co-occurrences of words instead of relying on the local context. GloVe proceeds as follows:

1. construct a co-occurrence matrix of dimensionality words x context

2. factor the matrix into a matrix of dimensionality word x features

In the initial matrix, the rows are words and the columns are word frequencies in a corpus. The factored matrix has a lower dimensionality, and the rows are the vector representations of the initial words.

GloVe can provide 100-dimensional dense vectors as word embeddings. However, there are two important limitations in GloVe. First, GloVe does not support OOV (Out of vocabulary) words. Second, GloVe does not support polysemy, which refers to words that have multiple meanings, which is determined by the context of the words in a sentence. Consider using models that provide support, such as ELMo and USE (Universal Sentence Encoder).

In case you're interested in the GloVe approach, the CoVe (McCann, 2017) is based on the GloVe algorithm. CoVe ("contextual vectors") uses machine translation to generate contextual vectors and does not use language modeling.

Working with GloVe

GloVe is a Python-based library (developed at Stanford University) for word embeddings, and it's an acronym for "Global Vectors [for word representation]".

`GloVe` performs unsupervised learning of word embeddings that is based on co-occurrence matrices. As such, GloVe combines two techniques:

1. Global Matrix Factorization (GMF)

2. Local Context Window (LCW)

In brief, *Global Matrix Factorization* uses matrix factorization methods from linear algebra that perform rank reduction on a large term-frequency matrix. Note that the matrices can represent term-document frequencies, in which case matrix rows are words and the matrix columns are documents (or paragraphs). Alternatively, matrices can represent term-term frequencies, with words on both axes and measure co-occurrence.

GMF applied to term-document frequency matrices is called *latent semantic analysis* (LSA), and the high-dimensional matrix in LSA is reduced via *singular value decomposition* (SVD). More details regarding matrix factorization are here:

https://machinelearningmastery.com/introduction-to-matrix-decompositions-for-machine-learning/

Local context window is a word embedding model that learns semantics by passing a window over the corpus line-by-line. This technique predicts the surroundings of a given word (e.g., skip-gram model) or predicts a word given its surroundings (e.g., `CBoW`).

The third important Python library for generating distributed word embeddings is `fastText`, which is the topic of the next section.

What is FastText?

Facebook developed the `fastText` NLP library, and you can install fastest with the following command:

```
pip3 install fasttext
```

The `fastText` library uses unsupervised learning to perform text clustering of data, which means that fastText uses a clustering algorithm. The `train_unsupervised()` method in `fastText` uses the skip-gram model in order to generate 100-dimensional vectors. In addition, `fastText` computes the similarity score between words, along with the `get_nearest_neighbors()` method to display the top 10 words that are the most similar to a given word. Similarity scores between pairs of words that are close to 1 indicates that the pair of words are more similar in meaning.

`FastText` leverages `word2vec` by learning vector representations for each word and the n-grams in each word. Next, a vector is created whose values are the average values of the representations during each training step. This step enables word embeddings to encode sub-word information. `FastText` vectors are more accurate than `word2vec` vectors based on various criteria. Moreover, `fastText` can handle OOV words, and the sub-word n-grams correspond to "intuition" (shown for multiple languages).

One useful advantage of vector generation techniques such as `fastText` is that no labeled data is required.

Comparison of Word Embeddings

This section contains a summary of the main features of three types of word embeddings. The first group consists of the simplest algorithms for producing word vectors for words: these algorithms were introduced in this chapter and the previous chapter. The second group consists of the earliest algorithms that use neural networks (i.e., `word2vec` and `fastText`) or matrix factorization (`gloVe`) (such as `word2vec`) for generating distributional word embeddings. The third group involves contextual algorithms for creating word embeddings, which are essentially state of the art algorithms. For your convenience, a bullet list for each of the three groups is given below:

- Group 1—Discrete word embeddings (BoW, tf, and tf-idf):

  Word vectors consist of integers, decimals, and decimals, respectively

  Key point: word embedding have zero context

- Group 2—Distributional word embeddings (word2vec, GloVe, fasttext):

  Based on shallow NN, MF, and NN, respectively

  Two words on the left and the right (bigrams) for word2vec

  Key point: only one embedding for each word (regardless of its context)

- Group 3—Contextual word representation (BERT et al):

  transformer architecture (no CNNs/RNNs/LSTMs)

  Pays "attention" to ALL words in a sentence

- *Key point: words can have multiple embeddings (depending on the context)*

As you can see, algorithms in group 1 provide one word embedding per word but no context is captured in the word embedding. Group 2 algorithms are an improvement because they provide context for word embeddings. Finally, group 3 algorithms generate multiple word embeddings for the same word that appears in multiple sentences. This feature is a significant improvement over group 2 algorithms, which in turn are a significant improvement over group 1 algorithms.

What is Topic Modeling?

Topic modeling is a technique for finding topics in one or more documents, and it's also a form of "dimensionality reduction." There are two underlying assumptions:

- Each document consists of a mixture of topics.
- Each topic consists of a collection of words.

Topic models assume that the semantics of a document are governed by so-called *latent variables* that are not immediately observable, which are topics that tend to be more abstract than the actual text. The goal of topic modeling is to uncover these latent variables (topics) that can reveal the primary content of a document or corpus.

Determining the main topics in documents can be performed in various ways, which is the topic of the next section.

Topic Modeling Algorithms

There are several well-known algorithms for topic modeling, some of which are listed below:

- Latent dirichlet analysis (LDA)
- Latent semantic indexing (LSI)
- Latent semantic analysis (LSA)

More details regarding LDA are in the next section, and you can perform an Internet search for details regarding LSI and LSA.

LDA and Topic Modeling

LDA is a dimensionality reduction technique that is well-suited for topic modeling. LDA is a generative model that assigns topic distributions to documents. Each document is described by a distribution of topics, and each topic is described by a distribution of words. Please keep in mind that the rest of this section contains a high-level description of LDA, which in turn involves concepts such as KL Divergence and the JS metric that are discussed in Appendix A.

LDA starts with a fixed set of topics, where each topic represents a set of words. Next, LDA maps documents to a set of topics, and document words are mapped to those topics.

LDA is also a clustering method that supports the concept of soft-clustering, which allows different cluster to overlap (so words can belong to multiple clusters). Soft clustering is advantageous because it's simpler to find similar words; however, it's more difficult to determine distinct clusters in LDA.

Note that LDA differs from the kMeans algorithm because the latter is based on hard-clustering, which means that each word belongs to a single cluster.

An LDA model assumes that documents contain several overlapping topics, along with the following:

- Topics are based on the words in each document.
- The actual topics may not be known in advance.
- The actual topics do not need to be specified.
- The number of topics must be specified in advance.

Recall that LDA supports soft clustering, and therefore the same word can appear in multiple topics (i.e., a topic has the role of a cluster). In addition, the LDA model is called "latent" because LDA generates the following latent (hidden) variables:

- a distribution over topics for each document
- a distribution over words for each topics

LDA uses the JS (Jenson-Shannon) metric, which is based on JS divergence, and the latter is based on KL divergence (more information about these topics in an appendix). Since JS divergence is a metric, it's also symmetric, which means that the similarity of two documents Doc1 and Doc2 is the same as the similarity of Doc2 and Doc1 (which is obviously a desirable property).

LDA uses the JS metric to determine which documents in a corpus are the most similar to document D by comparing the topic distribution of document D to the topic distributions of the documents in the corpus. As you might have already surmised, a smaller JS value for a pair of documents indicates greater similarity between the documents.

LDA is related to ANOVA as well as PCA (discussed in an appendix), but there are some differences. For instance, ANOVA uses categorical independent variables and a continuous dependent variable. By contrast, LDA involves the "reverse" of ANOVA: it uses continuous independent variables and a categorical dependent variable. Another key point: LDA assumes that the independent variables are normally distributed.

LDA and PCA share one particular aspect: both involve calculating linear combinations of variables. However, LDA tries to model the difference between the classes of data, whereas PCA ignores the difference in class.

Text Classification versus Topic Modeling

Text classification involves supervised learning on documents or articles with a known set of labels and classifies text into a single class. By contrast, topic modeling involves unsupervised learning, and it's a process of analyzing documents/articles. Topic modeling finds groups of co-occurring words in text documents, and co-occurring related words are "topics." In cases where the set of possible topics is unknown, topic modeling can be used to solve text classification problems to identify the topics in a document.

Language Models and NLP

In brief, a language model is a probability distribution (which is discussed in Appendix A) for sequences of words. Statistical language modeling refers to the creation of probabilistic models that predict the next word in a sequence based on the words that precede the predicted word. Calculating the probability of word occurrences involves examples of text. Models can be based on individual words, short sequences, sentences, or paragraphs.

Language models are used in machine learning and unsupervised learning (search/IR and clustering/topic modeling). A language model also tries to distinguish between similar sounding words. However, language models face some challenges, such as data sparsity and determining the likelihood of different phrases. One approach involves the use of n-gram models (described elsewhere in this chapter).

According to some NLP experts, language models learn only from co-occurrence patterns in the streams of symbols that they are trained on. Furthermore, there are at least two issues pertaining to language models:

- Symbol streams lack crucial information.
- Language models lack communicative intent.

Although pure language models do not have a counterpart to machine learning models that are trained via labeled datasets, some NLP experts believe that it's possible for language models to achieve language understanding.

How to Create a Language Model

There are three main ways to create a new language model in NLP for a given task:

- Create a new model "from scratch."
- Transfer learning (use a pretrained model).
- Transfer learning plus vocabulary enhancement.

Language models can also be classified into different subtypes. For example, neural language models (also called continuous space language models) are based on neural networks. Such models use continuous representations or embeddings of words to make their predictions. More details regarding language models are here:

https://en.wikipedia.org/wiki/Language_model

Language models are the intuition behind vector space models, which is the topic of the next section.

Vector Space Models

A *vector space model* (VSM) is based on a mathematical model called a vector space, in order to represent text documents as vectors of identifiers (for example, using `tf-idf` weights). If you are unfamiliar with vector spaces, there is a brief introduction to vector spaces in one of the appendices, and if need be, you can find additional information through an online search.

A VSM consists of a two-dimensional array of (usually) numeric values that are based on *frequencies*. The latter restriction on the data values creates a "link" between a VSM and the distributional hypothesis. A VSM whose values are based on sophisticated algorithms can overcome the shortcomings of losing semantics and feature sparsity in BoWs: *https:// en.wikipedia.org/wiki/Vector_space_model*

As a point of clarification, the following matrices do *not* represent vector space models:

- an arbitrary matrix
- an adjacency matrix for a tree or graph
- a feature matrix
- a covariance matrix
- a correlation matrix
- a recommender system

Recommender systems are included in the preceding list because they populate a user-item matrix whose cells contain a numeric rating of items; however, the data in such a matrix is *not* derived from event frequencies, which explains why recommender systems are not VSMs.

Now that you have seen examples of matrices that are not VSMs, the following list contains some examples of vector space models:

- a term-document matrix (discussed later)
- a context-document matrix
- a matrix based on `word2vec`
- the latent semantic analysis (LSA) algorithm
- a pair-pattern matrix

With the preceding in mind, here is a short list of some models that are based on (or extend) the VSM model:

- generalized vector space model
- latent semantic analysis (LSA)
- term discrimination

- Rocchio classification
- random indexing

Term-Document Matrix

A *term-document* matrix M is an mxn matrix where n is the number of documents and m is the number of unique words in the n documents. The value in a cell (i,j) in a term-document matrix M equals the number of times that the term i appears in document j. Moreover, the value in a cell (i,j) can be based on other calculations, such as tf (term frequency) or tf-idf values. Note that for a large corpus, the matrix M contains mainly zero values, which means that M is a sparse matrix (and operations are less efficient). Also keep in mind that a tf-idf vector is a vector representation of a *document* whereas a word2vec vector is a vector representation of a *word*.

There are two more points of interest regarding a term-document matrix M. First, if two documents are similar, then the two corresponding columns in M will tend to have similar patterns of numbers, which in turn means that their cosine similarity will be closer to 1. Second, instead of focusing on column vectors we can examine row vectors in order to measure word similarity.

We can also generalize the concept of a term-document matrix by expanding the meaning of a document to include phrases, sentences, paragraphs, and so forth. After doing so, the result is a *word-context* matrix.

Tradeoffs of the VSM

VSMs are not a perfect solution: some of the advantages and disadvantages of a VSM are related to the advantages and disadvantages of the algorithms that are used to compute the values in the cells of a VSM.

One advantage of a VSM model is because it's based on linear algebra. In addition, it's possible to compute a degree of similarity between queries and documents in a continuous fashion, which then enables you to rank documents according to their possible relevance. Furthermore, VSM models support partial matching.

However, long documents are poorly represented because they have poor similarity values (a small scalar product and a large dimensionality). Word substrings can result in a "false positive match," which means that search keywords must match document terms. Unfortunately, documents with similar context and also different term vocabulary won't be associated, which results in a "false negative match."

In addition, the order in which the terms appear in the document is not tracked in the vector space representation, along with the assumption that terms are statistically independent. Even so, some of the disadvantages can be ameliorated by using techniques such as singular value decomposition (SVD).

NLP and Text Mining

In high-level terms, text mining performs an analysis of large amounts of unstructured data in order to find patterns in that data. Text mining tasks involve finding keywords, topics, and patterns. The general sequence of steps (tasks) is shown here:

- preprocessing
- text transformation
- attribute selection
- visualization
- evaluation

Text mining also involves document classification whereby similar documents are placed in the same group. Text mining is useful for extracting product-related details, such as customer reviews, product issues, and so forth. Applications of text mining include spam detection, sentiment analysis, e-commerce and customer segmentation. The NLTK (Natural Language ToolKit) library is well-suited for text mining tasks, and you will see code samples in Chapter 6.

Text Extraction Preprocessing and N-Grams

As you learned earlier in this chapter n-grams are one type of language model that assigns numeric probabilities to word sequences. For example the 3-grams of a sentence is a set of tuples of length 3, where a tuple consists of three consecutive words in that sentence. Note that the terms unigram, bigram, and trigram are often used when n is 1, 2, or 3, respectively.

Relation Extraction and Information Extraction

In simplified terms, *relation extraction* (RE), *information extraction* (IE), and *relation classification* involve various aspects of searching a corpus to find subsets of text that describe relationships between words in those subsets of text. Relation extraction is a key component of NLU (Natural Language Understanding), and in general, relation extraction involves extracting relational triplets of text, such as (`founder, steve_jobs, apple`).

Although these three concepts overlap, they have significant differences. Relation extraction involves finding semantic relationships in a corpus. In addition, relation extraction is a subfield of information extraction, where the latter involves extracting structured information from natural language text. However, relation extraction differs in one important respect from IE: the latter also performs disambiguation. The `sense2vec` algorithm is one algorithm for word sense disambiguation that can be used with SpaCy:

https://github.com/explosion/sense2vec

As an example: if you have ever summarized a text document, you probably searched for the most important words (typically nouns) and the relationship between those words: this task is a form of IE. In fact, IE is relevant for multiple NLP tasks, including text summarization and question–answering systems.

On the other hand, *relation classification* is the task of identifying the semantic relation between two nominal entities in text. As you might have surmised, there is no one-size-fits-all solution that works for multiple domains (e.g., healthcare, biology, and chemistry).

One more point of interest is the "Never Ending Language Learning" (NELL) semantic machine learning system from Carnegie Mellon University that extracts relationships from the open Web:

https://en.wikipedia.org/wiki/Never-Ending_Language_Learning

What is a BLEU Score?

`BLEU` is an acronym for "bilingual evaluation understudy," which is a well-known NLP metric. A `BLEU` score involves a straightforward calculation, and since a BLEU score is typically published alongside NLP models, its inclusion has become standard practice.

However, `BLEU` was created in order to measure machine translation, and it's most reliable when it's calculated on an entire corpus instead of a sentence-by-sentence calculation. Perhaps the popularity of `BLEU` scores caused a side effect in which `BLEU` scores are assigned to NLP tasks where other measurement tools produce more accurate results.

BLEU has some significant limitations: it does not take into account sentence structure, which can vary significantly among different languages (see the section on "case endings" in Chapter 3), nor does it take into account the meaning of sentences.

In simplified terms, BLEU scores involve precision, n-grams, and exact matches with reference sentences. BLEU checks how many n-grams in the output also appear in the reference translation. However, BLEU does not recognize synonyms, which means that pairs of sentences that use closely related yet different verbs are not considered similar in BLEU. For example, three sentences that use the verbs "drink," "imbibe," and "consume" would probably be considered equivalent, especially in casual conversation, but BLEU does not recognize them as such.

ROUGE Score: An Alternative to BLEU

In brief, a ROUGE score is a variant of BLEU that involves *recall* (BLEU uses *precision*) and also determine the number of n-grams of the reference translation also appear in the output (BLEU does the opposite). More information about ROUGE is here:

https://www.aclweb.org/anthology/N03-1020/

There are also techniques that are unrelated to BLEU, such as perplexity, WER, and F1 score, all of which are discussed in an appendix. Perform an online search with the keywords "BLEU score alternatives" and you will find many articles that discuss other alternatives to BLEU.

Summary

This chapter started with a fast overview of language models, text encoding techniques, and two types of word context. Then you learned about word embeddings, which are highly useful in NLP. You also got an introduction to distance metrics, such as cosine similarity (for measuring the distance between two vectors) and document similarity. In addition, you learned about the concepts of vector space models (VSMs) and topic modeling.

CHAPTER 5

ALGORITHMS AND TOOLKITS (I)

This chapter contains Python code samples for some of the NLP-related concepts that were introduced in the previous chapter. You will see an assortment of code samples involving regular expressions, the Python library BeautifulSoup, Scrapy, and various NLP-related Python code samples that use the spaCy library.

As a quick reminder, there is an appendix devoted to regular expressions (Appendix C) and another appendix with a section that discusses Sklearn Python library (Appendix F), both of which are relevant for some of the code samples in this chapter.

The first part of this chapter contains some example of data cleaning that involve regular expressions. The second section contains some basic examples involving BoW, one-hot encoding, and word embeddings in Sklearn.

The third section discusses BeautifulSoup, which is a Python module for scraping HTML Web pages. This section contains some Python code samples that retrieve and then manipulate the contents of an HTML Web page from the GitHub code repository. This section also contains a brief introduction to Scrapy, which is a Python-based library that provides Web scraping functionality and various other APIs.

The fourth section introduces spaCy, which is a Python-based library for NLP, along with Python code samples that show you various features of spaCy.

Cleaning Data with Regular Expressions

This section contains a simple preview of what you can accomplish with regular expressions when you need to clean your data. If you are new to regular expressions, you can read Appendix C, which is devoted to this topic. The main concepts to understand for the code samples in this section are listed here:

- the range [A-Z] matches any uppercase letter
- the range [a-z] matches any lowercase letter
- the range [a-zA-Z] matches any lowercase or uppercase letter
- the range [^a-zA-Z] matches anything *except* lowercase or uppercase letters

Listing 5.1 displays the contents of text_clean_regex.py that illustrates how to remove any symbols that are not characters from a text string.

LISTING 5.1: text_clean_regex.py

```
import re # this is for regular expressions

text = "I have 123 apples for sale. Call me at 650-555-1212 or send me email at apples@acme.com."
print("text:")
print(text)
print()

# replace the '@' symbol with the string ' at ':
cleaned1 = re.sub('@', ' at ',text)
print("cleaned1:")
print(cleaned1)

# replace non-letters with ' ':
cleaned2 = re.sub('[^a-zA-Z]', ' ',cleaned1)
print("cleaned2:")
print(cleaned2)

# replace multiple adjacent spaces with a single ' ':
cleaned3 = re.sub('[ ]+', ' ',cleaned2)
print("cleaned3:")
print(cleaned3)
```

Listing 5.1 contains an `import` statement so that we can use regular expressions in the subsequent code. After initializing the variable `text` with a sentence and displaying its contents, the variable cleaned1 is defined, which involves replacing the "@" symbol with the text string " at. " (Notice the white space before and after the text "at"). Next, the variable cleaned2 is defined, which involves replacing anything that is not a letter with a white space. Finally, the variable cleaned3 is defined, which involves "squeezing" multiple white spaces into a single white space. Launch the code in Listing 5.1 and you will see the following output:

```
text:
I have 123 apples for sale. Call me at 650-555-1212 or send me
email at apples@acme.com.

cleaned1:
I have 123 apples for sale. Call me at 650-555-1212 or send me
email at apples at acme.com.
cleaned2:
I have     apples for sale  Call me at              or send me
email at apples at acme com
cleaned3:
I have apples for sale Call me at or send me email at apples
at acme com
```

Listing 5.2 displays the contents of text_clean_regex2.py that illustrates how to remove HTML tags from a text string.

LISTING 5.2: text_clean_regex2.py

```
import re # this is for regular expressions

# [^>]: matches anything except a '>'
# <[^>]: matches anything after '>' except a '>'
tagregex = re.compile(r'<[^>]+>')

def remove_html_tags(doc):
  return tagregex.sub(':', doc)

doc1 = "<html><head></head></body><p>paragraph1</p><div>div element</div></html>"

print("doc1:")
print(doc1)
print()

doc2 = remove_html_tags(doc1)
print("doc2:")
print(doc2)
```

Listing 5.2 contains an `import` statement, followed by the variable `tagregex`, which is a regular expression that matches a left angle bracket "<", followed by any character except for a right angle bracket ">". Next, the `Python` function `remove_html_tags()` removes all the HTML tags in a text string. The next portion of Listing 5.2 initializes the variable `doc1` as an HTML string and displays its contents. The final code block invokes the `Python` function `remove_html_tags()` to remove the HTML tags from `doc1`, and then prints the results. Launch the code in Listing 5.2 and you will see the following output:

```
doc1:
<html><head></head></body><p>paragraph1</p><div>div element</div></html>

doc2:
:::::paragraph1::div element::
```

The third (and final) code sample for this section also involves regular expressions, and it's useful when you need to remove contractions (e.g., replacing "that's" with "that is").

Listing 5.3 displays the contents of `text_clean_regex3.py` that illustrates how to replace contractions with the original words.

LISTING 5.3: text_clean_regex3.py

```
import re # this is for regular expressions

def clean_text(text):
  text = text.lower()

  text = re.sub(r"i'm",      "i am", text)
  text = re.sub(r"he's",     "he is", text)
  text = re.sub(r"she's",    "she is", text)
  text = re.sub(r"that's",   "that is", text)
  text = re.sub(r"what's",   "what is", text)
  text = re.sub(r"where's",  "where is", text)
  text = re.sub(r"how's",    "how is", text)
  text = re.sub(r"it's",     "it is", text)
  text = re.sub(r"\'ll",     " will", text)
  text = re.sub(r"\'ve",     " have", text)
  text = re.sub(r"\'re",     " are", text)
  text = re.sub(r"\'d",      " would", text)
  text = re.sub(r"n't",      "not", text)
  text = re.sub(r"won't",    "will not", text)
  text = re.sub(r"can't",    "can not", text)
```

```
    text = re.sub(r"[-()\"#/@;:<>{}`+=~|.!?,]", "", text)
    return text

sentences = ["It's a hot day and i'm sweating",
             "How's the zoom class going?",
             "She's smarter than me - that's a fact"]

for sent in sentences:
    print("Sentence:",sent)
    print("Cleaned: ",clean_text(sent))
    print("----------------")
```

Listing 5.3 contains an `import` statement, followed by the `Python` function `clean_text()` that performs a brute-force replacement of hyphenated strings with their unhyphenated counterparts. The final code snippet in this function also removes any special characters in a text string.

The next portion of Listing 5.3 initializes the variable `sentences` that contains multiple sentences, followed by a `for` loop that passes individual sentences to the Python `clean_text()` function. Launch the code in Listing 5.3 and you will see the following output:

```
Sentence: It's a hot day and i'm sweating
Cleaned:  it is a hot day and i am sweating
----------------
Sentence: How's the zoom class going?
Cleaned:  how is the zoom class going
----------------
Sentence: She's smarter than me - that's a fact
Cleaned:  she is smarter than me that is a fact
----------------
```

The `Python` package called `contractions` is an alternative to regular expressions for expanding contractions, an example of which is shown later in this chapter.

Listing 5.4 displays the contents of `remove_urls.py` that illustrates how to remove URLs from an array of strings.

LISTING 5.4: *remove_urls.py*

```
import re
import pandas as pd

arr1 = ["https://www.yahoo.com",
        "http://www.acme.com"]

data = pd.DataFrame(data=arr1)
```

```
print("before:")
print(data)
print()

no_urls = []
for url in arr1:
  clean = re.sub(r"http\S+", "", url)
  no_urls.append(clean)

data["cleaned"] = no_urls

print("after:")
print(data)
```

Listing 5.4 starts with two `import` statements, followed by the initialization of the variable `arr1` with two URLs. Next, the variable `data` is a `Pandas` data frame whose contents are based on the contents of `arr1`. The contents of `data` are displayed, followed by a `for` loop that removes the `http` prefix from each element of `arr1`. The last code section appends a new column called `cleaned` to the `data` data frame and then displays the contents of that data frame. Launch the code in Listing 5.4 and you will see the following output:

```
before:
                              0
0  https://www.yahoo.com web page
1   http://www.acme.com web page

after:
                              0   cleaned
0  https://www.yahoo.com web page  web page
1   http://www.acme.com web page   web page
```

This concludes the brief introduction to cleaning data with regular expressions, which are discussed in more detail (along with code samples) in one of the appendices.

Handling Contracted Words

The previous section showed you how to expand English contractions via regular expressions. This section contains an example of expanding contractions via the Python package `contractions` that is available here:

https://github.com/kootenpv/contractions

Install the contractions package with this command:

```
pip3 install contractions
```

Listing 5.5 displays the contents of contract.py that illustrates how to expand English contractions and also how to add custom expansion rules.

LISTING 5.5: *contract.py*

```
import contractions

sentences = ["what's new?",
             "how's the weather",
             "it's humid today",
             "we've been there before",
             "you should've been there!",
             "the sky's the limit"]
for sent in sentences:
  result = contractions.fix(sent)
  print("sentence:",sent)
  print("expanded:",result)
  print()

print("=> updating contraction rules...")
contractions.add("sky's", "sky is")

sent = "the sky's the limit"
result = contractions.fix(sent)
print("sentence:",sent)
print("expanded:",result)
print()
```

Listing 5.5 contains an import statement and then initializes the variable sentences to an array of text strings. The next portion of Listing 5.5 contains a loop that iterates through the array of strings in sentences, and then prints each sentence as well as the expanded version of the sentence.

As you will see in the output, the contraction sky's in the last sentence in the array sentences is not expanded, so let's add a new expansion rule, as shown here:

```
contractions.add("sky's", "sky is")
```

Now when we process this string again, the contraction sky's is expanded correctly. Launch the code in Listing 5.5 and you will see the following output:

```
sentence: what's new?
expanded: what is new?
```

```
sentence: how's the weather
expanded: how is the weather

sentence: it's humid today
expanded: it is humid today

sentence: we've been there before
expanded: we have been there before

sentence: you should've been there!
expanded: you should have been there!

sentence: the sky's the limit
expanded: the sky's the limit

=> updating contraction rules...
sentence: the sky's the limit
expanded: the sky is the limit
```

As an alternative, you can also write Python code to expand contractions, as shown in the following code block:

```
CONTRACT = {"how's":"how is", "what's":"what is", "it's":"it
is", "we've":"we have", "should've" :"should have", "sky's":
"sky is"}

sentences = ["what's new?",
             "how's the weather",
             "it's humid today",
             "we've been there before",
             "you should've been there!",
             "the sky's the limit"]

for sent in sentences:
  words = sent.split()
  expanded = [CONTRACT[w] if w in CONTRACT else w for w in words]
  new_sent = " ".join(expanded)
  print("sentence:",sent)
  print("expanded:",new_sent)
  print()
```

The next section contains some Python-based code samples that involve BoW (bag of words).

Python Code Samples of BoW

As you learned in Chapter 4, BoW is a technique for creating a numeric vector encoding of words. This section contains some simple Python-based code samples that illustrate how to perform this technique on a set of words.

The BoW algorithm counts how many times a word appears in a document, which generalizes a one-hot encoding of a set of words. Those word counts allow us to compare documents and gauge their similarities. The BoW algorithm can be used in applications like search, document classification and topic modeling. In addition, BoW can be used to prepare text for input in a deep learning neural network.

Listing 5.6 displays the contents of bow_to_vector1.py that illustrates how to create a one-dimensional numeric vector based on a given vocabulary.

LISTING 5.6: bow_to_vector1.py

```
VOCAB = ['dog', 'cheese', 'cat', 'mouse']
TEXT1 = 'the mouse ate the cheese'
TEXT2 = 'the horse ate the hay'

def to_bow(text):
  words = text.split(" ")
  return [1 if w in words else 0 for w in VOCAB]
  print("VOCAB: ",VOCAB)
  print("TEXT1:",TEXT1)
  print("BOW1: ",to_bow(TEXT1)) # [0, 1, 0, 1]
  print("")

  print("TEXT2:",TEXT2)
  print("BOW2: ",to_bow(TEXT2)) # [0, 0, 0, 0]
```

Listing 5.6 initializes the variables VOCAB, TEXT1, and TEXT2, followed by the Python function to_bow() that constructs a BoW representation for text strings. Next, this Python function is invoked twice: first with TEXT1 and then with TEXT2. Launch the code in Listing 5.6 and you will see the following output:

```
VOCAB:  ['dog', 'cheese', 'cat', 'mouse']
TEXT1: the mouse ate the cheese
BOW1:  [0, 1, 0, 1]

TEXT2: the horse ate the hay
BOW2:  [0, 0, 0, 0]
```

Listing 5.7 displays the contents of bow_to_vector2.py that illustrates how to create a one-dimensional numeric vector based on a given vocabulary.

LISTING 5.7: bow_to_vector2.py

```
VOCAB  = ['dog', 'cheese', 'cat', 'mouse']
MYTEXT = 'the mouse ate the cheese'

def to_bow(text):
  words = text.split(" ")
  found = [w if w in words else "MISS" for w in VOCAB]
  missing = [w if w not in words else "FOUND" for w in VOCAB]
  print("Found:",found)
  print("Missing:",missing)

  return [1 if w in words else 0 for w in VOCAB]

print("MYTEXT:",MYTEXT)
print("VOCAB: ",VOCAB)
print("MYTEXT:",to_bow(MYTEXT))   # [0, 1, 0, 1]
```

Listing 5.7 extends the code in Listing 5.6 by keeping track of the words in the vocabulary that are not included in a given sentence. Launch the code in Listing 5.7 and you will see the following output:

```
MYTEXT: the mouse ate the cheese
VOCAB:  ['dog', 'cheese', 'cat', 'mouse']
Found: ['MISS', 'cheese', 'MISS', 'mouse']
Missing: ['dog', 'FOUND', 'cat', 'FOUND']
MYTEXT: [0, 1, 0, 1]
```

Listing 5.8 displays the contents of count_vectorize.py that illustrates how to create a one-dimensional numeric vector based on a given vocabulary.

LISTING 5.8: count_vectorize.py

```
VOCAB = ['dog', 'cheese', 'cat', 'mouse']
TEXT1 = 'the mouse ate the cheese'
TEXT2 = 'the horse ate the hay'

from sklearn.feature_extraction.text import CountVectorizer
vectorizer = CountVectorizer(vocabulary=VOCAB)

result1 = vectorizer.transform([TEXT1]).todense() #
matrix([[0,1,0,1]])
result2 = vectorizer.transform([TEXT2]).todense() #
matrix([[0,1,0,1]])

print("VOCAB: ",VOCAB)
print("TEXT1:",TEXT1)
print("BOW1: ",result1)   # [0, 1, 0, 1]
print("")

print("TEXT2:",TEXT2)
```

```
print("BOW2: ",result2)    # [0, 1, 0, 1]
print()

print("=> contents of countvectorizer:")
print(vectorizer)
```

Listing 5.8 performs the same functionality as Listing 5.6 by means of the `CountVectorizer` class in `Sklearn` instead of the custom code in Listing 5.6. Launch the code in Listing 5.8 and you will see the following output, which is the same output that you saw in `bow_to_vector1.py`:

```
VOCAB:  ['dog', 'cheese', 'cat', 'mouse']
TEXT1: the mouse ate the cheese
BOW1:   [[0 1 0 1]]

TEXT2: the horse ate the hay
BOW2:   [[0 0 0 0]]

=> contents of countvectorizer:
CountVectorizer(analyzer='word', binary=False,
                decode_error='strict',
                dtype=<class 'numpy.int64'>, encoding='utf-8',
                input='content',
                lowercase=True, max_df=1.0, max_features=None,
                min_df=1,
                ngram_range=(1, 1), preprocessor=None,
                stop_words=None,
                strip_accents=None, token_pattern='(?u)\\
                b\\w\\w+\\b',
                tokenizer=None, vocabulary=['dog', 'cheese',
                'cat', 'mouse'])
```

As you can see from the preceding output, the vocabulary of the variable `vectorizer` matches the contents of the variable VOCAB.

Listing 5.9 contains a BoW example that illustrates how to use BoW with a Pandas data frame for an array of sentences.

LISTING 5.9: bow_pandas.py

```
import pandas as pd
from sklearn.feature_extraction.text import CountVectorizer

sent = ["this is a sentence with text and very simple",
        "a second sentence with text and listed second",
        "a third sentence with text and listed third",
        "a final sentence with text"]
```

```
print("=> list of sentences:")
for s in sent:
  print(s)
print()

bow = CountVectorizer()
bow_fit = bow.fit_transform(sent)
bag_words = pd.DataFrame(bow_fit.toarray())
bag_words.columns = bow.get_feature_names()
print("=> bag_words for the sentences:")
print(bag_words)
```

Listing 5.9 initializes the variable `sent` as an array of sentences that are subsequently displayed via a `for` loop. Next, the variable `bow` is initialized as an instance of the `CountVectorizer` class that is provided by the `Sklearn` library. The `bow_fit` variable is assigned the result of transforming and fitting the data in the `sent` variable. Next, the `bag_words` variable is initialized as a data frame that contains the data in `bow_fit`.

After specifying the column names for the `bag_words` dataframe, the contents of `bag_words` are displayed via a `print()` statement. Launch the code in Listing 5.9 and you will see the following output (unfortunately the output is wrapped because it's too wide for the page):

```
=> list of sentences:
this is a sentence with text and very simple
a second sentence with text and listed second
a third sentence with text and listed third
a final sentence with text

=> bag_words for the sentences:
   and final is listed second sentence simple text third this very with
0    1     0  1      0      0        1      1    1     0    1    1    1
1    1     0  0      1      2        1      0    1     0    0    0    1
2    1     0  0      1      0        1      0    1     2    0    0    1
3    0     1  0      0      0        1      0    1     0    0    0    1
```

In Chapter 7, you will see an example of creating a BoW model using the NLTK library, and in Chapter 9 you will see an example of BoW using TF2/Keras.

One-Hot Encoding Examples

Recall from Chapter 4 that a one-hot encoding for a set of words involves one numeric vector for each word, and each vector contains a single value of 1 and the other values are all 0. As a simple example, the sentence "I love thick pizza" can be tokenized as `["i", "love", "thick", "pizza"]`, and one-hot encoded as follows:

```
[1,0,0,0]
[0,1,0,0]
[0,0,1,0]
[0,0,0,1]
```

Based on the preceding one-hot encoding, the sentence "We also love thick pizza" can be encoded as:

```
[0,1,1,1] = [0,1,0,0] + [0,0,1,0] + [0,0,0,1]
```

As you can see, the left-side vector [0,1,1,1] is the sum of the three vectors that represent the one-hot encoding of the words, love, thick, and pizza, respectively. The first index of this vector is 0 because this sentence contains "we" instead of i."

Listing 5.10 displays the contents of onehot_encode.py that illustrates how to perform a one-hot encoding on a set of words.

LISTING 5.10: onehot_encode.py

```
import numpy as np

CLASSES = list(np.array([3, 1, 2]))

# The dataset labels
LABELS = np.array([1, 2, 3, 1, 2, 1, 1, 2, 3])
VALUES = [3, 3, 1, 1, 2, 2]
ONEHOT = np.zeros((len(LABELS), len(CLASSES)))

for idx, value in enumerate(LABELS):
  print("idx:",idx,"value:",value)
  ONEHOT[idx, CLASSES.index(value)] = 1

print("One-hot Encoding:")
print(ONEHOT)
```

Listing 5.10 initializes the variable CLASSES as a list created from a NumPy array that contains the numbers 3, 1, and 2. The next code block initializes the variables LABELS, VALUES, and ONEHOT, followed by a for loop that initializes each row of ONEHOT as a one-hot encoded vector. Launch the code in Listing 5.10 and you will see the following output:

```
idx: 0 value: 1
idx: 1 value: 2
idx: 2 value: 3
idx: 3 value: 1
```

```
idx: 4 value: 2
idx: 5 value: 1
idx: 6 value: 1
idx: 7 value: 2
idx: 8 value: 3
One-hot Encoding:
[[0. 1. 0.]
 [0. 0. 1.]
 [1. 0. 0.]
 [0. 1. 0.]
 [0. 0. 1.]
 [0. 1. 0.]
 [0. 1. 0.]
 [0. 0. 1.]
 [1. 0. 0.]]
```

Sklearn and Word Embedding Examples

Word embeddings pertain to algorithms that represent words (as well as documents) using a dense vector representation, which is a distributed representation. By contrast, vector representations refer to discrete representations, such as the use of the tf-idf values of words to generate vector representations of words.

Earlier in this chapter you saw an example of word vectorization, and this section contains a consolidated list of word embedding techniques, along with code samples that illustrate how to use these techniques:

Count Vectorizer
TF-IDF Vectorizer
Hashing Vectorizer
Word2Vec (gensim)

Listing 5.11 displays the contents of count_vectorize2.py that illustrates how to vectorize an array of sentences using the CountVectorizer class in Sklearn.

LISTING 5.11: count_vectorize2.py

```
from sklearn.feature_extraction.text import CountVectorizer
import matplotlib.pyplot as plt
import seaborn as sns

sentences = ['the mouse ate the cheese',
             'the horse ate the hay',
```

```
                'the mouse saw the horse',
                'the mouse scared the horse']

vectorizer = CountVectorizer()
sentence_vectors = vectorizer.fit_transform(sentences)

print("vectorized sentences:")
print(sentence_vectors.toarray())
print()

# learn vocabulary and store CountVectorizer
# sparse matrix in term_frequencies
term_frequencies = vectorizer.fit_transform(sentences)
vocab = vectorizer.get_feature_names()

# convert sparse matrix to numpy array
term_frequencies = term_frequencies.toarray()

# plot #1: visualize term frequencies
sns.heatmap(term_frequencies,annot=True,cbar=False,xticklabels
=vocab)
plt.show()

# plot #2: visualize "one hot" term frequencies
# one_hot_vectorizer = CountVectorizer(binary=True)
# one_hot = one_hot_vectorizer.fit_transform(sentences).toarray()
# vocab = one_hot_vectorizer.get_feature_names()
# sns.heatmap(one_hot,annot=True,cbar=False,xticklabels=vocab)
# plt.show()
```

Listing 5.11 contains several `import` statements, followed by the variable `sentences` that is initialized as an array of sentences. Next, the variable `vectorizer` is an instance of the `CountVectorizer` class in `Sklearn`, followed by assigning the result of fitting and transforming its contents to the variable `sentence_vectors`.

The next code snippet initializes the variable `term_frequencies` with the term frequencies of the contents of `sentences`. In addition, the variable `vocab` is assigned the array of unique words that appear in `sentences`. Launch the code in Listing 5.11 and you will see the following output:

```
vectorized sentences:
[[1 1 0 0 1 0 0 2]
 [1 0 1 1 0 0 0 2]
 [0 0 0 1 1 1 0 2]
 [0 0 0 1 1 0 1 2]]

vocabulary:
['ate', 'cheese', 'hay', 'horse', 'mouse', 'saw', 'scared', 'the']
```

As you can see in the preceding output, the word "the" appears twice in every row because this word occurs in every row of the variable sentences.

Figure 5.1 displays the term frequencies, where the rows are the "documents" in the variable `sentences`, and the columns are the distinct words.

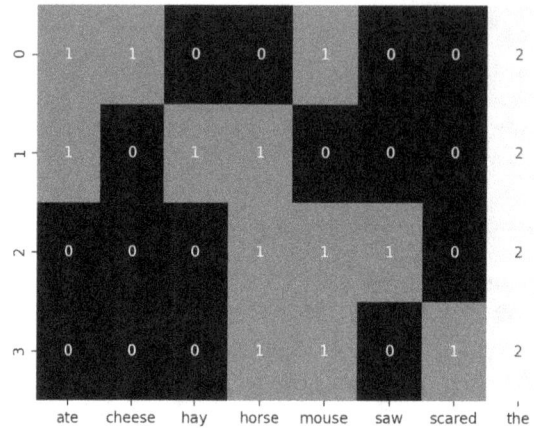

Figure 5.1. A Matrix with Term Frequencies.

Uncomment the final block of code in Listing 5.11 if you want to see the "one hot" encoding of the word frequencies.

Another way to vectorize an array of sentences involves the `HashingVectorizer` class.. Listing 5.12 displays the contents of `hashing_vectorize.py` that illustrates how to vectorize an array of sentences using the `HashingVectorizer` class in `Sklearn`.

LISTING 5.12: *hashing_vectorize.py*

```
from sklearn.feature_extraction.text import HashingVectorizer

sentences = ['the mouse ate the cheese',
             'the horse ate the hay',
             'the mouse saw the horse',
             'the mouse scared the horse']

vectorizer = HashingVectorizer(norm=None, n_features=8)

sentence_vectors = vectorizer.fit_transform(sentences)

print("vectorized sentences:")
print(sentence_vectors.toarray())
```

Listing 5.12 initializes the variable `vectorizer` as an instance of the `HashingVector` class in `Sklearn`, after which the variable `sentence_vectors` is assigned the result of transforming and fitting the contents of the `sentences` variable. Launch the code in Listing 5.12 and you will see the following output:

```
vectorized sentences:
[[ 0. -1.  0.  1.  1.  0. -2.  0.]
 [-2.  0.  0.  1.  0.  0. -2.  0.]
 [-1.  0.  0. -1.  1.  0. -2.  0.]
 [-1.  0. -1.  0.  1.  0. -2.  0.]]
```

A third way to vectorize an array of sentences involves the `TfidfVectorizer` class. Listing 5.13 displays the contents of `tfidf_vectorize.py` that illustrates how to vectorize an array of sentences using the `TfidfVectorizer` class in `Sklearn`.

LISTING 5.13: tfidf_vectorize.py

```
from sklearn.feature_extraction.text import TfidfVectorizer
import matplotlib.pyplot as plt
import seaborn as sns

sentences = ['the mouse ate the cheese',
             'the horse ate the hay',
             'the mouse saw the horse',
             'the mouse scared the horse']

vectorizer = TfidfVectorizer(norm=False, smooth_idf=False)
sentence_vectors = vectorizer.fit_transform(sentences)

print("vectorized sentences:")
print(sentence_vectors.toarray())

tfidf = vectorizer.fit_transform(sentences).toarray()

# display the tfidf frequencies:
sns.heatmap(tfidf,annot=True,cbar=False)
plt.show()
```

Listing 5.13 is similar to Listing 5.12, with the `TfidfVector` class in place of the `HashingVector` class. The other difference is the `Seaborn` Python library for visualization, which illustrates how to create a heat map in `Seaborn`. Note that Appendix F contains more information regarding `Seaborn`.

Now launch the code in Listing 5.13 and you will see the following output (numbers have been truncated from 8 decimal places to 3 decimal places to avoid "wrapping" the vectors on multiple lines):

```
vectorized sentences:
[[1.693 2.386 0.    0.    1.287 0.    0.    2. ]
 [1.693 0.    2.386 1.287 0.    0.    0.    2. ]
 [0.    0.    0.    1.287 1.287 2.386 0.    2. ]
 [0.    0.    0.    1.287 1.287 0.    2.386 2. ]]
```

Figure 5.2 displays the `tf-idf` frequencies, where the rows are the "documents" in the variable `sentences`, and the columns are the distinct words.

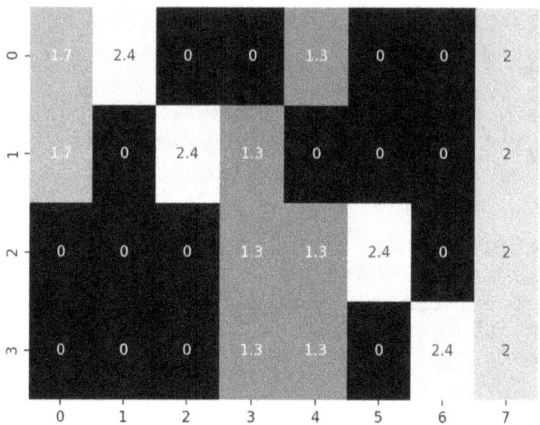

Figure 5.2: A Heatmap with tf-idf Frequencies.

Listing 5.14 displays the contents of `gensim_vectorize.py` that illustrates how to vectorize an array of sentences using the `word2vec` class in `gensim`.

LISTING 5.14: *gensim_vectorize.py*

```
from gensim.models import word2vec

sentences = ['the mouse ate the cheese',
             'the horse ate the hay',
             'the mouse saw the horse',
             'the mouse scared the horse']

for i, sentence in enumerate(sentences):
  tokenized = []
  for word in sentence.split(' '):
    tokenized.append(word)
  sentences[i] = tokenized

model = word2vec.Word2Vec(sentences,workers=1,size=2,min_count=1, window=3, sg=0)
```

```
word_list = model.wv.most_similar('mouse')
print("list of words:")
for word in word_list:
  print(word)
print()

similar_word = model.wv.most_similar('mouse')[0]
print("Most common word to mouse is: {}".format(similar_
word[0]))
```

Listing 5.14 initialize the variable `sentences` as an array of sentences, followed by a `for` loop that tokenizes each sentence in the variable `sentences`. Next, the variable `model` is initialized as an instance of the `Word2Vec` class that is available in the `word2vec` module in the `gensim` library.

The next code snippet initializes the variable `word_list` with the words that are most similar to the word `mouse` (which is a word that appears in `sentences`), followed by a loop that displays those words. Launch the code in Listing 5.14 and you will see the following output:

```
list of words:
('hay', 0.1007559671998024)
('the', -0.37532204389572144)
('saw', -0.528710126876831)
('horse', -0.7526397109031677)
('scared', -0.7596074342727661)
('ate', -0.9832854270935059)
('cheese', -0.9918226003646851)

Most common word to mouse is: hay
```

Listing 5.15 displays the contents of `tfidf_l1_l2.py` that illustrates how to specify L1 or L2 normalized frequencies when generating word embeddings of words in a corpus. *If you are unfamiliar with L1 or L2 normalization, you can treat this code sample as optional with no loss of continuity.*

LISTING 5.15: tfidf_l1_l2.py

```
from sklearn.feature_extraction.text import TfidfVectorizer
import pandas as pd

text = ['the mouse ate the cheese',
        'the horse ate the hay',
        'the mouse saw the horse',
        'the mouse scared the horse']

# use L1 penalty:
tfidf1 = TfidfVectorizer(binary=False,norm='l1',u
se_idf=False,smooth_idf=False,lowercase=True,stop_
```

```
words='english',min_df=1,max_df=1.0,max_features=None,ngram_
range=(1,1))

df = pd.DataFrame(tfidf1.fit_transform(text).
toarray(),columns=tfidf1.get_feature_names())

print("dataframe #1:")
print(df)
print()

# use L2 penalty:
tfidf2 = TfidfVectorizer(binary=False,norm='l2',u
se_idf=False,smooth_idf=False,lowercase=True,stop_
words='english',min_df=1,max_df=1.0,max_features=None,ngram_
range=(1,1))

df = pd.DataFrame(tfidf2.fit_transform(text).
toarray(),columns=tfidf2.get_feature_names())

print("dataframe #2:")
print(df)
print()
```

Listing 5.15 contains a variation of the TfidfVectorizer class (displayed in Listing 5.13) has that includes the parameter norm whose values can be either l1 or l2 that correspond to L1 or L2 normalization, respectively. The variables tfidf1 is initialized as an instance of TfidfVectorizer with norm set equal to l1, and then the data frame df is initialized with the result of transforming and fitting the contents of the array text (which is an array of sentences). The variable tfidf2 is similar to tfidf1, except that norm is set to the value l2 instead of l1. Launch the code in Listing 5.15 and you will see the following output:

```
dataframe #1:
        ate      cheese       hay      horse     mouse       saw     scared
0  0.333333    0.333333  0.000000  0.000000  0.333333  0.000000  0.000000
1  0.333333    0.000000  0.333333  0.333333  0.000000  0.000000  0.000000
2  0.000000    0.000000  0.000000  0.333333  0.333333  0.333333  0.000000
3  0.000000    0.000000  0.000000  0.333333  0.333333  0.000000  0.333333

dataframe #2:
       ate    cheese      hay    horse    mouse      saw   scared
0  0.57735   0.57735  0.00000  0.00000  0.57735  0.00000  0.00000
1  0.57735   0.00000  0.57735  0.57735  0.00000  0.00000  0.00000
2  0.00000   0.00000  0.00000  0.57735  0.57735  0.57735  0.00000
3  0.00000   0.00000  0.00000  0.57735  0.57735  0.00000  0.57735
```

What is BeautifulSoup?

`BeautifulSoup` is a very useful Python module that provides a plethora of APIs for retrieving the contents of HTML Web pages and extracting subsets of their content using `XPath`-based expressions. You need some familiarity with regular expressions, which are discussed in Appendix C. If need be, you can find online tutorials that discuss basic concepts of `XPath`.

This section contains three code samples: how to retrieve the contents of an HTML Web page, how to display the contents of HTML anchor ("a") tags, and how to remove non-alphanumeric characters from HTML anchor ("a") tags.

Listing 5.16 displays the contents of `scrape_text1.py` that illustrates how to retrieve the contents of the HTML Web page *https://www.github.com*.

LISTING 5.16: *scrape_text1.py*

```
import requests
import re
from bs4 import BeautifulSoup

src = "https://www.github.com"

# retrieve html web page as text
text = requests.get(src).text
#print("text:",text)

# parse into BeautifulSoup object
soup = BeautifulSoup(text, "html.parser")
print("soup:",soup)
```

Listing 5.16 contains `import` statements, followed by initializing the variable `src` as the URL for Github. Next, the variable `text` is initialized with the contents of the Github Web page, and then the variable `soup` is initialized as an instance of the `BeautifulSoup` class. Notice that `html.parser` is specified, which is why the HTML tags are removed. Launch the code in Listing 5.16 and you will see 1,036 lines of output, and only the first portion of the output is displayed below:

```
soup:
<!DOCTYPE html>

<html lang="en">
<head>
```

```
<meta charset="utf-8"/>
<link href="https://github.githubassets.com" rel="dns-
prefetch"/>
<link href="https://avatars0.githubusercontent.com"
rel="dns-prefetch"/>
<link href="https://avatars1.githubusercontent.com"
rel="dns-prefetch"/>
<link href="https://avatars2.githubusercontent.com"
rel="dns-prefetch"/>
<link href="https://avatars3.githubusercontent.com"
rel="dns-prefetch"/>
<link href="https://github-cloud.s3.amazonaws.com"
rel="dns-prefetch"/>
<link href="https://user-images.githubusercontent.com/"
rel="dns-prefetch"/>
<link crossorigin="anonymous" href="https://github.githu-
bassets.com/assets/frameworks-146fab5ea30e8afac08dd11013b-
b4ee0.css" integrity="sha512-FG+rXqMOivrAjdEQE7tO4BwM1poG-
mg70hJFTlNSxjX87grtrZ6UnPR8NkzwUHlQEGviu9XuRYeO8zH9YwvZhdg=="
media="all" rel="stylesheet">
```

Listing 5.17 displays the contents of `scrape_text2.py` that illustrates how to retrieve the contents of the HTML Web page *https://www.github.com* and display the contents of the HTML anchor ("a") tags. The new code is shown in bold.

LISTING 5.17: scrape_text2.py

```
import requests
import re
from bs4 import BeautifulSoup

src = "https://www.github.com"

# retrieve html web page as text
text = requests.get(src).text
#print("text:",text)

# parse into BeautifulSoup object
soup = BeautifulSoup(text, "html.parser")
print("soup:",soup)

# display contents of anchors ("a"):
for item in soup.find_all("a"):
  if len(item.contents) > 0:
    print("anchor:",item.get('href'))
```

Listing 5.17 contains three `import` statements and then initializes the variable src with the URL for Github. Next, the variable `text` is initialized with the contents of the Github page. The next snippet initializes the variable `soup` as an instance of the `BeautifulSoup` class. The final block of code is a `for` loop (shown in bold) that iterates through all the <a> elements in the variable `text`, and displays the `href` value embedded in each <a> element (after determining that its contents are non-empty).

Launch the code in Listing 5.17 and you will see 102 lines of output, and only the first portion of the output is displayed below:

```
anchor: #start-of-content
anchor: https://help.github.com/articles/supported-browsers
anchor: https://github.com/
anchor: /join?ref_cta=Sign+up&ref_loc=header+logged+out&ref_
page=%2F&source=header-home
anchor: /features
anchor: /features/code-review/
anchor: /features/project-management/
anchor: /features/integrations
anchor: /features/actions
anchor: /features/packages
anchor: /features/security
anchor: /features#team-management
anchor: /features#hosting
anchor: /customer-stories
anchor: /security
anchor: /team
```

Listing 5.18 displays the contents of `scrape_text3.py` that illustrates how to remove the nonalphanumeric characters from the HTML anchor ("a") tags in the HTML Web page *https://www.github.com*. The new code is shown in bold.

LISTING 5.18: scrape_text3.py

```
import requests
import re
from bs4 import BeautifulSoup

# removes non-alphanumeric characters
def remove_non_alpha_chars(text):
  # define the pattern to keep
  regex = r'[^a-zA-Z0-9]'
  return re.sub(regex, '', text)
```

```
src = "https://www.github.com"

# retrieve html web page as text
text = requests.get(src).text
#print("text:",text)

# parse into BeautifulSoup object
soup = BeautifulSoup(text, "html.parser")
print("soup:",soup)

# display contents of anchors ("a"):
for item in soup.find_all("a"):
  if len(item.contents) > 0:
    #print("anchor:",item.get('href'))
    cleaned = remove_non_alpha_chars(item.get('href'))
    print("cleaned:",cleaned)
```

Listing 5.18 is similar to Listing 5.16, and differs in the `for` loop (shown in bold) and that displays the `href` values after removing non-alphabetic characters and also all whitespaces. Launch the code in Listing 5.18 and you will see 102 lines of output, and only the first portion of the output is displayed below:

```
cleaned: startofcontent
cleaned: httpshelpgithubcomarticlessupportedbrowsers
cleaned: httpsgithubcom
cleaned: joinrefctaSignupreflocheaderloggedoutrefpage2Fsource-
         headerhome
cleaned: features
cleaned: featurescodereview
cleaned: featuresprojectmanagement
cleaned: featuresintegrations
cleaned: featuresactions
cleaned: featurespackages
cleaned: featuressecurity
cleaned: featuresteammanagement
cleaned: featureshosting
cleaned: customerstories
cleaned: security
cleaned: team
```

Web Scraping with Pure Regular Expressions

The previous section contains several examples of using `BeautifulSoup` to scrape HTML Web pages, and this section contains an example that involves only regular expressions. Once again, you need some familiarity with regular expressions, which are discussed in one of the appendices.

Listing 5.19 displays the contents of scrape_pure_regex.py that illustrates how to retrieve the contents of the HTML Web page *https://www.github.com* and remove the HTML tags with a single regular expression.

LISTING 5.19: *scrape_pure_regex.py*

```
import requests
import requests
import re
import os

src = "https://www.github.com"

# retrieve the web page contents:
r = requests.get(src)
print(r.text)

# remove HTML tags (notice the "?"):
pattern = re.compile(r'<.*?>')

cleaned = pattern.sub('', r.text)

#remove leading whitespaces:
cleaned = os.linesep.join([s.lstrip() for s in cleaned.splitlines() if s])

#remove embedded blank lines:
cleaned = os.linesep.join([s for s in cleaned.splitlines() if s])
print("cleaned text:")
print(cleaned)

#remove ALL whitespaces:
#cleaned = cleaned.replace(" ", "")

#this does not work:
#cleaned = cleaned.trim(" ", "")
```

Listing 5.19 also removes the HTML elements from the variable text that contains the contents of the Github Web page. However, there is a subtle yet very important detail regarding the regular expression <.*> versus the regular expression <.*?>.

The regular expression <.*> performs a *greedy* match, which means that it will continue matching characters until the right-most ">" is encountered. However, we want the greedy match to *stop* after finding the first ">" character, which matches the previous "<" character. The solution is simple: specify the regular expression <.*?>, which contains a question mark ("?") whose purpose is to disable the greedy matching nature of the metacharacter "*".

Launch the code in Listing 5.19 and you will see the following output (some output omitted for brevity):

```
<!DOCTYPE html>
<html lang="en">
  <head>
    <meta charset="utf-8">
    <link rel="dns-prefetch" href="https:
    //github.githubassets.com">
    <link rel="dns-prefetch" href="https:
    //avatars0.githubusercontent.com">
    <link rel="dns-prefetch" href="https:
    //avatars1.githubusercontent.com">
    <link rel="dns-prefetch" href="https:
    //avatars2.githubusercontent.com">
    <link rel="dns-prefetch" href="https:
    //avatars3.githubusercontent.com">
    <link rel="dns-prefetch" href="https:
    //github-cloud.s3.amazonaws.com">
    <link rel="dns-prefetch" href="https:
    //user-images.githubusercontent.com/">

    <link crossorigin="anonymous" media="all" integrity="sha512-/
    uy49LxdzjR0L36uT6CnmV1omP/8ZHxvOg4zq/dczzABHq9atntjJDmo5B7sV
    0J+AwVmv0fR0ZyW3EQawzdLFA==" rel="stylesheet" href="https://
    github.githubassets.com/assets/frameworks-feecb8f4bc5dce-
    34742f7eae4fa0a799.css" />
    <link crossorigin="anonymous" media="all" integrity="sha512-
    37pLQI8klDWPjWVVWFB9ITJLwVTTkp3Rt4bVf+yixrViURK9OoGHEJDbTLxBv/
    rTJhsLm8pb00H2H5AG3hUJfg==" rel="stylesheet" href="https://
    github.githubassets.com/assets/site-dfba4b408f2494358f8d655558
    507d21.css" />
    <meta name="viewport" content="width=device-width">

    <title>The world's leading software development platform ·
GitHub</title>

[details omitted for brevity]
      <div class="position-relative js-header-wrapper ">
        <a href="#start-of-content" class="px-2 py-4 bg-blue text-
        white show-on-focus js-skip-to-content">Skip to content</a>
```

```
      <span class="Progress progress-pjax-loader position-fixed
      width-full js-pjax-loader-bar">
        <span    class="progress-pjax-loader-bar    top-0    left-0"
        style="width: 0%;"></span>
      </span>
```
[details omitted for brevity]
cleaned text:
The world's leading software development platform · GitHub
Skip to content
GitHub no longer supports this web browser.
Learn more about the browsers we support.
```
<a href="/join?ref_cta=Sign+up&amp;ref_
loc=header+logged+out&amp;ref_page=%2F&amp;source=header-home"
```
[details omitted for brevity]

What is Scrapy?

In the previous section, you learned that BeautifulSoup is a Python-based library for scraping HTML Web pages. BeautifulSoup also supports XPath (which is an integral component of XSLT), whose APIs enable you to parse the scraped data, and also to extract portions of that data.

On the other hand, Scrapy is a Python-based library that provides data extraction and an assortment of additional APIs for a wide range of operations, including redirections, HTTP caching, filtering duplicated requests, preserving sessions/cookies across multiple requests, and various other features. Scrapy supports both CSS selectors and XPath expressions for data extraction. Moreover, you can also use BeautifulSoup or PyQuery as a data extraction mechanism.

Based on the preceding paragraph, you can probably see that while Scrapy and BeautifulSoup can do some of the same things (i.e., web scraping), they have fundamentally different purposes. As a rule of thumb: use BeautifulSoup if you need a "one-off" Web page scraper. However, if you need to perform web scraping and perform additional operations for one or more Web pages, then Scrapy is probably a better choice.

At the same time, keep in mind that Scrapy does have a steeper learning curve than BeautifulSoup, so decide whether or not the extra features of Scrapy are necessary for your requirements before you invest your time learning Scrapy. As a starting point, the Scrapy documentation Web page is here:

https://doc.scrapy.org/en/latest/intro/tutorial.html

What is SpaCy?

The `spaCy NLP` library is an efficient `Python`-based library that provides many useful features, and its home page is here: spacy.io

The `spaCy` library provides support for many `NLP`-related tasks, some of which are listed here:

- NER (named entity recognition)
- POS tagging
- Support for more than 60 languages
- More than 40 statistical models
- pretrained word vectors

You might encounter the following error message if you do not have the right components installed:

```
OSError: [E050] Can't find model 'en'. It doesn't seem to be
a shortcut link, a Python package or a valid path to a data
directory.
```

The solution for the preceding error is to open a command shell and launch the following command:

```
python3 -m spacy download en
```

After the preceding command has completed successfully you will see this message:

```
You can now load the model via spacy.load('en')
```

An important note: `SpaCy` version 3.0 was released as this book goes to print:

https://explosion.ai/blog/spacy-v3

The latest version contains significant new features, including transformer-based pipelines. The preceding link contains additional links that contain more information about the latest release.

SpaCy and Stop Words

Listing 5.20 displays the contents of `spacy_stopwords.py` that illustrates how to find the stop words in a sentence.

LISTING 5.20: spacy_stopwords.py

```
import spacy

import spacy
from spacy import displacy
from spacy.lang.en.stop_words import STOP_WORDS

sentence = "This simple sentence contains a stop word or two
            or more"

nlp = spacy.load('en')
doc = nlp(sentence)

print("sentence: ",sentence)
non_stop = []
for word in doc:
  if word.is_stop == True:
    print("stop word:",word)
  else:
    non_stop.append(word)
print("Non-stop: ",non_stop)
```

Listing 5.20 contains import statements for spaCy, displaCy (the latter is for visualization), and for English stop words. The next code snippet initializes three variables. First, the variable sentence is initialized as a text string. Second, nlp is initialized as an instance of the English language model. Next, the variable doc is initialized with the result of processing the text in the variable sentence.

The last portion of Listing 5.20 contains a loop that displays the stop words in the variable sentence. Launch the code in Listing 5.20 and you will see the following output:

```
sentence: This simple sentence contains a stop word or two or
more
stop word: This
stop word: a
stop word: or
stop word: two
stop word: or
stop word: more
Non-stop:  [simple, sentence, contains, stop, word]
```

The next section shows you how to perform tokenization with SpaCy.

SpaCy and Tokenization

Listing 5.21 displays the contents of spacy_tokenize.py that illustrates how to tokenize a sentence.

LISTING 5.21: *spacy_tokenize.py*

```
import spacy
nlp = spacy.load('en')

doc = nlp("I love Chicago deep dish pizza and Uno's as well.")

for token in doc:
  print(token)

print(f"Token \t\tLemma \t\tStopword".format('Token','Lemma',
'Stopword'))
print("-"*40)

for token in doc:
  print(f"{str(token)}\t\t{token.lemma_}\t\t{token.is_stop}")
```

Listing 5.21 contains an `import` statement followed by the initialization of the variable `nlp` as an instance of the English model in `spaCy`. Note that this code snippet will download the data model if it is not already present on your machine. The next portion of Listing 5.21 displays the tokens (words) in the initial text string, followed by a tabular display in which each row displays a token, its lemmatization, and whether or not it's a stop word. Launch the code in Listing 5.21 and you will see the following output:

```
I
love
Chicago
deep
dish
pizza
and
Uno
's
as
well
.
```

Token	Lemma	Stopword
I	-PRON-	True
love	love	False
Chicago	Chicago	False
deep	deep	False
dish	dish	False
pizza	pizza	False
and	and	True

Uno	Uno	False
's	's	True
as	as	True
well	well	True
.	.	False

SpaCy and Lemmatization

Listing 5.22 displays the contents of `spacy_lemma.py` that illustrates how to perform lemmatization in `spaCy`.

LISTING 5.22: *spacy_lemma.py*

```
import spacy

nlp = spacy.load("en_core_web_sm")

text = "I love Chicago deep dish pizza and Uno's as well."
doc = nlp(text)

print("=> text, lemma_, pos_, and is_stop:")
for token in doc:
  print(token.text, token.lemma_, token.pos_, token.is_stop)
print()

import pandas as pd

cols = ("text", "lemma", "POS", "explain", "stopword")
rows = []

for t in doc:
  row = [t.text, t.lemma_, t.pos_, spacy.explain(t.pos_),
         t.is_stop]
  rows.append(row)

df = pd.DataFrame(rows, columns=cols)
print("=> dataframe:")
print(df)
```

Listing 5.22 initializes the variable `nlp` with the `spaCy` model `en_core_web_sm` and the variable `text` with the same sentence as previous code samples. Next, the variable `doc` is instantiated by specifying the variable `text`, followed by a loop that displays the part of speech of each token (i.e., word) in the variable `text`.

The next portion of Listing 5.22 initializes the variable `cols` as the headings for the columns of a data frame, and the variable `rows` as an empty array. The following loop appends a row of attributes for each token in the variable `text`. Finally, the last code block initializes the data frame `df` with the contents of the variable `rows` and then displays its contents. Launch the code in Listing 5.22 and you will see the following output:

```
=> text, lemma_, pos_, and is_stop:
I -PRON- PRON True
love love VERB False
Chicago Chicago PROPN False
deep deep ADJ False
dish dish NOUN False
pizza pizza NOUN False
and and CCONJ True
Uno Uno PROPN False
's 's PART True
as as ADV True
well well ADV True
. . PUNCT False

=> dataframe:
        text   lemma    POS                 explain  stopword
0          I  -PRON-   PRON                 pronoun      True
1       love    love   VERB                    verb     False
2    Chicago Chicago  PROPN             proper noun     False
3       deep    deep    ADJ               adjective     False
4       dish    dish   NOUN                    noun     False
5      pizza   pizza   NOUN                    noun     False
6        and     and  CCONJ  coordinating conjunction     True
7        Uno     Uno  PROPN             proper noun     False
8         's      's   PART                particle      True
9         as      as    ADV                  adverb      True
10      well    well    ADV                  adverb      True
11         .       .  PUNCT             punctuation     False
```

SpaCy and NER

The code sample in this section shows you how to perform NER (Named Entity Recognition) in `spaCy`. Listing 5.23 displays the contents of `spacy_ner.py` that illustrates how to perform NER in `spaCy`.

LISTING 5.23: *spacy_ner.py*
```
import spacy

nlp = spacy.load('en_core_web_sm')
```

```
text = "Chicago style deep dish pizza, Uno's, and Nancy's pizza."
print("text:")
print(text)
print()

doc = nlp(text)

# Iterate over the entity text and label
for ent in doc.ents:
  print("text/label_:",ent.text, ent.label_)
```

Listing 5.23 is similar to Listing 5.21, except that this code only displays the `text` and `label_` values for each token in the string `text`. Launch the code in Listing 5.21 and you will see the following output:

```
text:
Chicago style deep dish pizza, Uno's, and Nancy's pizza.

text/label_: Chicago GPE
text/label_: Uno's ORG
text/label_: Nancy PERSON
```

Notice that Chicago is correctly identified as a location (`GPE`) and Uno's is correctly identified as an organization. However, Nancy's is identified as the person `Nancy` (which is actually correct), even though in this case the string Nancy's is the name of a pizza parlor in Chicago.

SpaCy Pipelines

`SpaCy` provides a pipeline class that enables you to specify a sequence of tasks to perform. The default pipeline consists of a tagger, a parser and an entity recognizer. The output of each task is a document, which becomes the input for the next task in the pipeline.

Listing 5.24 displays the contents of `spacy_pipeline.py` that illustrates how to use a `SpaCy` pipeline.

LISTING 5.24: *spacy_pipeline.py*

```
import spacy

sentences = [
  "We got a huge deep dish pizza from Pizzeria Uno.",
  "Supplemented with a couple of pitchers of beer.",
  "Then we went to the top of the Hancock building."
]
```

```
nlp = spacy.load("en_core_web_sm")

for doc in nlp.pipe(sentences, disable=["tagger", "parser"]):
  print("=> document:",doc)
  for ent in doc.ents:
    print("=> text:",ent.text,"=> label:",ent.label_)
  print()
```

Listing 5.24 initializes the variable `sentences` as an array of sentences and then initializes the variable `nlp` as an instance of a SpaCy model. The next portion of Listing 5.23 is a for loop that is based on `nlp.pipe()`, which in this example only processes the entity recognizer (the tagger and parser recognizers have been excluded).

Launch the code in Listing 5.24 and you will see the following output:

```
=> document: We got a huge deep dish pizza from Pizzeria Uno.
=> text: Pizzeria Uno => label: PERSON

=> document: Supplemented with a couple of pitchers of beer.

=> document: Then we went to the top of the Hancock building.
=> text: Hancock => label: GPE
```

As you can already see, pipelines are very flexible and convenient for processing text-based documents. More code samples and detailed information regarding `spaCy` pipelines is here:

https://spacy.io/usage/processing-pipelines

SpaCy and Word Vectors

Listing 5.25 displays the contents of `spacy_word_vectors.py` that illustrates word vectors for words.

LISTING 5.25: spacy_word_vectors.py

```
import spacy

nlp = spacy.load('en_core_web_lg')

nlp(u'pizza').vector

doc = nlp(u'We ate deep dish pizza with wine and beer.')
print("=> doc.vector:")
print(doc.vector)
print()
```

```
# find similar pairs of tokens:
tokens = nlp(u'wine beer soda')
for token1 in tokens:
  for token2 in tokens:
    print("=> token1.text, token2.text, token1.
similarity(token2):")
    print(token1.text, token2.text, token1.similarity(token2))
print()

# normalize tokens:
tokens = nlp(u'apple banana orange')
for token in tokens:
  print("=> token.text, token.has_vector, token.vector_norm,
token.is_oov:")
  print(token.text, token.has_vector, token.vector_norm,
token.is_oov)
print()

from scipy import spatial
cosine_similarity = lambda x, y: 1 - spatial.distance.
cosine(x, y)

queen = nlp.vocab['queen'].vector
woman = nlp.vocab['woman'].vector
man = nlp.vocab['man'].vector

# find the closest vector to "man" - "woman" + "queen"
new_vector = queen - woman + man
calc_similarities = []

for word in nlp.vocab:
  # Ignore words without vectors and mixed-case words:
  if word.has_vector:
    if word.is_lower:
      if word.is_alpha:
        similarity = cosine_similarity(new_vector, word.
                                       vector)
        calc_similarities.append((word, similarity))

calc_similarities = sorted(calc_similarities,
key=lambda item: -item[1])

print("=> [w[0].text for w in calc_similarities[:10]]:")
print([w[0].text for w in calc_similarities[:10]])
print()

doc = nlp(u'The quick brown fox jumped over the lazy dogs.')
print("doc:",doc)
print("doc.vector:",doc.vector)
```

Listing 5.25 initializes the variable doc as an instance of the nlp class, as well as the given text string, and then displays the contents of the associated word vector. Next, the variable `tokens` is initialized with three words, followed by a nested loop that displays the pair-wise similarity of the words in the `tokens` variable. The next portion of Listing 5.25 initializes the variable tokens with three different words, followed by a loop that displays various attributes these words.

The next portion of Listing 5.25 initializes the variable `cosine_similarity` as a lamb expression that calculates the cosine similarity between a pair of words. Then the variables queen, woman, and man are initializes, followed by the variable `new_vector` that is initialized as follows:

```
new_vector = queen - woman + man
```

Then another loop iterates through the words `nlp.vocab` and for each lower-case alphabetic word in `nlp.vocab`, computes the cosine similarity of that word with the variable `new_vector`. The resultant list of cosine similarities is sorted and then displayed. Launch the code in Listing 5.25 and you will see the following output:

```
=> doc.vector:
[-1.39887929e-01 -1.95095055e-02  8.34191069e-02 -2.64628291e-01
  2.40830615e-01  2.75315434e-01  2.51161046e-02  7.67326951e-02
  8.21892098e-02  1.90768397e+00 -2.59143114e-01  1.49312809e-01
 -6.83634281e-02 -1.11276604e-01 -1.17691800e-01 -2.02080399e-01
 -7.09474012e-02  1.21521211e+00 -1.57256007e-01 -2.19138991e-02
 // lines omitted for brevity
  3.04495007e-01 -1.26671968e-02  6.86664060e-02 -1.62135810e-01
 -6.57109767e-02  1.62497148e-01  4.26867157e-01  1.21716186e-01
  8.21024999e-02  2.98182011e-01  5.26543036e-02  2.68678162e-02
 -2.37585977e-01  1.15498960e-01 -1.25021964e-01 -1.34173691e-01
  9.52331945e-02 -1.57274202e-01  9.77694020e-02  1.11879949e-02]

tokens: wine beer soda

=> token1.text, token2.text, token1.similarity(token2):
wine wine 1.0
=> token1.text, token2.text, token1.similarity(token2):
wine beer 0.6600621
=> token1.text, token2.text, token1.similarity(token2):
wine soda 0.4345365
=> token1.text, token2.text, token1.similarity(token2):
beer wine 0.6600621
=> token1.text, token2.text, token1.similarity(token2):
beer beer 1.0
```

```
=> token1.text, token2.text, token1.similarity(token2):
beer soda 0.5788868
=> token1.text, token2.text, token1.similarity(token2):
soda wine 0.4345365
=> token1.text, token2.text, token1.similarity(token2):
soda beer 0.5788868
=> token1.text, token2.text, token1.similarity(token2):
soda soda 1.0

=> token.text, token.has_vector, token.vector_norm, token.is_oov:
apple True 7.1346846 False
=> token.text, token.has_vector, token.vector_norm, token.is_oov:
banana True 6.700014 False
=> token.text, token.has_vector, token.vector_norm, token.is_oov:
orange True 6.5420218 False

=> [w[0].text for w in calc_similarities[:10]]:
['queen', 'man', 'he', 'let', 'nothin', 'lovin', 'nuff', 'dare', 'doin',
'all']
```

The scispaCy Library (Optional)

The `scispaCy Python` library for NLP is based on `spaCy`, and it's used for processing biomedical text. This library performs common NLP tasks, such as NER, POS tagging, dependency parsing, and sentence segmentation.

The `scispaCy` library contains two primary packages that contain models: `en_core_sci_sm` (a smaller vocabulary without word vectors) and `en_core_sci_md` (a larger vocabulary with word vectors).

In particular, NER tasks play a key role in various types of biomedical data in datasets of differing sizes and number of entities (and their types) for different domains, such as cancer genetics, disease-drug interactions, pathway analysis and trial population extraction. The accuracy of `scispaCy` NER models is comparable to a decent number of other existing models. If this Python library interests you, more information regarding `scispaCy` is here:

https://arxiv.org/pdf/1902.07669.pdf

Summary

This chapter showed you how to perform data cleaning tasks that involve regular expressions. Then you learned about BoW, along with an explanation of word embeddings. In addition, you saw how to use `BeautifulSoup`, which is a `Python` module for scraping HTML Web pages.

Then you learned about `Scrapy`, which is a `Python`-based library that provides web scraping functionality and various other APIs. In addition, you were introduced to `spaCy`, which is a `Python`-based library for `NLP`, along with `Python` code samples that show you various features of `spaCy`.

You also learned about word embeddings and the fact that they provide context for words, which can yield more powerful models. Then you saw a Python code sample that involved `word2vec`, which is a `Python`-based library (discussed in Chapter 4) for `NLP`-related tasks that involve unstructured data as well as labeled data.

CHAPTER 6

ALGORITHMS AND TOOLKITS (II)

This chapter contains Python code samples that illustrate various NLP concepts that you learned in the previous two chapters. Since those chapters contain sufficient NLP-related theory, this chapter focuses almost exclusively on code samples. The majority of the code samples in this chapter involve NLTK (Natural Language Toolkit), along with several code samples that are based on gensim.

The first section (approximately two-thirds of this chapter) introduces NLTK and code samples that use NLTK with BoW, stemmers, and lemmatization. You will also see some examples of NLTK with Wordnet, lxml, XPath (not discussed in this book), n-grams, and skip-grams.

The second section introduces GloVe and gensim, which are very useful NLP Python libraries, along with some code samples.

What is NLTK?

Natural Language ToolKit (NLTK) is an open source Python library specifically for NLP-related tasks. Although NLTK does not provide SOTA (state-of-the-art) performance, it does provide a variety of solutions to many NLP tasks. This library was developed in 2002, and its home page is here:

www.nltk.org

NLTK provides support for many NLP-related tasks, such as stemmers, tokenization (words, sentences, and documents), lemmatization, chunking, and grammars. In particular, NLTK supports the SnowballStemmers that creates non-English stemmers for more than 10 languages: Danish, Dutch, English, French, German, Hungarian, Italian, Norwegian, Portuguese, Romanian, Russian, Spanish, and Swedish.

NLTK also supports n-grams, skip-grams, BoW, word2vec, parts of speech (POS), and named entity recognition (NER). In fact, NLTK enables you to define your own custom grammars and then parse sentences to determine if their structure conforms to a custom grammar.

NLTK is well-suited for various NLP tasks, such as recommendation systems and sentiment analysis, both of which are discussed in more detail in Chapter 9. NLTK also supports Wordnet, which enables you to find words (via Sysnet) and their homonyms and synonyms.

NLTK and BoW

Listing 6.1 displays the contents of ntk_bow.py that illustrates how to implement BoW in NLTK. Keep in mind that this code sample does involve regular expressions, also known as RegExs. If you are unfamiliar with RegExs, you can either "comment out" the two code snippets that involve regular expressions, or you can read the appendix that discusses this topic.

LISTING 6.1: nltk_bow.py

```
import nltk
import numpy as np
import re

text = 'the SF weather is hot and the LA weather is hotter'
ds = nltk.sent_tokenize(text)

# clean the words in the dataset:
for i in range(len(ds)):
  ds[i] = ds[i].lower()
  ds[i] = re.sub(r'\W', ' ', ds[i])
  ds[i] = re.sub(r'\s+', ' ', ds[i])

print("cleaned dataset:")
print(ds)
print()

# construct BoW model:
word2count = {}
for data in ds:
  words = nltk.word_tokenize(data)
  for word in words:
```

```
    if word not in word2count.keys():
      word2count[word] = 1
    else:
      word2count[word] += 1

# display word/frequency counts:
for word, freq in word2count.items():
  print(f'word: {word:8} frequency: {freq:3d}')
```

Listing 6.1 initializes the variable text with a string and then initializes the variable ds with the tokens of text. Next, a for loop iterates through the tokens and converts them to lowercase, removes all nonalphabetic characters, and replaces multiple whitespaces with a single whitespace.

Next, the cleaned data is displayed, followed by a loop that constructs a BoW model based on the tokens in the variable ds. Note that multiple occurrences of a token are taken into account when populating the dictionary word2count. The final portion of Listing 6.1 displays each word and its frequency. Launch the code in Listing 6.1 and you will see the following output:

```
cleaned dataset:
['the sf weather is hot and the la weather is hotter']

word: the       frequency:  2
word: sf        frequency:  1
word: weather   frequency:  2
word: is        frequency:  2
word: hot       frequency:  1
word: and       frequency:  1
word: la        frequency:  1
word: hotter    frequency:  1
```

NLTK and Stemmers

Listing 6.2 displays the contents of stem_documents1.py that illustrates how to perform stemming on a sentence with a PorterStemmer.

LISTING 6.2: stem_documents1.py

```
import nltk
from nltk.stem import PorterStemmer
from nltk.tokenize import sent_tokenize, word_tokenize

# read file contents:
file = open("data-science-wiki.txt")
```

```
my_lines_list = file.readlines()
#print("my_lines_list:")
#print(my_lines_list)

porter = PorterStemmer()

def stemSentence(sentence):
  token_words=word_tokenize(sentence)
  token_words
  stem_sentence = []

  for word in token_words:
    stem_sentence.append(porter.stem(word))
    stem_sentence.append(" ")

  return "".join(stem_sentence)

def saveStemmedLines():
  stem_file = open("stem-data-science-wiki.txt",mode="a+",
encoding="utf-8")
  for line in my_lines_list:
    stem_sentence = stemSentence(line)
    stem_file.write(stem_sentence)
  stem_file.close()

print(my_lines_list[0])
print("Stemmed sentence:")
x = stemSentence(my_lines_list[0])
print(x)
```

Listing 6.2 starts by reading the contents of a text file into the variable `my_lines_list`. Next, the variable `porter` is initialized as an instance of the `PorterStemmer` class that is available in NLTK. The next portion of Listing 6.2 is the definition of the Python function `stemSentence()` has that determines the stem of each word in the sentence that is passed into the function.

The next block defines the Python function `saveStemmedLines()` that contains a for loop that iterates through the sentences that have been processed by the function `stemSentence()`. The last portion of Listing 6.2 invokes the Python function `stemSentence()` with the first sentence in `my_lines_list`, displays the output, and then saves the stemmed text. Launch the code in Listing 6.2 and you will see the following output:

```
'data scienc is an interdisciplinari field that use scien-
tif method , process , algorithm and system to extract knowl-
edg and insight from data in variou form , both structur
and unstructur , [ 1 ] [ 2 ] similar to data mine . \n ' ,
'data scienc is a '' concept to unifi statist , data analysi
```

, machin learn and their relat method '' in order to '' understand and analyz actual phenomena '' with data . [3] It employ techniqu and theori drawn from mani field within the context of mathemat , statist , inform scienc , and comput scienc . \n ' ,

Listing 6.3 displays the contents of `porter_lancaster1.py` that illustrates how to invoke a `Porter` stemmer and a `Lancaster` stemmer to perform stemming on a set of words.

LISTING 6.3: porter_lancaster1.py

```
from nltk.stem import PorterStemmer
from nltk.stem import LancasterStemmer

# create two stemmers:
porter = PorterStemmer()
lancaster = LancasterStemmer()

#provide a word to be stemmed
print("Porter Stemmer:")
print(porter.stem("cats"))
print(porter.stem("trouble"))
print(porter.stem("troubling"))
print(porter.stem("troubled"))

print("Lancaster Stemmer:")
print(lancaster.stem("cats"))
print(lancaster.stem("trouble"))
print(lancaster.stem("troubling"))
print(lancaster.stem("troubled"))
```

Listing 6.3 is straightforward: the first portion displays the stemmed values that are determined by an instance of the `PorterStemmer` class, followed by another code block that performs the same calculations based on a `LancasterStemmer`. Launch the code in Listing 6.3 and you will see the following output:

```
Porter Stemmer:
cat
troubl
troubl
troubl
Lancaster Stemmer:
cat
troubl
troubl
troubl
```

Listing 6.4 displays the contents of porter_lancaster2.py that illustrates how to invoke a PorterStemmer and a LancasterStemmer to perform stemming on a set of words.

LISTING 6.4: porter_lancaster2.py

```
from nltk.stem import PorterStemmer
from nltk.stem import LancasterStemmer

# create two stemmers:
porter = PorterStemmer()
lancaster = LancasterStemmer()

word_list = ["friend", "friendship", "friends", "friendships",
"stabil","destabilize","misunderstanding","railroad","moonligh
t","football"]

print("{0:20}{1:20}{2:20}".format("Word","Porter
Stemmer","lancaster Stemmer"))

for word in word_list:      print("{0:20}{1:20}{2:20}".
format(word,porter.stem(word),lancaster.stem(word)))
```

Listing 6.4 initializes the variables porter and lancaster as instances of the classes PorterStemmer and LancasterStemmer, respectively, and then initializes the array word_list with a set of strings. The next portion of Listing 6.4 iterates through the words in the variable word_list and displays the stemmed values produced via the porter stemmer and the lancaster stemmer. Launch the code in Listing 6.4 and you will see the following output:

```
Word                Porter Stemmer      lancaster Stemmer
friend              friend              friend
friendship          friendship          friend
friends             friend              friend
friendships         friendship          friend
stabil              stabil              stabl
destabilize         destabil            dest
misunderstanding    misunderstand       misunderstand
railroad            railroad            railroad
moonlight           moonlight           moonlight
football            footbal             footbal
```

NLTK and Lemmatization

Listing 6.5 displays the contents of lemmatizer1.py that illustrates how to perform lemmatization on a sentence.

LISTING 6.5: *lemmatizer1.py*

```
import nltk
from nltk.stem import WordNetLemmatizer

wordnet_lemmatizer = WordNetLemmatizer()

sentence = "He eats Chicago deep dish pizzas, and lots of
pizzas from Pizzeria Uno!"
punctuations="?:!.,;"

sentence_words = nltk.word_tokenize(sentence)

for word in sentence_words:
  if word in punctuations:
    sentence_words.remove(word)

print("{0:20}{1:20}".format("Word","Lemma"))
for word in sentence_words:
  print ("{0:20}{1:20}".format(word,wordnet_lemmatizer.
lemmatize(word)))
```

Listing 6.5 initializes the variable `wordnet_lemmatizer` as an instance of the `WordNetLemmatizer` class that is available in NLTK. The variables `sentence` and `punctuations` are initialized, as well as the variable `sentence_words` that consists of the tokens in the variable `sentence`. Next, a loop that removes any punctuation symbols from the variable `sentence_words`. The final code block contains a loop that displays each word in `sentence_words`, along with its lemmatized value. Launch the code in Listing 6.5 and you will see the following output:

```
Word                Lemma
He                  He
eats                eats
Chicago             Chicago
deep                deep
dish                dish
pizzas              pizza
and                 and
lots                lot
of                  of
pizzas              pizza
from                from
Pizzeria            Pizzeria
Uno                 Uno
```

Listing 6.6 displays the contents of `lemmatizer2.py` that illustrates how to perform lemmatization on a sentence.

LISTING 6.6: lemmatizer2.py

```
import nltk
from nltk.stem import WordNetLemmatizer

wordnet_lemmatizer = WordNetLemmatizer()

sentence = "He eats Chicago deep dish pizzas, and lots of
pizzas from Pizzeria Uno!"
punctuations="?:!.,;"

sentence_words = nltk.word_tokenize(sentence)

for word in sentence_words:
  if word in punctuations:
    sentence_words.remove(word)

# display "part-of-speech" via pos="v"
print("{0:20}{1:20}".format("Word","Lemma"))
for word in sentence_words:
  print ("{0:20}{1:20}".format(word,wordnet_lemmatizer.
lemmatize(word, pos="v")))
```

Listing 6.6 is similar to Listing 6.5, with the addition of a `for` loop (shown in bold) that displays the displays the words in `sentence_words`, along with their lemmatized values. Launch the code in Listing 6.6 and you will see the following output:

```
Word                Lemma
He                  He
eats                eat
Chicago             Chicago
deep                deep
dish                dish
pizzas              pizzas
and                 and
lots                lot
of                  of
pizzas              pizzas
from                from
Pizzeria            Pizzeria
Uno                 Uno
```

NLTK and Stop Words

Listing 6.7 displays the contents of `nltk_newstop.py` that illustrates how to add new stop words to the default set of stop words.

LISTING 6.7: nltk_newstop.py

```
from sklearn.feature_extraction.text import CountVectorizer
from nltk.corpus import stopwords

newstop = set(stopwords.words('english')+['pasta','bliffet'])

print("new stopwords:")
print(newstop)
```

Listing 6.7 initializes the variable `newstop` with a pair of strings, after which the variable `cv` is initialized as an instance of the `CountVectorizer` class from Sklearn. Note that the latter initialization specifies the variable `newstop` as the set of stop words. Launch the code in Listing 6.7 and you will see the following output:

```
new stopwords:
{'couldn', 'hadn', 'theirs', 'shan', 'weren', 'having', 'y',
'between', 'before', 'can', 'other', 'all', 'wouldn', 'once',
'of', 'me', 'but', 'doing', 'because', 'own', 'mightn',
'hers', 'after', 'out', 'd', 'where', 'the', 'her', 'nor',
'him', 'below', 'both', 'do', "you'll", 'won', 'ourselves',
"needn't", 'ma', 'now', 'from', 'she', 'down', "you'd",
'an', "hadn't", 'should', 'were', 'you', 'it', 'such',
'their', 'bliffet', 'isn', 'who', 'had', "didn't", 'mustn',
'our', "you've", 'or', 'again', "aren't", "won't", 'itself',
'any', 'those', "don't", "isn't", 'am', "she's", 'how',
'than', 'be', 'as', 'has', 'being', 'each', 'doesn', 'wasn',
'ours', 'while', "hasn't", 'about', 'herself', 'with', 'on',
'them', 'shouldn', 'a', 'if', 'off', 'will', "wouldn't",
'over', 'some', 'these', 'there', 'why', 'yourself', 'too',
"doesn't", 'just', 'didn', "shouldn't", 'don', 'which',
'few', "mightn't", "you're", "haven't", 'my', 'i', 'and',
'then', 'only', 'by', 'your', 'what', 'when', 'up', 'here',
'o', 't', 'during', 'are', "couldn't", 'through', 'them-
selves', 'himself', 'until', 'did', 'against', 's', 'was',
'so', 'this', 'have', 'to', 'll', 'm', 'myself', 'at', 've',
'for', 'we', 'does', 'its', 're', 'needn', "mustn't", 'more',
'pasta', 'he', 'no', "shan't", 'his', 'above', 'that', 'un-
der', "weren't", 'whom', 'further', 'ain', 'is', 'into',
"should've", 'been', 'haven', 'yourselves', 'very', "wasn't",
'hasn', 'same', 'most', 'not', 'they', "that'll", "it's",
'yours', 'in', 'aren'}
```

What is Wordnet?

`Wordnet` is a corpus reader that is provided by `NLTK`, and you can use either of the following snippets to import `Wordnet`:

```
from nltk.corpus import wordnet
from nltk.corpus import wordnet as wn
```

`Wordnet` provides the `synsets()` function that enables you to search for words and display their `POS` (part of speech), as well as synonyms and antonyms of a given word.

`Wordnet` (via `NLTK`) provides the following similarity scorers (authors are in parentheses):

- jcn_similarity
- lch_similarity (Leacock-Chodorow)
- lin_similarity
- path_similarity
- res_similarity
- wup_similarity (Wu-Palmer)
- PPMI

Listing 6.8 displays the contents of `similarity1.py` that illustrates how to use `wup_similarity()` to find the similarity between a pair of words.

LISTING 6.8: similarity1.py

```
from nltk.corpus import wordnet as wn

# Wu and Palmer method to compare word similarity
w1 = wn.synset('ship.n.01')
w2 = wn.synset('boat.n.01')
print("=> similarity of ship and boat:")
print(w1.wup_similarity(w2))
print()

w1 = wn.synset('ship.n.01')
w2 = wn.synset('car.n.01')
print("=> similarity of ship and car:")
print(w1.wup_similarity(w2))
print()

w1 = wn.synset('ship.n.01')
w2 = wn.synset('dog.n.01')
```

```
print("=> similarity of ship and dog:")
print(w1.wup_similarity(w2))
print()
```

Listing 6.8 contains three blocks of code that compare the word *ship* with *boat*, *car*, and *dog*, respectively, using `wordnet`. Launch the code in Listing 6.8 and you will see the following output:

```
=> similarity of ship and boat:
0.9090909090909091

=> similarity of ship and car:
0.6956521739130435

=> similarity of ship and dog:
0.4
```

Listing 6.9 displays the contents of `wordnet1.py` that illustrates how to use `path_similarity()` to find the similarity between a pair of words.

LISTING 6.9: wordnet1.py

```
from nltk.corpus import wordnet as wn

# Multilingual WordNet (ISO-639 language codes):
print("=> sorted(wn.langs()):")
print(sorted(wn.langs()))
print()

drink = wn.lemma('drink.v.03.drink')
print("=> drink:",drink)
print("=> count:",drink.count())
print()

horse   = wn.synset('horse.n.01')
giraffe = wn.synset('giraffe.n.01')
zebra   = wn.synset('zebra.n.01')

print("=> horse.path_similarity(giraffe):")
print(horse.path_similarity(giraffe))
print()

print("=> horse.path_similarity(zebra):")
print(horse.path_similarity(zebra))
```

Listing 6.9 starts by displaying a sorted list of language code for supported languages, followed by the lemmatized value and frequency of the word *drink*. The next code snippet compares the word *horse* with the word *giraffe* and then with the word *zebra*, similar to the code in Listing 6.8. Launch the code in Listing 6.9 and you will see the following output:

```
=> sorted(wn.langs()):
['als', 'arb', 'bul', 'cat', 'cmn', 'dan', 'ell', 'eng',
'eus', 'fas', 'fin', 'fra', 'glg', 'heb', 'hrv', 'ind', 'ita',
'jpn', 'nld', 'nno', 'nob', 'pol', 'por', 'qcn', 'slv', 'spa',
'swe', 'tha', 'zsm']

=> drink: Lemma('toast.v.02.drink')
=> count: 1

=> horse.path_similarity(giraffe):
0.14285714285714285

=> horse.path_similarity(zebra):
0.3333333333333333
```

Synonyms and Antonyms

Listing 6.10 displays the contents of nltk_syn_ant.py that illustrates how to find synonyms and antonyms of a word using NLTK.

LISTING 6.10: nltk_syn_ant.py

```
from nltk.corpus import wordnet

word = "work"

synonyms = []
for syn in wordnet.synsets(word):
  for lemma in syn.lemmas():
    synonyms.append(lemma.name())

print("=> synonyms for",word,":")
print(synonyms)
print("------------------------")

antonyms = []
for syn in wordnet.synsets(word):
  for lemma in syn.lemmas():
    if lemma.antonyms():
      antonyms.append(lemma.antonyms()[0].name())

print("=> antonyms for",word,":")
print(antonyms)
```

Listing 6.10 starts with a loop that finds and displays the words that are synonyms for the word *work*. The next block of code in Listing 6.10 contains a loop that finds and displays the antonyms for the word *work*. Launch the code in Listing 6.10 and you will see the following output:

```
=> synonyms for work :
['work', 'work', 'piece_of_work', 'employment', 'work',
'study', 'work', 'work', 'workplace', 'work', 'oeuvre',
'work', 'body_of_work', 'work', 'work', 'do_work', 'work',
'act', 'function', 'work', 'operate', 'go', 'run', 'work',
'work_on', 'process', 'exercise', 'work', 'work_out', 'make',
'work', 'work', 'work', 'work', 'bring', 'work', 'play',
'wreak', 'make_for', 'work', 'put_to_work', 'cultivate',
'crop', 'work', 'work', 'influence', 'act_upon', 'work',
'work', 'work', 'work', 'work', 'shape', 'form', 'work',
'mold', 'mould', 'forge', 'work', 'knead', 'work', 'exploit',
'work', 'solve', 'work_out', 'figure_out', 'puzzle_out',
'lick', 'work', 'ferment', 'work', 'sour', 'turn', 'ferment',
'work', 'work']
------------------------
=> antonyms for work :
['idle', 'malfunction']
```

NLTK, lxml, and XPath

This section contains a code sample that combines NLTK, lxml, and XPath expressions. As a reminder, you can find online tutorials that discuss basic concepts of XPath if you are unfamiliar with XPath expressions.

NOTE *Make sure you invoke* `pip3 install lxml`

Listing 6.11 displays the contents of `nltk_xpath.py` that illustrates how to retrieve the contents of the HTML Web page *https://www.github.com*.

LISTING 6.11: *nltk_xpath.py*

```
import nltk
import lxml
from lxml import html
import requests

page = requests.get('https://www.ibm.com/events/think')
root = lxml.html.fromstring(page.content)
tree = html.fromstring(page.content)
data = tree.xpath('//*[@id="conference-overview"]/div/div[2]/
div/p')

print("root:")
print(root)
print("---------------------------\n")
```

```
print("data:")
print(data)
print("-------------------------\n")

items = []
for item in data:
  content = item.text_content()
  items.append(content)
  print("=> content:",item.text_content())
print("-------------------------\n")

print("items1:")
print(items)
print("-------------------------\n")
```

Listing 6.11 contains several `import` statements, followed by the initialization of several variables. The `page` variable is initialized with the contents of the URL in the `requests.get()` method. The variable `root` is assigned the top level node, and the `tree` variable is assigned the contents of the HTML Web page.

The fourth variable `data` is initialized with the result of an `XPath` expression, as shown here:

```
data = tree.xpath('//*[@id="conference-overview"]/div/div[2]/
                   div/p')
```

The left-most portion of the variable `data` consists of a tree of elements (starting from the `root` element) whose `id` value equals the string `conference-overview`. This tree is further pruned by selecting the leaf nodes of the preceding tree that have a descendant that matches the partial path `div/div[2]/div`. The preceding partial path involves (a) selecting elements that have a `<div>` element, then (b) navigating to the *second* `<div>` child element, and (c) further navigating to the `<div>` child elements of the elements in (b). The final step involves selecting the `<p>` elements that are child elements of the previous step.

The next section in Listing 6.11 displays the `root` element and the `data` element, followed by a `for` loop that iterates through the data subtree to append the text content of each element in the `data` variable. Launch the code in Listing 6.11 and you will see 102 lines of output, and only the first portion of the output is displayed below:

```
root:
<Element html at 0x1160ee778>
---------------------------
```

```
data:
[<Element p at 0x11613b138>, <Element p at 0x11613b048>, <Ele-
ment p at 0x11613b188>, <Element p at 0x11613b1d8>, <Element p
at 0x11613b228>]
---------------------------

=> content: As the evolving impacts of COVID-19 ripple through
our communities, we are all facing unforeseen challenges.
=> content: Gain new skills needed to adapt and evolve. Ex-
plore new ways of working and learn how to stabilize and pro-
tect your organization. Enhance IT resiliency, ensure business
continuity and most importantly, stay connected.
=> content: Sessions are on demand. Self-paced labs are avail-
able all day through Sunday, May 10.
=> content: Let's get thinking.
=> content: Watch now View self-paced labs
---------------------------

items1:
['As the evolving impacts of COVID-19 ripple through our com-
munities, we are all facing unforeseen challenges.', 'Gain new
skills needed to adapt and evolve. Explore new ways of work-
ing and learn how to stabilize and protect your organization.
Enhance IT resiliency, ensure business continuity and most
importantly, stay connected.', 'Sessions are on demand. Self-
paced labs are available all day through Sunday, May 10.',
"Let's get thinking.", 'Watch now View self-paced labs']
---------------------------
```

NLTK and n-grams

This section contains a code sample that uses NLTK in order to generate n-grams from a document. Listing 6.12 displays the contents of nltk_ngrams.py that illustrates how to extract the 5-grams from a string that represents a document.

LISTING 6.12: *nltk_ngrams.py*

```
import re
from nltk.util import ngrams

str = "Natural-language processing (NLP) is an area of com-
        puter science and artificial intelligence concerned with
        the interactions between computers and human (natural)
        languages."
```

```
str = str.lower()
str = re.sub(r'[^a-zA-Z0-9\s]', ' ', str)
tokens = [token for token in str.split(" ") if token != ""]
grams5 = list(ngrams(tokens, 5))

print("Generated 5-grams:")
print(grams5)
```

Listing 6.12 initializes the variable `str` with a text string, converts the text to lowercase, and then replaces every nonalphanumeric character with a single white space via a regular expression.

Next the `tokens` variable is initialized with the nonempty tokens in the `str` variable, followed by the variable `grams5` that is a list of 5 grams that are constructed from the `tokens` variable. Launch the code in Listing 6.12 and you will see 102 lines of output, and only the first portion of the output is displayed below:

```
Generated 5-grams:
[('natural', 'language', 'processing', 'nlp', 'is'), ('language', 'processing', 'nlp', 'is', 'an'), ('processing', 'nlp', 'is', 'an', 'area'), ('nlp', 'is', 'an', 'area', 'of'), ('is', 'an', 'area', 'of', 'computer'), ('an', 'area', 'of', 'computer', 'science'), ('area', 'of', 'computer', 'science', 'and'), ('of', 'computer', 'science', 'and', 'artificial'), ('computer', 'science', 'and', 'artificial', 'intelligence'), ('science', 'and', 'artificial', 'intelligence', 'concerned'), ('and', 'artificial', 'intelligence', 'concerned', 'with'), ('artificial', 'intelligence', 'concerned', 'with', 'the'), ('intelligence', 'concerned', 'with', 'the', 'interactions'), ('concerned', 'with', 'the', 'interactions', 'between'), ('with', 'the', 'interactions', 'between', 'computers'), ('the', 'interactions', 'between', 'computers', 'and'), ('interactions', 'between', 'computers', 'and', 'human'), ('between', 'computers', 'and', 'human', 'natural'), ('computers', 'and', 'human', 'natural', 'languages')]
```

NLTK and POS (1)

This section contains a code sample that uses NLTK in order to display the parts of speech for the words in a sentence.

Listing 6.13 displays the contents of `nltk_pos.py` that illustrates how to tokenize a sentence and then determine the parts of speech for each word in that sentence.

LISTING 6.13: *nltk_pos.py*

```
import nltk
from nltk.tokenize import word_tokenize
from nltk.corpus import wordnet

sentence = "I love pizza, and also pasta, what about you?"
split_words = sentence.split(" ")
print("sentence:")
print(sentence)
print()
print("split_words:")
print(split_words)
print()

word_tokenize(sentence)

w = word_tokenize(sentence)
pos = nltk.pos_tag(w)

print("tokenized:")
print(w)
print()

print("parts of speech:")
print(pos)
print()

syn = wordnet.synsets("spaceship")
print(syn)
print(syn[0].name())
print(syn[0].definition())

syn = wordnet.synsets("sleep")
print("examples of sleep:")
print(syn[0].examples())
print()
```

Listing 6.13 initializes the variable `sentence` to a text string and initializes the variable `split_words` with the tokens in the variable `sentence`. The next block of `print()` statements display the contents of `sentence` and `split_words`.

The next code snippet initializes the variable `w` with the result of passing `sentence` to the `word_tokenize` method from NLTK. The variable `pos` is then initialized with the parts of speech of the elements in `w`, followed by a block of `print()` statements that display their values as well as their parts of speech.

The final portion of Listing 6.13 invokes the `wordnet.synsets()` method to find the definitions of the word `spaceship` and the word `sleep`.

In both cases the definitions are displayed. Launch the code in Listing 6.14 and you will see the following output:

```
sentence:
I love pizza, and also pasta, what about you?

split_words:
['I', 'love', 'pizza,', 'and', 'also', 'pasta,', 'what',
'about', 'you?']

tokenized:
['I', 'love', 'pizza', ',', 'and', 'also', 'pasta', ',',
'what', 'about', 'you', '?']

parts of speech:
[('I', 'PRP'), ('love', 'VBP'), ('pizza', 'NN'), (',', ','),
('and', 'CC'), ('also', 'RB'), ('pasta', 'NN'), (',', ','),
('what', 'WP'), ('about', 'IN'), ('you', 'PRP'), ('?', '.')]

[Synset('starship.n.01')]
starship.n.01
a spacecraft designed to carry a crew into interstellar space
(especially in science fiction)

examples of sleep:
["he didn't get enough sleep last night", 'calm as a child in
dreamless slumber']
```

Listing 6.14 displays the contents of nltk_movie_reviews.py that illustrates how to tokenize a sentence and display relevant movie-related words.

LISTING 6.14: nltk_movie_reviews.py

```
import nltk
from nltk.corpus import movie_reviews
from nltk.corpus import stopwords
from nltk.tokenize import word_tokenize

print("first 16 English stop words:")
print(stopwords.words('english')[:16])
print()

para = "I started with Deep Learning, then proceeded to
Machine Learning, then NLP, and finally reached Deep
Reinforcement Learning. However, despite the preparatory
classes, the challenge of DRL was very steep."
```

```
words = word_tokenize(para)
print("tokenized words:")
print(words)
print()

useful_words = [word for word in words if word not in
stopwords.words('english')]
print("useful words:")
print(useful_words)
print()

print("movie reviews words:")
print(movie_reviews.words())
print()

print("movie reviews categories:")
print(movie_reviews.categories())
print()

print("movie reviews fileids:")
print(movie_reviews.fileids()[:4])
print()

all_words = movie_reviews.words()
freq_dist = nltk.FreqDist(all_words)
print("frequency distribution for 20 most common words:")
print(freq_dist.most_common(20))
print()
```

Listing 6.14 starts with several `import` statements, prints some stop words, and then initializes the variable `para` as a text string, which is tokenized and its tokens are then displayed. Next, the variable `useful_words` is initialized with the result of removing the stop words from the variable `words`.

The next code block in Listing 6.14 prints the nonstop words, followed by the movie-related words (from the `movie_reviews` class). The last portion of Listing 6.14 displays several file ids and then the distribution for the 20 most common words. Launch the code in Listing 6.14 and you will see the following output:

```
first 16 English stop words:
['i', 'me', 'my', 'myself', 'we', 'our', 'ours', 'ourselves',
'you', "you're", "you've", "you'll", "you'd", 'your', 'yours',
'yourself']

tokenized words:
['My', 'goal', 'was', 'simple', ':', 'learn', 'as', 'much',
'as', 'possible', 'about', 'Deep', 'Reinforcement', 'Learning',
'.', 'Even', 'after', 'studying', 'machine', 'learning', ',',
```

```
'deep', 'learning', ',', 'and', 'natural', 'language', 'pro-
cessing', ',', 'the', 'challenge', 'of', 'DRL', 'was', 'very',
'steep', '.']

useful words:
['My', 'goal', 'simple', ':', 'learn', 'much', 'possible',
'Deep', 'Reiforcement', 'Learning', '.', 'Even', 'studying',
'machine', 'learning', ',', 'deep', 'learning', ',', 'natu-
ral', 'language', 'processing', ',', 'challenge', 'DRL',
'steep', '.']

movie reviews words:
['plot', ':', 'two', 'teen', 'couples', 'go', 'to', ...]

movie reviews categories:
['neg', 'pos']

movie reviews fileids:
['neg/cv000_29416.txt', 'neg/cv001_19502.txt', 'neg/
cv002_17424.txt', 'neg/cv003_12683.txt']

frequency distribution for 20 most common words:
[(',', 77717), ('the', 76529), ('.', 65876), ('a', 38106),
('and', 35576), ('of', 34123), ('to', 31937), ('"', 30585),
('is', 25195), ('in', 21822), ("'s", 18513), ('"', 17612),
('it', 16107), ('that', 15924), ('-', 15595), (')', 11781),
('(', 11664), ('as', 11378), ('with', 10792), ('for', 9961)]
```

NLTK and POS (2)

This section contains a code sample that uses NLTK in order to display the parts of speech for the words in a sentence. Listing 6.15 displays the contents of nltk_entities.py that illustrates how to tokenize a sentence and then determine the parts of speech for each word in that sentence.

LISTING 6.15: nltk_entities.py

```
import nltk
from nltk.tokenize import sent_tokenize, word_tokenize
from nltk import ne_chunk, pos_tag

text = 'the SF weather is hot and the LA weather is hotter'
words = word_tokenize(text)
print("words:")
```

```
print(words)
print()

print("nltk.pos_tag(words):")
print(nltk.pos_tag(words))

def entities(text):
  return ne_chunk(pos_tag(word_tokenize(text)))

tree = entities(text)
print("tokenized:")
print(tree)
print("----------------")
tree.draw()
```

Listing 6.15 initializes the variable `text` with a text string, followed by the variable `words` that consists of the tokens of the variable `text`. Next, several `print()` statements display the contents of the variable `words` as well as the parts of speech of the tokens in the variable `words`.

The next portion of Listing 6.15 is a Python function `entities()` that returns the parts of speech of the tokens in the text string that is passed in to the `entities()` function. The final portion of Listing 6.15 invokes the `entities()` function, assigns the result to the variable `tree`, and then displays the contents of `tree`. Launch the code in Listing 6.15 and you will see the following output:

```
words:
['the', 'SF', 'weather', 'is', 'hot', 'and', 'the', 'LA',
'weather', 'is', 'hotter']

nltk.pos_tag(words):
[('the', 'DT'), ('SF', 'NNP'), ('weather', 'NN'), ('is',
'VBZ'), ('hot', 'JJ'), ('and', 'CC'), ('the', 'DT'), ('LA',
'NNP'), ('weather', 'NN'), ('is', 'VBZ'), ('hotter', 'RBR')]
tokenized:
(S
  the/DT
  (ORGANIZATION SF/NNP)
  weather/NN
  is/VBZ
  hot/JJ
  and/CC
  the/DT
  (ORGANIZATION LA/NNP)
  weather/NN
  is/VBZ
```

```
hotter/RBR)
----------------
```

Figure 6.1 displays the tree-like structure that is generated when you launch the code in Listing 6.16.

Figure 6.1. A Tree Structure with Named Entities.

NLTK and Tokenizers

This section contains a code sample that contains various tokenizers that are defined in NLTK. Listing 6.16 displays the contents of `nltk_tokenizers.py` that illustrates various ways of tokenizing the words in a sentence.

LISTING 6.16: nltk_tokenizers.py

```
import nltk

text = "I love deep dish pizza. Mainly from Chicago. Also with beer."

sents  = nltk.sent_tokenize(text)
words  = nltk.word_tokenize(text)
tokens = nltk.wordpunct_tokenize(text)
tags   = nltk.pos_tag(words)

print("text:   ",text)
print("sents:  ",sents)
print("words:  ",words)
print("tokens:",tokens)
print("tags:   ",tags)
```

Listing 6.16 initializes the variable `text` with a text string, followed by variables that are instances of various tokenizers that are available in NLTK. The block of `print()` statements displays the tokens that are produced by each of the tokenizers. Launch the code in Listing 6.16 and you will see the following output:

```
text:   I love deep dish pizza. Mainly from Chicago. Also with beer.
sents:  ['I love deep dish pizza.', 'Mainly from Chicago.',
         'Also with beer.']
words:  ['I', 'love', 'deep', 'dish', 'pizza', '.', 'Mainly',
         'from', 'Chicago', '.', 'Also', 'with', 'beer', '.']
```

```
tokens: ['I', 'love', 'deep', 'dish', 'pizza', '.', 'Mainly',
         'from', 'Chicago', '.', 'Also', 'with', 'beer', '.']
tags:   [('I', 'PRP'), ('love', 'VBP'), ('deep', 'JJ'),
         ('dish', 'JJ'), ('pizza', 'NN'), ('.', '.'),
         ('Mainly', 'RB'), ('from', 'IN'), ('Chicago', 'NNP'),
         ('.', '.'), ('Also', 'RB'), ('with', 'IN'), ('beer',
         'NN'), ('.', '.')]
```

The following URL contains a list of the terms in the preceding output, along with their corresponding parts of speech:

https://cs.nyu.edu/grishman/jet/guide/PennPOS.html

The next section provides another example of finding named entities using the NLTK library.

NLTK and Context-Free Grammars (Optional)

In simplified terms, a context-free grammar (CFG) is a set of rules or "productions" that are used to generate patterns of strings. Such rules are typically recursive, and they involve a set of terminal symbols, a set of nonterminal symbols, and an end symbol. There is also a start symbol that is a nonterminal symbol and appears in the initial string that is generated by a CFG. Depending on the complexity of the CFG, you will also see regular expressions in the productions.

While the preceding paragraph might seem esoteric or perhaps even pointless, you have already encountered CFGs: many popular programming languages, such as C, C++, and Java (but not Fortran) are context-free grammars. For example, the complete set of production rules for the C programming language is about five pages long.

As a simple example, here is a grammar that represents arithmetic expressions that contain any combination of the arithmetic operators *, /, +, and − (and numeric values as operands):

```
<expression> --> number
<expression> --> ( <expression> )
<expression> --> <expression> + <expression>
<expression> --> <expression> - <expression>
<expression> --> <expression> * <expression>
<expression> --> <expression> / <expression>
```

You might be surprised to discover that the NLTK library provides support for CFGs. Listing 6.17 displays the contents of nltk_grammar.py that illustrates how to specify a set of production rules for a simple context-free grammar. Note that it's more common to see the single letters N, V, and P used instead of noun, verb, and prep in CFGs: the latter are just to show you that you can be more "expressive" in the productions of a CFG.

LISTING 6.17: *nltk_grammar.py*

```
import re
import nltk
from nltk.parse import RecursiveDescentParser

# Define a CFG (Context Free Grammar):
mygrammar = nltk.CFG.fromstring("""
S -> NP VP
NP -> Art Noun | Art Noun PP
VP -> Verb | Verb NP | Verb NP PP
PP -> Prep NP

Art  -> 'a' | 'an' | 'the'
Noun -> 'boy' | 'ball' | 'apple' | 'hot' | 'dog'
Verb -> 'ate' | 'ran' | 'studied'
Prep -> 'in' | 'with'
""")

# a top-down parser:
rdstr = RecursiveDescentParser(mygrammar)

str1 = "the boy with the ball ate a hot dog"
str2 = "the boy ate an apple with the ball"

#display the grammar trees:
print("grammar trees for str1:")
for tree in rdstr.parse(str1.split()):
  print("tree:",tree)
print("-----------------------")

print("grammar trees for str2:")
for tree in rdstr.parse(str2.split()):
  print("tree:",tree)
```

Listing 6.17 initializes the variable `mygrammar` with 8 production rules that are used to determine whether or not a text string will parse correctly according to the given grammar. The next code snippet initializes the variable `rdstr` as an instance of the class `RecursiveDescentParser` (from NLTK) with the argument `mygrammar`.

The two variables `str1` and `str2` are initialized with text strings: one of them parses according to the grammar and one does not parse correctly. The two strings are very similar, and it's challenging to parse them visually against the grammar. However, the code in Listing 6.17 also contains two loops for displaying the parse tree for `str1` and `str2`. Notice that there is only a parse tree for `str2` because `str1` does not belong to the defined grammar. Launch the code in Listing 6.17 and you will see trees for the second sentence `str2` but not for `str1` (can you see why?):

```
grammar trees for str1:
----------------------
grammar trees for str2:
tree: (S
  (NP (Art the) (Noun boy))
  (VP
    (Verb ate)
    (NP
      (Art an)
      (Noun apple)
      (PP (Prep with) (NP (Art the) (Noun ball))))))
tree: (S
  (NP (Art the) (Noun boy))
  (VP
    (Verb ate)
    (NP (Art an) (Noun apple))
    (PP (Prep with) (NP (Art the) (Noun ball)))))
```

What is Gensim?

Gensim is an open source `Python`-based `NLP` library for performing `NLP`-related tasks, such as text processing, word embeddings and topic modeling, and its home page is here: *https://gensim.readthedocs.io/en/latest/index.html*.

`Gensim` supports unsupervised topic modeling and uses modern statistical machine learning. `Gensim` is also implemented in `Cython` (in addition to `Python`). `Gensim` works with word vector models, such as `Word2Vec` and `FastText`, and also supports `LDA` and `LSI` for topic modeling. Moreover, `Gensim` is compatible with `scipy` and `NumPy`, and provides functions to convert from/to `NumPy` arrays.

`Gensim` works with a single text-based document or a corpus (collection) of text-based documents. `Gensim` uses vectors to represent the words in a document, and its model is an algorithm for transforming vectors from one representation to another.

In addition, `Gensim` can create a `BoW` corpus, a `tf-idf` model, a `word2vec` model, and also `n-grams`. Moreover, `Gensim` computes similarity metrics. Now let's look at an example of `gensim` with `tf-idf` that is discussed in the next section.

Gensim and tf-idf Example

`Gensim` works with a single text-based document or a corpus (collection) of text-based documents. Listing 6.18 displays the contents of `gensim_tfidf.py` that illustrates how to combine `gensim` with `tf-idf`.

LISTING 6.18: gensim_tfidf.py

```
from gensim import models
from gensim import corpora
from gensim.utils import simple_preprocess
import numpy as np

documents = ["This is the first line",
             "This is the second sentence",
             "This third document"]

# Create the Dictionary and Corpus
mydict = corpora.Dictionary([simple_preprocess(line) for line
         in documents])
corpus = [mydict.doc2bow(simple_preprocess(line)) for line in
          documents]

# Show the Word Weights in Corpus
for doc in corpus:
    print([[mydict[id], freq] for id, freq in doc])

# Create the TF-IDF model
tfidf = models.TfidfModel(corpus, smartirs='ntc')

# Show the TF-IDF weights
for doc in tfidf[corpus]:
  print([[mydict[id], np.around(freq, decimals=2)] for id,
freq in doc])
```

Listing 6.18 starts with several `import` statements and then initializes the variable `documents` as an array of sentences. Next, the variable `mydict` is initialized as a dictionary that is based on the sentences in the `documents` variable. Notice that these sentences are first processed via the `simple_preprocess` class that tokenizes each sentence and converts the tokens to lowercase (and tokens are UTF-8 format).

The next code snippet instantiates the variable tfidf as an instance of the TfidfModel class. The final portion of Listing 6.18 displays the contents of tfidf.

Launch the code in Listing 6.19 and you will see the following output:

```
# [['first', 1], ['is', 1], ['line', 1], ['the', 1], ['this', 1]]
# [['is', 1], ['the', 1], ['this', 1], ['second', 1],
  ['sentence', 1]]
# [['this', 1], ['document', 1], ['third', 1]]

# [['first', 0.66], ['is', 0.24], ['line', 0.66], ['the', 0.24]]
# [['is', 0.24], ['the', 0.24], ['second', 0.66],
  ['sentence', 0.66]]
# [['document', 0.71], ['third', 0.71]]
```

Saving a Word2vec Model in Genism

Listing 6.19 displays the contents of `gensim_word2vec.py` that illustrates how to save a `word2vec` model in `gensim`.

LISTING 6.19: gensim_word2vec.py

```
from gensim.models import word2vec

corpus = [
        'Text of the first document.',
        'Text of the second document made longer.',
        'Number three.',
        'This is number four.',
]

# split sentences:
tokenized_sentences = [sentence.split() for sentence in corpus]

model = word2vec.Word2Vec(tokenized_sentences, min_count=1)
print("model:",model)

model.save("word2vec.model")
```

Listing 6.19 starts with an `import` statement and then initializes the variable `corpus` as an array of sentences. Next, the variable `tokenized_sentences` is initialized with the result of splitting `corpus` into sentences. The next code snippet instantiates the variable `model` as an instance of the `Word2Vec` class, along with the contents of the variable `tokenized_sentences`. The final portion of Listing 6.20 displays the contents of `model` and then saves the model in the file `word2vec.model`. Now launch the code in Listing 6.19 and you will see the following output:

```
model: Word2Vec(vocab=15, size=100, alpha=0.025)
```

An Example of Topic Modeling

Chapter 3 contains a high-level description of LDA (Latent Dirichlet Allocation), and this section contains a code sample for LDA. Listing 6.20 displays the contents of `lda_topic_modeling.py` that illustrates how to use LDA in order to perform topic modeling. Please keep in mind that the "documents" in this code sample are very short (and admittedly contrived), but you can replace them with your own set of documents and launch the code.

LISTING 6.20: lda_topic_modeling.py

```
# define a set of short documents:
doc1 = "Our plan was not without merit is similar in meaning
        to Our plan has merit."
doc2 = "I like the pizza toppings but I do not like the
        crust."
doc3 = "The only thing worse than being talked about, is not
        being talked about according to Oscar Wilde"
doc4 = "Everything is funny, as long as it's happening to
        somebody else according to Will Rogers"
doc5 = "When ignorance is bliss, 'tis folly to be wise by
        William Shakespeare and my favorite misquoted quote"
doc6 = "Good judgement is the result of experience and
        experience the result of bad judgement as Mark Twain
        astutely observed."

all_docs = [doc1, doc2, doc3, doc4, doc5, doc6]

from nltk.corpus import stopwords
from nltk.stem.wordnet import WordNetLemmatizer
import string

stop = set(stopwords.words('english'))
exclude = set(string.punctuation)
lemma = WordNetLemmatizer()

def clean_documents(doc):
  no_stop = ' '.join([i for i in doc.lower().split() if i not
           in stop])
  no_punct = ''.join([ch for ch in no_stop if ch not in
           exclude])
```

```
        normalized = ' '.join(lemma.lemmatize(word) for word in
                    no_punct.split())
        return normalized

cleaned_docs = [clean_documents(doc).split() for doc in
                all_docs]

import gensim
from gensim import corpora
dictionary = corpora.Dictionary(cleaned_docs)
doc_term_matrix = [dictionary.doc2bow(doc) for doc in cleaned_
                   docs]

# import and get an instance of the LdaModel:
Lda = gensim.models.ldamodel.LdaModel
ldamodel = Lda(doc_term_matrix, num_topics = 3,
               id2word = dictionary, passes=50)

print(ldamodel.print_topics(num_topics=3, num_words=3))
```

Listing 6.20 starts by initializing six variables `doc1` through `doc6` with a sentence, followed by the variable `all_docs` that is an array consisting of those six variables.

The next portion of 6.20 contains several `import` statements, after which the variables `stop`, `exclude`, and `lemma` are initialized appropriately. Then the `Python` function `clean_documents()` is defined, which removes stop words and punctuation, and returns the sentence `normalized` that contains the cleaned words.

Next, the `gensim` library is imported and the variables `dictionary` and `doc_term_matrix` are initialized as a dictionary from `cleaned_docs` and a document/term matrix from `cleaned_docs`, respectively.

The final code block in Listing 6.20 initializes the variable `Lda` as an instance of the class `LdaModel`. The final code snippet initializes the variable `ldamodel` as an instance of `Lda` with four parameters, as shown here:

```
ldamodel = Lda(doc_term_matrix, num_topics = 3,
               id2word = dictionary, passes=50)
```

Now launch the code in Listing 6.21 and you will see the following output:

```
model:
[
(0,'0.075*"experience" + 0.075*"result" + 0.075*"judgement"'),
(1,'0.060*"plan" + 0.060*"merit" + 0.034*"wise"'),
(2,'0.106*"talked" + 0.061*"according" + 0.061*"oscar"')
]
```

Notice that the final code snippet in Listing 6.20 specifies the value 3 for num_topics (the number of topics) and also for num_words. Hence, there are three elements in the preceding output: the first digit (shown in bold) of each element is the topic number. Each highlighted digit is followed by an element that is a linear combination of three strings: this is because the value of num_words is 3. The words in each linear combination are the most meaningful "topic" words, and the numeric coefficients indicate the relative weight (i.e., importance) of the associated word in the document.

Now change the number 3 to a 4 in the final line of code in Listing 6.20 as follows:

```
print(ldamodel.print_topics(num_topics=3, num_words=4))
```

Launch the code in Listing 6.21 and you will see the following output:

```
model:
[
(0,'0.067*"talked" + 0.067*"according" + 0.067*"like" +
0.038*"about"'),
(1,'0.065*"experience" + 0.065*"result" + 0.065*"judgement" +
0.037*"good"'),
(2,'0.111*"merit" + 0.111*"plan" + 0.063*"similar" +
0.063*"meaning"')
]
```

Compare the preceding output block with the first output block and observe the differences.

A Brief Comparison of Popular Python-Based NLP Libraries

This section contains information that you have seen in earlier sections and chapters, which is provided in a consolidated manner for your convenience.

Natural language toolkit NLTK is used for such tasks as tokenization, lemmatization, stemming, parsing, POS tagging, and so on. This library has tools for almost all NLP tasks.

SpaCy is the main competitor of the NLTK. These two libraries can be used for the same tasks.

Gensim is the package for topic and vector space modeling, document similarity.

`Sklearn` provides a large library for machine learning. The tools for text preprocessing are also presented here.

The general mission of the `Pattern` library is to serve as the Web mining module. So, it supports NLP only as a side task.

`Polyglot` is yet another `Python` package for NLP. It is not very popular but also can be used for a wide range of the NLP tasks.

Miscellaneous Libraries

This section contains task-specific libraries that can be used in NLP as well as non-NLP projects.

https://www.kdnuggets.com/2020/04/five-cool-python-libraries-data-science.html

1. Numerizer

https://github.com/jaidevd/numerizer

This library converts text numerics into int and float, and is installed via:

`pip3 install numerizer`

A simple example is shown here:

```
from numerizer import numerize
print(numerize('Eight fifty million'))
print(numerize('one two three'))
print(numerize('Fifteen hundred'))
print(numerize('Three hundred and Forty five'))
print(numerize('Six and one quarter'))
print(numerize('Jack is having fifty million'))
print(numerize('Three hundred billion'))
```

2. Missingo

This library provides a way to visualize missing values from an Excel spreadsheet, and is installed via:

`pip3 install missingno`

A simple example is shown here:

```
import pandas as pd
import missingno as mi
```

```
# reading the dummy dataset
data = pd.read_excel("dummy.xlsx")

# checking missing values
data.isnull().sum()

#Visualizing using missingno
print("Visualizing missing value using bar graph")
mi.bar(data, figsize = (10,5))
print("Visualizing missing value using matrix")
mi.matrix(data, figsize = (10,5))
```

3. Faker

This library generates various types of test data, and is installed via:

```
pip3 install faker
```

A simple example is shown here:

```
# Generating fake email
print (fake.email())
# Generating fake country name
print(fake.country())
# Generating fake name
print(fake.name())
# Generating fake text
print(fake.text())
# Generating fake lat and lon
print(fake.latitude(), fake.longitude())
# Generating fake url
print(fake.url())
# Generating fake profile
print(fake.profile())
# Generating random number
print(fake.random_number())
```

4. EMOT

This library can collect emojis (small images) and emoticons (keyboard-based characters), and then perform a sentiment-like analysis. Install this library via this command:

```
pip3 install emot
```

A simple example is shown here:

```
import re
# Function for converting emojis into word
from emot.emo_unicode import UNICODE_EMO, EMOTICONS

def convert_emojis(text):
  for emot in UNICODE_EMO:
    text = text.replace(emot, "_".join(UNICODE_EMO[emot].replace(",","").replace(":","").split()))
  return text# Example

text1 = "Awesome □üòÇ. The exhilaration from successfully completing my project □üòé, The euphoria is wonderfuls □üòí"
convert_emojis(text1)
```

5. Chartify

Chartify is a user-friendly visualization library for charts, and is installed via:

```
pip3 install chartify
```

A simple example is shown here:
```
import numpy as np
import pandas as pd
import chartify

#loading example dataset from chartify
data = chartify.examples.example_data()
data.head()

# Calculating total quantity for each fruits
quantity_by_fruit = (data.groupby('fruit')['quantity'].sum().reset_index())
ch = chartify.Chart(blank_labels=True, x_axis_type='categorical')
ch.set_title("Vertical bar plot.")
ch.set_subtitle("Automatically sorts by value counts.")

ch.plot.bar(
 data_frame=quantity_by_fruit,
 categorical_columns='fruit',
 numeric_column='quantity')
ch.show()
```

Summary

This chapter introduced you to `NLTK`, along with code samples of using `NLTK` with `lxml`, `XPath`, stemmers, lemmatization, and stop words. Then you learned about some of the features of `Wordnet`, such as finding synonyms and antonyms of words. You also learned about `NLTK` with `POS` (parts of speech), along with various tokenizers.

Next you learned how define a grammar in `NLTK` and determine whether or not a given sentence can be parsed with that grammar. Finally, you learned about `gensim` and its core concepts, with code samples that illustrate how to calculate `tf-idf` values in `gensim`, and how to save a `word2vec` model in `gensim`.

CHAPTER 7

INTRODUCTION TO MACHINE LEARNING

This chapter introduces numerous concepts in machine learning, such as feature selection, feature engineering, data cleaning, training sets, and test sets.

The first part of this chapter briefly discusses machine learning and the sequence of steps that are typically required in order to prepare a dataset. These steps include "feature selection" or "feature extraction" that can be performed using various algorithms.

The second section describes the types of data that you can encounter, issues that can arise with the data in datasets, and how to rectify them. You will also learn about the difference between "hold out" and "k-fold" when you perform the training step.

The third part of this chapter briefly discusses the basic concepts involved in linear regression. Although linear regression was developed more than 200 years ago, this technique is still one of the "core" techniques for solving (albeit simple) problems in Statistics and machine learning. In fact, the technique known as "mean squared error" (MSE) for finding a best-fitting line for data points in a 2D plane (or a hyperplane for higher dimensions) is implemented in Python and TensorFlow in order to minimize so-called "loss" functions.

The fourth section in this chapter contains additional code samples involving linear regression tasks using standard techniques in NumPy. Hence, if you are comfortable with this topic, you can probably skim quickly through the first two sections of this chapter. This section shows you how to solve linear regression using Keras.

One point to keep in mind is that some algorithms are mentioned without delving into details about them. For instance, the section pertaining to supervised learning contains a list of algorithms that appear later in the chapter in the section that pertains to classification algorithms. The algorithms that are displayed in bold in a list are the algorithms that are of greater interest for this book. In some cases the algorithms are discussed in greater detail in the next chapter; otherwise, you can perform an online search for additional information about the algorithms that are not discussed in detail in this book.

What is Machine Learning?

In high-level terms, machine learning is a subset of AI that can solve tasks that are infeasible or too cumbersome with traditional programming languages. A spam filter for email is an early example of machine learning. Machine learning generally supersedes the accuracy of older algorithms.

If you are a developer, you're probably accustomed to using an algorithmic approach to tasks, which often involves executing a sequence of steps in a deterministic manner. However, machine learning involves an approach that is similar to a forensic analysis because *the distribution of data in large datasets is often unknown and might even be impossible to determine with high accuracy*. As a result, it's difficult to apply a test-driven development (TDD) approach to training models on datasets. Moreover, the accuracy of a model that has been trained on a nontrivial dataset will never be 100%, which means that a lower percentage is the best that can be achieved.

How do you determine what level of accuracy is acceptable? First, you are unlikely to exceed the current SOTA ("state of the art"), unless you are implementing a new algorithm that has proven to be superior to all other existing algorithms for the task at hand. Second, this decision is likely to be a mixture of a technical decision and a business decision. For example, if your model achieves 90% accuracy and the State of the Art (SOTA) is 95%, is it worth investing the additional time and expense to improve the accuracy of your model, or is 90% "good enough" for your business needs?

Despite the variety of machine learning algorithms, the data is arguably more important than the selected algorithm. Many issues can arise with data, such as insufficient data, poor quality of data, incorrect data, missing data, irrelevant data, duplicate data values, and so forth. Later in this chapter you will see techniques that address many of these data-related issues.

If you are unfamiliar with machine learning terminology, a dataset is a collection of data values, which can be in the form of a csv file or a spreadsheet. Each column is called a feature, and each row is a datapoint that contains a set of specific values for each feature. If a dataset contains information about customers, then each row pertains to a specific customer.

One distinction to keep in mind is that machine learning differs from data mining: the latter is a manual process for making decisions, whereas machine learning involves training models on data sets by means of machine learning algorithms.

Learning Style of Machine Learning Algorithms

Here are the main types of machine learning (combinations of these are also possible) that you will encounter:

- supervised learning
- unsupervised learning
- semisupervised learning
- active learning
- self-supervised learning
- weakly supervised learning
- reinforcement learning

Supervised learning means that the datapoints in a dataset have a label that identifies its contents. For example, the MNIST dataset contains 28×28 PNG files, each of which contains a single hand-drawn digit (i.e., 0 through 9 inclusive). Every image with the digit 0 has the label 0; every image with the digit 1 has the label 1; all other images are labeled according to the digit that is displayed in those images.

As another example, the columns in the Titanic dataset are features about passengers, such as their gender, the cabin class, the price of their ticket, whether or not the passenger survived, and so forth. Each row contains information about a single passenger, including the value 1 if the passenger survived. The MNIST dataset and the Titanic dataset involve *classification* tasks: the goal is to train a model based on a training dataset and then predict the class of each row in a test dataset.

In general, the datasets for classification tasks have a small number of possible values: one of nine digits in the range of 0 through 9, one of four animals (dog, cat, horse, giraffe), one of two values (survived versus perished, purchased versus not purchased). As a rule of thumb, if the number of outcomes can be displayed "reasonably well" in a drop-down list, then it's probably a classification task.

In the case of a dataset that contains real estate data, each row contains information about a specific house, such as the number of bedrooms, the square feet of the house, the number of bathrooms, the price of the house, and so forth. In this dataset the price of the house is the label for each row. Notice that the range of possible prices is too large to fit "reasonably well" in a drop-down list. *A real estate dataset involves a* regression *task: the goal is to train a model based on a training dataset and then predict the price of each house in a test dataset.*

Unsupervised learning involves unlabeled data, which is typically the case for clustering algorithms (discussed later). Active learning is a subset of unsupervised learning, as described here:

https://www.kdnuggets.com/2018/10/introduction-active-learning.html

Self-supervised and weakly supervised learning:

https://towardsdatascience.com/weakly-and-self-supervised-learning-part-4-2fbfd10280b3

There is one more very important unsupervised task called *anomaly detection*. This task is relevant for fraud detection and detecting outliers (discussed later in more detail).

Semi-supervised learning is a combination of supervised and unsupervised learning: some data points are labeled and some are unlabeled. One technique involves using the labeled data in order to classify (i.e., label) the unlabeled data, after which you can apply a classification algorithm.

Reinforcement learning pertains to maximizing a reward, and this type of learning is beyond the scope of this book.

Types of Machine Learning Algorithms

This section contains lists of machine learning algorithms that includes algorithms that are accompanied by code samples later in this book. There are many algorithms that are not discussed in this book, however, they are included in case you decide to learn about them through self-study. Keep in mind that the lists of algorithms are not in increasing order of complexity of the algorithms.

One way to classify machine learning algorithms is based on how closely they perform the same task. A high-level list of various types of algorithms is given here:

- deep Learning algorithms
- instance-based algorithms
- Naive Bayes algorithms
- regression algorithms
- reinforcement learning algorithms
- tree-based algorithms

As you will see later in Chapter 8, machine learning uses various algorithms to find correlations (patterns) in datasets. Since the distribution of the data in a dataset is often unknown, it's virtually impossible to predict which algorithm will produce the best accuracy. Therefore, it's advisable to employ different algorithms on a given dataset and then see which one produces the best accuracy (along with an analysis of other metrics beyond accuracy).

There are three main types of algorithms in machine learning that you will learn about later in this book, and the choice of algorithm depends on the type of analysis that is required. For example, use *linear regression* algorithms when you need to predict numeric values: the price of a house in a real estate dataset, the temperature for the next day or week, and so forth. This type of algorithm belongs to "supervised learning" because you know the labels of the items in the dataset before you train a model on that dataset.

Classification algorithms (discussed in Chapter 8) are used when you have a dataset comprising labeled items and you need to make predictions about the label of unseen data items. For example, if you have a dataset consisting of pictures of dogs, cats, birds, and mice, then you can use convolutional neural networks (CNNs) to train a model with that dataset, after which the model can predict the "class" of an unseen photo containing either a dog, cat, bird, or a mouse. These algorithms also belong to "supervised learning."

A third type of algorithm involves *clustering*, which pertains to datasets that do *not* have labels. A clustering algorithm attempts to "partition" the data items into clusters, where the elements in each cluster have the same type. This type of algorithm is known as "unsupervised learning," and it's essentially an unsupervised classification task.

In the NLP world, datasets typically contain text-based data, and unsupervised learning algorithms help you find topics (aka topic modeling) in collections of documents.

In summary, this chapter and the next chapter group machine learning algorithms in the following categories:

- regression (e.g., linear regression)
- classification (e.g., kNN or k-nearest neighbor)
- clustering (e.g., kMeans)

Regression is a supervised learning technique to predict numerical quantities. An example of a regression task is predicting the value of a particular stock. Note that this task is different from predicting whether the value of a particular stock will increase or decrease tomorrow (or some other future time period). Another example of a regression task involves predicting the cost of a house in a real estate dataset. Both of these tasks are examples of a regression task.

Regression algorithms in machine learning include linear regression and generalized linear regression (also called multivariate analysis in traditional statistics).

Classification is also a supervised learning technique, but it's for predicting categorical quantities. An example of a classification task is detecting the occurrence of spam, fraud, or determining the digit in a PNG file (such as the MNIST dataset). In this case, the data is already labeled, so you can compare the prediction with the label that was assigned to the given PNG.

Classification algorithms in machine learning include the following list of algorithms (they are discussed in greater detail in the next chapter):

- decision trees (a single tree)
- random forests (multiple trees)
- kNN (k-nearest neighbor)
- logistic regression (despite its name)

- naïve Bayes
- SVM (support vector machines)

Some machine learning algorithms (such as SVMs, random forests, and kNN) support regression as well as classification. In the case of SVMs, the Sklearn implementation of this algorithm provides two APIs: SVC for classification and SVR for regression.

Each of the preceding algorithms involves a model that is trained on a dataset, after which the model is used to make a prediction. By contrast, a random forest consists of *multiple* independent trees (the number is specified by you), and each tree makes a prediction regarding the value of a feature. If the feature is numeric, take the mean or the mode (or perform some other calculation, such as SMOTE) in order to determine the "final" prediction. If the feature is categorical, use the mode (i.e., the most frequently occurring class) as the result; in the case of a tie you can select one of them in a random fashion.

Incidentally, the following link contains more information regarding the kNN algorithm for classification as well as regression:

http://saedsayad.com/k_nearest_neighbors_reg.htm

Clustering is an unsupervised learning technique for grouping similar data together. Clustering algorithms put data points in different clusters without knowing the nature of the data points. After the data has been separated into different clusters, you can use the SVM (support vector machine) algorithm to perform classification.

Some important unsupervised learning algorithms that involve *clustering* are listed below:

- k-Means
- meanshift
- hierarchical cluster analysis (HCA)
- expectation maximization

Keep in mind the following points. First, the value of k in k-Means is a hyperparameter, and it's usually an odd number to avoid ties between two classes. Next, the meanshift algorithm is a variation of the k-Means algorithm that does *not* require you to specify a value for k. In fact, the meanshift algorithm determines the optimal number of clusters. However, this algorithm does not scale well for large datasets.

If you are interested in learning more about clustering algorithms, the following link provides the details for ten clustering algorithms, including use-cases, scalability, and metric used in each algorithm:

https://scikit-learn.org/stable/modules/clustering.html

Some important machine learning algorithms that involve *dimensionality reduction* (discussed in more detail in Appendix A) are listed below:

- PCA (principal component analysis)
- kernel PCA
- LLE (locally linear embedding)
- t-SNE (t-distributed stochastic neighbor embedding)

Machine Learning Tasks

Unless you have a dataset that has already been sanitized, you need to examine the data in a dataset to make sure that it's in a suitable condition. The data preparation phase involves (a) examining the rows ("data cleaning") to ensure that they contain valid data (which might require domain-specific knowledge), and (b) examining the columns (feature selection or feature extraction) to determine if you can retain only the most important columns.

A high-level list of the sequence of machine learning tasks (some of which might not be required) is shown in the following list:

- obtain a dataset
- data cleaning
- feature selection
- dimensionality reduction
- algorithm selection
- train-versus-test data
- training a model
- testing a model
- fine-tuning a model
- obtain metrics for the model

First, you obviously need to obtain a dataset for your task. In the ideal scenario, this dataset already exists; otherwise, you need to cull the data from one or more data sources (e.g., a csv file, a relational database, a noSQL database, a Web service, and so forth).

Second, you need to perform *data cleaning*, which you can do via the following techniques:

- missing value ratio
- low variance filter
- high correlation filter

In general, data cleaning involves checking the data values in a dataset in order to resolve one or more of the following:

- Fix incorrect values.
- Resolve duplicate values.
- Resolve missing values.
- Decide what to do with outliers.

Use the *missing value ratio* technique if the dataset has too many missing values. In extreme cases, you might be able to drop features with a large number of missing values. Use the low variance filter technique to identify and drop features with constant values from the dataset. Use the high correlation filter technique to find highly correlated features, which increase multicollinearity in the dataset: such features can be removed from a dataset (but check with your domain expert before doing so).

Depending on your background and the nature of the dataset, you might need to work with a domain expert, which is a person who has a deep understanding of the contents of the dataset.

For example, you can use a statistical value (mean, mode, and so forth) to replace incorrect values with suitable values. Duplicate values can be handled in a similar fashion. You can replace missing numeric values with zero, the minimum, the mean, the mode, or the maximum value in a numeric column. You can replace missing categorical values with the mode of the categorical column.

If a row in a dataset contains a value that is an outlier, you have several options available:

- Delete the row.

- Keep the row.

- Replace the outlier with some other value (mean?).

When a dataset contains an outlier, you need to make a decision based on domain knowledge that is specific to the given dataset.

Suppose that a dataset contains stock-related information. As you know, there was a stock market crash in 1929, which you can view as an outlier. Such an occurrence is rare, but it can contain meaningful information. Incidentally, the source of wealth for some families in the 20th century was based on buying massive amounts of stock are very low prices during the Great Depression.

Preparing a Dataset and Training a Model

This section provides a list of general steps that are performed in machine learning, which includes data preparation and feature selection. Although portions of the details are included in Appendix A, it's worth emphasizing the frequent and common steps that you will perform, as shown in the following list:

Step 1: Collect data.
Step 2: Clean the data.
Step 3: Select or extract features.
Step 4: Select an algorithm.
Step 5: Inspect the results.
Step 6: Perform hyperparameter tuning.

The task of data collection might involve creating utilities (which might be a combination of shell scripts, Python scripts, and so forth) to extract data from multiple sources. There are many possible data repositories: `RDBMS`es, `NoSQL` databases, `Excel` spreadsheets, or text files in remote systems that are located behind firewalls.

Next, cleaning the data might require different types of data cleaning in different data files, such as removing duplicate data, checking for incorrect data values, and deciding what to do about missing values. For example, you can decide between populate missing values with the mean or mode of a feature, or perhaps dropping the row.

Step 3 might involve different formats for the same field that occurs in multiple data sources. For example, a currency field might have American currency in one data source and a European currency in another data source. You need to decide on a common currency format, as well as a common date format (and remember to take into account different taxes for different countries). Currency conversion also depends on the conversation rate, which can change on a daily basis.

Step 4 involves deciding which classification algorithms to use to train a model. When in doubt, try multiple algorithms to see which one produces the most desirable results.

Step 5 is where you can inspect a confusion matrix to see where misclassification has occurred. For example, if you have a target feature (i.e., the feature with labeled class values) with two possible values, then you can generate a 2×2 confusion matrix that contains four numeric values:

- the number of true positive values,
- the number of false positive values,
- the number of false negative values, and
- the number of true negative values.

Step 6 involves training the model with different values for hyperparameters. For example, the random forest algorithm requires specifying the number of trees in `n_components`; this algorithm has various other parameters with default values, and you can modify the latter before you train the model again.

Note that the task of hyperparameter tuning can be complex and time consuming and also expensive. Two possibilities to consider involve (1) using a pretrained model that requires a small amount of additional training data, or (2) using third-party services to perform hyperparameter tuning for your model.

Feature Engineering, Selection, and Extraction

In addition to creating a dataset and "cleaning" its values, generally you will examine the features in a dataset to determine which ones (if any) have little or no value and can be removed from the dataset. The process for doing so involves three main techniques:

- feature engineering
- feature selection
- feature extraction (aka feature projection)

Feature Engineering

Feature engineering is the process of determining a new set of features that are based on a combination of existing features in order to create a meaningful dataset for a given task. Domain expertise is often required for this process, even in cases of relatively simple datasets. Feature engineering can be tedious and expensive, and in some cases you might consider using automated feature learning. After you have created a dataset, it's a good idea to perform feature selection or feature extraction (or both) to ensure that you have a high quality dataset.

Feature Selection

Feature selection is also called variable selection, attribute selection or variable subset selection. Feature selection involves selecting a subset of the most relevant features in a dataset, which provides these advantages:

- reduced training time
- simpler models are easier to interpret
- avoidance of the curse of dimensionality
- better generalization due to a reduction in overfitting ("reduction of variance")

Feature selection techniques are often used in domains where there are many features and comparatively few samples (or data points). Keep in mind that a low-value feature can be redundant or irrelevant, which are two different concepts. For instance, a relevant feature might be redundant when it's combined with another strongly correlated feature.

Sometimes datasets contain a pair of features in which the categorical values of feature A are essentially a subset of the values in feature B. Determine whether or not there is no loss (or an acceptable loss) of information as a result of combining feature A and feature B into a single feature.

Another simple example involves splitting a feature into multiple features. For example, suppose that feature A contains the first name and last name of a set of customers. If you need to process that data based on a customer's last name, consider splitting feature A into two features (first name and last name). However, you might already have a pair of features for the first name and last name of customers, and merging them into one feature might be preferable (depends on the specific use-case).

Feature selection can be employed for performing regression tasks as well as classification tasks. Supervised feature selection techniques have the following properties:

- They take into account the target variable.
- Some remove irrelevant variables.
- Some use a filter strategy (e.g., information gain).
- Some use wrapper strategy (e.g., search guided by accuracy).
- Some use the embedded strategy.

In the embedded strategy, prediction errors are used to determine whether features are included or excluded while developing a model.

An example of a filter-based algorithm is XGBoost; examples of a wrapper-based algorithm include GA as well as the recursive feature elimination (RFE) feature selection technique; an example of an embedded-based algorithm is the L1 Lasso method.

A more recent technique for determining dependencies that works with numeric and categorical data is here:

https://phik.readthedocs.io/en/latest/#

One other point to keep in mind is that machine learning algorithms such as Lasso, decision trees, and random forests automatically perform feature selection during the training step of a given model.

By contrast, unsupervised feature selection techniques ignore the target variable, and some techniques remove redundant variables via correlation. Here is a list of several feature selection techniques available:

- Backward Feature Elimination
- Forward Feature Selection
- Factor Analysis
- Independent Component Analysis
- LOCO (Leave One Covariate Out)
- RFE (Recursive Feature Extraction)

Feature Extraction

Feature extraction creates new features from functions that produce combinations of the original features. By contrast, feature selection involves determining a subset of the existing features. The net effect of feature selection and feature extraction results in *dimensionality reduction* for a given dataset, which is discussed in Appendix A.

By contrast, feature exclusion involves retaining features that might be relevant for predicting the output. Moreover, feature exclusion involves dropping-versus-keeping features for training a model, whereas feature extraction involves as new (and ideally fewer) from the existing features.

After you have ascertained the most important features in a dataset (and also cleaned that dataset), the next step involves selecting a model, which is briefly discussed in the next section.

Model Selection

As you can probably infer, *model selection* refers to the steps involved in selecting a machine learning algorithm. Although there is no "silver bullet" with respect to model selection, here are some simple guidelines:

- Choose a model based on its expected performance.
- Prefer simpler models rather than complex models.
- Use a pretrained model.

Expected performance refers to highest accuracy or lowest prediction error, and simpler models generally make fewer assumptions. If you are fortunate, you might find a pretrained model that enables you to perform some additional training with your custom dataset. Despite these recommendations, always be prepared to try different algorithms and to change the values of some of the hyperparameters of those algorithms.

Working with Datasets

In addition to data cleaning, there are several other steps that you need to perform, such as selecting training data versus test data, and deciding whether to use "hold out" or cross-validation during the training process. More details are provided in the subsequent sections.

Training Data versus Test Data

After you have performed the tasks described earlier in this chapter (i.e., data cleaning and perhaps dimensionality reduction), you are ready to split the dataset into two parts. The first part is the *training set*, which is used to train a model, and the second part is the *test set*, which is used for "inferencing" (another term for making predictions). Make sure that you conform to the following guidelines for your test sets:

- the set is large enough to yield statistically meaningful results
- it's representative of the data set as a whole
- never train on test data
- never test on training data

What is Cross-Validation?

The purpose of cross-validation is to test a model with nonoverlapping test sets, which is performed in the following manner:

Step 1. Split the data into k subsets of equal size.
Step 2. Select one subset for testing and the others for training.
Step 3. Repeat step 2 for the other k-1 subsets.

This process is called *k-fold cross-validation*, and the overall error estimate is the average of the error estimates.

A standard method for evaluation involves 10-fold cross-validation. Extensive experiments have shown that 10 subsets is the best choice to obtain an accurate estimate. In fact, you can repeat 10-fold cross-validation 10 times and compute the average of the results, which helps to reduce the variance.

Specifically, the k-fold cross-validation is a technique that randomly partitions a dataset into `k` mutually exclusive subsets that have equal size (more or less). During the initial step, the first partition is used for testing and the remaining `(k-1)` partitions are used for training. When this step has completed, select the second partition for testing and the remaining `(k-1)` partitions for training. Continue this process until the `kth` partition is selected for testing and the remaining `(k-1)` partitions are used for training.

Overfitting versus Underfitting

Overfitting is a situation in which a model does not generalize well from the training data. When people say that a model "generalizes well" (after it has been trained), this means that the model can make predictions on other data sets with a high degree of accuracy that is comparable to the accuracy rate of trained model.

A symptom of overfitting is when the accuracy rate of the test data is significantly lower than the accuracy rate of the training data. Several techniques are available to address overfitting in a machine learning model, some of which are listed here (in no particular order):

- cross-validation
- remove features
- use more data
- proper normalization
- early stopping
- ensemble techniques
- regularization
- dropout technique
- boosting and bagging

The cross-validation technique is described in the previous section. Feature removal can also reduce overfitting, and there are various techniques for removing features from a dataset (and discussed earlier in this chapter). Increasing the size of the dataset is obviously constrained by the availability of suitable additional data.

Early stopping is a technique to stop the training process when the improvement in the accuracy falls below a small threshold value (specified by you). TF2/Keras has a nice mechanism for early stopping, and you can also specify what code to execute after the training process has terminated.

Ensemble techniques are discussed later in this chapter, and they include random forests, which are discussed in the next chapter. The next section discusses regularization, which is an important yet optional topic if you are primarily interested in TF2 code. If you plan to become proficient in machine learning, you will need to learn about regularization.

By contrast, *underfitting* occurs when the dataset is too small, which in turn results in a model that has lower accuracy. The obvious solution is to obtain more data; however, when it's not possible to do so, consider using data augmentation techniques such as generating synthetic data.

Please keep in mind that *oversampling* and *undersampling* (discussed in Appendix A) might sound similar to overfitting and underfitting, however they are different concepts.

What is Regularization?

Regularization helps to solve overfitting problem, which occurs when a model performs well on training data but poorly on validation or test data. Regularization solves this problem by adding a penalty term to the loss function, thereby controlling the model complexity with this penalty term. Regularization is generally useful for:

- a large number of variables
- a low ratio of (# observations)/(# of variables)
- a high multi-collinearity

There are two main types of regularization: the first type is L1 regularization (which is related to MAE, or the absolute value of differences) and the second type is L2 regularization (which is related to MSE, or the sum of the square of differences). In general, L2 performs better than L1, and L2 is also efficient in terms of computation.

L1 regularization, also called *Lasso regression*, adds a penalty term consisting of the sum of the absolute value of the weight estimates.

L2 regularization, which is also called *Ridge regression*, adds a penalty term to the loss function. The regularization term shrinks the weight estimates towards zero so that the regularized model is less affected by noise. The purpose of the regularization term is to reduce variance and increase bias.

ML and Feature Scaling

Feature scaling standardizes the range of features of data. Penalized estimation involves reducing the magnitude of the values of features by decreasing their corresponding coefficients. In particular, ridge regression and lasso regression are two examples of penalized estimation. This step is performed during the data preprocessing step, in part because gradient descent benefits from feature scaling.

In Chapter 8, you will see examples in which the training and test data is normalized, but not the label values because the latter values are already normalized.

Data Normalization Techniques

Data normalization in machine learning refers to transforming data to a common scale, which can improve the accuracy of algorithms that you adopt when you attempt to train a model on a dataset. Some common techniques include:

- standardization
- normalization
- min–max scaling
- mean normalization
- log transformation

Standardization assumes that the data in question conforms to a standard normal distribution, and standardization involves subtracting the mean and dividing by the standard deviation for every data point, which results in a $N(0,1)$ normal distribution. The relevant class from `sklearn` is here:

```
from sklearn.preprocessing import StandardScaler
```

Normalization (often confused with standardization) is a linear scaling technique. Let's assume that a dataset X has the values {X1, X2, . . . , Xn} and the terms `Minx` and `Maxx` are defined as follows:

```
Minx = minimum of Xi values
Maxx = maximum of Xi values
```

We normalize the elements of the dataset X by calculating a set of new `Xi` values as follows:

```
Xi = (Xi - Minx)/[Maxx - Minx]
```

The new Xi values are now scaled so that they are between 0 and 1. Note that some people refer this technique as *min max* scaling. The relevant class from `sklearn` is here:

```
from sklearn.preprocessing import Normalizer
```

The *mean normalization* for the elements of the set X involves calculating new values as follows:

```
Xi = (Xi - mean(Xi))/[max(Xi) - min(Xi)]
```

The new `xi` values are now scaled so that they are between -1 and 1, with a mean of 0. The relevant class from `sklearn` is here:

```
from sklearn.preprocessing import MinMaxScaler
```

Vector normalization is a technique that is used with vectors of real numbers. This technique divides each component of a vector by the length of the vector. If x is a vector, then the length of x is the square root of the sum of the squares of the components of x, which is a generalization of the Pythagorean theorem to more than two dimensions.

Specifically, if x is the vector (x1, x2, . . . , xn), then the length of x is the square root of the sum of its components, as shown here:

```
||X|| = sqrt(x1**2 + x2**2 + . . . + xn**2)
```

The normalized counterpart to the vector x is the vector x' whose components are shown here:

```
X' = (x1/||X||, x2/||X||, . . . , xn/||X||)
```

Notice that `||X'|| = 1`, which means that x' is a unit vector of dimension n.

Yet another technique is *log transformation* with data that does not have a normal distribution: this can help reduce the skewness of the data and also reduce the variability. Note that logarithms are only defined for positive numbers, so you might need to perform other transformations to the data before applying a log transformation.

Metrics in Machine Learning

There are several well-known metrics available in machine learning, such as a confusion matrix, ROC-AUC, and TOC that enables you to evaluate classifiers. These and other metrics are discussed in the following subsections.

R-Squared and its Limitations

One of the most frequently used metrics is R-squared, which measures how close the data is to the fitted regression line (regression coefficient). The R-squared value is always a percentage between 0 and 100%. The value 0% indicates that the model explains none of the variability of the response data around its mean. The value 100% indicates that the model explains all the variability of the response data around its mean. In general, a higher R-squared value indicates a better model.

Although high R-squared values are preferred, they are not necessarily always good values. Similarly, low R-squared values are not always bad. For example, an R-squared value for predicting human behavior is often less than 50%. Moreover, R-squared cannot determine whether the coefficient estimates and predictions are biased. In addition, an R-squared value does not indicate whether a regression model is adequate. Thus, it's possible to have a low R-squared value for a good model, or a high R-squared value for a poorly fitting model. Evaluate R-squared values in conjunction with residual plots, other model statistics, and subject area knowledge.

Confusion Matrix

The confusion matrix enables you to evaluate classifiers. The confusion matrix is suited for categorical data sets. For example, if you have a dataset that contains clinical trial data for cancer, you will be interested in four quantities: true positive, false positive, true negative, and false negative. A confusion matrix contains numeric (integer) values for these four quantities. By contrast, linear regression involves terms such as R and R^2 to help you evaluate the accuracy of a model.

In its simplest form, a confusion matrix (also called an error matrix) is a type of contingency table with two rows and two columns that contains the number of false positives, false negatives, true positives, and true negatives. Here is a 2×2 confusion matrix:

```
TP | FP
-------
FN | TN
```

The four entries in a 2×2 confusion matrix can be labeled as follows:

```
TP: True Positive
FP: False Positive
TN: True Negative
FN: False Negative
```

The diagonal values of the confusion matrix are correct, whereas the off-diagonal values are incorrect predictions. In general a lower FP value is better than a FN value. For example, an FP indicates that a healthy person was incorrectly diagnosed with a disease, whereas an FN indicates that an unhealthy person was incorrectly diagnosed as healthy.

Keep in mind that the confusion matrix can be an nxn matrix and not just a 2×2 matrix. For example, if a class has five possible values, then the confusion matrix is a 5×5 matrix, and the numbers on the main diagonal are the number of correct values for each class.

In addition, a type I error is the value FP (false positive), whereas a type II error is the value FN. The definition of accuracy is given by the following formula:

```
accuracy  = % of correct predictions
          = (TP + TN) / total cases
```

While accuracy can be a useful indicator, accuracy has limited (and perhaps misleading) value for imbalanced datasets. Accuracy can be an unreliable metric because it yields misleading results in unbalanced data sets. Classes with substantially different sizes are assigned equal importance to both false positive and false negative classifications. For example, declaring cancer as benign is worse than incorrectly informing patients that they are suffering from cancer. Unfortunately, accuracy won't differentiate between these two cases.

In this situation, you can inspect the values for precision, recall, and specificity, as discussed in the next section.

Precision, Recall, and Specificity

The definitions of precision, accuracy, and recall are given by the following formulas:

```
recall    = % of correctly identified positive cases
          = (TP/(TP + TN)

precision = % of correct positive predictions
          = (TP/(TP + FP)
```

Precision is the proportion of the samples that are actually positive in the set of positively predicted samples. Here is the formula for precision:

```
Precision = TP/[TP + FP]
```

Recall (also called *sensitivity*) is the proportion of the correctly predicted positive values in the set of actually positively labeled samples: this equals the fraction of the positively labeled samples that were correctly predicted by the model. Here is the formula for recall:

```
Recall = TP/[TP+FN]
```

Specificity is the proportion of negatively labeled samples that were predicted as negative. Here is the formula for specificity:

```
Specificity = TN/[TN+FP]
```

One way to remember precision and recall is to notice that:

- Both have the same numerator (=TP).
- The precision denominator is the sum of the first row.
- The recall denominator is the sum of the first column.

The *prevalence* is a fraction of total population that is labeled positive:

```
prevalence  = (TP+FN)/[TRP+TN+FP+FN]
FPR = proportion of negatively labeled samples that are incor-
rectly predicted positive
FPR = false positive rate
FPR = FP/[TN+FP]


NPV = Negative Predictive Value or NPV
NPV = proportion of negatively labeled samples that are cor-
rectly predicted negative
NPV = TN/[TN+FN]

FDR = false discovery rate = 1 - PPV = FP/[TP+FP]

FOR = false omission rate
FOR = 1 - NPV  = FN/[TN+FN]
```

The ROC Curve and AUC

The receiver operating characteristic (ROC) curve is a curve that plots the true negative rate (TP) on the horizontal axis and FP on the vertical axis, where TP and FP are defined in a previous section. Note that the TN is also called the specificity.

The ROC curve provides a visual comparison of classification models that shows the trade-off between the true positive rate and the false positive rate. Both axes have values between 0 and 1: the vertical axis is the true positive rate (TPR) whereas the horizontal axis is the false positive rate (FPR). The ROC curve provides a view of model performance at different threshold values.

The goal is to increase TPR while simultaneously maintaining a low FPR; however both values increase together, so it's a question of the tolerance level for false positives.

AUC is the area under ROC curve between (0,0) and (1,1), which aggregates the performance of the model at all threshold values. The area under the ROC curve (ROC-AUC) is a measure of the accuracy of the model. Models closer to the diagonal are less accurate and the models with perfect accuracy will have an area of 1.0.

The best possible value of AUC is 1 (a perfect classifier) and the worst value is 0 (if all the predictions are wrong). One other point to keep in mind is that the `AUC` is independent of the classification threshold value.

The following link contains a Python code sample using SkLearn and the `Iris` dataset, and also code for plotting the ROC:

https://scikit-learn.org/stable/auto_examples/model_selection/plot_roc.html

The following link contains an assortment of `Python` code samples for plotting the ROC:

https://stackoverflow.com/questions/25009284/how-to-plot-roc-curve-in-python

By contrast, a `TOC` graph plots the `(TP+FP)-TP` values on the horizontal axis and the `TP` values for the vertical axis. The interesting fact about a `TOC` graph is that it enables you to determine the confusion matrix for every point in `TOC` space.

Metrics for Model Evaluation and Selection

The metrics `AIC`, `AICc`, `BIC`, and `Mallows Cp` provide an unbiased estimate of the model prediction error `MSE` (lower values are better), and they are used for model evaluation and selection.

`AIC` is an acronym for Akaike's information criteria that adds a penalty to increase the error when additional terms are included. `AICc` is a variant of `AIC` that is specifically for small sample sizes. Bayesian information criteria (BIC), which is also a variant of AIC that involves a stronger penalty. Colin Mallows developed `Mallows Cp`, which is yet another variant of `AIC`. Perform an online search for more information regarding these metrics.

What is Linear Regression?

The goal of linear regression is to find the best fitting line that "represents" a dataset. Keep in mind two key points. First, the best fitting line does not necessarily pass through all (or even most of) the points in the dataset. The purpose of a best fitting line is to minimize the vertical distance of that line from the points in dataset. Second, linear regression does not determine the best-fitting polynomial: the latter involves finding a higher-degree polynomial that passes through the points in a dataset.

Moreover, a dataset in the plane can contain two or more points that lie on the same *vertical* line, which is to say that those points have the same x value. However, a function *cannot* pass through such a pair of points: if two points (x1,y1) and (x2,y2) have the same x value then they *must* have the same y value (i.e., y1=y2). However, a function can have two or more points that lie on the same *horizontal* line.

Now consider a scatter plot with many points in the plane that are sort of "clustered" in an elongated cloud-like shape: a best-fitting line will probably intersect only limited number of points (in fact, a best-fitting line might not intersect *any* of the points).

One other scenario to keep in mind: suppose a dataset contains a set of points that lie on the same line. For instance, let's suppose that the x values are in the set {1,2,3,...,10} and the corresponding y values are in the set {2,4,6,...,20}. Then the equation of the best-fitting line is y=2*x+0, which is a line of slope 2 that passes through the origin. In this scenario, all the points are *collinear*, which is to say that they lie on the same line.

Linear Regression versus Curve-Fitting

Suppose a dataset consists of n data points of the form (x, y), and no two of those data points have the same x value. Then according to a well-known result in mathematics, there is a polynomial of degree less than or equal to n-1 that passes through those n points (if you are really interested, you can find a mathematical proof of this statement in online articles). For example, a line is a polynomial of degree one and it can intersect any pair of non-vertical points in the plane. For any triple of points (that are not all on the same line) in the plane, there is a quadratic equation that passes through those points.

In addition, sometimes a lower degree polynomial is available. For instance, consider the set of 100 points in which the x value equals the y value: in this case, the line y = x (which is a polynomial of degree one) passes through all 100 points.

However, keep in mind that the extent to which a line "represents" a set of points in the plane depends on how closely those points can be which is measured by the residual errors of the points (the sum of the squares of vertical distances). The more collinear the points, the smaller the residual errors; conversely, the more "spread out" the points are, the larger the residual errors.

When are Solutions Exact Values?

Although statistics-based solutions provide closed-form solutions for linear regression, neural networks provide *approximate* solutions. This is due to the fact that machine learning algorithms for linear regression involve a sequence of approximations that "converges" to optimal values, which means that machine learning algorithms produce estimates of the exact values. For example, the slope m and y-intercept b of a best-fitting line for a set of points a 2D plane have a closed-form solution in statistics, but they can only be approximated via machine learning algorithms (exceptions do exist, but they are rare situations).

Keep in mind that even though a closed-form solution for "traditional" linear regression provides an exact value for both m and b, sometimes you can only use an approximation of the exact value. For instance, suppose that the slope m of a best-fitting line equals the square root of 3 and the y-intercept b is the square root of 2. If you plan to use these values in source code, you can only work with an approximation of these two numbers. In the same scenario, a neural network computes approximations for m and b, regardless of whether or not the exact values for m and b are irrational, rational, or integer values. However, machine learning algorithms are better suited for complex, nonlinear, multi-dimensional datasets, which is beyond the capacity of linear regression.

As a simple example, suppose that the closed form solution for a linear regression problem produces integer or rational values for both m and b. Specifically, let's suppose that a closed form solution yields the values 2.0 and 1.0 for the slope and y-intercept, respectively, of a best-fitting line. The equation of the line looks like this:

```
y = 2.0 * x + 1.0
```

However, the corresponding solution from training a neural network might produce the values 2.0001 and 0.9997 for the slope m and the y-intercept b, respectively, as the values of m and b for a best-fitting line. Always keep this point in mind, especially when you are training a neural network.

What is Multivariate Analysis?

Multivariate analysis generalizes the equation of a line in the Euclidean plane to higher dimensions, and it's called a *hyper plane* instead of a line.

The generalized equation has the following form:

```
y = w1*x1 + w2*x2 + . . . + wn*xn + b
```

In the case of 2D linear regression, you only need to find the value of the slope (m) and the y-intercept (b), whereas in multivariate analysis you need to find the values for `w1`, `w2`, . . ., `wn`. Note that multivariate analysis is a term from statistics, and in machine learning it's often referred to as "generalized linear regression."

Keep in mind that most of the code samples in this book that pertain to linear regression involve 2D points in the Euclidean plane.

Other Types of Regression

Linear regression finds the best fitting line that "represents" a dataset, but what happens if a line in the plane is not a good fit for the dataset? This is a relevant question when you work with datasets.

Some alternatives to linear regression include quadratic equations, cubic equations, or higher-degree polynomials. However, these alternatives involve trade-offs, as we'll discuss later.

Another possibility is a sort of hybrid approach that involves piece-wise linear functions, which comprises a set of line segments. If contiguous line segments are connected then it's a piece-wise linear continuous function; otherwise it's a piece-wise linear discontinuous function.

Thus, given a set of points in the plane, regression involves addressing the following questions:

- What type of curve fits the data well? How do we know?
- Does another type of curve fit the data better?
- What does "best fit" mean?

One way to check if a line fits the data involves a visual check, but this approach does not work for data points that are higher than two dimensions. Moreover, this is a subjective decision, as you will see in datasets displayed later in this chapter. By visual inspection of a dataset, you might decide that a quadratic or cubic (or even higher degree) polynomial has the potential of being a better fit for the data. However, visual inspection is probably limited to points in a 2D plane or in three dimensions.

Let's defer the nonlinear scenario and let's make the assumption that a line would be a good fit for the data. There is a well-known technique for finding the "best fitting" line for such a dataset that involves minimizing the Mean Squared Error (MSE) that we'll discuss later in this chapter.

The next section provides a quick review of linear equations in the plane, along with some images that illustrate examples of linear equations.

Working with Lines in the Plane (Optional)

This section contains a short review of lines in the Euclidean plane, so you can skip this section if you are comfortable with this topic. A minor point that's often overlooked is that lines in the Euclidean plane have infinite length. If you select two distinct points of a line, then all the points between those two selected points is a *line segment.* A *ray* is a "half infinite" line: when you select one point as an endpoint, then all the points on one side of the line constitutes a ray.

For example, the points in the plane whose y-coordinate is 0 is a line and also the x-axis, whereas the points between (0,0) and (1,0) on the x-axis form a line segment. In addition, the points on the x-axis that are to the right of (0,0) form a ray, and the points on the x-axis that are to the left of (0,0) also form a ray.

For simplicity and convenience, in this book we'll use the terms "line" and "line segment" interchangeably, and now let's delve into the details of lines in the Euclidean plane. Just in case you're a bit fuzzy on the details, here is the equation of a (nonvertical) line in the Euclidean plane:

```
y = m*x + b
```

The value of m is the slope of the line and the value of b is the y-intercept (i.e., the place where the line intersects the y-axis).

If need be, you can use a more general equation that can also represent vertical lines, as shown here:

```
a*x + b*y + c = 0
```

However, we won't be working with vertical lines, so we'll stick with the first formula.

Figure 7.1 displays three horizontal lines whose equations (from top to bottom) are y = 3, y = 0, and y = -3, respectively.

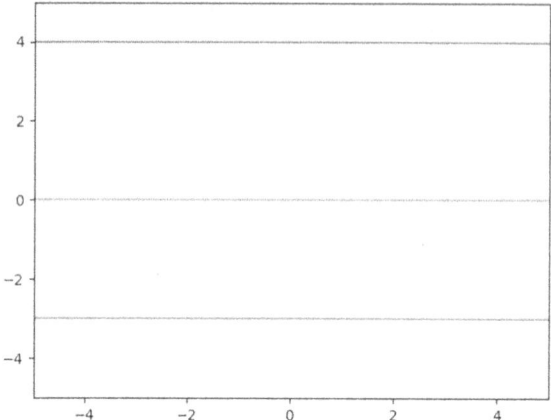

Figure 7.1. A Graph of Three Horizontal Line Segments.

Figure 7.2 displays two slanted lines whose equations are y = x and y = -x, respectively.

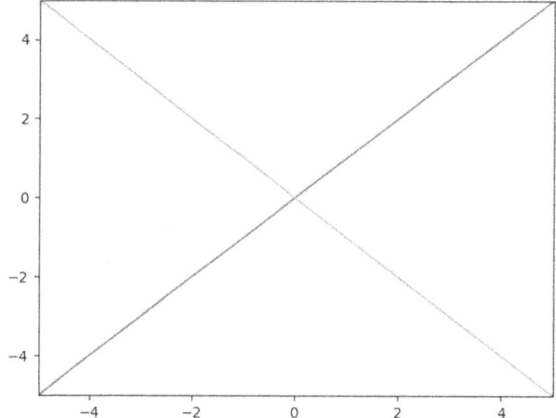

Figure 7.2. A Graph of Two Diagonal Line Segments.

Figure 7.3 displays two slanted parallel lines whose equations are y = 2*x and y = 2*x + 3, respectively.

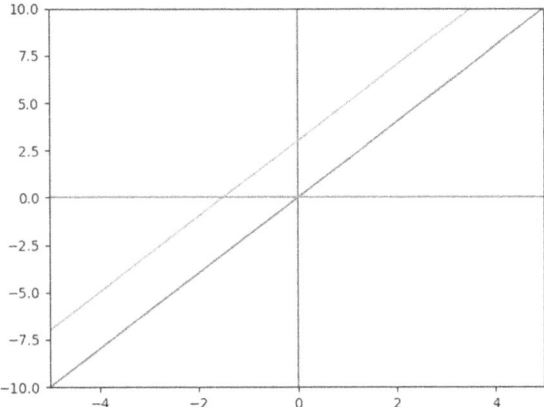

Figure 7.3. A Graph of Two Slanted Parallel Line Segments.

Figure 7.4 displays a piece-wise linear graph consisting of connected line segments.

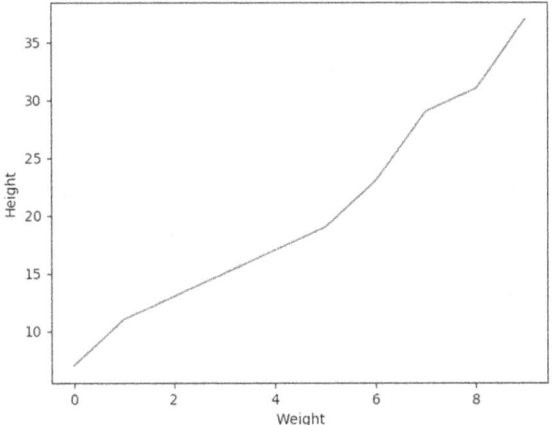

Figure 7.4. A PieceWise Linear Graph of Line Segments.

Now let's turn our attention to generating quasi-random data using a `NumPy` API, and then we'll plot the data using Matplotlib.

Scatter Plots with NumPy and Matplotlib (1)

Listing 7.1 displays the contents of `np_plot1.py` that illustrates how to use the `NumPy randn()` API to generate a dataset and then the `scatter()` API in Matplotlib to plot the points in the dataset.

One detail to note is that all the adjacent horizontal values are equally spaced, whereas the vertical values are based on a linear equation plus a "perturbation" value. This "perturbation technique" (which is not a standard term) is used in other code samples in this chapter in order to add a slightly randomized effect when the points are plotted. The advantage of this technique is that the best-fitting values for m and b are known in advance, and therefore we do not need to guess their values.

LISTING 7.1: *np_plot1.py*

```
import numpy as np
import matplotlib.pyplot as plt

x = np.random.randn(15,1)
y = 2.5*x + 5 + 0.2*np.random.randn(15,1)

print("x:",x)
print("y:",y)

plt.scatter(x,y)
plt.show()
```

Listing 7.1 contains two import statements and then initializes the array variable x with 15 random numbers between 0 and 1.

Next, the array variable y is defined in two parts: the first part is a linear equation 2.5*x + 5 and the second part is a "perturbation" value that is based on a random number. Thus, the array variable y simulates a set of values that closely approximate a line segment.

This technique is used in code samples that simulate a line segment, and then the training portion approximates the values of m and b for the best-fitting line. Obviously we already *know* the equation of the best fitting-line: the purpose of this technique is to compare the trained values for the slope m and y-intercept b with the known values (which in this case are 2.5 and 5).

A partial output from Listing 7.1 is here:

```
x: [[-1.42736308]
 [ 0.09482338]
 [-0.45071331]
 [ 0.19536304]
 [-0.22295205]
 // values omitted for brevity
y: [[1.12530514]
 [5.05168677]
```

```
[3.93320782]
[5.49760999]
[4.46994978]
// values omitted for brevity
```

Figure 7.5 displays a scatter plot of points based on the values of x and y.

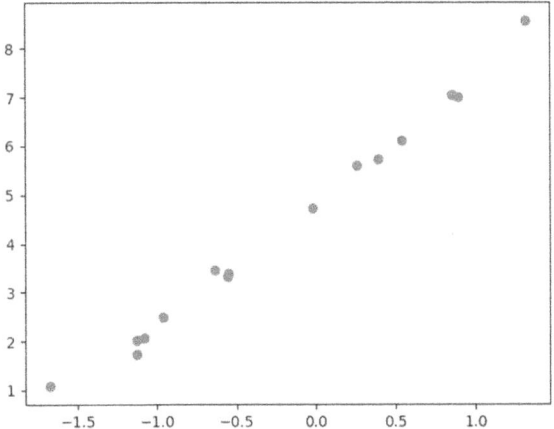

Figure 7.5. A Scatter Plot of Points for a Line Segment.

Why the "Perturbation Technique" is Useful

You already saw how to use the "perturbation technique" and by way of comparison, consider a dataset with the following points that are defined in the Python array variables X and Y:

```
X = [0,0.12,0.25,0.27,0.38,0.42,0.44,0.55,0.92,1.0]
Y = [0,0.15,0.54,0.51, 0.34,0.1,0.19,0.53,1.0,0.58]
```

If you need to find the best fitting line for the preceding dataset, how would you guess the values for the slope m and the y-intercept b? In most cases, you probably cannot guess their values. However, the "perturbation technique" enables you to "jiggle" the points on a line whose value for the slope m (and optionally the value for the y-intercept b) is specified in advance.

Keep in mind that the "perturbation technique" only works when you introduce small random values that do not result in different values for m and b.

Scatter Plots with NumPy and Matplotlib (2)

The code in Listing 7.1 assigned random values to the variable x, whereas a hard-coded value is assigned to the slope m. The y values are a hard-coded multiple of the x values, plus a random value that is calculated via the "perturbation technique." Hence we do not know the value of the y-intercept b.

In this section, the values for trainX are based on the np.linspace() API, and the values for trainY involve the "perturbation technique" that is described in the previous section.

The code in this example simply prints the values for trainX and trainY, which correspond to data points in the Euclidean plane. Listing 7.2 displays the contents of np_plot2.py that illustrates how to simulate a linear dataset in NumPy.

LISTING 7.2: np_plot2.py

```
import numpy as np

trainX = np.linspace(-1, 1, 11)
trainY = 4*trainX + np.random.randn(*trainX.shape)*0.5

print("trainX: ",trainX)
print("trainY: ",trainY)
```

Listing 7.2 initializes the NumPy array variable trainX via the NumPy linspace() API, followed by the array variable trainY that is defined in two parts. The first part is the linear term 4*trainX and the second part involves the "perturbation technique" that is a randomly generated number. The output from Listing 7.2 is here:

```
trainX:  [-1.  -0.8 -0.6 -0.4 -0.2  0.   0.2  0.4  0.6  0.8  1.]
trainY:  [-3.60147459 -2.66593108 -2.26491189 -1.65121314
-0.56454605  0.22746004 0.86830728  1.60673482  2.51151543
3.59573877  3.05506056]
```

The next section contains an example that is similar to Listing 7.2, using the same "perturbation technique" to generate a set of points that approximate a quadratic equation instead of a line segment.

A Quadratic Scatterplot with NumPy and Matplotlib

Listing 7.3 displays the contents of np_plot_quadratic.py that illustrates how to plot a quadratic function in the plane.

LISTING 7.3: np_plot_quadratic.py

```
import numpy as np
import matplotlib.pyplot as plt

#see what happens with this set of values:
#x = np.linspace(-5,5,num=100)

x = np.linspace(-5,5,num=100)[:,None]
y = -0.5 + 2.2*x +0.3*x**2 + 2*np.random.randn(100,1)
print("x:",x)

plt.plot(x,y)
plt.show()
```

Listing 7.3 initializes the variable x with the values that are generated via the np.linspace() API, which in this case is a set of 100 equally spaced decimal numbers between -5 and 5. Notice the snippet [:,None] in the initialization of x, which results in an array of elements, each of which is an array consisting of a single number.

The variable y is defined in two parts: the first part is a quadratic equation -0.5 + 2.2*x +0.3*x**2 and the second part is a "perturbation" value that is based on a random number (similar to the code in Listing 7.1). Thus, the array variable y simulates a set of values that approximates a quadratic equation. The output from Listing 7.3 is here:

```
x:
[[-5.        ]
 [-4.8989899 ]
 [-4.7979798 ]
 [-4.6969697 ]
 [-4.5959596 ]
 [-4.49494949]
 // values omitted for brevity
 [ 4.8989899 ]
 [ 5.        ]]
```

Figure 7.6 displays a scatter plot of points based on the values of x and y, which have an approximate shape of a quadratic equation.

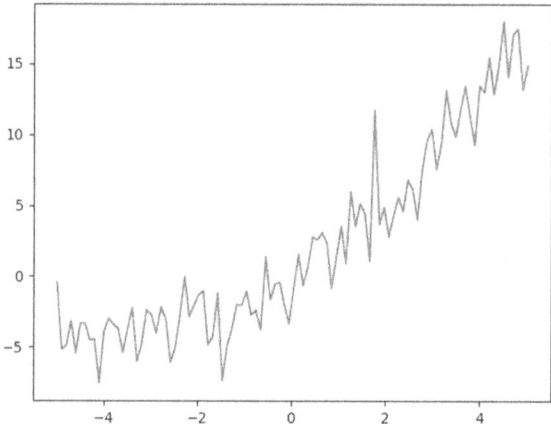

Figure 7.6. A Scatter Plot of Points for a Quadratic Equation.

The Mean Squared Error (MSE) Formula

In plain English, the MSE is the sum of the squares of the difference between an *actual* y value and its *predicted* y value, divided by the number of points. Notice that the predicted y value is the y value that each data point would have if that point were actually *on* the best-fitting line.

Although the MSE is popular for linear regression, there are other error types available, some of which are discussed briefly in the next section.

A List of Error Types

Although we will only discuss MSE for linear regression in this book, there are other types of formulas that you can use for linear regression, some of which are listed here:

- MSE
- RMSE
- RMSPROP
- MAE

The MSE is the basis for the preceding error types. For example, RMSE is "Root Mean Squared Error," which is the square root of MSE.

However, mean absolute error (MAE) is the sum of *the absolute value of the differences of the y terms* (*not* the square of the differences of the y terms), which is then divided by the number of terms.

The `RMSProp` optimizer utilizes the magnitude of recent gradients to normalize the gradients. Specifically, `RMSProp` maintain a moving average over the RMS (root mean squared) gradients, and then divides that term by the current gradient.

Although it's easier to compute the derivative of MSE, it's also true that MSE is more susceptible to outliers, whereas MAE is less susceptible to outliers. The reason is simple: a squared term can be significantly larger than the absolute value of a term. For example, if a difference term is 10, then a squared term of 100 is added to MSE, whereas only 10 is added to MAE. Similarly, if a difference term is -20, then a squared term 400 is added to MSE, whereas only 20 (which is the absolute value of -20) is added to MAE.

Nonlinear Least Squares

When predicting housing prices, where the dataset contains a wide range of values, techniques such as linear regression or random forests can cause the model to overfit the samples with the highest values in order to reduce quantities such as mean absolute error.

In this scenario, you probably want an error metric, such as relative error, that reduces the importance of fitting the samples with the largest values. This technique is called *nonlinear least squares*, which may use a log-based transformation of labels and predicted values.

The next section contains several code samples, the first of which involves calculating the MSE manually, followed by an example that uses `NumPy` formulas to perform the calculations. Finally, we'll look at a TensorFlow example for calculating the MSE.

Calculating the MSE Manually

This section contains two line graphs, both of which contain a line that approximates a set of points in a scatter plot.

Figure 7.7 displays a line segment that approximates a scatter plot of points (some of which intersect the line segment). The MSE for the line in Figure 7.7 is computed as follows:

```
MSE = (1*1 + (-1)*(-1) + (-1)*(-1) + 1*1)/7 = 4/7
```

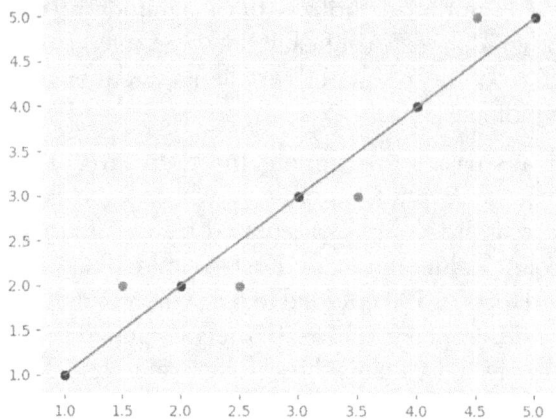

Figure 7.7. A Line Graph that Approximates Points of a Scatter Plot.

Figure 7.8 displays a set of points and a line that is a potential candidate for best-fitting line for the data. The MSE for the line in Figure 7.8 is computed as follows:

```
MSE = ((-2)*(-2) + 2*2)/7 = 8/7
```

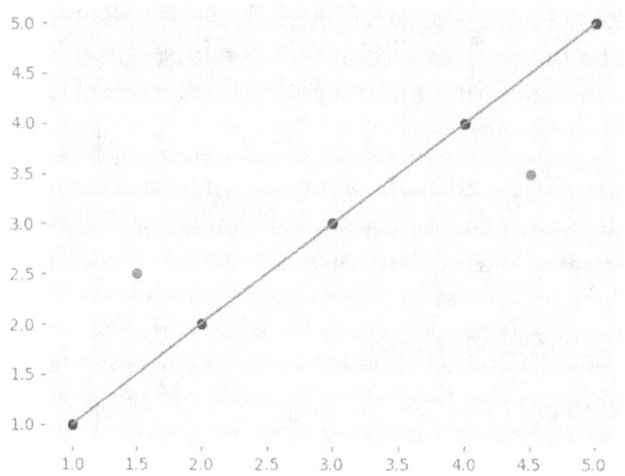

Figure 7.8. A Line Graph that Approximates Points of a Scatter Plot.

Thus, the line in Figure 7.7 has a smaller MSE than the line in Figure 7.8, which might have surprised you (or did you guess correctly?)

In these two figures we calculated the MSE easily and quickly, but in general it's significantly more difficult. For instance, if we plot 10 points in the Euclidean plane that do not closely fit a line, with individual terms that involve non-integer values, we would probably need a calculator.

A better solution involves NumPy functions, such as the `np.linspace()` API, as discussed in the next section.

Approximating Linear Data with `np.linspace()`

Listing 7.4 displays the contents of `np_linspace1.py` that illustrates how to generate some data with the `np.linspace()` API in conjunction with the "perturbation technique."

LISTING 7.4: *np_linspace1.py*

```
import numpy as np

trainX = np.linspace(-1, 1, 6)
trainY = 3*trainX+ np.random.randn(*trainX.shape)*0.5

print("trainX: ", trainX)
print("trainY: ", trainY)
```

The purpose of this code sample is merely to generate and display a set of randomly generated numbers. Later in this chapter we will use this code as a starting point for an actual linear regression task.

Listing 7.4 starts with the definition of the array variable `trainX` that is initialized via the `np.linspace()` API. Next, the array variable `trainY` is defined via the "perturbation technique" that you have seen in previous code samples. The output from Listing 7.4 is here:

```
trainX:  [-1.  -0.6 -0.2  0.2  0.6  1.]
trainY:  [-2.9008553  -2.26684745 -0.59516253  0.66452207
          1.82669051  2.30549295]
trainX:  [-1.  -0.6 -0.2  0.2  0.6  1.]
trainY:  [-2.9008553  -2.26684745 -0.59516253  0.66452207
          1.82669051  2.30549295]
```

What are Ensemble Methods?

In machine learning, *ensembles* refer to methods that combine predictions from multiple models. The underlying idea is to outperform a single classifier by combining the results of multiple trained classifiers; moreover, the worse ensemble outcome is probably no worse than the worst classifier in the ensemble. Although the preceding statement just a heuristic (there is no formal and rigorous proof), in practice it works rather well most of the time.

The outcome or prediction of an ensemble can be decided in various ways via a "combination" rule that can be any of the following (the average rule is the most common):

- majority vote
- mean value
- weighted average
- maximum value
- minimum value
- product

The two most common methods for ensembling are *bagging* and *boosting* (they use opposite approaches), and they are discussed later in this section.

Ensemble methods are meta-algorithms that combine several machine learning techniques into one predictive model because doing so decreases variance (bagging) or bias (boosting). These methods can also improve predictions (stacking). `Adaboost` (discussed later) is a type of sequential ensemble method.

Ensemble methods construct a set of classifiers and then they classify new data points by taking a (weighted) vote of their predictions. The original ensemble method is Bayesian averaging, and more recent algorithms include error-correcting output coding, bagging, and boosting.

The key idea is that the prediction of several models is better than the prediction of a single model. However, classifiers must be diverse enough in order for ensembling to produce good results. This can be accomplished in several ways:

- using different base classifiers
- training using different features
- training using different parts of the training set
- using different parameters

Stacking ensembles are a class of algorithms that involves training a metalearner to find the optimal combination of the base learners. Unlike bagging and boosting, the goal of stacking is to ensemble strong and diverse sets of learners.

Random forest ensembles are an ensemble learning method for classification, regression and other tasks that operate by constructing a multitude of decision trees at training time: they output the class that is the mode of the classes (classification) or mean prediction (regression).

Four Types of Ensemble Methods

Ensemble methods can be divided into the following four categories:

- bagging
- boosting
- stacking
- blending

The following subsections provides a brief introduction to each of the bullet items in the preceding list.

Bagging

Bagging ("boosted aggregation") trains many strong learners in a parallel fashion in order to reduce the chance of overfitting. The next step combines all the strong learners by averaging their predictions. Bagging reduces the variance of predictions by combining the result of multiple classifiers, each of which is modeled on different sub-samples of the same dataset.

A bagging model for random forests is an ensemble that is designed to prevent overfitting by using the predictions of several algorithms to calculate the final aggregated predictions in order to reduce the variance of the algorithms.

Boosting

Boosting involves so-called weak learners, which refers to classifiers that can involve a significant error rate. Boosting trains a large number of weak learners in a sequential manner in order to improve the predictions of simple models. Each weak model attempts to improve the prediction of its predecessor. Boosting then combines the weak learners into a strong learner.

Although boosting has better predictive accuracy than bagging, it also tends to overfit the training data. Several boosting algorithms are listed:

- AdaBoost
- Random Forest

- AdaBoost
- GBM
- XGB
- Light GBM
- CatBoost
- LPBoost
- TotalBoost
- BrownBoost
- xgboost
- MadaBoost
- LogitBoost

Adaptive boosting is a method of weighting training data points and hypotheses. Many boosting algorithms fit into the *AnyBoost* framework that shows that boosting performs gradient descent in a function space using a convex loss function.

The following steps describe the processing for finding weak rules:

1. Apply base learning (ML) algorithms with a different distribution
2. Each time the base learning algorithm is applied, a new weak prediction rule is generated
3. After many iterations, the boosting algorithm combines these weak rules into a single strong prediction rule.

A first predictor is learned on the whole data set, which starts by giving equal weights to each observation. If classes are predicted incorrectly using the first learner, then assign higher weight to missed classified observations.

The next predictors are learned on the training set based on the performance of previous one. Continue adding classifier learners and stop when a limit is reached in the number of models or accuracy.

Stacked Models and Blending Models

Stacked models involve the following steps:

1. Create several base models.

2. Gather the results from the base models.

3. Create a metamodel on top of the base models.

4. Produce final predictions.

Blending is similar to stacking, except for the difference in how the next layer is trained: stacking uses out-of-fold predictions, whereas blending uses a validation set (e.g., 10% of the training set).

What is Bootstrapping?

When you are given a population from which you can extract multiple same-sized samples, it's possible to use those samples in order to determine the distribution of the population.

However, if you only have a single sample available, you can use that sample in order to create multiple samples by replacement. Such samples are called *bootstrap samples* because they are obtained from the initial sample and not from the population. Since the bootstrap samples involve replacement, it's possible for a bootstrap sample to contain duplicates, and there will be some overlapping values in multiple bootstrap samples.

In essence, *bootstrapping* is a machine learning ensemble algorithm that reduces bias in supervised learning. The purpose of bootstrapping is to convert weak learners into strong learners. Note that random forests use replacement in order to construct multiple trees.

Keep in mind that "selection with replacement" is the opposite of "selection without replacement" technique for any card game. Each player is dealt a set of cards, and players do not have duplicate cards, nor is there any overlap in the cards held by any pair of players.

Common Boosting Algorithms

Most boosting algorithms consist of iteratively learning weak classifiers with respect to a distribution and adding them to a final strong classifier. The following list contains several well-known boosting algorithms for machine learning:

- AdaBoost
- Gradient Boosting
- XGBoost

AdaBoost ("Adaptive Boost") is a machine learning classification algorithm and also an ensemble algorithm that combines weak learners (decision trees) to produce one strong learner. AdaBoost is the first algorithm that adapted to weak learners. Adaboost uses bagging and also boosting methods to develop an enhanced predictor similar to random forests, which also involves Gini impurity scores and a bootstrapped dataset. However, AdaBoost differs from random forests in several ways:

1. AdaBoost creates a forest of stumps that are trees with a single node and two leaves.
2. The purpose of a given stump is to reduce the error of its predecessor.
3. The stumps are weighted differently during the final prediction: those with fewer errors are more significant.

Gradient boosting is another ensemble algorithm that uses boosting methods. Gradient boosting is a greedy algorithm that uses an iterative-based technique to create multiple models whose effect is to reduce the error after each step. Gradient boosting involves three elements:

1. It involves a loss function to be optimized.
2. It includes a weak learner to make predictions.
3. There is an additive model to add weak learners to minimize the loss function.

Note that gradient boosting can also quickly overfit a training dataset.

XGBoost is an open source gradient boosting framework for C++, Java, Python, R, and Julia that works on Linux, Windows, and macOS. XGBoost is a powerful and popular algorithm (often used in Kaggle competitions) that improves gradient boosting by using proportional shrinking of leaf nodes.

The initial implementation of gradient boosting constructed trees sequentially, whereas the XGBoost implementation parallelizes the tree building tasks, thereby reducing the training time. Installation details for XGBoost are here:

https://xgboost.readthedocs.io/en/latest/index.html

Hyperparameter Optimization

Hyperparameter optimization involves selecting a set of values for the hyperparameters of a machine learning model in such a way that its predictive accuracy is maximized. Fine tuning a model refers to hyperparameter optimization. The three main techniques for hyperparameter optimization are:

- grid search
- randomized search
- Bayesian optimization

Each of these techniques has advantages and disadvantages. For example, suppose that you want to find optimal values for two hyperparameters. For simplicity, we can assume that their values are comparable (or else they can be scaled), and represented in a two-dimensional grid in the Euclidean 2D plane.

Grid Search

A grid search is most effective when the pair of hyperparameters have similar importance. You can use the `GridSearchCV` class in `Sklearn` to perform a grid search. Simply specify which hyperparameters to select, along with a range of values for the hyperparameters. `GridSearch` uses cross-validation to evaluate the various combinations of hyperparameter values.

Randomized Search

If one hyperparameter has significantly greater importance than the second hyperparameter, a grid search can waste time searching and testing combinations that are far from the optimal combination. In this scenario a random search can converge to an optimal combination of values much faster than a grid search.

The grid search approach works well for a small number of combinations, whereas `RandomizedSearchCV` works better when the hyperparameter space is large.

This class evaluates random combinations by selecting a random value for each hyperparameter during each iteration, which is advantageous for two reasons. First, if randomized search runs for N iterations, it will explore N different values for each hyperparameter, whereas grid search only checks for several values. Second, the ability to specify the number of iterations gives you a finer-grained control over the hyperparameter search.

Bayesian Optimization

Bayesian Optimization is the third technique, which also has a good convergence rate for finding an optimal solution. The Python library `scikit-optimize` (`Skopt`) supports Bayesian optimization, and it's available here:

https://scikit-optimize.github.io

Skopt performs Bayesian Optimization via the class `BayesSearchCV` that has an interface that is similar to `GridSearchCV`. Install `Skopt` with the following command:

```
pip3 install scikit-optimize
```

Depending on the model that you are trying to optimize, hyperparameter tuning can be a time-consuming and expensive task. Keep in mind that randomized search is recommended when you have a large number of hyperparameters. Use grid search if you have a small number of hyperparameters.

AutoML, AutoML-Zero, and AutoNLP

`AutoML` is a system that automates and simplifies many of the underlying machine learning tasks that are involved in training a machine learning model. Although there are many various open-source tools for custom named entity recognition available, `AutoML` often provides higher accuracy (and is also good for other tasks).

One of the main advantages of `AutoML` is its ability to bring you to a production-ready model more quickly. However, there are shortcomings of `AutoML`, some of which appear in the following list:

- AutoML has no business intuition.
- AutoML cannot provide business justification or rationale for using ML.
- AutoML cannot select training data.

`AutoML` does not have the capacity to automate solutions to business problems or find useful data. Furthermore, `AutoML` does not provide ethics, marketing, alignment of stakeholders, or integration of a data model with other aspects of your business.

The key point is to leverage the strengths of `AutoML` that are relevant to your AI requirements and engage other resources to address the areas that AutoML does not provide.

A detailed tutorial regarding `AutoML` (as well as Jupyter notebooks) is available in the H2O documentation for `AutoML`:

https://docs.h2o.ai/h2o-tutorials/latest-stable/h2o-world-2017/automl/index.html

Another option is `AutoKeras` (`AutoML` for Keras): *https://autokeras.com*

If you want to explore something similar to `AutoML` for NLP, consider using `AutoNLP`, which is `AutoML` for NLP. Note that `AutoML` is included in the `AutoViML` framework, and you can install the latter as follows:

```
pip3 install autoviml
```

The Github repository for `AutoViML` is here:

https://github.com/AutoViML/Auto_ViML

Miscellaneous Topics

This final section in this chapter contains an assortment of topics that are of great interest to researchers and practitioners of machine learning. The topics are covered briefly, and the intent is to make you aware (if you aren't already) of aspects of machine learning that have not been fully answered.

What is Causality?

In its simplest form, causality is the extent to which one event influences another event. Machine learning models can reveal correlations, but they cannot determine causality. In simple terms, if A and B are two features, machine learning can determine if there is a correlation between A and B, but it cannot determine whether or not A causes B or B causes A.

What is Explainability?

The concept of explainability is simple: how can we explain the process by which a machine learning model makes predictions? Explainability in machine learning has financial implications. For example, the general data protection regulation (GDPR) in Europe does now allow the use of deep learning in financial transactions because deep learning models cannot explain how a given prediction was derived.

In particular, when people apply for a bank loan and the loan is declined, the bank must provide a reason (explanation) for rejecting the bank loan.

What is Interpretability?

Interpretability assists data scientists to explain, debug and validate their models, thus helping to build trust towards the model. InterpretML is an open-source Microsoft package that incorporates ultra-modern machine learning interpretability techniques and can be viewed as a valid source for explaining blackbox systems or glassbox models. The home page is here: *https://github.com/interpretml/interpret*

The `azureml.interpret` package supports developers using dataset formats such as `NumPy.array`, `pandas.DataFrame`, `iml.datatypes.DenseData`, and `scipy.sparse.csr_matrix`; furthermore, leverages libraries like `LIME`, `SHAP`, `SALib`, or `Plotly` and offers new interpretability algorithms like Explainable Boosting Machine (`EBM`).

The interpretability package can be useful for any data scientist, especially start-ups and companies as an essential tool for model debugging, detect fairness issues, understand regulatory compliance and the model's decisions to build trust amongst stakeholders and executives.

Summary

This chapter introduced you to machine learning and concepts such as feature selection, feature engineering, data cleaning, training sets, and test sets. Next, you learned about supervised, unsupervised, and semi-supervised learning. Then you learned regression tasks, classification tasks, and clustering, as well as the steps that are typically required in order to prepare a dataset. These steps include "feature selection" or "feature extraction" that can be performed using various algorithms. Then you learned about issue that can arise with the data in datasets, and how to rectify them.

In addition, you also learned about linear regression, along with a brief description of how to calculate a best-fitting line for a dataset of values in the Euclidean plane. You saw how to perform linear regression using NumPy in order to initialize arrays with data values, along with a "perturbation" technique that introduces some randomness for the y values. This technique is useful because you will know the correct values for the slope and y-intercept of the best-fitting line, which you can then compare with the trained values. Finally, you learned about `AutoML`, along with some of its advantages and disadvantages.

CHAPTER 8

CLASSIFIERS IN MACHINE LEARNING

This chapter is the second chapter that discusses machine learning, with a focus on classification algorithms because most tasks in machine learning involve classification or regression.

This chapter discusses classification algorithms, along with code samples that illustrate different values for the most important hyperparameters, would involve multiple chapters. As you know, the purpose of this book is to provide an introduction to many topics, and therefore this chapter provides a fast-paced overview of classifiers. If you plan to use machine learning classifiers, search for online resources that provide more detailed information regarding the algorithms that interest you; a good starting point is the online documentation pages for `Sklearn`.

Common classification algorithms includes the kNN (k nearest neighbor) algorithm, logistic regression (despite its name it *is* a classifier), decision trees, random forests, SVMs, and Bayesian classifiers. The emphasis on algorithms in this chapter is meant to introduce you to machine learning, which includes a tree-based code sample that relies on `Sklearn`. The latter portion of this chapter contains `Keras`-based code samples for standard datasets.

Due to space constraints, this chapter does not cover clustering algorithms. However, you can navigate to the following link where you will find an extensive list of such algorithms and their descriptions: *https://scikit-learn.org/stable/modules/clustering.html*.

With the preceding points in mind, the first section of this chapter briefly discusses the classifiers that are mentioned in the introductory paragraph. The second section, of this chapter provides an overview of activation functions, which will be very useful if you decide to learn about deep neural networks. In this section you will learn how and why they are used in neural networks. This section also contains a list of the `TensorFlow` APIs for activation functions, followed by a description of some of their merits.

The third section introduces *logistic regression*, which is a classifier (despite its name). Logistic regression relies on the sigmoid function, which is also used in recurrent neural networks (RNNs) and long short-term memory (LSTM). The fourth part of this chapter contains a code sample involving logistic regression and the `MNIST` dataset.

The final section in this chapter contains examples of linear regression using `Sklearn` as well as `Keras`.

Keep in mind that the section pertaining to activation functions does involve a basic understanding of hidden layers in a neural network. Depending on your comfort level, you might benefit from reading some preparatory material before diving into this section (there are many articles available online).

What is Classification?

Given a dataset that contains observations whose class membership is known, classification is the task of determining the class to which a new datapoint belongs. Classes refer to categories and are also called targets or labels. For example, spam detection in email service providers involves binary classification (only two classes). The `MNIST` dataset contain s a set of images, where each image is a single digit, which means there are 10 labels. Some applications in classification include: credit approval, medical diagnosis, and target marketing.

What are Classifiers?

In order to give you some context, classifiers are one of three major types of algorithms: regression algorithms (such as linear regression in Chapter 7), classification algorithms (discussed in this chapter), and clustering algorithms (such as `kMeans`, which is not discussed in this book).

In the previous chapter, you learned that linear regression uses supervised learning in conjunction with numeric data: the goal is to train a model that can make numeric predictions (e.g., the price of stock tomorrow, the temperature of a system, its barometric pressure, and so forth). By contrast, classifiers use supervised learning in conjunction with classes of data: the goal is to train a model to predict the correct labels for new data points.

For instance, suppose that each row in a dataset is a specific wine, and each column pertains to a specific wine feature (tannin, acidity, and so forth). Suppose further that there are five classes of wine in the dataset: for simplicity, let's label them A, B, C, D, and E. Given a new datapoint, which is to say a new row of data, a classifier for this dataset attempts to determine the label for this wine.

Some of the classifiers in this chapter can perform categorical classification and also make numeric predictions (i.e., they can be used for regression as well as classification).

Common Classifiers

Some of the most popular classifiers for machine learning are listed here (in no particular order):

- linear classifiers
- kNN
- logistic regression
- decision trees
- random forests
- SVMs
- Bayesian classifiers
- CNNs (deep learning)

Keep in mind that different classifiers have different advantages and disadvantages, which often involves a trade-off between complexity and accuracy, similar to algorithms in fields that are outside of AI.

In the case of deep learning, convolutional neural networks (CNNs) perform image classification, which makes them classifiers. (They can also be used for audio and text processing.)

The upcoming sections provide a brief description of the ML classifiers that are listed in the previous list.

Binary versus Multiclass Classification

Binary classifiers work with datasets that have two classes, whereas multiclass classifiers (sometimes called multinomial classifiers) distinguish more than two classes. Random forest classifiers, Naïve Bayes classifiers, and SVMs support multiple classes; although linear classifiers are binary classifiers, sometimes there are multi-class extensions.

In addition, there are techniques for multiclass classification that are based on binary classifiers: one-versus-all (OvA) and one-versus-one (OvO).

The OvA technique (also called one-versus-the-rest) involves multiple binary classifiers that is equal to the number of classes. For example, if a dataset has five classes, then OvA uses five binary classifiers, each of which detects one of the five classes. In order to classify a datapoint in this particular dataset, select the binary classifier whose output is the highest score.

The OvO technique also involves multiple binary classifiers, but in this case a binary classifier is used to train on a pair of classes. For instance, if the classes are A, B, C, D, and E, then 10 binary classifiers are required: one for A and B, one for A and C, one for A and D, and so forth, until the last binary classifier for D and E.

In general, if there are n classes, then `n*(n-1)/2` binary classifiers are required. Although the OvO technique requires considerably more binary classifiers (e.g., 190 are required for 20 classes) than the OvA technique (e.g., a mere 20 binary classifiers for 20 classes), the OvO technique has the advantage that each binary classifier is only trained on the portion of the dataset that pertains to its two chosen classes.

Multilabel Classification

Multilabel classification involves assigning multiple labels to an instance from a dataset. Hence, multilabel classification generalizes multiclass classification (discussed in the previous section), where the latter involves assigning a single label to an instance belonging to a dataset that has multiple classes. An article involving multilabel classification that contains `Keras`-based code can be found here:

https://medium.com/@vijayabhaskar96/multilabel-image-classification-tutorial-with-keras-imagedatagenerator-cd541f8eaf24

You can also perform an online search for articles that involve `Sklearn` or `PyTorch` for multilabel classification tasks.

What are Linear Classifiers?

A *linear classifier* separates a dataset into two classes. A linear classifier is a line for 2D points, a plane for 3D points, and a hyper plane (a generalization of a plane) for higher dimensional points.

Linear classifiers are often the fastest classifiers, so they are often used when the speed of classification is of high importance. Linear classifiers usually work well when the input vectors are sparse (i.e., mostly zero values) or when the number of dimensions is large.

What is kNN?

The kNN ("k Nearest Neighbor") algorithm is a classification algorithm. In brief, datapoints that are near each other are classified as belonging to the same class. When a new point is introduced, it's added to the class of the majority of its nearest neighbor. For example, suppose that k equals 3, and a new datapoint is introduced. Look at the class of its 3 nearest neighbors: let's say they are A, A, and B. Then by majority vote, the new datapoint is labeled as a datapoint of class A.

The kNN algorithm is essentially a heuristic and not a technique with complex mathematical underpinnings, and yet it's still an effective and useful algorithm. Try the kNN algorithm if you want to use a simple algorithm, or when you believe that the nature of your dataset is highly unstructured. The kNN algorithm can produce highly nonlinear decisions despite being very simple. You can use kNN in search applications where you are searching for "similar" items.

Measure similarity by creating a vector representation of the items, and then compare the vectors using an appropriate distance metric (such as Euclidean distance).

Some concrete examples of kNN search include searching for semantically similar documents.

How to Handle a Tie in kNN

An odd value for k is less likely to result in a tie vote, but it's possible. For example, suppose that k equals 7, and when a new datapoint is introduced, its seven nearest neighbors belong to the set {A,B,A,B,A,B,C}. As you can see, there is no majority vote, because there are three points in class A, 3 points in class B, and one point in class C.

There are several techniques for handling a tie in kNN, as listed here:

Assign higher weights to closer points.
Increase the value of k until a winner is determined.
Decrease the value of k until a winner is determined.
Randomly select one class.

If you reduce k until it equals 2, it's still possible to have a tie vote: there might be two points that are equally distant from the new point, so you need a mechanism for deciding which of those two points to select as the 2-neighbor.

If there is a tie between classes A and B, then randomly select either class A or class B. Another variant is to keep track of the "tie" votes, and alternate round-robin style to ensure a more even distribution.

SMOTE and kNN

One significant challenge involves imbalanced datasets, where the number of rows that belong to a particular class is much larger than the number of rows that belong to other classes. For example, a dataset involving healthy people and people with cancer might have 95% and 5%, respectively, of the rows in the dataset. Since classification algorithms tend to skew toward the dominant class in a dataset, we need a mechanism for balancing the dataset with more data that contains meaningful values.

One way to do so involves the synthetic minority oversampling technique (SMOTE) algorithm, which involves a heuristic that is based on the kNN algorithm. The intuition is straightforward: if two datapoints are very close to each other, then it's reasonable to perform linear interpolation with those two datapoints in order to generate synthetic data that is plausible as true datapoints. This process can be repeated with multiple pairs of highly similar datapoints in order to distribute the synthetic datapoints more proportionately.

Again, keep in mind that this technique is a heuristic, which means that it cannot guarantee that the synthetic data is actually valid data. In addition to kNN, SMOTE has also been implemented via SVMs. SMOTE is discussed briefly in appendix A, and you can perform an online search to find additional details regarding SMOTE.

kNN for Data Imputation

Data cleaning involves multiple subtasks, such as estimating values for missing data by calculating the mean in the case of numeric data and the mode for categorical data. You can also use kNN for data imputation (i.e., assigning values to missing data). The intuition of this technique is straightforward: datapoints that have the same (or similar) values can be interpolated in order to generate an appropriate value for another nearby datapoint that does not have a value assigned to a feature.

What are Decision Trees?

Decision trees are another type of classification algorithm that involves a tree-like structure. Some fields that benefit from applications of decision trees include:

- astronomy
- biomedical engineering
- financial analysis
- manufacturing
- medicine
- physics
- system control

A decision tree contains a root node with child nodes, each of which often contain their own child nodes. Some important aspects of a tree include the following: (Gini impurity and Gini entropy are discussed in Appendix A):

- the selection of a root node
- the depth (i.e., the number of layers) of the tree
- the number of elements in each node
- a rule for subdividing (splitting) a given node
- the choice of Gini impurity versus entropy

After a root node is selected, the next step involves adding child nodes, and the latter step is repeated until all the datapoints in the training set have been assigned to a node in the tree. Nodes that have no child nodes are called leaf nodes. Decision tree classification involves classifying new datapoints (such as those in the test data) by determining the leaf node to which they are most likely to belong.

In a "generic" tree, the placement of a datapoint is determined by simple conditional logic. As a simple illustration, suppose that a dataset contains a set of numbers that represent ages of people, and let's also suppose that the first number is 50. This number is chosen as the root of the tree, and all numbers that are smaller than 50 are added on the left branch of the tree, whereas all numbers that are greater than 50 are added on the right branch of the tree.

For example, suppose we have the sequence of numbers is {50, 25, 70, 40}. Then we can construct a tree as follows: 50 is the root node; 25 is the left child of 50; 70 is the right child of 50; and 40 is the right child of 25. Each additional numeric value that we add to this dataset is processed to determine which direction to proceed ("left" or "right") at each node in the tree.

Another point to keep in mind: most machine learning algorithms consider the entire dataset when the fit() method is invoked, and it's better to use binary variables for those algorithms.

By contrast, tree-based algorithms randomly select a subset of features from the dataset at each tree node (i.e., they do not evaluate the entire dataset during the training process). Hence, encode categorical variables into k binary variables if you want a tree-based algorithm to consider every category. Consider using k dummy variables if you are:

- building tree based algorithms
- performing recursive feature selection (RFE)
- evaluating the importance of individual categories

Also keep in mind that the Pandas get_dummies() method creates as many binary variables as categories in the variable.

Trade-offs with Decision Trees

Training a model with a decision tree involves trade-offs. First, decision trees are advantageous because they are:

- as good as other algorithms for simple datasets
- generally inexpensive to construct
- easy interpretability for smaller trees

However, keep in mind that decision trees have some disadvantages because they are:

- easy to overfit

- often biased toward features with many levels
- sensitive to small changes in the training data
- more difficult to interpret when they are large
- confined to decision boundaries that are parallel to attribute axes

Although decision trees have a tree-like structure, the logical conditions of decision nodes correspond to rectangular partitions of the Euclidean plane in the case of two dimensions.

Decision Tree Algorithms

There are multiple algorithms for constructing decision trees, some of which are listed here:

- ID3 (Iterative Dichotomiser 3)
- CART (Classification And Regression Tree)
- CHAID (Chi-square automatic interaction detection)

CHAID performs multilevel splits during the process of constructing classification trees. Try different algorithms to see which algorithm produces the best results for your model.

Appendix A discusses the `gini` index and entropy, and as you will see in a code sample in this chapter, both values can be specified as the value for the `criterion` parameter in `Sklearn` decision trees. In addition, decision tree algorithms use something called *information gain* in order to split a node, which can be calculated via the `gini` index or `entropy`. Moreover, the `gini` index used by CART algorithm and entropy used by ID3 algorithm. However, before delving into the details, let's look at an example of a `sklearn` decision tree that involves `gini` impurity, which is the default value for the `criterion` parameter.

Decision Tree Code Samples

Listing 8.1 displays the contents of `sklearn_tree2.py` that defines a set of 2D points in the Euclidean plane, along with their labels, and then predicts the label (i.e., the class) of several other 2D points in the Euclidean plane.

LISTING 8.1: sklearn_tree2.py

```
from sklearn import tree
```

```
# X = pairs of 2D points and Y = the class of each point
X = [[0, 0], [1, 1], [2,2]]
Y = [0, 1, 1]

tree_clf = tree.DecisionTreeClassifier()
tree_clf = tree_clf.fit(X, Y)

#predict the class of samples:
print("predict class of [-1., -1.]:")
print(tree_clf.predict([[-1., -1.]]))

print("predict class of [2., 2.]:")
print(tree_clf.predict([[2., 2.]]))

# the percentage of training samples of the same class
# in a leaf note equals the probability of each class
print("probability of each class in [2.,2.]:")
print(tree_clf.predict_proba([[2., 2.]]))
```

Listing 8.1 imports the `tree` class from `sklearn` and then initializes the arrays X and y with data values. Next, the variable `tree_clf` is initialized as an instance of the `DecisionTreeClassifier` class, after which it is trained by invoking the `fit()` method with the values of X and y.

Now launch the code in Listing 8.1 and you will see the following output:

```
predict class of [-1., -1.]:
[0]
predict class of [2., 2.]:
[1]
probability of each class in [2.,2.]:
[[0. 1.]]
```

As you can see, the points [-1,-1] and [2,2] are correctly labeled with the values 0 and 1, respectively, which is probably what you expected.

Listing 8.2 displays the contents of `sklearn_tree3.py` that extends the code in Listing 8.1 by adding a third label, and also by predicting the label of three points instead of two points in the Euclidean plane (the modifications are shown in bold).

LISTING 8.2: sklearn_tree3.py

```
from sklearn import tree

# X = pairs of 2D points and Y = the class of each point
X = [[0, 0], [1, 1], [2,2]]
Y = [0, 1, 2]
```

```
tree_clf = tree.DecisionTreeClassifier()
tree_clf = tree_clf.fit(X, Y)

#predict the class of samples:
print("predict class of [-1., -1.]:")
print(tree_clf.predict([[-1., -1.]]))

print("predict class of [0.8, 0.8]:")
print(tree_clf.predict([[0.8, 0.8]]))

print("predict class of [2., 2.]:")
print(tree_clf.predict([[2., 2.]]))

# the percentage of training samples of the same class
# in a leaf note equals the probability of each class
print("probability of each class in [2.,2.]:")
print(tree_clf.predict_proba([[2., 2.]]))
```

Now launch the code in Listing 8.2 and you will see the following output:

```
predict class of [-1., -1.]:
[0]
predict class of [0.8, 0.8]:
[1]
predict class of [2., 2.]:
[2]
probability of each class in [2.,2.]:
[[0. 0. 1.]]
```

As you can see, the points `[-1,-1]`, `[0.8, 0.8]`, and `[2,2]` are correctly labeled with the values 0, 1, and 2, respectively, which again is probably what you expected.

Listing 8.3 displays the dataset `partial_wine.csv`, which contains two features and a label column (there are three classes). The total row count for the complete dataset is 178.

LISTING 8.3: partial_wine.csv

```
Alcohol, Malic acid, class
14.23,1.71,1
13.2,1.78,1
13.16,2.36,1
14.37,1.95,1
13.24,2.59,1
14.2,1.76,1
```

Listing 8.4 displays contents of `tree_classifier.py` that uses a decision tree, with `entropy` as the value for the `criterion` parameter (and shown in bold), in order to train a model on the dataset `partial_wine.csv`.

LISTING 8.4: tree_classifier.py

```
import numpy as np
import matplotlib.pyplot as plt
import pandas as pd

# Importing the dataset
dataset = pd.read_csv('partial_wine.csv')
X = dataset.iloc[:, [0, 1]].values
y = dataset.iloc[:, 2].values

# split the dataset into a training set and a test set
from sklearn.model_selection import train_test_split
X_train, X_test, y_train, y_test = train_test_split(X, y,
test_size = 0.25, random_state = 0)

# Feature Scaling
from sklearn.preprocessing import StandardScaler
sc = StandardScaler()
X_train = sc.fit_transform(X_train)
X_test = sc.transform(X_test)

# ====> INSERT YOUR CLASSIFIER CODE HERE <====
from sklearn.tree import DecisionTreeClassifier
classifier = DecisionTreeClassifier(criterion='entropy',
                                    random_state=0)
classifier.fit(X_train, y_train)
# ====> INSERT YOUR CLASSIFIER CODE HERE <====

# predict the test set results
y_pred = classifier.predict(X_test)

# generate the confusion matrix
from sklearn.metrics import confusion_matrix
cm = confusion_matrix(y_test, y_pred)
print("confusion matrix:")
print(cm)
```

Listing 8.4 starts with `import` statements and then populates the variable `dataset` with the contents of the CSV file `partial_wine.csv`. Next, the variable `X` is initialized with the first two columns (and all the rows) of `dataset`, and the variable `y` is initialized with the third column (and all the rows) of dataset.

Next, the variables `X_train`, `X_test`, `y_train`, `y_test` are populated with data from `X` and `y` using a 75/25 split proportion. Notice that the variable `sc` (which is an instance of the `StandardScalar` class) performs a scaling operation on the variables `X_train` and `X_test`.

The code block shown in bold in Listing 8.4 is where we create an instance of the `DecisionTreeClassifier` class and then train the instance with the data in the variables `X_train` and `X_test`.

The next portion of Listing 8.4 populates the variable `y_pred` with a set of predictions that are generated from the data in the `X_test` variable. The last portion of Listing 8.4 creates a confusion matrix based on the data in `y_test` and the predicted data in `y_pred`.

Remember that all the diagonal elements of a confusion matrix are correct predictions (such as true positive and true negative); all the other cells contain a numeric value that specifies the number of predictions that are incorrect (such as false positive and false negative).

Now launch the code in Listing 8.4 and you will see the following output for the confusion matrix in which there are 36 correct predictions and nine incorrect predictions (with an accuracy of 80%):

```
confusion matrix:
[[13  1  2]
 [ 0 17  4]
 [ 1  1  6]]
from sklearn.metrics import confusion_matrix
```

The sum of the nonzero entries is 45 in the preceding 3×3 matrix, and the diagonal entries are correctly identified labels. Hence the accuracy is 36/45 = 0.80.

Decision Trees, Gini Impurity, and Entropy

In the previous chapter, you learned how to calculate values for `gini` impurity and `entropy`. As you now know, the `DecisionTreeClassifier` class has a `criterion` parameter whose value can be either `entropy` or `gini` (the latter is the default value).

Listing 8.5 displays the contents of `tree_iris_gini.py` that illustrates how to use the `DecisionTreeClassifier` class in `Sklearn` and specify `gini` as the `criterion` (which is specific in the code just for emphasis).

LISTING 8.5: tree_iris_gini.py

```
from sklearn.datasets import load_iris
from sklearn.tree import DecisionTreeClassifier
from sklearn.tree import export_graphviz
```

```
iris = load_iris()
X = iris.data[:, 2:]
y = iris.target

tree_clf = DecisionTreeClassifier(max_
depth=4,criterion='gini',random_state=10)

tree_clf.fit(X, y)

export_graphviz(
   tree_clf,
   out_file="iris_gini.dot",
   feature_names=iris.feature_names[2:],
   class_names=iris.target_names,
   rounded=True,
   filled=True)

plt.show()
```

Listing 8.5 starts with `import` statements and then initializes the variable `iris` as an instance of the `Iris` dataset that is available through Sklearn. The variable X is initialized with all the rows of `iris` and all columns except the first column. The variable y is initialized as the target column in `iris`, which is the label values. Note that the `data` and `target` components are defined in the `Iris` dataset that is built into `Sklearn`: if you download a CSV file containing the `Iris` dataset, it does not necessarily contain data and target components.

The next code snippet initializes the variable `tree_clf` as an instance of the `Sklearn` class `DecisionTreeClassifier`, after which the `fit()` method of `tree_clf` is invoked with X and y as arguments.

The last code block invokes the `export_graphviz()` method to generate a ".dot" file, and you can use the dot executable in `GraphViz` (after installing it on your machine) to create a PNG file with this command:

```
dot -Tpng iris_gini.dot -o iris_gini.png
```

Figure 8.1 displays a tree-based graph with `gini` impurity values for various nodes in the tree.

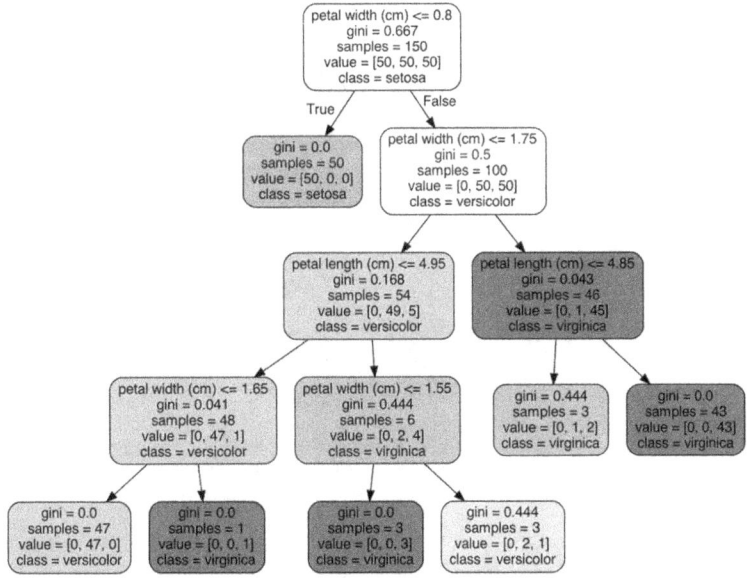

Figure 8.1. A Tree with `Gini` Impurity Values.

Listing 8.6 displays the contents of `tree_iris_entropy.py` that illustrates how to use the `DecisionTreeClassifier` class in `Sklearn` and specify `entropy` instead of `gini` as the value for the `criterion` parameter.

LISTING 8.6: *tree_iris_entropy.py*

```
from sklearn.datasets import load_iris
from sklearn.tree import DecisionTreeClassifier
from sklearn.tree import export_graphviz

iris = load_iris()
X = iris.data[:, 2:]
y = iris.target

tree_clf = DecisionTreeClassifier(max_depth=4,criterion='entro
py',random_state=10)
tree_clf.fit(X, y)

export_graphviz(
   tree_clf,
   out_file="iris_entropy.dot",
   feature_names=iris.feature_names[2:],
   class_names=iris.target_names,
   rounded=True,
   filled=True)

plt.show()
```

Listing 8.6 is based on Listing 8.5: simply change the occurrence of `gini` with `entropy` throughout the code and launch the code from the command line. See the comment after Listing 8.5 that explains how to generate a PNG file from a ".dot" file Figure 8.2 displays a tree-based graph with `entropy` values for various nodes in the tree.

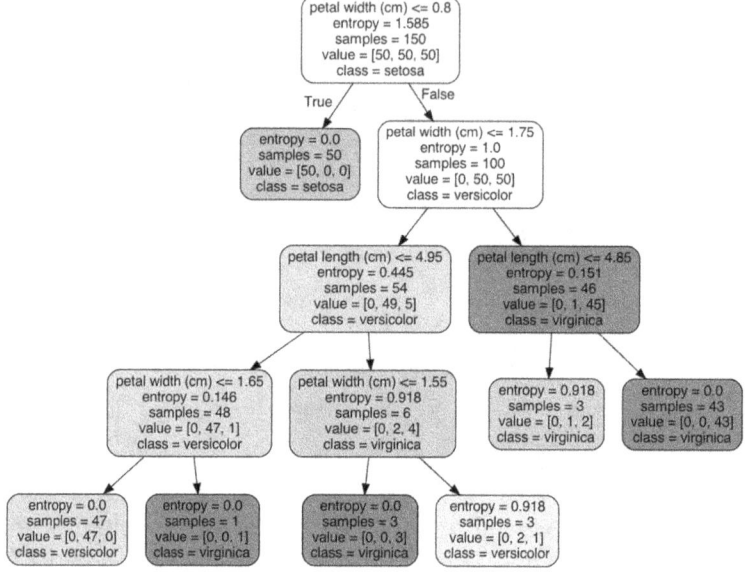

Figure 8.2. A Tree with Entropy Values.

What are Random Forests?

Random forests are a generalization of decision trees: this classification algorithm involves multiple trees. (The number is specified by you.) If the data involves making a numeric prediction, the average of the predictions of the trees is computed. If the data involves a categorical prediction, the mode of the predictions of the trees is determined.

By way of analogy, random forests operate in a manner similar to financial portfolio diversification: the goal is to balance the losses with higher gains. Random forests use a "majority vote" to make predictions, which operates under the assumption that selecting the majority vote is more likely to be correct (and more often) than any individual prediction from a single tree. Hence, random forests are a good choice, especially when a model that is based on a decision tree does not achieve the level of accuracy that you need.

You can easily modify the code in Listing 8.6 to use a random forest by replacing the two lines shown in bold with the following code:

```
from sklearn.ensemble import RandomForestClassifier
classifier = RandomForestClassifier(n_estimators = 10,
criterion='entropy', random_state = 0)
```

Make this code change, launch the code, and examine the confusion matrix to compare its accuracy with the accuracy of the decision tree in Listing 8.4.

What are Support Vector Machines?

Support vector machines (SVM) involve a supervised ML algorithm and can be used for classification or regression problems. SVM can work with nonlinearly separable data as well as linearly separable data. SVM uses a technique called the "kernel trick" to transform data and then finds an optimal boundary the transform involves higher dimensionality. This technique results in a separation of the transformed data, after which it's possible to find a hyperplane that separates the data into two classes.

SVMs are more common in classification tasks than regression tasks. Some use cases for SVMs include:

- text classification tasks: category assignment
- detecting spam/sentiment analysis
- used for image recognition: aspect-based recognition color-based classification
- handwritten digit recognition (postal automation)

Trade-offs of SVMs

Although SVMs are extremely powerful, there are trade-offs involved. Some of the advantages of SVMs are listed here:

- high accuracy
- works well on smaller cleaner datasets
- can be more efficient because it uses a subset of training points
- an alternative to CNNs in cases of limited datasets
- captures more complex relationships between datapoints

Some of the disadvantages of SVMs are listed here:

- not suitable for larger datasets (training time can be high)
- less effective on noisier datasets with overlapping classes

SVMs involve more parameters than decision trees and random forests.

Suggestion: modify Listing 8.4 to use an SVM by replacing the first two lines in Listing 8.4 (that are shown in bold) with the following two lines shown in bold:

```
from sklearn.svm import SVC
classifier = SVC(kernel = 'linear', random_state = 0)
```

You now have an SVM-based model, simply by making the previous code update! Make the code change, then launch the code and examine the confusion matrix in order to compare its accuracy with the accuracy of the decision tree model and the random forest model earlier in this chapter.

What is a Bayesian Classifier?

A naive Bayes (NB) classifier is a probabilistic classifier inspired by Bayes' theorem. An NB classifier assumes the attributes are conditionally independent and it works well even when assumption is not true. This assumption greatly reduces computational cost, and it's a simple algorithm to implement that only requires linear time. Moreover, an NB classifier is easily scalable to larger datasets and good results are obtained in most cases. Other advantages of an NB classifier include:

- can be used for binary and multiclass classification
- provides different types of NB algorithms
- good for text classification problems
- a popular choice for spam email classification
- can be easily trained on small datasets

As you can probably surmise, NB classifiers do have some disadvantages, as shown in the following list:

- All features are assumed unrelated.
- It cannot learn relationships between features.
- It can suffer from "the zero probability problem."

The "zero probability problem" refers to the case when the conditional probability is zero for an attribute: it fails to give a valid prediction. However, can be fixed explicitly using a `Laplacian` estimator whose details are outside the scope of this book.

Types of Naïve Bayes Classifiers

There are three major types of naive Bayes classifiers, as shown in the following list:

- Gaussian Naive Bayes
- MultinomialNB Naive Bayes
- Bernoulli Naive Bayes

Details of these classifiers are also beyond the scope of this chapter, but you can perform an online search for more information. Now that you are somewhat familiar with several classification algorithms in machine learning, let's turn our attention to different ways to train classifiers, which is the topic of the next section.

Training Classifiers

The *holdout method* is the most common method for training a classifier in machine learning, which starts by dividing the dataset into two partitions called `train` and `test` (80% and 20%, respectively). The train set is used for training the model, and the test data tests its predictive power.

The *k-fold cross-validation* technique is used to verify that the model is not overfitted. The dataset is randomly partitioned into k mutually exclusive subsets, where each partition has equal size. One partition is for testing and the other partitions are for training. Repeat this process whereby a different fold is designed the testing fold; since there are `k` folds, this process involves `k` iterations.

In addition to the k-fold cross-validation technique, there are other techniques that you can experiment with, as shown in the following list:

- stratified k-fold cross validation
- leave-one-out cross validation
- group k-fold cross validation

Listing 8.7 displays contents of `knn_classifier_cross_val.py` that illustrates several ways of performing cross validation.

LISTING 8.7: knn_classifier_cross_val.py

```
import pandas as pd
from sklearn import metrics
from sklearn.model_selection import ShuffleSplit
from sklearn.model_selection import cross_val_score

# Import the wine dataset:
dataset = pd.read_csv('wine.csv')
X = dataset.iloc[:, [0, 1]].values
y = dataset.iloc[:, 2].values

# split dataset into training and test sets:
from sklearn.model_selection import train_test_split

X_train, X_test, y_train, y_test = train_test_split(X, y,
test_size = 0.25, random_state = 0)

# scale the feature values between 0 and 1:
from sklearn.preprocessing import StandardScaler
sc = StandardScaler()
X_train = sc.fit_transform(X_train)
X_test = sc.transform(X_test)

# option 1: use cross validation
cv=8
from sklearn.neighbors import KNeighborsClassifier
classifier = KNeighborsClassifier(n_neighbors = 10,
metric='minkowski', p=2)
scores = cross_val_score(classifier, X_train, y_train, cv=cv)
print("=> option 1 default scores:")
print(scores)
print()

# option 2: use a scoring parameter
# The score at each CV iteration is the score method of the
# estimator that can be modified via the scoring parameter:
# more details here: https://scikit-learn.org/stable/modules/
model_evaluation.html#scoring-parameter

scores = cross_val_score(classifier, X_train, y_train, cv=cv,
                  scoring='f1_macro')
print("=> option 2 f1_macro scores:")
print(scores)
print()

# 3) pass a cross validation iterator:
```

```
# cross_val_score uses KFold or StratifiedKFold if cv is an
integer:
n_samples = X_train.shape[0]
cv = ShuffleSplit(n_splits=10, test_size=0.3, random_state=0)
print("=> option 3 ShuffleSplit scores:")
print(cross_val_score(classifier, X_train, y_train, cv=cv))
```
Launch the code in Listing 8.7 and you will see the following output:
```
=> option 1 default scores:
[0.64705882 0.76470588 0.82352941 0.82352941 0.82352941 0.8125
 0.8125     0.875     ]

=> option 2 f1_macro scores:
[0.63822844 0.76550117 0.80769231 0.81678322 0.81678322
 0.81818182 0.81111111 0.86666667]

=> option 3 ShuffleSplit scores:
[0.75 0.8   0.85  0.775 0.775 0.625 0.8   0.775 0.85  0.775]
```

Evaluating Classifiers

Whenever you select a classifier for a dataset, it's obviously important to evaluate the accuracy of that classifier. Some common techniques for evaluating classifiers are listed here:

- precision and recall
- ROC curve (receiver operating characteristics)

Precision and recall are discussed in an earlier chapter and they reproduced here for your convenience. First, let's define the following variables:

```
TP = the number of true positive results
FP = the number of false positive results
TN = the number of true negative results
FN = the number of false negative results
```

Then the definitions of precision, accuracy, and recall are given by the following formulas:

```
precision = TP/(TN + FP)
accuracy  = (TP + TN)/[P + N]
recall    = TP/[TP + FN]
```

The *receiver operating characteristics* (ROC) curve is used for visual comparison of classification models that shows the trade-off between the true positive rate and the false positive rate. The area under the ROC curve is a measure of the accuracy of the model. When a model is closer to the diagonal, it is less accurate and the model with perfect accuracy will have an area of 1.0.

The ROC curve plots the true positive rate (TPR) versus the false positive rate (FPR). Another type of curve is the PR curve that plots precision versus recall. When dealing with highly skewed datasets (strong class imbalance), precision-recall (PR) curves give better results.

Trade-offs for ML Algorithms

This section contains a brief description of the trade-offs of various ML algorithms that were discussed earlier in chapter.

In general, there is no *a priori* way to determine which algorithm works best for a given dataset. Hence, it's a good idea to try every model (or as many as are feasible), tune the hyperparameters accordingly, and analyze the errors carefully. If time and space are constraints, try using a subset of the original dataset (perhaps 25%), and after determining which algorithm produces the best results, use the same algorithm on the full dataset.

kNN best cases:

- kNN outperforms logistic regression and linear SVM when the data is not linear.
- There is no latency requirement; kNN performs well on data with few dimensions.
- Training is not required for the kNN, so new data can easily be handled by the model.

kNN limitations:

- kNN is not recommended for large datasets as kNN is a distance-based model: the cost of calculating the distance from query point to every point in data is very high.
- Make sure you standardize or normalize before distance measure.
- When data is imbalanced, kNN predicted values are biased toward the majority class.
- kNN doesn't work well on large dimensional data due to the curse of dimensionality.
- Performance gets worse with heavily randomized data.

Logistic regression best cases:

- It's very fast at the inference stage.
- Trained weights from logistic regression shows the importance of each feature.
- Output generated by logistic regression are probabilities, which is advantageous over models (such as SVM) that provide only labels as output.
- It's a recommended initial model that is simple and elegant to implement.

Logistic regression limitations:

- It behaves poorly with highly nonlinear data.
- Outliers can adversely affect the decision boundary.
- Collinearity affects the interpretability of weights for feature importance.

Decision trees best cases:

- There's no need for computation after training the model.
- There's support for multiclass classification and regression tasks with categorical and numerical data.
- Important features can be obtained.
- Scaling, standardization, or normalization of data is not required.

Decision trees limitations:

- They are computationally expensive for splitting tree nodes (based on all features and requires calculation of information gain).
- Decision trees have axis parallel boundaries: they are not well-suited for smooth boundaries.
- They do not perform as well when there are unrelated variables.

SVM best cases:

- It works well for small(er) datasets
- SVM is less susceptible to outliers.
- There is fast inference time.

SVM limitations:

- Selecting the correct kernel is not simple.
- It's computationally expensive for large data.
- It's difficult to interpret feature importance from the weights.

This concludes the portion of the chapter pertaining to statistical terms and techniques for measuring the validity of a dataset. Now let's look at activation functions in Machine learning, which is the topic of the next section.

What are Activation Functions?

An activation function is (usually) a nonlinear function that introduces nonlinearity into a neural network, thereby preventing a "consolidation" of the hidden layers in neural network. Specifically, suppose that every pair of adjacent layers in a neural network involves just a matrix transformation and no activation function. Such a network is a linear system, which means that its layers can be consolidated into a much smaller system.

First, the weights of the edges that connect the input layer with the first hidden layer can be represented by a matrix: let's call it `w1`. Next, the weights of the edges that connect the first hidden layer with the second hidden layer can also be represented by a matrix: let's call it `w2`. Repeat this process until we reach the edges that connect the final hidden layer with the output layer: let's call this matrix `wk`. Since we do not have an activation function, we can simply multiply the matrices `w1`, `w2`, ..., `wk` together and produce one matrix: let's call it `w`. We have now replaced the original neural network with an equivalent neural network that contains one input layer, a single matrix of weights `w`, and an output layer. In other words, we no longer have our original multilayered neural network!

Fortunately, we can prevent the previous scenario from happening when we specify an activation function between every pair of adjacent layers. In other words, *an activation function at each layer prevents this "matrix consolidation."* Hence, we can maintain all the intermediate hidden layers during the process of training the neural network.

For simplicity, let's assume that we have the same activation function between every pair of adjacent layers (we'll remove this assumption shortly).

The process for using an activation function in a neural network is a "three step," described as follows:

1. Start with an input vector x1 of numbers.

2. Multiply x1 by the matrix of weights W1 that represents the edges that connect the input layer with the first hidden layer: the result is a new vector x2.

3. "Apply" the activation function to each element of x2 to create another vector x3.

Now repeat steps 2 and 3, except that we use the "starting" vector x3 and the weights matrix W2 for the edges that connect the first hidden layer with the second hidden layer (or just the output layer if there is only one hidden layer).

After completing the preceding process, we have "preserved" the neural network, which means that it can be trained on a dataset. One other thing: instead of using the same activation function at each step, you can replace each activation function by a different activation function (the choice is yours).

Why Do we Need Activation Functions?

The previous section outlines the process for transforming an input vector from the input layer and then through the hidden layers until it reaches the output layer. The purpose of activation functions in neural networks is vitally important, so it's worth repeating here: activation functions "maintain" the structure of neural networks and prevent them from being reduced to an input layer and an output layer. In other words, if we specify a nonlinear activation function between every pair of consecutive layers, then the neural network cannot be "collapsed" to a neural network that contains fewer layers.

Without a nonlinear activation function, we simply multiply a weight matrix for a given pair of consecutive layers with the output vector that is produced from the previous pair of consecutive layers. We repeat this simple multiplication until we reach the output layer of the neural network. After reaching the output layer, we have effectively replaced multiple matrices with a single matrix that "connects" the input layer with the output layer.

How Do Activation Functions Work?

If this is the first time you have encountered the concept of an activation function, it's probably confusing, so here's an analogy that might be helpful.

Suppose you're driving your car late at night and there's nobody else on the highway. You can drive at a constant speed for as long as there are no obstacles (stop signs, traffic lights, and so forth). However, suppose you drive into the parking lot of a large grocery store. When you approach a speed bump you must slow down, cross the speed bump, and increase speed again, and repeat this process for every speed bump.

Think of the nonlinear activation functions in a neural network as the counterpart to the speed bumps: you simply cannot maintain a constant speed, which (by analogy) means that you cannot first multiply all the weight matrices together and "collapse" them into a single weight matrix. Another analogy involves a road with multiple toll booths: you must slow down, pay the toll, and then resume driving until you reach the next toll booth. These are only analogies (and hence imperfect) to help you understand the need for nonlinear activation functions.

Common Activation Functions

Although there are many activation functions (and you can define custom functions if you know how to do so), here is a list of common activation functions:

- Sigmoid
- Tanh
- ReLU
- ReLU6
- Leaky ReLU
- Parametric ReLU
- ELU
- SELU
- Mish
- Swish
- Softmax
- LogSoftmax
- Hardmax

The `sigmoid` activation function is based on Euler's constant e, with a range of values between 0 and 1, and its formula is shown here:

`1/[1+e^(-x)]`

The `tanh` activation function is also based on Euler's constant e, and its formula is shown here:

`[e^x - e^(-x)]/[e^x+e^(-x)]`

One way to remember the preceding formula is to note that the numerator and denominator have the same pair of terms: they are separated by a "-" sign in the numerator and a "+" sign in the denominator. The `tanh()` function has a range of values between -1 and 1.

The `mish` and `switch` activation functions involve the `tanh()` and `sigmoid()` functions, respectively, and they are defined as follows:

```
mish(x) = x * tanh(ln(1+e^x))
swish(x) = x * sigmoid(x)
```

In general, smooth activation functions seem to provide better information propagation more deeply into the neural network, thereby yielding higher accuracy and better generalization. Since the `mish` activation function is "extra" smooth when compared to other activation functions, perhaps this accounts for its higher accuracy.

More details about the `mish` and `swish` activation functions (along with a diagram of both) are available here:

https://towardsdatascience.com/mish-8283934a72df

The rectified linear unit (`ReLU`) activation function is straightforward: if x is negative then `ReLU(x)` is 0; for all other values of x, `ReLU(x)` equals x. `ReLU6` is specific to TensorFlow, and it's a variation of `ReLU(x)`: the additional constraint is that `ReLU(x)` equals 6 when x >= 6 (hence its name).

Keep in mind the following points regarding `ReLU` that could become problematic in your model:

- an unbounded gradient (which is addressed in ReLU6)
- a vanishing ReLU (activation=0) means that no learning occurs
- the mean and variance of activations is not 0 and 1.

The third item in the preceding list can be partially addressed by subtracting the value 0.5 from the activation.

Exponential linear unite (ELU) is the exponential "envelope" of ReLU, which replaces the two linear segments of ReLU with an exponential activation function that is differentiable for all values of x (including x = 0).

Scaled exponential linear unit (SELU) is slightly more complicated than the other activation functions (and used less frequently). For a thorough explanation of these and other activation functions (along with graphs that depict their shape), navigate to the following Wikipedia link:

https://en.wikipedia.org/wiki/Activation_function

The preceding link provides a long list of activation functions as well as their derivatives.

Activation Functions in Python

Listing 8.8 displays contents of the file `activations.py` that contains the formulas for various activation functions.

LISTING 8.8: activations.py

```
import numpy as np

# Python sigmoid example:
z = 1/(1 + np.exp(-np.dot(W, x)))

# Python tanh example:
z = np.tanh(np.dot(W,x))

# Python ReLU example:
z = np.maximum(0, np.dot(W, x))
```

Listing 8.8 contains Python code that use NumPy methods in order to define a sigmoid function, a tanh function, and a ReLU function. Note that you need to specify values for x and W in order to launch the code in Listing 8.8.

Keras Activation Functions

TensorFlow (and many other frameworks) provide implementations for many activation functions, which saves you the time and effort from writing your own implementation of activation functions.

Here is a list of TF2/Keras APIs activation functions that are located in the tf.keras.layers namespace:

- tf.keras.layers.leaky_relu
- tf.keras.layers.relu

- tf.keras.layers.relu6
- tf.keras.layers.selu
- tf.keras.layers.sigmoid
- tf.keras.layers.sigmoid_cross_entropy_with_logits
- tf.keras.layers.softmax
- tf.keras.layers.softmax_cross_entropy_with_logits_v2
- tf.keras.layers.softplus
- tf.keras.layers.softsign
- tf.keras.layers.softmax_cross_entropy_with_logits
- tf.keras.layers.tanh
- tf.keras.layers.weighted_cross_entropy_with_logits

The following subsections provide additional information regarding some of the activation functions in the preceding list. Keep the following point in mind: for simple neural networks, use ReLU as your first preference.

The ReLU and ELU Activation Functions

Currently `ReLU` is often the "preferred" activation function: previously the preferred activation function was `tanh` (and before `tanh` it was `sigmoid`). `ReLU` behaves close to a linear unit and provides the best training accuracy and validation accuracy.

`ReLU` is like a switch for linearity: it's "off" if you don't need it, and its derivative is 1 when it's active, which makes `ReLU` the simplest of all the current activation functions. Note that the second derivative of the function is 0 everywhere: it's a very simple function that simplifies optimization. In addition, the gradient is large whenever you need large values, and it never "saturates" (i.e., it does not shrink to zero on the positive horizontal axis).

Rectified linear units and generalized versions are based on the principle that linear models are easier to optimize. Use the `ReLU` activation function or one of its related alternatives (discussed later).

The Advantages and Disadvantages of ReLU

The following list contains the advantages of the ReLU activation function:

- It does not saturate in the positive region.
- It's very efficient in terms of computation.
- Models with `ReLUv` typically converge faster those with other activation functions.

However, `ReLU` does have a disadvantage when the activation value of a `ReLU` neuron becomes 0: then the gradients of the neuron will also be 0 during back-propagation. You can mitigate this scenario by judiciously assigning the values for the initial weights as well as the learning rate.

ELU

ELU is an acronym for *exponential linear unit* that is based on `ReLU`: the key difference is that ELU is differentiable at the origin (`ReLU` is a continuous function but *not* differentiable at the origin). However, keep in mind several points. First, ELUs trade computational efficiency for "immortality" (immunity to dying): read the following paper for more details: arxiv.org/abs/1511.07289. Secondly, `ReLU`s are still popular and preferred over ELU because the use of ELU introduces an additional new hyper-parameter.

Sigmoid, Softmax, and Hardmax Similarities

The `sigmoid` activation function has a range in (0,1), and it saturates and "kills" gradients. Unlike the `tanh` activation function, `sigmoid` outputs are not zero-centered. In addition, both `sigmoid` and `softmax` (discussed later) are discouraged for vanilla feed forward implementation (see Chapter 6 of the online book "Deep Learning" by Ian Goodfellow et al.). However, the `sigmoid` activation function is still used in LSTMs (specifically for the forget gate, input gate, and the output gate), gated recurrent units (GRUs), and probabilistic models. Moreover, some autoencoders have additional requirements that preclude the use of piecewise linear activation functions.

Softmax

The `softmax` activation function maps the values in a dataset to another set of values that are between 0 and 1, and whose sum equals 1. Thus, `softmax` creates a probability distribution. In the case of image classification with Convolutional Neural Networks (CNNs), the `softmax` activation function "maps" the values in the final hidden layer to the 10 neurons in the output layer. The index of the position that contains the largest probability is matched with the index of the number 1 in the one-hot encoding of the input image. If the index values are equal, then the image has been classified, otherwise it's considered a mismatch.

Softplus

The `softplus` activation function is a smooth (i.e., differentiable) approximation to the `ReLU` activation function. Recall that the origin is the only nondifferentiable point of the `ReLU` function, which is "smoothed" by the `softmax` activation whose equation is here:

```
f(x) = ln(1 + e^x)
```

Tanh

The `tanh` activation function has a range in (-1,1), whereas the `sigmoid` function has a range in (0,1). Both of these two activations saturate, but unlike the `sigmoid` neuron the `tanh` output is zero-centered. Therefore, in practice the `tanh` nonlinearity is always preferred to the `sigmoid` nonlinearity.

The `sigmoid` and `tanh` activation functions appear in LSTMs (sigmoid for the three gates and `tanh` for the internal cell state) as well as GRUs during the calculations pertaining to input gates, forget gates, and output gates (search online for tutorials with more details).

Sigmoid, Softmax, and HardMax Differences

This section briefly discusses some of the differences among these three functions. First, the `sigmoid` function is used for binary classification in logistic regression model, as well as the gates in LSTMs and GRUs. The `sigmoid` function is used as activation function while building neural networks, but keep in mind that the sum of the probabilities is *not* necessarily equal to 1.

Second, the `softmax` function generalizes the `sigmoid` function: it's used for multiclassification in logistic regression model. The `softmax` function is the activation function for the "fully connected layer" in CNNs, which is the right-most hidden layer and the output layer. Unlike the `sigmoid` function, the sum of the probabilities *must* equal 1. You can use either the `sigmoid` function or `softmax` for binary (n=2) classification.

Third, the so-called "`hardmax`" function assigns 0 or 1 to output values (similar to a step function). For example, suppose that we have three classes {c1, c2, c3} whose scores are [1, 7, 2], respectively. The `hardmax` probabilities are `[0, 1, 0]`, whereas the `softmax` probabilities are `[0.1, 0.7, 0.2]`. Notice that the sum of the `hardmax` probabilities is 1, which is also true of the sum of the `softmax` probabilities. However, the `hardmax` probabilities are all-or-nothing, whereas the `softmax` probabilities are analogous to receiving "partial credit."

Hyperparameters for Neural Networks

Neural networks require selecting values for several hyperparameters, including a loss function, an optimizer, a learning rate, and optionally the dropout rate. In brief, loss functions incorporate all the parameters of a neural network, and calculating the change in value for each parameter involves a partial derivative of the loss function, which means that loss functions need to be differentiable. There are several well-known loss functions, such as MSE (Mean Squared Error) and cross entropy.

The Loss Function Hyperparameter

Backward error propagation starts from the output layer and moves in a right-to-left toward the input layer and involves three hyperparameters. These hyperparameters are involved in the "heavy lifting" of machine learning frameworks: they compute the updates to the weights of the edges in neural networks.

The *loss function* is a function in multidimensional Euclidean space. For example the MSE loss function is a convex loss function, which means that it resembles a "bowl", so it has a global minimum. In general, the goal is to minimize the MSE function in order to minimize the cost, which in turn will help us maximize the accuracy of a model (but this is not guaranteed for other loss functions). However, sometimes a local minimum might be considered "good enough" instead of finding a global minimum: you must make this decision (i.e., it's not a purely programmatic decision).

Alas, loss functions for larger datasets tend to be very complex, which is necessary in order to detect potential patterns in datasets. Another loss function is the cross-entropy function, which involves maximizing the likelihood function (contrast this with MSE). Search for online articles (such as Wikipedia) for more details about loss functions.

The Optimizer Hyperparameter

An *optimizer* is an algorithm that is chosen in conjunction with a loss function, and its purpose is to converge to the minimum value of the loss function during the training phase (see the comment in the previous section regarding a local minimum). Different optimizers make different assumptions regarding the manner in which new approximations are calculated during the training process. Some optimizers involve only the most recent approximation, whereas other optimizers use a "rolling average" that takes into account several previous approximations.

There are several well-known optimizers, including `SGD`, `RMSprop`, `Adagrad`, `Adadelta`, and `Adam`. Check online for details regarding the advantages and trade-offs of these optimizers.

The Learning Rate Hyperparameter

The *learning rate* is a small number, often between 0.001 and 0.05, which affects the magnitude of number that is added to the current approximation in order to calculate the next approximation during the training process. The learning rate has a sort of "throttling effect." If the value is too large, the new approximation might "overshoot" the optimal point; if it's too small, the training time can increase significantly. By analogy, imagine you are in a passenger jet and you're 100 miles away from an airport. The speed of the airplane decreases as you approach the airport, which corresponds to decreasing the learning rate in a neural network.

The Dropout Rate Hyperparameter

The *dropout rate* is the eighth hyperparameter, which is a decimal value between 0 and 1, typically between 0.2 and 0.5. Multiply this decimal value with 100 to determine the percentage of randomly selected neurons to ignore during each forward pass in the training process. For example, if the dropout rate is 0.2, then 20% of the neurons are selected randomly *and ignored* during each step of the forward propagation. A different set of neurons is randomly selected whenever a new datapoint is processed in the neural network. Note that the neurons are not removed from the neural network: they still exist, and ignoring them during forward propagation has the effect of "thinning" the neural network. In TF 2 the `Keras tf.keras.layers.Dropout` class performs the task of "thinning" a neural network.

There are additional hyperparameters that you can specify, but they are optional and not required in order to understand ANNs.

What is Backward Error Propagation?

A neural network is typically drawn in a *left-to-right* fashion, where the left-most layer is the input layer. The output from each layer becomes the input for the next layer. The term forward propagation refers to supplying values to the input layer and progress through the hidden layers toward the output layer. The output layer contains the results (which are estimated numeric values) of the forward pass through the model.

Here is a key point: *backward error propagation involves the calculation of numbers that are used to update the weights of the edges in the neural network*. The update process is performed by means of a loss function (and an optimizer and a learning rate), starting from the output layer and then moving in a *right-to-left* fashion in order to update the weights of the edges between consecutive layers. This procedure trains the neural network, which involves reducing the loss between the estimated values at the output layer and the true values (in the case of supervised learning). This procedure is repeated for each datapoint in the training portion of the dataset.

The previous paragraph did not explain what the loss function is or how it's chosen: that's because the loss function and the optimizer and the learning rate are hyperparameters that are discussed in previous sections. However, two commonly used loss functions are MSE and cross entropy; a commonly used optimizer is Adam optimizer (and `SGD` and `RMSprop` and others); and a common value for the learning rate is 0.01.

This concludes the theoretical underpinnings of neural networks and the purpose of various hyperparameters. The next section discusses logistic regression, which (despite its name) is a well-known classification algorithm in machine learning.

What is Logistic Regression?

Despite its name, logistic regression is a classifier and a linear model with a binary output. Logistic regression works with multiple independent variables and involves a sigmoid function for calculating probabilities. Logistic regression is essentially the result of "applying" the `sigmoid` activation function to linear regression in order to perform binary classification.

Logistic regression is useful in a variety of unrelated fields. Such fields include machine learning, various medical fields, and social sciences. Logistic regression can be used to predict the risk of developing a given disease, based on various observed characteristics of the patient. Other fields that use logistic regression include engineering, marketing, and economics.

Logistic regression is binomial (two possible outcomes), and multinomial logistic regression (three or more possible outcomes) generalizes logistic regression to multiclass problems. For instance, suppose that a dataset consists of data that belong either to class A or to class B. If you are given a new datapoint, logistic regression predicts whether that new datapoint belongs to class A or to class B. By contrast, linear regression predicts a numeric value, such as the next-day value of a stock.

Setting a Threshold Value

The threshold value is a numeric value that determines which datapoints belong to class A and which points belong to class B. For instance, a pass/fail threshold might be 0.70. A pass/fail threshold for passing a writing driver's test in California is 0.85.

As another example, suppose that p = 0.5 is the "cutoff" probability. Then we can assign class A to the datapoints that occur with probability > 0.5 and assign class B to datapoints that occur with probability <= 0.5. Since there are only two classes, we do have a classifier.

A similar (yet slightly different) scenario involves tossing a well-balanced coin. We know that there is a 50% chance of throwing heads (let's label this outcome as class A) and a 50% chance of throwing tails (let's label this outcome as class B). If we have a dataset that consists of labeled outcomes, then we have the expectation that approximately 50% of them are class A and class B.

However, we have no way to determine (in advance) what percentage of people will pass their written driver's test, or the percentage of people who will pass their course. Datasets containing outcomes for these types of scenarios need to be trained, and logistic regression can be a suitable technique for doing so.

Logistic Regression: Important Assumptions

Logistic regression requires the observations to be independent of each other. In addition, logistic regression requires little or no multi collinearity among the independent variables. Logistic regression handles numeric, categorical, and continuous variables, and also assumes linearity of independent variables and log odds, which is defined here:

```
odds = p/(1-p) and logit = log(odds)
```

This analysis does not require the dependent and independent variables to be related linearly; however, another requirement is that independent variables are linearly related to the log odds.

Logistic regression is used to obtain odds ratio in the presence of more than one explanatory variable. The procedure is quite similar to multiple linear regression, with the exception that the response variable is binomial. The result is the impact of each variable on the odds ratio of the observed event of interest.

Linearly Separable Data

Linearly separable data is data that can be separated by a line (in 2D), a plane (in 3D), or a hyperplane (in higher dimensions). Linearly nonseparable data is data (clusters) that cannot be separated by a line or a hyperplane. For example, the XOR function involves datapoints that cannot be separated by a line. If you create a truth table for an XOR function with two inputs, the points (0,0) and (1,1) belong to class 0, whereas the points (0,1) and (1,0) belong to class 1 (draw these points in a 2D plane to convince yourself). The solution involves transforming the data in a higher dimension so that it becomes linearly separable, which is the technique used in SVMs (discussed earlier in this chapter).

Keras, Logistic Regression, and Iris Dataset

As this book goes to print, you need Python 3.7.x in order to install TensorFlow on your machine, and also to launch the code sample in this section.

Listing 8.9 displays the contents of tf2_keras_iris.py that defines a Keras-based model to perform logistic regression.

LISTING 8.9: tf2_keras_iris.py

```
import tensorflow as tf
import matplotlib.pyplot as plt

from sklearn.datasets import load_iris
from sklearn.model_selection import train_test_split
from sklearn.preprocessing import OneHotEncoder, StandardScaler

iris = load_iris()
X = iris['data']
y = iris['target']

#you can view the data and the labels:
#print("iris data:",X)
#print("iris target:",y)
```

```
# scale the X values so they are between 0 and 1
scaler = StandardScaler()
X_scaled = scaler.fit_transform(X)

X_train, X_test, y_train, y_test = train_test_split(X_scaled,
y, test_size = 0.2)

model = tf.keras.models.Sequential()
model.add(tf.keras.layers.Dense(activation='relu',
input_dim=4, units=4, kernel_initializer='uniform'))

model.add(tf.keras.layers.Dense(activation='relu', units=4,
                kernel_initializer='uniform'))

model.add(tf.keras.layers.Dense(activation='sigmoid', units=1,
                kernel_initializer='uniform'))
#model.add(tf.keras.layers.Dense(1, activation='softmax'))

model.compile(optimizer='adam', loss='mean_squared_error',
metrics=['accuracy'])

model.fit(X_train, y_train, batch_size=10, epochs=100)

# Predicting values from the test set
y_pred = model.predict(X_test)

# scatter plot of test values-vs-predictions
fig, ax = plt.subplots()
ax.scatter(y_test, y_pred)
ax.plot([y_test.min(), y_test.max()],
        [y_test.min(), y_test.max()], 'r*--')
ax.set_xlabel('Calculated')
ax.set_ylabel('Predictions')
plt.show()
```

Listing 8.9 starts with an assortment of import statements, and then initializes the variable iris with the Iris dataset. The variable X contains the first three columns (and all the rows) of the Iris dataset, and the variable y contains the fourth column (and all the rows) of the Iris dataset.

The next portion of Listing 8.9 initializes the training set and the test set using an 80/20 data split. Next, the Keras-based model contains three Dense layers, where the first two specify the relu activation function and the third layer specifies the sigmoid activation function.

The next portion of Listing 8.9 compiles the model, trains the model, and then calculates the accuracy of the model via the test data. Launch the code in Listing 8.9 and you will see the following output:

```
Train on 120 samples
Epoch 1/100
120/120 [==============================] - 0s 980us/sample -
                           loss: 0.9819 - accuracy: 0.3167
Epoch 2/100
120/120 [==============================] - 0s 162us/sample -
                           loss: 0.9789 - accuracy: 0.3083
Epoch 3/100
120/120 [==============================] - 0s 204us/sample -
                           loss: 0.9758 - accuracy: 0.3083
Epoch 4/100
120/120 [==============================] - 0s 166us/sample -
                           loss: 0.9728 - accuracy: 0.3083
Epoch 5/100
120/120 [==============================] - 0s 160us/sample -
                           loss: 0.9700 - accuracy: 0.3083
// details omitted for brevity
Epoch 96/100
120/120 [==============================] - 0s 128us/sample -
                           loss: 0.3524 - accuracy: 0.6500
Epoch 97/100
120/120 [==============================] - 0s 184us/sample -
                           loss: 0.3523 - accuracy: 0.6500
Epoch 98/100
120/120 [==============================] - 0s 128us/sample -
                           loss: 0.3522 - accuracy: 0.6500
Epoch 99/100
120/120 [==============================] - 0s 187us/sample -
                           loss: 0.3522 - accuracy: 0.6500
Epoch 100/100
120/120 [==============================] - 0s 167us/sample -
                           loss: 0.3521 - accuracy: 0.6500
```

Figure 8.3 displays a scatter plot of points based on the test values and the predictions for those test values.

The accuracy is admittedly poor (abysmal?), and yet it's quite possible that you will encounter this type of situation. Experiment with a different number of hidden layers and replace the final hidden layer with a Dense layer that specifies a softmax activation function—or some other activation function—to see if this change improves the accuracy.

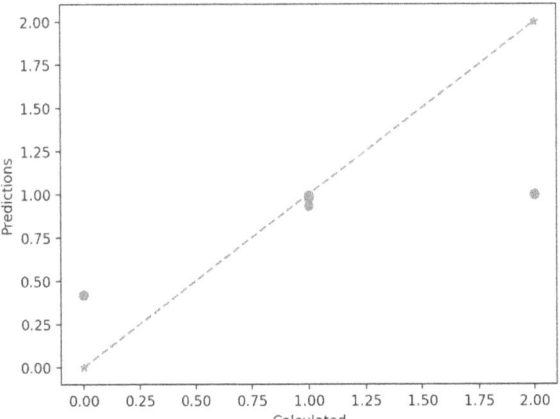

Figure 8.3. A Scatter Plot and a Best-Fitting Line.

Sklearn and Linear Regression

This optional section shows you how to perform linear regression on a set of randomly generated points in the Euclidean plane, and also how to render those points with a best-fitting line. However, there is no NLP-related functionality, which means that you can ignore this section with no loss of continuity. Later chapters discuss machine learning and machine learning classifiers. This code sample is one of the only code samples in this book that pertains to linear regression in machine learning.

Listing 8.10 displays the contents of sklearn_lin_reg.py that illustrates how to generate some random numbers in the Euclidean plane and then use linear regression in order to find the best-fitting line for those points.

LISTING 8.10: sklearn_lin_reg.py

```
import numpy as np
import pandas as pd
import matplotlib.pyplot as plt
from sklearn.linear_model import LinearRegression

x = 10*np.random.rand(100)
y = 5*x + 5*np.random.rand(100)

print("=> first 10 x values:")
print(x[0:10])
print("=> max x value:",x.max())
print()
print("=> first 10 y values:")
print(y[0:10])
```

```
print("=> max y value:",y.max())
print()

model = LinearRegression(fit_intercept=True)
X = x.reshape(-1, 1)
print("X.shape:",X.shape)

model.fit(X, y)

print("=> slope of line:", model.coef_[0])
print("=> y-intercept:  ", model.intercept_)

x_fit = np.linspace(-1,11)
X_fit = x_fit.reshape(-1,1)

y_fit = model.predict(X_fit)

# "random" points:
plt.scatter(x,y)

# best-fitting line:
plt.plot(x_fit,y_fit)
plt.show()
```

Listing 8.10 starts with some `import` statements and then initializes the variable `x` as a vector of 100 random floating point numbers between 0 and 10. The variable `y` is initialized as vector of 100 random floating point numbers, where each number is five times the corresponding value in the vector x, plus another random floating point number between 0 and 5.

The next portion of Listing 8.10 initializes the variable `model` as an instance of the `LinearRegression` class in `Sklearn`. Then the variable `X` is initialized as a 100×1 vector of values from the vector x.

The next code snippet invokes the `fit()` method of the variable `model`, after which the slope and y-intercept of the best fitting line are available. Now we can perform some predictions. Initialize the variable `x_fit` with a set of random numbers between -1 and 11, and initialize `X_fit` as a one-column vector whose values are from `x_fit`. Now we can get the predicted values from `X_fit` by invoking the `predict()` method of the variable `model`, as shown here:

```
y_fit = model.predict(X_fit)
```

Launch the code in Listing 8.10 and you will see the following output, along with a graph that displays the best fitting line for the set of random points:

```
=> first 10 x values:
[9.50318249  1.92716624  4.73429059  5.81910031  2.53858169
1.26370769 4.08290837 3.71162985 8.26798678 1.42404685]
```

```
=> max x value: 9.995419932716011

=> first 10 y values:
[49.94582654 11.9098716  25.61829038 32.7364018  17.18778012
  7.14293639 22.574198   20.62959673 42.65198716  7.71367233]
=> max y value: 54.255842476093875

X.shape: (100, 1)
=> slope of line: 5.070423937652158
=> y-intercept:   2.016428692525192
```

SciPy and Linear Regression

This section show you how to perform linear regression using SciPy. Since we have not discussed the SciPy Python library, this section is optional. However, the code sample uses the same datapoint as Listing 8.10 in the previous section, so you can compare the relative complexity of the two code samples.

Listing 8.11 displays the contents of `scipy_lin_reg.py` that illustrates how to generate some random numbers in the Euclidean plane and then use linear regression in order to find the best-fitting line for those points.

LISTING 8.11: scipy_lin_reg.py

```
import numpy as np
import matplotlib.pyplot as plt
from scipy import stats
from sklearn.metrics import r2_score

# same data as sklearn_lin_reg.py:
x = 10*np.random.rand(100)
y = 5*x + 5*np.random.rand(100)

# "linefit" uses the values slope and intercept:
slope, intercept, r_value, p_value, std_err = stats.
linregress(x,y)

print("slope:    ", slope)
print("intercept:", intercept)
print("r_value:  ", r_value)
print("p_value:  ", p_value)
print("std_err:  ", std_err)

def linefit(b):
  return intercept + slope * b

myline = linefit(x)
```

```
plt.scatter(x,y, color='b')
plt.plot(x,myline, color='r')
plt.show()
```

Listing 8.11 starts with some familiar `import` statements, and then initializes the variable x as a vector of 100 random floating point numbers between 0 and 10. The variable y is initialized as vector of 100 random floating point numbers, where each number is 5 times the corresponding value in the vector x, plus another random floating point number between 0 and 5.

The key code snippet in Listing 8.11 is shown in bold, which calculates the slope, y-intercept, r-value, p-value, and standard error for the best fitting line. If you need access to these quantities, then this type of code is more useful than the code in Listing 8.10.

Launch the code in Listing 8.11 and you will see the following output, along with a graph that displays the best fitting line for the set of random points:

```
slope:      5.008309175824397
intercept:  2.4242119308236134
r_value:    0.9960065560231295
p_value:    1.2047321054027177e-104
std_err:    0.04534930921236101
```

Figure 8.4 displays a scatter plot of points and the best-fitting line for those points.

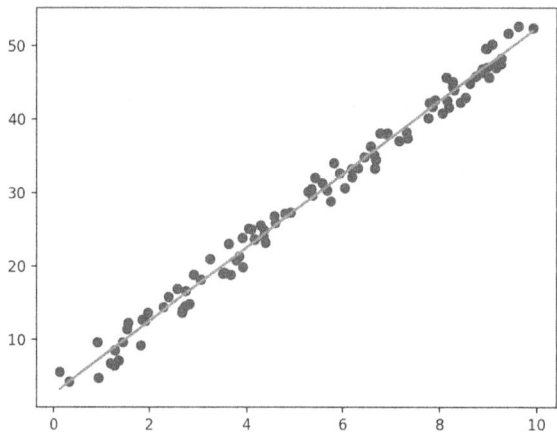

Figure 8.4. A Scatter Plot and a Best-Fitting Line.

Keras and Linear Regression

The code sample in this section contains primarily Keras code in order to perform linear regression. If you have read the previous examples in this chapter, this section will be easier for you to understand because the steps for linear regression are the same.

Listing 8.12 displays the contents of keras_linear_regression.py that illustrates how to perform linear regression in Keras.

LISTING 8.12: keras_linear_regression.py

```
###############################################################
#Keep in mind the following important points:
#1) Always standardize both input features and target
variable:
#doing so only on input feature produces incorrect predictions
#2) Data might not be normally distributed: check the data and
#based on the distribution apply StandardScaler, MinMaxScaler,
#Normalizer or RobustScaler
###############################################################

import tensorflow as tf
import numpy as np
import pandas as pd
import seaborn as sns
import matplotlib.pyplot as plt
from sklearn.preprocessing import MinMaxScaler
from sklearn.model_selection import train_test_split

df = pd.read_csv('housing.csv')
X  = df.iloc[:,0:13]
y  = df.iloc[:,13].values

mmsc = MinMaxScaler()
X  = mmsc.fit_transform(X)
y  = y.reshape(-1,1)
y  = mmsc.fit_transform(y)

X_train, X_test, y_train, y_test = train_test_split(X, y,
                                            test_size=0.3)

# this Python method creates a Keras model
def build_keras_model():
  model = tf.keras.models.Sequential()
  model.add(tf.keras.layers.Dense(units=13, input_dim=13))
  model.add(tf.keras.layers.Dense(units=1))
  model.compile(optimizer='adam',loss='mean_squared_error',
                metrics=['mae','accuracy'])
  return model
```

```
batch_size=32
epochs = 40

# specify the Python method 'build_keras_model' to create a
# Keras model
# using the implementation of the scikit-learn regressor API
# for Keras
model = tf.keras.wrappers.scikit_learn.KerasRegressor(build_
fn=build_keras_model, batch_size=batch_size,epochs=epochs)

# train ('fit') the model and then make predictions:
model.fit(X_train, y_train)
y_pred = model.predict(X_test)
#print("y_test:",y_test)
#print("y_pred:",y_pred)

# scatter plot of test values-vs-predictions
fig, ax = plt.subplots()
ax.scatter(y_test, y_pred)
ax.plot([y_test.min(), y_test.max()], [y_test.min(), y_test.
max()], 'r*--')
ax.set_xlabel('Calculated')
ax.set_ylabel('Predictions')
plt.show()
```

Listing 8.12 starts with multiple `import` statements and then initializes the data frame `df` with the contents of the CSV file `housing.csv` (a portion of which is shown in Listing 8.13 at the end of this section). Notice that the training set `X` is initialized with the contents of the first 13 columns of the dataset `housing.csv`, and the variable y contains the rightmost column of the dataset `housing.csv`.

The next section in Listing 8.12 uses the `MinMaxScaler` class to calculate the mean and standard deviation, and then invokes the `fit_transform()` method in order to update the `X` values and the `y` values so that they have a mean of 0 and a standard deviation of 1.

Next, the `build_keras_mode() Python` method creates a `Keras`-based model with two dense layers. Notice that the input layer has size 13, which is the number of columns in the data frame `X`. The next code snippet compiles the model with an `adam` optimizer, the MSE loss function, and also specifies the MAE and accuracy for the metrics. The compiled model is then returned to the caller.

The next portion of Listing 8.12 initializes the `batch_size` variable to 32 and the epochs variable to 40, and specifies them in the code snippet that creates the model, as shown here:

```
model = tf.keras.wrappers.scikit_learn.KerasRegressor(build_
fn=build_keras_model, batch_size=batch_size,epochs=epochs)
```

The short comment block that appears in Listing 8.12 explains the purpose of the preceding code snippet, which constructs our Keras model.

The next portion of Listing 8.12 invokes the fit() method to train the model and then invokes the predict() method on the X_test data to calculate a set of predictions and initialize the variable y_pred with those predictions.

The final portion of Listing 8.12 displays a scatter plot in which the horizontal axis is the values in y_test (the actual values from the CSV file housing.csv) and the vertical axis is the set of predicted values.

Figure 8.5 displays a scatter plot of points based on the test values and the predictions for those test values.

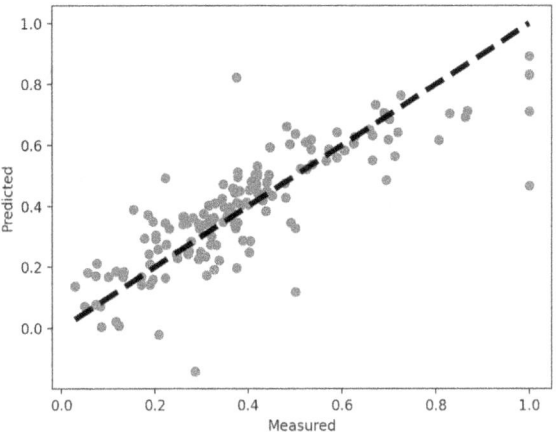

Figure 8.5. A Scatter Plot and a Best-Fitting Line.

Listing 8.13 displays the first four rows of the CSV file housing.csv used in the Python code in Listing 8.12.

LISTING 8.13: *housing.csv*
```
0.00632,18,2.31,0,0.538,6.575,65.2,4.09,1,296,15.3,396.9,4.98,24
0.02731,0,7.07,0,0.469,6.421,78.9,4.9671,2,242,17.8,396.9,9.14,21.6
0.02729,0,7.07,0,0.469,7.185,61.1,4.9671,2,242,17.8,392.83,4.03,34.7
0.03237,0,2.18,0,0.458,6.998,45.8,6.0622,3,222,18.7,394.63,2.94,33.4
```

Summary

This chapter started with an introduction to classification, followed by a brief explanation of commonly used classifiers in machine learning. In particular, you learned about kNN, logistic regression (despite its name it *is* a classifier), decision trees, random forests, SVMs, and Bayesian classifiers.

Next you learned about activation functions, why they are important in neural networks, and also how they are used in neural networks. Then you saw a list of the TF/Keras APIs for various activation functions, followed by a description of some of their merits.

Finally, you learned about logistic regression that involves the sigmoid activation function, followed by a Keras-based code sample involving logistic regression.

CHAPTER 9

NLP Applications

Chapters 5 and 6 provide a fast-paced introduction to several NLP-related Python libraries and related code samples. By contrast, this chapter is primarily about text classification, recommendation systems, and sentiment analysis.

The first section describes two main types of text summarization (extractive and abstractive), as well as text recommendation. This section also contains Python code samples that illustrate how to use gensim and spaCy to perform text classification.

The second section contains a brief overview of recommender systems, used in online reviews of books, movies, restaurants, and so forth. The optional portion of this section discusses how to use reinforcement learning in recommender systems.

The third section discusses sentiment analysis, which is actually a subset of text classification. In essence, sentiment analysis attempts to assess the mood (positive, negative, or neutral) of a document (such as a review). You will see Python code samples that perform sentiment analysis with Naïve Bayes, NLTK and VADER, and logistic regression.

The final part of this chapter contains a Python code sample involving a COVID-19 dataset, followed by a brief introduction to chatbots.

What is Text Summarization?

Text summarization can be informally described as producing a summary of the content of a block of text. Text summarization is similar to a synopsis or an executive summary of a document. In the NLP world, automatic text summarization involves generating a summary of text from various sources, such as a Web page, blog post, a document, or a set of documents.

There are two main categories of text summarization (the first is more complex than the second): abstractive summarization techniques and extractive summarization techniques. A high-level description of these summarization techniques is provided in the following subsections.

Extractive Text Summarization

Extractive text summarization algorithms extract keywords or sentences, without modifying any of the words in a document, which represent the content of a document. Examples of extractive text summarization tasks include producing book reviews, movie reviews, minutes of a meeting, document or blog post summary, and so forth.

Note that the extractive algorithms do not generate any new text from a document, and they typically involve smaller amounts of training data. Extractive text summarization has been extensively researched, and has reached a mature stage.

Extractive summarization algorithms perform three independent tasks:

- creating an intermediate representation of the text
- providing sentence ranks based on the representation
- creating a summary based on some of the sentences

A representation of the input text can use a frequency-based approach, such as calculating word frequencies via `tf-idf` scores. A topic-based approach involves finding topics in a document and then estimating the importance of each sentence based on the number of topic-related words that appear in a given sentence, or centroids from clusters that are formed by grouping similar data together. A score is assigned to each sentence based on how well it appears to explain the topics in a document. Finally, a summary is generated, based on the highest ranked sentences from the previous step.

Abstractive Text Summarization

Abstractive text summarization tasks are more difficult because they involve a more complex process that requires understanding the language and the context, after which they generate new sentences. These algorithms often require large amounts of data during the training step. Keep in mind that this type of text summarization involves generating new vocabulary that describes the content of a document in a concise and structured manner.

Two other points to keep in mind. First, text summarization tends to work better with documents that have a smaller number of distinct topics. For example, lengthy books and poems can contain a wide range of topics, which can pose a challenge for accurate text summarization.

Second, human speech tends to be more casual than written language, which means that errors occur when transcribing speech to text. However, the transcription accuracy continues to improve, which in turn means that it will become more feasible to apply extractive methods to text that has been transcribed from speech.

Text Summarization with gensim and SpaCy

This section contains `Python` code samples that combine `gensim` and `SpaCy` to perform text summarization, so now would be a good time to read the previous sections if you haven't done so already.

Listing 9.1 displays the contents of `text_summarization.py` that illustrates how to perform text summarization with `gensim` on a block of text.

LISTING 9.1: text_summarization.py

```
from gensim.summarization import summarize

mytext = """
Chapters five and six provide a fast-paced introduction
to several NLP-related Python libraries and related code
samples. By contrast, this chapter is primarily about text
classification, recommendation systems, and sentiment
analysis.
The first section discusses two main types of text
summarization (extractive and abstractive), as well as text
recommendation. This section also contains Python code samples
that illustrate how to use gensim and SpaCy to perform text
classification.
```

The second section contains a brief overview of recommender systems, which are used in online reviews of books, movies, restaurants, and so forth. You will also learn how to use the Python surprise library that provides a layer of abstraction above the tasks that are required for recommender systems. The final (optional) portion of this section discusses how to use reinforcement learning in recommender systems.
«»»

```
# Summarize the preceding text by passing it as
# an input to "summarize" that returns a summary
print("===> text summary:")
print(summarize(mytext))
print()

# the "split" option produces a list of strings
print("===> split the text summary:")
print(summarize(mytext, split=True))
print()

# 1) the "ratio" parameter changes the displayed text
# (default=20%)
# 2) the "word_count" parameter: the number of words to
# display
print("===> a 50-word summary:")
print(summarize(mytext, word_count=50))
print()

from gensim.summarization import keywords
print("===> keywords:")
print(keywords(mytext))
print()
```

Listing 9.1 initializes the variable `mytext` with a test string that is passed in to the `summary()` method provided by `gensim`, after which a summary of the contents of `mytext` is displayed.

The next portion of Listing 9.1 invokes the `summary()` method with `split=True`, in order to display the preceding output as a list of strings. The next code snippet invokes the `summary()` method again, this time with `word_count=50` in order to display a 50-word summary of the input text. Launch the code in Listing 9.1 and you will see the following output:

```
===> text summary:
You will also learn how to use the Python surprise library
that provides a layer of abstraction above the tasks that are
required for recommender systems.

===> split the text summary:
```

```
['You will also learn how to use the Python surprise library
that provides a layer of abstraction above the tasks that are
required for recommender systems.']

===> a 50-word summary:
This section also contains Python code samples that illustrate
how to use gensim and SpaCy to perform text classification.
You will also learn how to use the Python surprise library
that provides a layer of abstraction above the tasks that are
required for recommender systems.

===> keywords:
python
text
section
movies
optional
recommendation
recommender
```

Listing 9.2 displays the content of gensim_spacy.py that illustrates how to perform text summarization with gensim and SpaCy on text that is extracted from Wikipedia.

NOTE *Make sure that you invoke* pip3 install wikipedia

LISTING 9.2: gensim_spacy.py

```
import spacy

from gensim.summarization.summarizer import summarize
from gensim.summarization import keywords
import wikipedia

# Get wiki content for Japan:
wikisearch = wikipedia.page("Japan")
wikicontent = wikisearch.content

nlp = spacy.load('en_core_web_sm')
doc = nlp(wikicontent)

# Save the wiki content to a file:
f = open("wikicontent.txt", "w")
f.write(wikicontent)
f.close()
```

```
# Summary (0.5% of the original content):
summ_per = summarize(wikicontent, ratio = 0.05)
print("=> Percent summary:")
print(summ_per)
```

Listing 9.2 initializes the variable `wikisearch` with the result of invoking the `wikipedia.page()` method, followed by the variable `wikicontent` that contains the text from the variable `wikisearch`.

Next, the variable `nlp` is initialized as an instance of the small Web model from `spaCy`, and the variable `doc` is initialized with the result of passing `wikicontent` to the `nlp` variable. The `wikicontent` variable contains actual text, which is saved to a text file.

The final code block in Listing 9.2 provides a small (i.e., 0.5%) summary of the text in `wikicontent`. Launch the code in Listing 9.2 and you will see the following output:

=> Percent summary:

Japan (Japanese: 日本, Nippon [ɲippoꜜɴ] (listen) or Nihon [ɲihoꜜɴ] (listen)) is an island country in East Asia, located in the northwest Pacific Ocean. It is bordered on the west by the Sea of Japan, and extends from the Sea of Okhotsk in the north toward the East China Sea and Taiwan in the south. Part of the Ring of Fire, Japan spans an archipelago of 6852 islands covering 377,975 square kilometers (145,937 sq mi); the five main islands are Hokkaido, Honshu, Shikoku, Kyushu, and Okinawa. Tokyo is Japan's capital and largest city; other major cities include Yokohama, Osaka, Nagoya, Sapporo, Fukuoka, Kobe, and Kyoto.

Japan is the eleventh-most populous country in the world, as well as one of the most densely populated and urbanized. About three-fourths of the country's terrain is mountainous, concentrating its population of 125.71 million on narrow coastal plains. Japan is divided into 47 administrative prefectures and eight traditional regions. The Greater Tokyo Area is the most populous metropolitan area in the world, with more than 37.4 million residents.

[some content omitted for brevity]

=> Word count summary:
Although it has renounced its right to declare war, the country maintains Self-Defense Forces that are ranked as the world's fourth-most powerful military.

Ranked the second-highest country on the Human Development Index in Asia after Singapore, Japan has the world's second-highest life expectancy, though it is experiencing a decline in population.
Despite early resistance, Buddhism was promoted by the ruling class, including figures like Prince Shōtoku, and gained widespread acceptance beginning in the Asuka period (592-710).The far-reaching Taika Reforms in 645 nationalized all land in Japan, to be distributed equally among cultivators, and ordered the compilation of a household registry as the basis for a new system of taxation.
During the Meiji era (1868-1912), the Empire of Japan emerged as the most developed nation in Asia and as an industrialized world power that pursued military conflict to expand its sphere of influence.

[some content omitted for brevity]

What are Recommender Systems?

Recommender systems are a subset of information filtering systems that attempt to predict the "rating" or "preference" for items based on an analysis of a user's preferences. Such systems personalize the information supplied to users based on their interests, relevance of the information. Recommendation systems are used widely for many scenarios, such as the following:

- recommending movies
- articles
- restaurants
- places to visit
- items to buy

There are three major types of algorithms that are used for recommendation systems, as shown in the following list:

- collaborative filtering (similar users)
- content-based approaches (item features)
- a hybrid of the first two

In highly simplified terms, collaborative filtering makes recommendations to a user based on another user who has similar preferences. This technique obviously requires some users, and the initial absence of users is called the "cold start" problem. By contrast, a content-based approach recommends a new item to a user based on the similarity of the features of that item to an existing (and similar) item. A hybrid approach can start with a content-based approach (which does not suffer from the cold start problem), and then use a collaborative filtering approach.

These three approaches are discussed in greater detail in a subsequent section, after we explore some of the aspects of a movie recommender system, which is the topic of the next section.

Movie Recommender Systems

A movie recommender system is familiar to most people, and in simple terms, the goal of such a system is to create an accurate list of recommendations to its users. A recommendation list takes into account the movies that a user has seen, the ratings assigned to movies by each user, along with a mix of other factors.

Suppose that we have a matrix R with m rows (users) and n columns (movies), and each entry in matrix R is a movie rating, which can be a number between 1 and 5 inclusive or a floating point number between 0 and 1. Matrix R can have millions of rows and tens of thousands of movies. In addition, matrix R probably has some relationships that can provide useful information. For example, it's possible to have the following:

- two equal rows (two users have the same movie ratings)
- two equal columns (two movies have the same ratings by multiple users)
- a third row is the sum of two other rows (can you guess how?)

Here is an example of a matrix R that consists of four users and four movies, with movie ratings expressed as a floating point number between 0 and 1:

```
        M1   M2    M2   M4
Alice   1    -     0.2  -
Edward  -    0.5   -    0.3
Steve   1    -     1    -
David   1    -     -    0.4
```

As you can see, there are some missing entries in the preceding matrix: the goal of a recommender system is to infer values for the missing entries.

Now consider the following rating matrix R in which all numeric ratings are equal to 2, along with one missing value:

```
       M1  M2  M2  M4
Alice  2   2   2   2
Edward 2   2   2   2
Steve  2   2   2   ?
David  2   2   2   2
```

The obvious choice for the missing value in the preceding matrix R is 3. Now try to infer the missing value in the following matrix R:

```
       M1  M2  M2  M4
Alice  3   1   1   2
Edward 1   2   4   3
Steve  3   1   1   ?
David  4   3   5   4
```

What is the missing value in the preceding matrix? If you guessed 2, you are correct: this value is inferred from the fact that Alice and Steve have three identical ratings, and since Alice rated M4 with the value 2, we can infer that Steve would also rate this movie with a value of 2.

Factoring the Rating Matrix R

As you learned in a previous section, the rating matrix R can be massive, which will degrade performance when processing this matrix for information. Fortunately, we can avail ourselves of a technique called *matrix factorization*, which is discussed here (other online articles might be easier to read):

https://en.wikipedia.org/wiki/Matrix_factorization_(recommender_ systems)

Let's suppose that each row of R is a movie and there are 1,000 movies. In addition, suppose that each column of R is a user, and there are 2,000 users. Then the array R has 2,000,000 entries (and is also sparse).

However, we can decompose the matrix R into the product of two matrices M and U. Specifically, M is a 1000×100 matrix of consisting of movies and features for its rows and columns, respectively. In addition, matrix U is a 100×2000 matrix consisting of features and users for its rows and columns respectively. The matrices M and U are compatible, because their product is (1000×100) × (100×2000), which is a matrix of dimensionality 1000×2000: this is also the dimensionality of matrix R. Moreover, the content of the rows and columns of M*U matches the content of the rows and columns of matrix R.

The following section describes a new type of recommendation system, followed by the two main types of recommendation systems that were mentioned earlier in this chapter.

Content-Based Recommendation Systems

The premise of content-based recommendation systems is simple: if you like an item, you will probably like a "similar" item. In situations where it's easy to determine the context or properties of each item, a recommendation that's based on the similarity of the items generally works well. For example, recommending the same kind of item such as a movie, book, song, or restaurant recommendation.

Content-based recommendation systems are classified in two broad categories: (1) a technique that analyzes only the description of the content and (2) a technique that involves building user profiles and item profiles. Both techniques are discussed in the following subsections.

Analyzing only the Description of the Content

This technique is similar to item-based collaborative filtering: this means that the system recommends anything similar to previously items that are marked as "liked." The advantages of this technique are listed below:

- avoids the "new item problem" if descriptions are meaningful
- semantic information and inferences can be used
- easier to create more transparent systems

This technique also has the following disadvantages:

- content-based recommendation systems tend to overspecialize
- they will recommend items similar to those already consumed
- the preceding also has a tendency of creating a "filter bubble"

Building User Profiles and Item Profiles

One technique for creating use profiles utilizes a description or attributes from items the user has previously interacted with in order to recommend similar items. This technique depends only on the user previous choices. This technique is robust to avoid the cold-start problem," and it's also simple to use for textual items (such as articles, news, and books).

Collaborative Filtering Algorithm

The premise of collaborative algorithm can be illustrated with the following simple example. Suppose that person A likes items 1, 2, and 3, whereas person B likes items 2, 3, and 4. As you can see, A and B have similar interests, and so we infer that A would like item 4 (because B likes it) and that B would like item A (because A likes it).

As a concrete example, suppose you go to a restaurant and then you ask the wait staff (or someone in your group) for a recommendation: this is an example of collaborative filtering.

A few points to keep in mind regarding the collaborative filtering algorithm:

- The algorithm is entirely based on past behavior.
- It is not based on the context.
- It is independent of any other information.
- This is a commonly used algorithm.

User–User Collaborative Filtering

This technique involve searching for customers similar to a given customer, finding products that they like, and then suggesting those products to the given customer. This is a very effective algorithm that also requires a lot of time and resources because information about *every* customer pair must be determined. In case of very large platforms, this algorithm is difficult to implement without a very strong parallelizable system.

Item–Item Collaborative Filtering

This technique is similar to user–user collaborative filtering, with the following points:

find item lookalike instead of customer look alike
easy to recommend similar items to customers who have purchased items (when the item lookalike matrix is constructed)

This technique is far less resource consuming than user–user collaborative filtering. In fact, for new customers the item-item algorithm takes far lesser time than user-user collaborate as we don't need all similarity scores between customers. In the case of a fixed number of products, the product–

product look alike matrix is fixed over time. If need be, you can read the section in appendix A that discusses various types of distance metrics.

Recommender System with Surprise

`Surprise` is an acronym for simple Python recommendation system engine that is based on `Sklearn`. `Surprise` is an open source `Python` library for building and analyzing recommender systems.

`Surprise` provides built-in datasets, prediction algorithms, dimensionality reduction (PCA and SVD), and various metrics such as MAE, RMSE, and so forth. Navigate to its home page to learn about its features and code samples: *https://surpriselib.com*

Recommender Systems and Reinforcement Learning (Optional)

As you have already learned, traditional recommender systems typically involve either collaborative filtering or content-based systems. Another approach to implementing recommender systems involves reinforcement learning. Before we proceed with more details, let's take a short digression to provide a high-level description of reinforcement learning.

Basic Reinforcement Learning in Five Minutes

Reinforcement learning involves an "agent" seeks to maximize its expected future reward, which involves moving among various states, in a randomly selected fashion or in a deterministic fashion. Each state has a reward that can be a positive, zero, or negative value), and finding the optimal path often involves many, many iterations. *Keep in mind the following point: the agent (aka the learner) is not told which actions must be taken, and in which sequence they must be taken: the agent must discover those actions by itself.*

Here is another important point: *in general, greedy algorithms fail in reinforcement learning tasks, so a generalization called the "epsilon greedy" algorithm is employed.* This involves the following variables:

- an initial state S
- a variable `epsilon` with initial value equal to 1
- a variable `rnd` that is a randomly generated number between 0 and 1
- a Q table whose rows are states and columns are actions

If `rnd` is less than `epsilon`, then a random action **A** (that is defined for the current state) is selected; otherwise, an action is selected for which `Q(S,A)` has the maximum value. In either case, the selected action **A** is handed to the environment, which you can think of as an "oracle" that returns a new state, a reward, and a Boolean "done" flag that equals true when the current episode (or game) has concluded. Here is a sample of the type of code that determines the new state based on the current action, where the variable env is the "oracle":

```
import gym
# initialize state, action, epsilon, rnd, done, total_reward
# state = current state
# other details omitted

while(done=False):
  # find an action based on epsilon greedy algorithm:
  # details omitted...

  # get the next state and reward:
  next_state, reward, done, _ = env.step(action)

  # set the current state to the new state:
  state = next_state
  total_reward += reward
```

Note that the preceding code is inside a loop, which means that many actions are selected in order to arrive at different states.

Each time that a value is generated for `rnd`, the value of `epsilon` is decremented from 1 to a small number (typically 0.1). Hence, over the course of multiple iterations, the number of randomly selected actions (called "exploration") decreases and the number of greedy-style selections (called "exploitation") increases.

If `epsilon` is the constant 0, then the algorithm is simply a greedy algorithm, so the latter is actually a special case of the epsilon greedy algorithm. On the other hand, if `epsilon` is the constant 1, then the algorithm involves only randomly selected choices, which does not provide any meaningful value. When you think about it, the epsilon greedy algorithm is both clever and elegant in its ability to combine random choices with deterministic choices.

One well-known technique in reinforcement learning is called *q-learning* ("quality" learning) which involves a two-dimensional matrix (aka a "q-table") with states as rows and actions as columns. The matrix cells are (state, action) pairs that are initialized to 0. After each iteration of the loop containing the epsilon greedy algorithm, the currently selected (state, action) pair is updated with a new reward value, and the agent makes a transition to the newly selected state.

However, a q-table works when there is a *fixed* number of states and actions, such as tasks involving a maze or navigating around a rectangular grid. In the case of games such as Super Mario, each time Mario moves on the screen, the new set of pixels is treated as a new state. Thus, the number of states is treated as though it's continuous rather than discrete.

However, instead of appending each new state to a q-table, we use something called deep Q-learning (DQN), which involves passing the state as the input to a neural network, and the output layer is a set of possible actions. The neural network is trained via backward error propagation, and the action in the output layer that has the highest probability is selected.

One other scenario can arise: the number of states *and* the number of actions are both continuous. As an example, consider a moving vehicle: the number of states is continuous and the number of actions (such as turning the steering wheel) is also continuous. There are some deep reinforcement learning algorithms, such as soft actor critic (SAC) and twin delayed DDPG (TD3) that solve this type of task.

One other detail: almost every reinforcement learning task can be modeled as an Markov decision process (MDP), which is based on a Markov chain, and the latter is a nondeterministic finite automata (NFA) with probabilities for outgoing edges (whose sum equals one). Indeed, there are many concepts and algorithms in reinforcement learning, including:

- agent
- environment
- state
- state transitions
- actions (and probabilities)
- discount factor
- discounted future reward
- Markov chains

- MDPs
- on-policy versus off-policy
- model-based versus model-free
- Q-learning
- Bellman's equation
- policy gradient algorithms
- deep reinforcement learning algorithms

You can find plenty of online articles that discuss the topics in the preceding list, along with code samples for deep reinforcement learning algorithms.

What is RecSim?

`RecSim` is an open source platform that is based on reinforcement learning (RL) that creates simulations for collaborative interactive recommenders (CIRs). Recall from the previous section that RL involves an agent, a set of states, and a set of actions associated with each state that enables transitions between states. Moreover, some tasks use the epsilon greedy algorithm to select a state that is passed to the environment ("oracle") that returns a new state, a reward, and a Boolean "done" flag.

By contrast, a `RecSim` agent interacts with an environment that consists of a user model, a document model, and a user choice model. In RecSim, we can represent the state by the content, the action is the next best content, and the user satisfaction represents the reward. Moreover, we can use a vector embedding to represent the content. Without delving into many details, RL enables recommender systems to suggest new recommendations to users that are independent of earlier recommendations.

In fact, those new recommendations can contain random content that might be appealing to them. This approach provides users with opportunities to discover new interests that previously might not have interested them: after all, people's interests can (and do) change over time. Indeed, RL-based models continually learn and evolve as users' interests change.

This concludes the portion of the chapter pertaining to recommender systems. If you are interested in learning about recent trends in recommender systems, navigate to the following link:

https://aws.amazon.com/blogs/media/whats-new-in-recommender-systems/

The next section discusses sentiment analysis, along with a `Python` code sample that uses `NLTK` with sentiment analysis.

What is Sentiment Analysis?

The purpose of sentiment analysis is to determine the attitude of a person regarding a topic, the context of a document, or of a corpus of documents. In each case, sentiment analysis assesses whether or not the input text expresses a positive, negative, or neutral sentiment.

In high-level terms, sentiment analysis involves various steps for processing natural language, followed by training a model. The first stage processes text in a way that, when we are ready to train our model, we already know what variables the model needs to consider as inputs. The model learns how to determine the sentiment of a piece of text based on these variables.

Sentiment analysis can also be a binary classification task involving positive and negative sentiment. Sentiment analysis can be performed in many situations, some of which are listed here:

- the online sentiment for a particular product
- analyzing movie, book, and restaurant reviews
- issues logged at customer support centers

As you learned in Chapter 3, human languages are very flexible in that they enable people to express:

- a mix of positive and negative sentiments
- the use of sarcasm and its nuances
- the use of slang (a negative can mean a positive)

Moreover, language is fundamentally ambiguous because our emotions can convey sarcasm, irony, and plays on words, all of which pose challenges for NLP.

There are two main ways to perform sentiment analysis: a rule-based approach (older and less powerful) and also machine learning techniques.

The rule-based technique is straightforward: it counts the number of positive words and negative words in a document and whichever of these two numbers is larger determines the sentiment of the document.

However, the rule-based approach for sentiment analysis has a drawback: this method focuses on individual words and does not examine any context. More than likely, token-based algorithms will generate a highly negative ranking for sentences such as "The concert last night was the bomb."

The machine learning approach involves a classification model (chosen from various algorithms) that is trained with a labeled dataset of positive, negative, and neutral sentiments. Assign the values 1, -1, and 0 to these three sentiments, or assign a range of values that are in the interval [-1,1]. In the latter case, -1 is the most negative sentiment value and +1 is the most positive sentiment value.

As an exercise, see if you can assign a numeric value to the sentiment of each of the following sentences:

1. "Our plan was not without merit" is similar in meaning to "Our plan has merit."

2. "I like the pizza toppings, but I do not like the crust."

3. "The only thing worse than being talked about, is not being talked about" (Oscar Wilde).

4. "Everything is funny, as long as it's happening to somebody else" (Will Rogers).

5. "When ignorance is bliss, 'tis folly to be wise" (William Shakespeare).

6. "Good judgment is the result of experience and experience the result of bad judgement" (Mark Twain).

Here are some observations about the sentences in the preceding list. Example #1 contains two sentences that have approximately the same interpretation. However, the former sentence is close to a "double negative," which is a more difficult NLP sentiment analysis task. Depending on the Python library that you use, the second sentence is more likely to receive a higher positive sentiment than the first sentence.

In example #2 there is a positive and a negative sentiment: what numeric sentiment value would you assign to the entire sentence? If you compute the average of that +1 (for positive) and -1 (for negative) the result is 0, which suggests a neutral sentiment. Although the overall sentiment could be deemed neutral, the two parts of the sentence are not neutral.

Example #3 might be viewed as a pithy and ironic observation about people, and some might say that to varying degrees it's also somewhat rueful. This sentence expresses a sentiment of the form "B is worse than A," which implies that A is bad without explicitly expressing such an opinion.

Example #4 is an observation that tends to be true but it encompasses positive as well as negative events without the use of any negative words such as "not," "bad," "worse," and so forth.

Example #5 is a famous quote from William Shakespeare that is often misquoted as "ignorance is bliss," and the full quote obviously has a much different meaning. The words "ignorance" and "folly" are two words that express a negative sentiment.

Example #6 sounds paradoxical until you've gained enough experience and wisdom to understand its meaning. The words "good" and "bad" are the only two words that express any sentiment in this sentence. Later in this chapter you will see a Python code sample that performs sentiment analysis on the preceding list of sentences.

Useful Tools for Sentiment Analysis

The following list of sentiment analysis tools provide various features that might be well-suited for your NLP needs:

- IBM Watson Tone Analyzer
- OpenText
- Talkwalker
- Rapidminer
- Social Mention
- Textblob
- Vader

Perform an online search for documentation for these sentiment analysis tools to see which ones are suitable for your tasks.

Aspect-Based Sentiment Analysis

Aspect-based sentiment analysis is a more advanced technique than sentiment analysis: the latter only detects the sentiment of an overall corpus, whereas the former analyzes each text to identify various aspects and the corresponding sentiment for each text.

For example, sentiment analysis might determine that a comment is negative, whereas aspect-based sentiment analysis might determine that a customer is unhappy with the battery life of a specific product. Hence, aspect-based sentiment analysis produces finer-grained analysis of a corpus, which is obviously important when handling text-based customer feedback regarding products and services.

Note that aspect-based sentiment analysis can extract sentiments (i.e., positive or negative opinions about a particular aspect) as well as aspects (the item that is the current focus).

Several libraries provide the algorithmic building blocks of NLP in real-world applications. For instance, Algorithmia provides a free API endpoint for many of these algorithms, without ever having to setup or provision servers and infrastructure.

Another machine learning toolkit is `Apache OpenNLP` that provides tokenizers, sentence segmentation, part-of-speech tagging, named entity extraction, chunking, parsing, and coreference resolution.

Deep Learning and Sentiment Analysis

Deep Learning models such as RNNs and LSTMs can be combined with NLP-based sentiment analysis, such as gauging sentiment in tweets:

https://ieeexplore.ieee.org/stamp/stamp.jsp? arnumber=8244338

You can also combine RNNs with sentiment analysis, as discussed here:

https://blog.openai.com/unsupervised-sentiment-neuron/

https://github.com/openai/generating-reviews- discovering-sentiment

There are several details to keep in mind. First, distributed word vector techniques have been shown to outperform BoW models (as you would probably surmise). Second, the paragraph vector algorithm preserves word order information and produces state-of-the-art results. This algorithm performs better because vector averaging and clustering lose the word order. Third, it's worthwhile to acquaint yourself with the transformer architecture and BERT-based models that are discussed in Chapter 11 before you decide to use RNNs or LSTMs for sentiment analysis.

Sentiment Analysis with Naïve Bayes

Listing 9.3 displays the contents of `nb_sentiment.py` that illustrates how to perform sentiment analysis with NLTK.

LISTING 9.3: nb_sentiment.py

```python
import pandas as pd
import matplotlib.pyplot as plt
import nltk
from nltk.tokenize import RegexpTokenizer

from sklearn import metrics
from sklearn.feature_extraction.text import CountVectorizer
from sklearn.feature_extraction.text import TfidfVectorizer
from sklearn.model_selection import train_test_split
from sklearn.naive_bayes import MultinomialNB

data = pd.read_csv('train.tsv', sep='\t')
print(data.head())

print("=> Data information:")
data.info()
print("------------------------------")
print()

print("=> Sentiment value counts:")
print(data.Sentiment.value_counts())
print("------------------------------")
print()

#find alphanumeric patterns:
token = RegexpTokenizer(r'[a-zA-Z0-9]+')

cv = CountVectorizer(lowercase=True,stop_
words='english',ngram_range = (1,1),
tokenizer = token.tokenize)

phrase_counts = cv.fit_transform(data['Phrase'])

X_train, X_test, y_train, y_test = train_test_split(
  phrase_counts, data['Sentiment'], test_size=0.3,
  random_state=1)

# Multinomial Naive Bayes model:
clf = MultinomialNB().fit(X_train, y_train)
predicted = clf.predict(X_test)
print("=> MultinomialNB Accuracy:",
metrics.accuracy_score(y_test,predicted))
print("------------------------------")
print()

# second part: use tf-idf values
tf = TfidfVectorizer()
text_tf = tf.fit_transform(data['Phrase'])
print("text_tf:")
print(text_tf)
```

```
print("-------------------------------")
print()

X_train, X_test, y_train, y_test = train_test_split(
   text_tf, data['Sentiment'], test_size=0.3, random_state=123)

# Multinomial Naive Bayes model:
clf = MultinomialNB().fit(X_train, y_train)
predicted = clf.predict(X_test)
print("=> MultinomialNB Accuracy:",metrics.accuracy_score
(y_test,predicted))
print("-------------------------------")
```

Listing 9.3 contains two sections of code. The first section reads the contents of the TSV file train.tsv into the dataframe data, and then uses a combination of the classes RegexpTokenizer (performs tokenization based on a regular expression) and CountVectorizer (discussed in Chapter 4) to initialize the variables token and cv, respectively, in order to find alphabetic strings and determine the frequency of those strings. In addition, the training and test datasets are created from the Sentiment column of the data frame data, as shown here:

```
X_train, X_test, y_train, y_test = train_test_split(
  phrase_counts, data['Sentiment'], test_size=0.3, random_state=1)
```

Next, the variable clf is instantiated as an instance of the NaiveBayes classification algorithm. Notice that this code is similar to Listing 8.4 in Chapter 8 after replacing the instance of the DecisionTreeClassifier class with the following code snippet:

```
clf = MultinomialNB().fit(X_train, y_train)
```

The next portion of Listing 9.3 invokes the predict() method to make the predictions on the test-related data.

The next section of Listing 9.3 instantiates the variable tf as an instance of the TfidfVectorizer class, followed by the variable text_tf that is the result of transforming and fitting the data in the Phrase column. Once again, the training and test datasets are created from the Sentiment column of the data frame data, as shown here:

```
X_train, X_test, y_train, y_test = train_test_split(
  phrase_counts, data['Sentiment'], test_size=0.3, random_state=1)
```

The remaining code is a duplicate of the corresponding code in the first section of this code sample. Launch the code in Listing 9.4 and you will see the following output so that you can compare the accuracy of the two sections in Listing 9.3:

```
=> First five rows:
   PhraseId  ...  Sentiment
0         1  ...          1
1         2  ...          2
2         3  ...          2
3         4  ...          2
4         5  ...          2

[5 rows x 4 columns]

=> Data information:
<class 'pandas.core.frame.DataFrame'>
RangeIndex: 156060 entries, 0 to 156059
Data columns (total 4 columns):
PhraseId     156060 non-null int64
SentenceId   156060 non-null int64
Phrase       156060 non-null object
Sentiment    156060 non-null int64
dtypes: int64(3), object(1)
memory usage: 4.8+ MB
------------------------------

=> Sentiment value counts:
2    79582
3    32927
1    27273
4     9206
0     7072
Name: Sentiment, dtype: int64
------------------------------

=> MultinomialNB Accuracy: 0.6049169122986885
------------------------------
text_tf:
  (0, 12857)    0.12785637560254456
  (0, 8807)     0.1353879543646446
  (0, 13681)    0.07615285026452821
  (0, 593)      0.22068902883834374
  (0, 9085)     0.1898515417082945
  (0, 1879)     0.11034437734762885
  (0, 602)      0.26341877863818697
  (0, 9204)     0.19301332592202286
  (0, 14888)    0.28701927784529135
  (0, 12424)    0.1381592967010513
  (0, 5595)     0.265796263188737
```

```
(0, 529)        0.1614381914318891
(0, 5837)       0.22883807138484064
(0, 5323)       0.20344769269023563
(0, 5821)       0.2625302862532789
(0, 7217)       0.17522921677393963
(0, 14871)      0.1354415412970302
(0, 13503)      0.08982508036989033
(0, 288)        0.251134096800077
(0, 13505)      0.17690005957760713
(0, 3490)       0.2485059095620638
(0, 4577)       0.278538658922562
(0, 9227)       0.27061683772839323
(0, 11837)      0.1761994204821687
(1, 5837)       0.3782714454401254
// output omitted for brevity
(156050, 11465)     0.670263619653983
(156050, 625)   0.2115725833396903
(156050, 13505)     0.18632379802617538
(156051, 9193)  0.6987248068627274
(156051, 11465)     0.6822102168950972
(156051, 625)   0.21534359576868978
(156052, 11465)     0.953619269081851
(156052, 625)   0.3010154308931625
(156053, 2313)  0.4917001772764322
(156053, 1027)  0.4917001772764322
(156053, 6245)  0.45540097827929693
(156053, 5328)  0.3853824417825967
(156053, 1313)  0.40068964783307426
(156054, 2313)  0.5366653003868254
(156054, 1027)  0.5366653003868254
(156054, 6245)  0.4970466029897592
(156054, 5328)  0.4206249935248471
(156055, 6245)  1.0
(156056, 2313)  0.618474762808639
(156056, 1027)  0.618474762808639
(156056, 5328)  0.4847452274521073
(156057, 2313)  0.7071067811865476
(156057, 1027)  0.7071067811865476
(156058, 1027)  1.0
(156059, 2313)  1.0
-------------------------------
=> MultinomialNB Accuracy: 0.5865265496176684
-------------------------------
```

Sentiment Analysis in NLTK and VADER

This section contains two `Python` code samples that perform sentiment analysis. Listing 9.4 displays the contents of `vader_sentiment.py` that illustrates how to perform sentiment analysis with `Vader`.

NOTE *Make sure that you invoke the following two commands:*

- pip3 install vader
- pip3 install vaderSentiment

LISTING 9.4: *vader_sentiment.py*

```
# pip3 install vader
# pip3 install vaderSentiment

from vaderSentiment.vaderSentiment import
SentimentIntensityAnalyzer

sia = SentimentIntensityAnalyzer()

sent = "I love Chicago deep dish pizza."
print("=> Sentence:",sent)
word_probs = sia.polarity_scores(sent)
print("=> Sentiment:",str(word_probs))
print()

sent = "I love Chicago deep dish pizza!"
print("=> Sentence:",sent)
word_probs = sia.polarity_scores(sent)
print("=> Sentiment:",str(word_probs))
print()

sent = "I love Chicago deep dish pizza!!!"
print("=> Sentence:",sent)
word_probs = sia.polarity_scores(sent)
print("=> Sentiment:",str(word_probs))
print()
```

Listing 9.4 starts with an `import` statement and then initializes the variable `sia` as an instance of the class `SentimentIntensityAnalyzer` that is available from `vaderSentiment`.

The next three code blocks initialize the variable `sent` as a text string that contains zero, one, and three exclamation points, respectively. In each case, the variable `sent` is supplied to the method `polarity_scores()` to illustrate the effect of the exclamation points on the generated polarity value. Now launch the code in Listing 9.4 and you will see the following output:

```
=> Sentence: I love Chicago deep dish pizza.
=> Sentiment: {'neg': 0.0, 'neu': 0.543, 'pos': 0.457,
               'compound': 0.6369}

=> Sentence: I love Chicago deep dish pizza!
=> Sentiment: {'neg': 0.0, 'neu': 0.527, 'pos': 0.473,
               'compound': 0.6696}

=> Sentence: I love Chicago deep dish pizza!!!
=> Sentiment: {'neg': 0.0, 'neu': 0.496, 'pos': 0.504,
               'compound': 0.7249}
```

Notice how the positive sentiment in the preceding output increases when the number of exclamation points is increased; this makes sense because more exclamation points tends to make a statement or question more emphatic (be it positive or negative).

By comparison, Listing 9.5 displays the contents of the Python script Python script vader_nltk_sentiment.py that uses the SentimentIntensityAnalyzer class from NLTK instead of vaderSentiment to perform sentiment analysis with NLTK.

NOTE *The following code sample downloads a 266MB file (if it is not already available)* sentiment-en-mix-distillbert_3.1.pt *when you execute the code.*

LISTING 9.5: *vader_nltk_sentiment.py*

```
import nltk
#nltk.download('vader_lexicon')

from nltk.sentiment.vader import SentimentIntensityAnalyzer

sia = SentimentIntensityAnalyzer()
sent = "I love Chicago deep dish pizza."
print("=> sentence:",sent)
print(sia.polarity_scores(sent))
print()

sent = "I love Chicago deep dish pizza!"
print("=> sentence:",sent)
```

```
print(sia.polarity_scores(sent))
print()

sent = "I love Chicago deep dish pizza!!!"
print("=> sentence:",sent)
print(sia.polarity_scores(sent))
print()
```

Launch the code in Listing 9.5 and you will see the following output that you can compare with the output from launching Listing 9.5 in the previous section:

```
=> sentence: I love Chicago deep dish pizza.
{'neg': 0.0, 'neu': 0.488, 'pos': 0.512, 'compound': 0.6369}

=> sentence: I love Chicago deep dish pizza!
{'neg': 0.0, 'neu': 0.471, 'pos': 0.529, 'compound': 0.6696}

=> sentence: I love Chicago deep dish pizza!!!
{'neg': 0.0, 'neu': 0.441, 'pos': 0.559, 'compound': 0.7249}
```

Sentiment Analysis with Textblob

`Textblob` is an open source `Python`-based library that performs various NLP-tasks, including sentiment analysis. Specifically, `Textblob` provides a rule-based sentiment analyzer takes a text string as input and then returns two properties, both of which are floating point numbers:

1. *Polarity* is a number in the interval [-1,1], where -1 and +1 indicate negative and positive sentiment, respectively.

2. *Subjectivity* is number in the interval [0,1] that indicates the degree to which a sentence involves personal emotion, judgement, or opinion.

Listing 9.6 displays the contents of the Python script `textblob_sentiment.py` that uses the `Textblob` package to perform sentiment analysis.

LISTING 9.6: textblob_sentiment.py

```
# pip3 install textblob
from textblob import TextBlob

sent = "I love Chicago deep dish pizza."
tb_sent = TextBlob(sent)
print("sentence:",tb_sent)
print(tb_sent.sentiment)
print()
```

```
sent = "I love Chicago deep dish pizza!"
tb_sent = TextBlob(sent)
print("sentence:",tb_sent)
print(tb_sent.sentiment)
print()

sent = "I love Chicago deep dish pizza!!!"
tb_sent = TextBlob(sent)
print("sentence:",tb_sent)
print(tb_sent.sentiment)
print()
```

Listing 9.6 contains three code blocks, analogous to the contents of Listing 9.5, but with the variable `tb_sent` that is an instance of `Textblob`. Now launch the code in Listing 9.6 and compare this output with the output from Listing 9.5 and Listing 9.4:

```
sentence: I love Chicago deep dish pizza.
Sentiment(polarity=0.25, subjectivity=0.5)

sentence: I love Chicago deep dish pizza!
Sentiment(polarity=0.25, subjectivity=0.5)

sentence: I love Chicago deep dish pizza!!!
Sentiment(polarity=0.25, subjectivity=0.5)
```

Notice how the sentiment analysis in the preceding output is unaffected by the number of exclamation points in the input text.

Listing 9.7 displays the contents of `nltk_sentiment.py` that illustrates yet another example of performing sentiment analysis with NLTK.

LISTING 9.7: nltk_sentiment.py

```
import nltk
#nltk.download('vader_lexicon')
from nltk.sentiment.vader import SentimentIntensityAnalyzer
import pandas as pd

sentiment = SentimentIntensityAnalyzer()
sentence = "I love Chicago deep dish pizza."
print("=> sentence:",sentence)
print("=> polarity:",sentiment.polarity_scores(sentence))
print()

sentences = [
  "Our plan was not without merit",
  "I like the pizza toppings but I do not like the crust.",
```

```
    "The only thing worse than being talked about, is not being
talked about",
    "Everything is funny, as long as it's happening to somebody
else.",
    "When ignorance is bliss, 'tis folly to be wise.",
    "Good judgement is the result of experience and experience
the result of bad judgement."
    ]

scores = []
for sent in sentences:
  score = sentiment.polarity_scores(sent)
  scores.append(score)

df = pd.DataFrame(scores)
df['sentence'] = sentences
print("=> dataframe:",df)
print()

df['positive_sentiment'] = df['compound'] >= 0.5
print("=> dataframe:",df)
```

Listing 9.7 starts with two `import` statements and then initializes the variable `sentiment` as an instance of the class `SentimentIntensityAnalyzer` that is available from `nltk.sentiment.vader`.

The next code block initializes the variable `sentence` with a familiar string that you have seen in many code samples, and then displays the polarity of `sentence` by invoking the variable `sentiment` with the contents of `sentence`.

Next, the variable `sentences` is initialized as an array sentences, after which a `for` loop calculates the polarity score for each sentence and populates the array `scores` with those values.

The next portion of Listing 9.7 creates the data frame `df` with the contents of scores, and then appends the column `sentence` that is initialized with the contents of the variable `sentences`.

After displaying the contents of `df`, the final code snippet adds a new column called `positive_sentiment` consisting of the rows in `df` that have a positive sentiment (i.e., their value is at least 0.5) and then prints the new contents of `df`. Launch the code in Listing 9.7 and you will see the following output:

```
=> sentence: I love Chicago deep dish pizza.
=> polarity: {'neg': 0.0, 'neu': 0.488, 'pos': 0.512,
              'compound': 0.6369}
```

```
=> dataframe:        neg    neu   ...  compound  sentence
0    0.000   0.716   ...    0.2466   Our plan was not without merit
1    0.000   0.615   ...    0.6124   I like the pizza toppings but
                                     I do not like th...
2    0.205   0.795   ...   -0.4767   The only thing worse than
                                     being talked about, ...
3    0.000   0.775   ...    0.4404   Everything is funny, as long
as it's happening...
4    0.163   0.392   ...    0.6486   When ignorance is bliss,
                                     'tis folly to be wise.
5    0.190   0.652   ...   -0.1531   Good judgement is the result
                                     of experience and...

[6 rows x 5 columns]

=> dataframe:        neg   ...  positive_sentiment
0    0.000   ...              False
1    0.000   ...              True
2    0.205   ...              False
3    0.000   ...              False
4    0.163   ...              True
5    0.190   ...              False

[6 rows x 6 columns]
```

Sentiment Analysis with Flair

`Flair` is an open source `Python`-based library that performs various NLP-tasks, such as NER and POS tagging, and its home page is here:

https://github.com/flairNLP/flair

In addition to sentiment analysis, `Flair` provides the following functionality:

- a biomedical NER library
- a text embedding library
- a PyTorch NLP framework

The final example of sentiment analysis is Listing 9.8 that displays the contents of the `Python` script `flair_sentiment.py` that uses the `Flair` library to perform sentiment analysis. Make sure that you invoke `pip3 install flair`.

NOTE *You might need to use Python 3.7 instead of Python 3.9.x in order to install flair*

LISTING 9.8: flair_sentiment.py

```
# pip3 install flair

from flair.models import TextClassifier
from flair.data import Sentence

classifier = TextClassifier.load('en-sentiment')

sent = "I love Chicago deep dish pizza."
ssent = Sentence(sent)
classifier.predict(ssent)
print('Sentence:   ', sent)
print('Sentiment: ', ssent.labels)
print()

sent = "I love Chicago deep dish pizza!"
ssent = Sentence(sent)
classifier.predict(ssent)
print('Sentence:   ', sent)
print('Sentiment: ', ssent.labels)
print()

sent = "I love Chicago deep dish pizza!!!"
ssent = Sentence(sent)
classifier.predict(ssent)
print('Sentence:   ', sent)
print('Sentiment: ', ssent.labels)
```

Listing 9.8 starts with two `import` statements and then initializes several variables, starting with the variable `classifier` (which is a model) as an instance of the `TextClassifier` class.

The next three code blocks in the same style as the code in Listing 9.4 whereby the variable `sent` is initialized as three text strings containing zero, one, and three exclamation points, respectively, after which the sentiment of each sentence is calculated via the `predict()` method of the `classifier` variable and then displayed. Now launch the code in Listing 9.8 and you will see the following output:

```
Sentence:    I love Chicago deep dish pizza.
Sentiment:   [POSITIVE (0.999)]

Sentence:    I love Chicago deep dish pizza!
Sentiment:   [POSITIVE (0.9996)]

Sentence:    I love Chicago deep dish pizza!!!
Sentiment:   [POSITIVE (0.9997)]
```

Detecting Spam

Spam classification has been an on-going challenge ever since the introduction of email (or soon thereafter). Spam filters often use a Naïve Bayes classifier (discussed briefly in Chapter 6). However, the nature of spam evolves over time, which means that spam classifiers must also evolve in order to handle new types of spam.

A spam classifier involves the following set of steps that are common to machine learning tasks:

Step 1: a labeled training dataset
Step 2: determining a set of features
Step 3: splitting the dataset into train/validation/test
Step 4: training the classifier
Step 5: performs some predictions on new data

Step 1 involves a good mixture of legitimate email message as well as spam email messages. Step 2 involves the typical tasks that are described in Chapter 3 (such as removing stop words, stemming, and calculating word frequencies). Step 3 requires a decent sized dataset. If your dataset is small, you can split its content into train and test and omit the validation (not the best solution).

Step 4 is a standard step, and you can use k-fold cross validation, which involves dividing the dataset into subsets (such as ten "folds") and then repeating the training on nine of the ten folds, using the omitted fold as the test data. Calculate the average error after completing the cross fold validation. This technique is very handy for small datasets.

The final step involves making predictions and determining the accuracy of those predictions.

Logistic Regression and Sentiment Analysis

Recall that classification problems involve predicting discrete outcomes, whereas regression problems involve predicting a value of a continuous variable. As you learned in a previous chapter logistic regression is actually a classification algorithm (not a regression algorithm). Logistic regression works well when the features and the target have a relatively simple relationship.

The Sklearn `LogisticRegression` class has these arguments: `penalty, dual, tol, C, fit_intercept, intercept_scaling, class_weight,` random_state, solver, max_iter, verbose, warm_start, n_jobs, and l1_ratio.

Listing 9.9 displays the contents of log_reg_spam.py that illustrates how to perform sentiment analysis with NLTK.

LISTING 9.9: log_reg_spam.py

```
import numpy as np
import pandas as pd
from sklearn.feature_extraction.text import TfidfVectorizer

#for sklearn version 0.24.0:
from sklearn.linear_model import LogisticRegression

from sklearn.model_selection import train_test_split, cross_val_score

# you can download the SMSSpamCollection dataset here:
# https://archive.ics.uci.edu/ml/machine-learning-databases/00228
# NB: header "type\ttext" was manually added to
# SMSSpamCollection
df = pd.read_csv('SMSSpamCollection', delimiter='\t')

print("First five rows (before):")
print(df.head(5))
print("------------------------")

# map ham/spam to 0/1 values:
df['type'] = df['type'].map( {'ham':0 , 'spam':1} )

print("First five rows (after):")
print(df.head(5))
print("------------------------")

# X contains text and y contains labels:
X = df.iloc[:, 1].values
y = df.iloc[:, 0].values

# perform train/test split on the data (75/25):
X_train, X_test, y_train, y_test = train_test_split(X, y, test_size = 0.25, random_state = 0)
#print("X_train:",X_train)
#print("------------------------")

vectorizer = TfidfVectorizer()
X_train = vectorizer.fit_transform(X_train)
X_test  = vectorizer.transform(X_test)
```

```
# train an instance of the LogisticRegression class:
classifier = LogisticRegression()
classifier.fit(X_train, y_train)

# make predictions for the y_test data:
y_pred = classifier.predict(y_test)
print("predictions:",y_pred)
print("-------------------------")

# create the confusion matrix:
from sklearn.metrics import confusion_matrix
cm = confusion_matrix(y_test, y_pred)
print("confusion matrix:")
print(cm)

true_neg, false_pos = cm[0]
false_neg, true_pos = cm[1]
all_values = true_pos + true_neg + false_pos + false_neg

accuracy  = round((true_pos + true_neg) / all_values, 3)
precision = round((true_pos) / (true_pos + false_pos),3)
recall    = round((true_pos) / (true_pos + false_neg),3)
f1        = round(2 * (precision*recall) / (precision+recall),3)

print("-------------------------\n")
print('Accuracy:   {}'.format(accuracy))
print('Precision:  {}'.format(precision))
print('Recall:     {}'.format(recall))
print('F1 Score:   {}'.format(f1))
```

Listing 9.9 is similar to the logistic regression code sample in Chapter 8, using `sklearn` instead of `Keras`-based code. Specifically, the main difference involves the following code block instead of a `Keras`-based model from TensorFlow:

```
# train an instance of the LogisticRegression class:
classifier = LogisticRegression()
classifier.fit(X_train, y_train)
```

Launch the code in Listing 9.9 and you will see the following output:

```
=> First five rows (before):
    type                                               text
0   ham  Go until jurong point, crazy.. Available only ...
1   ham                      Ok lar... Joking wif u oni...
2  spam  Free entry in 2 a wkly comp to win FA Cup fina...
3   ham  U dun say so early hor... U c already then say...
4   ham  Nah I don't think he goes to usf, he lives aro...
------------------------
```

```
=> First five rows (after):
   type                                                    text
0     0  Go until jurong point, crazy.. Available only ...
1     0                      Ok lar... Joking wif u oni...
2     1  Free entry in 2 a wkly comp to win FA Cup fina...
3     0  U dun say so early hor... U c already then say...
4     0  Nah I don't think he goes to usf, he lives aro...
------------------------

=> predictions: [0 1 0 ... 0 0 0]

------------------------

=> confusion matrix:
[[1198    2]
 [  48  145]]

------------------------

Accuracy:  0.964
Precision: 0.986
Recall:    0.751
F1 Score:  0.853
```

Working with COVID-19

Listing 9.10 displays the contents of covid19.py that illustrates how to train a model on a Covid19 dataset.

LISTING 9.10: covid19.py

```
import numpy as np
import pandas as pd
from sklearn.ensemble import RandomForestClassifier
import matplotlib.pyplot as plt
import seaborn as sns

df = pd.read_csv("clean_covid19.csv", sep=",")

X = df.iloc[:, [0, 1, 2, 3]].values
y = df.iloc[:, 4].values
y = y.astype('int')

print("Number of rows and columns in dataset:")
print(df.shape)

# count the number of 0 and 1 values for y:
print(df.groupby('severity_illness').count())

# the count of y values: 8 and 3351
# the dataset is highly imbalanced
```

```
# balance the target data via SMOTE:
from collections import Counter
from imblearn.over_sampling import SMOTE

sm = SMOTE(random_state=42)
X, y = sm.fit_resample(X, y)

# split into training and test sets:
from sklearn.model_selection import train_test_split
X_train, X_test, y_train, y_test = train_test_split(X, y,
test_size = 0.25, random_state = 0)

# Feature Scaling
from sklearn.preprocessing import StandardScaler
sc = StandardScaler()
X_train = sc.fit_transform(X_train)
X_test = sc.transform(X_test)

# libraries for performance metrics:
from sklearn.metrics import make_scorer
from sklearn.metrics import accuracy_score
from sklearn.metrics import precision_score
from sklearn.metrics import recall_score
from sklearn.metrics import f1_score
from sklearn.model_selection import cross_validate

# dictionary with performance metrics:
scoring = {'accuracy':make_scorer(accuracy_score),
           'precision':make_scorer(precision_score),
           'recall':make_scorer(recall_score),
           'f1_score':make_scorer(f1_score)}

# instantiate classifier:
rfc_model = RandomForestClassifier()

# train model via cross-validation:
folds=10
rfc = cross_validate(rfc_model, X, y, cv=folds,
scoring=scoring)

print("accuracy: ",rfc['test_accuracy'].mean())
print("precision:",rfc['test_precision'].mean())
print("recall:   :",rfc['test_recall'].mean())
print("F1 score: ",rfc['test_f1_score'].mean())
```

Listing 9.10 is similar to Listing 8.4 in Chapter 8, albeit modified to use the following code block instead of a `DecisionTreeClassifier`:

from sklearn.ensemble import RandomForestClassifier

classifier = RandomForestClassifier(n_estimators = 10, criterion='entropy', random_state = 0)

In addition, notice that Listing 9.10 uses the `SMOTE` class in order to generate synthetic data because the `Covid19` dataset is highly imbalanced. Launch the code in Listing 9.10 and you will see the following output (truncated for ease of reading):

```
Number of rows and columns in dataset:
(3359, 5)

age    ...   severity_illness
0                            8
1                         3351

accuracy:   0.993136552705919
precision:  0.9920161922823759
recall:   : 0.9943283582089553
F1 score:   0.9931523221120553
```

What are Chatbots?

Chatbots are so ubiquitous that they touch many parts of our lives. In case you have not encountered chatbots, they have evolved into AI-based software programs that interact with users and attempt to provide them with satisfactory answers. Chatbots are available on devices (Siri, Alexa, Google Assistant, and so forth) and also in Websites. Chatbots can provide question-answer functionality or they provide task-oriented functionality, such as performing bookings for cars, airplanes, and hotels.

By today's standards, early chatbots had a rudimentary question–answer structure that tended to resemble flow charts. The response to a question was selected from a set of hard-coded answers, and if the answer did not satisfy the users, then the question was often routed to a human. Since chatbots vary in terms of quality and features, a metric called sensibleness and specificity average (SSA) was developed in order to rate chatbots.

Companies use chatbots to reduce the human-based interaction with customers with the goal of streamlining customers' interaction with a company's services. Some chatbot-based services include:

- providing product-related customer support
- providing flight information
- connecting customers and their finances

Open Domain Chatbots

There are several interesting open domain chatbots available, some of which are shown in the following list:

- Cleverbot
- DialoGPT
- Meena
- Mitsuku
- XiaoIce

Meena is optimized for multiturn conversation that scores well on the new metric (described earlier). Meena is a sequence-to-sequence model with an evolved transformer architecture that comprises 2.6 billion parameters. Meena predicts the actual response via perplexity (the latter is discussed in Appendix A): a measure of a language model's predictive ability perplexity is used as its loss function. Meena avoid generating repetitive responses: the model builds multiple candidate responses and uses a classifier to select the best one.

Perform an online search for information pertaining to the other open domain chatbots in the preceding list.

Chatbot Types

Chatbots can be classified into two main groups, which consists of *rule-based* chatbots and *self-learning* chatbots.

Rule-based chatbots are trained on rules that are also used in order to provide answers to questions. However, these chatbots work best for simple questions, and are less accurate for sophisticated questions.

By contrast, self-learning chatbots are trained via machine learning-based approaches and as you might expect, these chatbots provide better results. Moreover, self-learning chatbots can be divided into two broad categories that are called *retrieval-based* chatbots (which rely on heuristics to provide answers) and *generative* chatbots (which can generate answers beyond just predefined answers).

Logic Flow of Chatbots

Although chatbots can vary significantly in terms of their primary functionality, chatbots generally perform the following sequence of steps:

1. Prepare a corpus of text-based responses.
2. Clean the data (as described in earlier chapters).
3. Select a vectorizer (such as `CountVectorizer` or `TfidfVectorizer`).
4. Prompt users for a question/query.
5. Calculate the cosine similarity of the question with the sentences in the corpus.
6. Determine which sentence has the highest cosine similarity.
7. Use the previously selected sentence as a response to users.

As you can see, you already know how to perform all the steps in the preceding pseudo-code.

In case the highest cosine similarity is close to zero, then there is no meaningful response for the query, in which case you can route the users to a human agent. Of course, the threshold value for "close to zero" is a number that you decide in advance, and perhaps it can be determined through experimentation.

Chatbot Abuses

There have been some well-known cases of attempts to crowd-source the training of chatbots that have gone awry. One such chatbot is `Tay` from Microsoft, which some users trained to make various types of highly inappropriate remarks about certain groups of people.

Another (more recent) example is the chatbot `Lee Luda` from Korea, which was designed to emulate a Korean university student. However, this chatbot was removed from Facebook because some users trained the chatbot to make derogatory slurs and hate speech that were directed toward certain groups of people.

Unfortunately, chatbots are likely to encounter these sorts of issues when the enhancement of a chatbot's capabilities involve crowd-sourced contributions.

Useful Links

The definition of "useful" and "interesting" obviously varies among people, and you can peruse top-ten lists, which do not provide the breadth and diversity of existing chatbots. If you are unfamiliar with chatbots, navigate to the following link that has thousands of registered chatbots (sort of like a "play store" for chatbots):

https://botlist.co

Regarding specific chatbots: Microsoft developed and open-sourced `BlenderBot`, which at its peak was the largest state-of-the-art chatbot, which is available here:

https://ai.facebook.com/blog/state-of-the-art-open-source-chatbot/

`BlenderBot` was benchmarked (and is significantly better) against Google's `Meena` chatbot, and the latter is available here:

https://github.com/google-research/google-research/tree/master/meena

If you are interested in chatbots in the health-care field, here are two useful links:

https://topflightapps.com/ideas/chatbots-in-healthcare

https://emerj.com/ai-application-comparisons/chatbots-for-healthcare-comparison

If you plan to create a chatbot that is useful, then it probably needs to understand (human) natural language, and also solve a task that might require multiple steps.

Although there are online tools that enable you to create chatbots that connect to an AI backend system (such as IBM Watson), the following link explains how to build a chatbot in `Keras`:

https://www.kdnuggets.com/2019/08/deep-learning-nlp-creating-chatbot-keras.html

https://analyticsindiamag.com/how-does-a-simple-chatbot-with-nltk-work/

The following link shows you how to create a chatbot based on a pretrained transformers (discussed in Chapter 11) with PyTorch:

https://towardsdatascience.com/conversational-ai-chatbot-with-pretrained-transformers-using-pytorch-55b5e8882fd3

Finally, the following list of top chatbots of 2021 might provide ideas and helpful insights: *https://www.netomi.com/best-ai-chatbot*

Summary

This chapter started with a description of two types of text recommendation, along with some code samples using `gensim` and `spaCy`. Then you got a high-level description of recommendation systems, which is are used in online reviews of books, movies, restaurants, and so forth. Next, you learned about sentiment analysis, which is actually a subset of text classification. In essence, sentiment analysis attempts to assess the mood (positive, negative, or neutral) of a document (such as a review). Finally, you saw a `Python`-based code sample that uses logistic regression to predict spam email messages.

CHAPTER 10

NLP AND *TF2/KERAS*

This chapter contains machine learning `Python` code samples that involve `TF2/Keras`. The `NLP` concepts in the code samples were introduced in Chapter 3, and also written in various `NLP` toolkits that are discussed in Chapter 5 and Chapter 6.

The first section contains TensorFlow-based code samples that perform tokenization, encoding and word embeddings. The second section contains a Python code sample that uses the `kNN` machine learning algorithm to predict the category of a set of sentences, where the categories are a subset of a well-known set of 20 categories. This section also shows you how to modify the kNN-based code sample so that you can perform the same task using decision trees, random forests, SVC, and naïve Bayes. These code samples illustrated the fact that the accuracy can vary substantially among algorithms.

The third section contains several TensorFlow code samples for performing some NLP-related tasks. The last code sample in this chapter is an example of a Keras-based neural network that performed text summarization on the Reuters dataset.

One more thing to keep in mind: this chapter does not provide explanations of Tensorflow concepts. If you are unfamiliar with Tensorflow, please read Appendix E, Introduction to TensorFlow 2, so that you will be better prepared for the code samples in this chapter.

> **NOTE**
>
> 1. *As this book goes to print,* `Python` *3.7 works with the TF 2 code in this book, whereas Python 3.9.x does not work with TF 2.*
>
> 2. *For the* `Python` *file* `tf2_basic_nlp.py` *you need to run this command:*
>   `install tensorflow-text # <= note the "-" instead of "_"`

Term-Document Matrix

Suppose that `V` is a vocabulary of words and `D` is a set of documents. A *term-document matrix* for `D` and `V` is a `[|V|,|D|]` matrix (not the other way around) that contains |V| × |D| elements.

The cell in position `(i,j)` in D pertains to the ith word `vi` and the jth document `dj`. The value in cell `(i,j)` equals the number of occurrences of word `vi` in document `dj` (i.e., the term frequency). Each column in this matrix gives a vector of dimension |V| that represents a document. This matrix is a `BoW` representation of documents, except that `V` does not contain all words from the documents in `D`. In addition to specifying the number of occurrences of a word in cells, you can also use `tf-idf` values in the cells of this matrix, as well as other weighted scores.

The transpose of a term-document matrix is called a *document-term matrix*, which is a special case of a *document-feature matrix*, where a feature can be a property other than terms in documents. Check the `gensim` documentation for a description of efficient algorithms that construct term-document matrices.

Text Classification Algorithms in Machine Learning

There are many text classification algorithms available, some of which are listed here:

- kMeans (clustering algorithm)
- Multinomial naive Bayes (multiclass classification)
- Logistic regression (`sklearn` supports multilabel)
- SVMs (support vector machines)
- Random forests (ensemble method)
- GBM (gradient boosting machine [ensemble method])

Chapter 8 describes most of the algorithms in the preceding list, along with some code samples involving non-NLP datasets such as housing.csv and partial_wine.csv. In this chapter, you will see code samples that involve some of the algorithms in the preceding list in order to perform NLP-related tasks.

A Keras-Based Tokenizer

Listing 10.1 displays the contents of keras_tokenizer.py that shows you how to perform tokenization using Keras.

LISTING 10.1: keras_tokenizer.py

```
import tensorflow as tf
import numpy as np

# define documents
docs = ['Fantastic work this week!',
        'That was a really good job',
        'Jolly good work',
        'Super job in your work',
        'Awesome performance!',
        'Unsatisfactory job',
        'Mediocre results on this task',
        'This is not up to our standards',
        'This type of poor work looks bad',
        'Next time try to do a better job.']

# define class labels
labels = np.array([1,1,1,1,1,0,0,0,0,0])

# prepare tokenizer
t = tf.keras.preprocessing.text.Tokenizer()
t.fit_on_texts(docs)
vocab_size = len(t.word_index) + 1
print("vocab_size:",vocab_size)
print()

# integer encode the documents
encoded_docs = t.texts_to_sequences(docs)
print("encoded_docs:")
print(encoded_docs)
print()

# pad documents to a max length of 4 words
max_length = 4
padded_docs = tf.keras.preprocessing.sequence.pad_
sequences(encoded_docs, maxlen=max_length, padding='post')
```

```
print("padded_docs:")
print(padded_docs)
```

Listing 10.1 starts with `import` statements for `TensorFlow` and `NumPy`, followed by initializing the variable `docs` as an array of short strings that we will treat as documents in this code sample. Next, the variable `labels` is a `NumPy` array of 10 integers. The first five values are 1, followed by five 0s, which are the labels associated with the documents in the `docs` variable.

The next portion of Listing 10.1 initializes the variable `t` as an instance of the `Tokenizer` class in `TensorFlow`, after which the `fit_on_texts()` method is invoked in order to train the variable `t` on the `docs` dataset.

The next code block encodes the documents via the `texts_to_sequences()` method, which associates an integer-valued array of numbers for each document. The final code block in Listing 10.1 pads the shorter documents so that they have length 4, but does not perform any padding on documents that are exactly of length 4. Launch the code in Listing 10.1 and you will see the following output:

```
vocab_size: 38

encoded_docs:
[[7, 1, 2, 8], [9, 10, 4, 11, 5, 3], [12, 5, 1], [13, 3, 14, 15, 1], [16, 17], [18, 3], [19, 20, 21, 2, 22], [2, 23, 24, 25, 6, 26, 27], [2, 28, 29, 30, 1, 31, 32], [33, 34, 35, 6, 36, 4, 37, 3]]

padded_docs:
[[ 7  1  2  8]
 [ 4 11  5  3]
 [12  5  1  0]
 [ 3 14 15  1]
 [16 17  0  0]
 [18  3  0  0]
 [20 21  2 22]
 [25  6 26 27]
 [30  1 31 32]
 [36  4 37  3]]
```

Notice that each element in `encoded_docs` is the initial portion of the corresponding array of values in the padded documents, which have been padded with the value 0. The number of non-zero entries equals the number of tokens in each document. For example, the array [18, 3] is padded to become [18, 3, 0, 0], and [16, 17] is padded to become [16, 17, 0, 0].

TF2 and Tokenization

Listing 10.2 displays the contents of tf2_tokenization.py that shows you how to perform tokenization using TF2.

LISTING 10.2: *tf2_tokenization.py*

```
import tensorflow as tf
import tensorflow_text as text

sents = [["When ignorance is bliss."],
         ["Tis folly to be wise!"],
         ["According to the famous Bard."],]

docs = tf.data.Dataset.from_tensor_slices(sents)

tokenizer = text.WhitespaceTokenizer()
tokenized_docs = docs.map(lambda x: tokenizer.tokenize(x))

iterator = iter(tokenized_docs)
print(next(iterator).to_list())
print(next(iterator).to_list())
print()

tokenizer = text.WhitespaceTokenizer()
tokens = tokenizer.tokenize(sents)

print("tokens:")
print(tokens)
print()

print("Capitalized tokens:")
w1 = text.wordshape(tokens, text.WordShape.HAS_TITLE_CASE)
print(w1.to_list())
print()

print("Uppercase tokens:")
w2 = text.wordshape(tokens, text.WordShape.IS_UPPERCASE)
print(w2.to_list())
print()

print("tokens with punctuation:")
w3 = text.wordshape(tokens, text.WordShape.HAS_SOME_PUNCT_OR_SYMBOL)
print(w3.to_list())
print()

print("Numeric tokens:")
w4 = text.wordshape(tokens, text.WordShape.IS_NUMERIC_VALUE)
print(w4.to_list())
```

```
print()

tokenizer = text.WhitespaceTokenizer()
tokens = tokenizer.tokenize(sents)

bigrams = text.ngrams(tokens, 2, reduction_type=text.
Reduction.STRING_JOIN)
print("bigrams:")
print(bigrams.to_list())
print()
```

Listing 10.2 starts with `import` statements for `TensorFlow` and then initializes the variable `sents` as an array of short strings that we will treat as documents in this code sample. The next code snippet initializes the variable `docs` as a `TensorFlow` dataset, which is discussed in Appendix E.

The next portion of Listing 10.2 initializes the variables `tokenizer` as an instance of the `WhitespaceTokenizer` class, followed by the variable `tokens` that contains the tokens (words) in the `sents` array. The next significant portion of Listing 10.2 contains four code blocks that invoke the `wordshape()` method of the variable `text`. The variable `tokens` is the first value that is passed to the `wordshape()` method, followed by a term that specifies the type of tokens to successfully match.

For example, the following code snippet searches for all strings in the `tokens` variable that have uppercase letters, as shown here:

```
w1 = text.wordshape(tokens, text.WordShape.HAS_TITLE_CASE)
```

The final code block in Listing 10.2 finds the bigrams for the sentences in the variable `sent`. Launch the code in Listing 10.2 and you will see the following output:

```
[[b'When', b'ignorance', b'is', b'bliss.']]
[[b'Tis', b'folly', b'to', b'be', b'wise!']]

tokens: <tf.RaggedTensor [[[b'When', b'ignorance', b'is',
b'bliss.']], [[b'Tis', b'folly', b'to', b'be', b'wise!']],
[[b'According', b'to', b'the', b'famous', b'Bard.']]]>

Capitalized tokens: [[[True, False, False, False]], [[True,
False, False, False, False]], [[True, False, False, False,
True]]]

Uppercase tokens: [[[False, False, False, False]], [[False,
False, False, False, False]], [[False, False, False, False,
False]]]
```

```
tokens with punctuation: [[[False, False, False, True]], 
[[False, False, False, False, True]], [[False, False, False, 
False, True]]]

Numeric tokens: [[[False, False, False, False]], [[False, 
False, False, False, False]], [[False, False, False, False, 
False]]]

bigrams: [[[b'When ignorance', b'ignorance is', b'is 
bliss.']], [[b'Tis folly', b'folly to', b'to be', b'be 
wise!']], [[b'According to', b'to the', b'the famous', 
b'famous Bard.']]]
```

TF2 and Encoding

Listing 10.3 displays the contents of tf2_encoding.py that shows you how to perform encoding using TF2.

LISTING 10.3: tf2_encoding.py

```
import tensorflow as tf

train_data = [
  "I love deep dish pizza.",
  "I also eat vegetarian food.",
  "I enjoy garlic every day.",
  "I will get coffee later."
]

test_data = [
  "Enjoy coffee this morning.",
  "Long walks on the beach.",
  "Please add cream to my tea."
]

num_words = 1000
oov_token = '<UNK>'
pad_type = 'post'
trunc_type = 'post'

# Tokenize our training data
tokenizer = tf.keras.preprocessing.text.Tokenizer(num_
words=num_words, oov_token=oov_token)
tokenizer.fit_on_texts(train_data)

# Get our training data word index
word_index = tokenizer.word_index
```

```
# Encode training data sentences into sequences
train_sequences = tokenizer.texts_to_sequences(train_data)

# Get max training sequence length
maxlen = max([len(x) for x in train_sequences])

# Pad the training sequences
train_padded = tf.keras.preprocessing.sequence.pad_
sequences(train_sequences, padding=pad_type, truncating=trunc_
type, maxlen=maxlen)

# Output the results of our work
print("Word index:", word_index)
print()
print("Training sequences:\n", train_sequences)
print()
print("Padded training sequences:\n", train_padded)
print()
print("Padded training shape:", train_padded.shape)
print()
print("Training sequences data type:", type(train_sequences))
print()
print("Padded Training sequences data type:",
        type(train_padded))
```

Listing 10.3 starts with an `import` statement and then initializes the variables `train_data` and `test_data` with a set of short documents. The next code block initializes a set of scalar variables, as shown here:

```
num_words = 1000
oov_token = '<UNK>'
pad_type = 'post'
trunc_type = 'post'
```

The preceding variables specify the maximum length of a sentence (1000), the string <UNK> as the out of vocabulary (OOV) token, and also to perform padding and truncation on the right ("post") of documents.

The next portion of Listing 10.3 initializes the variable `tokenizer` as an instance of the `Tokenizer` class, which then invokes the `fit_on_texts()` method of the `tokenizer` variable in order to train on the training data.

Next, the variable `word_index` is initialized as a set of pairs consisting of a token and its numeric value, as shown here:

```
 {'<UNK>': 1, 'i': 2, 'love': 3, 'deep': 4, 'dish': 5,
'pizza': 6, 'also': 7, 'eat': 8, 'vegetarian': 9, 'food':
10, 'enjoy': 11, 'garlic': 12, 'every': 13, 'day': 14,
'will': 15, 'get': 16, 'coffee': 17, 'later': 18}
```

Now the variable `train_sequence` is initialized by replacing each word in the variable `train_data` by its corresponding index, which is available in the `word_index` variable. Next, a loop iterates through the sentences in `train_data` in order to determine the maximum sentence length and assign that value to the variable `max_len`.

One final initialization: the Keras method `pad_sequences()` that pads the sentences in `train_sequences` so that they all have length `max_len`, and assigns the result to the variable `train_padded`.

Finally, a set of `print()` statements displays the values of all the variables that have been described in the previous paragraphs. Launch the code in Listing 10.3 and you will see the following output:

```
Word index:
{'<UNK>': 1, 'i': 2, 'love': 3, 'deep': 4, 'dish': 5, 'pizza':
6, 'also': 7, 'eat': 8, 'vegetarian': 9, 'food': 10, 'enjoy':
11, 'garlic': 12, 'every': 13, 'day': 14, 'will': 15, 'get':
16, 'coffee': 17, 'later': 18}

Training sequences:
[[2, 3, 4, 5, 6], [2, 7, 8, 9, 10], [2, 11, 12, 13, 14],
[2, 15, 16, 17, 18]]

Padded training sequences:
 [[ 2  3  4  5  6]
  [ 2  7  8  9 10]
  [ 2 11 12 13 14]
  [ 2 15 16 17 18]]

Padded training shape: (4, 5)
Training sequences data type: <class 'list'>
Padded Training sequences data type: <class 'numpy.ndarray'>
```

A Keras-Based Word Embedding

Listing 10.4 displays the contents of `keras_word_embed.py` that shows you how to perform word embeddings using a Keras-based neural network.

LISTING 10.4: keras_word_embed.py

```
import tensorflow as tf
from numpy import array

# define documents
```

```
docs = ['Fantastic work this week!',
        'That was a really good job',
        'Jolly good work',
        'Super job in your work',
        'Awesome performance!',
        'Unsatisfactory job',
        'Mediocre results on this task',
        'This is not up to our standards',
        'This type of poor work looks bad',
        'Next time try to do a better job.']

# define class labels
labels = array([1,1,1,1,1,0,0,0,0,0])

# integer encode the documents
vocab_size = 50
encoded_docs = [tf.keras.preprocessing.text.one_hot(d, vocab_
                size) for d in docs]
print("encoded_docs:",encoded_docs)
print()

# pad documents to a max length of 4 words
max_length = 4
padded_docs = tf.keras.preprocessing.sequence.pad_
sequences(encoded_docs, maxlen=max_length, padding='post')
print("padded_docs:",padded_docs)
print()

# define the model
model = tf.keras.models.Sequential()
model.add(tf.keras.layers.Embedding(vocab_size, 8, input_
length=max_length))
model.add(tf.keras.layers.Flatten())
model.add(tf.keras.layers.Dense(1, activation='sigmoid'))

# compile the model
model.compile(optimizer='adam', loss='binary_crossentropy',
metrics=['acc'])

# summarize the model
print(model.summary())

# fit the model
model.fit(padded_docs, labels, epochs=50, verbose=0)

# evaluate the model
loss, accuracy = model.evaluate(padded_docs, labels,
verbose=0)
print('Accuracy: %f' % (accuracy*100))
```

The first part of Listing 10.4 starts with the same code as Listing 10.1, up to and including the `labels` variable. Next, the variable `encoded_docs` is initialized as a one-hot encoding of the documents in `docs`, where each encoding has length `vocab_size` that was initialized with the value 50.

The next code snippet pads the elements of `padded_docs` so that they all have length 4. Note that the padding operation occurs on the right with the value 0, which appears in all but the last document.

At this point we create a shallow `Keras`-based neural network that starts with an `Embed` layer, which is a `Keras` class that creates word vectors from tokens. The next layer involves the `tf.keras.layers.flatten()` that reshapes its input in order to reduce the dimensionality. For example, if the input to `flatten()` has shape `(batch_size,3,4)`, then the flatten() method returns an output with shape `(batch_size, 12)`.

The final layer in the model is the output layer, which is fully connected from the middle layer to a single output neuron. If you are unfamiliar with `Keras`, please read the material in Appendix D, Introduction to Keras.

Next, the `compile()` method of the model is invoked to compile the model, followed by the `fit()` method that trains the model on the training dataset. The final code snippet invokes the `evaluate()` method of the `model` variable in order to determine the accuracy of our model, as shown here:

```
# evaluate the model
loss, accuracy = model.evaluate(padded_docs, labels,
verbose=0)
```

Launch the code in Listing 10.4 and you will see the following output:

```
encoded_docs: [[41, 7, 14, 14], [7, 49, 45, 27, 1, 6], [21,
1, 7], [16, 6, 49, 38, 7], [38, 14], [26, 6], [9, 39, 18, 14,
13], [14, 25, 36, 29, 32, 39, 28], [14, 23, 13, 35, 7, 6, 13],
[46, 45, 15, 32, 31, 45, 31, 6]]

padded_docs: [[41  7 14 14]
 [45 27  1  6]
 [21  1  7  0]
 [ 6 49 38  7]
 [38 14  0  0]
 [26  6  0  0]
 [39 18 14 13]
 [29 32 39 28]
 [35  7  6 13]
 [31 45 31  6]]
```

```
Model: "sequential"
_____
Layer (type)                 Output Shape              Param #
=================================================================
embedding (Embedding)        (None, 4, 8)              400
_____
flatten (Flatten)            (None, 32)                0
_____
dense (Dense)                (None, 1)                 33
=================================================================
Total params: 433
Trainable params: 433
Non-trainable params: 0
_____
None
Accuracy: 100.000000
```

An Example of BoW with TF2

You have already seen code samples that use BoW, which is a very straightforward technique. Listing 10.5 displays the contents of tf2_simple_bow.py that shows you how to use BoW using TF2/Keras.

LISTING 10.5: tf2_simple_bow.py

```
import tensorflow as tf

docs = [
  'the city weather is hot',
  'the SF weather is hot and the LA weather is hotter',
  'hotter city weather last week',
  'weather next week hot and hotter',
]

# create a vocabulary:
tokenizer = tf.keras.preprocessing.text.Tokenizer()
tokenizer.fit_on_texts(docs)
print(f'Vocabulary: {list(tokenizer.word_index.keys())}')
print()

# count word occurrences:
vectors = tokenizer.texts_to_matrix(docs, mode='count')
print("Sentences as vectors:")
print(vectors)
```

Listing 10.5 initializes the variable docs as an array of documents, followed by some familiar code to initialize the variable tokenizer, and then the fit_on_texts() method is invoked to train on the docs variable.

The next `print()` statement displays the unique tokens in the vocabulary, followed by the variable `vectors` that is initialized with the result of converting the documents in the `docs` variable to an array via the `texts_to_matrix()` method. Launch the code in Listing 10.5 and you will see the following output:

```
Vocabulary: ['weather', 'the', 'is', 'hot', 'hotter', 'city',
'and', 'week', 'sf', 'la', 'last', 'next']

Sentences as vectors:
[[0. 1. 1. 1. 1. 0. 1. 0. 0. 0. 0. 0. 0.]
 [0. 2. 2. 2. 1. 1. 0. 1. 0. 1. 1. 0. 0.]
 [0. 1. 0. 0. 0. 1. 1. 0. 1. 0. 0. 1. 0.]
 [0. 1. 0. 0. 1. 1. 0. 1. 1. 0. 0. 0. 1.]]
```

The 20newsgroup Dataset

The `20newsgroups` dataset consists of approximately 18000 posts that are classified into 20 topics, each of which contains two subsets: one for training (or development) and the other one for testing (or for performance evaluation). The split between the train and test set is based upon a messages posted before and after a specific date.

The `sklearn.datasets.fetch_20newsgroups` function is a data fetching / caching function that downloads the data archive from the original 20 newsgroups website, extracts the archive contents and places them into the folder named `~/scikit_learn_data/20news_home` and calls the `sklearn.datasets.load_files` on either the training or testing set folder, or both of them.

Listing 10.6 displays the contents of `show_newsgroups.py` that shows you how to display all the newsgroups.

LISTING 10.6: knn_nlp_classify.py

```
from sklearn.datasets import fetch_20newsgroups
newsgroups_train = fetch_20newsgroups(subset='train')
from pprint import pprint

pprint(list(newsgroups_train.target_names))
```

Listing 10.6 is straightforward: the class `fetch_20newsgroups` is imported in order to load the names and the data in the 20 newsgroups, and assign the result to the variable `newsgroups_train`. The `pprint()` statement then displays the names of the 20 newsgroups. Launch the code in Listing 10.6 and you will see the following output:

```
['alt.atheism',
 'comp.graphics',
 'comp.os.ms-windows.misc',
 'comp.sys.ibm.pc.hardware',
 'comp.sys.mac.hardware',
 'comp.windows.x',
 'misc.forsale',
 'rec.autos',
 'rec.motorcycles',
 'rec.sport.baseball',
 'rec.sport.hockey',
 'sci.crypt',
 'sci.electronics',
 'sci.med',
 'sci.space',
 'soc.religion.christian',
 'talk.politics.guns',
 'talk.politics.mideast',
 'talk.politics.misc',
 'talk.religion.misc']
```

The code sample in the next section specifies some of the categories in the preceding list, along with the kNN machine learning algorithm to predict the category of a set of sentences.

Text Classification with the kNN Algorithm

Listing 10.7 displays the contents of knn_nlp_classify.py that illustrates how to perform text classification with the kNN algorithm.

LISTING 10.7: knn_nlp_classify.py

```
from sklearn.datasets import fetch_20newsgroups
from sklearn.feature_extraction.text import CountVectorizer
from sklearn.feature_extraction.text import TfidfTransformer
from sklearn.neighbors import KNeighborsClassifier
from sklearn.pipeline import Pipeline

# https://scikit-learn.org/0.19/datasets/twenty_newsgroups.html
my_cats = ['rec.sport.hockey', 'comp.sys.mac.hardware']
```

```
# load training/testing data from sklearn:
train_data = fetch_20newsgroups(subset='train',
            categories=my_cats, shuffle=True, random_state=42)

print("target_names:")
print(train_data.target_names)
print("------------------------\n")
print("\n".join(train_data.data[0].split("\n")[:3]))
print("------------------------\n")

print("First element of train_data target:")
print(train_data.target_names[train_data.target[0]])

# Initial training data points and their categories:
for t in train_data.target[:5]:
  print("target_name:",train_data.target_names[t])
print("------------------------\n")

#############################################
# 1) create a dictionary of features
# 2) transform documents to feature vectors
# 3) convert text documents to a matrix of
#    token counts (CountVectorizer)
#############################################
count_vect = CountVectorizer()
X_train_counts = count_vect.fit_transform(train_data.data)

# count matrix => normalized tf-idf representation:
tfidf_transformer = TfidfTransformer()
X_train_tfidf = tfidf_transformer.fit_transform(X_train_
counts)

# an instance of the sklearn KNN class:
n_neighbors = 9
knn = KNeighborsClassifier(n_neighbors=n_neighbors)

print("train_data.target:")
print(train_data.target)

# train_data.target has label data for each category in train
# data
clf = knn.fit(X_train_tfidf, train_data.target)

# predict the correct classes for these documents:
docs_new = ['My Macbook does not support Swift 5.',
            'I never played hockey',
            'Bobby Orr was the best NHL player']

# feature vector of our input:
X_new_counts = count_vect.transform(docs_new)
```

```
# invoke transform (feature vector is standardized):
X_new_tfidf = tfidf_transformer.transform(X_new_counts)

# predict the numeric categories for the documents:
predicted = clf.predict(X_new_tfidf)

for doc, category in zip(docs_new, predicted):
  print('%r: %s' % (doc, train_data.target_names[category]))

# Pipeline creates a single classifier:
# vectorizer -> transformer -> classifier
text_clf = Pipeline([
    ('vect', CountVectorizer()),
    ('tfidf', TfidfTransformer()),
    ('clf', knn),
])

# Fit the train data to the pipeline
text_clf.fit(train_data.data, train_data.target)

# Test data
test_data = fetch_20newsgroups(subset='test',
categories=my_cats, shuffle=True, random_state=42)

docs_test = test_data.data
predicted = text_clf.predict(docs_test)

from sklearn.metrics import confusion_matrix
cm = confusion_matrix(test_data.target, predicted)
print("confusion matrix:")
print(cm)

true_neg, false_pos = cm[0]
false_neg, true_pos = cm[1]

all_values = true_pos + true_neg + false_pos + false_neg

accuracy  = round((true_pos + true_neg) / all_values, 3)
precision = round((true_pos) / (true_pos + false_pos),3)
recall    = round((true_pos) / (true_pos + false_neg),3)
f1        = round(2 * (precision * recall) /
                  (precision + recall),3)

print("-------------------------\n")
print('Accuracy:  {}'.format(accuracy))
print('Precision: {}'.format(precision))
print('Recall:    {}'.format(recall
```

Listing 10.7 is a lengthy code sample that consists of three major sections. The first such section starts with various `import` statements, and then initializes `my_cats` with two categories `rec.sport.hockey` and `comp.sys.mac.hardware` from `20newsgroups`. Next, `train_data` is initialized with the data in those two newsgroups, after which their names are displayed.

The next section of code initializes `count_vect` as an instance of the class `CountVectorizer`, whose `fit_transform()` method transforms and trains the data in `train_data.data`. Next, the variable `tfidf_transformer` is initialized as an instance of the `TfidfTransformer` class, whose `fit_transform()` method is invoked to transform and train the data in `X_train_counts`.

The second major section in Listing 10.7 defines the variable `knn` as an instance of the class `KNeighborsClassifier`, whose `fit()` method is invoked on the data in `X_train_tfidf` with the labels in `train_data.target`, and the result is assigned to the variable `clf`.

The next block of code sets up the variables `docs_new`, `X_new_counts`, and `X_new_tfidf` that are counterparts to `docs`, `X_counts`, and `X_tfidf`, respectively. Then the `predict()` method of the `text_clf` variable is invoked on `X_new_tfidf` and the result is assigned to the variable `predicted`.

The third major section in Listing 10.7 defines the variable `text_clf` as a pipeline that invokes three classes sequentially: `CountVectorizer`, `TfidfTransformer`, and `knn`. Next, the `fit()` method of `text_clf` is invoked on the data in `train_data.data` and the labels in `train_data.target`.

The next code snippet initializes the variable `test_data` with the data in the two newsgroups that were specified at the beginning of this code sample. Next, the `docs_test` data is initialized with the data from `test_data.data`, and the `predict()` method of `text_clf` is invoked on the `docs_test` variable.

The next code block initializes the variable `cm` with the contents of the confusion matrix, based on `test_data.target` and the predictions in the variable `predicted`. Notice that the true negative and false positive are in the first element of `cm` (i.e., `cm[0]`) and the false negative and true positive values are in the second element of `cm` (i.e., `cm[1]`).

The final portion of Listing 10.7 performs some calculations to determine the values for the variables `accuracy`, `precision`, `recall`, and `f1`, followed by a block of `print()` statements that prints the values of these variables. Now launch the code in Listing 10.7 and you will see the following output:

```
target_names:
['comp.sys.mac.hardware', 'rec.sport.hockey']
------------------------

From: nhmas@gauss.med.harvard.edu (Mark Shneyder 432-4219)
Subject: Re: Playoff telecasts in Atlanta
Organization: HMS
------------------------

First element of train_data target:
rec.sport.hockey
target_name: rec.sport.hockey
target_name: comp.sys.mac.hardware
target_name: rec.sport.hockey
target_name: rec.sport.hockey
target_name: rec.sport.hockey
------------------------

train_data.target:
[1 0 1 ... 1 1 0]
'My Macbook does not support Swift 5.': comp.sys.mac.hardware
'I never played hockey': rec.sport.hockey
'Bobby Orr was the best NHL player': rec.sport.hockey
confusion matrix:
[[340  45]
 [  8 391]]
---------------------------

Accuracy:   0.932
Precision:  0.897
Recall:     0.98
F1 Score:   0.937
```

The following output displays the confusion matrix that is generated for different values of n_neighbors, with the highest accuracy shown in bold (n_neighbors=3).

```
Confusion matrix for neighbors=3:
[[352  33]
 [  9 390]]
```
Accuracy = 94.6428%

```
Confusion matrix for neighbors=5:
[[350  35]
 [  9 390]]
Accuracy = 94.3877%

Confusion matrix for neighbors=7:
[[344  41]
 [  7 392]]
Accuracy = 93.8775%

Confusion matrix for neighbors=9:
[[340  45]
 [  8 391]]
Accuracy = 93.2397%
```

Text Classification with a Decision Tree Algorithm

Listing 10.8 displays the contents of tree_nlp_classify.py that performs text classification with the DecisionTreeClassifier class in sklearn.

LISTING 10.8: tree_nlp_classify.py

```
from sklearn.datasets import fetch_20newsgroups
from sklearn.datasets import fetch_20newsgroups
from sklearn.feature_extraction.text import CountVectorizer
from sklearn.feature_extraction.text import TfidfTransformer
from sklearn.pipeline import Pipeline

# https://scikit-learn.org/0.19/datasets/twenty_newsgroups.html
my_cats = ['rec.sport.hockey', 'comp.sys.mac.hardware']

# load training/testing data from sklearn:
train_data = fetch_20newsgroups(subset='train',
                                categories=my_cats,
                                shuffle=True, random_state=42)

print("target_names:")
print(train_data.target_names)
print("-----------------------\n")

print("\n".join(train_data.data[0].split("\n")[:3]))
print("-----------------------\n")

print("First element of train_data target:")
print(train_data.target_names[train_data.target[0]])
```

```python
# Initial training data points and their categories:
for t in train_data.target[:5]:
  print("target_name:",train_data.target_names[t])
print("-----------------------\n")

##############################################
# 1) create a dictionary of features
# 2) transform documents to feature vectors
# 3) convert text documents to a matrix of
#    token counts (CountVectorizer)
##############################################
count_vect = CountVectorizer()
X_train_counts = count_vect.fit_transform(train_data.data)

# count matrix => normalized tf-idf representation:
tfidf_transformer = TfidfTransformer()
X_train_tfidf = tfidf_transformer.fit_transform(X_train_
counts)

# an instance of the sklearn DecisionTreeClassifier class:
from sklearn.tree import DecisionTreeClassifier
tree = DecisionTreeClassifier(criterion='entropy',random_
state=0)

print("train_data.target:")
print(train_data.target)
# train_data.target has label data for each category in train
data
clf = tree.fit(X_train_tfidf, train_data.target)

# predict the correct classes for these documents:
docs_new = ['My Macbook does not support Swift 5.',
            'I never played hockey',
            'Bobby Orr was the best NHL player']

# feature vector of our input:
X_new_counts = count_vect.transform(docs_new)

# invoke transform (feature vector is standardized):
X_new_tfidf = tfidf_transformer.transform(X_new_counts)

# predict the numeric categories for the documents:
predicted = clf.predict(X_new_tfidf)

for doc, category in zip(docs_new, predicted):
  print('%r: %s' % (doc, train_data.target_names[category]))

# Pipeline creates a single classifier:
# vectorizer -> transformer -> classifier
text_clf = Pipeline([
    ('vect', CountVectorizer()),
    ('tfidf', TfidfTransformer()),
    ('clf', tree),
```

```
])

# Fit the train data to the pipeline
text_clf.fit(train_data.data, train_data.target)

# Test data
test_data = fetch_20newsgroups(subset='test',
categories=my_cats, shuffle=True, random_state=42)

docs_test = test_data.data
predicted = text_clf.predict(docs_test)

from sklearn.metrics import confusion_matrix
cm = confusion_matrix(test_data.target, predicted)
print("confusion matrix:")
print(cm)

true_neg, false_pos = cm[0]
false_neg, true_pos = cm[1]

all_values = true_pos + true_neg + false_pos + false_neg

accuracy  = round((true_pos + true_neg) / all_values, 3)
precision = round((true_pos) / (true_pos + false_pos),3)
recall    = round((true_pos) / (true_pos + false_neg),3)
f1        = round(2 * (precision * recall) / (precision +
                  recall),3)

print("--------------------------\n")
print('Accuracy:  {}'.format(accuracy))
print('Precision: {}'.format(precision))
print('Recall:    {}'.format(recall
```

Listing 10.8 contains code that is very similar to Listing 10.7. The only differences occur in the following locations that are shown in bold:

```
# count matrix => normalized tf-idf representation:
tfidf_transformer = TfidfTransformer()
X_train_tfidf = tfidf_transformer.fit_transform(X_train_counts

# an instance of the sklearn DecisionTreeClassifier class:
from sklearn.tree import DecisionTreeClassifier
tree = DecisionTreeClassifier(criterion='entropy',
                              random_state=0)

print("train_data.target:")
print(train_data.target)
# train_data.target has label data for each category in train
# data
clf = tree.fit(X_train_tfidf, train_data.target)
```

```
// some code omitted
# Pipeline creates a single classifier:
# vectorizer -> transformer -> classifier
text_clf = Pipeline([
    ('vect', CountVectorizer()),
    ('tfidf', TfidfTransformer()),
    ('clf', tree),
])
```

As you can see, Listing 10.8 differs from Listing 10.7 primarily in its use of the `DecisionTreeClassifier` class. Launch the code in Listing 10.8 and you will see the following output:

```
target_names:
target_names:
['comp.sys.mac.hardware', 'rec.sport.hockey']
------------------------

From: nhmas@gauss.med.harvard.edu (Mark Shneyder 432-4219)
Subject: Re: Playoff telecasts in Atlanta
Organization: HMS
------------------------

First element of train_data target:
rec.sport.hockey
target_name: rec.sport.hockey
target_name: comp.sys.mac.hardware
target_name: rec.sport.hockey
target_name: rec.sport.hockey
target_name: rec.sport.hockey
------------------------

train_data.target:
[1 0 1 ... 1 1 0]
'My Macbook does not support Swift 5.': comp.sys.mac.hardware
'I never played hockey': rec.sport.hockey
'Bobby Orr was the best NHL player': rec.sport.hockey
confusion matrix:
[[359  26]
 [ 31 368]]
--------------------------

Accuracy:  0.927
Precision: 0.934
```

```
Recall:    0.922
F1 Score:  0.928
```

Based on the preceding confusion matrix, the accuracy for this example is 92.87%, which is the best accuracy thus far (but the SVC model has an even higher accuracy).

Text Classification with a Random Forest Algorithm

Listing 10.9 displays the contents of `forest_nlp_classify.py` that performs text classification with a random forest algorithm.

LISTING 10.9: *forest_nlp_classify.py*

```
from sklearn.datasets import fetch_20newsgroups
from sklearn.datasets import fetch_20newsgroups
from sklearn.feature_extraction.text import CountVectorizer
from sklearn.feature_extraction.text import TfidfTransformer
from sklearn.pipeline import Pipeline

# https://scikit-learn.org/0.19/datasets/twenty_newsgroups.html
my_cats = ['rec.sport.hockey', 'comp.sys.mac.hardware']

# load training/testing data from sklearn:
train_data = fetch_20newsgroups(subset='train',
            categories=my_cats, shuffle=True, random_state=42)

print("target_names:")
print(train_data.target_names)
print("------------------------\n")

print("\n".join(train_data.data[0].split("\n")[:3]))
print("------------------------\n")

print("First element of train_data target:")
print(train_data.target_names[train_data.target[0]])

# Initial training data points and their categories:
for t in train_data.target[:5]:
  print("target_name:",train_data.target_names[t])
print("------------------------\n")

###############################################
# 1) create a dictionary of features
# 2) transform documents to feature vectors
# 3) convert text documents to a matrix of
#    token counts (CountVectorizer)
###############################################
```

```python
count_vect = CountVectorizer()
X_train_counts = count_vect.fit_transform(train_data.data)

# count matrix => normalized tf-idf representation:
tfidf_transformer = TfidfTransformer()
X_train_tfidf = tfidf_transformer.fit_transform(X_train_
counts)

# an instance of the sklearn RandomForestClassifier class:
n_estimators = 10
from sklearn.ensemble import RandomForestClassifier
randomforest = RandomForestClassifier(n_estimators =
n_estimators, criterion='entropy', random_state = 0)

print("train_data.target:")
print(train_data.target)
# train_data.target has label data for each category in train data
clf = randomforest.fit(X_train_tfidf, train_data.target)

# predict the correct classes for these documents:
docs_new = ['My Macbook does not support Swift 5.',
            'I never played hockey',
            'Bobby Orr was the best NHL player']

# feature vector of our input:
X_new_counts = count_vect.transform(docs_new)

# invoke transform (feature vector is standardized):
X_new_tfidf = tfidf_transformer.transform(X_new_counts)

# predict the numeric categories for the documents:
predicted = clf.predict(X_new_tfidf)

for doc, category in zip(docs_new, predicted):
  print('%r: %s' % (doc, train_data.target_names[category]))

# Pipeline creates a single classifier:
# vectorizer -> transformer -> classifier
text_clf = Pipeline([
    ('vect', CountVectorizer()),
    ('tfidf', TfidfTransformer()),
    ('clf', randomforest),
])

# Fit the train data to the pipeline
text_clf.fit(train_data.data, train_data.target)

# Test data
test_data = fetch_20newsgroups(subset='test',
categories=my_cats, shuffle=True, random_state=42)
```

```
docs_test = test_data.data
predicted = text_clf.predict(docs_test)

from sklearn.metrics import confusion_matrix
cm = confusion_matrix(test_data.target, predicted)
print("confusion matrix:")
print(cm)

true_neg, false_pos = cm[0]
false_neg, true_pos = cm[1]

all_values = true_pos + true_neg + false_pos + false_neg

accuracy  = round((true_pos + true_neg) / all_values, 3)
precision = round((true_pos) / (true_pos + false_pos),3)
recall    = round((true_pos) / (true_pos + false_neg),3)
f1        = round(2 * (precision * recall) /
                  (precision + recall),3)

print("--------------------------\n")
print('Accuracy:   {}'.format(accuracy))
print('Precision:  {}'.format(precision))
print('Recall:     {}'.format(recall
```

Listing 10.9 is also similar to Listing 10.8: the three main differences are shown in bold in the code, which uses an instance of the `RandomForestClassifier` class instead of an instance of the `DecisionTreeClassifier` class. Launch the code in Listing 10.9 and you will see the following output:

```
target_names:
['comp.sys.mac.hardware', 'rec.sport.hockey']
------------------------

From: nhmas@gauss.med.harvard.edu (Mark Shneyder 432-4219)
Subject: Re: Playoff telecasts in Atlanta
Organization: HMS
------------------------

First element of train_data target:
rec.sport.hockey
target_name: rec.sport.hockey
target_name: comp.sys.mac.hardware
target_name: rec.sport.hockey
target_name: rec.sport.hockey
target_name: rec.sport.hockey
------------------------

train_data.target:
[1 0 1 ... 1 1 0]
'My Macbook does not support Swift 5.': comp.sys.mac.hardware
'I never played hockey': rec.sport.hockey
```

```
'Bobby Orr was the best NHL player': rec.sport.hockey
confusion matrix:
[[378   7]
 [ 36 363]]
-------------------------

Accuracy:   0.963
Precision:  0.979
Recall:     0.947
F1 Score:   0.963
```

Based on the preceding confusion matrix, the accuracy for this example is 96.3%, which is even better than the tree-based code sample in the previous section.

If you modify the code in Listing 10.9 to specify the value 20 for the `n_estimators` hyperparameter (i.e., 20 trees instead of 10) and you launch the code, you will see the following values in the confusion matrix:

```
confusion matrix:
[[377   8]
 [ 21 378]]
```

The preceding confusion matrix has an accuracy of 92.4479%, which is lower than the accuracy of the previous confusion matrix that is generated when `n_estimators` equals 10. This example illustrates that "more trees is better" isn't necessarily true.

Text Classification with the SVC Algorithm

Listing 10.10 displays the contents of `svc_nlp_classify.py` that performs text classification with the SVC algorithm (i.e., the SVM classifier).

LISTING 10.10: *svc_nlp_classify.py*

```python
from sklearn.datasets import fetch_20newsgroups
from sklearn.feature_extraction.text import CountVectorizer
from sklearn.feature_extraction.text import TfidfTransformer
#from sklearn.neighbors import KNeighborsClassifier
from sklearn.pipeline import Pipeline

# https://scikit-learn.org/0.19/datasets/twenty_newsgroups.html
my_cats = ['rec.sport.hockey', 'comp.sys.mac.hardware']

# load training/testing data from sklearn:
train_data = fetch_20newsgroups(subset='train',
            categories=my_cats, shuffle=True, random_state=42)
```

```python
print("target_names:")
print(train_data.target_names)
print("-----------------------\n")

print("\n".join(train_data.data[0].split("\n")[:3]))
print("-----------------------\n")

print("First element of train_data target:")
print(train_data.target_names[train_data.target[0]])

# Initial training data points and their categories:
for t in train_data.target[:5]:
  print("target_name:",train_data.target_names[t])
print("-----------------------\n")

##############################################
# 1) create a dictionary of features
# 2) transform documents to feature vectors
# 3) convert text documents to a matrix of
#    token counts (CountVectorizer)
##############################################
count_vect = CountVectorizer()
X_train_counts = count_vect.fit_transform(train_data.data)

# count matrix => normalized tf-idf representation:
tfidf_transformer = TfidfTransformer()
X_train_tfidf = tfidf_transformer.fit_transform(X_train_counts)

# an instance of the sklearn SVC class:
from sklearn.svm import SVC
svc = SVC(kernel = 'linear', random_state = 0)
#svc = SVC(kernel = 'sigmoid', random_state = 0)
#svc = SVC(kernel = 'poly', random_state = 0)
#svc = SVC(random_state = 0)

print("train_data.target:")
print(train_data.target)
# train_data.target has label data for each category in train data
clf = svc.fit(X_train_tfidf, train_data.target)

# predict the correct classes for these documents:
docs_new = ['My Macbook does not support Swift 5.',
            'I never played hockey',
            'Bobby Orr was the best NHL player']

# feature vector of our input:
X_new_counts = count_vect.transform(docs_new)
```

```
# invoke transform (feature vector is standardized):
X_new_tfidf = tfidf_transformer.transform(X_new_counts)

# predict the numeric categories for the documents:
predicted = clf.predict(X_new_tfidf)

for doc, category in zip(docs_new, predicted):
  print('%r: %s' % (doc, train_data.target_names[category]))

# Pipeline creates a single classifier:
# vectorizer -> transformer -> classifier
text_clf = Pipeline([
    ('vect', CountVectorizer()),
    ('tfidf', TfidfTransformer()),
    ('clf', svc),
])

# Fit the train data to the pipeline
text_clf.fit(train_data.data, train_data.target)

# Test data
test_data = fetch_20newsgroups(subset='test',
categories=my_cats, shuffle=True, random_state=42)

docs_test = test_data.data
predicted = text_clf.predict(docs_test)

from sklearn.metrics import confusion_matrix
cm = confusion_matrix(test_data.target, predicted)
print("confusion matrix:")
print(cm)

true_neg, false_pos = cm[0]
false_neg, true_pos = cm[1]

all_values = true_pos + true_neg + false_pos + false_neg

accuracy  = round((true_pos + true_neg) / all_values, 3)
precision = round((true_pos) / (true_pos + false_pos),3)
recall    = round((true_pos) / (true_pos + false_neg),3)
f1        = round(2 * (precision * recall) /
                  (precision + recall),3)

print("-------------------------\n")
print('Accuracy:  {}'.format(accuracy))
print('Precision: {}'.format(precision))
print('Recall:    {}'.format(recall
```

As you can see in the first new block of code in Listing 10.10, there are five different kernels that you can specify in the svc (as well as the svm) algorithm, in addition to many other hyperparameters.

Listing 10.10 is another example that is similar to Listing 10.7: the three main differences are shown in bold. As you can see, this code sample uses an instance of the SVC class instead of `DecisionTreeClassifier` or `RandomForestClassifier`. Launch the code in Listing 10.10 and you will see the following portion of output:

```
confusion matrix:
[[145 238   2]
 [155   1 243]
 [  0   0   0]]
```

The accuracy is 98.8520%, which is the best accuracy thusfar, and we have one more classification algorithm to try: Naïve Bayes, which is discussed in the next section.

Text Classification with the Naïve Bayes Algorithm

Listing 10.11 displays the contents of `nbayes_nlp_classify.py` that performs text classification with the naïve Bayes algorithm.

LISTING 10.11: nbayes_nlp_classify.py

```
import numpy as np
from sklearn.datasets import fetch_20newsgroups
from sklearn.feature_extraction.text import CountVectorizer
from sklearn.feature_extraction.text import TfidfTransformer
#from sklearn.neighbors import KNeighborsClassifier
from sklearn.pipeline import Pipeline

# https://scikit-learn.org/0.19/datasets/twenty_newsgroups.html
my_cats = ['rec.sport.hockey', 'comp.sys.mac.hardware']

# load training/testing data from sklearn:
train_data = fetch_20newsgroups(subset='train',
                                categories=my_cats,
                                shuffle=True, random_state=42)

print("target_names:")
print(train_data.target_names)
print("------------------------\n")

print("\n".join(train_data.data[0].split("\n")[:3]))
print("------------------------\n")

print("First element of train_data target:")
print(train_data.target_names[train_data.target[0]])
```

```python
# Initial training data points and their categories:
for t in train_data.target[:5]:
  print("target_name:",train_data.target_names[t])
print("-----------------------\n")

##############################################
# 1) create a dictionary of features
# 2) transform documents to feature vectors
# 3) convert text documents to a matrix of
#    token counts (CountVectorizer)
##############################################
count_vect = CountVectorizer()
X_train_counts = count_vect.fit_transform(train_data.data)

# count matrix => normalized tf-idf representation:
tfidf_transformer = TfidfTransformer()
X_train_tfidf = tfidf_transformer.fit_transform(X_train_
counts)

# an instance of the sklearn MultinomialNB class:
from sklearn.naive_bayes import MultinomialNB
nbayes = MultinomialNB()

print("train_data.target:")
print(train_data.target)

# train_data.target has label data for each category in train
data
clf = nbayes.fit(X_train_tfidf, train_data.target)

# predict the correct classes for these documents:
docs_new = ['My Macbook does not support Swift 5.',
            'I never played hockey',
            'Bobby Orr was the best NHL player']

# feature vector of our input:
X_new_counts = count_vect.transform(docs_new)

# invoke transform (feature vector is standardized):
X_new_tfidf = tfidf_transformer.transform(X_new_counts)

# predict the numeric categories for the documents:
predicted = clf.predict(X_new_tfidf)

#for doc, category in zip(docs_new, predicted):
#  print('%r: %s' % (doc, train_data.target_names[category]))

# Pipeline creates a single classifier:
# vectorizer -> transformer -> classifier
text_clf = Pipeline([
    ('vect', CountVectorizer()),
    ('tfidf', TfidfTransformer()),
    ('clf', nbayes),
```

```
])

# Fit the train data to the pipeline
text_clf.fit(train_data.data, train_data.target)

# Test data
test_data = fetch_20newsgroups(subset='test',
categories=my_cats, shuffle=True, random_state=42)

docs_test = test_data.data
predicted = text_clf.predict(docs_test)

from sklearn.metrics import confusion_matrix
cm = confusion_matrix(test_data.target, predicted)
print("confusion matrix:")
print(cm)

true_neg, false_pos = cm[0]
false_neg, true_pos = cm[1]

all_values = true_pos + true_neg + false_pos + false_neg

accuracy  = round((true_pos + true_neg) / all_values, 3)
precision = round((true_pos) / (true_pos + false_pos),3)
recall    = round((true_pos) / (true_pos + false_neg),3)
f1        = round(2 * (precision * recall) /
                  (precision + recall),3)

print("-------------------------\n")
print('Accuracy:  {}'.format(accuracy))
print('Precision: {}'.format(precision))
print('Recall:    {}'.format(recall))
print('F1 Score:  {}'.format(f1))
```

Listing 10.11 is also similar to Listing 10.7: the three main differences are shown in bold in the code. Launch the code in Listing 10.11 and you will see the following output:

```
confusion matrix:
target_names:
['comp.sys.mac.hardware', 'rec.sport.hockey']
-----------------------

From: nhmas@gauss.med.harvard.edu (Mark Shneyder 432-4219)
Subject: Re: Playoff telecasts in Atlanta
Organization: HMS
-----------------------

First element of train_data target:
rec.sport.hockey
```

```
target_name: rec.sport.hockey
target_name: comp.sys.mac.hardware
target_name: rec.sport.hockey
target_name: rec.sport.hockey
target_name: rec.sport.hockey
------------------------

train_data.target:
[1 0 1 ... 1 1 0]
confusion matrix:
[[378   7]
 [  1 398]]
-------------------------

Accuracy:   0.99
Precision:  0.983
Recall:     0.997
F1 Score:   0.99
```

The accuracy is 99%, which is the best accuracy of all the classification algorithms that we have seen: kNN, decision trees, random forests, and SVC.

This concludes the portion of the chapter that performs text classification with machine learning classifiers. The next section shows you how to perform text classification with the kMeans algorithm, which is an unsupervised clustering algorithm.

Text Classification with the kMeans Algorithm

This section contains a brief description of the kMeans clustering algorithm, followed by a code sample that uses kMeans to perform text classification.

The intuition for the kMeans algorithm involves first selecting a set of points (called "centroids"), and second for each point in the dataset, determine its closest centroid. A more detailed description of the kMeans algorithm is shown here:

1. Specify a value for k (typically an odd number).

2. Initialize a set of randomly selected points as the centroids.

3. Assign each datapoint to the closest centroid.

4. Recompute the centroid for each cluster.

5. Perform steps 3 and 4 again for each n-tuple.

6. Repeat until the centroids no longer change.

Here are some details to keep in mind regarding the `kMeans` algorithm:

1. The initial centroids can be any points (including points in the dataset).

2. The number of centroids is a hyperparameter.

3. This algorithm involves in-memory calculations.

4. All datapoints must fit into memory.

The `meanShift` algorithm is another clustering algorithm that does not require you to specify the number of clusters, but it's not scalable for very large datasets (which is also true of `kMeans` itself).

One technique for finding the optimal number of clusters involves the minimization of the within-cluster sum of squares (WSS). The value of WSS for a given cluster equals the sum of the distances between each datapoint in the cluster and the cluster centroid. In general, lower WSS values occur when observations are closer to their respective centroids, which in turn indicates a better fit.

In the extreme case in which each datapoint is its own cluster, the value of WSS is zero and hence it's minimized. At the other extreme, if we have a single cluster, then the value of WSS is maximized. Hence, it's necessary to find the right balance the value of WSS and the number of clusters.

The concept of "prediction strength" is way to evaluate clustering algorithms and to find the optimal number of clusters, which also involves WSS and the "elbow" technique, as discussed here:

https://towardsdatascience.com/prediction-strength-a-simple-yet-relatively-unknown-way-to-evaluate-clustering-2e5eaf56643

Now that you have a rudimentary understanding of the `kMeans` clustering algorithm, let's look at a code sample.

Listing 10.12 displays the contents of `kmeans_nlp_classify.py` that performs text classification with the `kMeans` clustering algorithm.

LISTING 10.12: *kmeans_nlp_classify.py*

```
from sklearn.datasets import fetch_20newsgroups
from sklearn.feature_extraction.text import CountVectorizer
```

```
from sklearn.feature_extraction.text import TfidfTransformer
from sklearn.cluster import KMeans
from sklearn.pipeline import Pipeline

# https://scikit-learn.org/0.19/datasets/twenty_newsgroups.html
my_cats = ['rec.sport.hockey', 'comp.sys.mac.hardware']

# load training/testing data from sklearn:
train_data = fetch_20newsgroups(subset='train',
          categories=my_cats, shuffle=True, random_state=42)

print("target_names:")
print(train_data.target_names)
print("------------------------\n")

print("\n".join(train_data.data[0].split("\n")[:3]))
print("------------------------\n")

print("First element of train_data target:")
print(train_data.target_names[train_data.target[0]])

# Initial training data points and their categories:
for t in train_data.target[:5]:
  print("target_name:",train_data.target_names[t])
print("------------------------\n")

#############################################
# 1) create a dictionary of features
# 2) transform documents to feature vectors
# 3) convert text documents to a matrix of
#    token counts (CountVectorizer)
#############################################
count_vect = CountVectorizer()
X_train_counts = count_vect.fit_transform(train_data.data)

# count matrix => normalized tf-idf representation:
tfidf_transformer = TfidfTransformer()
X_train_tfidf = tfidf_transformer.fit_transform(X_train_
counts)

# an instance of the sklearn KMeans class:
n_clusters = 3
kmeans = KMeans(n_clusters=n_clusters, init='k-means++',
max_ iter=10, n_init=10)

print("train_data.target:")
print(train_data.target)
# train_data.target has label data for each category in train
data
clf = kmeans.fit(X_train_tfidf, train_data.target)
```

```python
# predict the correct classes for these documents:
docs_new = ['My Macbook does not support Swift 5.',
            'I never played hockey',
            'Bobby Orr was the best NHL player']

# feature vector of our input:
X_new_counts = count_vect.transform(docs_new)

# invoke transform (feature vector is standardized):
X_new_tfidf = tfidf_transformer.transform(X_new_counts)

# predict the numeric categories for the documents:
predicted = clf.predict(X_new_tfidf)

#for doc, category in zip(docs_new, predicted):
#  print('%r: %s' % (doc, train_data.target_names[category]))

# Pipeline creates a single classifier:
# vectorizer -> transformer -> classifier
text_clf = Pipeline([
    ('vect', CountVectorizer()),
    ('tfidf', TfidfTransformer()),
    ('clf', kmeans),
])

# Fit the train data to the pipeline
text_clf.fit(train_data.data, train_data.target)

# Test data
test_data = fetch_20newsgroups(subset='test',
categories=my_cats, shuffle=True, random_state=42)

docs_test = test_data.data
predicted = text_clf.predict(docs_test)

from sklearn.metrics import confusion_matrix
cm = confusion_matrix(test_data.target, predicted)
print("confusion matrix:")
print(cm)

true_neg, false_pos = cm[0]
false_neg, true_pos = cm[1]

all_values = true_pos + true_neg + false_pos + false_neg

accuracy  = round((true_pos + true_neg) / all_values, 3)
precision = round((true_pos) / (true_pos + false_pos),3)
recall    = round((true_pos) / (true_pos + false_neg),3)
f1        = round(2 * (precision * recall) /
                  (precision + recall),3)
```

```
print("------------------------\n")
print('Accuracy:   {}'.format(accuracy))
print('Precision:  {}'.format(precision))
print('Recall:     {}'.format(recall
```

Listing 10.12 is similar to Listing 10.11: this time the differences involve four blocks of code that are shown in bold. Launch the code in Listing 10.12 and you will see the following portion of output:

```
confusion matrix:
[[145 238   2]
 [155   1 243]
 [  0   0   0]]
```

Notice that the confusion matrix is a 3×3 matrix because the number of clusters is 3, whereas the confusion matrix for the kNN code sample is a 2×2 matrix.

However, the accuracy in this code sample equals 18.6224%, which is dramatically lower than the accuracy obtained for four different values of k in the kNN code sample.

Here are the contents of the confusion matrix when the number of clusters equals 5:

```
confusion matrix:
[[205 180   0   0   0]
 [136   1  24   4 234]
 [  0   0   0   0   0]
 [  0   0   0   0   0]
 [  0   0   0   0   0]]
```

The accuracy in this case equals 26.2755, which is a modest improvement over the accuracy when the number of clusters is 3.

Here are the contents of the confusion matrix when the number of clusters equals 7:

```
confusion matrix:
[[  2   1 180   0  22 180   0]
 [207  68  95   4   0   1  24]
 [  0   0   0   0   0   0   0]
 [  0   0   0   0   0   0   0]
 [  0   0   0   0   0   0   0]
 [  0   0   0   0   0   0   0]
 [  0   0   0   0   0   0   0]]
```

The accuracy in this case equals 8.9285%, which is truly abysmal. The key point to keep in mind is that different algorithms can yield much different accuracy values, which means that it's important to try multiple algorithms (with different hyperparameter values) on the same dataset.

TF2/Keras and Word Tokenization

This section contains the Python script tf2_basic_nlp.py as well as the Jupyter notebook tf2_basic_nlp.ipynb. If you encounter issues when you attempt to install tensorflow-text on your machine, you can upload and launch the Jupyter notebook in Google Colaboratory (which contains the same code). If need be, you can read Appendix E regarding TensorFlow concepts, some of which are included in the code sample in this section.

Listing 10.13 displays the contents of tf2_basic_nlp.py that illustrates how to tokenize the words in a collection of sentences, and perform basic operations such as checking whether or not words are uppercase, contain punctuation, and so forth.

LISTING 10.13: tf2_basic_nlp.py

```
import tensorflow as tf
import tensorflow_text as text

sents = [["When ignorance is bliss."],
         ["Tis folly to be wise!"],
         ["According to the famous Bard!"],]

docs = tf.data.Dataset.from_tensor_slices(sents)

tokenizer = text.WhitespaceTokenizer()
tokenized_docs = docs.map(lambda x: tokenizer.tokenize(x))

iterator = iter(tokenized_docs)
print(next(iterator).to_list())
print(next(iterator).to_list())
print()

tokenizer = text.WhitespaceTokenizer()
tokens = tokenizer.tokenize(sents)

print("tokens:")
print(tokens)
print()

print("Capitalized tokens:")
w1 = text.wordshape(tokens, text.WordShape.HAS_TITLE_CASE)
print(w1.to_list())
print()

print("Uppercase tokens:")
```

```
w2 = text.wordshape(tokens, text.WordShape.IS_UPPERCASE)
print(w2.to_list())
print()

print("tokens with punctuation:")
w3 = text.wordshape(tokens, text.WordShape.HAS_SOME_PUNCT_OR_
SYMBOL)
print(w3.to_list())
print()

print("Numeric tokens:")
w4 = text.wordshape(tokens, text.WordShape.IS_NUMERIC_VALUE)
print(w4.to_list())
print()

tokenizer = text.WhitespaceTokenizer()
tokens = tokenizer.tokenize(sents)

bigrams = text.ngrams(tokens, 2, reduction_type=text.
Reduction.STRING_JOIN)
print("bigrams:")
print(bigrams.to_list())
print()
```

Listing 10.13 starts with `import` statements and then initializes the variables `sents` and `docs` as an array of documents and a `tf.data.Dataset` instance, respectively. Next the variable `tokenizer` is an instance of the TensorFlow WhitespaceTokenizer class, and the variable `tokenized_docs` is initialized with the result of tokenizing all the documents in the `docs` variable (using a combination of the `map()` method and a `lambda` expression).

Next, the variable `iterator` is initialized, and then the first two elements of the `sents` variable are displayed. The next four blocks of code invoke the `wordshape()` method of the `TensorFlow text` class in order to display capitalized tokens, upper case tokens, tokens with punctuation, and numeric tokens.

The last portion of Listing 10.13 invokes the `ngrams()` method of the built-in `text` class to initialize the variable `bigrams` with the bigrams in the `tokens` variable and then display the results. Launch the code in Listing 10.13 and you will see the following output:

```
[[b'When', b'ignorance', b'is', b'bliss.']]
[[b'Tis', b'folly', b'to', b'be', b'wise!']]

tokens:
<tf.RaggedTensor [[[b'When', b'ignorance', b'is', b'bliss.']],
[[b'Tis', b'folly', b'to', b'be', b'wise!']],
[[b'According', b'to', b'the', b'famous', b'Bard!']]]>
```

```
Capitalized tokens:
[[[True, False, False, False]], [[True, False, False, False,
False]], [[True, False, False, False, True]]]

Uppercase tokens:
[[[False, False, False, False]], [[False, False, False, False,
False]], [[False, False, False, False, False]]]

tokens with punctuation:
[[[False, False, False, True]], [[False, False, False, False,
True]], [[False, False, False, False, True]]]

Numeric tokens:
[[[False, False, False, False]], [[False, False, False, False,
False]], [[False, False, False, False, False]]]

bigrams:
[[[b'When ignorance', b'ignorance is', b'is bliss.']],
[[b'Tis folly', b'folly to', b'to be', b'be wise!']],
[[b'According to', b'to the', b'the famous', b'famous Bard!']]]
```

TF2/Keras and Word Encodings

Listing 10.14 displays the contents of tf2_encoding.py that illustrates how to tokenize a sentence.

LISTING 10.14: *tf2_encoding.py*

```
import tensorflow as tf

train_data = [
  "I enjoy coffee.",
  "I enjoy tea.",
  "I dislike milk.",
  "I am going to the supermarket later this morning for some
coffee."
]

test_data = [
  "Enjoy coffee this morning.",
  "I enjoy going to the supermarket.",
  "Want some milk for your coffee?"
]
```

```
num_words = 1000
oov_token = '<UNK>'
pad_type = 'post'
trunc_type = 'post'

# Tokenize our training data
tokenizer = tf.keras.preprocessing.text.Tokenizer(num_
words=num_words, oov_token=oov_token)
tokenizer.fit_on_texts(train_data)

# Get our training data word index
word_index = tokenizer.word_index

# Encode training data sentences into sequences
train_sequences = tokenizer.texts_to_sequences(train_data)

# Get max training sequence length
maxlen = max([len(x) for x in train_sequences])

# Pad the training sequences
train_padded = tf.keras.preprocessing.sequence.pad_
sequences(train_sequences, padding=pad_type,
truncating=trunc_type, maxlen=maxlen)

# Output the results of our work
print("Word index:\n", word_index)
print("\nTraining sequences:\n", train_sequences)
print("\nPadded training sequences:\n", train_padded)
print("\nPadded training shape:", train_padded.shape)
print("Training sequences data type:", type(train_sequences))
print("Padded Training sequences data type:",
type(train_padded))
```

Listing 10.14 starts with `import` statements and then initializes the variables `train_data` and `test_data` with a set of documents. The remaining code is very similar to the contents of Listing 10.3, which will not be duplicated here.

One other point to keep in mind: The `pad_type` parameter specifies how to pad sentences so that they will have the same length: the padding can be performed at the beginning of a sentence ("pre-pad") or at the end of a sentence ("post-pad"). Now launch the code in Listing 10.14 and you will see the following output:

```
Word index:
{'<UNK>': 1, 'i': 2, 'enjoy': 3, 'coffee': 4, 'tea': 5,
'dislike': 6, 'milk': 7, 'am': 8, 'going': 9, 'to': 10, 'the':
11, 'supermarket': 12, 'later': 13, 'this': 14, 'morning':
15, 'for': 16, 'some': 17}
```

```
Training sequences:
[[2, 3, 4], [2, 3, 5], [2, 6, 7], [2, 8, 9, 10, 11, 12, 13,
 14, 15, 16, 17, 4]]

Padded training sequences:
[[ 2  3  4  0  0  0  0  0  0  0  0  0]
 [ 2  3  5  0  0  0  0  0  0  0  0  0]
 [ 2  6  7  0  0  0  0  0  0  0  0  0]
 [ 2  8  9 10 11 12 13 14 15 16 17  4]]

Padded training shape: (4, 12)
Training sequences data type: <class 'list'>
Padded Training sequences data type: <class 'numpy.ndarray'>
```

Text Summarization with TF2/Keras and Reuters Dataset

Listing 10.15 displays the contents of reuters_mlp.py that illustrates how to perform text summarization with a Keras-based MLP in TF2. This code sample has been adapted from reuters_mlp.py that is part of the standalone Keras distribution:

https://github.com/keras-team/keras/blob/master/examples/reuters_mlp.py

LISTING 10.15: reuters_mlp.py

```
#Train/evaluate an MLP on the Reuters dataset
from __future__ import print_function

import tensorflow as tf
import numpy as np

max_words = 1000
batch_size = 32
epochs = 5

print('Loading data...')
(x_train, y_train), (x_test, y_test) = tf.keras.datasets.
reuters.load_data(num_words=max_words, test_split=0.2)

print(len(x_train), 'train sequences')
print(len(x_test), 'test sequences')

num_classes = np.max(y_train) + 1
print(num_classes, 'classes')

print('Vectorizing sequence data...')
```

```
tokenizer = tf.keras.preprocessing.text.Tokenizer(num_
words=max_words)

x_train = tokenizer.sequences_to_matrix(x_train, mode='binary')
x_test = tokenizer.sequences_to_matrix(x_test, mode='binary')

print('x_train shape:', x_train.shape)
print('x_test shape:', x_test.shape)

print('Convert class vector to binary class matrix '
      '(for use with categorical_crossentropy)')

y_train = tf.keras.utils.to_categorical(y_train, num_classes)
y_test  = tf.keras.utils.to_categorical(y_test, num_classes)

print('y_train shape:', y_train.shape)
print('y_test shape:', y_test.shape)

print('Building Keras-based model...')
model = tf.keras.models.Sequential()
model.add(tf.keras.layers.Dense(512,
          input_shape=(max_words,)))
model.add(tf.keras.layers.Activation('relu'))
model.add(tf.keras.layers.Dropout(0.5))
model.add(tf.keras.layers.Dense(num_classes))
model.add(tf.keras.layers.Activation('softmax'))

print("Compilation step...")
model.compile(loss='categorical_crossentropy',
              optimizer='adam',
              metrics=['accuracy'])

print("Training step...")
history = model.fit(x_train, y_train,
                    batch_size=batch_size,
                    epochs=epochs,
                    verbose=1,
                    validation_split=0.1)

print("Evaluation step...")
score = model.evaluate(x_test, y_test,
                       batch_size=batch_size, verbose=1)

print('Test score:   ', score[0])
print('Test accuracy:', score[1])
```

Listing 10.15 starts with an `import` statement and then initializes four variables with data from the built-in Reuters dataset, as shown here:

```
(x_train, y_train), (x_test, y_test) = tf.keras.datasets.
reuters.load_data(num_words=max_words, test_split=0.2)
```

Next, the variable `tokenizer` is initialized as you have seen in previous examples, and then the variables `x_train_` and `x_test` are converted to 2D arrays via the method `tokenizer.sequences_to_matrix()`, followed by the variables `y_train` and `y_test` that are converted from vectors to binary class matrices. Note that in this code sample the vectors are integer-valued, but the vectors can be floating point values for other types of tasks (such as image classification).

The next portion of Listing 10.15 initializes the variable `model`, which is a Keras-based neural network consisting of various layers. If you are unfamiliar with Keras, Appendix D contains the details regarding the construction of neural networks in Keras.

After the model is compiled via `model.compile()` and trained via `model.fit()`, the `score` variable is initialized with the result of invoking the `model.evaluate()` on the test data contained in `x_test` and `y_test`. Please refer to Appendix D for more details regarding these methods.

The final section of Listing 10.15 displays the test score and the test accuracy. Launch the code in Listing 10.15 and you will see the following output:

```
Loading data...
8982 train sequences
2246 test sequences
46 classes

Vectorizing sequence data...
x_train shape: (8982, 1000)
x_test shape: (2246, 1000)

Convert class vector to binary class matrix (for use with cat-
egorical_crossentropy)

y_train shape: (8982, 46)
y_test shape: (2246, 46)

Building Keras-based model...

Compilation step...

Training step...
Train on 8083 samples, validate on 899 samples
Epoch 1/5
```

```
8083/8083 [==============================] - 2s 254us/sample
- loss: 1.4200 - accuracy: 0.6850 - val_loss: 1.0709 - val_ac-
curacy: 0.7686
Epoch 2/5
8083/8083 [==============================] - 1s 180us/sample -
loss: 0.7741 - accuracy: 0.8212 - val_loss:
0.9344 - val_accuracy: 0.7964
Epoch 3/5
8083/8083 [==============================] - 2s 189us/sample -
loss: 0.5363 - accuracy: 0.8668 - val_loss:
0.8815 - val_accuracy: 0.7953
Epoch 4/5
8083/8083 [==============================] - 1s 179us/sample -
loss: 0.4098 - accuracy: 0.9005 - val_loss:
0.8717 - val_accuracy: 0.8087
Epoch 5/5
8083/8083 [==============================] - 2s 187us/sample -
loss: 0.3241 - accuracy: 0.9167 - val_loss:
0.9160 - val_accuracy: 0.8031
Evaluation step...
2246/2246 [==============================] - 0s 99us/sample -
loss: 0.8997 - accuracy: 0.7916

Test score:     0.8997269553577698
Test accuracy:  0.79162955
```

Summary

This chapter introduced you to `NLP` and `TF2/Keras`, with code samples that illustrate various topics that were introduced in Chapter 3.

You saw an example of using the `kNN` algorithm to perform text classification on a set of documents (albeit very short documents). In addition, you saw how to modify the `kNN` code sample to solve the same task using decision trees, random forests, SVC, Naïve Bayes, and the `kMeans` algorithm. These code samples illustrated the fact that the accuracy can vary substantially among different machine learning algorithms.

Next, you saw several TensorFlow code samples for performing some NLP-related tasks. Finally, you saw an example of a Keras-based neural network that performed text summarization on the Reuters dataset.

CHAPTER 11

TRANSFORMER, BERT, AND GPT

This chapter covers the concept of attention, the transformer architecture, the pretrained BERT model and its variants, and features of GPT-2 and GPT-3 from OpenAI. If you are familiar with some of these topics, feel free to skim through the material in this chapter and peruse the Python-based code samples.

The first part of this chapter contains a brief introduction to the concept of attention, which is a powerful mechanism for generating word embeddings that contain context-specific information for words in sentences. The concept of attention is a key aspect of the transformer architecture. This section also contains a summary of the distinguishing characteristics of three types of word embeddings, in which the most powerful technique is the attention-based approach.

The second part of this chapter provides an overview of the transformer architecture that was developed by Google and released in late 2017. This section also discusses the T5 (text-to-text transfer transformer) model that converts all NLP tasks into a text-to-text format.

The third part of this chapter introduces you to BERT, along with various code samples that illustrate how to invoke some of the BERT APIs. Note that this section relies on the installation of the HuggingFace transformers Python library.

The fourth part of this chapter contains a list of several BERT-based trained models, along with brief description of their functionality. Some of the models that are discussed include `DistilledBERT`, `CamemBERT`, and `FlauBERT`. The final part of this chapter introduces you to the GPT-based models from OpenAI, along with some of the amazing features in GPT-3.

What is Attention?

Attention is a mechanism by which contextual word embeddings are determined for words in a corpus. Unlike `word2vec` or `gloVe`, the attention mechanism takes into account *all* the words in a sentence during the process of creating a word embedding for a given word. As a result, the same word that is used in multiple sentences will have a different word embedding in each of those sentences.

Prior to the attention mechanism, popular architectures were based on RNNs, LSTMs, or bi-LSTMs. In fact, the attention mechanism was first used in conjunction with RNNs or LSTMs. However, the Google team performed some experiments involving machine translation tasks on models that relied on the attention mechanism and the transformer architecture, and discovered that those models achieved higher performance that models that included CNNs, RNNs, or LSTMs. This result led to the expression "attention is all you need." The seminal paper regarding the transformer architecture is here:

https://papers.nips.cc/paper/2017/file/3f5ee243547dee91fbd053c1c4a845 aa-Paper.pdf

As a quick review, and before delving into details of the attention mechanism, let's look at a summary of the main types of word embeddings that we have encountered in this book, as discussed in the next section.

Types of Word Embeddings

This section contains a summary of the main features of three types of word embeddings. The first group consists of the simplest algorithms for word embeddings that have been discussed in previous chapters. The second group consists of the earliest algorithms that use neural networks (`word2vec` and `fasttext`) or matrix factorization (`gloVe`) for generating word embeddings. The third group involves contextual algorithms for creating contextual word representations, which are essentially state of the art algorithms. Here is the summary:

1. Discrete word embeddings (BoW, tf, and tf-idf):

Word vectors consist of integers, decimals, and decimals, respectively
Key point: word embedding have zero context

2. Distributional word embeddings (word2vec, GloVe, fasttext):
   Based on shallow NN, MF, and NN, respectively
   Two words on the left and the right (bi-grams) for word2vec
   Key point: a single word embedding for each word that is used for every occurrence of that word, regardless of its context.

3. Contextual word representations (BERT et al):
   Transformer architecture (no CNNs/RNNs/LSTMs required)
   Pays "attention" to ALL words in a sentence
   Key point: words can have multiple embeddings (depending on the context)

Types of Attention and Algorithms

There are several types of attention mechanisms, three of which are listed here:

1. self-attention

2. global/soft

3. local/hard

Self-attention tries to determine how words in a sentence are interconnected with each other. Multiheaded attention uses a block of multiple self-attention instead of just one self-attention. However, each head processes a different section of the embedding vector.

In addition to the preceding attention mechanisms, there are also several attention algorithms available:

- additive
- content-based
- dot product
- general
- location-based
- scaled dot product <= transformer uses this technique

The formulas for attention mechanisms can be divided into two broad types: formulas that involve a dot product of vectors (and sometimes with a scaling factor), and formulas that apply a `softmax` function or a `tanh` function to products of matrices and vectors.

Keep in mind that the transformer model uses a scaled dot-product mechanism in order to calculate the attention. If you want more detailed information regarding attention types, the following link contains a list of more than 20 attention types:

https://paperswithcode.com/methods/category/attention-mechanisms-1

An Overview of the Transformer Architecture

The transformer architecture differs from other architectures in the following important ways:

- It's primarily based on an "attention" mechanism.
- Model training can be parallelized.
- No CNN/RNN/LSTMs are required.

Due to the last point in the preceding list, the encoder-decoder construction differs from a `seq2seq` model that often contains RNNs or LSTMs.

The `Transformer` architecture has two main components: an *encoder* and a *decoder*. The encoder component has six (sometimes more) concatenated encoder elements. Each encoder element has *two* layers, and the output of the first layer is the input for the second layer (like a miniature pipeline). The final output of the sixth (or in some cases, the twelfth) encoder component is then passed to *every* decoder element in the decoder component.

Similarly, the decoder component also has six (sometimes more) concatenated decoder elements, where the output of one element in the input for the next element. However, each decoder element consists of *three* sub-elements, one of which is the output from the encoder.

The overall `Transformer` architecture consists of an encoder component that contains six "sub" encoder, as well as a decoder component that also contains six "sub" decoders. Loosely speaking, these structures somewhat analogous to filter elements in a CNN.

The input for the encoder is a set of word embeddings that encode the words in a sentence. The word embeddings are constructed via the so-called "attention" mechanism, which means that every embedding is based on all the words in a given sentence. Hence, a word that appears in two different sentences can have two different word embeddings for both of those sentences. Given a sentence with n tokens, the construction of each word embedding involves the remaining (n-1) words. Hence, the attention-based mechanism has order `O(N^2)`, where `N` is the number of unique tokens in the corpus.

The actual input vector for an encoder is called a *context vector*. This is a crucial detail: by contrast, `word2vec` constructs a single word embedding for every word, regardless of whether or not a given word has a different context in different sentences.

The Transformers Library from HuggingFace

HuggingFace created a `transformers` library and an open-source repository to develop models based on the transformer architecture that you can access here:

https://github.com/huggingface/transformers

The library provides pretrained models for NLU and NLG. In fact, HuggingFace provides more than 30 pretrained models for more than 100 languages, along with operability between TensorFlow 2 and PyTorch. Furthermore, HuggingFace supports not only BERT-related models, but also GPT-2/GPT-3, XLNet, and others.

HuggingFace is an excellent resource with numerous models, some of which are listed here:

- BART (from Facebook)
- BERT (from Google)
- Blenderbot (from Facebook)
- CamemBERT (from Inria/Facebook/Sorbonne)
- CTRL (from Salesforce)
- DeBERTa (from Microsoft Research)
- DistilBERT (from HuggingFace)
- ELECTRA (from Google Research/Stanford University)
- FlauBERT (from CNRS)
- GPT-2 (from OpenAI)
- Longformer (from AllenAI)
- LXMERT (from UNC Chapel Hill)

- Pegasus (from Google)
- Reformer (from Google Research)
- RoBERTa (from Facebook)
- SqueezeBert
- T5 (from Google AI)
- Transformer-XL (from Google/CMU)
- XLM-RoBERTa (from Facebook AI)
- XLNet (from Google/CMU)

Check the online documentation more information regarding these architectures.

Transformers are well-suited for various tasks, such as text generation, text summarization, and language translation. The next several sections contain several short code samples that illustrate how to use the `HuggingFace` transformer to perform NLP-related tasks. Specifically, you will see how to perform NER, QnA, and sentiment analysis using the `HuggingFace` transformer.

Transformer and NER Tasks

Listing 11.1 displays the contents of `hf_transformer_ner.py` that illustrates how to perform an NER task with the `HuggingFace` transformer.

LISTING 11.1: hf_transformer_ner.py

```
from transformers import pipeline

nlp = pipeline('ner')
result = nlp("I am a UCSC instructor and my name is Oswald")

print("result:",result)
```

Listing 11.1 starts with an `import` statement and then initializes the variable `nlp` as an instance of the `pipeline` class, with `ner` as a parameter. Next, the variable `nlp` is invoked with a hard-coded sample sentence. The output is assigned to the variable `result`, whose contents are then displayed. Launch the code in Listing 11.1 and you will see the following output:

```
result: [{'word': 'UC', 'score': 0.9993938207626343,
'entity': 'I-ORG', 'index': 4}, {'word': '##SC', 'score':
```

```
0.9974051713943481, 'entity': 'I-ORG', 'index': 5},
{'word': 'Oswald', 'score': 0.9988114833831787, 'entity':
'I-PER', 'index': 11}]
```

Transformer and QnA Tasks

Listing 11.2 displays the contents of `hf_transformer_qa.py` that illustrates how to perform a question-and-answer task with the `HuggingFace` transformer.

LISTING 11.2: hf_transformer_qa.py

```
from transformers import pipeline

nlp = pipeline('question-answering')

result = nlp({
 'question': "Do you know my name?",
 'context': "My name is Oswald"
})

print("result:",result)
```

Listing 11.2 starts with an `import` statement and then initializes the variable `nlp` as an instance of the `pipeline` class, with `question-answering` as a parameter. Next, the variable `nlp` is invoked with a question/context pair. The output is assigned to the variable `result`, whose contents are then displayed. Launch the code in Listing 11.2 and you will see the following output:

```
result: [{'word': 'UC', 'score': 0.9993938207626343,
'entity': 'I-ORG', 'index': 4}, {'word': '##SC', 'score':
0.9974051713943481, 'entity': 'I-ORG', 'index': 5},
{'word': 'Oswald', 'score': 0.9988114833831787, 'entity':
'I-PER', 'index': 11}]
```

Transformer and Sentiment Analysis Tasks

Listing 11.3 displays the contents of `hf_transformer_sentiment.py` that illustrates how to perform a sentiment analysis task with the `HuggingFace` transformer.

LISTING 11.3: hf_transformer_sentiment.py

```
from transformers import pipeline

nlp = pipeline('sentiment-analysis')
comment = "Great news that we have pipelines in transformers"
```

```
result = nlp(comment)

print("comment:",comment)
print("sentiment:",result)
```

Listing 11.3 starts with an `import` statement and then initializes the variable `nlp` as an instance of the pipeline class, with `sentiment-analysis` as a parameter. Next, the variable comment is initialized with a test string, which is supplied to the variable `nlp`. The output is assigned to the variable `result`, whose contents are displayed. Launch the code in Listing 11.3 and you will see the following output:

```
comment: Great news that we have pipelines in transformers
sentiment: [{'label': 'POSITIVE', 'score': 0.9985968470573425}]
```

Transformer and Mask Filling Tasks

Listing 11.4 displays the contents of `hf_transformer_mask.py` that illustrates how to perform a mask-filling task with the `HuggingFace` transformer.

LISTING 11.4: hf_transformer_mask.py

```
from transformers import pipeline

nlp = pipeline('fill-mask')
result = nlp("I hope that you <mask> the movie")

print("result:",result)
```

Listing 11.4 starts with an `import` statement and then initializes the variable `nlp` as an instance of the pipeline class, with `fill-mask` as a parameter. Next, the variable `nlp` is invoked with a hard-coded sample sentence. The output is assigned to the variable `result`, whose contents are then displayed. Launch the code in Listing 11.4 and you will see the following output:

```
result: [{'sequence': '<s>I hope that you enjoyed the movie</
s>', 'score': 0.5466918349266052, 'token': 3776, 'token_str':
'Ġenjoyed'}, {'sequence': '<s>I hope that you enjoy the mov-
ie</s>', 'score': 0.36409610509872437, 'token': 2254, 'to-
ken_str': 'Ġenjoy'}, {'sequence': '<s>I hope that you liked
the movie</s>', 'score': 0.06604353338479996, 'token': 6640,
'token_str': 'Ġliked'}, {'sequence': '<s>I hope that you like
the movie</s>', 'score': 0.008552208542823792, 'token': 101,
'token_str': 'Ġlike'}, {'sequence': '<s>I hope that you loved
the movie</s>', 'score': 0.003726127091795206, 'token': 2638,
'token_str': 'Ġloved'}]
```

This concludes the section of the chapter pertaining to the HuggingFace transformer code samples. The next section briefly discusses T5, which is another powerful NLP model created by Google.

What is T5?

Text-to-text transfer transformer (T5) is an encoder-decoder model that converts all NLP tasks into a text-to-text format, and its downloadable code is here:

https://github.com/google-research/text-to-text-transfer-transformer

You can also install T5 by invoking the following command:

```
pip install t5[gcp]
```

T5 is pretrained on a multitask mixture of unsupervised and supervised tasks, and it works well on various tasks, such as translation. T5 is trained using a technique called "teacher forcing," which means that an input sequence and a target sequence are always required for training. The input sequence is designated with input_ids, whereas the target sequence is designated with output_ids and then passed to the decoder.

Since all tasks (such as classification, question answering, and translation) involve this input/output mechanism, the same model can be used for multiple tasks.

T5 provides several useful classes when working with T5 models. For example, the class `transformers.T5Config` enables you to specify configuration information, whose default values are similar to the `t5-small` architecture. Another useful class is `transformers.T5Tokenizer` that enables you to construct a T5 tokenizer.

T5 does differ from BERT in two significant ways that will become clearer after you read the BERT related material later in this chapter:

The inclusion of a causal decoder
The use of pretraining tasks instead of a fill-in-the-blank task

Although you can download code samples for T5, initially it might be simpler to experiment with T5 in this Google Colaboratory notebook (make sure to select a TPU for execution):

https://tiny.cc/t5-colab

More information about T5 and details regarding the preceding T5 classes (and other classes) is here:

https://huggingface.co/transformers/model_doc/t5.html

The next section briefly discusses BERT, along with some details regarding the way that BERT is trained and some BERT-based pretrained models.

What is BERT?

BERT is a pretrained model that is based on the transformer architecture that was developed in 2017 by Google. There are two versions of BERT called BERT Base and BERT Large. BERT Base consists of twelve layers (transformer blocks), twelve attention heads, and 110 million parameters. BERT Large is a larger pretrained model that consists of 24 layers (transformer blocks), sixteen attention heads, and 340 million parameters.

BERT can be used in conjunction with the Transformers library (discussed earlier in this chapter) that provide classes to perform various tasks, such as question answering and sequence classification.

BERT Features

BERT has a set of approximately 30,000 learned raw vectors. Moreover, just under 80% of those raw vectors correspond to "normal" words (i.e., they exist in an English dictionary). The remaining 20% are subwords that are created by WordPiece: these subwords have the form "##s" or "##ed". The latter subwords are useful for detecting the past tense of a verb in a sentence. In addition, the BERT vocabulary consists of 45% uppercase and 25% lowercase terms (approximately).

How is BERT Trained?

BERT is trained by performing a pretraining step, followed by a fine-tuning step. The pretraining step involves task-specific data. For example, if you want to perform sentiment analysis using BERT, you need a corpus of labeled data that specifies whether a sentence has positive or negative sentiment. As you would expect, the dataset is split into a training portion and a test portion, just as you have seen in code samples in previous chapters.

The fine-tuning step involves training the model on a large set of sample tasks. For example, if you want to train BERT to perform a question-answering task, then start with the pretrained model (that was trained on sentiment analysis) and fine-tune that model by training the model on a corpus of question/answer data.

How BERT Differs from Earlier NLP Techniques

There are several important aspects of BERT that differentiate BERT from algorithms such as word2vec. First, BERT does not perform a stemming operation. Instead, BERT performs subword tokenization via WordPiece (discussed later in this chapter).

Second, BERT creates contextual word embeddings whereas word2vec creates distributional word embeddings. Specifically, BERT uses all the words in a sentence in order to generate a word embedding for each word in a given sentence. As a result, the same word that is used in a different context in two sentences will have different word embeddings. However, word2vec uses bigrams to calculate word embeddings.

Third, BERT does *not* use cosine similarity in order to determine the extent to which two words are similar to each other. However, it's possible to use BERT with cosine similarity, provided that you fine-tune BERT on suitable data, such as the data and code samples in the following repository:

https://github.com/UKPLab/sentence-transformers

The Inner Workings of BERT

BERT implements a number of interesting techniques, some of which are listed here:

- MLM (masked language model)
- NSP (next sentence prediction)
- Special tokens ([CLS] and [SEP])
- Language mask
- Wordpiece (subword tokenization)
- SentencePiece

Each topic in the preceding list is discussed briefly in the following subsections.

What is MLM?

MLM is an acronym for masked language model. MLM is a BERT pretraining task, during which BERT processed the contents of Wikipedia (and also the BookCorpus). In this task, 15% of the words were replaced with the [MASK] token, and BERT then predicted the missing words.

Note that this task was performed on "chunks" of data that were submitted to BERT.

Many words in Wikipedia involve dates, names of people, and names of locations, some of which were replaced by the [MASK] token. During the training process, BERT ascertained the missing tokens correctly.

What is NSP?

In addition to MLM, BERT uses NSP, which is an acronym for next sentence prediction. NSP combines pairs of sentences in the following way:

- The second sentence is logically related to the first sentence in 50% of the pairs
- The second sentence is not logically related to the first sentence in the other 50% of the pairs

One of the tasks of BERT is to identify which pairs of sentences are correct and which pairs of sentences are incorrect.

Special Tokens

BERT uses two special tokens: [CLS] to indicate the start of a text string and [SEP] to separate sentences. For example, consider the following sentence:

```
Pizza with four toppings and trimmings.
```

The BERT tokenization of the preceding sentence is here:

```
['[CLS]', 'pizza', 'with', 'four', 'topping', '##s', 'and',
'trim', '##ming', '##s', '.', '[SEP]']
```

Listing 11.5 displays the contents of bert_special_tokens.py that illustrates how to display the special tokens in BERT.

LISTING 11.5: bert_special_tokens.py

```
import transformers
import numpy as np

# instantiate a BERT tokenizer and model:
print("creating tokenizer...")
tokenizer = transformers.BertTokenizer.from_pretrained('bert-base-uncased', do_lower_case=True)

print("creating model...")
```

```
nlp = transformers.TFBertModel.from_pretrained('bert-base-
                                                uncased')

# hidden layer with embeddings:
text1       = "cell phone"
input_ids1 = np.array(tokenizer.encode(text1))[None,:]
embedding1 = nlp(input_ids1)

print("input_ids1:")
print(input_ids1)
print()

print("tokenizer.sep_token:    ",tokenizer.sep_token)
print("tokenizer.sep_token_id:",tokenizer.sep_token_id)
print("tokenizer.cls_token:    ",tokenizer.cls_token)
print("tokenizer.cls_token_id:",tokenizer.cls_token_id)
print("tokenizer.pad_token:    ",tokenizer.pad_token)
print("tokenizer.pad_token_id:",tokenizer.pad_token_id)
print("tokenizer.unk_token:    ",tokenizer.unk_token)
print("tokenizer.unk_token_id:",tokenizer.unk_token_id)
print()
```

Listing 11.5 starts with two import statements and then initializes the variable `tokenizer` as an instance from a pretrained model. Next, the variable nlp is initialized as an instance of a pretrained model.

The next portion of Listing 11.5 initializes the variable `text1` as a two-word string, followed by the variable input-ids1 that consists of the tokens for the two words, along with two special tokens.

The final code block consists of a set of `print()` statements that display several special tokens and their token_id values. Launch the code in Listing 11.5 and you will see the following output:

```
creating tokenizer...
creating model...
input_ids1:
[[ 101 3526 3042  102]]

tokenizer.sep_token:     [SEP]
tokenizer.sep_token_id: 102
tokenizer.cls_token:     [CLS]
tokenizer.cls_token_id: 101
tokenizer.pad_token:     [PAD]
tokenizer.pad_token_id: 0
tokenizer.unk_token:     [UNK]
tokenizer.unk_token_id: 100
```

BERT Encoding: Sequence of Steps

BERT performs the following sequence of steps, all of which have been illustrated via code snippets in previous sections:

Step 1: Tokenize the text.
Step 2: Map the tokens to their IDs.
Step 3: Add the special [CLS] and [SEP] tokens.

As a simple example, the sentence "I got a book" has a total of six tokens (four word tokens, and the start and end tokens), along with the following indices:

```
[CLS]       101
i           1,045
got         2,288
a           1,037
book        2,338
[SEP]       101
```

Listing 11.6 displays the contents of bert_encoding_plus.py that illustrates how to display the special tokens in BERT.

LISTING 11.6: bert_encoding_plus.py

```
import transformers
import numpy as np

# instantiate a BERT tokenizer and model:
print("creating tokenizer...")
tokenizer = transformers.BertTokenizer.from_pretrained('bert-
base-uncased', do_lower_case=True)
print("creating model...")
nlp = transformers.TFBertModel.from_pretrained('bert-base-
uncased')

text="When were you last outside? I have been inside for 2
weeks."

encoding = tokenizer.encode_plus(
  text,
  max_length=32,
  add_special_tokens=True, # Add '[CLS]' and '[SEP]'
  return_token_type_ids=False,
  pad_to_max_length=True,
  return_attention_mask=True,
  return_tensors='pt',  # Return PyTorch tensors
)

print("encoding.keys():")
```

```
print(encoding.keys())
print()

print("len(encoding['input_ids'][0]):")
print(len(encoding['input_ids'][0]))
print()

print("encoding['input_ids'][0]:")
print(encoding['input_ids'])
print()

print("len(encoding['attention_mask'][0]):")
print(len(encoding['attention_mask'][0]))
print()

print("encoding['attention_mask']:")
print(encoding['attention_mask'])
print()

print("tokenizer.convert_ids_to_tokens(encoding['input_ids']
      [0]):")
print(tokenizer.convert_ids_to_tokens(encoding['input_ids']
      [0]))
print()
```

Listing 11.6 starts with two import statements and then initializes the variables tokenizer and nlp in the same fashion as previous code samples. Next, the variable text is initialized as a text string, followed by the variable encoding that acts as a configuration-like "holder" of parameters and their values.

The final portion of Listing 11.6 consists of six pairs of print() statements, each of which displays a parameter/value pair that is defined in the encoding variable. Launch the code in Listing 11.6 and you will see the following output:

```
creating tokenizer...
creating model...

encoding.keys():
dict_keys(['input_ids', 'attention_mask'])

len(encoding['input_ids'][0]):
32

encoding['input_ids'][0]:
tensor([[ 101, 2043, 2020, 2017, 2197, 2648, 1029, 1045, 2031,
         2042, 2503, 2005, 1016, 3134, 1012,  102, 0, 0, 0, 0, 0, 0, 0, 0,
         0, 0, 0, 0, 0, 0, 0, 0]])
```

```
len(encoding['attention_mask'][0]):
32

encoding['attention_mask']:
tensor([[1, 1, 1, 1, 1, 1, 1, 1, 1, 1, 1, 1, 1, 1, 1, 1, 0, 0,
0, 0, 0, 0, 0, 0, 0, 0, 0, 0, 0, 0, 0, 0]])

tokenizer.convert_ids_to_tokens(encoding['input_ids'][0]):
['[CLS]', 'when', 'were', 'you', 'last', 'outside', '?', 'i',
'have', 'been', 'inside', 'for', '2', 'weeks', '.', '[SEP]',
'[PAD]', '[PAD]', '[PAD]', '[PAD]', '[PAD]', '[PAD]', '[PAD]',
'[PAD]', '[PAD]', '[PAD]', '[PAD]', '[PAD]', '[PAD]', '[PAD]',
'[PAD]', '[PAD]']
```

Subword Tokenization

Out of vocabulary (OOV) refers to words in a corpus that do not belong to a vocabulary. When an OOV word is encountered, BERT splits the word into subwords, which is known as *subword tokenization*. The same process is applied to rare words.

Subword tokenization algorithms are based on a heuristic (something that's intuitive and often produces the correct answer). Specifically, words that appear more frequently words are assigned unique ids. However, lower frequency words are split into subwords that retain the meaning of the lower frequency words. The following list contains four important subword tokenization algorithms:

- byte-pair encoding (BPE)
- sentencepiece
- unigram language model
- wordpiece (used in BERT)

Byte-pair encoding for subwords represents frequent words with fewer symbols and less frequent words with more symbols. BPE is a bottom-up subword tokenization algorithm that learns a subword vocabulary of a certain size (the vocabulary size is a hyperparameter).

The first step in this technique involves splitting every word into unicode characters, each of which corresponds to a symbol in the final vocabulary. Now perform the following sequence of steps repeatedly:

1. Find the most frequent symbol bigram (pair of symbols).

2. Merge those symbols to create a new symbol and add this to the vocabulary.

3. Repeat the preceding steps until a maximum vocabulary size is reached.

In addition, GPT-2 views text input as a sequence of bytes instead of unicode characters; furthermore, an id is allocated to every byte in the sequence.

Wordpiece is a subword tokenization algorithm that is very similar to BPE. The main difference pertains to the specific manner in which bigrams are selected for the merging step. Interestingly, RoBERTa (which is based on BERT) also involves the use of wordpiece. Here are some example of subword tokenization in BERT:

```
"toppings"   is split into "topping" and "##s"
"trimmings"  is split into "trim", "##ming", and "##s"
"misspelled" is split into "mis", "##spel", and "##led"
```

However, keep in mind that BERT does *not* provide a mechanism to reconstruct the original word from its word pieces. Note that ELMo provides word-level (not subword) contextual representations for words, which is different from BERT. Later in this chapter you will see code samples that create BERT tokens from English sentences (that include toppings and trimmings).

Since word2vec and GloVe don't compute contextual word embeddings, the similarity between two embedded vectors may be of limited value.

Byte pair encoding (BPE) is one of the algorithms that is used in the GPT family of models. BPE (also known as diagram coding) is a data compression algorithm that uses the following technique: given a text string the most common pair of consecutive bytes of data is replaced with a byte that does exist in the text string. Each replacement is stored in a look-up table, which means that the table can be used to create the original text string. The models in the GPT family utilize a modified version of BPE.

For example, suppose we wanted to encode the data consisting of the following string:

```
aaabdaaabac
```

Since the byte pair aa occurs most often, we will replace it with a character that does not appear in the string, such as the letter z. Perform the replacement, which results in the following text string:

```
ZabdZabac (where Z=aa)
```

Repeat the substitution step, this time with the pair ab, and replace this pair with the letter Y:

```
ZYdZYac (where Y=ab Z=aa)
```

At this point we can continue the preceding procedure by selecting ZY (which appears twice) and replacing this string with the letter X, as shown here:

```
XdXac (where X=ZY Y=ab Z=aa)
```

SentencePiece is another subword tokenizer and a detokenizer for NLP that performs subword segmentation. SentencePiece also supporting BPE and unigram language model. The original arxiv paper that describes sentencepiece in detail is here:

https://arxiv.org/abs/1808.06226v1

Sentence Similarity in BERT

As you learned in a previous chapter, word2vec and GloVe use word embeddings to find the semantic similarity between two words. However, sentences contain additional information as well as relationships between multiple words.

A well-known example the need for contextual awareness is illustrated in the following pair of sentences:

The dog did not cross the street because it was too narrow.
The dog did not cross the street because it was too tired.

One technique for sentence similarity involves computing the average of the word embeddings of the words in each sentence and then computing the cosine similarity of the resulting pair of word embeddings. Alternatively, you can use tf-idf instead of word embeddings, and other techniques are also available. In all of these cases, word order is not taken into account, and the word embeddings are determined in an unsupervised fashion.

Word Context in BERT

Listing 11.7 displays the contents of `bert_context.py` that illustrates how BERT generates a different word vector for the same word that is used in a different context.

If you do not already have the `transformers` library installed, launch the following command in a command shell:

```
pip3 install transformers
```

> **NOTE** *This code downloads a 536M BERT model*

LISTING 11.7: bert_context.py

```
import transformers

text1 = "cell phone"

# instantiate a BERT tokenizer and model:
tokenizer = transformers.BertTokenizer.from_pretrained('bert-base-uncased', do_lower_case=True)

nlp = transformers.TFBertModel.from_pretrained('bert-base-uncased')

# hidden layer with embeddings:
input_ids1 = np.array(tokenizer.encode(text1))[None,:]
embedding1 = nlp(input_ids1)

# display text1 and its context:
print("text1:",text1)
print("embedding1[0][0]:")
print(embedding1[0][0])
print()

text2 = "prison cell"
# hidden layer with embeddings:
input_ids2 = np.array(tokenizer.encode(text2))[None,:]
embedding2 = nlp(input_ids2)

# display text2 and its context:
print("text2:",text2)
print("embedding2[0][0]:")
print(embedding2[0][0])
```

Listing 11.7 starts with import statements and then initializes the variables tokenizer, nlp, input_ids1, and embedding1 in exactly the same manner that you have seen in previous code samples. The next block of code displays the values of text1 and embedding1[0][0].

The next portion of Listing 11.7 is virtually the same as the previous code block, based on the replacement of text1 with text2. The output of Listing 11.7 is here:

```
input sentence #1:
text1: cell phone
embedding1[0][0]:
tf.Tensor(
[[-0.30501425  0.14509355 -0.18064171 ... -0.3127299
 -0.12173399 -0.09033043]
```

```
[ 0.80547976 -0.15233847  0.61319923 ... -0.7498784
  0.00167803 -0.11698578]
[ 1.0339862  -0.66511637 -0.17642722 ... -0.24407595
  0.03978422 -0.8694502 ]
[ 0.87851435  0.10932285 -0.27658027 ...  0.18180653
 -0.5829581  -0.34113947]], shape=(4, 768), dtype=float32)

text2: cell mate
embedding2[0][0]:
tf.Tensor(
[[-0.24141303  0.1146469  -0.13710016 ... -0.2908613
  -0.04577148  0.2965925 ]
 [ 0.05608664 -1.0035615   0.12738925 ... -0.30271983
   0.17530476  0.7245784 ]
 [ 0.2818157  -0.28047347 -0.6547173  ...  0.04996978
   0.01698243  0.03285426]
 [ 1.039136    0.12364347 -0.2661501  ...  0.09439699
  -0.7794917  -0.24966209]], shape=(4, 768), dtype=float32)
```

Listing 11.7 also generates the following informative message:

```
Some weights of the model checkpoint at bert-base-uncased were
not used when initializing TFBertModel: ['nsp___cls',
'mlm___cls']
- This IS expected if you are initializing TFBertModel from
the checkpoint of a model trained on another task or with an-
other architecture (e.g. initializing a BertForSequenceClassi-
fication model from a BertForPretraining model).
- This IS NOT expected if you are initializing TFBertModel
from the checkpoint of a model that you expect to be exactly
identical (initializing a BertForSequenceClassification model
from a BertForSequenceClassification model).
All the weights of TFBertModel were initialized from the model
checkpoint at bert-base-uncased.
If your task is similar to the task the model of the ckeck-
point was trained on, you can already use TFBertModel for pre-
dictions without further training.
```

Now that you have seen an example where BERT generates a different word vector for a word that is used in a different context, let's look at BERT tokens, which is the topic of the next section.

Generating BERT Tokens (1)

Listing 11.8 displays the contents of bert_tokens1.py that illustrates how to convert a text string to a BERT-compatible string and then tokenize the latter string into BERT tokens.

LISTING 11.8: bert_tokens1.py

```
from transformers import BertTokenizer, BertModel

tokenizer = BertTokenizer.from_pretrained('bert-base-uncased')

text1 = "Pizza with four toppings and trimmings."
marked_text1 = "[CLS] " + text1 + " [SEP]"
tokenized_text1 = tokenizer.tokenize(marked_text1)

print("input sentence #1:")
print(text1)
print()

print("Tokens from input sentence #1:")
print(tokenized_text1)
print()

print("Some tokens in BERT:")
print(list(tokenizer.vocab.keys())[1000:1020])
print()
```

Listing 11.8 imports BertTokenizer and BertModel, and uses the former to initialize the variable tokenizer. Next, the variable text1 is initialized to a text string, and marked_text1 prepends [CLS] to text1 and then appends [SEP] to text1. The last variable that is initialized is tokenized_text1, which is assigned the result of invoking the tokenizer() method on the variable marked_text1. The next three blocks of print() statements display the contents of text1, tokenized_text1, and a range of 20 BERT tokens, respectively. Launch the code in Listing 11.8 and you will see the following output:

```
input sentence #1:
Pizza with four toppings and trimmings.

Tokens from input sentence #1:
['[CLS]', 'pizza', 'with', 'four', 'topping', '##s', 'and',
'trim', '##ming', '##s', '.', '[SEP]']

Some tokens in BERT:
['"', '#', '$', '%', '&', "'", '(', ')', '*', '+', ',', '-',
'.', '/', '0', '1', '2', '3', '4', '5']
```

Generating BERT Tokens (2)

Listing 11.9 displays the contents of bert_tokens2.py that illustrates how to convert a text string to a BERT-compatible string and then tokenize the latter string into BERT tokens.

LISTING 11.9: bert_tokens2.py

```
from transformers import BertTokenizer, BertModel

tokenizer = BertTokenizer.from_pretrained('bert-base-uncased')

text2 = "I got a book and after I book for an hour, it's time
to book it."
marked_text2 = "[CLS] " + text2 + " [SEP]"
tokenized_text2 = tokenizer.tokenize(marked_text2)

print("input sentence #2:")
print(text2)
print()

print("Tokens from input sentence #2:")
print(tokenized_text2)
print()

# Map token strings to their vocabulary indices:
indexed_tokens2 = tokenizer.convert_tokens_to_ids(tokenized_
text2)

# Display the words with their indices:
for pair in zip(tokenized_text2, indexed_tokens2):
  print('{:<12} {:>6,}'.format(pair[0], pair[1]))
```

The first half of Listing 11.9 is almost identical to the first half of Listing 11.8, using the variable `text2` instead of `text1`.

The next portion of Listing 11.9 contains two blocks of `print()` statements that display the contents of `text2` and `tokenized_text2`, respectively. The next code snippet initializes the variable `indexed_tokens2` to the result of converting the tokens in `tokenized_text2` to `id` values.

The final portion of Listing 11.9 contains a loop that displays tokens and their associated `id` values. The output of Listing 11.9 is here:

```
input sentence #2:
I got a book and after I book for an hour, it's time to book
it.

Tokens from input sentence #2:
['[CLS]', 'i', 'got', 'a', 'book', 'and', 'after', 'i',
'book', 'for', 'an', 'hour', ',', 'it', "'", 's', 'time',
'to', 'book', 'it', '.', '[SEP]']

[CLS]            101
i              1,045
```

```
got         2,288
a           1,037
book        2,338
and         1,998
after       2,044
i           1,045
book        2,338
for         2,005
an          2,019
hour        3,178
,           1,010
it          2,009
'           1,005
s           1,055
time        2,051
to          2,000
book        2,338
it          2,009
.           1,012
[SEP]         102
```

The BERT Family

BERT has spawned a remarkable set of variations of the original BERT model, each of which provides some interesting features. Some of those variations are listed here:

- ALBERT
- DistilBERT
- CamemBERT
- FlauBERT
- RoBERTa
- BioBERT
- DocBERT
- ClinicalBERT
- German BERT

A lite BERT for self-supervised learning of language representations (ALBERT) was created by Google Research and Toyota Technological

Institute. Like RoBERTa, ALBERT is significantly smaller than BERT, and it's also more capable than BERT.

Keep in mind that ALBERT (unlike BERT) shares its parameters in all layers, which reduces the number of parameters, but has no effect on the training and inference time. In addition, ALBERT uses embedding matrix factorization, which further reduces the number of parameters. Furthermore, ALBERT uses sentence-order prediction (SOP), which is an improvement over next sentence prediction (NSP). Finally, ALBERT does not use a dropout rate, which also increases the model capacity.

ALBERT uses both whole-word masking and "n-gram masking," where the latter refers to masking multiple sequential words. Here is a code snippet for ALBERT:

```
from transformers import AlbertForMaskedLM, AlbertTokenizer

model1 = AlbertForMaskedLM.from_pretrained('albert-xxlarge-v1')
tokenizer = AlbertTokenizer.from_pretrained('albert-xxlarge-v1')

model2 = AlbertForMaskedLM.from_pretrained('albert-xxlarge-v2')
tokenizer = AlbertTokenizer.from_pretrained('albert-xxlarge-v2')
```

DistilBERT is a smaller version of BERT that contains 66 million parameters, which is 40% of the number of parameters of BERT Base (which has 110 million parameters). Even so, DistilBERT achieves 97% of BERT accuracy and is 60% faster than BERT Base, which makes DistilBERT useful for transfer learning.

As an aside, *knowledge distillation* involves a small model (called the "student") that is trained to mimic a larger model or an ensemble of models (called the "teacher"). DistilBERT is an example of a distilled network that is also used in production.

To give you an idea of the type of code required for DistilBERT, here is an example of instantiating a DistilBERT tokenizer:

```
import transformers
tokenizer = transformers.AutoTokenizer.from_
pretrained('distilbert-base-uncased', do_lower_case=True)
```

Here is another example of instantiating a DistilBERT tokenizer:

```
from transformers import DistilBertTokenizer:
tokenizer = DistilBertTokenizer.from.pretrained('distilbert-
base-uncased')
```

RoBERTa (from Facebook) leverages BERT's language masking strategy, along with some modifications of BERT's hyperparameters. Note that RoBERTa was trained on a corpus that is at least 10 times larger than the corpus for BERT.

Unlike BERT, RoBERTa does *not* use an NSP (Next Sentence Prediction) task. Instead, RoBERTa uses something called dynamic masking, whereby a masked token is actually modified during the training process.

Perform an online search to find more detailed information about the list of BERT-related models in the first part of this section.

Surpassing Human Accuracy: deBERTa

The deBERTa model from Microsoft recently surpassed human accuracy, as described in the following link:

https://www.microsoft.com/en-us/research/blog/microsoft-deberta-surpasses-human-performance-on-the-superglue-benchmark/

The architecture for this model comprises 48 Transformer layers with 1.5 billion parameters. This model has a GLUE score of 90.8, and a SuperGLUE score of 89.9, which manages to exceed the human performance score of 89.8.

Microsoft intends to integrate DeBERTa with the Turing natural language representation model Turing NLRv4 (also from Microsoft). The Turing models are ubiquitous in the Microsoft ecosystem, including products such as Bing and Azure Cognitive Services.

What is Google Smith?

The SMITH model from Google is a model for analyzing documents. In a very simplified description, the SMITH model is trained to understand passages within the context of the entire document. By contrast, BERT is trained to understand words within the context of sentences. However, the SMITH model (which outperforms BERT) supplements BERT by performing major operations that are not possible in BERT.

This concludes the BERT-specific portion of the chapter. The next section introduces GPT, followed by sections that contain details regarding GPT-2 (and code samples) as well as GPT-3.

Introduction to GPT

Generative pretraining (GPT), or sometimes called generative pretraining transformers, is a pretrained NLP-based model that was developed by OpenAI. GPT is trained with unlabeled data via unsupervised pretraining (also known as self-supervision).

GPT is based on the transformer architecture and takes advantage of the self-attention mechanism of the transformer. There are several versions of GPT, which includes GPT-2 (developed in 2019) and GPT-3 (the most recent version) that was released in June, 2020. Both GPT-2 and GPT-3 are discussed later in this chapter.

Lottery Ticket Hypothesis: In every sufficiently deep neural network, there is a smaller subnetwork that can perform just as well as the whole neural network.

Installing the Transformers Package

The installation process involves the following command:

```
pip3 install transformers
```

You can perform an upgrade of transformers by invoking the following command:

```
pip3 install -U transformers
```

However, you might encounter the following error message:

```
ERROR: After October 2020 you may experience errors when in-
stalling or updating packages. This is because pip will change
the way that it resolves dependency conflicts.

We recommend you use --use-feature=2020-resolver to test your
packages with the new resolver before it becomes the default.

sentence-transformers 0.3.7.2 requires transform-
ers<3.4.0,>=3.1.0, but you'll have transformers 4.1.1 which is
incompatible.
```

Working with GPT-2

This section contains `Python` code samples that use GPT-2 in order to perform sentiment analysis, question-and-answer, and there are some tasks that you can perform in GPT-2 that are comparable in GPT-3.

NOTE *The `Python` code samples in this section work with `Python` 3.7.9 but not with `Python` 3.6 or `Python` 3.8 (it's possible that other `Python` 3.7.x versions will work as well)*

If you need to install `Python` 3.7.9, you will also need to execute the following commands to install transformers, tensorflow, and scipy:

```
pip3 install transformers
pip3 install tensorflow
pip3 install scipy
```

Listing 11.10 displays the contents of `gpt2_sentiment.py` that illustrates how to perform sentiment analysis in GPT2.

LISTING 11.10: gpt2_sentiment.py

```
# pip3 install transformers
from transformers import pipeline

# pipeline for sentiment-analysis:
cls = pipeline('sentiment-analysis')

text1 = "I love deep dish Chicago pizza."
sentiment1 = cls(text1)
print("sentence: ",text1)
print("sentiment:",sentiment1)
print()

text2 = "I dislike anchovies."
sentiment2 = cls(text2)
print("sentence: ",text2)
print("sentiment:",sentiment2)
print()

text3 = "I dislike anchovies but I like pickled herring."
sentiment3 = cls(text3)
print("sentence: ",text3)
print("sentiment:",sentiment3)
```

Listing 11.10 contains an `import` statement and then initializes the variable `cls` as an instance of the `pipeline` class by specifying sentiment-analysis (which is the task for this code sample).

The next three code blocks perform sentiment analysis on the text strings `text1`, `text2`, and `text3`, respectively. Launch the code and you will see the following output:

```
sentence:  I love deep dish Chicago pizza.
sentiment: [{'label': 'POSITIVE', 'score': 0.9985044598579407}]
```

```
sentence:   I dislike anchovies.
sentiment: [{'label': 'NEGATIVE', 'score':
0.9982384443283081}]

sentence:   I dislike anchovies but I like pickled herring.
sentiment: [{'label': 'POSITIVE', 'score':
0.7346124649047852}]
```

Listing 11.11 displays the contents of gpt2_qna.py that illustrates how to perform sentiment analysis in GPT2.

Note that this Python code sample will not work on Python 3.8.x: you must use Python 3.7.

LISTING 11.11: gpt2_qna.py

```
from transformers import pipeline

# pipeline for question-answering:
qna = pipeline('question-answering')

qc_pair = {
   'question': 'What is the name of the repository ?',
   'context': 'Pipeline have been included in the huggingface/
              transformers repository'
}

if __name__ == "__main__":
 result = qna (qc_pair)
 print("result:")
 print(result)
```

Listing 11.11 starts with an `import` statement and then initializes the variable `qna` as an instance of the `pipeline` class from the `transformers` library, with `question-answering` as a parameter. Next, the variable `gc_pair` is initialized as a pair of question/answer strings.

Next, the variable `result` is initialized with the result of invoking Ana with `gc_pair`, and then the contents of `result` are displayed. Now launch the code and you will see the following output:

```
result:
{'score': 0.5135953426361084, 'start': 35, 'end': 59,
'answer': 'huggingface/transformers'}
```

In case you're wondering why Listing 11.11 contains an `if` statement, you might see the following error message if you remove the `if` statement:

```
#output:
   raise RuntimeError('''
RuntimeError:
        An attempt has been made to start a new process before
the current process has finished its bootstrapping phase.

        This probably means that you are not using fork to
start your child processes and you have forgotten to use the
proper idiom in the main module:

             if __name__ == '__main__':
                freeze_support()
                ...

        The "freeze_support()" line can be omitted if the program
        is not going to be frozen to produce an executable.
```

Listing 11.12 displays the contents of gpt2_text_gen.py that illustrates how to use generate text from an input string in GPT2. Note that the default model for the text generation pipeline is GPT-2.

LISTING 11.12: gpt2_text_gen.py

```
from transformers import pipeline

text_gen = pipeline("text-generation")

# specify a max_length of 50 tokens and sampling "off":
prefix_text = "What a wonderful"
generated_text = text_gen(prefix_text, max_length=50,
do_sample=False)[0]

print("=> #1 generated_text['generated_text']:")
print(generated_text['generated_text'])
print("------------------------------\n")

prefix_text = "Once in a "
generated_text = text_gen(prefix_text, max_length=50,
do_sample=False)[0]

print("=> #2 generated_text['generated_text']:")
print(generated_text['generated_text'])
print("------------------------------\n")

prefix_text = "Once in a blue "
generated_text = text_gen(prefix_text, max_length=50,
do_sample=False)[0]

print("=> #3 generated_text['generated_text']:")
print(generated_text['generated_text'])
```

```
print("-------------------------------\n")
```

Listing 11.12 starts with an `import` statement and then initializes the variable `text_gen` as an instance of the `pipeline` class by specifying `text-generation` (which is the task for this code sample). The next three blocks of code display the completion of the text in prefix_text, where the latter is assigned three different text strings. Launch the code in Listing 11.12 and you will see the following output:

```
=> #1 generated_text['generated_text']:
What a wonderful thing about this is that it's a very simple
and simple way to get your hands on a new game.

The game is a simple, simple game. It's a simple game. It's a
simple game. It's
-------------------------------

=> #2 generated_text['generated_text']:
Once in a vernacular, the word "carnage" is used to describe a
large, open, and well-lit place.

The word "carnage" is used to describe a large, open, and well-
-------------------------------

=> #3 generated_text['generated_text']:
Once in a blue urn, you can see the "C" in the center of the
"C" and the "A" in the bottom right corner.

The "C" is the "A" and the "A" are
-------------------------------
```

Listing 11.13 displays the contents of `gpt2_qna.py` that illustrates how to perform sentiment analysis in GPT2. Note that this `Python` code sample will not work on `Python` 3.8.x: you must use `Python` 3.7.

LISTING 11.13: *gpt2_auto.py*

```
from transformers import AutoTokenizer, TFAutoModel

tokenizer = AutoTokenizer.from_pretrained("bert-base-uncased")
mymodel = TFAutoModel.from_pretrained("bert-base-uncased")

inputs = tokenizer("I love deep dish Chicago pizza", return_tensors="tf")
```

```
outputs = mymodel(**inputs)

print("inputs:   ",inputs)
print("outputs: ",outputs)
```

Listing 11.13 starts with an `import` statement and then initializes the variable `tokenizer` as a generic tokenizer class from `bert-base-uncased` by invoking the `from_pretrained()` method of the `AutoTokenizer` class that belongs to the `transformers` library. Similarly, `mymodel` is a general model class from `bert-base-uncased` by invoking the `from_pretrained()` method of the `TFAutoModel` class that belongs to the `transformers` library.

Next, the variable `inputs` is initialized with the result of passing a hard-coded string to the `tokenizer` variable. Then the variable `outputs` is initialized with the result of passing `inputs` to the variable `mymodel`. The last portion of Listing 11.13 displays the contents of inputs and outputs. Launch the code and you will see the following output:

```
inputs:    {'input_ids': <tf.Tensor: shape=(1, 8), dtype=int32,
numpy=array([[  101,  1045,  2293,  2784,  9841,  3190, 10733,
  102]],
      dtype=int32)>, 'token_type_ids': <tf.Tensor: shape=(1,
8), dtype=int32, numpy=array([[0, 0, 0, 0, 0, 0, 0, 0]],
dtype=int32)>, 'attention_mask': <tf.Tensor: shape=(1,
8), dtype=int32, numpy=array([[1, 1, 1, 1, 1, 1, 1, 1]],
dtype=int32)>}
outputs:   TFBaseModelOutputWithPooling(last_hidden_state=<tf.
Tensor: shape=(1, 8, 768), dtype=float32, numpy=
array([[[-0.00286604,  0.22725284,  0.0192489 , ...,
         -0.16997483,  0.22732456,  0.2084062 ],
        [ 0.37293857,  0.18514417, -0.1804212 , ...,
         -0.02841423,  0.92029154,  0.08076832],
        [ 1.0605763 ,  0.68393016,  0.3488946 , ...,
          0.23068337,  0.57474136, -0.2725499 ],
        ...,
        [ 0.36834046,  0.09277615, -0.49751407, ...,
         -0.21702018, -0.15317607, -0.17662546],
        [ 0.2218363 , -0.1452129 , -0.6224062 , ...,
          0.19659105,  0.0055675 ,  0.05520308],
        [ 0.38959947,  0.1536812 , -0.2523777 , ...,
          0.3461408 , -0.5905776 , -0.2758692 ]]],
dtype=float32)>, pooler_output=<tf.Tensor: shape=(1, 768),
dtype=float32,
...
numpy=array([[-8.23929489e-01, -2.69686729e-01,  2.79440969e-01,
         5.52639008e-01, -5.11318594e-02, -8.98018852e-02,
         7.92447925e-01,  1.49121523e-01,  4.11069989e-02,
        -9.99752760e-01,  2.84106694e-02,  4.69654143e-01,
```

```
              9.74410057e-01, -2.57081628e-01,  9.02504683e-01,
         -4.83381122e-01,  3.19796950e-02, -5.14692605e-01,
...
              3.13184172e-01,  3.45878363e-01,  7.98233569e-01,
              4.64420468e-01,  6.13458335e-01,  4.65085119e-01,
              2.03554392e-01, -5.93035281e-01,  8.85935843e-01]],
dtype=float32)>, hidden_states=None, attentions=None)
```

Listing 11.14 displays the contents of `pytorch_gpt_next_word.py` that illustrates how to predict the next word in a sentence.

LISTING 11.14: *pytorch_gpt_next_word.py*

```
import torch
from pytorch_transformers import GPT2Tokenizer,
GPT2LMHeadModel

# Load pre-trained GPT-2 tokenizer model:
tokenizer = GPT2Tokenizer.from_pretrained('gpt2')

# encode the words in a sentence:
text = "What is the fastest car in the"
indexed_tokens = tokenizer.encode(text)

# convert tokens to a PyTorch tensor:
tokens_tensor = torch.tensor([indexed_tokens])

# load pre-trained model (weights)
model = GPT2LMHeadModel.from_pretrained('gpt2')

# "eval" mode deactivates the DropOut modules:
model.eval()

# Predict each token:
with torch.no_grad():
 outputs = model(tokens_tensor)
 predictions = outputs[0]

print("=> list of predictions:")
print(predictions[0, -1, :])
print()

print("=> argmax of predictions:")
print(torch.argmax(predictions[0, -1, :]).item())
print()

# Get the predicted next sub-word
predicted_index = torch.argmax(predictions[0, -1, :]).item()
predicted_text = tokenizer.decode(indexed_tokens +
[predicted_index])
```

```
# Print the predicted word
print("=> initial text:")
print(text)
print()

print("=> Predicted next word:")
print(predicted_text)
```

Listing 11.14 starts with two `import` statements, the second of which is sort of like the counterpart to the `import` statement in Listing 11.13:

```
from transformers import AutoTokenizer, TFAutoModel
```

Next, the variable `tokenizer` is created as an instance of a generic `gpt2` model. Then the variable `text` is initialized as a text string and passed as a parameter to the `encode()` method of the variable `tokenizer`, with the result assigned to the variable `indexed_tokens`.

The next portion of Listing 11.14 creates the variable `tokens_tensor`, which is a `Torch`-based tensor that is created from `indexed_tokens`. Now we can instantiate the variable `model` as generic instance of the `gpt2` model.

The second half of Listing 11.14 starts by initializing the variables `outputs` and `predictions`, followed by blocks of `print()` statements that display the values of `predictions` and the index position with the maximum value. Then the initial text is displayed, followed by the initial text concatenated with the predicted word **world** (that is shown in bold in the following output).

The output of Listing 11.14 is here (this might take a minute or two when you launch it the first time due to a file download):

```
=> list of predictions:
tensor([ -96.1219,  -94.2472,  -96.9560,   ..., -103.5570,
        -100.5182,  -95.6672])

=> argmax of predictions:
995

=> initial text:
What is the fastest car in the

=> Predicted next word:
What is the fastest car in the world
```

What is GPT-3?

GPT-3 is an extension of the GPT-2 model that also involves more layers and data. For example, the largest model has 96 attention layers, each of which contains 96×128 dimension heads. GPT-3 consists of 175 billion parameters and was trained on hundreds of gigabytes of text in order to learn how to predict the next word in a user-supplied text string.

Give GPT-3 an initial sequence of words and GPT-3 will generate various responses, such as code generation, news articles, poems, and even make jokes.

GPT-3 generated an interesting poem about Elon Musk ("your tweets are a blight"), part of which you can read here:

https://www.businessinsider.com/elon-musk-poem-tweets-gpt-3-openai-2020-8

GPT-3 caught the world by surprise, and the response to GPT-3 ranges from shock, skepticism, anxiety, and amazement.

The GPT-3 model with 175 billion parameters was trained on an unlabeled dataset consisting of almost 500 billion tokens from a variety of sources. The key differentiator of GPT-3 is its ability to perform specific tasks without the need for fine-tuning, whereas other models tend to require task-specific datasets, and they generally do not perform as well on other tasks.

GPT-2 and GPT-3 have similar architectures, which is to say, they both have a "vanilla" transformer. GPT-2 has 1.5 billion parameters whereas GPT-3 has 175 billion parameters, which is more than 100 times larger than GPT-2.

One of the distinguishing characteristics of GPT-3 is its ability to solve unseen NLP tasks: this is due to the fact that GPT-3 was trained on a very large corpus. GPT-3 also uses "few shot" learning (discussed later in this chapter) and can perform the following tasks:

- translate natural language into code for websites
- solve complex medical question-and-answer problems
- create tabular financial reports
- write code to train machine learning models

The GPT-3 API involves setting the temperature parameter as well as the response length parameter. The temperature parameter (whose default value is 0.7) affects how much randomness the system uses in generating its replies. The response length parameter yields an approximate number of "words" the system generates in its response.

GPT-3 has surprised people with its capacity to generate prose as well as poetry. In case you didn't already know, Elon Musk is one of the founding members of OpenAI that created GPT-3, which generated the following poem about Elon Musk. [1]

> *The SEC said, "Musk,/your tweets are a blight. / They really could cost you your job, / if you don't stop / all this tweeting at night." / ... Then Musk cried, "Why? / The tweets I wrote are not mean, / I don't use all caps / and I'm sure that my tweets are clean." / "But your tweets can move markets / and that's why we're sore. / You may be a genius / and a billionaire, / but that doesn't give you the right to be a bore!"*

What is the Goal?

The aim of the GPT-3 pretrained model is to directly evaluate the model on the test-related data of new tasks; i.e., GPT-3 essentially skips the training-related data of new tasks and focuses directly on the test-related data, in its capacity as a "few shot" learner (discussed later).

By way of comparison, GPT-3 has 175 billion parameters, whereas GPT-2 has 1.5 billion parameters, and BERT Large has 340 million parameters. GPT-3 and was trained entirely on publicly available datasets, on nearly 500,000,000,000 words (some of which might contain offensive content). GPT-3 achieved state of the art performance on several NLP tasks without fine-tuning, at the cost of over USD 10,000,000. Some of the datasets that were used to train GPT-3 are downloadable from this read-only Github repository:

https://github.com/openai/gpt-3

GPT-3 has caught the attention of many people because of various tasks that it has performed, including automatic code generation. For example, one user typed a paragraph of text describing the following Web application:

- a button that increments a total by USD 3
- a button that decrements a total by USD 5
- a button that displays the current total

---

[1] *https://www.businessinsider.com/elon-musk-poem-tweets-gpt-3-openai-2020-8*

GPT-3 then created a React application with the preceding functionality, which prompted a variety of reactions: some people were amused by such a simplistic application, whereas others contemplated their future job security.

GPT-3 Task Strengths and Mistakes

GPT-3 has the ability to perform text generation that is close to human-level quality. For example, suppose that GPT-3 is given a title and a subtitle, along with the word "article" that serves as a prompt. GPT-3 can then write brief articles that often seem to be written by humans.

However, any trained model has limitations, including GPT-3. Keep in mind that bias exists in the corpus that was used to train GPT-3. According to the following article, one way in which GPT-3 can misclassify results is to include bias toward women and minorities:

https://techcrunch.com/2020/08/07/here-are-a-few-ways-gpt-3-can-go-wrong/

A more significant example is the use of GPT-3 in a medical chatbot, that told a fake patient (who expressed suicidal thoughts) to kill himself:

https://artificialintelligence-news.com/2020/10/28/medical-chatbot-openai-gpt3-patient-kill-themselves/

GPT-3 Architecture

GPT-3 has eight different model sizes (from 125M to 175B parameters), and the smallest GPT-3 model is about the size of BERT-Base and RoBERTa-Base, with twelve attention layers that in turn have 12×64 dimension heads. However, the largest GPT-3 model is ten times larger than T5-11B (the previous record holder), and has 96 attention layers, which in turn have 96×128 dimension heads.

GPT versus BERT

There are some important differences between GPT-2 and BERT. Specifically, GPT-2 is *not* bidirectional and has no concept of masking. In addition, GPT-2 is based on transformer decoder blocks. Moreover, GPT-2 involves supervised fine-tuning and outputs only one token at a time.

By contrast, BERT adds the NSP task during training and also has a segment embedding. BERT uses transformer encoder blocks (not the decoder blocks) and also requires pretraining. Moreover, the fine-tuning process necessitates task-specific sample data.

Zero-Shot, One-Shot, and Few Shot Learners

These three types of learners differ in the number of task examples that they are given and also the number of gradient updates that they perform.

Specifically, a *zero-shot* learner is a model that predicts an answer based solely on an NLP description of the task: *no gradient updates are performed*.

A *one-shot* learner is a model that (a) sees a description of the task and (b) one example of the task: *no gradient updates are performed*.

A *few-shot* learner is a model that (a) sees a description of the task and (b) a few examples of the task: *no gradient updates are performed*, and a "few" examples can involve between ten and 100 examples of the task.

With the preceding points in mind, GPT-3 is a "few shot" learner because GPT-3 is fine-tuned on a small set of samples. By contrast, most other models (including BERT) require an elaborate fine-tuning step.

GPT Task Performance

For most models, the task of translating sentences from English to Italian involves thousands of sentence pairs in order for those models to learn how to perform translation. By comparison, GPT-3 does not require a fine-tuning step: it can handle custom language tasks without training data.

Thus, GPT-3 has the ability to perform specific tasks without any special tuning, which is something that other models cannot do well. For example, GPT-3 can be trained to translate text, generate code, or even write poetry. Moreover, GPT-3 can do so with no more than ten training examples.

One other point to keep in mind: GPT-3 is not only a few-short learner, but it can also perform as a zero-short learner and a one-shot learner. By way of comparison, GPT-3 as a zero-shot learner has higher accuracy than a fine-tuned RoBERTa model (which previously had SOTA performance).

In terms of reading comprehension, GPT-3 performs best on free-form conversational datasets, and performs its worst on datasets that involve modeling structured dialog. However, as a few-shot learner for this task, GPT-3 outperforms the fine-tuned baseline of BERT. In addition, GPT-3 performs well on the SQuAD 2.0 dataset from Stanford, but under performs on multiple-choice test questions.

The Switch Transformer: One Trillion Parameters

As this book goes to print, Google researchers announced an NLP model with one trillion parameters, which is almost six times as large as GPT-3 (175 billion parameters). This model is the largest model ever created, and as much as four times faster than T5-XXL (a previous largest language model from Google).

Instead of using complicated algorithms, the researchers combined a simple architecture in conjunction with large datasets and parameter counts. Since large-scale training is computationally intensive, they adopted a `Switch Transformer`, which is a technique that uses only a subset of the parameters of a model. In addition to the model's sparseness, the Switch Transformer adroitly takes advantage of GPUs and TPUs for intense matrix multiplications operations.

Looking Ahead

Several important topic are not discussed in this book. For example, the topic of ethics is much more visible than it was even just a few years ago. Various questions have become more prominent in AI, such as the ethical concerns associated with large-scale deployment of AI system, how algorithms contribute decision-making processes, the source of data and the extent of biases in that data.

In health care, questions arise regarding AI-controlled robots prescribing medicine and performing surgery. Moreover, there are legal issues and accountability when robots make mistakes, such as who is responsible (the owner or the robot manufacturer?) and determining the type of penalty to impose (deactivate one robot or every robot in the same series?).

In parallel with the preceding issues, recent developments in AI are creating a sense of optimism that breakthroughs may well be on the event horizon. Recently OpenAI created DALL-E (coined from Salvador Dali and Pixar's WALL-E), which is 12-billion parameter variation of GPT-3: *https://openai.com/blog/dall-e/*

In addition, DeepMind developed AlphaFold that made a significant contribution toward solving the so-called *protein folding* problem, which has been called a "50-year-old problem in biology," and AlphaFold handily won a competition (by a substantial margin) over the competition.

To give you an idea of the impact of AlphaFold, Andrei Lupas, who is an evolutionary biologist at the Max Planck Institute for Developmental Biology in Tübingen, Germany, stated "The [AlphaFold] model from group 427 gave us our structure in half an hour, after we had spent a decade trying everything."[2]

Indeed, the future of NLP and AI in general looks both challenging and promising, guided by ethical principles that may lead us to a more mindful way of life.

Summary

This chapter started with an introduction to the concept of attention, followed by the transformer architecture that was developed by Google and released in late 2017. You also learned how to use the transformer model from HuggingFace to perform tasks such as NER, QnA, Sentiment Analysis, and mask-filling Tasks.

Next, you learned about `BERT`, which is a pretrained NLP model that is based on the transformer architecture, along with some of its features. You also saw how to perform sentence similarity in `BERT`, and how to generate `BERT` tokens. Then you learned about several `BERT`-based trained models, including `DistilledBERT`, `CamemBERT`, and `FlauBERT`.

In the final portion of this chapter you learned about GPT-3 and some of its remarkable features, and its strengths as well as its weaknesses. You also learned about various types of learners and how GPT-3 was trained.

Congratulations! You have reached the end of a fast-paced introduction to NLP, and now you are in a good position to use the knowledge that you acquired in this book as a stepping stone to further your understanding of NLP.

---

[2] *https://www.nature.com/articles/d41586-020-03348-4*

APPENDIX A

DATA AND STATISTICS

This appendix contains a wide assortment of topics of varying degrees of complexity. The first part is devoted to explanations about data types, scaling data values, techniques for dealing with missing data values, and several dimensionality reduction algorithms. The second part is primarily about probability and statistical concepts such as Gini impurity, entropy, perplexity, cross-entropy, and KL divergence. This section also contains brief introduction to distance metrics and Sklearn (and some of its built-in datasets).

Given the diverse set of topics in this appendix, it might be easier to focus on a subset of topics containing what is unfamiliar to you instead of reading the appendix in its entirety. Whichever approach you adopt, be assured that it's *not* necessary to understand everything in this appendix. In fact, there are topics in this appendix that you might rarely encounter until you have gained several years of experience in machine learning. At the same time, it's a good idea to read as much material as you can absorb, and perhaps opting to skip the optional sections and the dimensionality reduction algorithms during your first pass through this appendix.

The first part of this appendix contains an overview of different types of data, and an explanation of how to normalize and standardize a set of numeric values by calculating the mean and standard deviation of a set of numbers. You will see how to map categorical data to a set of integers and how to perform a one-hot encoding. This section also contains details about anomalies and outliers, and how you can handle them.

The second part discusses imbalanced datasets as well as SMOTE for generating synthetic data. This section also discusses LIME and ANOVA, which are two ways to analyze classifiers.

The third section introduces probability and how to calculate expected values. This section also introduces discrete and continuous random variables, followed by statistical concepts (mean, median, mode, and standard deviation). In addition, you will learn about the central limit theory and the bias-variance trade-off.

The fourth section introduces many concepts, including Gini impurity, entropy, perplexity, cross-entropy, and Kullback-Leibler (KL) divergence. Moreover, you will learn about covariance matrices, and correlation matrices.

The fifth section introduces principal component analysis (PCA), which involves concepts from linear algebra, such as eigenvalues and eigenvectors. Then you will learn about algorithms such as singular value decomposition (SVD) and t-SNE. The last part of this section discusses various types of distance metrics.

The sixth section of this appendix introduces Sklearn, which is a very powerful Python library for machine learning. You will see an example of combining Sklearn with Pandas and the Iris dataset, as well as how to use Sklearn for outlier detection.

The final section contains a mixture of topics, starting with Bayes' theorem, the topic of statistical test, and a description of vector spaces that are relevant for VSMs (vector space models) that are discussed in Chapter 4.

What are Datasets?

In simple terms, a dataset is a source of data (such as a text file) that contains rows and columns of data. Each row is typically called a *datapoint*, and each column is called a *feature*. The goal is to clean the data, determine the most important features, and define a model (based on an algorithm) and then train the model on the dataset.

A dataset can be a CSV, TSV, Excel spreadsheet, a table in an RDMBS, a document in a NoSQL database, the output from a Web service, and so forth. As you will see, someone needs to analyze the dataset to determine which features are the most important and which features can be safely ignored in order to train a model with the given dataset.

A dataset can vary from very small (a couple of features and 100 rows) to very large (more than 1,000 features and more than one million rows). If you are unfamiliar with the problem domain, then you might struggle to determine the most important features in a large dataset. In this situation, you might need a "domain expert" who understands the importance of the features, their inter-dependencies (if any), and whether or not the data values for the features are valid. In addition, there are algorithms (called dimensionality reduction algorithms) that can help you determine the most important features. For example, Principal Component Analysis (PCA) s one such algorithm, which is discussed in more detail later in this appendix.

Data Preprocessing

Data preprocessing is the initial step that involves validating the contents of a dataset, which involves making decisions about missing and incorrect data values:

- dealing with missing data values
- cleaning "noisy" text-based data
- removing HTML tags
- dealing with emojis/emoticons
- filtering data
- grouping data
- handling currency and date formats (i18n)

Cleaning data is a subset of data wrangling that involves removing unwanted data as well as handling missing data. In the case of text-based data, you might need to remove HTML tags, punctuation, and so forth. In the case of numeric data, it's less likely (although still possible) that alphabetic characters are mixed together with numeric data. However, a dataset with numeric features might have incorrect values or missing values (discussed later). In addition, calculating the minimum, maximum, mean, median, and standard deviation of the values of a feature obviously pertain only to numeric values.

After the preprocessing step is completed, data wrangling is performed, which refers to transforming data into a new format. For example, you might have to combine data from multiple sources into a single dataset. For example, you might need to convert between different units of measurement (such as date formats, currency values, and so forth so that the data values can be represented in a consistent manner in a dataset.

In case you didn't already know, currency and date values are part of something that is called `i18n` (internationalization), whereas `l10n` (localization) targets a specific nationality, language, or region. Hard-coded values (such as text strings) can be stored as resource strings in a file that's often called a resource bundle, where each string is referenced via a code. Each language has its own resource bundle.

Data Types

If you have written computer programs, then you know that explicit data types exist in many programming languages, such as `C`, `C++`, `Java`, `TypeScript`, and so forth. Some programming languages, such as `JavaScript` and `awk`, do not require initializing variables with an explicit type: the type of a variable is inferred dynamically via an implicit type system (i.e., one that is not directly exposed to a developer).

In machine learning, datasets can contain features that have different types of data, such as a combination of one or more of the following:

- numeric data (integer/floating point and discrete/continuous)
- character/categorical data (different languages)
- date-related data (different formats)
- currency data (different formats)
- binary data (yes/no, 0/1, and so forth)
- nominal data (multiple unrelated values for identification)
- ordinal data (multiple and related values for ordering)

Consider a dataset that contains real-estate data, which can have as many as 30 columns (or even more), often with the following features:

- the number of bedrooms in a house: numeric value and a discrete value
- the number of square feet: a numeric value and (probably) a continuous value
- the name of the city: character data
- the construction date: a date value

- the selling price: a currency value and probably a continuous value
- the "for sale" status: binary data (either "yes" or "no")

Nominal data is qualitative, which includes: categories, colors, names, labels, and yes/no values. Another example of nominal data is a set of colors such as {red, green, blue}. A third example of nominal data is the seasons in a year: although many (most?) countries have four distinct seasons, some countries have two distinct seasons. However, keep in mind that seasons can be associated with different temperature ranges (summer versus winter). An example of ordinal data is an employee pay grade: 1=entry level, 2=one year of experience, and so forth. Just to add a bit more emphasis to three types of numeric data:

> *nominal data* involving numbers simply name or identify something (such as members of a team or a particular zip code) without reference to quantity or rank
> *ordinal data* involves numbers that indicate the order or rank of items (such as third place or second in a queue)
> *cardinal data* involves numbers that indicate quantity (such as 8 employees)

An example of binary data is the pair {male, female}, and in some (many?) cases, this feature needs to be included during the training of a model. The solution involves converting {male, female} to a numeric counterpart, such as {0,1}. If you needed to do so with the previous set of colors, you could use {0,1,2} as the counterparts for {red, green, blue}. Categorical data is discussed in more detail later in this chapter.

Preparing Datasets

If you have the good fortune to inherit a dataset that is in pristine condition, then data-cleaning tasks (discussed later) are vastly simplified: in fact, it might not be necessary to perform *any* data cleaning for the dataset. However, if you need to create a dataset that combines data from multiple datasets that contain different formats for dates and currency, then you need to perform a conversion to a common format.

If you need to train a model that includes features that have categorical data, then you need to convert that categorical data to numeric data. For instance, the `Titanic` dataset contains a feature called "gender," which is either male or female. As you will see later in this appendix, `Pandas` makes it extremely simple to "map" male to 0 and female to 1.

Continuous versus Discrete Data

As a simple rule of thumb: *discrete data* is a set of values that can be counted whereas *continuous data* must be measured. Discrete data can "reasonably" fit in a drop-down list of values, but there is no exact value for making such a determination. One person might think that a list of 500 values is discrete, whereas another person might think it's continuous.

For example, the list of provinces of Canada and the list of states of the United States are discrete data values, but is the same true for the number of countries in the world (roughly 200) or for the number of languages in the world (more than 7,000)?

However, values for temperature, humidity, and barometric pressure are considered continuous. Currency is also treated as continuous, even though there is a measurable difference between two consecutive values. The smallest unit of currency for US currency is one penny, which is 1/100th of a dollar (accounting-based measurements use the "mil," which is 1/1,000th of a dollar).

Continuous data types can have subtle differences. For example, someone who is 200 centimeters tall is twice as tall as someone who is 100 centimeters tall; similarly for 100 kilograms versus 50 kilograms. However, temperature is different: 80 degrees Fahrenheit is not twice as hot as 40 degrees Fahrenheit.

Furthermore, keep in mind that the word "continuous" has a different meaning in mathematics is not necessarily the same as continuous in machine learning. In the former, a continuous variable (let's say in the 2D Euclidean plane) can have an uncountably infinite number of values. However, a feature in a dataset that can have more values that can be "reasonably" displayed in a drop down list is treated *as though* it's a continuous variable.

For instance, values for stock prices are discrete: they must differ by at least a penny (or some other minimal unit of currency), which is to say, it's meaningless to say that the stock price changes by one-millionth of a penny. However, since there are "so many" possible stock values, it's treated as a continuous variable. The same comments apply to car mileage, ambient temperature, barometric pressure, and so forth.

"Binning" Continuous Data

With the previous section in mind, the concept of "binning" refers to subdividing a set of values into multiple intervals, and then treating all the numbers in the same interval as though they had the same value.

As a simple example, suppose that a feature in a dataset contains the age of people in a dataset. The range of values is approximately between 0 and 120, and we could "bin" them into 12 equal intervals, where each consists of 10 values: 0 through 9, 10 through 19, 20 through 29, and so forth.

However, partitioning the values of people's age as described in the preceding paragraph can be problematic. Suppose that person A, person B, and person C are 29, 30, and 39 years of age, respectively. Person A and person B are probably more similar to each other than person B and person C, but because of the way in which the ages are partitioned, B is classified as closer to C than to A. In fact, binning can increase Type I errors (false positive) and Type II errors (false negative), as discussed in this blog post:

https://medium.com/@peterflom/why-binning-continuous-data-is-almost-always-a-mistake-ad0b3a1d141f

Fortunately, there are several alternatives to binning that you can explore, such as:

- probability mass function
- cumulative distribution function
- kernel density estimate

You can perform an online search for more details regarding the preceding methods.

As another example, using quartiles is even more coarse-grained than the earlier age-related binning example. The issue with binning pertains to the consequences of classifying people in different bins, even though they are in close proximity to each other. For instance, some people struggle financially because they earn a meager wage, and they are disqualified from financial assistance because their salary is higher than the cut-off point for receiving any assistance.

Scaling Numeric Data via Normalization

A range of values can vary significantly and it's important to note that they often need to be scaled to a smaller range, such as values in the range [-1,1] or [0,1], which you can do via the `tanh` function or the sigmoid function, respectively.

For example, measuring a person's height in terms of meters involves a range of values between 0.50 meters and 2.5 meters (in the vast majority of cases), whereas measuring height in terms of centimeters ranges between

50 centimeters and 250 centimeters: these two units differ by a factor of 100. A person's weight in kilograms generally varies between 4 kilograms (newborn babies) and 200 kilograms (or even higher), whereas measuring weight in grams differs by a factor of 1,000. Distances between objects can be measured in meters or in kilometers, which also differ by a factor of 1,000.

In general, use units of measure so that the data values in multiple features are belong to a similar range of values. In fact, some machine learning algorithms require scaled data, often in the range of [0,1] or [-1,1]. In addition to the `tanh` and `sigmoid` functions, there are other techniques for scaling data, such as "standardizing" data (think Gaussian distribution) and "normalizing" data (linearly scaled so that the new range of values is in (0,1)).

The following examples involve a floating point variable x with different ranges of values that will be scaled so that the new values are in the interval [0,1].

Example 1: if the values of x are in the range [0,2], then `x/2` is in the range [0,1].

Example 2: if the values of x are in the range [3,6], then `x-3` is in the range [0,3], and (X-3)/3 is in the range [0,1].

Example 3: if the values of x are in the range [-10,20], then X+10 is in the range [0,30], and (X+10)/30 is in the range of [0,1].

In general, suppose that x is a random variable (discussed in more detail later) this whose values are in the range [a,b], where a < b. You can scale the data values by performing two steps:

Step 1: X-a is in the range [0,b-a]

Step 2: (X-1)/(b-a) is in the range [0,1]

If x is a random variable that has the values {`x1`, `x2`, `x3`, . . ., `xn`}, then the formula for normalization involves mapping each `xi` value to `(xi - min)/(max - min)`, where min is the minimum value of x and max is the maximum value of X.

As a simple example, suppose that the random variable x has the values {-1, 0, 1}. Then `min` and `max` are 1 and -1, respectively, and the normalization of {-1, 0, 1} is the set of values {(-1-(-1))/2, (0-(-1))/2, (1-(-1))/2}, which equals (0, 1/2, 1}.

Scaling Numeric Data via Standardization

The standardization technique involves finding the mean mu and the standard deviation sigma, and then mapping each xi value to (xi - mu)/sigma. Recall the following formulas:

```
mu = [SUM (x) ]/n
variance(x) = [SUM (x - xbar)*(x-xbar)]/n
sigma = sqrt(variance)
```

As a simple illustration of standardization, suppose that the random variable x has the values {-1, 0, 1}. Then mu, variance, and sigma are calculated as follows:

```
mu       = (SUM xi)/n = (-1 + 0 + 1)/3 = 0

variance = [SUM (xi- mu)^2]/n
         = [(-1-0)^2 + (0-0)^2 + (1-0)^2]/3
         = 2/3

sigma    = sqrt(2/3) = 0.816 (approximate value)
```

Hence, the standardization of {-1, 0, 1} is {-1/0.816, 0/0.816, 1/0.816}, which in turn equals the set of values {-1.2254, 0, 1.2254}.

As another example, suppose that the random variable x has the values {-6, 0, 6}. Then mu, variance, and sigma are calculated as follows:

```
mu       = (SUM xi)/n = (-6 + 0 + 6)/3 = 0

variance = [SUM (xi- mu)^2]/n
         = [(-6-0)^2 + (0-0)^2 + (6-0)^2]/3
         = 72/3
         = 24

sigma    = sqrt(24) = 4.899 (approximate value)
```

Hence, the standardization of {-6, 0, 6} is {-6/4.899, 0/4.899, 6/4.899}, which in turn equals the set of values {-1.2247, 0, 1.2247}.

In the preceding two examples, the mean equals 0 in both cases but the variance and standard deviation are significantly different. In addition, the normalization of a set of values *always* produces a set of numbers between 0 and 1.

However, the standardization of a set of values can generate numbers that are less than -1 and greater than 1: this will occur when sigma is less than the minimum value of every term |mu − xi|, where the latter is the absolute value of the difference between mu and each xi value. In the preceding example, the minimum difference equals 1, whereas sigma is 0.816, and therefore the largest standardized value is greater than 1.

What to Look for in Categorical Data

This section contains various suggestions for handling inconsistent data values, and you can determine which ones to adopt based on any additional factors that are relevant to your particular task. For example, consider dropping columns that have very low cardinality (equal to or close to 1), as well as numeric columns with zero or very low variance.

Next, check the contents of categorical columns for inconsistent spellings or errors. A good example pertains to the gender category, which can consist of a combination of the following values:

male
Male
female
Female
m
f
M
F

The preceding categorical values for gender can be replaced with two categorical values (unless you have a valid reason to retain some of the other values). Moreover, if you are training a model whose analysis involves a single gender, then you need to determine which rows (if any) of a dataset must be excluded. Also check categorical data columns for redundant or missing whitespaces.

Check for data values that have multiple data types, such as numerical column with numbers as numerals and some numbers as strings or objects. Also ensure consistent data formats: numbers as integer or floating numbers and ensure that dates have the same format (for example, do not mix `mm/dd/yyyy` with another format such as `dd/mm/yyyy`).

Mapping Categorical Data to Numeric Values

Character data is often called categorical data, examples of which include people's names, home or work addresses, email addresses, and so forth. Many types of categorical data involve short lists of values. For example, the days of the week and the months in a year involve seven and twelve distinct values, respectively. Notice that the days of the week have a relationship: Each day has a previous day and a next day, and similarly for the months of a year.

However, the colors of an automobile are independent of each other: The color red is not "better" or "worse" than the color blue. Yet, cars of a certain color can have a statistically higher number of accidents, but we won't address this case here.

There are several well-known techniques for mapping categorical values to a set of numeric values. A simple example where you need to perform this conversion involves the gender feature in the Titanic dataset. This feature is one of the relevant features for training a machine learning model. The gender feature has {M, F} as its set of possible values. As you will see later in this appendix, `Pandas` makes it very easy to convert the set of values {M, F} to the set of values {0,1}.

Another mapping technique involves mapping a set of categorical values to a set of consecutive integer values. For example, the set {red, green, blue} can be mapped to the set of integers {0,1,2}. The set {male, female} can be mapped to the set of integers {0,1}. The days of the week can be mapped to {0,1,2,3,4,5,6}. Note that the first day of the week depends on the country: in some cases it's Sunday and in other cases its Monday.

Another technique is called *one-hot encoding*, which converts each value to a *vector* (check online if you need to refresh your memory about vectors). Thus, {Male, Female} can be represented by the vectors [1,0] and [0,1], and the colors {red, green, blue} can be represented by the vectors [1,0,0], [0,1,0], and [0,0,1].

If you vertically "line up" the two vectors for gender, they form a 2×2 identity matrix, and doing the same for the colors will form a 3×3 identity matrix, as shown here:

[1,0,0]
[0,1,0]
[0,0,1]

If you are familiar with matrices, you probably noticed that the preceding set of vectors looks like the 3×3 identity matrix. In fact, this technique generalizes in a straightforward manner. Specifically, if you have n distinct categorical values, you can map each of those values to one of the vectors in an nxn identity matrix.

As another example, the set of titles {"Intern," "Junior," "Mid-Range," "Senior," "Project Leader," "Dev Manager"} have a hierarchical relationship in terms of their salaries (which can also overlap, but we'll gloss over that detail for now).

Another set of categorical data involves the season of the year: {"Spring," "Summer," "Autumn," "Winter"} and while these values are generally independent of each other, there are cases in which the season is significant. For example, the values for the monthly rainfall, average temperature, crime rate, foreclosure rate can depend on the season, month, week, or even the day of the year.

If a feature has a large number of categorical values, then a one-hot encoding will produce many additional columns for each datapoint. Since the majority of the values in the new columns equal 0, this can increase the sparsity of the dataset, which in turn can result in more overfitting and hence adversely affect the accuracy of machine learning algorithms that you adopt during the training process.

Another solution is to use a sequence-based solution in which N categories are mapped to the integers 1, 2, . . ., N. Another solution involves examining the row frequency of each categorical value. For example, suppose that N equals 20, and there are 3 categorical values occur in 95% of the values for a given feature. You can try the following:

Assign the values 1, 2, and 3 to those three categorical values.
Assign numeric values that reflect the relative frequency of those categorical values.
Assign the category "OTHER" to the remaining categorical values.
Aelete the rows that whose categorical values belong to the 5%.

Working with Dates

The format for a calendar dates varies among different countries, and this belongs to something called localization of data (not to be confused with i18n, which is data internationalization). Some examples of date formats are shown below (and the first four are probably the most common):

MM/DD/YY
MM/DD/YYYY
DD/MM/YY
DD/MM/YYYY
YY/MM/DD
M/D/YY
D/M/YY
YY/M/D

MMDDYY
DDMMYY
YYMMDD

If you need to combine data from datasets that contain different date formats, then converting the disparate date formats to a single common date format will ensure consistency.

Working with Currency

The format for currency also among different countries, and the use of a "," and "." have opposite meanings in various languages. For example, 1,124.78 equals "one thousand one hundred twenty four point seven eight" in the United States, whereas 1.124,78 has the same meaning in Europe (i.e., the "." symbol and the "," symbol are interchanged).

If you need to combine data from datasets that contain different currency formats, then you probably need to convert all the disparate currency formats to a single common currency format. There is another detail to consider: currency exchange rates can fluctuate on a daily basis, which in turn can affect the calculation of taxes, late fees, and so forth. Although you might be fortunate enough where you won't have to deal with these issues, it's still worth being aware of them.

Missing Data, Anomalies, and Outliers

How you handle missing data depends on the specific dataset. Here are some ways to handle missing data (the first three techniques are manual techniques and the other techniques are algorithms):

- replace missing data with the mean/median/mode value
- infer ("impute") the value for missing data
- delete rows with missing data
- isolation forest (tree-based algorithm)
- minimum covariance determinant
- local outlier factor
- one-class SVM

In general, replace a missing numeric value with zero is a risky choice: This value is obviously incorrect if the values of a feature are between 1,000 and

5,000. For a feature that has numeric values, replacing a missing value with the average value is better than the value zero (unless the average equals zero); also consider using the median value. For categorical data, consider using the mode to replace a missing value.

If you are not confident that you can impute a "reasonable" value, consider dropping the row with a missing value, and then train a model with the imputed value and also with the deleted row.

One problem that can arise after removing rows with missing values is that the resulting dataset is too small. In this case, consider using Synthetic Minority Oversampling Technique (SMOTE), which is discussed in Chapter 5, in order to generate synthetic data.

Anomalies and Outliers

In simplified terms, an outlier is an abnormal data value that is outside the range of "normal" values. For example, a person's height in centimeters is typically between 30 centimeters and 230 centimeters. Hence, a datapoint (e.g., a row of data in a spreadsheet) with a height of 5 centimeters or a height of 500 centimeters is an outlier. The consequences of these outlier values are unlikely to involve a significant financial or physical loss (although they could have an adverse effect the accuracy of a trained model).

Anomalies are also outside the "normal" range of values (just like outliers), and they are typically more problematic than outliers: anomalies can have more "severe" consequences than outliers. For example, consider the scenario in which someone who lives in California suddenly makes a credit card purchase in New York. If the person is on vacation or on a business trip in New York, then the purchase is an outlier. (It's "outside" the typical purchasing pattern), but it's not an issue. However, if that person was in California when the credit card purchase was made, then it's most likely to be credit card fraud, as well as an anomaly.

Unfortunately, there is no simple way to *decide* how to deal with anomalies and outliers in a dataset. Although you can drop rows that contain outliers, keep in mind that doing so might deprive the dataset—and therefore the trained model—of valuable information. You can try modifying the data values (described in the following section), but again, this might lead to erroneous inferences in the trained model.

Another possibility is to train a model with the dataset that contains anomalies and outliers, and then train a model with a dataset from which the anomalies and outliers have been removed. Compare the two results and see if you can infer anything meaningful regarding the anomalies and outliers.

Outlier Detection

Although the decision to keep or drop outliers is your decision to make, there are some techniques available that help you detect outliers in a dataset. This section contains a short list of some techniques, along with a very brief description and links for additional information.

Perhaps *trimming* is the simplest technique (apart from dropping outliers), which involves removing rows whose feature value is in the upper 5% range or the lower 5% range.

Winsorizing the data is an improvement over trimming: set the values in the top 5% range equal to the maximum value in the 95th percentile, and set the values in the bottom 5% range equal to the minimum in the 5th percentile.

The *minimum covariance determinant* is a covariance-based technique, and a Python-based code sample that uses this technique is downloadable here:

https://scikit-learn.org/stable/modules/outlier_detection.html

The *local outlier factor* (LOF) technique is an unsupervised technique that calculates a local anomaly score via the kNN (k nearest neighbor) algorithm. Some documentation and short code samples that use LOF are here:

https://scikit-learn.org/stable/modules/generated/Sklearn.neighbors.LocalOutlierFactor.html

Two other techniques involve the *Huber* and the *Ridge* classes, both of which are included as part of Sklearn. Huber error is less sensitive to outliers because it's calculated via linear loss, similar to Mean Absolute Error (MAE) that is discussed in Chapter 7. A code sample that compares Huber and Ridge is downloadable here:

https://scikit-learn.org/stable/auto_examples/linear_model/plot_huber_vs_ridge.html

You can also explore the Theil-Sen estimator and RANSAC that are "robust" against outliers, and additional information is here:

https://scikit-learn.org/stable/auto_examples/linear_model/plot_theilsen.html

Four algorithms for outlier detection are discussed here:

https://www.kdnuggets.com/2018/12/four-techniques-outlier-detection.html

One other scenario involves "local" outliers. For example, suppose that you use kMeans (or some other clustering algorithm) and determine that a value that is an outlier with respect to one of the clusters. While this value is not necessarily an "absolute" outlier, detecting such a value might be important for your use case.

Yet another option to explore is the open source Python toolkit PyOD that performs outlier detection for multivariate data, and its home page is here:

https://pyod.readthedocs.io/en/latest/

Missing Data: MCAR, MAR, and MNAR

Donald Rubin proposed a classification system for missing data based on whether or not such missing data is due to random factors. According to his classification system, missing data can belong to one the following categories:

1. MCAR (missing completely at random)

2. MAR (missing at random)

3. MNAR (missing not at random)

Type #1 suggests that missing data is due to factors that are unrelated to the data. Type #2 applies to when there is equal probability of missing data that occurs within groups of the defined data. Type #3 refers to data (outside of type #1 or type #2) that is missing due to unknown reasons. More information about this classification system can be found here: *https://academic.oup.com/biomet/article-abstract/63/3/581/270932?redirectedFrom=fulltext*

What is Data Drift?

Strictly speaking, data drift is not directly related to missing data; however, before you handle such missing data issues it's important to ensure that that data is meaningful. Specifically, the value of data is based on its accuracy, its relevance, and its age. *Data drift* refers to data that has become less relevant over time (sometimes called stale data). Such data can be due to a change in the distribution of the data over time.

For example, online purchasing patterns in 2010 are probably not as relevant as data from 2020 because of various factors (such as the profile of different types of customers). Keep in mind that multiple factors can influence data drift in a specific dataset.

If this topic interests you, there are two techniques that can assist in detecting data drift, known as *domain classifier* and the *black-box shift detector*, both of which are discussed here:

https://blog.dataiku.com/towards-reliable-mlops-with-drift-detectors

What is Imbalanced Classification?

Imbalanced classification involves datasets with imbalanced classes. For example, suppose that class A has 99% of the data and class B has 1%. Which classification algorithm would you use? Unfortunately, classification algorithms don't work so well with this type of imbalanced dataset. Here is a list of several well-known techniques for handling imbalanced datasets:

- random resampling rebalances the class distribution
- random oversampling duplicates data in the minority class
- random undersampling deletes examples from the majority class
- SMOTE (synthetic minority oversampling technique)

Several of the technique in the preceding list are discussed in the following subsections.

Undersampling and Oversampling

Undersampling refers to methods whose purpose is to balance the class distribution for a classification dataset that has a skewed class distribution. These methods focus on a subset of the larger class and are applied to a training dataset, after which a model can be trained on the dataset.

Random undersampling also involves randomly selecting examples; however, the random samples are taken from the majority class and then deleted them from the training dataset, thereby reducing the imbalance in the dataset.

Random oversampling focuses on randomly selecting (and replacing) examples from the minority class in order to reduce the class imbalance in the training dataset.

Random resampling transforms the training dataset into a new dataset, which is quite effective for imbalanced classification problems.

The *random undersampling* technique removes samples from the dataset, and involves the following:

- randomly remove samples from majority class
- can be performed with or without replacement
- alleviates imbalance in the dataset
- may increase the variance of the classifier
- may discard useful or important samples

However, random under sampling does not work so well with a dataset that has a 99%/1% split into two classes. Moreover, undersampling can result in losing information that is useful for a model.

Instead of random unders ampling, another approach involves generating new samples from a minority class. The first technique involves the following:

- oversample examples in the minority class:
- duplicate examples from the minority class
- can balance distribution (no new information)

The second technique is better than the preceding technique, which involves the following:

- synthesize new examples from minority class
- a type of data augmentation for tabular data
- this technique can be very effective
- generate new samples from minority class

Another option is the Python package imbalanced-learn that provides various re-sampling techniques for datasets that exhibit class imbalance. This package is available in the `scikit-learn-contrib` project. More details can be found here:

https://github.com/scikit-learn-contrib/imbalanced-learn

Limitations of Resampling

Many techniques for handling imbalanced datasets typically involve either generating more samples for the under-represented class (such as SMOTE that is discussed in the next section) or reducing the number of samples selected from the dominant class.

However, some datasets are fundamentally imbalanced due to the nature of the data in the datasets. For example, datasets contain far fewer people with cancer, diabetes, or other life-threatening disease than the number of healthy people in the dataset. Similarly, datasets containing credit card fraud also have a very low percentage of fraud, and therefore are fundamentally imbalanced.

Unfortunately, oversampling the smaller class can lead to overfitting, and under sampling the dominant class can lead to underfitting. Moreover, machine learning algorithms differ in terms of their sensitivity to imbalanced datasets. For example, logistic regression is less sensitive to class imbalance than a decision tree, whereas ensemble models are more impervious to overfitting.

What is SMOTE?

SMOTE (Synthetic Minority Oversampling Technique) is a technique for synthesizing new samples for a dataset, which is data augmentation (i.e., synthesizing new data samples) will before you use a classification algorithm. SMOTE was initially developed by means of the kNN algorithm (other options are available), and it can be an effective technique for handling imbalanced classes. This technique is based on linear interpolation:

Step 1: Select samples that are close in the feature space.
Step 2: Draw a line between the samples in the feature space.
Step 3: Draw a new sample at a point along that line.

The following is a more detailed explanation of the SMOTE algorithm:

1. Select a random sample "a" from the minority class.

2. Find k nearest neighbors for that example.

3. Select a random neighbor "b" from the nearest neighbors.

4. Create a line L that connects "a" and "b."

5. Randomly select one or more points "c" on line L.

If need be, you can repeat this process for the other (k-1) nearest neighbors in order to distribute the synthetic values more evenly among the nearest neighbors.

SMOTE Extensions

The initial SMOTE algorithm is based on the kNN classification algorithm, which has been extended in various ways, such as replacing kNN with SVM. A list of SMOTE extensions is as follows:

Borderline-SMOTE (kNN)
Borderline-SMOTE (SVM)
Adaptive Synthetic Sampling (ADASYN)
DBSMOTE

Perform an Internet search for more details about these algorithms, and also navigate to the following URL:

https://en.wikipedia.org/wiki/Oversampling_and_undersampling_in_data_analysis

Analyzing Classifiers

Several well-known techniques are available for analyzing the quality of machine learning classifiers. Two techniques are LIME and ANOVA, both of which are discussed in the following subsections.

What is LIME?

LIME is an acronym for local interpretable model-agnostic explanations. LIME is a model-agnostic technique that can be used with machine learning models. The intuition for this technique is straightforward: make small random changes to data samples and then observe the manner in which predictions change (or not). In other words, change the output (slightly) and see what happens to the output.

By way of analogy, consider food inspectors who test for bacteria in truckloads of perishable food. Clearly it's not feasible to test every food item in a truck (or a train car), so inspectors perform "spot checks" that involve testing randomly selected items. In an analogous fashion, LIME makes small changes to input data in random locations and then analyzes the changes in the associated output values.

However, there are two caveats to keep in mind when you use LIME with input data for a given model:

1. The actual changes to input values is model-specific.

2. This technique works on input that is interpretable.

Examples of interpretable input include machine learning classifiers (such as trees and random forests) and NLP techniques such as BoW. Noninterpretable input involves "dense" data, such as a word embedding (which is a vector of floating point numbers).

You could also substitute your model with another model that involves interpretable data, but then you need to evaluate how accurate the approximation is to the original model.

What is ANOVA?

ANOVA is an acronym for analysis of variance, which attempts to analyze the differences among the mean values of a sample that's taken from a population. ANOVA enables you to test if multiple mean values are equal. More importantly, ANOVA can assist in reducing Type I (false positive) errors and Type II errors (false negative) errors. If you are unfamiliar with this terminology, suppose that person A and person B are tested for cancer, and the results of the test are erroneous: they indicate that person A has cancer. Obviously a test result of false positive is *much* preferable to a test result of false negative.

ANOVA pertains to the design of experiments and hypothesis testing, which can produce meaningful results in various situations. For example, suppose that a dataset contains a feature that can be partitioned into several "reasonably" homogenous groups. Next, analyze the variance in each group and perform comparisons with the goal of determining different sources of variance for the values of a given feature.

For more information about ANOVA, navigate to the following link:

https://en.wikipedia.org/wiki/Analysis_of_variance

The next portion of this appendix discusses some concepts in probability, followed by a longer section that discusses basic concepts in statistics.

What is a Probability?

If you have ever performed a science experiment (perhaps in high school), you might remember that measurements have some uncertainty. In general, we assume that there is a correct value, and we endeavor to find the best estimate of that value.

The *probability* of an event is the frequency with which you expect that event to occur, and it's typically expressed as a real number in the interval [0,1]. You will also see the probability expressed as a fraction, such as 1/2.

The *likelihood* of an event is the probability expressed as a percentage, such as the probability of 0.75 is equivalent to the likelihood of 75%.

The *odds* of an event occurring is calculated by computing the ratio of the probability e that event E will occur, divided by the probability (1-e) that E will not occur. For example, if e equals 0.75, then 1-e equals 0.25, and so the odds of the event E occurring equals 0.75/0.25 = 3. In the addition, the odds are expressed in the form of "m to n," which in this case would be "3 to 1." If the first number is smaller than the second, then the odds are against the occurrence of an event.

If the odds are a fraction or a mixed number, then the odds are expressed as a ratio of two integers. For example, if the odds are 1.25, the latter is the same as decimal value is the same as 5/4, and so the odds are "5 to 4."

When we work with an event that can have multiple outcomes, we try to define the probability of an outcome as the chance that it will occur, which is calculated as follows:

```
p(outcome) = # of times outcome occurs/(total number of outcomes)
```

For example, in the case of a single balanced coin, the probability of tossing a head H or a tail T is equal, as shown here:

```
p(H) = 1/2 p(T) = 1/2
```

The set of probabilities associated with the outcomes {H, T} is shown here:

```
P = {1/2, 1/2}
```

Some experiments involve replacement while others involve non-replacement. For example, suppose that an urn contains 10 red balls and 10 green balls. What is the probability that a randomly selected ball is red? The answer is 10/(10+10) = 1/2. What is the probability that the second ball is also red?

There are two scenarios and therefore two different answers. If each ball is selected with replacement, then each ball is returned to the urn after selection, which means that the urn always contains 10 red balls and 10 green balls. In this case, the answer is 1/2 * 1/2 = 1/4. In fact, the probability of any event is independent of all previous events.

However, if balls are selected without replacement, then the answer is 10/20 * 9/19. As you undoubtedly know, card games are also examples of selecting cards without replacement.

One other concept is called conditional probability, which refers to the likelihood of the occurrence of event E1 given that event E2 has occurred.

Calculating the Expected Value

Consider the following scenario involving a well-balanced coin: Whenever a head appears you earn $1, and whenever a tail appears you earn $1. If you toss the coin 100 times, how much money do you expect to earn? Since you will earn $1 regardless of the outcome, the expected value (in fact, the guaranteed value) is 100.

Now consider this scenario: whenever a head appears, you earn $1 and whenever a tail appears, you earn 0 dollars. If you toss the coin 100 times, how much money do you expect to earn? You probably determined the value 50 (which is the correct answer) by making a quick mental calculation. The more formal derivation of the value of E (the expected earning) is here:

```
E = 100 *[1 * 0.5 + 0 * 0.5] = 100 * 0.5 = 50
```

The quantity **1** ∗ 0.5 + **0** ∗ 0.5 is the amount of money you expected to earn during each coin toss, and multiplying this number by 100 is the expected earning after 100 coin tosses.

As another example, suppose that you earn $3 whenever a head appears, and you *lose* $1.50 dollars whenever a tail appears. Then the expected earning E after 100 coin tosses is shown here:

```
E = 100 *[3 * 0.5 - 1.5 * 0.5] = 100 * 1.5 = 150
```

We can generalize the preceding calculations as follows. Let P = {p1,..., pn} be a probability distribution, which means that the values in P are non-negative and their sum equals 1. In addition, let R = {R1,..., Rn} be a set of rewards, where reward Ri is received with probability pi. Then the expected value E after N trials is shown here:

```
E = N * [SUM pi*Ri]
```

In the case of a single balanced die, we have the following probabilities:

```
p(1) = 1/6
p(2) = 1/6
p(3) = 1/6
p(4) = 1/6
p(5) = 1/6
p(6) = 1/6
P = { 1/6, 1/6, 1/6, 1/6, 1/6, 1/6}
```

Suppose that the earnings are {3, 0, -1, 2, 4, -1} when the values 1,2,3,4,5,6, respectively, appear when tossing the single die. Then after 100 trials our expected earnings are shown here:

```
E = 100 * [3 + 0 + -1 + 2 + 4 + -1]/6 = 100 * 3/6 = 50
```

In the case of two balanced dice, we have the following probabilities:

```
p(2) = 1/36
p(3) = 2/36
...
p(12) = 1/36
P = {1/36,2/36,3/36,4/36,5/36,6/36,5/36,4/36,3/36,2/36,1/36}
```

Random Variables

A random variable is a variable that can have multiple values, and where each value has an associated probability of occurrence. For example, if we let x be a random variable whose values are the outcomes of tossing a well-balanced die, then the values of x are the numbers in the set {1,2,3,4,5,6}. Moreover, each of those values can occur with equal probability (which is 1/6).

In the case of two well-balanced dice, the random variable x can have any of the values in the set {2,3,4, ... , 12}, and the associated probabilities are listed in the previous section.

Discrete versus Continuous Random Variables

The preceding section contains examples of *discrete* random variables because the list of possible values is either finite or countably infinite (such as the set of integers). As an aside, the set of rational numbers is also countably infinite, but the set of irrational numbers and also the set of real numbers are both uncountably infinite (proofs are available online). As pointed out earlier, the associated set of probabilities must form a probability distribution, which means that the probability values are nonnegative and their sum equals 1.

A *continuous* random variable whose values can be *any* number in an interval, which can be an uncountably infinite number of values. For example, the amount of time required to perform a task is represented by a continuous random variable.

A continuous random variable also has a probability distribution that is represented as a continuous function. The constraint for such a variable is that the area under the curve (which is sometimes calculated via an integral) equals 1.

Well-Known Probability Distributions

There are many probability distributions, and some well-known probability distributions are listed here:

- Gaussian distribution
- Poisson distribution
- chi-squared distribution
- binomial distribution

The Gaussian distribution is named after Karl F Gauss, and it is sometimes called a normal distribution or a bell curve. The distribution of IQ scores follows a curve that is similar to a Gaussian distribution.

However, the `Poisson` distribution is useful for counting the number of times that something occurs during a specified period of time. For example, frequency of traffic at a given point in a road follows a `Poisson` distribution. Interestingly, if you count the number of people who go to a public pool based on five-degree (Fahrenheit) increments of the temperature, that set of numbers follows a Poisson distribution.

Perform an Internet search for each of the bullet items in the preceding list and you will find numerous articles, along with images, that contain details about these (and other) probability distributions.

Fundamental Concepts in Statistics

This section contains several subsections that discuss the mean, median, mode, variance, and standard deviation. Feel free to skim (or skip) this section if you are already familiar with these concepts. As a start point, let's suppose that we have a set of numbers $X = \{x1, \ldots, xn\}$ that can be positive, negative, integer-valued or decimal values.

The Mean

The *mean* of the numbers in the set cx is the average of the values. For example, if the set x consists of $\{-10, 35, 75, 100\}$, then the *mean* mu equals $(-10 + 35 + 75 + 100)/4 = 50$. If the set x consists of $\{2, 2, 2, 2\}$, then the *mean* mu equals $(2+2+2+2)/4 = 2$. As you can see, the mean value is not necessarily one of the values in the set.

Keep in mind that the mean is sensitive to outliers. For example, the mean of the set of numbers $\{1,2,3,4\}$ is 2.5, whereas the mean of the set of number {1,2,3,4,1000} is 202. Since the formulas for the variance and standard deviation involve the mean of a set of numbers, both of these terms are also more sensitive to outliers.

The Median

The *median* of the numbers (sorted in increasing or decreasing order) in the set X is the middle value in the set of values, which means that half the numbers in the set are less than the median and half the numbers in the set are greater than the median. For example, if the set x consists of {-10,35,75,100}, then the *median* equals 55 because 55 is the average of the two numbers 35 and 75. As you can see, half the numbers are less than 55 and half the numbers are greater than 55. If the set x consists of {2,2,2,2}, then the *median* equals 2.

By contrast, the median is much less sensitive to outliers than the mean. For example, the median of the set of numbers {1,2,3,4} is 2.5, and the median of the set of numbers {1,2,3,4,1000} is 3.

The Mode

The *mode* of the numbers (sorted in increasing or decreasing order) in the set x is the most frequently occurring value, which means that there can be more than one such value. If the set x consists of {2,2,2,2}, then the *mode* equals 2.

If x is the set of numbers {2,4,5,5,6,8}, then the number 5 occurs twice and the other numbers occur only once, so the *mode* equals 5.

If x is the set of numbers {2,2,4,5,5,6,8}, then the numbers 2 and 5 occur twice and the other numbers occur only once, so the *mode* equals 2 and 5. A set that has two modes is called *bimodal*, and a set that has more than two modes is called multimodal.

One other scenario involves sets that have numbers with the same frequency and they are all different. In this case, the mode does not provide meaningful information, and one alternative is to partition the numbers into subsets and then select the largest subset. For example, if set x has the values {1,2,15,16,17,25,35,50}, we can partition the set into subsets whose elements are in range that are multiples of 10, which results in the subsets {1,2}, {15,16,17}, {25}, {35}, and {50}. The largest subset is {15,16,17}, so we could select the number 16 as the mode.

As another example, if set x has the values {-10,35,75,100}, then partitioning this set does not provide any additional information, so it's probably better to work with either the mean or the median.

The Variance and Standard Deviation

The *variance* is the average of the sum of the squares of the difference between the numbers in x and the mean mu of the set x, divided by the number of value in x, as shown here:

```
variance = [SUM (xi - mu)**2 ] / n
```

For example, if the set x consists of {-10,35,75,100}, then the *mean* equals (-10 + 35 + 75 + 100)/4 = 50, and the variance is computed as follows:

```
variance = [(-10-50)**2 + (35-50)**2 + (75-50)**2 +
           (100-50)**2]/4
         = [60**2 + 15**2 + 25**2 + 50**2]/4
         = [3600 + 225 + 625 + 2500]/4
         = 6950/4 = 1,737
```

The standard deviation std is the square root of the variance:

```
std = sqrt(1737) = 41.677
```

If the set x consists of {2,2,2,2}, then the *mean* equals (2+2+2+2)/4 = 2, and the variance is computed as follows:

```
variance = [(2-2)**2 + (2-2)**2 + (2-2)**2 + (2-2)**2]/4
         = [0**2 + 0**2 + 0**2 + 0**2]/4
         = 0
```

The standard deviation std is the square root of the variance:

```
std = sqrt(0) = 0
```

Population, Sample, and Population Variance

The population specifically refers to the entire set of entities in a given group, such as the population of a country, the people over 65 years old in the United States, or the number of first-year students in a university.

However, in many cases statistical quantities are calculated on samples instead of an entire population. Thus, a sample is (a much smaller) subset of the given population. See the central limit theorem regarding the distribution of the mean of a set of sample of a population (which need not be a population with a Gaussian distribution).

If you want to learn about techniques for sampling data, here is a list of three different techniques that you can investigate:

1. stratified sampling

2. cluster sampling

3. quota sampling

One other important point: The population variance is calculated by multiplying the sample variance by n/(n-1), as shown here:

```
population variance = [n/(n-1)]*variance
```

Chebyshev's Inequality

Chebyshev's inequality provides a very simple way to determine the minimum percentage of data that lies within k standard deviations. Specifically, this inequality states that for any positive integer k greater than 1, the amount of data in a sample that lies within k standard deviations is at least 1 - 1/k**2. For example, if k = 2, then at least 1 - 1/2**2 = 3/4 of the data must lie within 2 standard deviations.

The interesting part of this inequality is that it's been mathematically proven to be true; that is, it's not an empirical or heuristic-based result. An extensive description regarding Chebyshev's inequality (including some advanced mathematical explanations) can be found here:

https://en.wikipedia.org/wiki/Chebyshev%27s_inequality

What is a p-Value?

The null hypothesis states that there is no correlation between a dependent variable (such as `y`) and an independent variable (such as `x`). The `p-value` is used to reject the null hypothesis if the `p-value` is small enough (< 0.005) which indicates a higher significance. The threshold value for `p` is typically 1% or 5%.

There is no straightforward formula for calculating p-values, which are values that are always between 0 and 1. In fact, `p-values` are statistical quantities to evaluate the null hypothesis, and they are calculated by means of `p-value` tables or via spreadsheet/statistical software.

The Moments of a Function (Optional)

The previous sections describe several statistical terms that is sufficient for the material in this book. However, several of those terms can be viewed from the perspective of different moments of a function. In brief, the moments of a function are measures that provide information regarding the shape of the graph of a function. In the case of a probability distribution, the first four moments are defined as follows:

1. The mean is the first central moment.

2. The variance is the second central moment.

3. The skewness (discussed later) is the third central moment.

4. The kurtosis (discussed later) is the fourth central moment.

More detailed information (including the relevant integrals) regarding moments of a function is available here:

https://en.wikipedia.org/wiki/Moment_(mathematics)#Variance

Skewness

Skewness is a measure of the asymmetry of a probability distribution. A Gaussian distribution is symmetric, which means that its skew value is zero (it's not exactly zero, but close enough for our purposes). Specifically, the skewness of a distribution is the *third* moment of the distribution. A *left-sided skew* means that the long tail is on the left side of the curve, with the following relationships:

```
mean < median < mode
```

By contrast, a *right-sided skew* means that the long tail is on the right side of the curve, with the following relationships (compare with the left-sided skew):

```
mode < median < mean
```

If need be, you can transform skewed data to a normally distributed dataset using one of the following techniques (which depends on the specific use-case):

- exponential transform
- log transform
- power transform

Perform an online search for more information regarding the preceding transforms and when to use each of these transforms.

Kurtosis

Kurtosis is related to the skewness of a probability distribution, in the sense that both of them assess the asymmetry of a probability distribution.

The kurtosis of a distribution is a scaled version of the *fourth* moment of the distribution, whereas its skewness is the *third* moment of the distribution. Note that the kurtosis of a univariate distribution equals 3.

Standardized values that lie within one standard deviation of the mean have negligible impact on the kurtosis. Indeed, the values beyond one standard deviation (including outliers) affect the kurtosis.

If you are interested in learning about additional kurtosis-related concepts, you can perform an online search for information regarding mesokurtic, leptokurtic, and platykurtic types of so-called "excess kurtosis."

Data and Statistics

This section contains various subsections that briefly discuss some of the challenges and obstacles that you might encounter when working with datasets. This section and subsequent sections introduce you to the following concepts:

- The central limit theorem
- correlation versus causation
- statistical inferences

First, keep in mind that statistics typically involves data *samples*, which are subsets of observations of a population. The goal is to find well-balanced samples provide a good representation of the entire population.

This goal can be very difficult to achieve, yet it's also possible to achieve highly accurate results with a very small sample size. For example, the Harris poll in the United States has been used for decades to analyze political trends. This poll computes percentages that indicate the favorability rating of political candidates, and it's usually within 3.5% of the correct percentage values. What's remarkable about the Harris poll is the fact that its sample size is a mere 4,000 people that are from the US population that is greater than 325,000,000 people.

Another aspect to consider is that each sample has a mean and variance, which do not necessarily equal the mean and variance of the actual population. However, the expected value of the sample mean and variance equal the mean and variance, respectively, of the population.

The Central Limit Theorem

Samples of a population have an interesting property. Suppose that you take a set of samples {S1, S3, …, Sn} of a population and you calculate the mean of those samples, which is {m1, m2, …, mn}. The central limit theorem is remarkable: given a set of samples of a population and the mean value of those samples, the distribution of the mean values can be approximated by a Gaussian distribution. Moreover, as the number of samples increases, the approximation becomes more accurate.

Correlation versus Causation

In general, datasets have some features (columns) that are more significant in terms of their set of values, and some features only provide additional information that does not contribute to potential trends in the dataset. For example, the passenger names in the list of passengers on the Titanic are unlikely to affect the survival rate of those passengers, whereas the gender of the passengers is likely to be an important factor.

In addition, a pair of significant features may also be "closely coupled" in terms of their values. For example, a real estate dataset for a set of houses will contain the number of bedrooms and the number of bathrooms for each house in the dataset. As you know, these values tend to increase together and also decrease together.

Extreme combinations of these two features is rare. For example, have you ever seen a house that has 10 bedrooms and 1 bathroom, or a house that has 10 bathrooms and 1 bedroom? If you did find such a house, would you purchase that house as your primary residence?

The extent to which the values of two features change is called their correlation, which is a number between -1 and 1. Two "perfectly" correlated features have a correlation of 1, and two features that are not correlated have a correlation of 0. In addition, if the values of one feature decrease when the values of another feature increase, and vice versa, then their correlation is closer to -1 (and might also equal -1).

However, causation between two features means that the values of one feature can be used to calculate the values of the second feature (within some margin of error).

Keep in mind this fundamental point about machine learning models: they can provide correlation but they cannot provide causation.

Statistical Inferences

Statistical thinking related processes and statistics, whereas statistical inference refers to the process by which the inferences that you make regarding a population. Those inferences are based on statistics that are derived from samples of the population. The validity and reliability of those inferences depend on random sampling in order to reduce bias. There are various metrics that you can calculate to help you assess the validity of a model that has been trained on a particular dataset.

This concludes the brief introduction to data types, categorical data, normalization and standardization of numeric data, and concepts related to samples of a population.

The Bias-Variance Trade-off

Bias in machine learning can be due to an error from wrong assumptions in a learning algorithm. High bias might cause an algorithm to miss relevant relations between features and target outputs (underfitting). Prediction bias can occur because of "noisy" data, an incomplete feature set, or a biased training sample.

Error due to bias is the difference between the expected (or average) prediction of your model and the correct value that you want to predict. Repeat the model building process multiple times, and gather new data each time, and also perform an analysis to produce a new model. The resulting models have a range of predictions because the underlying datasets have a degree of randomness. Bias measures the extent to the predictions for these models are from the correct value.

Variance in machine learning is the expected value of the squared deviation from the mean. High variance can/might cause an algorithm to model the random noise in the training data, rather than the intended outputs (aka overfitting)

Adding parameters to a model increases its complexity, increases the variance, and decreases the bias. Dealing with bias and variance is dealing with underfitting and overfitting.

Error due to variance is the variability of a model prediction for a given datapoint. As before, repeat the entire model building process, and the variance is the extent to which predictions for a given point vary among different "instances" of the model.

If you have worked with datasets and performed data analysis, you already know that finding well-balanced samples can be difficult or highly impractical. Moreover, performing an analysis of the data in a dataset is vitally important, yet there is no guarantee that you can produce a dataset that is 100% "clean."

A biased statistic is a statistic that is systematically different from the entity in the population that is being estimated. In more casual terminology, if a data sample "favors" or "leans" toward one aspect of the population, then the sample has bias. For example, if you prefer movies that are comedies more so than any other type of movie, then clearly you are more likely to select a comedy instead of a dramatic movie or a science fiction movie. Thus, a frequency graph of the movie types in a sample of your movie selections will be more closely "clustered" around comedies.

However, if you have a wide-ranging set of preferences for movies, then the corresponding frequency graph will be more varied, which is to say, have a larger spread of values.

As a simple example, suppose that you are given an assignment that involves writing a term paper on a controversial subject, which has many opposing viewpoints. Since you want your bibliography to support your well-balanced term paper that takes into account multiple viewpoints, your bibliography will contain a wide variety of sources. Hence, your bibliography will have a larger variance and a smaller bias: if all the references in your bibliography espouses the same point of view, then you will have a smaller variance and a larger bias (it's just an analogy, so it's not a perfect counterpart to bias-versus-variance).

The *bias-variance* trade-off can be stated very simply: in general, reducing the bias in samples can increase the variance, and conversely, reducing the variance tends to increase the bias.

Types of Bias in Data

In addition to the bias-variance trade-off that is discussed in the previous section, there are several types of bias, some of which are listed below:

- availability bias
- onfirmation bias
- false causality

- sunk cost fallacy
- survivorship bias

Availability bias is akin to making a "rule" based on an exception. For example, there is a known link between smoking cigarettes and cancer, but there are exceptions. If you find someone who has smoked three packs of cigarettes on a daily basis for 4 decades and is still healthy, can you assert that smoking does not lead to cancer?

Confirmation bias refers to the tendency to focus on data that confirms their beliefs and simultaneously ignore data that contradicts a belief.

False causality occurs when you incorrectly assert that the occurrence of a particular event causes another event to occur as well. One of the most well-known examples involves ice cream consumption and violent crime in New York during the summer. Since more people eat ice cream in the summer, that "causes" more violent crime, which is a false causality. Other factors, such as the increase in temperature, may be linked to the increase in crime. However, it's important to distinguish between correlation and causality: the latter is a much stronger link than the former, and it's also more difficult to establish causality instead of than just correlation.

Sunk cost refers to something (often money) that has been spent or incurred that cannot be recouped. A common example pertains to gambling at a casino: people fall into the pattern of spending more money in order to recoup a substantial amount of money that has already been lost. While there are cases in which people do recover their money, in many (most?) cases people simply incur an even greater loss because they continue to spend their money. Hence the expression, "it's time to cut your losses and walk away."

Survivorship bias refers to analyzing a particular subset of "positive" data while ignoring the "negative" data. This bias occurs in various situations, such as being influenced by individuals who recount their rags-to-riches success story ("positive" data) while ignoring the fate of the people (which is often a very high percentage) who did not succeed (the "negative" data) in a similar quest. So, while it's certainly possible for an individual to overcome many difficult obstacles in order to succeed, is the success rate one in one thousand (or even lower)?

Gini Impurity, Entropy, and Perplexity

The first two concepts are useful for some machine learning algorithms. For example, the decision tree algorithm has a hyperparameter whose values can be either *Gini impurity* or *entropy*, both of which are used during the construction of a decision tree. *Perplexity* is a measurement of how well a probability distribution predicts a sample.

Before we discuss the details of Gini impurity, let's introduce the concept of a *probability distribution* `P`, which means (in the finite case) that `P` is a set of non-negative numbers `{p1, p2, …, pn}` such that the sum of all the numbers in the set `P` equals 1.

As a simple example, P = {1/2, 1/2} and P = {1/6, 1/6, 1/6, 1/6, 1/6, 1/6} are both probability distributions: the first set is the set of probabilities associated with tossing a fair coin, and the second set is the probability of seeing one of the integers 1 through 6 as a result of tossing a fair die. Let's use the letter `p` to designate a probability distribution of a set `P` of numbers.

Now suppose that the set K contains a total of 10 balls, with 2 red balls, 3 green balls, and 5 yellow balls. As you can see, the set P consisting of {2/10,3/10,5/10} is a probability distribution.

In the general case, suppose that the set K contains a total of M elements, with k1 elements from class S1, k2 elements from class S2, . . ., and kn elements from class Sn. Compute the fractional representation for each class as follows:

```
p1 = k1/M, p2 = k2/M, . . ., pn = kn/M
```

As you can surmise, the values in the set `{p1, p2, …, pn}` form a probability distribution. We're going to use the preceding values in the following subsections.

What is Gini Impurity?

The Gini impurity is defined as follows, where `{p1,p2,…,pn}` is a probability distribution:

```
Gini = 1 - [p1*p1 + p2*p2 + . . . + pn*pn]
     = 1 - SUM pi*pi (for all i, where 1<=I<=n)
```

Since each pi is between 0 and 1, then pi*pi <= pi, which means that:

```
1 = p1 + p2 + . . . + pn
 >= p1*p1 + p2*p2 + . . . + pn*pn
  = Gini impurity
```

Since the `gini impurity` is the sum of the squared values of a set of probabilities, the `gini impurity` cannot be negative. Hence we have derived the following result:

```
0 <= Gini impurity <= 1
```

What is Entropy?

A formal definition of entropy is: a measure of the expected ("average") number of bits required to encode the outcome of a random variable. The calculation for the entropy H is defined via the following formula:

```
H = (-1)*[p1*log p1 + p2 * log p2 + . . . + pn * log pn]
  = (-1)* SUM pi * log(pi) (for all i, where 1<=i<=n)
```

Calculating Gini Impurity and Entropy Values

Let's start with an example involving two classes A and B and a cluster of 10 elements with 8 elements from class A and 2 elements from class B. Therefore p1 and p2 are 8/10 and 2/10, respectively. We can compute the `gini impurity` as follows:

```
Gini = 1 - [p1*p1 + p2*p2]
     = 1 - [64/100 + 04/100]
     = 1 - 68/100
     = 32/100
     = 0.32
```

We can also calculate the `entropy H` for this example as follows:

```
H = (-1)*[p1 * log p1 + p2 * log p2]
  = (-1)*[0.8 * log 0.8 + 0.2 * log 0.2]
  = (-1)*[0.8 * (-0.322) + 0.2 * (-2.322)]
  = 0.8 * 0.322 + 0.2 * 2.322
  = 0.7220
```

As a second example, suppose that we have *three* classes A, B, C and a cluster of 10 elements with 5 elements from class A, 3 elements from class B, and 2 elements from class C. Therefore p1, p2, and p3 are 5/10, 3/10, and 2/10, respectively. We can compute the `gini impurity` as follows:

```
Gini = 1 - [p1*p1 + p2*p2 + p3*p3]
     = 1 - [25/100 + 9/100 + 04/100]
     = 1 - 38/100
     = 62/100
     = 0.62
```

We can also calculate the `entropy H` for this example as follows:

```
H = (-1)*[p1 * log p1 + p2 * log p2]
  = (-1)*[0.5*log0.5 + 0.3*log0.3 + 0.2*log0.2]
  = (-1)*[-1 + 0.3*(-1.737) + 0.2*(-2.322)]
  = 1 + 0.3*1.737 + 0.2*2.322
  = 1.9855
```

In both of the preceding examples the `gini impurity` is between 0 and 1. Contrastingly, the entropy is between 0 and 1 in the first example, but it's greater than 1 in the second example (which was the rationale for showing you two examples).

Keep in mind that a set whose elements belong to the same class has `gini impurity` equal to 0 and also its entropy equal to 0. For example, if a set has 10 elements that belong to class S1, then:

```
Gini = 1 - SUM pi*pi
     = 1 - p1*p1
     = 1 - (10/10)*(10/10)
     = 1 - 1 = 0

H = (-1)*SUM pi*log pi
  = (-1) * p1*log pi
  = (-1) * (10/10) * log(10/10)
  = (-1)*1*0  = 0
```

Chapter 8 contains an example that uses a `DecisionTreeClassifier` with `gini` impurity to train a model on the `Iris` dataset, and another example that uses entropy instead of `gini` impurity.

Multidimensional Gini Index

The `gini` index is a one-dimensional index that works well because the value is uniquely defined. However, when working with multiple factors, we need a multidimensional index. Unfortunately, the multidimensional gini index (MGI) is not uniquely defined. While there have been various attempts to define an MGI that has unique values, they tend to be nonintuitive and mathematically much more complex. More information about MGI is here:

https://link.springer.com/appendix/10.1007/978-981-13-1727-9_5

What is Perplexity?

Suppose that `q` and `p` are two probability distributions, and `{x1, x2, …, xN}` is a set of sample values that is drawn from a model whose probability distribution is `p`. In addition, suppose that `b` is a positive integer (it's usually equal to 2). Now define the variable s as the following sum (logarithms are in base b not 10):

```
S = (-1/N) * [log q(x1) + log q(x2) + . . . + log q(xN)]
  = (-1/N) * SUM log q(xi)
```

The formula for the perplexity PERP of the model q is b raised to the power s, as shown here:

```
PERP = b**s
```

If you compare the formula for entropy with the formula for s, you can see that the formulas is similar, so the perplexity of a model is somewhat related to the entropy of a model.

Cross-Entropy and KL Divergence

Cross-entropy is useful for understanding machine learning algorithms, and frameworks such as TensorFlow, which supports multiple APIs that involve cross entropy. *KL divergence* is relevant in machine learning, deep learning, and reinforcement learning, and you will see it in numerous *arXiv* papers.

As an interesting example, consider the credit assignment problem, which involves assigning credit to different elements or steps in a sequence. Case in point, suppose that users arrive at a Web page by clicking on a previous page, which was also reached by clicking on yet another Web page. Then on the final Web page users click on an ad. How much credit is given to the first and second Web pages for the selected ad? You might be surprised to discover that one solution to this problem involves KL divergence.

What is Cross Entropy?

In an earlier section, you learned that for a probability distribution P with values {p1,p2,... pn}, its entropy is H defined as follows:

```
H(P) = (-1)*SUM pi*log(pi)
```

Now let's introduce another probability distribution Q whose values are {q1,q2,..., qn}, which means that the entropy for Q is defined as follows:

```
H(Q) = (-1)*SUM qi*log(qi)
```

Now we can define the cross entropy CE of Q and P as follows (notice the `log qi` and `log pi` terms):

```
CE(Q,P) = SUM pi*log qi - SUM pi*log pi
        = SUM (pi*log qi - pi*log pi)
        = SUM pi*(log qi - log pi)
        = SUM pi*(log qi/pi)
```

What is KL Divergence?

Now we can define the KL divergence of the probability distributions Q and P as follows:

$$KL(P\|Q) = CE(P,Q) - H(P)$$

The definitions of entropy H, cross entropy CE, and KL divergence in this appendix involve discrete probability distributions P and Q. However, these concepts have counterparts in continuous probability density functions. The mathematics (which is beyond the scope of this book) involves the concept of a *Lebesgue* measure on *Borel* sets that are described here:

https://en.wikipedia.org/wiki/Lebesgue_measure
https://en.wikipedia.org/wiki/Borel_set

In addition to KL divergence, there is also Jenson-Shannon (JS) divergence was developed by Johan Jensen and Claude Shannon (Claude and his wife defined the formula for entropy). JS divergence is based on KL divergence, and it has some differences: JSdivergence is symmetric and a true metric, whereas KL divergence is neither. More information regarding JS divergence is available here:

https://en.wikipedia.org/wiki/Jensen–Shannon_divergence

What's their Purpose?

The *Gini* impurity is often used to obtain a measure of the homogeneity of a set of elements in a decision tree. The entropy of that set is an alternative to its `gini` impurity, and you will see both of these quantities used in machine learning models.

The *perplexity* value in NLP is one way to evaluate language models, which are probability distributions over sentences or texts. This value provides an estimate for the encoding size of a set of sentences.

Cross entropy is used in various methods in the TensorFlow framework, and the *KL divergence* is used in various algorithms, such as the dimensionality reduction algorithm `t-SNE`. For more information about any of these terms, perform an online search and you will find numerous online tutorials that provide more detailed information.

Covariance and Correlation Matrices

This section explains two important matrices: the covariance matrix and the correlation matrix. Although these are relevant for PCA that is discussed later, these matrices are not specific to PCA, which is the rationale for discussing them in a separate section. If you are familiar with these matrices, feel free to skim through this section.

Covariance Matrix

As a reminder, the statistical quantity called the variance of a random variable x is defined as follows:

```
variance(x) = [SUM (x - xbar)*(x-xbar)]/n
```

A *covariance matrix* C is an nxn matrix whose values on the main diagonal are the variance of the variables $x_1, x_2, \ldots, x_n$. The other values of C are the covariance values of each pair of variables x_i and x_j.

The formula for the covariance of the variables x and y is a generalization of the variance of a variable, and the formula is shown here:

```
covariance(X, Y) = [SUM (x - xbar)*(y-ybar)]/n
```

Notice that you can reverse the order of the product of terms (multiplication is commutative), and therefore the covariance matrix C is a symmetric matrix:

```
covariance(X, Y) = covariance(Y,X)
```

Suppose that a CSV file contains four numeric features, all of which have been scaled appropriately, and let's call them x1, x2, x3, and x4. Then the covariance matrix C is a 4×4 square matrix that is defined as follows:

$$\begin{bmatrix} cov(x1, x1) & cov(x1, x2) & cov(x1, x3) & cov(x1, x4) \\ cov(x2, x1) & cov(x2, x2) & cov(x2, x3) & cov(x2, x4) \\ cov(x3, x1) & cov(x3, x2) & cov(x3, x3) & cov(x3, x4) \\ cov(x4, x1) & cov(x4, x2) & cov(x4, x3) & cov(x4, x4) \end{bmatrix}$$

Note that the following is true for the diagonal entries in the preceding covariance matrix C:

```
var(x1,x1) = cov(x1,x1)
var(x2,x2) = cov(x2,x2)
var(x3,x3) = cov(x3,x3)
var(x4,x4) = cov(x4,x4)
```

In addition, C is a symmetric matrix, which is to say that the transpose of matrix C (rows become columns and columns become rows) is identical to the matrix C. The latter is true because (as you saw in the previous section) cov(x,y) = cov(y,x) for any feature x and any feature y.

Covariance Matrix: An Example

Suppose we have the two-column matrix A defined as follows:

$$A = \begin{matrix} x & y \\ \begin{bmatrix} 1 & 1 \\ 2 & 1 \\ 3 & 2 \\ 4 & 2 \\ 5 & 3 \\ 6 & 3 \end{bmatrix} \end{matrix} \Leftarrow \text{6x2 matrix}$$

The mean x_bar of column x is (1+2+3+4+5+6)/6 = 3.5, and the mean y_bar of column y is (1+1+2+2+3+3)/6 = 2. Now subtract x_bar from column x and subtract y_bar from column y and we get matrix B, as shown here:

$$B = \begin{bmatrix} -2.5 & -1 \\ -1.5 & -1 \\ -0.5 & 0 \\ 0.5 & 0 \\ 1.5 & 1 \\ 2.5 & 1 \end{bmatrix} \Leftarrow \text{6x2 matrix}$$

Let Bt indicate the transpose of the matrix B, which means that Bt is a 2 x 6 matrix, as shown here:

$$Bt = \begin{bmatrix} -2.5 & -1.5 & -0.5 & 0.5 & 1.5 & 2.5 \\ -1 & -1 & 0 & 0 & 1 & 1 \end{bmatrix}$$

The covariance matrix C is the product of Bt and B, as shown here:

$$C = Bt * B = \begin{bmatrix} 15.25 & 4 \\ 4 & 8 \end{bmatrix}$$

Note that if the units of measure of features x and y do not have a similar scale, then the covariance matrix is adversely affected. In this case, the solution is simple: use the correlation matrix, which defined in the next section.

However, if the units of measure of features x and y do not have a similar scale, then the covariance matrix is adversely affected. The solution is simple: use the correlation matrix, which defined in the next section.

Correlation Matrix

As you learned in the preceding section, if the units of measure of features x and y do not have a similar scale, then the covariance matrix is adversely affected. The solution involves the *correlation matrix*, which equals the covariance values `cov(x,y)` divided by the standard deviation `stdx` and `stdy` of x and y, respectively, as shown here:

`corr(x,y) = cov(x,y)/[stdx * stdy]`

The correlation matrix no longer has units of measure, and we can use this matrix to find the eigenvalues and eigenvectors.

Eigenvalues and Eigenvectors

According to a well-known theorem in mathematics (which you can find online), the eigenvalues of a symmetric matrix are real numbers. Consequently, the eigenvectors of C are vectors in a Euclidean vector space (not a complex vector space).

In case you're wondering, a non-zero vector x' is an eigenvector of the matrix C if there is a non-zero scalar lambda such that C*x' = lambda * x'

Now suppose that the eigenvalues of C are b1, b2, b3, and b4, in decreasing numeric order from left-to-right, and that the corresponding eigenvectors of C are the vectors w1, w2, w3, and w4. These vectors form the principal components of the new matrix.

Now that you understand how to calculate the covariance matrix and the correlation matrix, you are ready for an example of calculating eigenvalues and eigenvectors, which are the topic of the next section.

Calculating Eigenvectors: A Simple Example

As a simple illustration of calculating eigenvalues and eigenvectors, suppose that the square matrix C is defined as follows:

$$C = \begin{bmatrix} 1 & 3 \\ 3 & 1 \end{bmatrix}$$

Let I denote the 2×2 identity matrix, and let b' be an eigenvalue of C, which means that there is an eigenvector x' such that:

```
C* x' = b' * x', or
(C-b*I)*x' = 0 (the right side is a 2x1 vector)
```

Since x' is non-zero, that means the following is true (where `det` refers to the *determinant* of a matrix):

$$\det(C-b*I) = \det\begin{bmatrix} 1-b & 3 \\ 3 & 1-b \end{bmatrix} = (1-b)*(1-b) - 9 = 0$$

We can expand the quadratic equation in the preceding line to get:

```
det(C-b*I) = (1-b)*(1-b) - 9
           = 1 - 2*b + b*b - 9
           = -8 - 2*b + b*b
           = b*b - 2*b - 8
```

Use the quadratic formula (or perform factorization by visual inspection) to determine that the solution for `det(C-b*I) = 0` is `b = -2` or `b = 4`. Next, substitute `b = -2` into `(C-b*I)x' = 0` and we get the following result:

$$\begin{bmatrix} 1-(-2) & 3 \\ 3 & 1-(-2) \end{bmatrix}\begin{bmatrix} x1 \\ x2 \end{bmatrix} = \begin{bmatrix} 0 \\ 0 \end{bmatrix}$$

The preceding reduces to the following identical equations:

```
3*x1 + 3*x2 = 0
3*x1 + 3*x2 = 0
```

The general solution is `x1 = -x2`, and we can choose any non-zero value for x2, so let's set `x2 = 1` (any other non-zero value will do just fine), which yields `x1 = -1`. Therefore, the eigenvector [-1, 1] is associated with the eigenvalue -2. In a similar fashion, if x' is an eigenvector whose eigenvalue is 4, then [1,1] is an eigenvector.

Notice that the eigenvectors [-1, 1] and [1,1] are orthogonal because their inner product is zero, as shown here:

```
[-1,1] * [1,1] = (-1)*1 + (1)*1 = 0
```

In fact, the set of eigenvectors of a square matrix (whose eigenvalues are real) are always orthogonal, regardless of the dimensionality of the matrix.

Gauss Jordan Elimination (Optional)

This simple technique enables you to find the solution to systems of linear equations "in place," which involves a sequence of arithmetic operations to transform a given matrix to an identity matrix.

The following example combines the Gauss-Jordan elimination technique (which finds the solution to a set of linear equations) with the "bookkeeper's method," which determines the inverse of an invertible matrix (its determinant is non-zero).

This technique involves two adjacent matrices: the left-side matrix is the initial matrix and the right-side matrix is an identity matrix. Next, perform various linear operations on the left-side matrix to reduce it to an identity matrix: the matrix on the right side equals its inverse. For example, consider the following pair of linear equations whose solution is x = 1 and y = 2:

```
2*x + 2*y = 6
4*x - 1*y = 2
```

Step 1: create a 2×2 matrix with the coefficients of x in column 1 and the coefficients of y in column two, followed by the 2×2 identity matrix, and finally a column from the numbers on the right of the equals sign:

$$\begin{bmatrix} 2 & 2 \\ 4 & -1 \end{bmatrix} \begin{bmatrix} 1 & 0 \\ 0 & 1 \end{bmatrix} \begin{bmatrix} 6 \\ 2 \end{bmatrix}$$

Step 2: add (-2) times the first row to the second row:

$$\begin{bmatrix} 2 & 2 \\ 0 & -5 \end{bmatrix} \begin{bmatrix} 1 & 0 \\ -2 & 1 \end{bmatrix} \begin{bmatrix} 6 \\ -10 \end{bmatrix}$$

Step 3: divide the second row by 5:

$$\begin{bmatrix} 2 & 2 \\ 0 & -1 \end{bmatrix} \begin{bmatrix} 1 & 0 \\ -2/5 & 1/5 \end{bmatrix} \begin{bmatrix} 6 \\ -10/5 \end{bmatrix}$$

Step 4: add 2 times the second row to the first row:

$$\begin{bmatrix} 2 & 0 \\ 0 & -1 \end{bmatrix} \begin{bmatrix} 1/5 & 2/5 \\ -2/5 & 1/5 \end{bmatrix} \begin{bmatrix} 2 \\ -2 \end{bmatrix}$$

Step 5: divide the first row by 2:

$$\begin{bmatrix} 1 & 0 \\ 0 & -1 \end{bmatrix} \begin{bmatrix} -2/10 & 2/10 \\ -2/5 & 1/5 \end{bmatrix} \begin{bmatrix} 1 \\ -2 \end{bmatrix}$$

Step 6: multiply the second row by (-1):

$$\begin{bmatrix} 1 & 0 \\ 0 & 1 \end{bmatrix} \begin{bmatrix} -2/10 & 2/10 \\ 2/5 & -1/5 \end{bmatrix} \begin{bmatrix} 1 \\ 2 \end{bmatrix}$$

As you can see, the left-side matrix is the 2×2 identity matrix, the right-side matrix is the inverse of the original matrix, and the right-most column is the solution to the original pair of linear equations (x=1 and y=2).

Principal Component Analysis (PCA)

PCA is a linear dimensionality reduction technique for determining the most important features in a dataset. This section discusses PCA because it's a very popular technique that you will encounter frequently. Other techniques (such as SVD) also discussed later) are more efficient than PCA, so it's worthwhile to learn other dimensionality reduction techniques as well.

Keep in mind the following points regarding the PCA technique:

PCA is a variance-based algorithm.
PCA creates variables that are linear combinations of the original variables.
The new variables are all pair-wise orthogonal.
PCA can be a useful preprocessing step before clustering.
PCA is generally preferred for data reduction.

PCA can be useful for variables that are strongly correlated. If most of the coefficients in the correlation matrix are smaller than 0.3, PCA is not helpful. PCA provides some advantages: less computation time for training a model (for example, using only five features instead of 100 features), a simpler model, and the ability to render the data visually when two or three features are selected. Here is a key point regarding PCA:

PCA calculates the eigenvalues and the eigenvectors of the covariance (or correlation) matrix C.

If you have four or five components, you won't be able to display them visually, but you could select subsets of three components for visualization, and perhaps gain some additional insight into the dataset.

The PCA algorithm involves the following sequence of steps:

1. calculate the correlation matrix (from the covariance matrix) C of a dataset.

2. Find the eigenvalues of C.

3. Find the eigenvectors of C.

4. Construct a new matrix that comprises the eigenvectors.

The covariance matrix and correlation matrix were explained in a previous section. You also saw the definition of eigenvalues and eigenvectors, along with an example of calculating eigenvalues and eigenvectors.

The eigenvectors are treated as column vectors that are placed adjacent to each other in decreasing order (from left-to-right) with respect to their associated eigenvectors.

PCA uses the variance as a measure of information: the higher the variance, the more important the component. In fact, just to jump ahead slightly: PCA determines the eigenvalues and eigenvectors of a covariance matrix (discussed in a previous section), and constructs a new matrix whose columns are eigenvectors, ordered from left-to-right based on the maximum eigenvalue in the left-most column, decreasing until the right-most eigenvector also has the smallest eigenvalue.

Alternatively, there is an interesting theorem in linear algebra: if C is a symmetric matrix, then there is a diagonal matrix D and an orthogonal matrix P (the columns are pair-wise orthogonal, which means their pair-wise inner product is zero), such that the following holds:

`C = P * D * Pt (where Pt is the transpose of matrix P)`

In fact, the diagonal values of D are eigenvalues, and the columns of P are the corresponding eigenvectors of the matrix C.

Fortunately, we can use `NumPy` and `Pandas` to calculate the mean, standard deviation, covariance matrix, correlation matrix, as well as the matrices D and P in order to determine the eigenvalues and eigenvectors.

As an interesting point: any positive definite square matrix has real-valued eigenvectors, which also applies to the covariance matrix C because it is a real-valued symmetric matrix.

The New Matrix of Eigenvectors

The previous section described how the matrices D and P are determined. The left-most eigenvector of D has the largest eigenvalue, the next eigenvector has the second-largest eigenvalue, and so forth. This fact is very convenient: the eigenvector with the highest eigenvalue is the principal component of the dataset. The eigenvector with the second-highest eigenvalue is the second principal component, and so forth. You specify the number of principal components that you want via the `n_components` hyperparameter in the PCA class of Sklearn.

As a simple and minimalistic example, consider the following code block that uses PCA for a (somewhat contrived) dataset:

```
import numpy as np
from Sklearn.decomposition import PCA
data = np.array([[-1,-1], [-2,-1], [-3,-2], [1,1], [2,1], [3,2]])
pca = PCA(n_components=2)
pca.fit(X)
```

Note that a trade-off here: we greatly reduce the number of components, which reduces the computation time and the complexity of the model, but we also lose some accuracy. However, if the unselected eigenvalues are small, we lose only a small amount of accuracy.

Now let's define the variables `NM`, `NMt`, `PC`, `SD`, and `SDt` as follows:

`NM` denotes the matrix with the new principal components
`NMt` is the transpose of `NM`
`PC` is the matrix of the subset of selected principal components
`SD` is the matrix of scaled data from the original dataset
`SDt` is the transpose of `SD`

Then the matrix `NM` can be expressed via the following formula:

```
NM = PCt * SDt
```

Although `PCA` is a very nice technique for dimensionality reduction, keep in mind the following limitations of `PCA`:

less suitable for data with nonlinear relationships
less suitable for special classification problems

A related algorithm is called `Kernel PCA`, which is an extension of `PCA` that introduces a nonlinear transformation so you can still use the `PCA` approach.

Dimensionality Reduction

The previous section described various types of feature selection techniques, whereas dimensionality reduction involves a transformation of the data (such as `PCA`) or a projection of the data. Some of the well-known algorithms that perform dimensionality reduction are listed here:

- principal component analysis (PCA)
- kernel PCA
- graph-based kernel PCA
- singular value decomposition (SVD)
- nonnegative matrix factorization (NMF)
- linear discriminant analysis (LDA)
- generalized discriminant analysis (GDA)
- isomap embedding

- locally linear embedding
- modified locally linear embedding
- variational autoencoders (VAEs)

VAEs (the last item in the preceding list) are deep learning models that have a number of use cases. Although VAEs are beyond the scope of this book, a comparison of PCA and VAEs is here:

https://towardsdatascience.com/dimensionality-reduction-pca-versus-autoencoders-338fcaf3297d

The following algorithms combine feature extraction and dimensionality reduction (some of which belong to both lists):

- PCA (principal component analysis)
- LDA (linear discriminant analysis)
- CCA (canonical correlation analysis)
- NMF (non-negative matrix factorization)

These algorithms can be used during a preprocessing step before using clustering or some other algorithm (such as kNN) on a dataset.

One other group of algorithms involves methods based on projections, which includes t-distributed stochastic neighbor embedding (t-SNE) as well as UMAP.

Dimensionality Reduction Techniques

In simplified terms, dimensionality reduction refers to reducing a high-dimensional vector space to a lower dimensional vector space. There are several techniques that perform dimensionality reduction (such as PCA in the previous section), as listed here:

- principal component analysis (PCA)
- singular value decomposition (SVD)
- locally linear embedding (LLE)
- UMAP
- t-SNE
- PHATE

The previous section discussed PCA because PCA is a common algorithm for dimensionality reduction in machine learning. The other algorithms in the preceding list are discussed in a high-level fashion in the following subsections.

Dimensionality reduction techniques belong to different categories, such as matrix factorization (PCA and SVD), model-based reduction (LDA), and manifold learning (SOM and t-SNE).

The Curse of Dimensionality

This term refers to the following phenomenon: as you increase the number of dimensions in a dataset, the datapoints in the dataset tend to be farther apart, which in turn increases the possibility of overfitting. In a perfect world, the datapoints in a dataset are evenly distributed (how wonderful this would be!), but in reality, different features have different distributions. One feature might be almost constant, a second feature might have a Gaussian distribution, a third feature might be bi-modal, and so forth.

Nevertheless, many dimensionality reduction algorithms involve projecting datapoints in a dataset to a lower-dimensional space (the other technique is discussed later).

What are Manifolds (Optional)?

Although this is a concept in topology, which might seem wildly out of place in this book, it's a concept that is useful for understanding the second popular dimensionality reduction technique called *manifold learning*.

As a simple example, walking on a sidewalk or driving a car feels like movement in two dimensions. In reality, you are moving along a sphere-like object (the Earth), which means that you are actually moving in three dimensions. Obviously the third component (i.e., the height) is extremely small: in fact, it's so small that you don't even notice its effect, which is why this movement feels as though it's happening in two dimensions.

Another way to say the same thing is that a three-dimensional sphere is locally "similar" a two-dimensional plane (as described in the preceding paragraph). In general, a manifold is a topological space that locally resembles Euclidean space for points that are "close" together. In mathematical terms, given any point of an n-dimensional manifold, there is a neighborhood of that point that is homeomorphic to Euclidean space of the same dimensionality.

In the walking/driving example, we noted that if we are standing at a point and we walk or drive away from that point, it feels as though we are moving in two dimensions, even though we are moving in three dimensions.

Some simple examples: lines and circles are one-manifolds but a "figure eight" is not a one-manifold. Two dimensional manifolds (also called surfaces) include planes, spheres, and the torus ("donut").

Singular Value Decomposition (SVD)

SVD is a technique in linear algebra that factors any mxn matrix A into the product of three matrices U, S, and V, as shown here:

```
A = U*S*Vt
```

The preceding formula is true for any matrix A (square, rectangular, invertible, or non-invertible), and the matrices U, S, and V are as follows:

```
U: (mxm) is orthogonal (U*Ut = I) with left singular vectors
V: (nxn) is orthogonal (V*Vt = I) with right singular vectors
S: (mxn) is diagonal with "singular values"
```

Recall that if B, C, and D are compatible matrices, then the following transpose rules are true:

```
(B*C)t = Ct * Bt
(B*C*D)t = Dt * Ct * Bt
```

Now we can determine the nature of the matrices U and V by computing At*A and A*At, as shown below:

```
At*A = (V*S*Ut)*(U*S*Vt) = V*S^2*Vt (because Ut*U = I)
```

In fact, V is the matrix of eigenvectors for At*A, and S^2 is the matrix of eigenvalues for At*A. Now let's compute A*At, as shown below:

```
A*At = (U*S*Vt)*(V*S*Ut) = U*S^2*Ut (because Vt*V = I)
```

Now U is the matrix of eigenvectors for A*At, and S^2 is the matrix of eigenvalues for At*A. Since S^2 is a diagonal matrix of eigenvalues, the diagonal matrix S consists of the square root of the eigenvalues.

Keep in mind that there are some scalability and performance-related issues regarding SVD, as follows:

Complexity is $O(m*n^2)$ when n < m (n x m matrix).
It's not scalable for millions of words/documents.
It's difficult to incorporate new words/documents.

In case you're wondering, one application of SVD is the decomposition of the ratings matrix in recommender systems into a product of three matrices.

Another application of SVD pertains to gene expression, which is discussed in the following link:

http://homepages.math.uic.edu/~friedlan/svdwvumerge.pdf

There are several variants of SVD that might be of interest, and perhaps better suited to your particular needs. For example, Truncated SVD reduces dimensionality by selecting only the largest singular values, keeping the first t columns of U and V. Details for Truncated SVD as well as Thin SVD and Compact SVD are provided here: *https://en.wikipedia.org/wiki/Singular_value_decomposition*

Another variant of SVD is SVDpp (sometimes called SVD++), which is described here:

https://surprise.readthedocs.io/en/stable/matrix_factorization.html

Finally, HybridSVD, PureSVD, SVDpp, and timeSVDpp are additional variations of SVD, and you can perform an online search for additional information.

Locally Linear Embedding (LLE)

LLE is a nonlinear dimensionality reduction technique that is based on the following two tasks:

1. Compute the linear distance of a datapoint to its nearest neighbor.

2. Attempt to determine a lower-dimensional representation of the datapoints such that the local relationships are preserved.

Thus, the intuition of LLE is similar to the intuition of t-SNE. An example of using LocallyLinearEmbedding with Sklearn is here:

https://scikit-learn.org/stable/modules/generated/Sklearn.manifold.LocallyLinearEmbedding.html

UMAP

UMAP is an acronym for Uniform Manifold Approximation and Projection, and it's a nonlinear dimensionality reduction technique. Although it is similar to the t-SNE algorithm (discussed in the next section), UMAP makes the assumption that the data is uniformly distributed on a locally connected Riemannian manifold and that the Riemannian metric is locally constant or approximately locally constant. A detailed discussion regarding Riemannian metrics is here:

https://arxiv.org/pdf/1212.2474.pdf

t-SNE ("tee-snee")

The `t-SNE` (T-distributed stochastic neighbor embedding) algorithm is a nonlinear dimensionality reduction technique in machine learning algorithm for visualization.

The goal of `t-SNE` is to perform the following:

1. Map similar objects to nearby points.

2. Map dissimilar objects to more distant points.

The `t-SNE` algorithm is a non-linear dimensionality reduction technique in machine learning algorithm for visualization. The key idea of t-SNE is to perform the following:

1. Map similar objects to nearby points.

2. Map dissimilar objects to more distant points.

The implementation of `t-SNE` involves two probability distributions: one for pairs of high-dimensional objects that performs #1, and another for pairs of low-dimensional objects that performs #2. The next step involves minimizing the KL divergence for these two probability distributions.

Note that `PCA` is a much older technique (1930s) whereas `t-SNE` was developed more recently (2008). `PCA` performs linear dimension reduction that (a) maximizes variance, and (b) preserves large pair-wise distances. As a result, different datapoints will be moved farther apart in `PCA`, which might not work as well with non-linear data.

By contrast, `t-SNE` preserves small pair-wise distances by means of an algorithm that calculates a similarity measure between datapoints in the high dimensional space as well as in the low dimensional space. In addition, `t-SNE` uses a cost function in order to optimize similarity measures.

PHATE

`PHATE` is an acronym for potential of heat-diffusion affinity-based transition embedding. `PHATE` is a visualization and dimensionality reduction technique that does resemble `t-SNE`: both are sensitive to local and global relationships and attempt to preserve relationships among close objects and distant objects.

Note that this technique shows up in biological data, which is not discussed in this book. However, more information about `PHATE` is available here:

https://www.biorxiv.org/content/10.1101/120378v1.full.pdf

Linear Versus Nonlinear Reduction Techniques

One detail that has been glossed over is the difference between linear dimensionality reduction versus non-linear dimensionality reduction algorithms. Before discussing those two types of algorithms, a mathematical definition is required.

Suppose that T is a mapping from vector space U to the vector space V (which can have different dimensions), denoted as T:U->V. Then T is a *linear transformation* if the following are both true for any vectors u1 and u2 in U and any real number a:

```
   T(u1+u2) = T(u1) + T(u2)
2) T(a*u)   = a*T(u)
```

For example, rotating a vector in the plane or scaling a vector in the plane is a linear transformation: shifting a vector in the plane is not a linear transformation (it's an *affine transformation*).

If the dimension of U and V are the same and equal n, then a linear transformation T can be represented as an nxn invertible matrix (i.e., it has an inverse). If the dimension of V is lower than the dimension of U, then the linear transformation T involves a *projection*. If the dimension of V is higher than the dimension of U, then the transformation T involves an *embedding*.

For example, if T doubles the size of the components of vectors in two-dimensional Euclidean space, then T can be represented by the following matrix:

$$\begin{bmatrix} 2 & 0 \\ 0 & 2 \end{bmatrix}$$

If T halves the first component and triples the second component of vectors in two-dimensional space, then T can be represented by the following matrix:

$$\begin{bmatrix} 0.5 & 0 \\ 0 & 3 \end{bmatrix}$$

If T maps the vector of the form (x,y,z) to a vector of the form (x,y,0), then T is a projection, and T can be represented by the following matrix:

$$\begin{bmatrix} 1 & 0 & 0 \\ 0 & 1 & 0 \\ 0 & 0 & 0 \end{bmatrix}$$

Based on the definition of a linear transformation that you saw in the beginning of this section, `PCA` is a *linear* dimensionality reduction algorithm, whereas `kernel PCA` is a *non-linear* dimensionality reduction algorithm.

Linear reduction involves computing a linear combination of features or performing a linear transformation. An example of the latter transforming a spanning set of vectors by a non-singular matrix. Specifically, suppose that the set B of vectors {v1, v2, . . . , vn} are orthogonal and they form a basis for an n-dimensional vector space V. In addition, suppose that M is an nxn non-singular matrix. (Its determinant is non-zero). Then {Mv1, Mv2, . . ., Mvn} is a linear transformation of the basis B that also spans the vector space V.

By contrast, nonlinear (NL) dimensionality reduction techniques perform non-linear transformations. However, in many cases, NL dimensionality reduction techniques are related to linear methods, and they tend to belong to one of two groups:

- NL techniques that provide high-to-low mapping (or vice versa)
- NL techniques that provide visualization

Mapping methods are used to perform an initial feature extraction step, after which machine learning algorithms can perform pattern recognition. However, NL techniques that provide visualization perform calculations involving the distance between objects.

Types of Distance Metrics

Nonlinear dimensionality reduction techniques can also have different distance metrics. For example, linear reduction techniques can use the Euclidean distance metric (based on the Pythagorean theorem). However, you need to use a different distance metric to measure the distance between two points on a sphere (or some other curved surface). In the case of NLP, the *cosine similarity* metric is used to measure the distance between word embeddings (which are vectors of floating point numbers that represent words or tokens).

Distance metrics are used for measuring physical distances, and some well-known distance metrics are listed here:

- Euclidean distance
- Manhattan distance
- Chebyshev distance

The Euclidean algorithm also obeys the *triangle inequality*, which states that for any triangle in the Euclidean plane, the sum of the lengths of any pair of sides must be greater than the length of the third side.

In spherical geometry, you can define the distance between two points as the arc of a great circle that passes through the two points (always selecting the smaller of the two arcs when they are different).

In addition to physical metrics, there are algorithms that implement the concept of "edit distance" (the distance between strings), as listed here:

- Hamming distance
- Jaro–Winkler distance
- Lee distance
- Levenshtein distance
- Mahalanobis distance metric
- Wasserstein metric

The *Mahalanobis* metric is based on an interesting idea: given a point P and a probability distribution D, this metric measures the number of standard deviations that separate point P from distribution D. More information about Mahalanobis is here:

https://en.wikipedia.org/wiki/Mahalanobis_distance

In the branch of mathematics called topology, a metric space is a set for which distances between all members of the set are defined. Various metrics are available (such as the *Hausdorff* metric), depending on the type of topology.

The *Wasserstein* metric measures the distance between two probability distributions over a metric space X. This metric is also called the "earth mover's metric" for the following reason: given two unit piles of dirt, it's the measure of the minimum cost of moving one pile on top of the other pile.

KL divergence bears some superficial resemblance to the Wasserstein metric. However, there are some important differences between them. Specifically, the Wasserstein metric has the following properties:

- It is a metric.
- It is symmetric.
- It satisfies the triangle inequality.

However, KL divergence has the following properties:

- It is not a metric (it's a divergence).
- It is not symmetric: KL(P,Q) != KL(Q,P).
- It does not satisfy the triangle inequality.

Note that JS (Jenson-Shannon) divergence (which is based on KL divergence) is a true metric, which would enable a more meaningful comparison with other metrics (such as the Wasserstein metric).

Other Well-Known Distance Metrics

Chapter 9 discusses recommendation systems, which involve finding similarities between users or items and then making recommendations. There are several similarity metrics available, such as item similarity metrics, Jaccard (user-based) similarity, and cosine similarity (which is used to compare vectors of numbers). The following subsections introduce you to these similarity metrics.

Another well-known distance metric is the so-called "taxicab" metric, which is also called the Manhattan distance metric. Given two points A and B in a rectangular grid, the taxicab metric calculates the distance between two points by counting the number of "blocks" that must be traversed in order to reach B from A (the other direction has the same taxicab metric value). For example, if you need to travel two blocks north and then three blocks east in a rectangular grid, then the Manhattan distance is 5.

In fact, there are various other metrics available, which you can learn about by searching Wikipedia. In the case of NLP, the most frequently used distance metric is calculated via the cosine similarity of two vectors, and it's derived from the formula for the inner ("dot") product of two vectors.

Pearson Correlation Coefficient

Pearson similarity is the Pearson coefficient between two vectors. Given random variables X and Y, and the following terms:

```
std(X)    = standard deviation of X
std(Y)    = standard deviation of Y
cov(X,Y)  = covariance of X and Y
```

Then the Pearson correlation coefficient `rho(X,Y)` is defined as follows:

$$\text{rho}(X, Y) = \frac{\text{cov}(X, Y)}{\text{std}(X) * \text{std}(Y)}$$

Keep in mind that the Pearson coefficient is limited to items of the same type. More information about the Pearson correlation coefficient is here:

https://en.wikipedia.org/wiki/Pearson_correlation_coefficient

Jaccard Index (or Similarity)

The *Jaccard similarity* is based on the number of users which have rated item A and B divided by the number of users who have rated either A or B. Jaccard similarity is based on unique words in a sentence and is unaffected by duplicates, whereas cosine similarity is based on the length of all word vectors (which changes when duplicates are added). The choice between cosine similarity and Jaccard similarity depends on whether or not word duplicates are important.

The following `Python` method illustrates how to compute the Jaccard similarity of two sentences:

```
def get_jaccard_sim(str1, str2):
set1 = set(str1.split())
set2 = set(str2.split())
set3 = set1.intersection(set2)
# (size of intersection) / (size of union):
return float(len(set3)) / (len(set1) + len(set2) - len(set3))
```

Jaccard similarity can be used in situations involving boolean values, such as product purchases (true/false), instead of numeric values. More information is available here: *https://en.wikipedia.org/wiki/Jaccard_index*

Local Sensitivity Hashing (Optional)

If you are familiar with hash algorithms, you know that they are algorithms that create a hash table that associate items with a value. The advantage of hash tables is that the lookup time to determine whether or not an item exists in the hash table is constant. Of course, it's possible for two items to "collide," which means that they both occupy the same bucket in the hash table. In this case, a bucket can consist of a list of items that can be searched in more or less constant time. If there are too many items in the same bucket, then a different hashing function can be selected to reduce the number of collisions. The goal of a hash table is to minimize the number of collisions.

The local sensitivity hashing (LSH) algorithm hashes similar input items into the same "buckets." In fact, the goal of LSH is to maximize the number of collisions, whereas traditional hashing algorithms attempt to minimize the number of collisions.

Since similar items end up in the same buckets, LSH is useful for data clustering and nearest neighbor searches. Moreover, LSH is a dimensionality reduction technique that places datapoints of high dimensionality closer together in a lower-dimensional space, while simultaneously preserving the relative distances between those datapoints.

More details about LSH are here:

https://en.wikipedia.org/wiki/Locality-sensitive_hashing

What is Sklearn?

Before we discuss any code samples, please keep in mind that `Sklearn` is an immensely useful `Python` library that supports a huge number of machine learning algorithms. In particular, `Sklearn` supports many classification algorithms, such as logistic regression, naive Bayes, decision trees, random forests, and SVMs (support vector machines). Chapter 8 provides a high-level description of most of these classification algorithms. Although entire books are available that are dedicated to `Sklearn`, this appendix contains only a few pages of `Sklearn` material.

One-hot encoding and label encoding and `Sklearn SimpleImputer` class:

https://www.kdnuggets.com/2020/07/easy-guide-data-preprocessing-python.html

The following link contains a list of some of the best new features in version 0.25 of `Sklearn`:

https://towardsdatascience.com/the-10-best-new-features-in-scikit-learn-0-24-f45e49b6741b

If you decide that you want to acquire a deep level of knowledge about `Sklearn`, navigate to the Web pages that contain very detailed documentation for `Sklearn`. Moreover, if you have "how to" questions involving `Sklearn`, you can almost always find suitable answers on stackoverflow.

In addition to support for machine learning algorithms, `Sklearn` provides various built-in datasets that you can access with literally one line of code. In fact, Listing A.1 displays the contents of `sklearn_iris1.py` that illustrates how you can easily load the `Iris` dataset into a `Pandas` data frame.

LISTING A.1: sklearn_iris1.py

```
import numpy as np
import pandas as pd
from sklearn.datasets import load_iris

iris = load_iris()

print("=> iris keys:")
for key in iris.keys():
print(key)
print()

#print("iris dimensions:")
#print(iris.shape)
#print()

print("=> iris feature names:")
for feature in iris.feature_names:
print(feature)
print()

X = iris.data[:, [2, 3]]
y = iris.target
print('=> Class labels:', np.unique(y))
print()

print("=> target:")
print(iris.target)
print()

print("=> all data:")
print(iris.data)
```

Listing A.1 starts with several `import` statements and then initializes the variable `iris` with the `Iris` dataset. Next, a loop displays the keys in dataset, followed by another loop that displays the feature names.

The next portion of Listing A.1 initializes the variable X with the feature values in columns 2 and 3, and then initializes the variable y with the values of the `target` column. Now launch the code in Listing A.1 and you will see the following output (truncated to save space):

```
Pandas df1:

iris keys:
data
target
target_names
DESCR
```

```
feature_names
filename

iris feature names:
sepal length (cm)
sepal width (cm)
petal length (cm)
petal width (cm)

Class labels: [0 1 2]

target:
[0 0 0 0 0 0 0 0 0 0 0 0 0 0 0 0 0 0 0 0 0 0 0 0 0 0 0 0 0 0
 0 0 0 0 0 0
 0 0 0 0 0 0 0 0 0 0 0 0 0 0 1 1 1 1 1 1 1 1 1 1 1 1 1 1 1 1
 1 1 1 1 1 1
 1 1 1 1 1 1 1 1 1 1 1 1 1 1 1 1 1 1 1 1 1 1 1 1 1 1 2 2 2 2
 2 2 2 2 2 2
 2 2 2 2 2 2 2 2 2 2 2 2 2 2 2 2 2 2 2 2 2 2 2 2 2 2 2 2 2 2
 2 2 2 2 2 2
 2 2]

all data:
[[5.1 3.5 1.4 0.2]
 [4.9 3.  1.4 0.2]
 [4.7 3.2 1.3 0.2]
 // details omitted for brevity
 [6.5 3.  5.2 2. ]
 [6.2 3.4 5.4 2.3]
 [5.9 3.  5.1 1.8]]
```

Sklearn, Pandas, and the IRIS Dataset

Listing A.2 displays the contents of pandas_iris1.py that illustrates how to load the contents of the Iris dataset (from Sklearn) into a Pandas data frame.

LISTING A.2: pandas_iris1.py

```
import numpy as np
import pandas as pd
from Sklearn.datasets import load_iris

iris = load_iris()

print("=> IRIS feature names:")
for feature in iris.feature_names:
print(feature)
print()
```

```
# Create a dataframe with the feature variables
df = pd.DataFrame(iris.data, columns=iris.feature_names)

print("=> number of rows:")
print(len(df))
print()

print("=> number of columns:")
print(len(df.columns))
print()

print("=> number of rows and columns:")
print(df.shape)
print()

print("=> number of elements:")
print(df.size)
print()

print("=> IRIS details:")
print(df.info())
print()

print("=> top five rows:")
print(df.head())
print()

X = iris.data[:, [2, 3]]
y = iris.target
print('=> Class labels:', np.unique(y))
```

Listing A.2 starts with several `import` statements and then initializes the variable `iris` with the `Iris` dataset. Next, a loop displays the feature names. The next code snippet initializes the variable `df` as a `Pandas` data frame that contains the data from the `Iris` dataset.

The next block of code invokes some attributes and methods of a `Pandas` data frame to display the number of row, columns, and elements in the data frame, as well as the details of the `Iris` dataset, the first five rows, and the unique labels in the `Iris` dataset. Launch the code in Listing A.2 and you will see the following output:

```
IRIS feature names:
sepal length (cm)
sepal width (cm)
petal length (cm)
petal width (cm)

number of rows:
150
```

```
number of columns:
4

number of rows and columns:
(150, 4)

number of elements:
600

IRIS details:
<class 'pandas.core.frame.DataFrame'>
RangeIndex: 150 entries, 0 to 149
Data columns (total 4 columns):
sepal length (cm)    150 non-null float64
sepal width (cm)     150 non-null float64
petal length (cm)    150 non-null float64
petal width (cm)     150 non-null float64
dtypes: float64(4)
memory usage: 4.8 KB
None

top five rows:
   sepal length (cm)  sepal width (cm)  petal length (cm)  petal width (cm)
0                5.1               3.5                1.4               0.2
1                4.9               3.0                1.4               0.2
2                4.7               3.2                1.3               0.2
3                4.6               3.1                1.5               0.2
4                5.0               3.6                1.4               0.2

Class labels: [0 1 2]
```

Sklearn and Outlier Detection

Listing A.3 displays the contents of elliptic_envelope.py that illustrates how to use the EllipticEnvelope class in Sklearn in order to detect outliers in a dataset.

LISTING A.3: elliptic_envelope.py

```
import numpy as np

import matplotlib.pyplot as plt
import numpy as np
import pandas as pd
from sklearn.covariance import EllipticEnvelope

datapoints = [[-1,1], [1,1], [1,-1], [-1,-1], [2,2]]
columns = ["x", "y"]
index = [0,1,2,3,4]
```

```
df = pd.DataFrame(np.array(datapoints),columns=columns,index=i
ndex)

# display datapoints in a scatterplot:
plt.scatter(df["x"], df["y"], color = "r")
plt.grid()

data = df[['x', 'y']].values

# the contamination parameter defines the proportion of values
# that will be identified as outliers: values are in [0, 0.5]
model1 = EllipticEnvelope(contamination = 0.1)
model1.fit(data)

# new data for prediction:
pred_data = [[3,3], [1.5,1.5], [-2,-2], [-3,-3]]
new_data = np.array(pred_data)

#print("new_data[:,0]:", new_data[:,0])
#print("new_data[:,1]:", new_data[:,1])

# display new datapoints in a scatterplot:
plt.scatter(new_data[:,0], new_data[:,1], s=100, color = "b")

# predict on new data:
pred1 = model1.predict(new_data)

# negative values are outliers:
print("negative predicted values are outliers:")
print(pred1)

for i in range(new_data.shape[0]):
    print("new_data[",i,"] = ",new_data[i],"is an
outlier:",pred1[i]==-1)

#plt.show()
```

Listing A.3 starts with several `import` statements and then initializes the variable datapoint with an array of 2D points in order to define the `Pandas` data frame `df`.

The next section displays a scatter plot of the datapoints (drawn in red), and then initializes the variable `model1` as an instance of the `EllipticEnvelope` class. The `fit()` method of `model1` is invoked in order to train the model on the datapoints

Next, the variable `pred_data` is initialized with a different set of datapoints, and their values will be examined in order to determine if any of them are outliers. After the points in `pred_data` are added to the scatter plot (and drawn in blue), the `predict()` method of the variable `model1` is invoked with `pred_data` and the result is assigned to the variable `pred1`. Finally, a loop iterates through the contents of `pred1`, and a predicted value of -1 indicates an outlier. Now launch the code in Listing A.3 and you will see the following output:

```
negative predicted values are outliers:
[-1  1 -1 -1]
new_data[ 0 ] = [3. 3.] is an outlier: True
new_data[ 1 ] = [1.5 1.5] is an outlier: False
new_data[ 2 ] = [-2. -2.] is an outlier: True
```

Uncomment the last code snippet in Listing A.3 and you will see the initial datapoint displayed in red and the test-related points in blue.

What is Bayesian Inference?

Bayesian inference is an important technique in statistics that involves statistical inference and Bayes' theorem to update the probability for a hypothesis as more information becomes available. Bayesian inference is often called "Bayesian probability," and it's important in dynamic analysis of sequential data.

Bayes Theorem

Given two sets A and B, let's define the following numeric values (all of them are between 0 and 1):

P(A) = probability of being in set A

P(B) = probability of being in set B

P(Both) = probability of being in A intersect B

P(A|B) = probability of being in A (given you're in B)

P(B|A) = probability of being in B (given you're in A)

Then the following formulas are also true:

```
P(A|B) = P(Both)/P(B)  (#1)
P(B|A) = P(Both)/P(A)  (#2)
```

Multiply the preceding pair of equations by the term that appears in the denominator and we get these equations:

```
P(B)*P(A|B) = P(Both)  (#3)
P(A)*P(B|A) = P(Both)  (#4)
```

Now set the left-side of equations #3 and #4 equal to each another and that gives us this equation:

```
P(B)*P(A|B) = P(A)*P(B|A)   (#5)
```

Divide both sides of #5 by P(B) and we get this well-known equation:

```
P(A|B) = P(A)*P(A|B)/P(B)   (#6)
```

Some Bayesian Terminology

In the previous section, we derived the following relationship:

```
P(h|d) = (P(d|h) * P(h)) / P(d)
```

Each of the four terms in the preceding equation has a name.

First, the *posterior probability* is `P(h|d)`, which is the probability of hypothesis h given the data d.

Second, `P(d|h)` is the probability of data d given that the hypothesis h was true.

Third, the *prior probability* of h is `P(h)`, which is the probability of hypothesis h being true (regardless of the data).

Finally, `P(d)` is the probability of the data (regardless of the hypothesis)

We are interested in calculating the posterior probability of P(h|d) from the prior probability p(h) with P(D) and P(d|h).

What is MAP?

The maximum a posteriori (MAP) hypothesis is the hypothesis with the highest probability, which is the maximum probable hypothesis. This can be written as follows:

```
MAP(h) = max(P(h|d))
```

or:

```
MAP(h) = max((P(d|h) * P(h)) / P(d))
```

or:

```
MAP(h) = max(P(d|h) * P(h))
```

Why Use Bayes Theorem?

Bayes' Theorem describes the probability of an event based on the prior knowledge of the conditions that might be related to the event. If we know the conditional probability, we can use Bayes rule to find out the reverse probabilities. The previous statement is the general representation of the Bayes rule.

What are Vector Spaces?

This section is intended primarily for the section about VSMs (vector space models) in Chapter 4; if you are already familiar with vector spaces, feel free to quickly skim through this section.

A *vector space* is a mathematical construct whose elements are *vectors* that typically consist of a tuple of numbers. A real-valued vector space contains vectors of real numbers, whereas a complex vector space contains vectors of complex numbers. The dimensionality of numeric vector spaces is the minimum number of linearly independent vectors. For example, the vector **u** = [2,3] in the Euclidean plan is a real-valued two-dimensional vector, whereas the vector **v** = [2+5i,4-7j] in the complex plane is a complex two-dimensional vector.

Every vector in a numeric vector space can be expressed as a linear combination of the vectors in a basis. A *spanning set* is a superset of a basis, which means that some vectors in the spanning set are a linear combination of the other vectors in the spanning set: those vectors are dependent vectors. If the dependent vectors are removed from a spanning set, the remaining vectors form a basis. As a side note: the vectors in a basis are not required to be unit vectors nor must they be orthogonal to each other (examples shown later).

The real number line can be viewed as a one-dimensional vector space. The vector **i** = [1,0] is a unit vector that forms a so-called basis for this vector space because any other vector is a multiple of the vector i.

The Euclidean plane can be viewed as a two-dimensional vector space. The unit vectors **i** = [1,0] and **j** = [0,1] are unit vectors that form a basis for this vector space because any other vector is a linear combination of the vectors **i** and **j**. Notice that the dot product of i and j is 0, which means that they are orthogonal. However, the vectors in the set {2∗**i**, 3∗**j**} are not unit vectors, and yet they form a basis for the Euclidean plan.

As another example, the vectors in the set {**i**+**j**, **i**} also form a basis, even though they are not orthogonal and one of them is not a unit vector. However, any basis can be transformed into any other basis for a given vector space, which means that any basis can be transformed into a basis that consists of orthonormal unit vectors (search online for a proof of this statement).

In the three-dimensional Euclidean space, the set of vectors {**i**,**j**,**k**} form an orthonormal basis, where the unit vectors **i**, **j**, and **k** are [1,0,0], [0,1,0], and [0,0,1], respectively.

In general, an n-dimensional vector space V has a basic S that consists of n orthonormal vectors. If you create a matrix M whose rows are the vectors in a basis, then the inverse of matrix M exists because the rows are linearly independent.

In fact, a set of n linear equations in n unknowns has a unique solution if (and only if) the associated matrix M is invertible. Statistical packages contain one or more algorithms for solving systems of linear equations.

Summary

This appendix started with an explanation of datasets and various types of data. Then you learned about techniques for scaling numeric data, such as normalization and standardization. You saw how to convert categorical data to numeric values, and how to handle dates and currency.

Then you learned some of the nuances of missing data, anomalies, and outliers.

You also learned about the bias-variance trade-off, types of bias, skewness, and kurtosis.

Moreover, you saw how to handle imbalanced datasets via SMOTE, details about LIME and ANOVA, followed by covariance and correlation matrices.

In addition, you learned about an assortment of statistical terms, including: F1 scores, p-values, gini impurity, entropy, perplexity, cross-entropy, and KL divergence.

Then you saw how to compute eigenvalues and eigenvectors of square matrices that is a key aspect of PCA, which is an SVD algorithm. Finally, you got a very brief introduction to Sklearn and you saw a code sample that combines Pandas and built-in datasets in Sklearn.

APPENDIX B

INTRODUCTION TO PYTHON

This appendix contains an introduction to Python, with information about useful tools for installing Python modules, basic Python constructs, and how to work with some data types in Python.

The first part of this appendix covers how to install Python, some Python environment variables, and how to use the Python interpreter. You will see Python code samples and also how to save Python code in text files that you can launch from the command line. The second part of this appendix shows you how to work with simple data types, such as numbers, fractions, and strings. The final part of this appendix discusses exceptions and how to use them in Python scripts.

NOTE *The* Python *code samples in this volume are for* Python *3.x.*

Tools for Python

The Anaconda Python distribution available for Windows, Linux, and Mac, and it's downloadable here:

http://continuum.io/downloads

Anaconda is well-suited for modules such as NumPy (the latter is discussed in Chapter 1)and scipy (not discussed in this book), and if you are a Windows user, Anaconda appears to be a better alternative.

easy_install and pip

Both `easy_install` and `pip` are very easy to use when you need to install `Python` modules.

Whenever you need to install a `Python` module (and there are many in this book), use either `easy_install` or `pip` with the following syntax:

```
easy_install <module-name>
pip install <module-name>
```

NOTE *`Python`-based modules are easier to install, whereas modules with code written in C are usually faster but more difficult in terms of installation.*

virtualenv

The `virtualenv` tool enables you to create isolated Python environments, and its home page is here:

http://www.virtualenv.org/en/latest/virtualenv.html

The tool `virtualenv` addresses the problem of preserving the correct dependencies and versions (and indirectly permissions) for different applications. If you are a `Python` novice you might not need `virtualenv` right now, but keep this tool in mind.

IPython

Another very good tool is `IPython` (which won a Jolt award), and its home page is here:

http://ipython.org/install.html

Type `ipython` to invoke IPython from the command line:

```
ipython
```

The preceding command displays the following output:

```
Python 3.9.1 (default, Feb  3 2021, 07:04:15)
Type 'copyright', 'credits' or 'license' for more information
IPython 7.22.0 -- An enhanced Interactive Python. Type '?' for help.

In [1]:
```

Now type a question mark ("?") at the prompt and you will see some useful information, a portion of which is here:

```
IPython -- An enhanced Interactive Python
=========================================

IPython offers a fully compatible replacement for the standard
Python interpreter, with convenient shell features, special
commands, command history mechanism and output results
caching.

At your system command line, type 'ipython -h' to see the
command line options available. This document only describes
interactive features.

GETTING HELP
------------

Within IPython you have various way to access help:

  ?         -> Introduction and overview of IPython's features
(this screen).
  object?   -> Details about 'object'.
  object??  -> More detailed, verbose information about 'object'.
  %quickref -> Quick reference of all IPython specific syntax
and magics.
  help      -> Access Python's own help system.

If you are in terminal IPython you can quit this screen by
pressing 'q'.
```

Finally, simply type `quit` at the command prompt and you will exit the ipython shell.

The next section shows you how to check whether or not `Python` is installed on your machine, and also where you can download `Python`.

Python Installation

Before you download anything, check if you already have `Python` installed on your machine (which is likely if you have a Macbook or a Linux machine) by typing the following command in a command shell:

```
python -V
```

The output for the Macbook used in this book is here:

```
Python 3.9.1
```

NOTE *Install Python 3.9 (or as close as possible to this version) on your machine so that you will have the same version of* `Python` *that was used to test the* `Python` *scripts in this book.*

If you need to install Python on your machine, navigate to the Python home page and select the downloads link or navigate directly to this Website:

http://www.python.org/download

In addition, PythonWin is available for Windows, and its home page is here:

http://www.cgl.ucsf.edu/Outreach/pc204/pythonwin.html

Use any text editor that can create, edit, and save Python scripts and save them as plain text files.

After you have Python installed and configured on your machine, you are ready to work with the Python scripts in this book.

Setting the PATH Environment Variable (Windows Only)

The PATH environment variable specifies a list of directories that are searched whenever you specify an executable program from the command line. A very good guide to setting up your environment so that the Python executable is always available in every command shell is to follow the instructions here:

http://www.blog.pythonlibrary.org/2011/11/24/python-101-setting-up-python-on-windows/

Launching Python on Your Machine

There are three different ways to launch Python:

- Use the Python interactive interpreter.
- Launch Python scripts from the command line.
- Use an integrated development environment (IDE).

The next section shows you how to launch the Python interpreter from the command line, and later in this appendix you will learn how to launch Python scripts from the command line and also about Python IDEs.

NOTE *The emphasis in this book is to launch* Python *scripts from the command line or to enter code in the Python interpreter.*

The Python Interactive Interpreter

Launch the Python interactive interpreter from the command line by opening a command shell and typing the following command:

```
python
```

You will see the following prompt (or something similar):

```
Python 3.9.1 (default, Feb  3 2021, 07:04:15)
[Clang 12.0.0 (clang-1200.0.32.2)] on darwin
```

Type "help", "copyright", "credits" or "license" for more information.

```
>>>
```

Now type the expression 2 + 7 at the prompt:

```
>>> 2 + 7
```

Python displays the following result:

```
9
>>>
```

Type quit() to exit the Python shell.

You can launch any Python script from the command line by preceding it with the word "python." For example, if you have a Python script myscript.py that contains Python commands, launch the script as follows:

```
python myscript.py
```

As a simple illustration, suppose that the Python script myscript.py contains the following Python code:

```
print('Hello World from Python')
print('2 + 7 = ', 2+7)
```

When you launch the preceding Python script you will see the following output:

```
Hello World from Python
2 + 7 = 9
```

Python Identifiers

A Python identifier is the name of a variable, function, class, module, or other Python object, and a valid identifier conforms to the following rules:

- It starts with a letter A to Z or a to z or an underscore (_).
- It includes zero or more letters, underscores, and digits (0 to 9).

NOTE *Python identifiers cannot contain characters such as @, $, and %.*

Python is a case-sensitive language, so Abc and abc different identifiers in Python.

In addition, `Python` has the following naming convention:

- Class names start with an uppercase letter and all other identifiers with a lowercase letter.
- An initial underscore is used for private identifiers.
- Two initial underscores is used for strongly private identifiers.

A `Python` identifier with two initial underscore and two trailing underscore characters indicates a language-defined special name.

Lines, Indentation, and Multilines

Unlike other programming languages (such as Java or Objective-C), `Python` uses indentation instead of curly braces for code blocks. Indentation must be consistent in a code block, as shown here:

```
if True:
    print("ABC")
    print("DEF")
else:
    print("ABC")
    print("DEF")
```

Multi-line statements in `Python` can terminate with a new line or the backslash ("\") character, as shown here:

```
total = x1 + \
        x2 + \
        x3
```

Obviously you can place `x1`, `x2`, and `x3` on the same line, so there is no reason to use three separate lines; however, this functionality is available in case you need to add a set of variables that do not fit on a single line.

You can specify multiple statements in one line by using a semicolon (";") to separate each statement, as shown here:

```
a=10; b=5; print(a); print(a+b)
```

The output of the preceding code snippet is here:

```
10
15
```

NOTE *The use of semi-colons and the continuation character are discouraged in Python.*

Quotation and Comments in Python

`Python` allows single ('), double (") and triple (''' or """) quotes for string literals, provided that they match at the beginning and the end of the string. You can use triple quotes for strings that span multiple lines. The following examples are legal Python strings:

```
word = 'word'
line = "This is a sentence."
para = """This is a paragraph. This paragraph contains
more than one sentence."""
```

A string literal that begins with the letter "r" (for "raw") treats everything as a literal character and "escapes" the meaning of meta characters, as shown here:

```
a1 = r'\n'
a2 = r'\r'
a3 = r'\t'
print('a1:',a1,'a2:',a2,'a3:',a3)
```

The output of the preceding code block is here:

```
a1: \n a2: \r a3: \t
```

You can embed a single quote in a pair of double quotes (and vice versa) in order to display a single quote or a double quote. Another way to accomplish the same result is to precede a single or double quote with a backslash ("\") character. The following code block illustrates these techniques:

```
b1 = "'"
b2 = '"'
b3 = '\''
b4 = "\""
print('b1:',b1,'b2:',b2)
print('b3:',b3,'b4:',b4)
```

The output of the preceding code block is here:

```
b1: ' b2: "
b3: ' b4: "
```

A hash sign (#) that is not inside a string literal is the character that indicates the beginning of a comment. Moreover, all characters after the # and up to the physical line end are part of the comment (and ignored by the `Python` interpreter). Consider the following code block:

```
#!/usr/bin/python
```

```
# First comment
print("Hello, Python!")   # second comment
```

This will produce following result:

```
Hello, Python!
```

A comment may be on the same line after a statement or expression:

```
name = "Tom Jones"  # This is also comment
```

You can comment multiple lines as follows:

```
# This is comment one
# This is comment two
# This is comment three
```

A blank line in Python is a line containing only whitespace, a comment, or both.

Saving Your Code in a Module

Earlier you saw how to launch the Python interpreter from the command line and then enter Python commands. However, everything that you type in the Python interpreter is only valid for the current session: if you exit the interpreter and then launch the interpreter again, your previous definitions are no longer valid. Fortunately, Python enables you to store code in a text file, as discussed in the next section.

A *module* in Python is a text file that contains Python statements. In the previous section, you saw how the Python interpreter enables you to test code snippets whose definitions are valid for the current session. If you want to retain the code snippets and other definitions, place them in a text file so that you can execute that code outside of the Python interpreter.

The outermost statements in a Python are executed from top to bottom when the module is imported for the first time, which will then set up its variables and functions.

A Python module can be run directly from the command line, as shown here:

```
python First.py
```

As an illustration, place the following two statements in a text file called First.py:

```
x = 3
print(x)
Now type the following command:
```

```
python First.py
```

The output from the preceding command is 3, which is the same as executing the preceding code from the Python interpreter.

When a Python module is run directly, the special variable __name__ is set to __main__. You will often see the following type of code in a Python module:

```
if __name__ == '__main__':
   # do something here
   print('Running directly')
```

The preceding code snippet enables Python to determine if a Python module was launched from the command line or imported into another Python module.

Some Standard Modules in Python

The Python Standard Library provides many modules that can simplify your own Python scripts. A list of the Standard Library modules is here:

http://www.python.org/doc

Some of the most important Python modules include cgi, math, os, pickle, random, re, socket, sys, time, and urllib.

The code samples in this book use the modules math, os, random, re, socket, sys, time, and urllib. You need to import these modules in order to use them in your code. For example, the following code block shows you how to import four standard Python modules:

```
import datetime
import re
import sys
import time
```

The code samples in this book import one or more of the preceding modules, as well as other Python modules.

The `help()` and `dir()` Functions

An Internet search for Python-related topics usually returns a number of links with useful information. Alternatively, you can check the official Python documentation site: *docs.python.org*

In addition, Python provides the help() and dir() functions that are accessible from the Python interpreter. The help() function displays documentation strings, whereas the `dir()` function displays defined symbols.

For example, if you type `help(sys)` you will see documentation for the `sys` module, whereas `dir(sys)` displays a list of the defined symbols.

Type the following command in the `Python` interpreter to display the string-related methods in `Python`:

```
>>> dir(str)
```

The preceding command generates the following output:

```
['__add__', '__class__', '__contains__', '__delattr__', '__doc__', '__eq__', '__format__', '__ge__', '__getattribute__', '__getitem__', '__getnewargs__', '__getslice__', '__gt__', '__hash__', '__init__', '__le__', '__len__', '__lt__', '__mod__', '__mul__', '__ne__', '__new__', '__reduce__', '__reduce_ex__', '__repr__', '__rmod__', '__rmul__', '__setattr__', '__sizeof__', '__str__', '__subclasshook__', '_formatter_field_name_split', '_formatter_parser', 'capitalize', 'center', 'count', 'decode', 'encode', 'endswith', 'expandtabs', 'find', 'format', 'index', 'isalnum', 'isalpha', 'isdigit', 'islower', 'isspace', 'istitle', 'isupper', 'join', 'ljust', 'lower', 'lstrip', 'partition', 'replace', 'rfind', 'rindex', 'rjust', 'rpartition', 'rsplit', 'rstrip', 'split', 'splitlines', 'startswith', 'strip', 'swapcase', 'title', 'translate', 'upper', 'zfill']
```

The preceding list gives you a consolidated "dump" of built-in functions (including some that are discussed later in this appendix). Although the `max()` function obviously returns the maximum value of its arguments, the purpose of other functions such as `filter()` or `map()` is not immediately apparent (unless you have used them in other programming languages). In any case, the preceding list provides a starting point for finding out more about various Python built-in functions that are not discussed in this appendix.

Note that while `dir()` does not list the names of built-in functions and variables, you can obtain this information from the standard module `__builtin__` that is automatically imported under the name `__builtins__`:

```
>>> dir(__builtins__)
```

The following command shows you how to get more information about a function:

```
help(str.lower)
```

The output from the preceding command is here:

```
Help on method_descriptor:

lower(...)
    S.lower() -> string

    Return a copy of the string S converted to lowercase.
(END)
```

Check the online documentation and also experiment with `help()` and `dir()` when you need additional information about a particular function or module.

Compile Time and Runtime Code Checking

`Python` performs some compile-time checking, but most checks (including type, name, and so forth) are *deferred* until code execution. Consequently, if your `Python` code references a user-defined function that that does not exist, the code will compile successfully. In fact, the code will fail with an exception *only* when the code execution path references the nonexistent function.

As a simple example, consider the following `Python` function `myFunc` that references the nonexistent function called `DoesNotExist`:

```
def myFunc(x):
    if x == 3:
        print(DoesNotExist(x))
    else:
        print('x: ',x)
```

The preceding code will only fail when the `myFunc` function is passed the value 3, after which `Python` raises an error.

Now that you understand some basic concepts (such as how to use the `Python` interpreter) and how to launch your custom `Python` modules, the next section discusses primitive data types in Python.

Simple Data Types in Python

`Python` supports primitive data types, such as numbers (integers, floating point numbers, and exponential numbers), strings, and dates. `Python` also supports more complex data types, such as lists (or arrays), tuples, and dictionaries. The next several sections discuss some of the `Python` primitive data types, along with code snippets that show you how to perform various operations on those data types.

Working with Numbers

`Python` provides arithmetic operations for manipulating numbers a straightforward manner that is similar to other programming languages. The following examples involve arithmetic operations on integers:

```
>>> 2+2
4
>>> 4/3
1
>>> 3*8
24
```

The following example assigns numbers to two variables and computes their product:

```
>>> x = 4
>>> y = 7
>>> x * y
28
```

The following examples demonstrate arithmetic operations involving integers:

```
>>> 2+2
4
>>> 4/3
1
>>> 3*8
24
```

Notice that division ("/") of two integers is actually truncation in which only the integer result is retained. The following example converts a floating point number into exponential form:

```
>>> fnum = 0.00012345689000007
>>> "%.14e"%fnum
'1.23456890000070e-04'
```

You can use the `int()` function and the `float()` function to convert strings to numbers:

```
word1 = "123"
word2 = "456.78"
var1 = int(word1)
```

```
var2 = float(word2)
print("var1: ",var1," var2: ",var2)
The output from the preceding code block is here:
var1:  123   var2:  456.78
Alternatively, you can use the eval() function:
word1 = "123"
word2 = "456.78"
var1 = eval(word1)
var2 = eval(word2)
print("var1: ",var1," var2: ",var2)
```

If you attempt to convert a string that is not a valid integer or a floating point number, `Python` raises an exception, so it's advisable to place your code in a `try/except` block (discussed later in this appendix).

Working with Other Bases

Numbers in `Python` are in base 10 (the default), but you can easily convert numbers to other bases. For example, the following code block initializes the variable x with the value `1234`, and then displays that number in base `2`, `8`, and `16`, respectively:

```
>>> x = 1234
>>> bin(x) '0b10011010010'
>>> oct(x) '0o2322'
>>> hex(x) '0x4d2'
```

Use the `format()` function if you want to suppress the `0b`, `0o`, or `0x` prefixes, as shown here:

```
>>> format(x, 'b') '10011010010'
>>> format(x, 'o') '2322'
>>> format(x, 'x') '4d2'
```

Negative integers are displayed with a negative sign:

```
>>> x = -1234
>>> format(x, 'b') '-10011010010'
>>> format(x, 'x') '-4d2'
```

The chr() Function

The `Python` `chr()` function takes a positive integer as a parameter and converts it to its corresponding alphabetic value (if one exists). The letters A through Z have decimal representation of `65` through `91` (which corresponds to hexadecimal `41` through `5b`), and the lowercase letters a through z have decimal representation `97` through `122` (hexadecimal `61` through `7b`).

Here is an example of using the `chr()` function to print uppercase A:

```
>>> x=chr(65)
>>> x
'A'
```

The following code block prints the ASCII values for a range of integers:

```
result = ""
for x in range(65,91):
  print(x, chr(x))
  result = result+chr(x)+' '
print("result: ",result)
```

NOTE Python 2 uses ASCII strings whereas Python 3 uses UTF-8.

You can represent a range of characters with the following line:

```
for x in range(65,91):
```

However, the following equivalent code snippet is more intuitive:

```
for x in range(ord('A'), ord('Z')):
```

If you want to display the result for lowercase letters, change the preceding range from (65,91) to either of the following statements:

```
for x in range(65,91):
for x in range(ord('a'), ord('z')):
```

The round() Function in Python

The Python `round()` function enables you to round decimal values to the nearest precision:

```
>>> round(1.23, 1)
1.2
>>> round(-3.42,1)
-3.4
```

Formatting Numbers in Python

Python allows you to specify the number of decimal places of precision to use when printing decimal numbers, as shown here:

```
>>> x = 1.23456
>>> format(x, '0.2f')
'1.23'
>>> format(x, '0.3f')
'1.235'
>>> 'value is {:0.3f}'.format(x) 'value is 1.235'
>>> from decimal import Decimal
>>> a = Decimal('4.2')
```

```
>>> b = Decimal('2.1')
>>> a + b
Decimal('6.3')
>>> print(a + b)
6.3
>>> (a + b) == Decimal('6.3')
True
>>> x = 1234.56789
>>> # Two decimal places of accuracy
>>> format(x, '0.2f')
'1234.57'
>>> # Right justified in 10 chars, one-digit accuracy
>>> format(x, '>10.1f')
'    1234.6'
>>> # Left justified
>>> format(x, '<10.1f') '1234.6    '
>>> # Centered
>>> format(x, '^10.1f') '  1234.6  '
>>> # Inclusion of thousands separator
>>> format(x, ',')
'1,234.56789'
>>> format(x, '0,.1f')
'1,234.6'
```

Working with Fractions

Python supports the Fraction() function (which is define in the fractions module) that accepts two integers that represent the numerator and the denominator (which must be non-zero) of a fraction. Several example of defining and manipulating fractions in Python are shown here:

```
>>> from fractions import Fraction
>>> a = Fraction(5, 4)
>>> b = Fraction(7, 16)
>>> print(a + b)
27/16
>>> print(a * b) 35/64
>>> # Getting numerator/denominator
>>> c = a * b
>>> c.numerator
35
>>> c.denominator 64
>>> # Converting to a float >>> float(c)
0.546875
>>> # Limiting the denominator of a value
>>> print(c.limit_denominator(8))
4
>>> # Converting a float to a fraction >>> x = 3.75
>>> y = Fraction(*x.as_integer_ratio())
>>> y
Fraction(15, 4)
```

Before delving into `Python` code samples that work with strings, the next section briefly discusses `Unicode` and UTF-8, both of which are character encodings.

Unicode and UTF-8

A `Unicode` string consists of a sequence of numbers that are between 0 and `0x10ffff`, where each number represents a group of bytes. An encoding is the manner in which a `Unicode` string is translated into a sequence of bytes. Among the various encodings, unicode transformation format (`UTF-8`) is perhaps the most common, and it's also the default encoding for many systems. The digit 8 in `UTF-8` indicates that the encoding uses 8-bit numbers, whereas `UTF-16` uses 16-bit numbers (but this encoding is less common).

The ASCII character set is a subset of `UTF-8`, so a valid ASCII string can be read as a `UTF-8` string without any reencoding required. In addition, a Unicode string can be converted into a `UTF-8` string.

Working with Unicode

Python supports `Unicode`, which means that you can render characters in different languages. `Unicode` data can be stored and manipulated in the same way as strings. Create a `Unicode` string by prepending the letter "u," as shown here:

```
>>> u'Hello from Python!'
u'Hello from Python!'
```

Special characters can be included in a string by specifying their `Unicode` value. For example, the following `Unicode` string embeds a space (which has the `Unicode` value 0x0020) in a string:

```
>>> u'Hello\u0020from Python!'
u'Hello from Python!'
```

Listing B.1 displays the contents of `Unicode1.py` that illustrates how to display a string of characters in Japanese and another string of characters in Chinese (Mandarin).

LISTING B.1: Unicode1.py

```
chinese1 = u'\u5c07\u63a2\u8a0e HTML5 \u53ca\u5176\u4ed6'
hiragana = u'D3 \u306F \u304B\u3063\u3053\u3043\u3043 \u3067\
u3059!'
```

```
print('Chinese:',chinese1)
print('Hiragana:',hiragana)
The output of Listing B.1 is here:
Chinese: 將探討 HTML5 及其他
Hiragana: D3 は かっこいい です!
```

The next portion of this appendix shows you how to "slice and dice" text strings with built-in `Python` functions.

Working with Strings

A string in `Python2` is a sequence of ASCII-encoded bytes. You can concatenate two strings using the "+" operator. The following example prints a string and then concatenates two single-letter strings:

```
>>> 'abc'
'abc'
>>> 'a' + 'b'
'ab'
```

You can use "+" or "*" to concatenate identical strings, as shown here:

```
>>> 'a' + 'a' + 'a'
'aaa'
>>> 'a' * 3
'aaa'
```

You can assign strings to variables and print them using the `print()` statement:

```
>>> print('abc')
abc
>>> x = 'abc'
>>> print(x)
abc
>>> y = 'def'
>>> print(x + y)
abcdef
```

You can "unpack" the letters of a string and assign them to variables, as shown here:

```
>>> str = "World"
>>> x1,x2,x3,x4,x5 = str
>>> x1
'W'
>>> x2
'o'
>>> x3
```

```
'r'
>>> x4
'l'
>>> x5
'd'
```

The preceding code snippets shows you how easy it is to extract the letters in a text string. You can extract substrings of a string as shown in the following examples:

```
>>> x = "abcdef"
>>> x[0]
'a'
>>> x[-1]
'f'
>>> x[1:3]
'bc'
>>> x[0:2] + x[5:]
'abf'
```

However, you will cause an error if you attempt to subtract two strings, as would be expected:

```
>>> 'a' - 'b'
```

Traceback (most recent call last):

```
    File "<stdin>", line 1, in <module>
TypeError: unsupported operand type(s) for -: 'str' and 'str'
```

The `try/except` construct in `Python` (discussed later in this appendix) enables you to handle the preceding type of exception more gracefully.

Comparing Strings

You can use the methods `lower()` and `upper()` to convert a string to lowercase and uppercase, respectively, as shown here:

```
>>> 'Python'.lower()
'python'
>>> 'Python'.upper()
'PYTHON'
>>>
```

The methods `lower()` and `upper()` are useful for performing a case insensitive comparison of two ASCII strings. Listing B.2 displays the contents of `Compare.py` that uses the `lower()` function in order to compare two ASCII strings.

LISTING B.2: Compare.py

```
x = 'Abc'
y = 'abc'

if(x == y):
  print('x and y: identical')
elif (x.lower() == y.lower()):
  print('x and y: case insensitive match')
else:
  print('x and y: different')
```

Since x contains mixed case letters and y contains lowercase letters, Listing B.2 displays the following output:

```
x and y: different
```

Formatting Strings in Python

Python provides the functions `string.lstring()`, `string.rstring()`, and `string.center()` for positioning a text string so that it is left-justified, right-justified, and centered, respectively. As you saw in a previous section, Python also provides the `format()` method for advanced interpolation features.

Now enter the following commands in the Python interpreter:

```
import string

str1 = 'this is a string'
print(string.ljust(str1, 10))
print(string.rjust(str1, 40))
print(string.center(str1,40))
The output is shown here:
this is a string
                        this is a string
            this is a string
```

Uninitialized Variables and the Value None in Python

Python distinguishes between an uninitialized variable and the value None. The former is a variable that has not been assigned a value, whereas the value None is a value that indicates "no value." Collections and methods often return the value None, and you can test for the value None in conditional logic.

The next portion of this appendix shows you how to "slice and dice" text strings with built-in Python functions.

Slicing and Splicing Strings

`Python` enables you to extract substrings of a string (called "slicing") using array notation. Slice notation is `start:stop:step`, where the start, stop, and step values are integers that specify the start value, end value, and the increment value. The interesting part about slicing in `Python` is that you can use the value `-1`, which operates from the right-side instead of the left-side of a string.

Some examples of slicing a string are here:

```
text1 = "this is a string"
print('First 7 characters:',text1[0:7])
print('Characters 2-4:',text1[2:4])
print('Right-most character:',text1[-1])
print('Right-most 2 characters:',text1[-3:-1])
```

The output from the preceding code block is here:

```
First 7 characters: this is
Characters 2-4: is
Right-most character: g
Right-most 2 characters: in
```

Later in this appendix you will see how to insert a string in the middle of another string.

Testing for Digits and Alphabetic Characters

`Python` enables you to examine each character in a string and then test whether that character is a bona fide digit or an alphabetic character. This section provides a simple introduction to regular expressions.

Listing B.3 displays the contents of `CharTypes.py` that illustrates how to determine if a string contains digits or characters. Although we have not discussed conditional logic in `Python` yet, the examples in Listing B.3 are straightforward.

LISTING B.3: CharTypes.py

```
str1 = "4"
str2 = "4234"
str3 = "b"
str4 = "abc"
str5 = "a1b2c3"

if(str1.isdigit()):
  print("this is a digit:",str1)
```

```
if(str2.isdigit()):
  print("this is a digit:",str2)

if(str3.isalpha()):
  print("this is alphabetic:",str3)

if(str4.isalpha()):
  print("this is alphabetic:",str4)

if(not str5.isalpha()):
  print("this is not pure alphabetic:",str5)

print("capitalized first letter:",str5.title())
```

Listing B.3 initializes some variables, followed by 2 conditional tests that check whether or not `str1` and `str2` are digits using the `isdigit()` function. The next portion of Listing B.3 checks if `str3`, `str4`, and `str5` are alphabetic strings using the `isalpha()` function. The output of Listing B.3 is here:

```
this is a digit: 4
this is a digit: 4234
this is alphabetic: b
this is alphabetic: abc
this is not pure alphabetic: a1b2c3
capitalized first letter: A1B2C3
```

Search and Replace a String in Other Strings

`Python` provides methods for searching and also for replacing a string in a second text string. Listing B.4 displays the contents of `FindPos1.py` that shows you how to use the find function to search for the occurrence of one string in another string.

LISTING B.4: FindPos1.py

```
item1 = 'abc'
item2 = 'Abc'
text = 'This is a text string with abc'

pos1 = text.find(item1)
pos2 = text.find(item2)

print('pos1=',pos1)
print('pos2=',pos2)
```

Listing B.4 initializes the variables `item1`, `item2`, and `text`, and then searches for the index of the contents of `item1` and `item2` in the string text. The `Python` `find()` function returns the column number where the first successful match occurs; otherwise, the `find()` function returns a -1 if a match is unsuccessful. The output from launching Listing B.4 is here:

```
pos1= 27
pos2= -1
```

In addition to the `find()` method, you can use the `in` operator when you want to test for the presence of an element, as shown here:

```
>>> lst = [1,2,3]
>>> 1 in lst
True
```

Listing B.5 displays the contents of `Replace1.py` that shows you how to replace one string with another string.

LISTING B.5: Replace1.py

```
text = 'This is a text string with abc'
print('text:',text)
text = text.replace('is a', 'was a')
print('text:',text)
```

Listing B.5 starts by initializing the variable text and then printing its contents. The next portion of Listing B.5 replaces the occurrence of "is a" with "was a" in the string text, and then prints the modified string. The output from launching Listing B.5 is here:

```
text: This is a text string with abc
text: This was a text string with abc
```

Remove Leading and Trailing Characters

`Python` provides the functions `strip()`, `lstrip()`, and `rstrip()` to remove characters in a text string. Listing B.6 displays the contents of `Remove1.py` that shows you how to search for a string.

LISTING B.6 Remove1.py

```
text = '   leading and trailing white space   '
print('text1:','x',text,'y')

text = text.lstrip()
print('text2:','x',text,'y')
```

```
text = text.rstrip()
print('text3:','x',text,'y')
```

Listing B.6 starts by concatenating the letter x and the contents of the variable `text`, and then printing the result. The second part of Listing B.6 removes the leading white spaces in the string `text` and then appends the result to the letter x. The third part of Listing B.6 removes the trailing white spaces in the string `text` (note that the leading white spaces have already been removed) and then appends the result to the letter x.

The output from launching Listing B.6 is here:

```
text1: x   leading and trailing white space   y
text2: x leading and trailing white space   y
text3: x leading and trailing white space y
```

If you want to remove extra white spaces inside a text string, use the `replace()` function as discussed in the previous section. The following example illustrates how this can be accomplished, which also contains the `re` module for regular expressions:

```
import re
text = 'a    b'
a = text.replace(' ', '')
b = re.sub('\s+', ' ', text)

print(a)
print(b)
```

The result is here:

```
ab
a b
```

Printing Text without NewLine Characters

If you need to suppress white space and a newline between objects output with multiple print statements, you can use concatenation or the `write()` function.

The first technique is to concatenate the string representations of each object using the `str()` function prior to printing the result. For example, run the following statement in Python:

```
x = str(9)+str(0xff)+str(-3.1)
print('x: ',x)
```

The output is shown here:

```
x:   9255-3.1
```

The preceding line contains the concatenation of the numbers 9 and 255 (which is the decimal value of the hexadecimal number 0xff) and -3.1.

Incidentally, you can use the `str()` function with modules and user-defined classes. An example involving the Python built-in module `sys` is here:

```
>>> import sys
>>> print(str(sys))
<module 'sys' (built-in)>
```

The following code snippet illustrates how to use the `write()` function to display a string:

```
import sys
write = sys.stdout.write
write('123')
write('123456789')
```

The output is here:

```
1233
1234567899
```

Text Alignment

Python provides the methods `ljust()`, `rjust()`, and `center()` for aligning text. The `ljust()` and `rjust()` functions left justify and right justify a text string, respectively, whereas the `center()` function will center a string. An example is shown in the following code block:

```
text = 'Hello World'
text.ljust(20)
'Hello World         '
>>> text.rjust(20)
'         Hello World'
>>> text.center(20)
'    Hello World     '
```

You can use the Python `format()` function to align text. Use the <, >, or ^ characters, along with a desired width, in order to right justify, left justify, and center the text, respectively. The following examples illustrate how you can specify text justification:

```
>>> format(text, '>20')
'         Hello World'
```

```
>>>
>>> format(text, '<20')
'Hello World         '
>>>
>>> format(text, '^20')
'    Hello World     '
>>>
```

Working with Dates

`Python` provides a rich set of date-related functions that are documented here:

http://docs.python.org/2/library/datetime.html

Listing B.7 displays the contents of the `Python` script `Datetime2.py` that displays various date-related values, such as the current date and time; the day of the week, month, and year; and the time in seconds since the epoch.

LISTING B.7: Datetime2.py

```
import time
import datetime

print("Time in seconds since the epoch: %s" %time.time())
print("Current date and time: " , datetime.datetime.now())
print("Or like this: " ,datetime.datetime.now().strftime("%y-%m-%d-%H-%M"))

print("Current year: ", datetime.date.today().strftime("%Y"))
print("Month of year: ", datetime.date.today().strftime("%B"))
print("Week number of the year: ", datetime.date.today().strftime("%W"))
print("Weekday of the week: ", datetime.date.today().strftime("%w"))
print("Day of year: ", datetime.date.today().strftime("%j"))
print("Day of the month : ", datetime.date.today().strftime("%d"))
print("Day of week: ", datetime.date.today().strftime("%A"))
```
Listing B.8 displays the output generated by running the code in Listing B.7.

LISTING B.8: datetime2.out

```
Time in seconds since the epoch: 1375144195.66
Current date and time:  2013-07-29 17:29:55.664164
Or like this:  13-07-29-17-29
Current year:  2013
Month of year:  July
Week number of the year:  30
```

```
Weekday of the week:   1
Day of year:   210
Day of the month :   29
Day of week:   Monday
```

`Python` also enables you to perform arithmetic calculates with date-related values, as shown in the following code block:

```
>>> from datetime import timedelta
>>> a = timedelta(days=2, hours=6)
>>> b = timedelta(hours=4.5)
>>> c = a + b
>>> c.days
2
>>> c.seconds
37800
>>> c.seconds / 3600
10.5
>>> c.total_seconds() / 3600
58.5
```

Converting Strings to Dates

Listing B.9 displays the contents of `String2Date.py` that illustrates how to convert a string to a date, and also how to calculate the difference between two dates.

LISTING B.9: String2Date.py

```
from datetime import datetime

text = '2014-08-13'
y = datetime.strptime(text, '%Y-%m-%d')
z = datetime.now()
diff = z - y
print('Date difference:',diff)
```

The output from Listing B.9 is shown here:

```
Date difference: -210 days, 18:58:40.197130
```

Exception Handling in Python

Unlike `JavaScript` you cannot add a number and a string in `Python`. However, you can detect an illegal operation using the `try/except` construct in `Python`, which is similar to the `try/catch` construct in languages such as JavaScript and Java.

An example of a `try/except` block is here:

```
try:
```

```
  x = 4
  y = 'abc'
  z = x + y
except:
  print 'cannot add incompatible types:', x, y
```

When you run the preceding code in Python, the print statement in the except code block is executed because the variables x and y have incompatible types.

Earlier in this appendix you also saw that subtracting two strings throws an exception:

```
>>> 'a' - 'b'
```

Traceback (most recent call last):

```
  File "<stdin>", line 1, in <module>
```

TypeError: unsupported operand type(s) for -: 'str' and 'str'

A simple way to handle this situation is to use a try/except block:

```
>>> try:
...   print('a' - 'b')
... except TypeError:
...   print('TypeError exception while trying to subtract two
          strings')
... except:
...   print('Exception while trying to subtract two strings')
...
```

The output from the preceding code block is here:

```
TypeError exception while trying to subtract two strings
```

As you can see, the preceding code block specifies the finer-grained exception called TypeError, followed by a "generic" except code block to handle all other exceptions that might occur during the execution of your Python code. This style is similar to the exception handling in Java code.

Listing B.10 displays the contents of Exception1.py that illustrates how to handle various types of exceptions.

LISTING B.10: Exception1.py

```
import sys

try:
    f = open('myfile.txt')
    s = f.readline()
```

```
        i = int(s.strip())
except IOError as err:
    print("I/O error: {0}".format(err))
except ValueError:
    print("Could not convert data to an integer.")
except:
    print("Unexpected error:", sys.exc_info()[0])
    raise
```

Listing B.10 contains a `try` block followed by three `except` statements. If an error occurs in the `try` block, the first `except` statement is compared with the type of exception that occurred. If there is a match, then the subsequent `print()` statement is executed, and the program terminates. If not, a similar test is performed with the second `except` statement. If neither `except` statement matches the exception, the third `except` statement handles the exception, which involves printing a message and then "raising" an exception.

Note that you can also specify multiple exception types in a single statement, as shown here:

```
except (NameError, RuntimeError, TypeError):
    print('One of three error types occurred')
```

The preceding code block is more compact, but you do not know which of the three error types occurred. Python allows you to define custom exceptions, but this topic is beyond the scope of this book.

Handling User Input

`Python` enables you to read user input from the command line via the `input()` function or the `raw_input()` function. Typically you assign user input to a variable, which will contain all characters that users enter from the keyboard. User input terminates when users press the `<return>` key (which is included with the input characters). Listing B.11 displays the contents of `UserInput1.py` that prompts users for their name and then uses interpolation to display a response.

LISTING B.11: *UserInput1.py*

```
userInput = input("Enter your name: ")
print ("Hello %s, my name is Python" % userInput)
```

The output of Listing B.11 is here (assume that the user entered the word Dave):

```
Hello Dave, my name is Python
```

The `print()` statement in Listing B.11 uses string interpolation via `%s`, which substitutes the value of the variable after the `%` symbol. This functionality is obviously useful when you want to specify something that is determined at runtime.

User input can cause exceptions (depending on the operations that your code performs), so it's important to include exception-handling code.

Listing B.12 displays the contents of `UserInput2.py` that prompts users for a string and attempts to convert the string to a number in a `try/except` block.

LISTING B.12: UserInput2.py

```
userInput = input("Enter something: ")

try:
  x = 0 + eval(userInput)
  print('you entered the number:',userInput)
except:
  print(userInput,'is a string')
```

Listing B.12 adds the number `0` to the result of converting a user's input to a number. If the conversion was successful, a message with the user's input is displayed. If the conversion failed, the `except` code block consists of a `print` statement that displays a message.

NOTE *This code sample uses the `eval()` function, which should be avoided so that your code does not evaluate arbitrary (and possibly destructive) commands.*

Listing B.13 displays the contents of `UserInput3.py` that prompts users for two numbers and attempts to compute their sum in a pair of `try/except` blocks.

LISTING B.13: UserInput3.py

```
sum = 0

msg = 'Enter a number:'
val1 = input(msg)

try:
  sum = sum + eval(val1)
except:
```

```
  print(val1,'is a string')

msg = 'Enter a number:'
val2 = input(msg)

try:
  sum = sum + eval(val2)
except:
  print(val2,'is a string')

print('The sum of',val1,'and',val2,'is',sum)
```

Listing B.13 contains two `try` blocks, each of which is followed by an `except` statement. The first `try` block attempts to add the first user-supplied number to the variable `sum`, and the second `try` block attempts to add the second user-supplied number to the previously entered number. An error message occurs if either input string is not a valid number; if both are valid numbers, a message is displayed containing the input numbers and their sum. Be sure to read the caveat regarding the `eval()` function that is mentioned earlier in this appendix.

Python and Emojis (Optional)

Listing B.14 displays the contents `remove_emojis.py` that illustrates how to remove emojis from a text string.

LISTING B.14: remove_emojis.py

```
import re
import emoji

text = "I want a Chicago deep dish pizza tonight \U0001f600"
print("text:")
print(text)
print()

emoji_pattern = re.compile("[" "\U0001F1E0-\U0001F6FF" "]+",
flags=re.UNICODE)
text = emoji_pattern.sub(r"", text)
text = "".join([x for x in text if x not in emoji.UNICODE_EMOJI])
print("text:")
print(text)
print()
```

Listing B.14 starts with two `import` statements, followed by initializing the variable `text` with a text string, whose contents are displayed. The next portion of Listing B.14 defines the variable `emoji_pattern` as a regular expression that represents a range of Unicode values for emojis.

The next portion of Listing B.14 sets the variable `text` equal to the set of nonemoji characters contained in the previously initialized value for `text` and then displays its contents. Launch the code in Listing B.14 and you will see the following output:

```
text:
I want a Chicago deep dish pizza tonight

text:
I want a Chicago deep dish pizza tonight
```

Command-Line Arguments

`Python` provides a `getopt` module to parse command-line options and arguments, and the `Python sys` module provides access to any command-line arguments via the `sys.argv`. This serves two purposes:

* `sys.argv` is the list of command-line arguments
* `len(sys.argv)` is the number of command-line arguments

Here `sys.argv[0]` is the program name, so if the `Python` program is called `test.py`, it matches the value of `sys.argv[0]`.

Now you can provide input values for a `Python` program on the command line instead of providing input values by prompting users for their input.

As an example, consider the script `test.py` shown here:

```
#!/usr/bin/python
import sys
print('Number of arguments:',len(sys.argv),'arguments')
print('Argument List:', str(sys.argv))
```

Now run above script as follows:

```
python test.py arg1 arg2 arg3
```

This will produce following result:

```
Number of arguments: 4 arguments.
Argument List: ['test.py', 'arg1', 'arg2', 'arg3']
```

The ability to specify input values from the command line provides useful functionality. For example, suppose that you have a custom `Python` class that contains the methods `add` and `subtract` to add and subtract a pair of numbers.

You can use command-line arguments in order to specify which method to execute on a pair of numbers, as shown here:

```
python MyClass add 3 5
python MyClass subtract 3 5
```

This functionality is very useful because you can programmatically execute different methods in a `Python` class, which means that you can write unit tests for your code as well.

Listing B.15 displays the contents of `Hello.py` that shows you how to use `sys.argv` to check the number of command line parameters.

LISTING B.15: Hello.py

```
import sys

def main():
  if len(sys.argv) >= 2:
    name = sys.argv[1]
  else:
    name = 'World'
  print('Hello', name)

# Standard boilerplate to invoke the main() function
if __name__ == '__main__':
  main()
```

Listing B.15 defines the `main()` function that checks the number of command-line parameters: if this value is at least 2, then the variable `name` is assigned the value of the second parameter (the first parameter is `Hello.py`), otherwise `name` is assigned the value `Hello`. The `print` statement then prints the value of the variable `name`.

The final portion of Listing B.15 uses conditional logic to determine whether or not to execute the `main()` function.

Summary

This appendix showed you how to work with numbers and perform arithmetic operations on numbers, and then you learned how to work with strings and use string operations. The next appendix introduces you to data and how to perform various data-related operations.

APPENDIX C

INTRODUCTION TO REGULAR EXPRESSIONS

This appendix introduces you to regular expressions, which is a very powerful language feature in Python. Since regular expressions are available in other programming languages (such as JavaScript and Java), the knowledge that you gain from the material in this appendix will be useful to you outside of Python. This appendix contains a mixture of code blocks and complete code samples, with varying degrees of complexity, that are suitable for beginners as well as people who have had some exposure to regular expressions.

In fact, you have probably used (albeit simple) regular expressions in a command line on a laptop, whether it be Windows, Unix, or Linux-based systems. In this appendix you will learn how to define and use more complex regular expressions than the regular expressions that you have used from the command line. Recall that in Chapter 1 you learned about some basic metacharacters, and you can use them as part of regular expressions in order to perform sophisticated search-and-replace operations involving text strings and text files.

The first part of this appendix shows you how to define regular expressions with digits and letters (uppercase as well as lowercase), and also how to use character classes in regular expressions. You will also learn about character sets and character classes.

The second portion discusses the Python re module, which contains several useful methods, such as the re.match() method for matching groups of characters, the `re.search()` method to perform searches in character strings, and the `findAll()` method. You will also learn how to use character classes (and how to group them) in regular expressions.

The final portion of this appendix contains an assortment of code samples, such as modifying text strings, splitting text strings with the `re.split()` method, and substituting text strings with the `re.sub()` method.

As you read the code samples in this appendix, some concepts and facets of regular expressions might make you feel overwhelmed with the density of the material if you are a novice. However, practice and repetition will help you become comfortable with regular expressions.

Finally, please keep in mind that the code samples are for `Python` 3.x, which might require some modification if you need to use them with `Python` 2.x.

What are Regular Expressions?

Regular expressions are referred to as REs, or regexes, or regex patterns, and they enable you to specify expressions that can match specific "parts" of a string. For instance, you can define a regular expression to match a single character or digit, a telephone number, a zip code, or an email address. You can use metacharacters and character classes (defined in the next section) as part of regular expressions to search text documents for specific patterns. As you learn how to use RE you will find other ways to use them as well.

The `re` module (added in `Python` 1.5) provides `Perl`-style regular expression patterns. Note that earlier versions of `Python` provided the `regex` module that was removed in `Python` 2.5. The `re` module provides an assortment of methods (discussed later in this appendix) for searching text strings or replacing text strings, which is similar to the basic search and/or replace functionality that is available in word processors (but usually without regular expression support). The `re` module also provides methods for splitting text strings based on regular expressions.

Before delving into the methods in the `re` module, you need to learn about metacharacters and character classes, which are the topic of the next section.

Metacharacters in Python

`Python` supports a set of *metacharacters*, most of which are the same as the metacharacters in other scripting languages such as `Perl`, as well as programming languages such as `JavaScript` and `Java`. The complete list of metacharacters in Python is here:

. ^ $ * + ? { } [ ] \ | ( )

The meaning of the preceding metacharacters is here:

? (matches 0 or 1): the expression `a?` matches the string `a` (but not `ab`)
* (matches 0 or more): the expression `a*` matches the string `aaa` (but not `baa`)
+ (matches 1 or more): the expression a+ matches aaa (but not baa)
^ (beginning of line): the expression `^[a]` matches the string `abc` (but not `bc`)
$ (end of line): `[c]$` matches the string `abc` (but not `cab`)
. (a single dot): matches any character (except newline)

Sometimes you need to match the metacharacters themselves rather than their representation, which can be done in two ways. The first way involves by "escaping" their symbolic meaning with the backslash ("\") character. Thus, the sequences `\?, \*, \+, \^, \$, and \.` represent the literal characters instead of their symbolic meaning. You can also "escape" the backslash character with the sequence "\\". If you have two consecutive backslash characters, you need an additional backslash for each of them, which means that "\\\\" is the "escaped" sequence for "\\".

The second way is to list the metacharacters inside a pair of square brackets. For example, `[+?]` treats the two characters "+" and "?" as literal characters instead of metacharacters. The second approach is obviously more compact and less prone to error (it's easy to forget a backslash in a long sequence of metacharacters). As you might surmise, the methods in the `re` module support metacharacters.

> **NOTE** *The "^" character that is to the left (and outside) of a sequence in square brackets (such as `^[A-Z]`) "anchors" the regular expression to the beginning of a line, whereas the "^" character that is the first character inside a pair of square brackets negates the regular expression (such as `[^A-Z]`) inside the square brackets.*

The interpretation of the "^" character in a regular expression depends on its location in a regular expression, as shown here:

"`^[a-z]`" means any string that starts with any lowercase letter
"`[^a-z]`" means any string that does *not* contain any lowercase letters
"`^[^a-z]`" means any string that starts with anything *except* a lowercase letter

"`^[a-z]$`" means a single lowercase letter

"`^[^a-z]$`" means a single character (including digits) that is *not* a lowercase letter

As a quick preview of the `re` module that is discussed later in this appendix, the `re.sub()` method enables you to remove characters (including metacharacters) from a text string. For example, the following code snippet removes all occurrences of a forward slash ("/") and the plus sign ("+") from the variable `str`:

```
>>> import re
>>> str  = "this string has a / and + in it"
>>> str2 = re.sub("[/]+","",str)
>>> print('original:',str)
original: this string has a / and + in it
>>> print('replaced:',str2)
replaced: this string has a  and + in it
```

We can easily remove occurrences of other metacharacters in a text string by listing them inside the square brackets, just as we have done in the preceding code snippet.

Listing C.1 displays the contents of `RemoveMetaChars1.py` that illustrates how to remove other metacharacters from a line of text.

LISTING C.1: RemoveMetaChars1.py

```
import re

text1 = "meta characters ? and / and + and ."
text2 = re.sub("[/\.*?=+]+","",text1)

print('text1:',text1)
print('text2:',text2)
```

The regular expression in Listing C.1 might seem daunting if you are new to regular expressions, but let's demystify its contents by examining the entire expression and then the meaning of each character. First of all, the term `[/\.*?=+]` matches a forward slash ("/"), a dot ("."), a question mark ("?"), an equals sign ("="), or a plus sign ("+"). Notice that the dot "." is preceded by a backslash character "\". Doing so "escapes" the meaning of the "." metacharacter (which matches any single nonwhitespace character) and treats it as a literal character.

Thus the term `[/\.*?=+]+` means "one or more occurrences of *any* of the metacharacters—treated as literal characters—inside the square brackets."

Consequently, the expression re.sub("[/\.*?=+]+","",text1) matches any occurrence of the previously listed metacharacters, and then replaces them with an empty string in the text string specified by the variable text1. The output from Listing C.1 is here:

text1: meta characters ? and / and + and .

text2: meta characters and and and

Later in this appendix you will learn about other functions in the re module that enable you to modify and split text strings.

Character Sets in Python

A single digit in base 10 is a number between 0 and 9 inclusive, which is represented by the sequence [0-9]. Similarly, a lowercase letter can be any letter between a and z, which is represented by the sequence [a-z]. An uppercase letter can be any letter between A and Z, which is represented by the sequence [A-Z].

The following code snippets illustrate how to specify sequences of digits and sequences of character strings using a short-hand notation that is much simpler than specifying every matching digit:

[0-9] matches a single digit
[0-9][0-9] matches 2 consecutive digits
[0-9]{3} matches 3 consecutive digits
[0-9]{2,4} matches 2, 3, or 4 consecutive digits
[0-9]{5,} matches 5 or more consecutive digits
^[0-9]+$ matches a string consisting solely of digits

You can define similar patterns using uppercase or lowercase letters in a way that is much simpler than explicitly specifying every lowercase letter or every uppercase letter:

[a-z][A-Z] matches a single lowercase letter that is followed by 1 uppercase letter
[a-zA-Z] matches any upper- or lowercase letter

Working with "^" and "\"

The purpose of the "^" character depends on its context in a regular expression. For example, the following expression matches a text string that starts with a digit:

^[0-9].

However, the following expression matches a text string that does *not* start with a digit because of the "^" metacharacter that is at the beginning of an expression in square brackets as well as the "^" metacharacter that is to the left (and outside) the expression in square brackets (which you learned in a previous note):

`^[^0-9]`

Thus, the "^" character inside a pair of matching square brackets ("[]") negates the expression immediately to its right that is also located inside the square brackets.

The backslash ("\") allows you to "escape" the meaning of a metacharacter. Consequently, a dot "." matches a single character (except for whitespace characters), whereas the sequence "\." matches the dot "." character. Other examples involving the backslash metacharacter are here:

`\.H.*` matches the string `.Hello`
`H.*` matches the string `Hello`
`H.*\.` matches the string `Hello.`
`.ell` matches the string `Hello`
`.*` matches the string `Hello`
`\..*` matches the string `.Hello`

Character Classes in Python

Character classes are convenient expressions that are shorter and simpler than their "bare" counterparts that you saw in the previous section. Some convenient character sequences that express patterns of digits and letters:

`\d` matches a single digit
`\w` matches a single character (digit or letter)
`\s` matches a single whitespace (space, newline, return, or tab)
`\b` matches a boundary between a word and a nonword
`\n`, `\r`, `\t` represent a newline, a return, and a tab, respectively
`\` "escapes" any character

Based on the preceding definitions, `\d+` matches one or more digits and `\w+` matches one or more characters, both of which are more compact expressions than using character sets. In addition, we can reformulate the expressions in the previous section:

`\d` is the same as `[0-9]` and `\D` is the same as `[^0-9]`

\s is the same as `[ \t\n\r\f\v]` and it matches any nonwhitespace character, whereas \S is the opposite (it matches `[^ \t\n\r\f\v]`)
\w is the same as `[a-zA-Z0-9_]` and it matches any alphanumeric character, whereas \W is the opposite (it matches `[^a-zA-Z0-9_]`)

Additional examples are here:

\d{2} is the same as `[0-9][0-9]`
\d{3} is the same as `[0-9]{3}`
\d{2,4} is the same as `[0-9]{2,4}`
\d{5,} is the same as `[0-9]{5,}`
^\d+$ is the same as `^[0-9]+$`

The curly braces ("{}") are called quantifiers, and they specify the number (or range) of characters in the expressions that precede them.

Matching Character Classes with the `re` Module

The `re` module provides the following methods for matching and searching one or more occurrences of a regular expression in a text string:

`match()`: Determine if the RE matches at the *beginning* of the string.
`search()`: Scan through a string, looking for *any* location where the RE matches.
`findall()`: Find *all* substrings where the RE matches and return them as a list.
`finditer()`: Find all substrings where the RE matches and return them as an iterator.

NOTE *The `match()` function only matches pattern to the start of string.*

The next section shows you how to use the `match()` function in the `re` module.

Using the `re.match()` Method

The `re.match()` method attempts to match RE pattern in a text string (with optional flags), and it has the following syntax:

`re.match(pattern, string, flags=0)`

The `pattern` parameter is the regular expression that you want to match in the `string` parameter. The flags parameter allows you to specify multiple flags using the bitwise OR operator that is represented by the pipe "|" symbol.

The `re.match` method returns a match object on success and `None` on failure. Use `group(num)` or `groups()` function of the match object to get a matched expression.

`group(num=0)`: This methods returns entire match (or specific subgroup `num`)

`groups()`: This method returns all matching subgroups in a tuple (empty if there weren't any)

> **NOTE** *The `re.match()` method only matches patterns from the start of a text string, which is different from the `re.search()` method discussed later in this appendix.*

The following code block illustrates how to use the `group()` function in regular expressions:

```
>>> import re
>>> p = re.compile('(a(b)c)de')
>>> m = p.match('abcde')
>>> m.group(0)
'abcde'
>>> m.group(1)
'abc'
>>> m.group(2)
'b'
```

Notice that the higher numbers inside the `group()` method match more deeply nested expressions that are specified in the initial regular expression.

Listing C.2 displays the contents of `MatchGroup1.py` that illustrates how to use the `group()` function to match an alphanumeric text string and an alphabetic string.

LISTING C.2: MatchGroup1.py

```
import re

line1 = 'abcd123'
line2 = 'abcdefg'
mixed = re.compile(r"^[a-z0-9]{5,7}$")
line3 = mixed.match(line1)
line4 = mixed.match(line2)

print('line1:',line1)
print('line2:',line2)
print('line3:',line3)
print('line4:',line4)
print('line5:',line4.group(0))
```

```
line6 = 'a1b2c3d4e5f6g7'
mixed2 = re.compile(r"^([a-z]+[0-9]+){5,7}$")
line7 = mixed2.match(line6)

print('line6:',line6)
print('line7:',line7.group(0))
print('line8:',line7.group(1))

line9 = 'abc123fgh4567'
mixed3 = re.compile(r"^([a-z]*[0-9]*){5,7}$")
line10 = mixed3.match(line9)
print('line9:',line9)
print('line10:',line10.group(0))
The output from Listing C.2 is here:
line1: abcd123
line2: abcdefg
line3: <_sre.SRE_Match object at 0x100485440>
line4: <_sre.SRE_Match object at 0x1004854a8>
line5: abcdefg
line6: a1b2c3d4e5f6g7
line7: a1b2c3d4e5f6g7
line8: g7
line9: abc123fgh4567
line10: abc123fgh4567
```

Notice that `line3` and `line7` involve two similar but different regular expressions. The variable `mixed` specifies a sequence of lowercase letters followed by digits, where the length of the text string is also between 5 and 7. The string `'abcd123'` satisfies all of these conditions.

However, `mixed2` specifies a pattern consisting of one or more pairs, where each pair contains one or more lowercase letters followed by one or more digits, where the length of the matching pairs is also between 5 and 7. In this case, the string `'abcd123'` as well as the string `'a1b2c3d4e5f6g7'` both satisfy these criteria.

The third regular expression `mixed3` specifies a pair such that each pair consists of zero or more occurrences of lowercase letters and zero or more occurrences of a digit, and also that the number of such pairs is between 5 and 7. As you can see from the output, the regular expression in `mixed3` matches lowercase letters and digits in any order.

In the preceding example, the regular expression specified a range for the length of the string, which involves a lower limit of five and an upper limit of seven.

However, you can also specify a lower limit without an upper limit (or an upper limit without a lower limit).

Listing C.3 displays the contents of MatchGroup2.py that illustrates how to use a regular expression and the group() function to match an alphanumeric text string and an alphabetic string.

LISTING C.3: MatchGroup2.py

```
import re

alphas = re.compile(r"^[abcde]{5,}")
line1 = alphas.match("abcde").group(0)
line2 = alphas.match("edcba").group(0)
line3 = alphas.match("acbedf").group(0)
line4 = alphas.match("abcdefghi").group(0)
line5 = alphas.match("abcdefghi abcdef")

print('line1:',line1)
print('line2:',line2)
print('line3:',line3)
print('line4:',line4)
print('line5:',line5)
```

Listing C.3 initializes the variable alphas as a regular expression that matches any string that starts with one of the letters a through e, and consists of at least five characters. The next portion of Listing C.3 initializes the four variables line1, line2, line3, and line4 by means of the alphas RE that is applied to various text strings. These four variables are set to the first matching group by means of the expression group(0).

The output from Listing C.3 is here:

```
line1: abcde
line2: edcba
line3: acbed
line4: abcde
line5: <_sre.SRE_Match object at 0x1004854a8>
```

Listing C.4 displays the contents of MatchGroup3.py that illustrates how to use a regular expression with the group() function to match words in a text string.

LISTING C.4: MatchGroup3.py

```
import re

line = "Giraffes are taller than elephants";

matchObj = re.match( r'(.*) are(\.*)', line, re.M|re.I)
```

```
if matchObj:
   print("matchObj.group()   : ", matchObj.group())
   print("matchObj.group(1)  : ", matchObj.group(1))
   print("matchObj.group(2)  : ", matchObj.group(2))
else:
   print("matchObj does not match line:", line)
The code in Listing C.4 produces the following output:
matchObj.group()   :   Giraffes are
matchObj.group(1)  :   Giraffes
matchObj.group(2)  :
```

Listing C.4 contains a pair of delimiters separated by a pipe ("|") symbol. The first delimiter is `re.M` for "multiline," which has no effect in this example because it contains only a single line of text. The second delimiter `re.I` means "ignore case" during the pattern matching operation. The `re.match()` method supports additional delimiters, as discussed in the next section.

Options for the `re.match()` Method

The `match()` method supports various optional modifiers that affect the type of matching that will be performed. As you saw in the previous example, you can also specify multiple modifiers separated by the OR ("|") symbol. Additional modifiers that are available for RE are shown here:

`re.I` performs case-insensitive matches (see previous section)
`re.L` interprets words according to the current locale
`re.M` makes $ match the end of a line and makes ^ match the start of any line
`re.S` makes a period (".") match any character (including a newline)
`re.U` interprets letters according to the Unicode character set

Experiment with these modifiers by writing Python code that uses them in conjunction with different text strings.

Matching Character Classes with the `re.search()` Method

As you saw earlier in this appendix, the `re.match()` method only matches from the beginning of a string, whereas the `re.search()` method can successfully match a substring anywhere in a text string.

The `re.search()` method takes two arguments: a regular expression pattern and a string and then searches for the specified pattern in the given string. The `search()` method returns a match object (if the search was successful) or `None`.

As a simple example, the following searches for the pattern `tasty` followed by a five-letter word:

```
import re

str = 'I want a tasty pizza'
match = re.search(r'tasty \w\w\w\w\w', str)

if match:
  ## 'found tasty pizza'
  print('found', match.group())
else:
  print('Nothing tasty here')
```

The output of the preceding code block is here:

```
found tasty pizza
```

The following code block further illustrates the difference between the `match()` method and the `search()` methods:

```
>>> import re
>>> print(re.search('this', 'this is the one').span())
(0, 4)
>>>
>>> print(re.search('the', 'this is the one').span())
(8, 11)
>>> print(re.match('this', 'this is the one').span())
(0, 4)
>>> print(re.match('the', 'this is the one').span())
```

Traceback (most recent call last):

```
File "<stdin>", line 1, in <module>
AttributeError: 'NoneType' object has no attribute 'span'
```

Matching Character Classes with the `findAll()` Method

Listing C.5 displays the contents of the `Python` script `RegEx1.py` that illustrates how to define simple character classes that match various text strings.

LISTING C.5: RegEx1.py

```
import re

str1 = "123456"
matches1 = re.findall("(\d+)", str1)
print('matches1:',matches1)
```

```
str1 = "123456"
matches1 = re.findall("(\d\d\d)", str1)
print('matches1:',matches1)

str1 = "123456"
matches1 = re.findall("(\d\d)", str1)
print('matches1:',matches1)

print
str2 = "1a2b3c456"
matches2 = re.findall("(\d)", str2)
print('matches2:',matches2)

print
str2 = "1a2b3c456"
matches2 = re.findall("\d", str2)
print('matches2:',matches2)

print
str3 = "1a2b3c456"
matches3 = re.findall("(\w)", str3)
print('matches3:',matches3)
```

Listing C.5 contains simple regular expressions (which you have seen already) for matching digits in the variables `str1` and `str2`. The final code block of Listing C.5 matches every character in the string `str3`, effectively "splitting" `str3` into a list where each element consists of one character. The output from Listing C.5 is here (notice the blank lines after the first three output lines):

```
matches1: ['123456']
matches1: ['123', '456']
matches1: ['12', '34', '56']

matches2: ['1', '2', '3', '4', '5', '6']

matches2: ['1', '2', '3', '4', '5', '6']

matches3: ['1', 'a', '2', 'b', '3', 'c', '4', '5', '6']
```

Finding Capitalized Words in a String

Listing C.6 displays the contents of the Python script FindCapitalized.py that illustrates how to define simple character classes that match various text strings.

LISTING C.6: FindCapitalized.py

```
import re

str = "This Sentence contains Capitalized words"
```

```
caps = re.findall(r'[A-Z][\w\.-]+', str)

print('str: ',str)
print('caps:',caps)
```

Listing C.6 initializes the string variable `str` and the RE `caps` that matches any word that starts with a capital letter because the first portion of `caps` is the pattern [A-Z] that matches any capital letter between A and Z inclusive. The output of Listing C.6 is here:

```
str:  This Sentence contains Capitalized words
caps: ['This', 'Sentence', 'Capitalized']
```

Additional Matching Function for Regular Expressions

After invoking any of the methods `match()`, `search()`, `findAll()`, or `finditer()`, you can invoke additional methods on the "matching object." An example of this functionality using the `match()` method is here:

```
import re

p1 = re.compile('[a-z]+')
m1 = p1.match("hello")
```

In the preceding code block, the `p1` object represents the compiled regular expression for one or more lowercase letters, and the "matching object" `m1` object supports the following methods:

    `group()` return the string matched by the RE
    `start()` return the starting position of the match
    `end()` return the ending position of the match
    `span()` return a tuple containing the (start, end) positions of the match

As a further illustration, Listing C.7 displays the contents of `SearchFunction1.py` that illustrates how to use the `search()` method and the `group()` method.

LISTING C.7: SearchFunction1.py

```
import re

line = "Giraffes are taller than elephants";

searchObj = re.search( r'(.*) are(\.*)', line, re.M|re.I)

if searchObj:
   print("searchObj.group()  : ", searchObj.group()
```

```
    print("searchObj.group(1) : ", searchObj.group(1)
    print("searchObj.group(2) : ", searchObj.group(2)
else:
    print("searchObj does not match line:", line
```

Listing C.7 contains the variable `line` that represents a text string and the variable `searchObj` is an RE involving the `search()` method and pair of pipe-delimited modifiers (discussed in more detail in the next section). If `searchObj` is not null, the `if/else` conditional code in Listing C.7 displays the contents of the three groups resulting from the successful match with the contents of the variable line. The output from Listing C.7 is here:

```
searchObj.group()  : Giraffes are
searchObj.group(1) : Giraffes
searchObj.group(2) :
```

Grouping with Character Classes in Regular Expressions

In addition to the character classes that you have seen earlier in this appendix, you can specify subexpressions of character classes.

Listing C.8 displays the contents of `Grouping1.py` that illustrates how to use the `search()` method.

LISTING C.8: Grouping1.py

```
import re

p1 = re.compile('(ab)*')
print('match1:',p1.match('abababab').group()
print('span1: ',p1.match('abababab').span()

p2 = re.compile('(a)b')
m2 = p2.match('ab')
print('match2:',m2.group(0)
print('match3:',m2.group(1)
```

Listing C.8 starts by defining the RE `p1` that matches zero or more occurrences of the string `ab`. The first `print()` statement displays the result of using the `match()` function of `p1` (followed by the `group()` function) against a string, and the result is a string. This illustrates the use of "method chaining," which eliminates the need for an intermediate object (as shown in the second code block). The second `print()` statement displays the result of using the `match()` function of `p1`, followed by applying the `span()` function, against a string. In this case the result is a numeric range (see output in the following paragraph).

The second part of Listing C.8 defines the RE `p2` that matches an optional letter a followed by the letter `b`. The variable `m2` invokes the match method on `p2` using the string `ab`. The third `print(` statement displays the result of invoking `group(0)` on `m2`, and the fourth `print(` statement displays the result of involving group(1) on m2. Both results are substrings of the input string `ab`. Recall that `group(0)` returns the highest level match that occurred, and `group(1)` returns a more "specific" match that occurred, such as one that involves the parentheses in the definition of `p2`. The higher the value of the integer in the expression `group(n)`, the more specific the match. The output from Listing C.8 is here:

```
match1: abababab
span1:  (0, 10)
match2: ab
match3: a
```

Using Character Classes in Regular Expressions

This section contains some examples that illustrate how to use character classes to match various strings and also how to use delimiters in order to split a text string. For example, one common date string involves a date format of the form MM/DD/YY. Another common scenario involves records with a delimiter that separates multiple fields. Usually such records contain one delimiter, but as you will see, Python makes it very easy to split records using multiple delimiters.

Matching Strings with Multiple Consecutive Digits

Listing C.9 displays the contents of the `Python` script `MatchPatterns1.py` that illustrates how to define simple regular expressions in order to split the contents of a text string based on the occurrence of one or more consecutive digits.

Although the regular expressions `\d+/\d+/\d+` and `\d\d/\d\d/\d\d\d\d` both match the string `08/13/2014`, the first regular expression matches more patterns than the second regular expression which is an "exact match" with respect to the number of matching digits that are allowed.

LISTING C.9: MatchPatterns1.py

```
import re

date1 = '02/28/2013'
date2 = 'February 28, 2013'
```

```
# Simple matching: \d+ means match one or more digits
if re.match(r'\d+/\d+/\d+', date1):
  print('date1 matches this pattern')
else:
  print('date1 does not match this pattern')

if re.match(r'\d+/\d+/\d+', date2):
  print('date2 matches this pattern')
else:
  print('date2 does not match this pattern')
```

The output from launching Listing C.9 is here:

```
date1 matches this pattern
date2 does not match this pattern
```

Reversing Words in Strings

Listing C.10 displays the contents of the `Python` script `ReverseWords1.py` that illustrates how to reverse a pair of words in a string.

LISTING C.10: ReverseWords1.py

```
import re

str1 = 'one two'
match = re.search('([\w.-]+) ([\w.-]+)', str1)

str2 = match.group(2) + ' ' + match.group(1)
print('str1:',str1)
print('str2:',str2)
The output from Listing C.10 is here:
str1: one two
str2: two one
```

Now that you understand how to define regular expressions for digits and letters, let's look at some more sophisticated regular expressions.

For example, the following expression matches a string that is any combination of digits, uppercase letters, or lowercase letters (i.e., no special characters):

```
^[a-zA-Z0-9]$
```

Here is the same expression rewritten using character classes:

```
^[\w\W\d]$
```

Modifying Text Strings with the `re` Module

The Python `re` module contains several methods for modifying strings. The `split()` method uses a regular expression to "split" a string into a list. The `sub()` method finds all substrings where the regular expression matches, and then replaces them with a different string. The `subn()` performs the same functionality as `sub()`, and also returns the new string and the number of replacements. The following subsections contain examples that illustrate how to use the functions `split()`, `sub()`, and `subn()` in regular expressions.

Splitting Text Strings with the `re.split()` Method

Listing C.11 displays the contents of the Python script `RegEx2.py` that illustrates how to define simple regular expressions in order to split the contents of a text string.

LISTING C.11: RegEx2.py

```
import re

line1 = "abc def"
result1 = re.split(r'[\s]', line1)
print('result1:',result1)

line2 = "abc1,abc2:abc3;abc4"
result2 = re.split(r'[,:;]', line2)
print('result2:',result2)

line3 = "abc1,abc2:abc3;abc4 123 456"
result3 = re.split(r'[,:;\s]', line3)
print('result3:',result3)
```

Listing C.11 contains three blocks of code, each of which uses the `split()` method in the `re` module in order to tokenize three different strings. The first regular expression specifies a whitespace, the second regular expression specifies three punctuation characters, and the third regular expression specifies the combination of the first two regular expressions.

The output from launching `RegEx2.py` is here:

```
result1: ['abc', 'def']
result2: ['abc1', 'abc2', 'abc3', 'abc4']
result3: ['abc1', 'abc2', 'abc3', 'abc4', '123', '456']
```

Splitting Text Strings Using Digits and Delimiters

Listing C.12 displays the contents of `SplitCharClass1.py` that illustrates how to use regular expression consisting of a character class, the "." character, and a whitespace to split the contents of two text strings.

LISTING C.12: SplitCharClass1.py

```
import re

line1 = '1. Section one 2. Section two 3. Section three'
line2 = '11. Section eleven 12. Section twelve 13. Section thirteen'

print(re.split(r'\d+\. ', line1))
print(re.split(r'\d+\. ', line2))
```

Listing C.12 contains two text strings that can be split using the same regular expression '\d+\. '. Note that if you use the expression '\d\. ' only the first text string will split correctly. The result of launching Listing C.12 is here:

```
['', 'Section one ', 'Section two ', 'Section three']
['', 'Section eleven ', 'Section twelve ', 'Section thirteen']
```

Substituting Text Strings with the `re.sub()` Method

Earlier in this appendix you saw a preview of using the `sub()` method to remove all the metacharacters in a text string. The following code block illustrates how to use the `re.sub()` method to substitute alphabetic characters in a text string.

```
>>> import re
>>> p = re.compile( '(one|two|three)')
>>> p.sub( 'some', 'one book two books three books')
'some book some books some books'
>>>
>>> p.sub( 'some', 'one book two books three books', count=1)
'some book two books three books'
```

The following code block uses the `re.sub()` method in order to insert a line feed after each alphabetic character in a text string:

```
>>> line = 'abcde'
>>> line2 = re.sub('', '\n', line)
>>> print('line2:',line2)
line2:
a
b
```

```
c
d
e
```

Matching the Beginning and the End of Text Strings

Listing C.13 displays the contents of the `Python` script `RegEx3.py` that illustrates how to find substrings using the `startswith()` function and `endswith()` function.

LISTING C.13: RegEx3.py

```
import re

line2 = "abc1,Abc2:def3;Def4"
result2 = re.split(r'[,:;]', line2)

for w in result2:
  if(w.startswith('Abc')):
    print('Word starts with Abc:',w)
  elif(w.endswith('4')):
    print('Word ends with 4:',w)
  else:
    print('Word:',w)
```

Listing C.13 starts by initializing the string `line2` (with punctuation characters as word delimiters) and the RE `result2` that uses the `split()` function with a comma, colon, and semicolon as "split delimiters" in order to tokenize the string variable `line2`.

The output after launching Listing C.13 is here:

```
Word: abc1
Word starts with Abc: Abc2
Word: def3
Word ends with 4: Def4
```

Listing C.14 displays the contents of the `Python` script `MatchLines1.py` that illustrates how to find substrings using character classes.

LISTING C.14: MatchLines1.py

```
import re

line1 = "abcdef"
line2 = "123,abc1,abc2,abc3"
line3 = "abc1,abc2,123,456f"

if re.match("^[A-Za-z]*$", line1):
  print('line1 contains only letters:',line1
```

```
# better than the preceding snippet:
line1[:-1].isalpha()
  print('line1 contains only letters:',line1

if re.match("^[\w]*$", line1):
  print('line1 contains only letters:',line1

if re.match(r"^[^\W\d_]+$", line1, re.LOCALE):
  print('line1 contains only letters:',line1
print

if re.match("^[0-9][0-9][0-9]", line2):
  print('line2 starts with 3 digits:',line2

if re.match("^\d\d\d", line2):
  print('line2 starts with 3 digits:',line2
print

# the initial ".*" is required in this RE:
if re.match(".*[0-9][0-9][0-9][a-z]$", line3):
  print('line3 ends with 3 digits and 1 char:',line3

# the initial ".*" is required in this RE:
if re.match(".*[a-z]$", line3):
  print('line3 ends with 1 char:',line3
```

Listing C.14 starts by initializing 3 string variables line1, line2, and line3. The first RE contains an expression that matches any line containing uppercase or lowercase letters (or both):

```
if re.match("^[A-Za-z]*$", line1):
```

The following two snippets also test for the same thing:

```
line1[:-1].isalpha()
```

The preceding snippet starts from the right-most position of the string and checks if each character is alphabetic. The next snippet checks if line1 can be tokenized into words (whereas a word contains only alphabetic characters):

```
if re.match("^[\w]*$", line1):
```

The next portion of Listing C.14 checks if a string contains three consecutive digits:

```
if re.match("^[0-9][0-9][0-9]", line2):
  print('line2 starts with 3 digits:',line2

if re.match("^\d\d\d", line2):
```

The first snippet uses the pattern [0-9] to match a digit, whereas the second snippet uses the expression \d to match a digit.

The output from Listing C.14 is here:

```
line1 contains only letters: abcdef
line1 contains only letters: abcdef
line1 contains only letters: abcdef
line1 contains only letters: abcdef

line2 starts with 3 digits: 123,abc1,abc2,abc3
line2 starts with 3 digits: 123,abc1,abc2,abc3
```

Compilation Flags

Compilation flags modify the manner in which regular expressions work. Flags are available in the re module as a long name (such as IGNORECASE) and a short, one-letter form (such as I). The short form is the same as the flags in pattern modifiers in Perl. You can specify multiple flags by using the "|" symbol. For example, re.I | re.M sets both the I and M flags.

You can check the online Python documentation regarding all the available compilation flags in Python.

Compound Regular Expressions

Listing C.15 displays the contents of MatchMixedCase1.py that illustrates how to use the pipe ("|") symbol to specify two regular expressions in the same match() function.

LISTING C.15: MatchMixedCase1.py

```
import re

line1 = "This is a line"
line2 = "That is a line"

if re.match("^[Tt]his", line1):
  print('line1 starts with This or this:'
  print(line1
else:
  print('no match'

if re.match("^This|That", line2):
  print('line2 starts with This or That:'
  print(line2
else:
  print('no match'
```

Listing C.15 starts with two string variables line1 and line2, followed by an if/else conditional code block that checks if line1 starts with the RE [Tt]his, which matches the string This as well as the string this.

The second conditional code block checks if `line2` starts with the string `This` or the string `That`. Notice the "^" metacharacter, which in this context anchors the RE to the beginning of the string. The output from Listing C.15 is here:

```
line1 starts with This or this:
This is a line
line2 starts with This or That:
That is a line
```

Counting Character Types in a String

You can use a regular expression to check whether a character is a digit, a letter, or some other type of character. Listing C.16 displays the contents of `CountDigitsAndChars.py` that performs this task.

LISTING C.16: CountDigitsAndChars.py

```
import re

charCount  = 0
digitCount = 0
otherCount = 0

line1 = "A line with numbers: 12 345"

for ch in line1:
   if(re.match(r'\d', ch)):
      digitCount = digitCount + 1
   elif(re.match(r'\w', ch)):
      charCount = charCount + 1
   else:
      otherCount = otherCount + 1

print('charcount:',charCount)
print('digitcount:',digitCount)
print('othercount:',otherCount)
```

Listing C.16 initializes three numeric counter-related variables, followed by the string variable `line1`. The next part of Listing C.16 contains a `for` loop that processes each character in the string `line1`. The body of the `for` loop contains a conditional code block that checks whether the current character is a digit, a letter, or some other nonalphanumeric character. Each time there is a successful match, the corresponding "counter" variable is incremented.

The output from Listing C.16 is here:

```
charcount: 16
digitcount: 5
othercount: 6
```

Regular Expressions and Grouping

You can also "group" subexpressions and even refer to them symbolically. For example, the following expression matches zero or one occurrences of three consecutive (uppercase or lowercase) letters or digits (such as az4, P2c, 73X, and so forth):

```
^([a-zA-Z0-9]{3,3})?
```

The following expression matches a telephone number (such as 650-555-1212) in the USA:

```
^\d{3,3}[-]\d{3,3}[-]\d{4,4}
```

The following expression matches a zip code (such as `67827` or `94343-04005`) in the USA:

```
^\d{5,5}([-]\d{5,5})?
```

The following code block partially matches an email address:

```
str = 'john.doe@google.com'
  match = re.search(r'\w+@\w+', str)
  if match:
    print(match.group()   ## 'doe@google'
```

Exercise: use the preceding code block as a starting point in order to define a regular expression for email addresses.

Simple String Matches

Listing C.17 displays the contents of the Python script RegEx4.py that illustrates how to define regular expressions that match various text strings.

LISTING C.17: RegEx4.py

```
import re

searchString = "Testing pattern matches"

expr1 = re.compile( r"Test" )
expr2 = re.compile( r"^Test" )
expr3 = re.compile( r"Test$" )
expr4 = re.compile( r"\b\w*es\b" )
```

```
expr5 = re.compile( r"t[aeiou]", re.I )

if expr1.search( searchString ):
   print('"Test" was found.'

if expr2.match( searchString ):
   print('"Test" was found at the beginning of the line.'

if expr3.match( searchString ):
   print('"Test" was found at the end of the line.'

result = expr4.findall( searchString )

if result:
   print('There are %d words(s) ending in "es":' % \
      ( len( result ) ),

   for item in result:
      print(" " + item,

print

result = expr5.findall( searchString )
if result:
   print('The letter t, followed by a vowel, occurs %d times:' % \
      ( len( result ) ),

   for item in result:
      print(" "+item,

print
```

Listing C.17 starts with the variable searchString that specifies a text string, followed by the REs expr1, expr2, expr3. The RE expr1 matches the string Test that occurs anywhere in searchString, whereas expr2 matches Test if it occurs at the beginning of searchString, and expr3 matches Test if it occurs at the end of searchString. The RE expr matches words that end in the letters es, and the RE expr5 matches the letter t followed by a vowel. The output from Listing C.17 is here:

```
"Test" was found.
"Test" was found at the beginning of the line.
There are 1 words(s) ending in "es":  matches
The letter t, followed by a vowel, occurs 3 times:  Te  ti  te
```

Additional Topics for Regular Expressions

In addition to the Python-based search/replace functionality that you have seen in this appendix, you can also perform a greedy search and substitution. Perform an internet search to learn what these features are and how to use them in Python code.

Summary

This appendix showed you how to create various types of regular expressions. First you learned how to define primitive regular expressions using sequences of digits, lowercase letters, and uppercase letters. Next you learned how to use character classes, which are more convenient and simpler expressions that can perform the same functionality. You also learned how to use the `Python re` library in order to compile regular expressions and then use them to see if they match substrings of text strings.

Exercises

1. Given a text string, find the list of words (if any) that start or end with a vowel, and treat upper- and lowercase vowels as distinct letters. Display this list of words in alphabetical order, and also in descending order based on their frequency.

2. Given a text string, find the list of words (if any) that contain lowercase vowels or digits or both, but no uppercase letters. Display this list of words in alphabetical order, and also in descending order based their frequency.

3. There is a spelling rule in English specifying that "the letter i is before e, except after c," which means that "receive" is correct but "recieve" is incorrect. Write a Python script that checks for incorrectly spelled words in a text string.

4. Subject pronouns cannot follow a preposition in the English language. Thus, "between you and me" and "for you and me" are correct whereas "between you and I" and "for you and I" are incorrect. Write a Python script that checks for incorrect grammar in a text string, and search for the prepositions "between," "for," and "with." In addition, search for the subject pronouns "I," "you," "he," and "she." Modify and display the text with the correct grammar usage.

5. Find the words in a text string whose length is at most four and then print(all) the substrings of those characters. For example, if a text string contains the word "text," then print the strings "t," "te," "tex," and "text."

APPENDIX D

INTRODUCTION TO KERAS

This appendix introduces you to `Keras` along with code samples that illustrate how to define basic neural networks, as well as deep neural networks with various datasets with `MNIST` and `Cifar10`.

The first part of this appendix briefly discusses some of the important namespaces (e.g., `tf.keras.layers`) and their contents, as well as a simple `Keras`-based model.

The second section contains an example of performing linear regression with `Keras` and a simple CSV file. You will also see a `Keras`-based MLP neural network that is trained on the `MNIST` dataset.

The third section contains a simple example of training a neural network with the `cifar10` dataset. This code sample is similar to training a neural network on the `MNIST` dataset and requires a very small code change.

The final section contains two examples of `Keras`-based models that perform "early stopping," which is convenient when the model exhibits minimal improvement (that is specified by you) during the training process.

What is Keras?

If you are already comfortable with `Keras`, you can skim this section to learn about the new namespaces and what they contain, and then proceed to the next section that includes details for creating a `Keras`-based model.

If you are new to Keras, you might be wondering why this section is included in this appendix. First, Keras is well-integrated into TF 2, and it's in the tf.keras namespace. Second, Keras is well-suited for defining models to solve a myriad of tasks such as linear regression and logistic regression, as well as deep learning tasks involving CNNs, RNNs, and LSTMs that are discussed in the appendix.

The next several subsections contain lists of bullet items for various Keras-related namespaces, and they will be very familiar if you have worked with TF 1.x. If you are new to TF 2, you'll see examples of some of the classes in subsequent code samples.

Working with Keras Namespaces in TF 2

TF 2 provides the tf.keras namespace, which in turn contains the following namespaces:

- tf.keras.layers
- tf.keras.models
- tf.keras.optimizers
- tf.keras.utils
- tf.keras.regularizers

The preceding namespaces contain various layers in Keras models, different types of Keras models, optimizers (Adam et al), utility classes, and regularizers (such as L1 and L2), respectively.

Currently there are three ways to create Keras-based models:

- Sequential class
- functional API
- model class

The Keras-based code samples in this book use primarily the Sequential class (it's the most intuitive and straightforward). The Sequential class enables you to specify a list of layers, most of which are available in the tf.keras.layers namespace (discussed later).

The Keras-based models that use the functional API involve specifying layers that are passed as function-like elements in a "pipeline-like" fashion. Although the functional API provides some additional flexibility, you will probably use the `Sequential` class to define `Keras`-based models if you are a TF 2 beginner.

The model class provides the greatest flexibility, and it involves defining a `Python` class that encapsulates the semantics of your `Keras` model. This class is a subclass of the `tf.model.Model` class, and you must implement the two methods `__init__` and `call` in order to define a `Keras` model in this subclass.

Perform an online search for more details regarding the functional API and the model class.

Working with the tf.keras.layers Namespace

The most common (and also the simplest) `Keras`-based model is the `Sequential` class that is in the `tf.keras.models` namespace. This model is comprised of various layers that belong to the `tf.keras.layers` namespace, as shown here:

- tf.keras.layers.Conv2D()
- tf.keras.layers.MaxPooling2D()
- tf.keras.layers.Flatten()
- tf.keras.layers.Dense()
- tf.keras.layers.Dropout()
- tf.keras.layers.BatchNormalization()
- tf.keras.layers.embedding()
- tf.keras.layers.RNN()
- tf.keras.layers.LSTM()
- tf.keras.layers.Bidirectional (ex: BERT)

The `Conv2D()` and `MaxPooling2D()` classes are used in `Keras`-based models for CNNs, which are discussed in Chapter 5. Generally speaking, the next six classes in the preceding list can appear in models for CNNs as well as models for machine learning. The `RNN()` class is for simple RNNs and the `LSTM` class is for `LSTM`-based models. The `Bidirectional()` class is a bidirectional `LSTM` that you will often see in models for solving natural language processing (NLP) tasks. One very important NLP model is BERT (from Google), which is based on the Transformer architecture (also from Google).

Working with the tf.keras.activations Namespace

Machine learning and deep learning models require activation functions. For `Keras`-based models, the activation functions are in the `tf.keras.activations` namespace, some of which are listed here:

- `tf.keras.activations.relu`
- `tf.keras.activations.selu`
- `tf.keras.activations.linear`
- `tf.keras.activations.elu`
- `tf.keras.activations.sigmoid`
- `tf.keras.activations.softmax`
- `tf.keras.activations.softplus`
- `tf.keras.activations.tanh`
- Others

The ReLU/SELU/ELU functions are closely related, and they often appear in artificial neural networks (ANNs) and CNNs. Before the `relu()` function became popular, the `sigmoid()` and `tanh()` functions were used in ANNs and CNNs. However, they are still important and they are used in various gates in GRUs and LSTMs. The `softmax()` function is typically used in the pair of layers consisting of the right-most hidden layer and the output layer.

Working with the keras.tf.datasets Namespace

For your convenience, TF 2 provides a set of built-in datasets in the `tf.keras.datasets` namespace, some of which are listed here:

- `tf.keras.datasets.boston_housing`
- `tf.keras.datasets.cifar10`
- `tf.keras.datasets.cifar100`
- `tf.keras.datasets.fashion_mnist`
- `tf.keras.datasets.imdb`
- `tf.keras.datasets.mnist`
- `tf.keras.datasets.reuters`

The preceding datasets are popular for training models with small datasets. The mnist dataset and fashion_mnist dataset are both popular when training CNNs, whereas the boston_housing dataset is popular for linear regression. The Titanic dataset is also popular for linear regression, but it's not currently supported as a default dataset in the tf.keras.datasets namespace.

Working with the tf.keras.experimental Namespace

The contrib namespace in TF 1.x has been deprecated in TF 2, and its successor is the tf.keras.experimental namespace, which contains the following classes (among others):

- tf.keras.experimental.CosineDecay
- tf.keras.experimental.CosineDecayRestarts
- tf.keras.experimental.LinearCosineDecay
- tf.keras.experimental.NoisyLinearCosineDecay
- tf.keras.experimental.PeepholeLSTMCell

If you are a beginner, you probably won't use any of the classes in the preceding list. Although the PeepholeLSTMCell class is a variation of the LSTM class, there are limited use cases for this class.

Working with Other tf.keras Namespaces

TF 2 provides a number of other namespaces that contain useful classes, some of which are listed here:

- tf.keras.callbacks   (early stopping)
- tf.keras.optimizers   (Adam et al.)
- tf.keras.regularizers   (L1 and L2)
- tf.keras.utils   (to_categorical)

The tf.keras.callbacks namespace contains a class that you can use for "early stopping," which is to say that it's possible to terminate the training process if there is insufficient reduction in the loss function in two successive iterations.

The tf.keras.optimizers namespace contains the various optimizers that are available for working in conjunction with loss functions, which includes the popular Adam optimizer.

The `tf.keras.regularizers` namespace contains two popular regularizers: the L1 regularizer (also called `LASSO` in machine learning) and the L2 regularizer (also called the `Ridge` regularizer in machine learning). L1 is for mean absolute error (`MAE`) and L2 is for mean squared error (`MSE`).. Both of these regularizers act as "penalty" terms that are added to the chosen cost function in order to reduce the "influence" of features in a machine learning model. Note that `LASSO` can drive values to zero, with the result that features are actually eliminated from a model, and hence is related to something called *feature selection* in machine learning.

The `tf.keras.utils` namespace contains an assortment of functions, including the `to_categorical()` function for converting a class vector into a binary class.

Although there are other namespaces in TF 2, the classes listed in all the preceding subsections will probably suffice for the majority of your tasks if you are a beginner in TF 2 and machine learning.

TF 2 Keras versus "Standalone" Keras

The original `Keras` is actually a specification, with various "backend" frameworks such as TensorFlow, Theano, and CNTK. Currently `Keras` standalone does not support TF 2, whereas the implementation of `Keras` in `tf.keras` has been optimized for performance.

`Keras` standalone will live in perpetuity in the `keras.io` package, which is discussed in detail at the `Keras` Website: `keras.io`.

Now that you have a high-level view of the TF 2 namespaces for `Keras` and the classes that they contain, let's find out how to create a `Keras`-based model, which is the subject of the next section.

Creating a Keras-Based Model

The following list of steps describe the high-level sequence involved in creating, training, and testing a `Keras` model:

Step 1: Determine a model architecture (the number of hidden layers, various activation functions, and so forth).
Step 2: Invoke the `compile()` method.
Step 3: Invoke the `fit()` method to train the model.
Step 4: Invoke the `evaluate()` method to evaluate the trained model.
Step 5: Invoke the `predict()` method to make predictions.

Step 1 involves determining the values of a number of hyperparameters, including the following list:

- the number of hidden layers
- the number of neurons in each hidden layer
- the initial values of the weights of edges
- the cost function
- the optimizer
- the learning rate
- the dropout rate
- the activation function(s)

Steps 2 through 4 involve the training data, whereas step 5 involves the test data, which are included in the following more detailed sequence of steps for the preceding list:

- Specify a dataset (if necessary, convert data to numeric data).
- Split the dataset into training data and test data (usually 80/20 split).
- Define the Keras model (e.g., the `tf.keras.models.Sequential()` API).
- Compile the Keras model (the `compile()` API).
- Train (fit) the Keras model (the `fit()` API).
- Make a prediction (the `prediction()` API).

Note that the preceding bullet items skip some steps that are part of a real `Keras` model, such as evaluating the Keras model on the test data, as well as dealing with issues such as overfitting.

The first bullet item states that you need a dataset, which can be as simple as a `CSV` file with 100 rows of data and just three columns (or even fewer). In general, a dataset is substantially larger: it can be a file with 1,000,000 rows of data and 10,000 columns in each row. We'll look at a concrete dataset in a subsequent section.

Next, a `Keras` model is in the `tf.keras.models` namespace, and the simplest (and also very common) `Keras` model is `tf.keras.models.Sequential`. In general, a `Keras` model contains layers that are in the `tf.keras.layers` namespace, such as `tf.keras.Dense` (which means that two adjacent layers are completely connected).

The activation functions that are referenced in `Keras` layers are in the `tf.nn` namespace, such as the `tf.nn.ReLU` for the `ReLU` activation function.

Here's a code block of the `Keras` model that's described in the preceding paragraphs (which covers the first four bullet points):

```
import tensorflow as tf

model = tf.keras.models.Sequential([
  tf.keras.layers.Dense(512, activation=tf.nn.relu),
])
```

We have three more bullet items to discuss, starting with the compilation step. `Keras` provides a `compile()` API for this step, an example of which is here:

```
model.compile(optimizer='adam',
              loss='sparse_categorical_crossentropy',
              metrics=['accuracy'])
```

Next we need to specify a training step, and `Keras` provides the `fit()` API (as you can see, it's not called `train()`), an example of which is here:

```
model.fit(x_train, y_train, epochs=5)
```

The final step is the prediction that is performed via the `predict()` API, an example of which is here:

```
pred = model.predict(x)
```

Keep in mind that the `evaluate()` method is used for evaluating a trained model, and the output of this method is accuracy or loss. However, the `predict()` method makes predictions from the input data.

Listing D.1 displays the contents of `tf2_basic_keras.py` that combines the code blocks in the preceding steps into a single code sample.

LISTING D.1: tf2_basic_keras.py

```
import tensorflow as tf

# NOTE: we need the train data and test data

model = tf.keras.models.Sequential([
  tf.keras.layers.Dense(1, activation=tf.nn.relu),
])

model.compile(optimizer='adam',
              loss='sparse_categorical_crossentropy',
              metrics=['accuracy'])
```

```
model.fit(x_train, y_train, epochs=5)
model.evaluate(x_test, y_test)
```

Listing D.1 contains no new code, and we've essentially glossed over some of the terms such as the optimizer (an algorithm that is used in conjunction with a cost function), the loss (the type of loss function) and the metrics (how to evaluate the efficacy of a model).

Thorough explanations for these details cannot be condensed into a few paragraphs (alas), but the good news is that you can find a plethora of detailed online blog posts that discuss these terms.

Keras and Linear Regression

This section contains a simple example of creating a Keras-based model in order to solve a task involving linear regression: given a positive number representing kilograms of pasta, predict its corresponding price. Listing D.2 displays the contents of pasta.csv and Listing D.3 displays the contents of keras_pasta.py that performs this task.

LISTING D.2: pasta.csv

```
weight,price
5,30
10,45
15,70
20,80
25,105
30,120
35,130
40,140
50,150
```

LISTING D.3: keras_pasta.py

```
import tensorflow as tf
import numpy as np
import pandas as pd
import matplotlib.pyplot as plt

# price of pasta per kilogram
df = pd.read_csv("pasta.csv")

weight = df['weight']
price  = df['price']

model = tf.keras.models.Sequential([
    tf.keras.layers.Dense(units=1,input_shape=[1])
```

```
])

# MSE loss function and Adam optimizer
model.compile(loss='mean_squared_error',
              optimizer=tf.keras.optimizers.Adam(0.1))

# train the model
history = model.fit(weight, price, epochs=100, verbose=False)

# graph the # of epochs versus the loss
plt.xlabel('Number of Epochs')
plt.ylabel("Loss Values")
plt.plot(history.history['loss'])
plt.show()

print("Cost for 11kg:",model.predict([11.0]))
print("Cost for 45kg:",model.predict([45.0]))
```

Listing D.3 initializes the Pandas data frame df with the contents of the CSV file pasta.csv, and then initializes the variables weight and cost with the first and second columns, respectively, of df.

The next portion of Listing D.3 defines a Keras-based model that consists of a single Dense layer. This model is compiled and trained, and then a graph is displayed that shows the "number of epochs" on the horizontal axis and the corresponding value of the loss function for the vertical axis. Launch the code in Listing D.3 and you will see the following output:

```
Cost for 11kg: [[41.727108]]
Cost for 45kg: [[159.02121]]
```

Figure D.1 displays a graph of epochs versus loss during the training process.

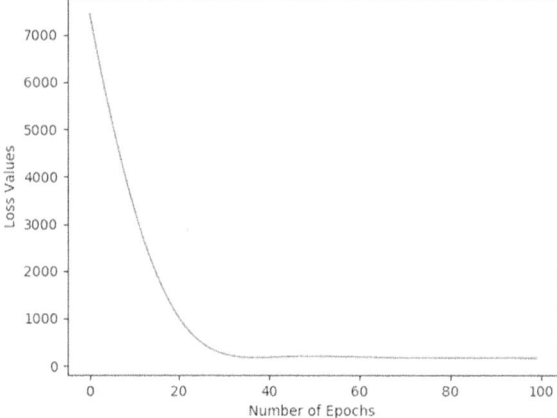

Figure D.1. A Graph of Epochs versus Loss.

Keras, MLPs, and MNIST

This section contains a simple example of creating a `Keras`-based MLP neural network that will be trained with the `MNIST` dataset. Listing D.4 displays the contents of `keras_mlp_mnist.py` that performs this task.

LISTING D.4: keras_mlp_mnist.py

```
import tensorflow as tf
import numpy as np

# instantiate mnist and load data:
mnist = tf.keras.datasets.mnist
(x_train, y_train), (x_test, y_test) = mnist.load_data()

# one-hot encoding for all labels to create 1x10
# vectors that are compared with the final layer:
y_train = tf.keras.utils.to_categorical(y_train)
y_test  = tf.keras.utils.to_categorical(y_test)

image_size = x_train.shape[1]
input_size = image_size * image_size

# resize and normalize the 28x28 images:
x_train = np.reshape(x_train, [-1, input_size])
x_train = x_train.astype('float32') / 255
x_test  = np.reshape(x_test, [-1, input_size])
x_test  = x_test.astype('float32') / 255

# initialize some hyper-parameters:
batch_size = 128
hidden_units = 128
dropout_ratea = 0.20

# define a Keras-based model:
model = tf.keras.models.Sequential()
model.add(tf.keras.layers.Dense(hidden_units, input_dim=input_size))
model.add(tf.keras.layers.Activation('relu'))
model.add(tf.keras.layers.Dropout(dropout_rate))
model.add(tf.keras.layers.Dense(hidden_units))
model.add(tf.keras.layers.Activation('relu'))
model.add(tf.keras.layers.Dense(10))
model.add(tf.keras.layers.Activation('softmax'))

model.summary()

model.compile(loss='categorical_crossentropy',
              optimizer='adam',
              metrics=['accuracy'])
```

```
# train the network on the training data:
model.fit(x_train, y_train, epochs=10, batch_size=batch_size)

# calculate and then display the accuracy:
loss, acc = model.evaluate(x_test, y_test, batch_size=batch_size)
print("\nTest accuracy: %.1f%%" % (100.0 * acc))
```

Listing D.4 contains the usual `import` statements and then initializes the variable `mnist` as a reference to the `MNIST` dataset. The next portion of Listing D.4 contains some typical code that populates the training dataset and the test dataset and converts the labels to numeric values via the technique known as "one-hot" encoding.

Next, several hyperparameters are initialized, and a `Keras`-based model is defined that specifies three `Dense` layers and the `relu` activation function. This model is compiled and trained, and the accuracy on the test dataset is computed and then displayed. Launch the code in Listing D.4 and you will see the following output:

```
Model: "sequential"
_____
Layer (type)                 Output Shape              Param #
=================================================================
dense (Dense)                (None, 256)               200960
_____
activation (Activation)      (None, 256)               0
_____
dropout (Dropout)            (None, 256)               0
_____
dense_1 (Dense)              (None, 256)               65792
_____
activation_1 (Activation)    (None, 256)               0
_____
dropout_1 (Dropout)          (None, 256)               0
_____
dense_2 (Dense)              (None, 10)                2570
_____
activation_2 (Activation)    (None, 10)                0
=================================================================
Total params: 269,322
Trainable params: 269,322
Non-trainable params: 0

Train on 60000 samples
Epoch 1/10
60000/60000 [==============================] - 4s 74us/sample
- loss: 0.4281 - accuracy: 0.8683
Epoch 2/10
60000/60000 [==============================] - 4s 66us/sample
- loss: 0.1967 - accuracy: 0.9417
```

```
Epoch 3/10
60000/60000 [==============================] - 4s 63us/sample
- loss: 0.1507 - accuracy: 0.9547
Epoch 4/10
60000/60000 [==============================] - 4s 63us/sample
- loss: 0.1298 - accuracy: 0.9600
Epoch 5/10
60000/60000 [==============================] - 4s 60us/sample
- loss: 0.1141 - accuracy: 0.9651
Epoch 6/10
60000/60000 [==============================] - 4s 66us/sample
- loss: 0.1037 - accuracy: 0.9677
Epoch 7/10
60000/60000 [==============================] - 4s 61us/sample
- loss: 0.0940 - accuracy: 0.9702
Epoch 8/10
60000/60000 [==============================] - 4s 61us/sample
- loss: 0.0897 - accuracy: 0.9718
Epoch 9/10
60000/60000 [==============================] - 4s 62us/sample
- loss: 0.0830 - accuracy: 0.9747
Epoch 10/10
60000/60000 [==============================] - 4s 64us/sample
- loss: 0.0805 - accuracy: 0.9748
10000/10000 [==============================] - 0s 39us/sample
- loss: 0.0654 - accuracy: 0.9797

Test accuracy: 98.0%
```

Keras, CNNs, and cifar10

This section contains a simple example of training a neural network with the cifar10 dataset. This code sample is similar to training a neural network on the MNIST dataset, and requires a very small code change.

Keep in mind that images in MNIST have dimensions 28×28, whereas images in cifar10 have dimensions 32×32. Always ensure that images have the same dimensions in a dataset, otherwise the results can be unpredictable.

NOTE *Make sure that the images in your dataset all have the same dimensions.*

Listing D.5 displays the contents of keras_cnn_cifar10.py that trains a CNN with the cifar10 dataset.

LISTING D.5: keras_cnn_cifar10.py

```
import tensorflow as tf

batch_size = 32
num_classes = 10
```

```python
epochs = 100
num_predictions = 20

cifar10 = tf.keras.datasets.cifar10

# The data, split between train and test sets:
(x_train, y_train), (x_test, y_test) = cifar10.load_data()
print('x_train shape:', x_train.shape)
print(x_train.shape[0], 'train samples')
print(x_test.shape[0], 'test samples')

# Convert class vectors to binary class matrices
y_train = tf.keras.utils.to_categorical(y_train, num_classes)
y_test = tf.keras.utils.to_categorical(y_test, num_classes)

model = tf.keras.models.Sequential()
model.add(tf.keras.layers.Conv2D(32, (3, 3), padding='same',
                 input_shape=x_train.shape[1:]))

model.add(tf.keras.layers.Activation('relu'))
model.add(tf.keras.layers.Conv2D(32, (3, 3)))
model.add(tf.keras.layers.Activation('relu'))
model.add(tf.keras.layers.MaxPooling2D(pool_size=(2, 2)))
model.add(tf.keras.layers.Dropout(0.25))

# you can also duplicate the preceding code block here

model.add(tf.keras.layers.Flatten())
model.add(tf.keras.layers.Dense(512))
model.add(tf.keras.layers.Activation('relu'))
model.add(tf.keras.layers.Dropout(0.5))
model.add(tf.keras.layers.Dense(num_classes))
model.add(tf.keras.layers.Activation('softmax'))

# use RMSprop optimizer to train the model
model.compile(loss='categorical_crossentropy',
              optimizer=opt,
              metrics=['accuracy'])

x_train = x_train.astype('float32')
x_test = x_test.astype('float32')
x_train /= 255
x_test /= 255

model.fit(x_train, y_train,
          batch_size=batch_size,
          epochs=epochs,
          validation_data=(x_test, y_test),
          shuffle=True)

# evaluate and display results from test data
scores = model.evaluate(x_test, y_test, verbose=1)
```

```
print('Test loss:', scores[0])
print('Test accuracy:', scores[1])
```

Listing D.5 contains the usual `import` statement and then initializes the variable `cifar10` as a reference to the `cifar10` dataset. The next section of code is similar to the contents of Listing D.4, however the main difference is that this `Keras`-based model defines a CNN instead of an MLP. Hence, the first layer is a convolutional layer, as shown here:

```
model.add(tf.keras.layers.Conv2D(32, (3, 3), padding='same',
                input_shape=x_train.shape[1:]))
```

Note that a generic CNN involves a convolutional layer (which is the purpose of the preceding code snippet), followed by the `ReLU` activation function, and a max pooling layer, both of which are displayed in Listing D.5. In addition, the final layer of the `Keras` model is the `softmax` activation function, which converts the ten numeric values in the "fully connected" layer to a set of ten nonnegative numbers between 0 and 1, whose sum equals 1 (this gives us a probability distribution).

This model is compiled and trained, and then evaluated on the test dataset. The last portion of Listing D.5 displays the value of the test-related loss and accuracy, both of which are calculated during the preceding evaluation step. Launch the code in Listing D.5 and you will see the following output. (Note that the code was stopped after partially completing the second epoch.)

```
x_train shape: (50000, 32, 32, 3)
50000 train samples
10000 test samples

Epoch 1/100
50000/50000 [==============================] - 285s 6ms/sample
- loss: 1.7187 - accuracy: 0.3802 - val_loss: 1.4294 - val_
accuracy: 0.4926
Epoch 2/100
 1888/50000 [>.............................] - ETA: 4:39 -
loss: 1.4722 - accuracy: 0.4635
```

Resizing Images in Keras

Listing D.6 displays the contents of `keras_resize_image.py` that illustrates how to resize an image in `Keras`.

LISTING D.6: keras_resize_image.py

```
import tensorflow as tf
```

```
import numpy as np
import imageio
import matplotlib.pyplot as plt

# use any image that has 3 channels
inp = tf.keras.layers.Input(shape=(None, None, 3))
out = tf.keras.layers.Lambda(lambda image: tf.image.
resize(image, (128, 128)))(inp)

model = tf.keras.Model(inputs=inp, outputs=out)
model.summary()

# read the contents of a PNG or JPG
X = imageio.imread('sample3.png')

out = model.predict(X[np.newaxis, ...])

fig, axes = plt.subplots(nrows=1, ncols=2)
axes[0].imshow(X)
axes[1].imshow(np.int8(out[0,...]))

plt.show()
```

Listing D.6 contains the usual `import` statements and then initializes the variable `inp` so that it can accommodate a color image, followed by the variable `out` that is the result of resizing `inp` so that it has dimensions 28×23. Next, `inp` and `out` are specified as the values of `inputs` and `outputs`, respectively, for the Keras model, as shown in this code snippet:

```
model = tf.keras.Model(inputs=inp, outputs=out)
```

Next, the variable X is initialized as a reference to the result of reading the contents of the image `sample3.png`. The remainder of Listing D.6 involves displaying two images: the original image and the resized image. Launch the code in Listing D.6 and you will see a graph of an image and its resized image as shown in Figure D.2.

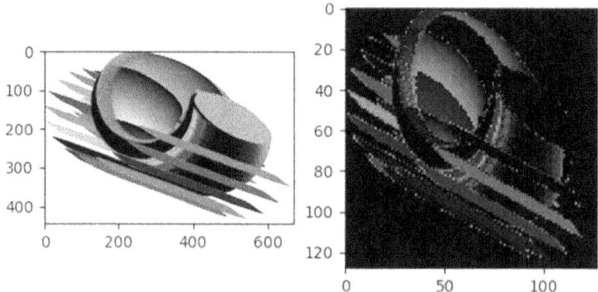

Figure D.2 A Graph of an Image and its Resized Image.

Keras and Early Stopping (1)

After specifying the training set and the test set from a dataset, you also decide on the number of training epochs. A value that's too large can lead to overfitting, whereas a value that's too small can lead to underfitting. Moreover, model improvement can diminish and subsequent training iterations become redundant.

Early stopping is a technique that allows you to specify a large value for the number of epochs, and yet the training will stop if the model performance improvement drops below a threshold value.

There are several ways that you can specify early stopping, and they involve the concept of a *callback function*. Listing D.7 displays the contents of tf2_keras_callback.py that performs early stopping via a callback mechanism.

LISTING D.7: tf2_keras_callback.py

```
import tensorflow as tf
import numpy as np

model = tf.keras.Sequential()
model.add(tf.keras.layers.Dense(64, activation='relu'))
model.add(tf.keras.layers.Dense(64, activation='relu'))
model.add(tf.keras.layers.Dense(10, activation='softmax'))

model.compile(optimizer=tf.keras.optimizers.Adam(0.01),
              loss='mse',       # mean squared error
              metrics=['mae'])  # mean absolute error

data   = np.random.random((1000, 32))
labels = np.random.random((1000, 10))

val_data   = np.random.random((100, 32))
val_labels = np.random.random((100, 10))

callbacks = [
  # stop training if "val_loss" stops improving for over 2
    epochs
  tf.keras.callbacks.EarlyStopping(patience=2,
  monitor='val_loss'),
  # write TensorBoard logs to the ./logs directory
  tf.keras.callbacks.TensorBoard(log_dir='./logs')
]

model.fit(data, labels, batch_size=32, epochs=50,
callbacks=callbacks,
```

```
            validation_data=(val_data, val_labels))
model.evaluate(data, labels, batch_size=32)
```

Listing D.7 defines a `Keras`-based model with three hidden layers and then compiles the model. The next portion of Listing D.7 uses the `np.random.random` function in order to initialize the variables `data`, `labels`, `val_data`, and `val_labels`.

The interesting code involves the definition of the `callbacks` variable that specifies `tf.keras.callbacks.EarlyStopping` class with a value of 2 for `patience`, which means that the model will stop training if there is an insufficient reduction in the value of `val_loss`. The `callbacks` variable includes the class `tf.keras.callbacks.TensorBoard` to specify the logs subdirectory as the location for the `TensorBoard` files.

Next, the `model.fit()` method is invoked with a value of 50 for epochs (shown in bold), followed by the `model.evaluate()` method. Launch the code in Listing D.7 and you will see the following output:

```
Epoch 1/50
1000/1000 [==============================] - 0s 354us/sample
- loss: 0.2452 - mae: 0.4127 - val_loss: 0.2517 - val_mae:
0.4205
Epoch 2/50
1000/1000 [==============================] - 0s 63us/sample
- loss: 0.2447 - mae: 0.4125 - val_loss: 0.2515 - val_mae:
0.4204
Epoch 3/50
1000/1000 [==============================] - 0s 63us/sample
- loss: 0.2445 - mae: 0.4124 - val_loss: 0.2520 - val_mae:
0.4209
Epoch 4/50
1000/1000 [==============================] - 0s 68us/sample
- loss: 0.2444 - mae: 0.4123 - val_loss: 0.2519 - val_mae:
0.4205
1000/1000 [==============================] - 0s 37us/sample -
loss: 0.2437 - mae: 0.4119
(1000, 10)
```

Notice that the code stopped training after four epochs, even though 50 epochs are specified in the code.

Keras and Early Stopping (2)

The previous section contains a code sample with minimalistic functionality with respect to the use of callback functions in `Keras`. However, you can also define a custom class that provides finer-grained functionality that uses a callback mechanism.

Listing D.8 displays the contents of tf2_keras_callback2.py that performs early stopping via a callback mechanism (the new code is shown in bold).

LISTING D.8: *tf2_keras_callback2.py*

```
import tensorflow as tf
import numpy as np

model = tf.keras.Sequential()
model.add(tf.keras.layers.Dense(64, activation='relu'))
model.add(tf.keras.layers.Dense(64, activation='relu'))
model.add(tf.keras.layers.Dense(10, activation='softmax'))

model.compile(optimizer=tf.keras.optimizers.Adam(0.01),
              loss='mse',       # mean squared error
              metrics=['mae'])  # mean absolute error

data   = np.random.random((1000, 32))
labels = np.random.random((1000, 10))

val_data   = np.random.random((100, 32))
val_labels = np.random.random((100, 10))

class MyCallback(tf.keras.callbacks.Callback):
  def on_train_begin(self, logs={}):
    print("on_train_begin")

  def on_train_end(self, logs={}):
    print("on_train_begin")
    return

  def on_epoch_begin(self, epoch, logs={}):
    print("on_train_begin")
    return

  def on_epoch_end(self, epoch, logs={}):
    print("on_epoch_end")
    return

  def on_batch_begin(self, batch, logs={}):
    print("on_batch_begin")
    return

  def on_batch_end(self, batch, logs={}):
    print("on_batch_end")
    return
```

```
callbacks = [MyCallback()]
model.fit(data, labels, batch_size=32, epochs=50,
callbacks=callbacks,
          validation_data=(val_data, val_labels))
model.evaluate(data, labels, batch_size=32)
```

The new code in Listing D.8 differs from Listing D.7 in that it is limited to the code block that is displayed in bold in Listing D.8. This new code defines a custom `Python` class with several methods, each of which is invoked during the appropriate point during the `Keras` lifecycle execution. The six methods consists of three pairs of methods for the start event and end event associated with training, epochs, and batches, as listed here:

- `def on_train_begin()`
- `def on_train_end()`
- `def on_epoch_begin()`
- `def on_epoch_end()`
- `def on_batch_begin()`
- `def on_batch_end()`

The preceding methods contain just a `print()` statement in Listing D.8, and you can insert any code you wish in any of these methods. Launch the code in Listing D.8 and you will see the following output:

```
on_train_begin
on_train_begin
Epoch 1/50
on_batch_begin
on_batch_end
  32/1000 [..............................] - ETA: 4s - loss:
0.2489 - mae: 0.4170on_batch_begin
on_batch_end
on_batch_begin on_batch_end
// details omitted for brevity
on_batch_begin
on_batch_end
on_batch_begin
on_batch_end
992/1000 [=============================>.] - ETA: 0s - loss:
0.2468 - mae: 0.4138on_batch_begin
on_batch_end
on_epoch_end
```

```
1000/1000 [==============================] - 0s 335us/sample
- loss: 0.2466 - mae: 0.4136 - val_loss: 0.2445 - val_mae:
0.4126
on_train_begin
Epoch 2/50
on_batch_begin
on_batch_end
  32/1000 [..............................] - ETA: 0s - loss:
0.2465 - mae: 0.4133on_batch_begin
on_batch_end
on_batch_begin
on_batch_end
// details omitted for brevity
on_batch_end
on_epoch_end
1000/1000 [==============================] - 0s 51us/sample
- loss: 0.2328 - mae: 0.4084 - val_loss: 0.2579 - val_mae:
0.4241
on_train_begin
  32/1000 [..............................] - ETA: 0s - loss:
0.2295 - mae: 0.4030
1000/1000 [==============================] - 0s 22us/sample -
loss: 0.2313 - mae: 0.4077
(1000, 10)
```

Keras and Metrics

Many `Keras`-based models only specify "accuracy" as the metric for evaluating a trained model, as shown here:

```
model.compile(optimizer='adam',
              loss='sparse_categorical_crossentropy',
              metrics=['accuracy'])
```

However, there are many other built-in metrics available, each of which is encapsulated in a `Keras` class in the `tf.keras.metrics` namespace. An inventory of many such metrics are displayed in the following list:

- class Accuracy: how often predictions match labels
- class BinaryAccuracy: how often predictions match labels
- class CategoricalAccuracy: how often predictions match labels
- class FalseNegatives: the number of false negatives
- class FalsePositives: the number of false positives
- class Mean: the (weighted) mean of the given values
- class Precision: the precision of the predictions wrt the labels

- class Recall: the recall of the predictions wrt the labels
- class TrueNegatives: the number of true negatives
- class TruePositives: the number of true positives

Earlier in this chapter you learned about the "confusion matrix" that provides numeric values for TP, TN, FP, and FN; each of these values has a corresponding Keras class TruePositive, TrueNegative, FalsePositive, and FalseNegative, respectively. Perform an online search for code samples that use the metrics in the preceding list.

Saving and Restoring Keras Models

Listing D.9 displays the contents of tf2_keras_save_model.py that creates, trains, and saves a Keras-based model, then creates a new model that is populated with the data from the saved model.

LISTING D.9: tf2_keras_save_model.py

```
import tensorflow as tf
import os
def create_model():
  model = tf.keras.models.Sequential([
    tf.keras.layers.Flatten(input_shape=(28, 28)),
    tf.keras.layers.Dense(512, activation=tf.nn.relu),
    tf.keras.layers.Dropout(0.2),
    tf.keras.layers.Dense(10, activation=tf.nn.softmax)
  ])

  model.compile(optimizer=tf.keras.optimizers.Adam(),
         loss=tf.keras.losses.sparse_categorical_
         crossentropy,metrics=['accuracy'])

  return model

# Create a basic model instance
model = create_model()
model.summary()

checkpoint_path = "checkpoint/cp.ckpt"
checkpoint_dir = os.path.dirname(checkpoint_path)

# Create checkpoint callback
cp_callback = tf.keras.callbacks.ModelCheckpoint(checkpoint_
         path, save_weights_only=True, verbose=1)
```

```
# => model #1: create the first model
model = create_model()

mnist = tf.keras.datasets.mnist
(X_train, y_train),(X_test, y_test) = mnist.load_data()

X_train, X_test = X_train / 255.0, X_test / 255.0
print("X_train.shape:",X_train.shape)

model.fit(X_train, y_train,  epochs = 2,
          validation_data = (X_test,y_test),
          callbacks = [cp_callback])
          # pass callback to training

# => model #2: create a new model and load saved model
model = create_model()
loss, acc = model.evaluate(X_test, y_test)
print("Untrained model, accuracy: {:5.2f}%".format(100*acc))

model.load_weights(checkpoint_path)
loss,acc = model.evaluate(X_test, y_test)
print("Restored model, accuracy: {:5.2f}%".format(100*acc))
```

Listing D.8 starts with the create_model() Python function that creates and compiles a Keras-based model. The next portion of Listing D.8 defines the location of the file that will be saved as well as the checkpoint callback, as shown here:

```
checkpoint_path = "checkpoint/cp.ckpt"
checkpoint_dir = os.path.dirname(checkpoint_path)

# Create checkpoint callback
cp_callback = tf.keras.callbacks.ModelCheckpoint(checkpoint_
path, save_weights_only=True, verbose=1)
```

The next portion of Listing D.8 trains the current model using the MNIST dataset, and also specifies cp_callback so that the model can be saved.

The final code block in Listing D.8 creates a new Keras-based model by invoking the Python method create_model() again, evaluating this new model on the test-related data, and displaying the value of the accuracy. Next, the model is loaded with the saved model weights via the load_weights() API. The relevant code block is reproduced here:

```
model = create_model()
loss, acc = model.evaluate(X_test, y_test)
print("Untrained model, accuracy: {:5.2f}%".format(100*acc))

model.load_weights(checkpoint_path)
```

```
loss,acc = model.evaluate(X_test, y_test)
print("Restored model, accuracy: {:5.2f}%".format(100*acc))
```
Now launch the code in Listing D.8 and you will see the following output:
```
on_train_begin
Model: "sequential"
_____
Layer (type)                 Output Shape              Param #
=================================================================
flatten (Flatten)            (None, 784)               0
_____
dense (Dense)                (None, 512)               401920
_____
dropout (Dropout)            (None, 512)               0
_____
dense_1 (Dense)              (None, 10)                5130
=================================================================
Total params: 407,050
Trainable params: 407,050
Non-trainable params: 0

Train on 60000 samples, validate on 10000 samples
Epoch 1/2
59840/60000 [=============================>.] - ETA:
0s - loss: 0.2173 - accuracy: 0.9351
Epoch 00001: saving model to checkpoint/cp.ckpt
60000/60000 [==============================] - 10s 168us/
sample - loss: 0.2170 - accuracy: 0.9352 - val_loss:
0.0980 - val_accuracy: 0.9696
Epoch 2/2
59936/60000 [=============================>.] - ETA:
0s - loss: 0.0960 - accuracy: 0.9707
Epoch 00002: saving model to checkpoint/cp.ckpt
60000/60000 [==============================] - 10s 174us/
sample - loss: 0.0959 - accuracy: 0.9707 - val_loss:
0.0735 - val_accuracy: 0.9761
10000/10000 [==============================] -
1s 86us/sample - loss: 2.3986 - accuracy: 0.0777
Untrained model, accuracy:  7.77%
10000/10000 [==============================] -
1s 67us/sample - loss: 0.0735 - accuracy: 0.9761
Restored model, accuracy: 97.61%
```

The directory where you launched this code sample contains a new subdirectory called `checkpoint` whose contents are shown here:

```
-rw-r--r--  1 owner   staff      1222 Aug 17 14:34 cp.ckpt.index
-rw-r--r--  1 owner   staff   4886716 Aug 17 14:34 cp.ckpt.data-00000-of-00001
-rw-r--r--  1 owner   staff        71 Aug 17 14:34 checkpoint
```

Summary

This appendix introduced you to some of the features of `Keras` and an assortment of `Keras`-based code samples involving basic neural networks with the `MNIST` and `cifar10` datasets. You learned about some of the important namespaces (such as `tf.keras.layers`) and their contents.

Next, you saw an example of performing linear regression with `Keras` and a simple `CSV` file. Then you learned how to create a `Keras`-based MLP neural network that is trained on the `MNIST` dataset.

In addition, you saw examples of `Keras`-based models that perform "early stopping," which is convenient when the model exhibits minimal improvement (that is specified by you) during the training process.

APPENDIX E

INTRODUCTION TO TENSORFLOW 2

Welcome to TensorFlow 2! This appendix introduces you to various features of TensorFlow 2 (abbreviated as TF 2), as well as some of the TF 2 tools and projects that are covered under the TF 2 "umbrella." You will see TF 2 code samples that illustrate new TF 2 features (such as tf.GradientTape and the @tf.function decorator), plus an assortment of code samples that illustrate how to write code "the TF 2 way." Despite the simplicity of many topics in this appendix, they provide you with a foundation for TF 2.

Keep in mind that the TensorFlow 1.x releases are considered legacy code after the production release of TF 2. Google will provide only security-related updates for TF 1.x (i.e., no new code development), and support TensorFlow 1.x for at least another year beyond the initial production release of TF 2. For your convenience, TensorFlow provides a conversion script to facilitate the automatic conversion of TensorFlow 1.x code to TF 2 code in many cases (details provided later in this appendix).

As you saw in the Preface, this appendix contains several sections regarding TF 1.x, all of which are placed near the end of this appendix. If you do not have TF 1.x code, obviously these sections are optional (and they are labeled as such).

The first part of this appendix briefly discusses some TF 2 features and some of the tools that are included under the TF 2 "umbrella." The second section of this appendix shows you how to write TF 2 code involving TF constants and TF variables.

The third section digresses a bit: you will learn about the new TF 2 `Python` function decorator `@tf.function` that is used in many code samples in this appendix. Although this decorator is not always required, it's important to become comfortable with this feature, and there are some nonintuitive caveats regarding its use that are discussed in this section.

The fourth section of this appendix shows you how to perform typical arithmetic operations in TF 2, how to use some of the built-in TF 2 functions, and how to calculate trigonometric values. If you need to perform scientific calculations, see the code samples that pertain to the type of precision that you can achieve with floating point numbers in TF 2. This section also shows you how to use `for` loops and how to calculate exponential values.

The fifth section contains TF 2 code samples involving arrays, such as creating an identity matrix, a constant matrix, a random uniform matrix, and a truncated normal matrix, along with an explanation about the difference between a truncated matrix and a random matrix. This section also shows you how to multiply second-order tensors in TF 2 and how to convert `Python` arrays to second-order tensors in TF 2. The sixth section contains code samples that illustrate how to use some of the new features of TF 2, such as `tf.GradientTape`. Although the TF 2 code samples in this book use `Python` 3.x, it's possible to modify the code samples in order to run under `Python` 2.7.

NOTE *As this book goes to print, `Python` 3.7 works with the TF 2 code in this book, whereas Python 3.9.x does not work with TF 2.*

With all the preceding points in mind, the next section discusses a few details of TF 2, its architecture, and some of its features.

What is TF 2?

TF 2 is an open source framework from Google and the newest version of TensorFlow. The TF 2 framework is a modern framework that's well-suited for machine learning and deep learning, and it's available through an Apache license. Interestingly, TensorFlow surprised many people, perhaps even members of the TF team, in terms of the creativity and plethora of use cases for TF in areas such as art, music, and medicine. For a variety of reasons, the TensorFlow team created TF 2 with the goal of consolidating the TF APIs, eliminating duplication of APIs, enabling rapid prototyping, and making debugging an easier experience.

There is good news if you are a fan of Keras: improvements in TF 2 are partially due to the adoption of Keras as part of the core functionality of TF 2. In fact, TF 2 extends and optimizes Keras so that it can take advantage of all the advanced features in TF 2.

If you work primarily with deep learning models (CNNs, RNNs, LSTMs, and so forth), you'll probably use some of the classes in the tf.keras namespace, which is the implementation of Keras in TF 2. Moreover, tf.keras.layers provides several standard layers for neural networks. As you'll see later, there are several ways to define Keras-based models, via the tf.keras.Sequential class, a functional style definition, and via a subclassing technique. Alternatively, you can still use lower-level operations and automatic differentiation if you wish to do so.

Furthermore, TF 2 removes duplicate functionality, provides a more intuitive syntax across APIs, and also compatibility throughout the TF 2 ecosystem. TF 2 even provides a backward compatibility module called tf.compat.v1 (which does not include tf.contrib), and a conversion script tf_upgrade_v2 to help users migrate from TF 1.x to TF 2.

Another significant change in TF 2 is eager execution as the default mode (not deferred execution), with new features such as the @tf.function decorator and TF 2 privacy-related features. Here is a condensed list of some TF 2 features and related technologies:

- support for tf.keras: a specification for high-level code for ML and DL
- tensorflow.js v1.0: TF in modern browsers
- TensorFlow Federated: an open source framework for ML and decentralized data
- ragged Tensors: nested variable-length ("uneven") lists
- TensorFlow Probability: probabilistic models combined with deep learning
- Tensor2Tensor: a library of DL models and datasets

TF 2 also supports a variety of programming languages and hardware platforms, including:

- support for Python, Java, C++
- desktop, server, mobile device (TF Lite)
- CPU/GPU/TPU support

- Linux and Mac OS X support
- VM for Windows

Navigate to the TF 2 home page, where you will find links to many resources for TF 2: *https://www.tensorflow.org*

TF 2 Use Cases

TF 2 is designed to solve tasks that arise in a plethora of use cases, some of which are listed here:

- image recognition
- computer vision
- voice/sound recognition
- time series analysis
- language detection
- language translation
- text-based processing
- handwriting recognition

The preceding list of use cases can be solved in TF 1.x as well as TF 2, and in the latter case, the code tends to be simpler and cleaner compared to their TF 1.x counterpart.

TF 2 Architecture: The Short Version

TF 2 is written in C++ and supports operations involving primitive values and tensors (discussed later). The default execution mode for TF 1.x is *deferred execution* whereas TF 2 uses *eager execution* (think "immediate mode"). Although TF 1.4 introduced eager execution, the vast majority of TF 1.x code samples that you will find online use deferred execution.

TF 2 supports arithmetic operations on tensors (i.e., multi-dimensional arrays with enhancements) as well as conditional logic, "for" loops, and "while" loops. Although it's possible to switch between eager execution mode and deferred mode in TF 2, all the code samples in this book use eager execution mode.

Data visualization is handled via `TensorBoard` that is included as part of TF 2. As you will see in the code samples in this book, TF 2 APIs are available in `Python` and can therefore be embedded in `Python` scripts.

So, enough already with the high-level introduction: let's learn how to install TF 2, which is the topic of the next section.

TF 2 Installation

Install TensorFlow by issuing the following command from the command line:

```
Pip3 install tensorflow
```

If you want to install a specific version (let's say version 2.3) of TF 2, type the following command:

```
Pip3 install --upgrade tensorflow==2.3
```

You can also downgrade the installed version: `pip3` will uninstall your current version and install the version that you specified (i.e., 2.4).

As a sanity check, create a `Python` script with the following three line of code to determine the version number of TF that is installed on your machine:

```
import tensorflow as tf
print("TF Version:",tf.__version__)
print("eager execution:",tf.executing_eagerly())
```

Launch the preceding code and you ought to see something similar to the following output:

```
TF version: 2.0.0-beta1
eager execution: True
```

As a simple example of TF 2 code, place this code snippet in a text file:

```
import tensorflow as tf
print("1 + 2 + 3 + 4 =", tf.reduce_sum([1, 2, 3, 4]))
```

Launch the preceding code from the command line and you should see the following output:

```
1 + 2 + 3 + 4 = tf.Tensor(10, shape=(), dtype=int32)
```

TF 2 and the Python REPL

In case you aren't already familiar with the `Python REPL` (read-eval-print-loop), it's accessible by opening a command shell and then typing the following command:

```
python
```

As a simple illustration, access TF 2-related functionality in the `REPL` by importing the TF 2 library as follows:

```
>>> import tensorflow as tf
```

Now check the version of TF 2 that is installed on your machine with this command:

```
>>> print('TF version:',tf.__version__)
```

The output of the preceding code snippet is shown here (the number that you see depends on which version of TF 2 that you installed):

```
TF version: 2.0.0-beta1
```

Although the `REPL` is useful for short code blocks, the TF 2 code samples in this book are `Python` scripts that you can launch with the `c` executable.

Other TF 2-Based Toolkits

In addition to providing support for TF 2-based code on multiple devices, TF 2 also provides the following toolkits:

- TensorBoard for visualization (included as part of TensorFlow)
- TensorFlow Serving (hosting on a server)
- TensorFlow Hub
- TensorFlow Lite (for mobile applications)
- Tensorflow.js (for Web pages and NodeJS)

TensorBoard is a graph visualization tool that runs in a browser. Launch TensorBoard from the command line as follows: open a command shell and type the following command to access a saved TF graph in the subdirectory `/tmp/abc` (or a directory of your choice):

```
tensorboard -logdir /tmp/abc
```

Note that there are two consecutive dashes ("-") that precede the `logdir` parameter in the preceding command. Now launch a browser session and navigate to this URL: `localhost:6006`

After a few moments you will see a visualization of the TF 2 graph that was created in your code and then saved in the directory `/tmp/abc`.

TensorFlow Serving is a cloud-based flexible, high-performance serving system for machine learning models that is designed for production environments. TensorFlow Serving makes it easy to deploy new algorithms and experiments, while keeping the same server architecture and APIs. More information is here: *https://www.TF 2.org/serving/*

TensorFlow Lite was specifically created for mobile development (both Android and iOS). Please keep in mind that TensorFlow Lite supersedes TF 2 Mobile, which was an earlier SDK for developing mobile applications. TensorFlow Lite supports on-device ML inference with low latency and a small binary size. Moreover, TensorFlow Lite supports hardware acceleration with the Android Neural Networks API. More information about TensorFlow Lite is here:

https://www.tensorflow.org/lite/

Another addition is tensorflow.js that provides JavaScript APIs to access TensorFlow in a Web page. The tensorflow.js toolkit was previously called deeplearning.js. You can also use tensorflow.js with NodeJS. More information about tensorflow.js is here: *https://js.tensorflow.org*

TF 2 Eager Execution

TF 2 eager execution mode makes TF 2 code much easier to write compared to TF 1.x code (which used deferred execution mode). You might be surprised to discover that TF introduced "eager execution" as an alternative to deferred execution in version 1.4.1, but this feature was vastly underutilized. With TF 1.x code, TensorFlow creates a dataflow graph that consists of (a) a set of tf.Operation objects that represent units of computation, and (b) tf.Tensor objects that represent the units of data that flow between operations.

However, TF 2 evaluates operations immediately without instantiating a Session object or a creating a graph. Operations return concrete values instead of creating a computational graph. TF 2 eager execution is based on Python control flow instead of graph control flow. Arithmetic operations are simpler and intuitive, as you will see in code samples later in this appendix. Moreover, TF 2 eager execution mode simplifies the debugging process. However, keep in mind that there isn't a 1:1 relationship between a graph and eager execution.

TF 2 Tensors, Data Types, and Primitive Types

In simplified terms, a TF 2 tensor is an n-dimensional array that is similar to a NumPy ndarray. A TF 2 tensor is defined by its dimensionality, as illustrated here:

scalar number: a zeroth-order tensor
vector: a first-order tensor
matrix: a second-order tensor
3-dimensional array: a 3rd order tensor

The next section discusses some of the data types that are available in TF 2, followed by a section that discusses TF 2 primitive types.

TF 2 Data Types

TF 2 supports the following data types (similar to the supported data types in TensorFlow 1.x):

- tf.float32
- tf.float64
- tf.int8
- tf.int16
- tf.int32
- tf.int64
- tf.uint8
- tf.string
- tf.bool

The data types in the preceding list are self-explanatory: two floating point types, four integer types, one unsigned integer type, one string type, and one Boolean type. As you can see, there is a 32-bit and a 64-bit floating point type, and integer types that range from 8-bit through 64-bit.

TF 2 Primitive Types

TF 2 supports `tf.constant()` and `tf.Variable()` as primitive types. Notice the capital "V" in `tf.Variable()`: this indicates a TF 2 class (which is not the case for lowercase initial letter such as `tf.constant()`).

A TF 2 *constant* is an immutable value, and a simple example is shown here:

```
aconst = tf.constant(3.0)
```

A TF 2 *variable* is a "trainable value" in a TF 2 graph. For example, the slope m and y-intercept b of a best-fitting line for a dataset consisting of points in the Euclidean plane are two examples of trainable values. Some examples of TF variables are shown here:

```
b = tf.Variable(3, name="b")
x = tf.Variable(2, name="x")
z = tf.Variable(5*x, name="z")

W = tf.Variable(20)
lm = tf.Variable(W*x + b, name="lm")
```

Notice that b, x, and z are defined as TF variables. In addition, b and x are initialized with numeric values, whereas the value of the variable z is an expression that depends on the value of x (which equals 2).

Constants in TF 2

Here is a short list of some properties of TF 2 constants:

- initialized during their definition
- cannot change its value ("immutable")
- can specify its name (optional)
- the type is required (ex: tf.float32)
- not modified during training

Listing E.1 displays the contents of tf2_constants1.py that illustrates how to assign and print the values of some TF 2 constants.

LISTING E.1: tf2_constants1.py

```
import tensorflow as tf

scalar = tf.constant(10)
vector = tf.constant([1,2,3,4,5])
matrix = tf.constant([[1,2,3],[4,5,6]])
cube   = tf.constant([[[1],[2],[3]],[[4],[5],[6]],[[7],[8],[9]]])

print(scalar.get_shape())
print(vector.get_shape())
print(matrix.get_shape())
print(cube.get_shape())
```

Listing E.1 contains four tf.constant() statements that define TF 2 tensors of dimension 0, 1, 2, and 3, respectively. The second part of Listing

E.1 contains four `print()` statements that display the shape of the four TF 2 constants that are defined in the first section of Listing E.1. The output from Listing E.1 is here:

```
()
(5,)
(2, 3)
(3, 3, 1)
```

Listing E.2 displays the contents of `tf2_constants2.py` that illustrates how to assign values to TF 2 constants and then print those values.

LISTING E.2: tf2_constants2.py

```
import tensorflow as tf

x = tf.constant(5,name="x")
y = tf.constant(8,name="y")

@tf.function
def calc_prod(x, y):
  z = 2*x + 3*y
  return z

result = calc_prod(x, y)
print('result =',result)
```

Listing E.2 defines a "decorated" (shown in bold) `Python` function `calc_prod()` with TF 2 code that would otherwise be included in a TF 1.x `tf.Session()` code block. Specifically, `z` would be included in a `sess.run()` statement, along with a `feed_dict` that provides values for `x` and `y`. Fortunately, a decorated `Python` function in TF 2 makes the code look like "normal" `Python` code.

Variables in TF 2

TF 2.0 eliminates global collections and their associated APIs, such as `tf.get_variable`, `tf.variable_scope`, and `tf.initializers.global_variables`. Whenever you need a `tf.Variable` in TF 2, construct and initialize it directly, as shown here:

```
tf.Variable(tf.random.normal([2, 4]))
```

Listing E.3 displays the contents of `tf2_variables.py` that illustrates how to compute values involving TF constants and variables in a `with` code block.

LISTING E.3: tf2_variables.py

```
import tensorflow as tf

v = tf.Variable([[1., 2., 3.], [4., 5., 6.]])
print("v.value():", v.value())
print("")
print("v.numpy():", v.numpy())
print("")

v.assign(2 * v)
v[0, 1].assign(42)
v[1].assign([7., 8., 9.])
print("v:",v)
print("")

try:
  v[1] = [7., 8., 9.]
except TypeError as ex:
  print(ex)
```

Listing E.3 defines a TF 2 variable v and prints its value. The next portion of Listing E.3 updates the value of v and prints its new value. The last portion of Listing E.3 contains a try/except block that attempts to update the value of v[1]. The output from Listing E.3 is here:

```
v.value(): tf.Tensor(
[[1. 2. 3.]
 [4. 5. 6.]], shape=(2, 3), dtype=float32)

v.numpy(): [[1. 2. 3.]
 [4. 5. 6.]]

v: <tf.Variable 'Variable:0' shape=(2, 3) dtype=float32, numpy=
array([[ 2., 42.,  6.],
       [ 7.,  8.,  9.]], dtype=float32)>

"ResourceVariable" object does not support item assignment
```

This concludes the quick tour involving TF 2 code that contains various combinations of TF constants and TF variables. The next few sections delve into more details regarding the TF primitive types than what appeared in the preceding sections.

The `tf.rank()` API

The *rank* of a TF 2 tensor is the dimensionality of the tensor, whereas the *shape* of a tensor is the number of elements in each dimension. Listing

E.4 displays the contents of tf2_rank.py that illustrates how to find the rank of TF 2 tensors.

LISTING E.4: tf2_rank.py

```
import tensorflow as tf # tf2_rank.py

A = tf.constant(3.0)
B = tf.fill([2,3], 5.0)
C = tf.constant([3.0, 4.0])

@tf.function
def show_rank(x):
  return tf.rank(x)

print('A:',show_rank(A))
print('B:',show_rank(B))
print('C:',show_rank(C))
```

Listing E.4 contains familiar code for defining the TF constant A, followed by the TF tensor B, which is a 2×3 tensor in which every element has the value 5. The TF tensor C is a 1×2 tensor with the values 3.0 and 4.0.

The next code block defines the decorated Python function show_rank() that returns the rank of its input variable. The final section invokes show_rank() with A and then with B. The output from Listing E.4 is here:

```
A: tf.Tensor(0, shape=(), dtype=int32)
B: tf.Tensor(2, shape=(), dtype=int32)
C: tf.Tensor(1, shape=(), dtype=int32)
```

The tf.shape() API

The *shape* of a TF 2 tensor is the number of elements in each dimension of a given tensor. Listing E.5 displays the contents of tf2_getshape.py that illustrates how to find the shape of TF 2 tensors.

LISTING E.5: tf2_getshape.py

```
import tensorflow as tf

a = tf.constant(3.0)
print("a shape:",a.get_shape())

b = tf.fill([2,3], 5.0)
print("b shape:",b.get_shape())
```

```
c = tf.constant([[1.0,2.0,3.0], [4.0,5.0,6.0]])
print("c shape:",c.get_shape())
```

Listing E.5 contains the definition of the TF constant a whose value is 3.0. Next, the TF variable b is initialized as a 1×2 vector with the value [[2,3], 5.0], followed by the constant c whose value is [[1.0,2.0,3.0],[4.0,5.0,6.0]]. The three print() statements display the values of a, b, and c. The output from Listing E.5 is here:

```
a shape: ()
b shape: (2, 3)
c shape: (2, 3)
```

Shapes that specify a 0-D Tensor (scalar) are numbers (9, -5, 2.34, and so forth), [], and (). As another example, Listing E.6 displays the contents of tf2_shapes.py that contains an assortment of tensors and their shapes.

LISTING E.6: tf2_shapes.py

```
import tensorflow as tf

list_0 = []
tuple_0 = ()
print("list_0:",list_0)
print("tuple_0:",tuple_0)

list_1 = [3]
tuple_1 = (3)
print("list_1:",list_1)
print("tuple_1:",tuple_1)

list_2 = [3, 7]
tuple_2 = (3, 7)
print("list_2:",list_2)
print("tuple_2:",tuple_2)

any_list1  = [None]
any_tuple1 = (None)
print("any_list1:",any_list1)
print("any_tuple1:",any_tuple1)

any_list2 = [7,None]
any_list3 = [7,None,None]
print("any_list2:",any_list2)
print("any_list3:",any_list3)
```

Listing E.6 contains simple lists and tuples of various dimensions in order to illustrate the difference between these two types. The output from Listing E.6 is probably what you would expect, and it's shown here:

```
list_0: []
tuple_0: ()
list_1: [3]
tuple_1: 3
list_2: [3, 7]
tuple_2: (3, 7)
any_list1: [None]
any_tuple1: None
any_list2: [7, None]
any_list3: [7, None, None]
```

Variables in TF 2 (Revisited)

TF 2 variables can be updated during backward error propagation. TF 2 variables can also be saved and then restored at a later point in time. The following list contains some properties of TF 2 variables:

- initial value is optional
- must be initialized before graph execution
- updated during training
- constantly recomputed
- they hold values for weights and biases
- in-memory buffer (saved/restored from disk)

Here are some simple examples of TF 2 variables:

```
b = tf.Variable(3, name='b')
x = tf.Variable(2, name='x')
z = tf.Variable(5*x, name="z")

W = tf.Variable(20)
lm = tf.Variable(W*x + b, name="lm")
```

Notice that the variables b, x, and W specify constant values, whereas the variables z and lm specify expressions that are defined in terms of other variables. If you are familiar with linear regression, you undoubtedly noticed that the variable lm ("linear model") defines a line in the Euclidean plane. Other properties of TF 2 variables are listed below:

- a tensor that's updateable via operations
- exist outside the context of session.run
- like a "regular" variable

- holds the learned model parameters
- variables can be shared (or nontrainable)
- used for storing/maintaining state
- internally stores a persistent tensor
- you can read/modify the values of the tensor
- multiple workers see the same values for `tf.Variables`
- the best way to represent shared persistent state manipulated by your program

TF 2 also provides the method `tf.assign()` in order to modify values of TF 2 variables; be sure to read the relevant code sample later in this appendix so that you learn how to use this API correctly.

TF 2 Variables versus Tensors

Keep in mind the following distinction between TF variables and TF tensors:

TF *variables* represent your model's trainable parameters (ex: weights and biases of a neural network), whereas TF *tensors* represents the data fed into your model and the intermediate representations of that data as it passes through your model.

In the next section, you will learn about the `@tf.function` "decorator" for Python functions and how it can improve performance.

What is `@tf.function` in TF 2?

TF 2 introduced the `@tf.function` "decorator" for Python functions that defines a graph and performs session execution: it's sort of a "successor" to `tf.Session()` in TF 1.x. Since graphs can still be useful, `@tf.function` transparently converts Python functions into functions that are "backed" by graphs. This decorator also converts tensor-dependent Python control flow into TF control flow, and also adds control dependencies to order read and write operations to TF 2 state. Remember that `@tf.function` works best with TF 2 operations instead of NumPy operations or Python primitives.

In general, you won't need to decorate functions with @tf.function; use it to decorate high-level computations, such as one step of training, or the forward pass of a model.

Although TF 2 eager execution mode facilitates a more intuitive user interface, this ease-of-use can be at the expense of decreased performance. Fortunately, the `@tf.function` decorator is a technique for generating graphs in TF 2 code that execute more quickly than eager execution mode.

The performance benefit depends on the type of operations that are performed: matrix multiplication does not benefit from the use of `@tf.function`, whereas optimizing a deep neural network can benefit from `@tf.function`.

How Does `@tf.function` Work?

Whenever you decorate a Python function with `@tf.function`, TF 2 automatically builds the function in graph mode. If a `Python` function that is decorated with `@tf.function` invokes other `Python` functions that are not decorated with `@tf.function`, then the code in those "nondecorated" `Python` functions will also be included in the generated graph.

Another point to keep in mind is that a `tf.Variable` in eager mode is actually a "plain" `Python` object: this object is destroyed when it's out of scope. However, a `tf.Variable` object defines a persistent object if the function is decorated via `@tf.function`. In this scenario, eager mode is disabled and the `tf.Variable` object defines a node in a persistent TF 2 graph. Consequently, a function that works in eager mode without annotation can fail when it is decorated with `@tf.function`.

A Caveat about `@tf.function` in TF 2

If constants are defined *before* the definition of a decorated `Python` function, you can print their values inside the function using the Python `print()` function. However, if constants are defined *inside* the definition of a decorated `Python` function, you can print their values inside the function using the TF 2 `tf.print()` function. Consider this code block:

```
import tensorflow as tf

a = tf.add(4, 2)

@tf.function
def compute_values():
  print(a) # 6

compute_values()

# output:
# tf.Tensor(6, shape=(), dtype=int32)
```

As you can see, the correct result is displayed (shown in bold). However, if you define constants *inside* a decorated `Python` function, the output contains types and attributes but *not* the execution of the addition operation. Consider the following code block:

```
import tensorflow as tf

@tf.function
def compute_values():
  a = tf.add(4, 2)
  print(a)

compute_values()

# output:
# Tensor("Add:0", shape=(), dtype=int32)
```

The zero in the preceding output is part of the tensor name and not an outputted value. Specifically, `Add:0` is output zero of the `tf.add()` operation. Any additional invocation of `compute_values()` prints nothing. If you want actual results, one solution is to return a value from the function, as shown here:

```
import tensorflow as tf

@tf.function
def compute_values():
  a = tf.add(4, 2)
  return a

result = compute_values()
print("result:", result)
```

The output from the preceding code block is here:

```
result: tf.Tensor(6, shape=(), dtype=int32)
```

A second solution involves the TF `tf.print()` function instead of the `Python` `print()` function, as shown in bold in this code block:

```
@tf.function
def compute_values():
  a = tf.add(4, 2)
  tf.print(a)
```

A third solution is to cast the numeric values to Tensors if they do not affect the shape of the generated graph, as shown here:

```
import tensorflow as tf
```

```
@tf.function
def compute_values():
  a = tf.add(tf.constant(4), tf.constant(2))
  return a

result = compute_values()
print("result:", result)
```

The `tf.print()` Function and Standard Error

There is one more detail to remember: the `Python print()` function "sends" output to something called "standard output" that is associated with a file descriptor whose value is 1; However, `tf.print()` sends output to "standard error" that is associated with a file descriptor whose value is 2. In programming languages such as C, only errors are sent to standard error, so keep in mind that the behavior of `tf.print()` differs from the convention regarding standard out and standard error. The following code snippets illustrate this difference:

```
python3 file_with_print.py     1>print_output
python3 file_with_tf.print.py  2>tf.print_output
```

If your `Python` file contains both `print()` and `tf.print()` you can capture the output as follows:

```
python3 both_prints.py 1>prnt_output 2>tf.print_output
```

However, keep in mind that the preceding code snippet might also redirect *real* error messages to the file `tf.print_output`.

Working with `@tf.function` in TF 2

The preceding section explained how the output will differ depending on whether you use the `Python print()` function versus the `tf.print()` function in TF 2 code, where the latter function also sends output to standard error instead of standard output.

This section contains several examples of the `@tf.function` decorator in TF 2 to show you some nuances in behavior that depend on where you define constants and whether you use the `tf.print()` function or the `Python print()` function. Also keep in mind the comments in the previous section regarding `@tf.function`, as well as the fact that you don't need to use `@tf.function` in all your `Python` functions.

An Example without `@tf.function`

Listing E.7 displays the contents of `tf2_simple_function.py` that illustrates how to define a `Python` function with TF 2 code.

LISTING E.7: tf2_simple_function.py

```python
import tensorflow as tf

def func():
  a = tf.constant([[10,10],[11.,1.]])
  b = tf.constant([[1.,0.],[0.,1.]])
  c = tf.matmul(a, b)
  return c

print(func().numpy())
```

The code in Listing E.7 is straightforward: a Python function func() defines two TF 2 constants, computes their product, and returns that value.

Since TF 2 works in eager mode by default, the Python function func() is treated as a "normal" function. Launch the code and you will see the following output:

```
[[20. 30.]
 [22. 3.]]
```

An Example with `@tf.function`

Listing E.8 displays the contents of tf2_at_function.py that illustrates how to define a decorated Python function with TF code.

LISTING E.8: tf2_at_function.py

```python
import tensorflow as tf

@tf.function
def func():
  a = tf.constant([[10,10],[11.,1.]])
  b = tf.constant([[1.,0.],[0.,1.]])
  c = tf.matmul(a, b)
  return c

print(func().numpy())
```

Listing E.8 defines a decorated Python function: the rest of the code is identical to Listing E.7. However, because of the @tf.function annotation, the Python func() function is "wrapped" in a tensorflow.python.eager.def_function.Function object. The Python function is assigned to the .python_function property of the object.

When func() is invoked, the graph construction begins. Only the Python code is executed, and the behavior of the function is traced so that TF 2 can collect the required data to construct the graph. The output is shown here:

```
[[20. 30.]
 [22.  3.]]
```

Overloading Functions with `@tf.function`

If you have worked with programming languages such as `Java` and `C++`, you are already familiar with the concept of "overloading" a function. If this term is new to you, the idea is simple: an overloaded function is a function that can be invoked with different data types. For example, you can define an overloaded "add" function that can add two numbers as well as "add" (i.e., concatenate) two strings.

If you're curious, overloaded functions in various programming languages are implemented via "name mangling," which means that the signature (the parameters and their data types for the function) are appended to the function name in order to generate a unique function name. This happens "under the hood," which means that you don't need to worry about the implementation details.

Listing E.9 displays the contents of `tf2_overload.py` that illustrates how to define a decorated `Python` function that can be invoked with different data types.

LISTING E.9: *tf2_overload.py*

```
import tensorflow as tf

@tf.function
def add(a):
  return a + a

print("Add 1:             ", add(1))
print("Add 2.3:           ", add(2.3))
print("Add string tensor:", add(tf.constant("abc")))

c = add.get_concrete_function(tf.TensorSpec(shape=None,
dtype=tf.string))
c(a=tf.constant("a"))
```

Listing E.9 defines a decorated `Python` function `add()` is preceded by a `@tf.function` decorator. This function can be invoked by passing an integer, a decimal value, or a TF 2 tensor and the correct result is calculated. Launch the code and you will see the following output:

```
Add 1:              tf.Tensor(2, shape=(), dtype=int32)
Add 2.3:            tf.Tensor(4.6, shape=(), dtype=float32)
Add string tensor: tf.Tensor(b'abcabc', shape=(), dtype=string)
c: <tensorflow.python.eager.function.ConcreteFunction object at
0x1209576a0>
```

What is AutoGraph in TF 2?

`AutoGraph` refers to the conversion from `Python` code to its graph representation, which is a significant new feature in TF 2. In fact, `AutoGraph` is automatically applied to functions that are decorated with `@tf.function`; this decorator creates callable graphs from `Python` functions.

`AutoGraph` transforms a subset of `Python` syntax into its portable, high-performance and language agnostic graph representation, thereby bridging the gap between TF 1.x and TF 2.0. In fact, autograph allows you to inspect its autogenerated code with this code snippet. For example, if you define a `Python` function called `my_product()`, you can inspect its autogenerated code with this snippet:

```
print(tf.autograph.to_code(my_product))
```

In particular, the `Python for/while` construct in implemented in TF 2 via `tf.while_loop` (break and continue are also supported). The `Python if` construct is implemented in TF 2 via `tf.cond`. The `"for _ in dataset"` is implemented in TF 2 via `dataset.reduce`.

`AutoGraph` also has some rules for converting loops. A `for` loop is converted if the iterable in the loop is a Tensor, and a `while` loop is converted if the `while` condition depends on a Tensor. If a loop is converted, it will be dynamically "unrolled" with `tf.while_loop`, as well as the special case of a `for x in tf.data.Dataset` (the latter is transformed into `tf.data.Dataset.reduce`). If a loop is not converted, it will be statically unrolled.

`AutoGraph` supports control flow that is nested arbitrarily deep, so you can implement many types of machine learning programs. Check the online documentation for more information regarding `AutoGraph`.

Arithmetic Operations in TF 2

Listing E.10 displays the contents of `tf2_arithmetic.py` that illustrates how to perform arithmetic operations in a TF 2.

LISTING E.10: tf2_arithmetic.py

```
import tensorflow as tf

@tf.function # replace print() with tf.print()
def compute_values():
  a = tf.add(4, 2)
  b = tf.subtract(8, 6)
  c = tf.multiply(a, 3)
  d = tf.math.divide(a, 6)
```

```
print(a) # 6
print(b) # 2
print(c) # 18
print(d) # 1

compute_values()
```

Listing E.10 defines the decorated `Python` function `compute_values()` with simple code for computing the sum, difference, product, and quotient of two numbers via the `tf.add()`, `tf.subtract()`, `tf.multiply()`, and the `tf.math.divide()` APIs, respectively. The four `print()` statements display the values of a, b, c, and d. The output from Listing E.10 is here:

```
tf.Tensor(6,    shape=(), dtype=int32)
tf.Tensor(2,    shape=(), dtype=int32)
tf.Tensor(18,   shape=(), dtype=int32)
tf.Tensor(1.0,  shape=(), dtype=float64)
```

Caveats for Arithmetic Operations in TF 2

As you can probably surmise, you can also perform arithmetic operations involves TF 2 constants and variables. Listing E.11 displays the contents of `tf2_const_var.py` that illustrates how to perform arithmetic operations involving a TF 2 constant and a variable.

LISTING E.11: tf2_const_var.py

```
import tensorflow as tf

v1 = tf.Variable([4.0, 4.0])
c1 = tf.constant([1.0, 2.0])

diff = tf.subtract(v1,c1)
print("diff:",diff)
```

Listing E.11 computes the difference of the TF variable `v1` and the TF constant `c1`, and the output is shown here:

```
diff: tf.Tensor([3. 2.], shape=(2,), dtype=float32)
```

However, if you update the value of `v1` and then print the value of `diff`, it will *not* change. You must reset the value of `diff`, just as you would in other imperative programming languages.

Listing E.12 displays the contents of `tf2_const_var2.py` that illustrates how to perform arithmetic operations involving a TF 2 constant and a variable.

LISTING E.12: tf2_const_var2.py

```
import tensorflow as tf

v1 = tf.Variable([4.0, 4.0])
c1 = tf.constant([1.0, 2.0])

diff = tf.subtract(v1,c1)
print("diff1:",diff.numpy())

# diff is NOT updated:
v1.assign([10.0, 20.0])
print("diff2:",diff.numpy())

# diff is updated correctly:
diff = tf.subtract(v1,c1)
print("diff3:",diff.numpy())
```

Listing E.12 recomputes the value of diff in the final portion of Listing E.11, after which it has the correct value. The output is shown here:

```
diff1: [3. 2.]
diff2: [3. 2.]
diff3: [9. 18.]
```

TF 2 and Built-In Functions

Listing E.13 displays the contents of tf2_math_ops.py that illustrates how to perform additional arithmetic operations in a TF graph.

LISTING E.13: tf2_math_ops.py

```
import tensorflow as tf

PI = 3.141592

@tf.function # replace print() with tf.print()
def math_values():
  print(tf.math.divide(12,8))
  print(tf.math.floordiv(20.0,8.0))
  print(tf.sin(PI))
  print(tf.cos(PI))
  print(tf.math.divide(tf.sin(PI/4.), tf.cos(PI/4.)))

math_values()
```

Listing E.13 contains a hard-coded approximation for PI, followed by the decorated Python function math_values() with five print() statements that display various arithmetic results. Note in particular the third output value is a very small number (the correct value is zero). The output from Listing E.13 is here:

```
1.5
tf.Tensor(2.0,              shape=(), dtype=float32)
tf.Tensor(6.2783295e-07,    shape=(), dtype=float32)
tf.Tensor(-1.0,             shape=(), dtype=float32)
tf.Tensor(0.99999964,       shape=(), dtype=float32)
```

Listing E.14 displays the contents of tf2_math-ops_pi.py that illustrates how to perform arithmetic operations in TF 2.

LISTING E.14: tf2_math_ops_pi.py

```
import tensorflow as tf
import math as m

PI = tf.constant(m.pi)

@tf.function # replace print() with tf.print()
def math_values():
  print(tf.math.divide(12,8))
  print(tf.math.floordiv(20.0,8.0))
  print(tf.sin(PI))
  print(tf.cos(PI))
  print(tf.math.divide(tf.sin(PI/4.), tf.cos(PI/4.)))

math_values()
```

Listing E.14 is almost identical to the code in Listing E.13: the only difference is that Listing E.14 specifies a hard-coded value for PI, whereas Listing E.14 assigns m.pi to the value of PI. As a result, the approximated value is one decimal place closer to the correct value of zero. The output from Listing E.14 follows, and notice how the output format differs from Listing E.13 due to the Python print() function:

```
1.5
tf.Tensor(2.0,              shape=(), dtype=float32)
tf.Tensor(-8.742278e-08,    shape=(), dtype=float32)
tf.Tensor(-1.0,             shape=(), dtype=float32)
tf.Tensor(1.0,              shape=(), dtype=float32)
```

Calculating Trigonometric Values in TF 2

Listing E.15 displays the contents of tf2_trig_values.py that illustrates how to compute values involving trigonometric functions in TF 2.

LISTING E.15: tf2_trig_values.py

```
import tensorflow as tf
import math as m

PI = tf.constant(m.pi)

a = tf.cos(PI/3.)
b = tf.sin(PI/3.)
c = 1.0/a # sec(60)
d = 1.0/tf.tan(PI/3.) # cot(60)

@tf.function # this decorator is okay
def math_values():
  print("a:",a)
  print("b:",b)
  print("c:",c)
  print("d:",d)

math_values()
```

Listing E.15 is straightforward: there are several of the same TF 2 APIs that you saw in Listing E.14. In addition, Listing E.15 contains the `tf.tan()` API, which computes the tangent of a number (in radians). The output from Listing E.15 is here:

```
a: tf.Tensor(0.49999997, shape=(), dtype=float32)
b: tf.Tensor(0.86602545, shape=(), dtype=float32)
c: tf.Tensor(2.0000002,  shape=(), dtype=float32)
d: tf.Tensor(0.57735026, shape=(), dtype=float32)
```

Calculating Exponential Values in TF 2

Listing E.16 displays the contents of `tf2_exp_values.py` that illustrates how to compute values involving additional trigonometric functions in TF 2.

LISTING E.16: tf2_exp_values.py

```
import tensorflow as tf

a  = tf.exp(1.0)
b  = tf.exp(-2.0)
s1 = tf.sigmoid(2.0)
s2 = 1.0/(1.0 + b)
t2 = tf.tanh(2.0)

@tf.function # this decorator is okay
def math_values():
  print('a: ', a)
  print('b: ', b)
```

```
print('s1:', s1)
print('s2:', s2)
print('t2:', t2)
```

math_values()

Listing E.16 starts with the TF 2 APIs `tf.exp()`, `tf.sigmoid()`, and `tf.tanh()` that compute the exponential value of a number, the sigmoid value of a number, and the hyperbolic tangent of a number, respectively. The output from Listing E.16 is here:

```
a:  tf.Tensor(2.7182817,   shape=(), dtype=float32)
b:  tf.Tensor(0.13533528,  shape=(), dtype=float32)
s1: tf.Tensor(0.880797,    shape=(), dtype=float32)
s2: tf.Tensor(0.880797,    shape=(), dtype=float32)
t2: tf.Tensor(0.9640276,   shape=(), dtype=float32)
```

Working with Strings in TF 2

Listing E.17 displays the contents of `tf2_strings.py` that illustrates how to work with strings in TF 2.

LISTING E.17: tf2_strings.py

```
import tensorflow as tf

x1 = tf.constant("café")
print("x1:",x1)
tf.strings.length(x1)
print("")

len1 = tf.strings.length(x1, unit="UTF8_CHAR")
len2 = tf.strings.unicode_decode(x1, "UTF8")

print("len1:",len1.numpy())
print("len2:",len2.numpy())
print("")

# String arrays
x2 = tf.constant(["Café", "Coffee", "caffè", "咖啡"])
print("x2:",x2)
print("")

len3 = tf.strings.length(x2, unit="UTF8_CHAR")
print("len2:",len3.numpy())
print("")

r = tf.strings.unicode_decode(x2, "UTF8")
print("r:",r)
```

Listing E.17 defines the TF 2 constant x1 as a string that contains an accent mark. The first `print()` statement displays the first three characters of x1, followed by a pair of hexadecimal values that represent the accented "e" character. The second and third `print()` statements display the number of characters in x1, followed by the UTF8 sequence for the string x1.

The next portion of Listing E.17 defines the TF 2 constant x2 as a first-order TF 2 tensor that contains four strings. The next `print()` statement displays the contents of x2, using UTF8 values for characters that contain accent marks.

The final portion of Listing E.17 defines r as the Unicode values for the characters in the string x2. The output from Listing E.17 is here:

```
x1: tf.Tensor(b'caf\xc3\xa9', shape=(), dtype=string)

len1: 4
len2: [ 99  97 102 233]

x2: tf.Tensor([b'Caf\xc3\xa9' b'Coffee' b'caff\xc3\xa8' b'\
xe5\x92\x96\xe5\x95\xa1'], shape=(4,), dtype=string)

len2: [4 6 5 2]

r: <tf.RaggedTensor [[67, 97, 102, 233], [67, 111, 102, 102,
101, 101], [99, 97, 102, 102, 232], [21654, 21857]]>
```

Working with Tensors and Operations in TF 2

Listing E.18 displays the contents of `tf2_tensors_operations.py` that illustrates how to use various operators with tensors in TF 2.

LISTING E.18: tf2_tensors_operations.py

```
import tensorflow as tf

x = tf.constant([[1., 2., 3.], [4., 5., 6.]])

print("x:", x)
print("")
print("x.shape:", x.shape)
print("")
print("x.dtype:", x.dtype)
print("")
print("x[:, 1:]:", x[:, 1:])
print("")
print("x[..., 1, tf.newaxis]:", x[..., 1, tf.newaxis])
print("")
print("x + 10:", x + 10)
```

```
print("")
print("tf.square(x):", tf.square(x))
print("")
print("x @ tf.transpose(x):", x @ tf.transpose(x))

m1 = tf.constant([[1., 2., 4.], [3., 6., 12.]])
print("m1:              ", m1 + 50)
print("m1 + 50:         ", m1 + 50)
print("m1 * 2:          ", m1 * 2)
print("tf.square(m1):   ", tf.square(m1))
```

Listing E.18 defines the TF tensor x that contains a 2×3 array of real numbers. The bulk of the code in Listing E.18 illustrates how to display properties of x by invoking `x.shape` and `x.dtype`, as well as the TF function `tf.square(x)`. The output from Listing E.18 is here:

```
x: tf.Tensor(
[[1. 2. 3.]
 [4. 5. 6.]], shape=(2, 3), dtype=float32)

x.shape: (2, 3)

x.dtype: <dtype: 'float32'>

x[:, 1:]: tf.Tensor(
[[2. 3.]
 [5. 6.]], shape=(2, 2), dtype=float32)

x[..., 1, tf.newaxis]: tf.Tensor(
[[2.]
 [5.]], shape=(2, 1), dtype=float32)

x + 10: tf.Tensor(
[[11. 12. 13.]
 [14. 15. 16.]], shape=(2, 3), dtype=float32)

tf.square(x): tf.Tensor(
[[ 1.  4.  9.]
 [16. 25. 36.]], shape=(2, 3), dtype=float32)

x @ tf.transpose(x): tf.Tensor(
[[14. 32.]
 [32. 77.]], shape=(2, 2), dtype=float32)

m1:              tf.Tensor(
[[51. 52. 54.]
 [53. 56. 62.]], shape=(2, 3), dtype=float32)

m1 + 50:         tf.Tensor(
[[51. 52. 54.]
 [53. 56. 62.]], shape=(2, 3), dtype=float32)
```

```
m1 * 2:          tf.Tensor(
[[  2.   4.   8.]
 [  6.  12.  24.]], shape=(2, 3), dtype=float32)

tf.square(m1):   tf.Tensor(
[[  1.   4.  16.]
 [  9.  36. 144.]], shape=(2, 3), dtype=float32)
```

Second-Order Tensors in TF 2 (1)

Listing E.19 displays the contents of tf2_elem2.py that illustrates how to define a second-order TF tensor and access elements in that tensor.

LISTING E.19: tf2_elem2.py

```
import tensorflow as tf

arr2 = tf.constant([[1,2],[2,3]])

@tf.function
def compute_values():
  print('arr2: ',arr2)
  print('[0]:  ',arr2[0])
  print('[1]:  ',arr2[1])

compute_values()
```

Listing E.19 contains the TF constant arr1 that is initialized with the value [[1,2],[2,3]]. The three print() statements display the value of arr1, the value of the element whose index is 1, and the value of the element whose index is [1,1]. The output from Listing E.19 is here:

```
arr2:   tf.Tensor(
[[1 2]
 [2 3]], shape=(2, 2), dtype=int32)
[0]:    tf.Tensor([1 2], shape=(2,), dtype=int32)
[1]:    tf.Tensor([2 3], shape=(2,), dtype=int32)
```

Second-Order Tensors in TF 2 (2)

Listing E.20 displays the contents of tf2_elem3.py that illustrates how to define a second-order TF 2 tensor and how to access elements in that tensor.

LISTING E.20: tf2_elem3.py

```
import tensorflow as tf

arr3 = tf.constant([[[1,2],[2,3]],[[3,4],[5,6]]])
```

```
@tf.function # replace print() with tf.print()
def compute_values():
  print('arr3:    ',arr3)
  print('[1]:     ',arr3[1])
  print('[1,1]:   ',arr3[1,1])
  print('[1,1,0]:',arr3[1,1,0])

compute_values()
```

Listing E.20 contains the TF constant `arr3` that is initialized with the value `[[[1,2],[2,3]],[[3,4],[5,6]]]`. The four `print()` statements display the value of `arr3`, the value of the element whose index is 1, the value of the element whose index is `[1,1]`, and the value of the element whose index is `[1,1,0]`. The output from Listing E.20 (adjusted slightly for display purposes) is here:

```
arr3:      tf.Tensor(
[[[1 2]
  [2 3]]

 [[3 4]
  [5 6]]], shape=(2, 2, 2), dtype=int32)
[1]:       tf.Tensor(
[[3 4]
 [5 6]], shape=(2, 2), dtype=int32)
[1,1]:     tf.Tensor([5 6], shape=(2,), dtype=int32)
[1,1,0]: tf.Tensor(5, shape=(), dtype=int32)
```

Multiplying Two Second-Order Tensors in TF

Listing E.21 displays the contents of `tf2_mult.py` that illustrates how to multiply Second-order tensors in TF 2.

LISTING E.21: tf2_mult.py

```
import tensorflow as tf

m1 = tf.constant([[3., 3.]])    # 1x2
m2 = tf.constant([[2.],[2.]])   # 2x1
p1 = tf.matmul(m1, m2)          # 1x1

@tf.function
def compute_values():
  print('m1:',m1)
  print('m2:',m2)
  print('p1:',p1)

compute_values()
```

Listing E.21 contains two TF constant `m1` and `m2` that are initialized with the value `[[3., 3.]]` and `[[2.],[2.]]`. Due to the nested square brackets, `m1` has shape `1x2`, whereas `m2` has shape `2x1`. Hence, the product of `m1` and `m2` has shape `(1,1)`.

The three `print()` statements display the value of `m1`, `m2`, and `p1`. The output from Listing E.21 is here:

```
m1: tf.Tensor([[3. 3.]], shape=(1, 2), dtype=float32)
m2: tf.Tensor(
[[2.]
 [2.]], shape=(2, 1), dtype=float32)
p1: tf.Tensor([[12.]], shape=(1, 1), dtype=float32)
```

Convert Python Arrays to TF Tensors

Listing E.22 displays the contents of `tf2_convert_tensors.py` that illustrates how to convert a Python array to a TF 2 tensor.

LISTING E.22: tf2_convert_tensors.py

```python
import tensorflow as tf
import numpy as np

x1 = np.array([[1.,2.],[3.,4.]])
x2 = tf.convert_to_tensor(value=x1, dtype=tf.float32)

print ('x1:',x1)
print ('x2:',x2)
```

Listing E.22 is straightforward, starting with an `import` statement for TensorFlow and one for `NumPy`. Next, the `x_data` variable is a `NumPy` array, and `x` is a TF tensor that is the result of converting `x_data` to a TF tensor. The output from Listing E.22 is here:

```
x1: [[1. 2.]
 [3. 4.]]
x2: tf.Tensor(
[[1. 2.]
 [3. 4.]], shape=(2, 2), dtype=float32)
```

Conflicting Types in TF 2

Listing E.23 displays the contents of `tf2_conflict_types.py` that illustrates what happens when you try to combine incompatible tensors in TF 2.

LISTING E.23: tf2_conflict_types.py

```
import tensorflow as tf

try:
  tf.constant(1) + tf.constant(1.0)
except tf.errors.InvalidArgumentError as ex:
  print(ex)

try:
  tf.constant(1.0, dtype=tf.float64) + tf.constant(1.0)
except tf.errors.InvalidArgumentError as ex:
  print(ex)
```

Listing E.23 contains two `try/except` blocks. The first block adds two constants 1 and 1.0, which are compatible. The second block attempts to add the value 1.0 that's declared as a `tf.float64` with 1.0, which are not compatible tensors. The output from Listing E.23 is here:

```
cannot compute Add as input #1(zero-based) was expected to be
a int32 tensor but is a float tensor [Op:Add] name: add/
cannot compute Add as input #1(zero-based) was expected to be
a double tensor but is a float tensor [Op:Add] name: add/
```

Differentiation and `tf.GradientTape` in TF 2

Automatic differentiation (i.e., calculating derivatives) is useful for implementing ML algorithms such as back propagation for training various types of neural networks. During eager execution, the TF 2 context manager `tf.GradientTape` traces operations for computing gradients. This context manager provides a `watch()` method for specifying a tensor that will be differentiated (in the mathematical sense of the word).

The `tf.GradientTape` context manager records all forward-pass operations on a "tape." Next, it computes the gradient by "playing" the tape backward, and then discards the tape after a single gradient computation. Thus, a `tf.GradientTape` can only compute one gradient: subsequent invocations throw a runtime error. Keep in mind that the `tf.GradientTape` context manager only exists in eager mode.

Why do we need the `tf.GradientTape` context manager? Consider deferred execution mode, where we have a graph in which we know how nodes are connected. The gradient computation of a function is performed in two steps: 1) backtracking from the output to the input of the graph, and 2) computing the gradient to obtain the result.

By contrast, in eager execution the only way to compute the gradient of a function using automatic differentiation is to construct a graph. After constructing the graph of the operations executed within the tf.GradientTape context manager on some "watchable" element (such as a variable), we can instruct the tape to compute the required gradient. If you want a more detailed explanation, the tf.GradientTape documentation page contains an example that explains how and why tapes are needed.

The default behavior for tf.GradientTape is to "play once and then discard." However, it's possible to specify a persistent tape, which means that the values are persisted and therefore the tape can be "played" multiple times. The next section contains several examples of tf.GradientTape, including an example of a persistent tape.

Examples of tf.GradientTape

Listing E.24 displays the contents of tf2_gradient_tape1.py that illustrates how to invoke tf.GradientTape in TF 2. This example is one of the simplest examples of using tf.GradientTape in TF 2.

LISTING E.24: tf2_gradient_tape1.py

```
import tensorflow as tf

w = tf.Variable([[1.0]])

with tf.GradientTape() as tape:
  loss = w * w

grad = tape.gradient(loss, w)
print("grad:",grad)
```

Listing E.24 defines the variable w, followed by a with statement that initializes the variable loss with expression w*w. Next, the variable grad is initialized with the derivative that is returned by the tape, and then evaluated with the current value of w.

As a reminder, if we define the function z = w*w, then the first derivative of z is the term 2*w, and when this term is evaluated with the value of 1.0 for w, the result is 2.0. Launch the code in Listing E.24 and you will see the following output:

```
grad: tf.Tensor([[2.]], shape=(1, 1), dtype=float32)
Using the watch() Method of tf.GradientTape
```

Listing E.25 displays the contents of tf2_gradient_tape2.py that also illustrates the use of tf.GradientTape with the watch() method in TF 2.

LISTING E.25: tf2_gradient_tape2.py

```
import tensorflow as tf

x = tf.constant(3.0)

with tf.GradientTape() as g:
  g.watch(x)
  y = 4 * x * x

dy_dx = g.gradient(y, x)
```

Listing E.25 contains a similar with statement as Listing E.24, but this time a watch() method is also invoked to "watch" the tensor x. As you saw in the previous section, if we define the function y = 4*x*x, then the first derivative of y is the term 8*x; when the latter term is evaluated with the value 3.0, the result is 24.0.

Launch the code in Listing E.25 and you will see the following output:

```
dy_dx: tf.Tensor(24.0, shape=(), dtype=float32)
```

Using Nested Loops with tf.GradientTape

Listing E.26 displays the contents of tf2_gradient_tape3.py that also illustrates how to define nested loops with tf.GradientTape in order to calculate the first and the second derivative of a tensor in TF 2.

LISTING E.26: tf2_gradient_tape3.py

```
import tensorflow as tf

x = tf.constant(4.0)
with tf.GradientTape() as t1:
  with tf.GradientTape() as t2:
    t1.watch(x)
    t2.watch(x)
    z = x * x * x
  dz_dx = t2.gradient(z, x)
d2z_dx2 = t1.gradient(dz_dx, x)

print("First  dz_dx:  ",dz_dx)
print("Second d2z_dx2:",d2z_dx2)

x = tf.Variable(4.0)
```

```
with tf.GradientTape() as t1:
  with tf.GradientTape() as t2:
    z = x * x * x
  dz_dx = t2.gradient(z, x)
d2z_dx2 = t1.gradient(dz_dx, x)

print("First  dz_dx:  ",dz_dx)
print("Second d2z_dx2:",d2z_dx2)
```

The first portion of Listing E.26 contains a nested loop, where the outer loop calculates the first derivative and the inner loop calculates the second derivative of the term x*x*x when x equals 4. The second portion of Listing E.26 contains another nested loop that produces the same output with slightly different syntax.

In case you're a bit rusty regarding derivatives, the next code block shows you a function z, its first derivative z', and its second derivative z'':

```
z    = x*x*x
z'   = 3*x*x
z''  = 6*x
```

When we evaluate z, z', and z'' with the value 4.0 for x, the result is 64.0, 48.0, and 24.0, respectively. Launch the code in Listing E.25 and you will see the following output:

```
First  dz_dx:    tf.Tensor(48.0, shape=(), dtype=float32)
Second d2z_dx2: tf.Tensor(24.0, shape=(), dtype=float32)
First  dz_dx:    tf.Tensor(48.0, shape=(), dtype=float32)
Second d2z_dx2: tf.Tensor(24.0, shape=(), dtype=float32)
```

Other Tensors with `tf.GradientTape`

Listing E.27 displays the contents of tf2_gradient_tape4.py that illustrates how to use tf.GradientTape in order to calculate the first derivative of an expression that depends on a 2×2 tensor in TF 2.

LISTING E.27: tf2_gradient_tape4.py

```
import tensorflow as tf

x = tf.ones((3, 3))

with tf.GradientTape() as t:
  t.watch(x)
  y = tf.reduce_sum(x)
  print("y:",y)
  z = tf.multiply(y, y)
  print("z:",z)
```

```
z = tf.multiply(z, y)
print("z:",z)

# the derivative of z with respect to y
dz_dy = t.gradient(z, y)
print("dz_dy:",dz_dy)
```

In Listing E.27, y equals the sum of the elements in the 3×3 tensor x, which is 9.

Next, z is assigned the term `y*y` and then multiplied again by y, so the final expression for z (and its derivative) is here:

```
z  = y*y*y
z' = 3*y*y
```

When z' is evaluated with the value 9 for y, the result is 3*9*9, which equals 243. Launch the code in Listing E.27 and you will see the following output (slightly reformatted for readability):

```
y: tf.Tensor(9.0,        shape=(), dtype=float32)
z: tf.Tensor(81.0,       shape=(), dtype=float32)
z: tf.Tensor(729.0,      shape=(), dtype=float32)
dz_dy: tf.Tensor(243.0,  shape=(), dtype=float32)
```

A Persistent Gradient Tape

Listing E.28 displays the contents of `tf2_gradient_tape5.py` that illustrates how to define a persistent gradient tape in order to with `tf.GradientTape` in order to calculate the first derivative of a tensor in TF 2.

LISTING E.28: tf2_gradient_tape5.py

```
import tensorflow as tf

x = tf.ones((3, 3))

with tf.GradientTape(persistent=True) as t:
  t.watch(x)
  y = tf.reduce_sum(x)
  print("y:",y)
  w = tf.multiply(y, y)
  print("w:",w)
  z = tf.multiply(y, y)
  print("z:",z)
  z = tf.multiply(z, y)
  print("z:",z)

# the derivative of z with respect to y
dz_dy = t.gradient(z, y)
```

```
print("dz_dy:",dz_dy)
dw_dy = t.gradient(w, y)
print("dw_dy:",dw_dy)
```

Listing E.28 is almost the same as Listing E.27: the new sections are displayed in bold. Note that w is the term `y*y` and therefore the first derivative w ' is `2*y`. Hence, the values for w and w ' are 81 and 18, respectively, when they are evaluated with the value 9.0. Launch the code in Listing E.28 and you will see the following output (slightly reformatted for readability), where the new output is shown in bold:

```
y:     tf.Tensor(9.0,     shape=(), dtype=float32)
w:     tf.Tensor(81.0,    shape=(), dtype=float32)
z:     tf.Tensor(81.0,    shape=(), dtype=float32)
z:     tf.Tensor(729.0,   shape=(), dtype=float32)
dz_dy: tf.Tensor(243.0,   shape=(), dtype=float32)
dw_dy: tf.Tensor(18.0,    shape=(), dtype=float32)
```

What is Trax?

`Trax` is a deep learning library (maintained by the Google Brain team) that "focuses on clear code and speed," and the `Trax` documentation is here:

https://trax.readthedocs.io/en/latest/

`Trax` is similar to `Keras`, and can handle resources such as `Jax` and `TF-NumPy`. Moreover, `Trax` models can be easily converted to `Keras`-based models. The `Trax` code samples are available in this Github repository:

https://github.com/Sirsirious/trax_start/blob/colabs/TraxStart.ipynb

In particular, the `Trax` repository provides code samples that implement the following:

- Seq2Seq models
- Transformer models
- BERT
- Reformer (based on Transformer)

`Trax` provides predefined layers, such as LSTM cells, dense layers, and so forth. In addition, `Trax` enables you to define custom layers in two ways. One way is to inherit from an existing layer, and another way is to provide a function to the following:

```
trax.layers.PureLayer(forward_fn = your_function_here
```

After specifying a custom function you can add it as a layer in a neural network.

`Trax` supports various Tensorflow utilities, such as Tensorflow Datasets. For example, the following code snippet download the IMDB dataset in TFDS:

```
imdb = data.TFDS('imdb_reviews',keys=('text','label'),
train=True)
```

Google Colaboratory

Depending on the hardware, GPU-based TF 2 code can be as much as 15 times faster than CPU-based TF 2 code. However, the cost of a good GPU can be a significant factor. Although NVIDIA provides GPUs, those consumer-based GPUs are not optimized for multi-GPU support (which *is* supported by TF 2).

Fortunately Google Colaboratory is an affordable alternative that provides free GPU and TPU support, and also runs as a `Jupyter` notebook environment. In addition, Google Colaboratory executes your code in the cloud and involves zero configuration, and it is available here:

https://colab.research.google.com/notebooks/welcome.ipynb

This `Jupyter` notebook is suitable for training simple models and testing ideas quickly. Google Colaboratory makes it easy to upload local files, install software in `Jupyter` notebooks, and even connect Google Colaboratory to a `Jupyter` runtime on your local machine.

Some of the supported features of Colaboratory include TF 2 execution with GPUs, visualization using Matplotlib, and the ability to save a copy of your Google Colaboratory notebook to Github by using `File > Save a copy to GitHub`.

Moreover, you can load any Jupyter notebook on GitHub by just adding the path to the following URL `colab.research.google.com/github/`

(See the Colaboratory website for details.)

Google Colaboratory has support for other technologies such as HTML and SVG, enabling you to render SVG-based graphics in notebooks that are in Google Colaboratory. One point to keep in mind: any software that you install in a Google Colaboratory notebook is only available on a per-session basis: if you log out and log in again, you need to perform the same installation steps that you performed during your earlier Google Colaboratory session.

As mentioned earlier, there is one other *very* nice feature of Google Colaboratory: you can execute code on a GPU for up to 12 hours per day for free. This free GPU support is extremely useful for people who don't have a suitable GPU on their local machine (which is probably the majority of users), and now they launch TF 2 code to train neural networks in less than 20 or 30 minutes that would otherwise require multiple hours of CPU-based execution time.

In case you're interested, you can launch Tensorboard inside a Google Colaboratory notebook with the following command (replace the specified directory with your own location):

```
%tensorboard --logdir /logs/images
```

Keep in mind the following details about Google Colaboratory. First, whenever you connect to a server in Google Colaboratory, you start what's known as a *session*. You can execute the code in a session with a GPU or a TPU, and you can execute your code without any time limit for your session. However, if you select the GPU option for your session, *only the first 12 hours of GPU execution time are free*. Any additional GPU time during that same session incurs a small charge (see the Website for those details).

The other point to keep in mind is that any software that you install in a Jupyter notebook during a given session will *not* be saved when you exit that session. For example, the following code snippet installs TFLearn in a Jupyter notebook:

```
!pip3 install tflearn
```

When you exit the current session and at some point later you start a new session, you need to install TFLearn again, as well as any other software (such as Github repositories) that you also installed in any previous session.

Incidentally, you can also run TF 2 code and TensorBoard in Google Colaboratory, with support for CPUs and GPUs (and support for TPUs will be available later). Navigate to this link for more information:

https://www.tensorflow.org/tensorboard/r2/tensorboard_in_notebooks

Other Cloud Platforms

Google Cloud Platform (GCP) is a cloud-based service that enables you to train TF 2 code in the cloud. GCP provides deep learning DL images (similar in concept to Amazon AMIs) that are available here:

https://cloud.google.com/deep-learning-vm/docs

The preceding link provides documentation, and also a link to DL images based on different technologies, including TF 2 and PyTorch, with GPU and CPU versions of those images. Along with support for multiple versions of Python, you can work in a browser session or from the command line.

GCP SDK

Install the GCloud SDK on a Mac-based laptop by downloading the software at this link: *https://cloud.google.com/sdk/docs/quickstart-macos*

You will also receive USD 300 dollars worth of credit (over one year) if you have never used Google cloud.

TF2 and `tf.data.Dataset`

The remaining portion of this appendix discusses the TF 2 `tf.data.Dataset` namespace and the classes therein that support a rich set of operators for processing very large datasets (i.e., datasets that are too large to fit in memory). You will learn about so-called lazy operators (such as `filter()` and `map()`) that you can invoke via "method chaining" to extract a desired subset of data from a dataset. In addition, you'll learn about TF 2 `Estimators` (in the `tf.estimator` namespace) and TF 2 `layers` (in the `tf.keras.layers` namespace).

Please note that the word "dataset" in this appendix refers to a TF 2 class in the `tf.data.Dataset` namespace. Such a dataset acts as a "wrapper" for actual data, where the latter can be a CSV file or some other data source. This appendix does not cover TF 2 built-in datasets of "pure" data, such as `MNIST`, `CIFAR`, and `IRIS`, except for cases in which they are part of code samples that involve TF 2 lazy operators.

If you have worked with lambda expressions (discussed later) and functional reactive programming, the material in this section will be very familiar to you. In fact, the code samples will be very straightforward if you already have experience with `Observables` in `RxJS`, `RxAndroid`, `RxJava`, or some other environment that involves lazy execution.

The first part of this appendix briefly introduces you to TF 2 `Datasets` and *lambda expressions*, along with some simple code samples. You will learn about `iterators` that work with TF 1.x `tf.data.Datasets`, and also TF 2 *generators* (which are Python functions with a `@tf.function` decorator).

The TF 2 `tf.data.Dataset`

Before we delve into this topic, we need to make sure that the following distinction is clear: a "dataset" contains rows of data (often in a flat file), where the columns are called "features" and the rows represent an "instance" of the dataset. By contrast, a TF 2 `Dataset` refers to a class in the `tf.data.Dataset` namespace that acts like a "wrapper" around a "regular" dataset that contains rows of data.

You can also think of a TF 2 `Dataset` as being analogous to a `Pandas` data frame. Again, if you are familiar with `Observables` in Angular (or something similar), you can perform a quick knowledge transfer as you learn about TF 2 `Dataset`s.

TF 2 `tf.data.Dataset`s are well-suited for creating asynchronous and optimized data pipelines. In brief, the TF 2 `Dataset` API loads data from the disk (both images and text), applies optimized transformations, creates batches, and sends the batches to the GPU. In fact, the TF 2 `Dataset` API is well-suited for better GPU utilization. In addition, use `tf.functions` in TF 2.0 to fully utilize dataset asynchronous prefetching/streaming features.

According to the TF 2 documentation: "A Dataset can be used to represent an input pipeline as a collection of elements (nested structures of tensors) and a 'logical plan' of transformations that act on those elements."

A TF 2 `tf.data.Dataset` is designed to handle very large datasets. A TF 2 `Dataset` can also represent an input pipeline as a collection of elements (i.e., a nested structure of tensors), along with a "logical plan" of transformations that act on those elements. For example, you can define a TF 2 `Dataset` that initially contains the lines of text in a text file, then extract the lines of text that start with a "#" character, and then display only the first three matching lines. Creating this pipeline is easy: create a TF 2 `Dataset` and then chain the lazy operators `filter()` and `take()`, which is similar to an example that you will see later in this appendix.

Creating a Pipeline

Think of a dataset as a pipeline that starts with a source, which can be a `NumPy` array, tensors in memory, or some other source. If the source involves tensors, use `tf.data.Dataset.from_tensors()` to combine the input, otherwise use `tf.data.Dataset.from_tensor_slices()` if you want a separate row for each input tensor. On the other hand, if the input data is located on disk in a `TFRecord` format (which is recommended), construct a `tf.data.TFRecordDataset`.

The difference between the first two APIs is shown below:

```
#combine the input into one element => [[1, 2], [3, 4]]
t1 = tf.constant([[1, 2], [3, 4]])
ds1 = tf.data.Dataset.from_tensors(t1)

#a separate element for each item: [1, 2], [3, 4]
t2 = tf.constant([[1, 2], [3, 4]])
ds2 = tf.data.Dataset.from_tensor_slices(t2)
for item in ds1:
  print("1item:",item)

print("--------------")

for item in ds2:
  print("2item:",item)
The output from the preceding code block is here:
1item: tf.Tensor(
[[1 2]
 [3 4]], shape=(2, 2), dtype=int32)
--------------
2item: tf.Tensor([1 2], shape=(2,), dtype=int32)
2item: tf.Tensor([3 4], shape=(2,), dtype=int32)
```

The TF 2 `from_tensors()` API also requires compatible dimensions, which means that the following code snippet causes an error:

```
# exception: ValueError: Dimensions 10 and 9 are not
compatible
ds1 = tf.data.Dataset.from_tensor_slices(
    (tf.random_uniform([10, 4]), tf.random_
uniform([9])))
```

However, the TF 2 from_tensor_slices() API does not have a compatibility restriction, so the following code snippet works correctly:

```
ds2 = tf.data.Dataset.from_tensors(
    (tf.random_uniform([10, 4]), tf.random_uniform([9])))
```

Another situation in which there are differences in these two APIs involves the use of lists, as shown here:

```
ds1 = tf.data.Dataset.from_tensor_slices(
    [tf.random_uniform([2, 3]), tf.random_uniform([2, 3])])

ds2 = tf.data.Dataset.from_tensors(
    [tf.random_uniform([2, 3]), tf.random_uniform([2, 3])])

print(ds1) # shapes: (2, 3)
print(ds2) # shapes: (2, 2, 3)
```

In the preceding code block, the TF 2 `from_tensors()` API creates a 3D tensor whose shape is (2,2,3), whereas the TF 2 `from_tensor_slices()` API merges the input tensor and produces a tensor whose shape is (2,3).

As a further illustration of these two APIs, consider the following code block:

```
import tensorflow as tf

ds1 = tf.data.Dataset.from_tensor_slices(
    (tf.random.uniform([3, 2]), tf.random.uniform([3])))

ds2 = tf.data.Dataset.from_tensors(
    (tf.random.uniform([3, 2]), tf.random.uniform([3])))
print('----------------------------')
for i, item in enumerate(ds1):
  print('elem1: ' + str(i + 1), item[0], item[1])

print('----------------------------')
for i, item in enumerate(ds2):
  print('elem2: ' + str(i + 1), item[0], item[1])
print('----------------------------')
```

Launch the preceding code and you will see the following output:

```
----------------------------
elem1: 1 tf.Tensor([0.965013  0.8327141], shape=(2,),
dtype=float32) tf.Tensor(0.03369963, shape=(), dtype=float32)
elem1: 2 tf.Tensor([0.2875235  0.11409616], shape=(2,),
dtype=float32) tf.Tensor(0.05131495, shape=(), dtype=float32)
elem1: 3 tf.Tensor([0.08330548 0.13498652], shape=(2,),
dtype=float32) tf.Tensor(0.3145547, shape=(), dtype=float32)
----------------------------

elem2: 1 tf.Tensor(
[[0.9139079  0.13430142]
 [0.9585271  0.58751714]
 [0.4501326  0.8380357 ]], shape=(3, 2), dtype=float32)
tf.Tensor([0.00776255 0.2655964  0.61935973], shape=(3,),
dtype=float32)
----------------------------
zzzzz
```

Perform the following three steps in order to create and process the contents of a TF 2 `Dataset`:

1. Create or import data.

2. Define a generator (`Python` function).

3. Consume the data.

There are many ways to populate a TF 2 `Dataset` from multiple sources. For simplicity, the code samples in the first part of this appendix perform the following steps: start by creating a TF 2 `Dataset` instance with an initialized `NumPy` array of data; second, define a Python function in order to iterate through the TF 2 `Dataset`; and third, access the elements of the dataset (and in some cases, supply those elements to a TF 2 model).

TF 2 uses *generators* with `Datasets`. TF 2 uses generators because eager execution (the default execution mode for TF 2) does not support iterators.

A Simple TF 2 `tf.data.Dataset`

Listing E.29 displays the contents of `tf2_numpy_dataset.py` that illustrates how to create a very basic TF 2 `tf.data.Dataset` from a `NumPy` array of numbers. Although this code sample is minimalistic, it's the initial code block that appears in other code samples in this appendix.

LISTING E.29: tf2_numpy_dataset.py

```
import tensorflow as tf
import numpy as np

x = np.arange(0, 10)

# make a dataset from a numpy array
ds = tf.data.Dataset.from_tensor_slices(x)
```

Listing E.29 contains two familiar `import` statements and then initializes the variable `x` as a `NumPy` array with the integers from 0 through 9 inclusive. The variable `ds` is initialized as a TF 2 `Dataset` that's based on the contents of the variable `x`.

Note that nothing else happens in Listing E.29, and no output is generated. Later you will see more meaningful code samples involving TF 2 `Datasets`.

What are Lambda Expressions?

In brief, a *lambda expression* is an anonymous function. Use lambda expressions to define local functions that can be passed as arguments, returned as the value of function calls, or used as "one-off" function definitions.

Informally, a lambda expression takes an input variable and performs some type of operation (specified by you) on that variable. For example, here's a "bare bones" lambda expression that adds the number 1 to an input variable x:

```
lambda x: x + 1
```

The term on the left of the ":" is x, and it's just a formal variable name that acts as the input (you can replace x with another string that's convenient for you). The term on the right of the ":" is x+1, which simply increments the value of the input x.

As another example, the following lambda expression doubles the value of the input parameter:

```
lambda x: 2*x
```

You can also define a lambda expression in a valid TF 2 code snippet, as shown here (ds is a TF 2 Dataset that is defined elsewhere):

```
ds.map(lambda x: x + 1)
```

Even if you are unfamiliar with TF 2 Datasets or the map() operator, you can still understand the preceding code snippet. Later in this appendix you'll see other examples of lambda expressions that are used in conjunction with lazy operators.

The next section contains a complete TF 2 code sample that illustrates how to define a generator (which is a Python function) that adds the number 1 to the elements of a TF 2 Dataset.

Working with Generators in TF 2

Listing E.30 displays the contents of tf2_plusone.py that illustrates how to use a lambda expression to add the number 1 to the elements of a TF 2 Dataset.

LISTING E.30: tf2_plusone.py

```
import tensorflow as tf
import numpy as np

x = np.arange(0, 10)

def gener():
  for i in x:
    yield (i+1)

ds = tf.data.Dataset.from_generator(gener, (tf.int64))
```

```
#for value in ds.take(len(x)):
for value in ds:
  print("1value:",value)

for value in ds.take(2*len(x)):
  print("2value:",value)
```

Listing E.30 initializes the variable x as a NumPy array consisting of the integers from 0 through 9 inclusive. Next, the variable ds is initialized as a TF 2 Dataset that is created in the Python function gener(), which returns the input value incremented by 1. As you can see, the Python function gener() does *not* have a @tf.function() decorator: even so, this function is treated as a generator because it's specified as such in the from_generator() API.

The next portion of Listing E.30 contains two for loops that iterate through the elements of ds and displays their values. Since the first for loop does not specify the number of elements in ds, that for loop will process all the numbers in ds.

Here's an important detail regarding generators in TF 2: *they only emit a single value when they are invoked*. This means that the for loop in the Python gener() function does *not* execute 10 times: it executes only *once* when it is invoked, and then it "waits" until the gener() function is invoked again.

In case it's helpful, you can think of the gener() function as a "writer" that prints a single value to a pipe, and elsewhere there is some code that acts like a "reader" that reads a data value from the pipe. The code that acts as a reader is the first for loop that is reproduced here:

```
for value in ds:
  print("1value:",value)
```

How does the preceding code block invoke the gener() function when it doesn't even appear in the code? The answer is simple: the preceding code block indirectly invokes the gener() function because it's specified in the definition of ds, as shown here in bold:

ds = tf.data.Dataset.**from_generator(gener,** (tf.int64))

To summarize, each time that the preceding loop executes, it invokes the Python gener() function, which in turn prints a value and then "waits" until it is invoked again.

The second for loop also acts as a "reader," and this time the code invokes the take() operator (it will "take" data from the dataset) that specifies *twice* the length of the NumPy array x. Why would anyone specify a length that is greater than the number of elements in the underlying array? There may be various reasons (perhaps it was accidental), so it's good to know what will happen in this situation (see if you can correctly guess the result). The output from launching the code in Listing E.30 is here:

```
1value: tf.Tensor(1,  shape=(), dtype=int64)
1value: tf.Tensor(2,  shape=(), dtype=int64)
1value: tf.Tensor(3,  shape=(), dtype=int64)
1value: tf.Tensor(4,  shape=(), dtype=int64)
1value: tf.Tensor(5,  shape=(), dtype=int64)
1value: tf.Tensor(6,  shape=(), dtype=int64)
1value: tf.Tensor(7,  shape=(), dtype=int64)
1value: tf.Tensor(8,  shape=(), dtype=int64)
1value: tf.Tensor(9,  shape=(), dtype=int64)
1value: tf.Tensor(10, shape=(), dtype=int64)
2value: tf.Tensor(1,  shape=(), dtype=int64)
2value: tf.Tensor(2,  shape=(), dtype=int64)
2value: tf.Tensor(3,  shape=(), dtype=int64)
2value: tf.Tensor(4,  shape=(), dtype=int64)
2value: tf.Tensor(5,  shape=(), dtype=int64)
2value: tf.Tensor(6,  shape=(), dtype=int64)
2value: tf.Tensor(7,  shape=(), dtype=int64)
2value: tf.Tensor(8,  shape=(), dtype=int64)
2value: tf.Tensor(9,  shape=(), dtype=int64)
2value: tf.Tensor(10, shape=(), dtype=int64)
```

Summary

This appendix introduced you to TF 2, a very brief view of its architecture, and some of the tools that are part of the TF 2 "family." Then you learned how to write basic `Python` scripts containing TF 2 code with TF constants and variables. You also learned how to perform arithmetic operations and also some built-in TF functions.

Next, you learned how to calculate trigonometric values, how to use for loops, and how to calculate exponential values. You also saw how to perform various operations on second-order TF 2 tensors. In addition, you saw code samples that illustrate how to use some of the new features of TF 2, such as the `@tf.function` decorator and `tf.GradientTape`.

Then you got an introduction to Google Colaboratory, which is a cloud-based environment for machine learning and deep learning. This environment is based on `Jupyter` notebooks, with support for Python and various other languages. Google Colaboratory also provides up to 12 hours of free GPU use on a daily basis, which is a very nice feature.

APPENDIX F

DATA VISUALIZATION

This appendix introduces data visualization, along with an eclectic collection of Python-based code samples that use various visualization tools (including Matplotlib and Seaborn) to render charts and graphs. You will also see Python code samples that combine Pandas, Matplotlib, and Sklearn built-in datasets.

In case you are wondering why this appendix contains an introduction to Sklearn when the title of the appendix is data visualization. The reason is straightforward: you will get an easy introduction to some Sklearn functionality without going through a more formal learning process: this knowledge will bode well if you decide to delve into machine learning (and perhaps this section will provide additional motivation to do so). However, if you are not interested in learning about Sklearn at this point in time, you can skip this section and perhaps return to it when you are ready for this material.

The first part of this appendix briefly discusses data visualization, a short list of some data visualization tools, and a list of various types of visualization (bar graphs, pie charts, and so forth).

The second part of this appendix introduces you to Matplotlib, which is an open source Python library that is modeled after MatLab. The code samples in this section involve plotting lines (horizontal, vertical, and diagonal) in the Euclidean plane.

The third part of the appendix introduces you to `Sklearn`, which is a very powerful `Python` library that supports many machine learning algorithms and also supports visualization. If you are new to machine learning, fear not: *this section does not require a background in machine learning in order to understand the Python code samples.*

The fourth part of the appendix introduces you to `Seaborn` for data visualization, which is a layer above `Matplotlib`. Although `Seaborn` does not have all of the features that are available in `Matplotlib`, `Seaborn` provides an easier set of APIs for rendering charts and graphs.

What is Data Visualization?

Data visualization refers to presenting data in a graphical manner, such as bar charts, line graphs, heat maps, and many other specialized representations. As you probably know, big data comprises massive amounts of data, which leverages data visualization tools to assist in making better decisions.

A key role for good data visualization is to tell a meaningful story that involves focusing on useful information that resides in datasets that can contain billions of rows of data. Another aspect of data visualization is its effectiveness: how well does it convey the trends that might exist in the dataset?

There are many open source data visualization tools available, some of which are listed here (many others are available):

- Matplotlib
- Seaborn
- Bokeh
- YellowBrick
- Tableau
- D3.js (JavaScript and SVG)

In case you have not already done so, make sure you have the following `Sklearn` libraries installed (using `pip3`) on your computer so that you can launch the code samples in this appendix:

pip3 install matplotlib
pip3 install seaborn

pip3 install bokeh
pip3 install yellowbrick

Types of Data Visualization

Bar graphs, line graphs, and pie charts are common ways to present data, and yet many other types exist, some of which are listed here:

- 2D/3D Area Chart
- bar chart
- Gantt chart
- heat map
- histogram
- polar area
- ccatter plot (2D or 3D)
- timeline

The `Python` code samples in the next several sections illustrate how to renders contain some rudimentary APIs from `matplotlib`.

What is `Matplotlib`?

`Matplotlib` is a plotting library that supports `NumPy`, `SciPy`, and toolkits such as `wxPython` (among others). `Matplotlib` supports only version 3 of `Python`: support for version 2 of `Python` was available only through 2020. `Matplotlib` is a multiplatform library that is built on NumPy arrays.

You can use the `plt.style` directive to specify a style for figures. The following code snippet specifies the classic style of `Matplotlib`:

```
plt.style.use('classic')
```

The plotting-related code samples in this appendix use `pyplot`, which is a `Matplotlib` module that provides a MATLAB-like interface. Here is an example of using `pyplot` to plot a smooth curve based on negative powers of Euler's constant e:

```
import matplotlib.pyplot as plt
import numpy as np
num_list = np.linspace(0, 10, 100)
exp_num_list = np.exp(-num_list)
plt.plot(num_list, exp_num_list)
plt.show()
```

The `Python` code samples for visualization in this appendix use primarily `Matplotlib`, along with some code samples that use Seaborn. Keep in mind that the code samples that plot line segments assume that you are familiar with the equation of a (nonvertical) line in the plane: y = m*x + b, where m is the slope and b is the y-intercept.

Furthermore, some code samples use `NumPy` APIs such as `np.linspace()`, `np.array()`, `np.random.rand()`, and `np.ones()` that are discussed in Chapter 1, so you can refresh your memory regarding these APIs.

Now let's proceed with a fast-paced set of rudimentary code samples that display various types of line segments, starting with the next section.

Horizontal Lines in `Matplotlib`

Listing F.1 displays the contents of `hlines1.py` that illustrates how to plot horizontal lines using `Matplotlib`. Recall that the equation of a nonvertical line in the 2D plane is y = m*x + b, where m is the slope of the line and b is the y-intercept of the line.

LISTING F.1: hlines1.py

```
import numpy as np
import matplotlib.pyplot as plt

# top line
x1 = np.linspace(-5,5,num=200)
y1 = 4 + 0*x1

# middle line
x2 = np.linspace(-5,5,num=200)
y2 = 0 + 0*x2

# bottom line
x3 = np.linspace(-5,5,num=200)
y3 = -3 + 0*x3

plt.axis([-5, 5, -5, 5])
plt.plot(x1,y1)
plt.plot(x2,y2)
plt.plot(x3,y3)
plt.show()
```

Listing F.1 uses the `np.linspace()` API in order to generate a list of 200 equally spaced numbers for the horizontal axis, all of which are between -5 and 5. The three lines defined via the variables y1, y2, and y3, are defined in terms of the variables x1, x2, and x3, respectively.

Figure F.1 displays three horizontal line segments whose equations are contained in Listing F.1.

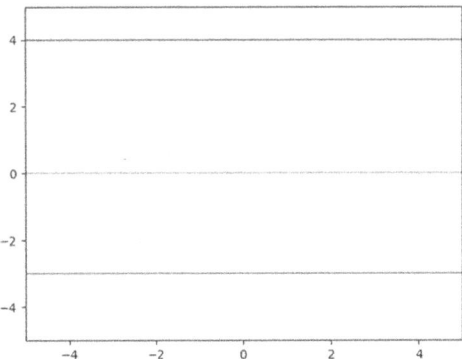

Figure F.1. A Graph of Three Horizontal Line Segments.

Slanted Lines in `Matplotlib`

Listing F.2 displays the contents of diagonallines.py that illustrates how to plot slanted lines.

LISTING F.2: diagonallines.py

```
import matplotlib.pyplot as plt
import numpy as np

x1 = np.linspace(-5,5,num=200)
y1 = x1

x2 = np.linspace(-5,5,num=200)
y2 = -x2

plt.axis([-5, 5, -5, 5])
plt.plot(x1,y1)
plt.plot(x2,y2)
plt.show()
```

Listing F.2 defines two lines using the technique that you saw in Listing F.1, except that these two lines define y1 = x1 and y2 = -x2, which produces slanted lines instead of horizontal lines.

Figure F.2 displays two slanted line segments whose equations are defined in Listing F.2.

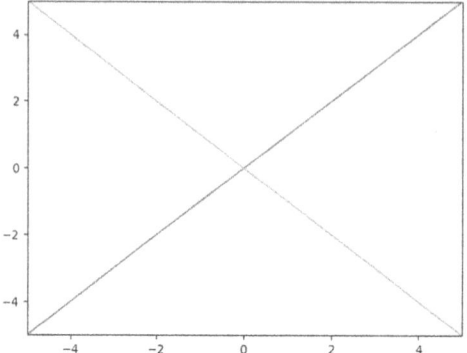

Figure F.2. A Graph of Two Slanted Line Segments.

Parallel Slanted Lines in `Matplotlib`

If two lines in the Euclidean plane have the same slope then they are parallel. Listing F.3 displays the contents of `parallellines1.py` that illustrates how to plot parallel slanted lines.

LISTING F.3: parallellines1.py

```
import matplotlib.pyplot as plt
import numpy as np

# lower line
x1 = np.linspace(-5,5,num=200)
y1 = 2*x1

# upper line
x2 = np.linspace(-5,5,num=200)
y2 = 2*x2 + 3

# horizontal axis
x3 = np.linspace(-5,5,num=200)
y3 = 0*x3 + 0

# vertical axis
plt.axvline(x=0.0)

plt.axis([-5, 5, -10, 10])
plt.plot(x1,y1)
plt.plot(x2,y2)
plt.plot(x3,y3)
plt.show()
```

Listing F.3 defines three lines using the technique that you saw in Listing F.1, where these three lines are slanted and also parallel to each other.

Figure F.3 displays two slanted and also parallel line segments whose equations are defined in Listing F.3.

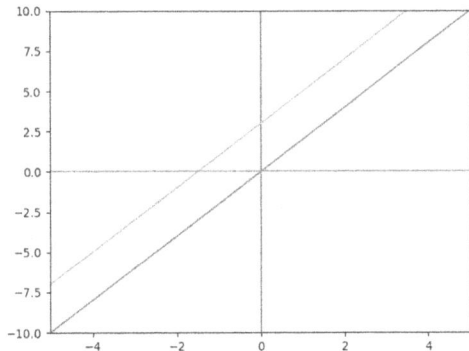

Figure F.3. A Graph of Two Slanted Parallel Line Segments.

A Grid of Points in Matplotlib

Listing F.4 displays the contents of plotgrid.py that illustrates how to plot a simple grid.

LISTING F.4: plotgrid.py

```
import numpy as np
from itertools import product
import matplotlib.pyplot as plt

points = np.array(list(product(range(3),range(4))))

plt.plot(points[:,0],points[:,1],'ro')
plt.show()
```

Listing F.4 defines the NumPy variable points that defines a 2D list of points with three rows and four columns. The Pyplot API plot() uses the points variable to display a grid-like pattern.

Figure F.4 displays a grid of points as defined in Listing F.4.

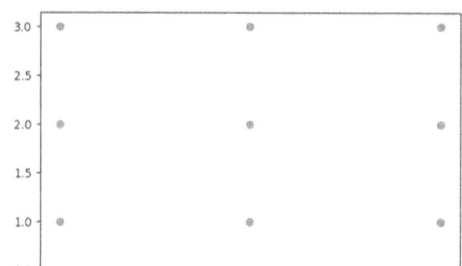

Figure F.4. A Grid of Points.

A Dotted Grid in `Matplotlib`

Listing F.5 displays the contents of `plotdottedgrid1.py` that illustrates how to plot a "dotted" grid pattern.

LISTING F.5: *plotdottedgrid1.py*

```
import numpy as np
import pylab
from itertools import product
import matplotlib.pyplot as plt

fig = pylab.figure()
ax = fig.add_subplot(1,1,1)

ax.grid(which='major', axis='both', linestyle='--')

[line.set_zorder(3) for line in ax.lines]
fig.show() # to update

plt.gca().xaxis.grid(True)
plt.show()
```

Listing F.5 is similar to the code in Listing F.5 in that both of them plot a grid-like pattern; however, the former renders a "dotted" grid pattern whereas the latter renders a "dotted" grid pattern by specifying the value `'--'` for the `linestyle` parameter.

The next portion of Listing F.5 invokes the `set_zorder()` method that controls which items are displayed on top of other items, such as dots on top of lines, or vice versa. The final portion of Listing F.5 invokes the `gca()`. `xaxis.grid(True)` chained methods to display the vertical grid lines.

Figure F.5 displays a "dashed" grid pattern based on the code in Listing F.5.

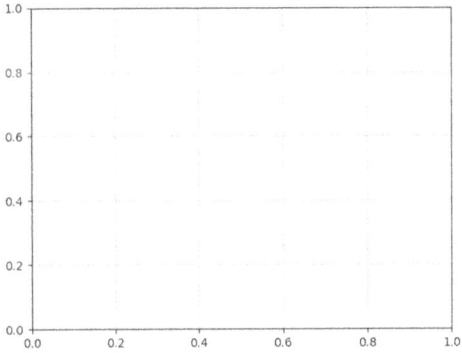

Figure F.5. A "Dashed" Grid Pattern.

Lines in a Grid in `Matplotlib`

Listing F.6 displays the contents of `plotlinegrid2.py` that illustrates how to plot lines in a grid.

LISTING F.6: plotlinegrid2.py

```
import numpy as np
import pylab
from itertools import product
import matplotlib.pyplot as plt

fig = plt.figure()
graph = fig.add_subplot(1,1,1)
graph.grid(which='major', linestyle='-', linewidth='0.5',
color='red')

x1 = np.linspace(-5,5,num=200)
y1 = 1*x1
graph.plot(x1,y1, 'r-o')

x2 = np.linspace(-5,5,num=200)
y2 = -x2
graph.plot(x2,y2, 'b-x')

fig.show() # to update
plt.show()
```

Listing F.6 defines the `NumPy` variable `points` that defines a 2D list of points with three rows and four columns. The `Pyplot` API `plot()` uses the `points` variable to display a grid-like pattern.

Figure F.6 displays a set of "dashed" line segment whose equations are contained in Listing F.6.

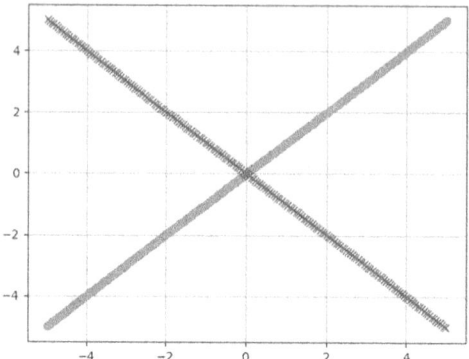

Figure F.6. A Grid of Line Segments.

A Colored Grid in `Matplotlib`

Listing F.7 displays the contents of `plotgrid2.py` that illustrates how to display a colored grid.

LISTING F.7: plotgrid2.py

```
import matplotlib.pyplot as plt
from matplotlib import colors
import numpy as np

data = np.random.rand(10, 10) * 20

# create discrete colormap
cmap = colors.ListedColormap(['red', 'blue'])
bounds = [0,10,20]
norm = colors.BoundaryNorm(bounds, cmap.N)

fig, ax = plt.subplots()
ax.imshow(data, cmap=cmap, norm=norm)

# draw gridlines
ax.grid(which='major', axis='both', linestyle='-', color='k', linewidth=2)
ax.set_xticks(np.arange(-.5, 10, 1));
ax.set_yticks(np.arange(-.5, 10, 1));

plt.show()
```

Listing F.7 defines the `NumPy` variable `data` that defines a 2D set of points with ten rows and ten columns. The `Pyplot` API `plot()` uses the `data` variable to display a colored grid-like pattern.

Figure F.7 displays a colored grid whose equations are contained in Listing F.7.

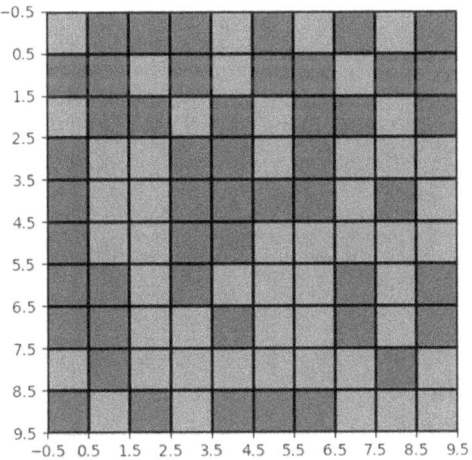

Figure F.7. A Colored Grid of Line Segments.

A Colored Square in an Unlabeled Grid in Matplotlib

Listing F.8 displays the contents of plotgrid3.py that illustrates how to display a colored square inside a grid.

LISTING F.8: plotgrid3.py

```
import matplotlib.pyplot as plt
import numpy as np
from itertools import product
import Matplotlib.pyplot as plt
import Matplotlib.colors as colors

N = 15
# create an empty data set
data = np.ones((N, N)) * np.nan

# fill in some fake data
for j in range(3)[::-1]:
   data[N//2 - j : N//2 + j +1, N//2 - j : N//2 + j +1] = j

# make a figure + axes
fig, ax = plt.subplots(1, 1, tight_layout=True)

# make color map
my_cmap = colors.ListedColormap(['r', 'g', 'b'])
```

```
# set the 'bad' values (nan) to be white and transparent
my_cmap.set_bad(color='w', alpha=0)

# draw the grid
for x in range(N + 1):
  ax.axhline(x, lw=2, color='k', zorder=5)
  ax.axvline(x, lw=2, color='k', zorder=5)

# draw the boxes
ax.imshow(data, interpolation='none', cmap=my_cmap, extent=[0,
N, 0, N], zorder=0)

# turn off the axis labels
ax.axis('off')
plt.show()
```

Listing F.8 defines the `NumPy` variable `data` that defines an NxN set of 2D points, followed by a loop that initializes the variable `data` as a 15×15 array of `np.nan` values. The `Pyplot` API `plot()` uses the `data` variable to display a colored square inside a grid-like pattern.

Figure F.8 displays a colored square in a grid whose equations are contained in Listing F.8.

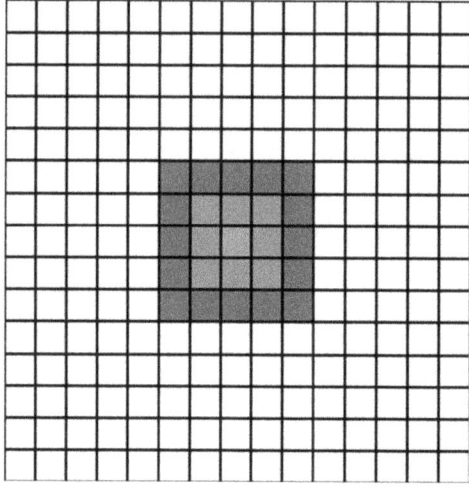

Figure F.8. A Colored Square in a Grid of Line Segments.

Randomized Data Points in `Matplotlib`

Listing F.9 displays the contents of `lin_reg_plot.py` that illustrates how to plot a graph of random points.

LISTING F.9: lin_plot_reg.py

```
import numpy as np
import matplotlib.pyplot as plt

trX = np.linspace(-1, 1, 101) # Linear space of 101 and [-1,1]

#Create the y function based on the x axis
trY = 2*trX + np.random.randn(*trX.shape)*0.4+0.2

#create figure and scatter plot of the random points
plt.figure()
plt.scatter(trX,trY)

# Draw one line with the line function
plt.plot (trX, .2 + 2 * trX)
plt.show()
```

Listing F.9 defines the NumPy variable trX that contains 101 equally spaced numbers that are between -1 and 1 (inclusive). The variable trY is defined in two parts: the first part is 2*trX and the second part is a random value that is partially based on the length of the one-dimensional array trX.

The variable trY is the sum of these two "parts," which creates a "fuzzy" line segment. The next portion of Listing F.9 creates a scatterplot based on the values in trX and trY, followed by the Pyplot API plot() that renders a line segment

Figure F.9 displays a random set of points based on the code in Listing F.9.

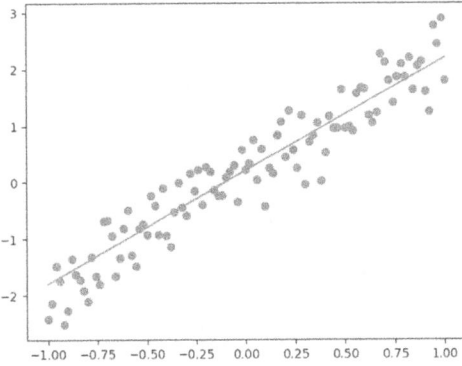

Figure F.9. A Random Set of Points.

A Histogram in `Matplotlib`

Listing F.10 displays the contents of `histogram1.py` that illustrates how to plot a histogram using `Matplotlib`.

LISTING F.10: histogram1.py

```
import numpy as np
import matplotlib.pyplot as plt

apples  = 500
bananas = 500

appl_height = 28 + 4 * np.random.randn(apples)
bana_height = 24 + 4 * np.random.randn(bananas)

plt.hist([appl_height, bana_height],stacked=True,
      color=['r','b'])
plt.show()
```

Listing F.10 is straightforward: the `NumPy` variables `appl_height` and `bana_height` contain a random set of values whose upper bound are `apples` and `bananas`, respectively. The `Pyplot` API `hist()` uses the points `appl_height` and `bana_height` in order to display a histogram.

Figure F.10 displays a histogram whose shape is based on the code in Listing F.10.

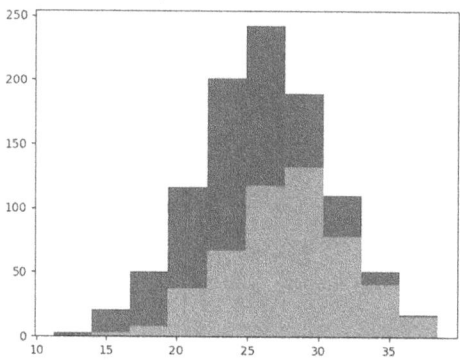

Figure F.10. A Histogram Based on Random Values.

A Set of Line Segments in `Matplotlib`

Listing F.11 displays the contents of `line_segments.py` that illustrates how to plot a set of connected line segments in `Matplotlib`.

LISTING F.11: line_segments.py

```
import numpy as np
import matplotlib.pyplot as plt

x = [7,11,13,15,17,19,23,29,31,37]

plt.plot(x) # OR: plt.plot(x, 'ro-') or bo
plt.ylabel('Height')
plt.xlabel('Weight')
plt.show()
```

Listing F.11 defines the array x that contains a hard-coded set of values. The Pyplot API plot() uses the variable x to display a set of connected line segments. Figure F.11 displays the result of launching the code in Listing F.11.

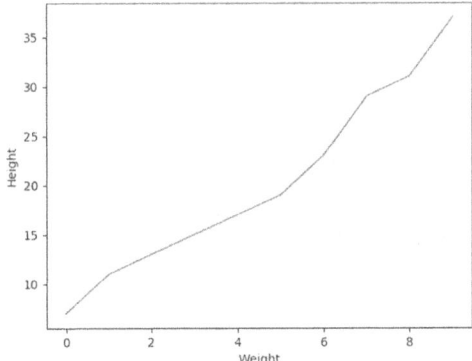

Figure F.11. A Set of Connected Line Segments.

Plotting Multiple Lines in Matplotlib

Listing F.12 displays the contents of plt_array2.py that illustrates the ease with which you can plot multiple lines in Matplotlib.

LISTING F.12: plt_array2.py

```
import matplotlib.pyplot as plt

x = [7,11,13,15,17,19,23,29,31,37]
data = [[8, 4, 1], [5, 3, 3], [6, 0, 2], [1, 7, 9]]
plt.plot(data, 'd-')
plt.show()
```

Listing F.12 defines the array data that contains a hard-coded set of values. The Pyplot API plot() uses the variable data to display a line segment. Figure F.12 displays multiple lines based on the code in Listing F.12.

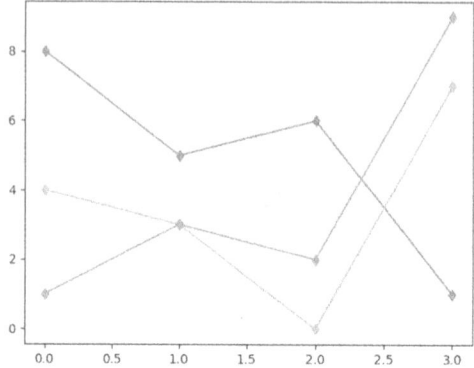

Figure F.12. Multiple Lines in Matplotlib.

Trigonometric Functions in `Matplotlib`

In case you're wondering, you can display the graph of trigonometric functions as easily as you can render "regular" graphs using `Matplotlib`. Listing F.13 displays the contents of `sincos.py` that illustrates how to plot a sine function and a cosine function in `Matplotlib`.

LISTING F.13: sincos.py

```
import numpy as np
import math

x = np.linspace(0, 2*math.pi, 101)
s = np.sin(x)
c = np.cos(x)

import matplotlib.pyplot as plt
plt.plot (s)
plt.plot (c)
plt.show()
```

Listing F.13 defines the `NumPy` variables x, s, and c using the `NumPy` APIs `linspace()`, `sin()`, and `cos()`, respectively. Next, the `Pyplot` API `plot()` uses these variables to display a sine function and a cosine function.

Figure F.13 displays a graph of two trigonometric functions based on the code in Listing F.13.

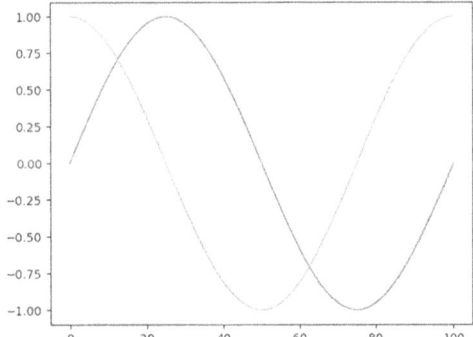

Figure F.13 Sine and Cosine Trigonometric Functions.

Now let's look at a simple dataset consisting of discrete data points, which is the topic of the next section.

Display IQ Scores in `Matplotlib`

Listing F.14 displays the contents of `iq_scores.py` that illustrates how to plot a histogram that displays IQ scores (based on a normal distribution).

LISTING F.14: iq_scores.py

```
import numpy as npf
import matplotlib.pyplot as plt

mu, sigma = 100, 15
x = mu + sigma * np.random.randn(10000)

# the histogram of the data
n, bins, patches = plt.hist(x, 50, normed=1, facecolor='g',
alpha=0.75)

plt.xlabel('Intelligence')
plt.ylabel('Probability')
plt.title('Histogram of IQ')
plt.text(60, .025, r'$\mu=100,\ \sigma=15$')
plt.axis([40, 160, 0, 0.03])
plt.grid(True)
plt.show()
```

Listing F.14 defines the scalar variables `mu` and `sigma`, followed by the NumPy variable `x` that contains a random set of points. Next, the variables `n`, `bins`, and `patches` are initialized via the return values of the NumPy `hist()` API. Finally, these points are plotted via the usual `plot()` API to display a histogram.

Figure F.14 displays a histogram whose shape is based on the code in Listing F.14.

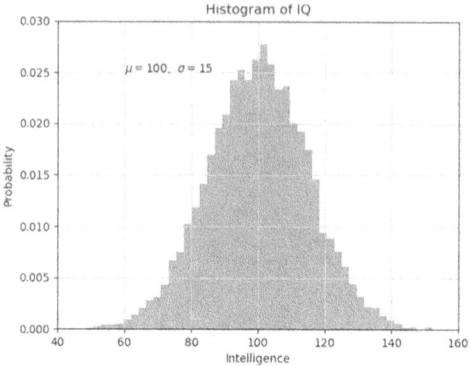

Figure F.14. A Histogram to Display IQ Scores.

Plot a Best-Fitting Line in `Matplotlib`

Listing F.15 displays the contents of `plot_best_fit.py` that illustrates how to plot a best-fitting line in `Matplotlib`.

LISTING F.15: plot-best-fit2.py

```
import numpy as np

xs = np.array([1,2,3,4,5], dtype=np.float64)
ys = np.array([1,2,3,4,5], dtype=np.float64)

def best_fit_slope(xs,ys):
  m = (((np.mean(xs)*np.mean(ys))-np.mean(xs*ys)) /
       ((np.mean(xs)**2) - np.mean(xs**2)))
  b = np.mean(ys) - m * np.mean(xs)

  return m, b

m,b = best_fit_slope(xs,ys)
print('m:',m,'b:',b)

regression_line = [(m*x)+b for x in xs]

import matplotlib.pyplot as plt
from matplotlib import style
style.use('ggplot')

plt.scatter(xs,ys,color='#0000FF')
plt.plot(xs, regression_line)
plt.show()
```

Listing F.15 defines the `NumPy` array variables `xs` and `ys` that are passed into the `Python` function `best_fit_slope()` that calculates the slope m and the y-intercept b for the best-fitting line. The `Pyplot` API `scatter()` displays a scatter plot of the points `xs` and `ys`, followed by the `plot()` API that displays the best-fitting line. Figure F.15 displays a simple line based on the code in Listing F.15.

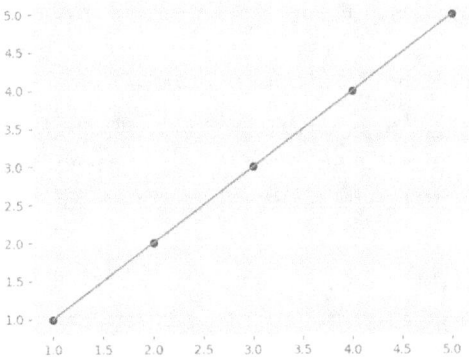

Figure F.15. A Best-Fitting Line for a 2D Dataset.

This concludes the portion of the appendix that is specifically about `NumPy` and `Matplotlib`.

The next section introduces you to `Sklearn`, which is a powerful `Python`-based library that supports many algorithms for machine learning. After you have read the short introduction, subsequent sections contain `Python` code samples that combine `Pandas`, `Matplotlib`, and `Sklearn` built-in datasets.

Introduction to Sklearn (scikit-learn)

`Sklearn` (which is installed as `Sklearn`) is Python's premier general-purpose machine learning library, and its home page is here:

https://scikit-learn.org/stable

Before we discuss any code samples, please keep in mind that `Sklearn` is an immensely useful `Python` library that supports a huge number of machine learning algorithms. In particular, `Sklearn` supports many classification algorithms, such as logistic regression, naive Bayes, decision trees, random forests, and support vector machines (SVMs). Chapter 8 provides a high-level description of most of these classification algorithms. Although entire books are available that are dedicated to `Sklearn`, this Appendix contains only a few pages of `Sklearn` material.

If you decide that you want to acquire a deep level of knowledge about `Sklearn`, navigate to the Web pages that contain very detailed documentation for `Sklearn`. Moreover, if you have "how to" questions involving `Sklearn`, you can almost always find suitable answers on *stackoverflow.com*.

`Sklearn` is well-suited for classification tasks as well as regression and clustering tasks in machine learning. `Sklearn` supports a vast collection of machine learning algorithms, including linear regression, logistic regression, `kNN` ("k nearest neighbor"), `kMeans`, decision trees, random forests, multilayer perceptions (MLPs), and support vector machines (SVMs).

Moreover, `Sklearn` supports dimensionality reduction techniques such as principal component analysis (PCA), "hyper parameter" tuning, methods for scaling data, and is suitable for preprocessing data, cross-validation, and so forth.

Machine learning code samples often contain a combination of `Sklearn`, `NumPy`, `Pandas`, and `Matplotlib`. In addition, `Sklearn` provides various built-in datasets that we can display visually. The next section of this appendix provides several `Python` code samples that contain a combination of `Pandas`, `Matplotlib`, and the `Sklearn` built-in `Digits` dataset.

The Digits Dataset in `Sklearn`

The `Digits` dataset in `Sklearn` comprises 1,797 small 8×8 images: each image is a hand-written digit, which is also the case for the `MNIST` dataset. Listing F.16 displays the contents of `load_digits1.py` that illustrates how to plot the `Digits` dataset.

LISTING F.16: load_digits1.py

```
from sklearn import datasets

# Load in the 'digits' data
digits = datasets.load_digits()

# Print the 'digits' data
print(digits)
```

Listing F.16 is very straightforward: after importing the `datasets` module, the variable `digits` is initialized with the contents of the `Digits` dataset. The `print()` statement displays the contents of the `digits` variable, which is displayed here:

```
{images': array(
      [[[0.,    0.,    5., ...,    1.,    0.,    0.],
        [0.,    0.,   13., ...,   15.,    5.,    0.],
        [0.,    3.,   15., ...,   11.,    8.,    0.],
        ...,
        [0.,    4.,   11., ...,   12.,    7.,    0.],
        [0.,    2.,   14., ...,   12.,    0.,    0.],
        [0.,    0.,    6., ...,    0.,    0.,    0.]]]),
'target': array([0, 1, 2, ..., 8, 9, 8]), 'frame': None,
'feature_names': ['pixel_0_0', 'pixel_0_1', 'pixel_0_2',
'pixel_0_3', 'pixel_0_4', 'pixel_0_5', 'pixel_0_6',
'pixel_0_7', 'pixel_1_0', 'pixel_1_1', 'pixel_1_2',
'pixel_1_3', 'pixel_1_4', 'pixel_1_5', 'pixel_1_6',
'pixel_1_7', 'pixel_2_0', 'pixel_2_1', 'pixel_2_2',
'pixel_2_3', 'pixel_2_4', 'pixel_2_5', 'pixel_2_6',
'pixel_2_7', 'pixel_3_0', 'pixel_3_1', 'pixel_3_2',
'pixel_3_3', 'pixel_3_4', 'pixel_3_5', 'pixel_3_6',
'pixel_3_7', 'pixel_4_0', 'pixel_4_1', 'pixel_4_2',
'pixel_4_3', 'pixel_4_4', 'pixel_4_5', 'pixel_4_6',
'pixel_4_7', 'pixel_5_0', 'pixel_5_1', 'pixel_5_2',
'pixel_5_3', 'pixel_5_4', 'pixel_5_5', 'pixel_5_6',
'pixel_5_7', 'pixel_6_0', 'pixel_6_1', 'pixel_6_2',
'pixel_6_3', 'pixel_6_4', 'pixel_6_5', 'pixel_6_6',
'pixel_6_7', 'pixel_7_0', 'pixel_7_1', 'pixel_7_2',
'pixel_7_3', 'pixel_7_4', 'pixel_7_5', 'pixel_7_6',
'pixel_7_7'], 'target_names': array([0, 1, 2, 3, 4, 5, 6, 7,
8, 9]), 'images': array([[[ 0.,    0.,    5., ...,    1.,    0.,    0.],
         [ 0.,    0.,   13., ...,   15.,    5.,    0.],
         [ 0.,    3.,   15., ...,   11.,    8.,    0.],
// data omitted for brevity
])}
```

Listing F.17 displays the contents of `load_digits2.py` that illustrates how to plot one of the Digits dataset (which you can change in order to display a different digit).

LISTING F.17: load_digits2.py

```
from sklearn.datasets import load_digits
from matplotlib import pyplot as plt

digits = load_digits()
#set interpolation='none'

fig = plt.figure(figsize=(3, 3))
plt.imshow(digits['images'][66], cmap="gray",
interpolation='none')
plt.show()
```

Listing F.17 imports the `load_digits` class from `Sklearn` in order to initialize the variable `digits` with the contents of the `Digits` dataset that is available in `Sklearn`. The next portion of Listing F.17 initializes the variable `fig` and invokes the method `imshow()` of the `plt` class in order to display a number in the digits dataset.

Figure F.16 displays a plot of one of the digits in the `Digits` dataset based on the code in Listing F.17.

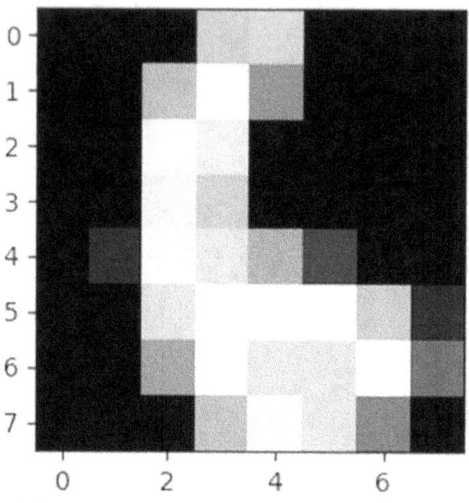

Figure F.16. A Digit in the Sklearn Digits Dataset.

Listing F.18 displays the contents of `sklearn_digits.py` that illustrates how to access the `Digits` dataset in `Sklearn`.

LISTING F.18: sklearn_digits.py

```
from sklearn import datasets

digits = datasets.load_digits()
print("digits shape:",digits.images.shape)
print("data    shape:",digits.data.shape)

n_samples, n_features = digits.data.shape
print("(samples,features):", (n_samples, n_features))

import matplotlib.pyplot as plt
#plt.imshow(digits.images[-1], cmap=plt.cm.gray_r)
#plt.show()

plt.imshow(digits.images[0], cmap=plt.cm.binary,
interpolation='nearest')
plt.show()
```

Listing F.18 starts with one `import` statement followed by the variable `digits that` contains the `Digits` dataset. The output from Listing F.18 is here:

```
digits shape: (1797, 8, 8)
data   shape: (1797, 64)
(samples,features): (1797, 64)
```

Figure F.17 displays the images in the `Digits` dataset based on the code in Listing F.18.

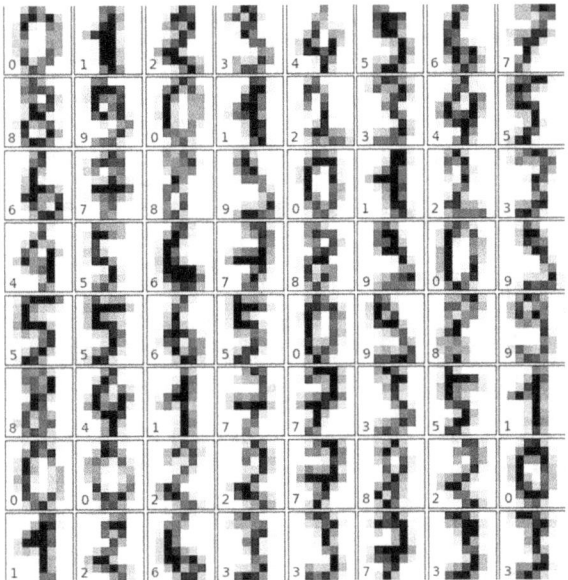

Figure F.17. The Digits in the Digits Dataset.

The Iris Dataset in `Sklearn`

Listing F.19 displays the contents of `sklearn_iris1.py` that illustrates how to access the `Iris` dataset in `Sklearn`.

In addition to support for machine learning algorithms, `Sklearn` provides various built-in datasets that you can access with literally one line of code. In fact, Listing F.19 displays the contents of `sklearn_iris1.py` that illustrates how you can easily load the `Iris` dataset into a `Pandas` data frame.

LISTING F.19: sklearn_iris1.py

```
import numpy as np
import pandas as pd
from sklearn.datasets import load_iris

iris = load_iris()

print("=> iris keys:")
for key in iris.keys():
  print(key)
print()

#print("iris dimensions:")
#print(iris.shape)
#print()

print("=> iris feature names:")
for feature in iris.feature_names:
  print(feature)
print()

X = iris.data[:, [2, 3]]
y = iris.target
print('=> Class labels:', np.unique(y))
print()

print("=> target:")
print(iris.target)
print()

print("=> all data:")
print(iris.data)
```

Listing F.19 contains several `import` statements and then initializes the variable `iris` with the Iris dataset. Next, a for loop displays the keys in dataset, followed by another for loop that displays the feature names.

The next portion of Listing F.19 initializes the variable x with the feature values in columns 2 and 3, and then initializes the variable y with the values of the `target` column.

Launch the code in Listing F.19 and you will see the following output (truncated to save space):

```
Pandas df1:

=> iris keys:
data
target
target_names
```

```
DESCR
feature_names
filename

=> iris feature names:
sepal length (cm)
sepal width (cm)
petal length (cm)
petal width (cm)

=> Class labels: [0 1 2]

=> target:
[0 0 0 0 0 0 0 0 0 0 0 0 0 0 0 0 0 0 0 0 0 0 0 0 0 0 0 0 0 0
 0 0 0 0 0 0
 0 0 0 0 0 0 0 0 0 0 0 0 0 0 1 1 1 1 1 1 1 1 1 1 1 1 1 1 1 1
 1 1 1 1 1 1
 1 1 1 1 1 1 1 1 1 1 1 1 1 1 1 1 1 1 1 1 1 1 1 1 1 1 2 2 2 2
 2 2 2 2 2 2
 2 2 2 2 2 2 2 2 2 2 2 2 2 2 2 2 2 2 2 2 2 2 2 2 2 2 2 2 2 2
 2 2 2 2 2 2
 2 2]

=> all data:
[[5.1 3.5 1.4 0.2]
 [4.9 3.  1.4 0.2]
 [4.7 3.2 1.3 0.2]
 // details omitted for brevity
 [6.5 3.  5.2 2. ]
 [6.2 3.4 5.4 2.3]
 [5.9 3.  5.1 1.8]]
```

Sklearn, Pandas, and the Iris Dataset

Listing F.20 displays the contents of `pandas_iris1.py` that illustrates how to load the contents of the `Iris` dataset (from `Sklearn`) into a `Pandas` data frame.

LISTING F.20: pandas_iris1.py

```
import numpy as np
import pandas as pd
from sklearn.datasets import load_iris

iris = load_iris()

print("=> IRIS feature names:")
for feature in iris.feature_names:
  print(feature)
print()
```

```
# Create a dataframe with the feature variables
df = pd.DataFrame(iris.data, columns=iris.feature_names)

print("=> number of rows:")
print(len(df))
print()

print("=> number of columns:")
print(len(df.columns))
print()

print("=> number of rows and columns:")
print(df.shape)
print()

print("=> number of elements:")
print(df.size)
print()

print("=> IRIS details:")
print(df.info())
print()

print("=> top five rows:")
print(df.head())
print()

X = iris.data[:, [2, 3]]
y = iris.target
print('=> Class labels:', np.unique(y))
```

Listing F.20 contains several `import` statements and then initializes the variable `iris` with the `Iris` dataset. Next, a `for` loop displays the feature names. The next code snippet initializes the variable `df` as a `Pandas` data frame that contains the data from the `Iris` dataset.

The next block of code invokes some methods of a `Pandas` data frame to display the number of row, columns, and elements in the data frame, as well as the details of the `Iris` dataset, the first five rows, and the unique labels in the `Iris` dataset. Launch the code in Listing F.20 and you will see the following output:

```
=> IRIS feature names:
sepal length (cm)
sepal width (cm)
petal length (cm)
petal width (cm)

=> number of rows:
```

```
150

=> number of columns:
4

=> number of rows and columns:
(150, 4)

=> number of elements:
600

=> IRIS details:
<class 'pandas.core.frame.DataFrame'>
RangeIndex: 150 entries, 0 to 149
Data columns (total 4 columns):
sepal length (cm)    150 non-null float64
sepal width (cm)     150 non-null float64
petal length (cm)    150 non-null float64
petal width (cm)     150 non-null float64
dtypes: float64(4)
memory usage: 4.8 KB
None

=> top five rows:
   sepal length (cm)  sepal width (cm)  petal length (cm)  petal width (cm)
0                5.1               3.5                1.4               0.2
1                4.9               3.0                1.4               0.2
2                4.7               3.2                1.3               0.2
3                4.6               3.1                1.5               0.2
4                5.0               3.6                1.4               0.2

=> Class labels: [0 1 2]
```

The Iris Dataset in Sklearn (Optional)

The `Iris` dataset in `Sklearn` consists of the lengths of three different types of `Iris`-based petals and sepals: Setosa, Versicolour, and Virginica. These numeric values are stored in a 150x4 `NumPy.ndarray`.

Note that the rows in the `Iris` dataset are the sample images, and the columns consist of the values for the Sepal Length, Sepal Width, Petal Length, and Petal Width of each image. Listing F.21 displays the contents of `sklearn_iris.py` that illustrates how to display detailed information about the `Iris` dataset.

LISTING F.21: sklearn_iris.py

```
from sklearn import datasets
from sklearn.model_selection import train_test_split
```

```python
iris = datasets.load_iris()
data = iris.data

print("iris data shape:  ",data.shape)
print("iris target shape:",iris.target.shape)
print("first 5 rows iris:")
print(data[0:5])
print("keys:",iris.keys())
print("")

n_samples, n_features = iris.data.shape
print('Number of samples: ', n_samples)
print('Number of features:', n_features)
print("")

print("sepal length/width and petal length/width:")
print(iris.data[0])

import numpy as np
np.bincount(iris.target)

print("target names:",iris.target_names)

print("mean: %s " % data.mean(axis=0))
print("std:  %s " % data.std(axis=0))

#print("mean: %s " % data.mean(axis=1))
#print("std:  %s " % data.std(axis=1))

# load the data into train and test datasets:

X_train, X_test, y_train, y_test = train_test_split(iris.data,
iris.target, random_state=0)

from sklearn.preprocessing import StandardScaler
scaler = StandardScaler()
scaler.fit(X_train)

# rescale the train datasest:
X_train_scaled = scaler.transform(X_train)
print("X_train_scaled shape:",X_train_scaled.shape)

print("mean : %s " % X_train_scaled.mean(axis=0))
print("standard deviation : %s " % X_train_scaled.std(axis=0))

import matplotlib.pyplot as plt

x_index = 3
colors = ['blue', 'red', 'green']
```

```
for label, color in zip(range(len(iris.target_names)), colors):
  plt.hist(iris.data[iris.target==label, x_index],
         label=iris.target_names[label],
         color=color)

plt.xlabel(iris.feature_names[x_index])
plt.legend(loc='upper right')
plt.show()
```

Listing F.21 starts with an `import` statement followed by the variables `iris` and `data`, where the latter contains the `Iris` dataset. The first half of Listing F.21 consists of self-explanatory code, such as displaying the number of images and the number of features in the `Iris` dataset.

The second portion of Listing F.21 imports the `StandardScaler` class in `Sklearn`, which rescales each value in `x_train` by subtracting the mean and then dividing by the standard deviation. The final block of code in Listing F.21 generates a histogram that displays some of the images in the `Iris` dataset. The output from Listing F.26 is here:

```
iris data shape:    (150, 4)
iris target shape: (150,)
first 5 rows iris:
[[5.1 3.5 1.4 0.2]
 [4.9 31.4 0.2]
 [4.7 3.2 1.3 0.2]
 [4.6 3.1 1.5 0.2]
 [53.6 1.4 0.2]]
keys: dict_keys(['target', 'target_names', 'data',
'feature_names', 'DESCR'])

Number of samples:  150
Number of features: 4

sepal length/width and petal length/width:
[5.1 3.5 1.4 0.2]
target names: ['setosa' 'versicolor' 'virginica']
mean: [5.84333333 3.054      3.75866667 1.19866667]
std:  [0.82530129 0.43214658 1.75852918 0.76061262]
X_train_scaled shape: (112, 4)
mean : [ 1.21331516e-15 -4.41115398e-17  7.13714802e-17
2.57730345e-17]
standard deviation : [1. 1. 1. 1.]
```

Figure F.18 displays the images in the `Iris` dataset based on the code in Listing F.21.

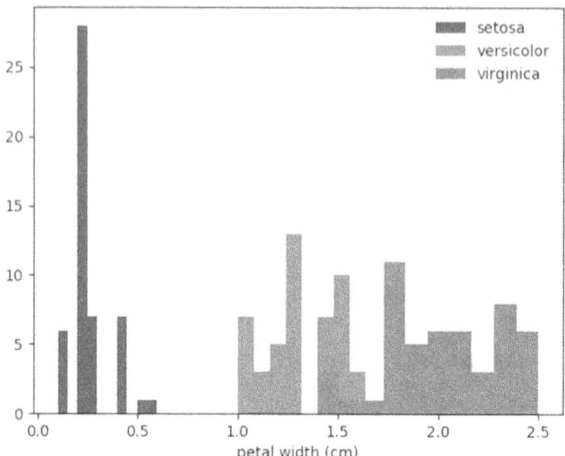

Figure F.18. The Iris Dataset.

The `faces` Dataset in `Sklearn` (Optional)

The `Olivetti Faces` dataset contains a set of face images that were taken between April 1992 and April 1994 at AT&T Laboratories Cambridge. As you will see in Listing F.22, the `Sklearn.datasets.fetch_olivetti_faces` function is the data fetching and caching function that downloads the data archive from AT&T.

Listing F.22 displays the contents of `sklearn_faces.py` that displays the contents of the `Faces` dataset in `Sklearn`.

LISTING F.22: sklearn_faces.py

```
import Sklearn
from sklearn.datasets import fetch_olivetti_faces

faces = fetch_olivetti_faces()

import matplotlib.pyplot as plt

# display figures in inches
fig = plt.figure(figsize=(6, 6))
fig.subplots_adjust(left=0, right=1, bottom=0, top=1,
hspace=0.05, wspace=0.05)

# plot the faces:
for i in range(64):
    ax = fig.add_subplot(8, 8, i + 1, xticks=[], yticks=[])
```

```
    ax.imshow(faces.images[i], cmap=plt.cm.bone,
interpolation='nearest')

plt.show()
```

Listing F.22 starts with `import` statements and then initializes the variable `faces` with the contents of the `Olivetti Faces` dataset. The next portion of Listing F.22 contains some plot-related code, followed by a `for` loop that displays 64 images in an 8×8 grid pattern (similar to an earlier code sample).

Launch Listing F.22 and you will see the plotted image as shown in Figure F.19.

Figure F.19. The Sklearn Faces Dataset.

Now that you have seen some of the `Sklearn` datasets, along with code samples for displaying their contents, let's turn our attention to `Seaborn`, which is a very nice data visualization package for `Python`.

Working with `Seaborn`

`Seaborn` is a `Python` package for data visualization that also provides a high-level interface to `Matplotlib`. `Seaborn` is easier to work with than `Matplotlib`, and actually extends `Matplotlib`. However, keep in mind that `Seaborn` is not as powerful as `Matplotlib`.

`Seaborn` addresses two challenges of `Matplotlib`. The first involves the default `Matplotlib` parameters. `Seaborn` works with different parameters, which provides greater flexibility than the default rendering of `Matplotlib` plots. `Seaborn` addresses the limitations of the `Matplotlib` default values for features such as colors, tick marks on the upper and right axes, and the style (among others).

In addition, `Seaborn` makes it easier to plot entire data frames (somewhat like pandas) than doing so in `Matplotlib`. Nevertheless, since `Seaborn` extends `Matplotlib`, knowledge of the latter is advantageous and will simplify your learning curve.

Features of Seaborn

Some of the features of `Seaborn` include:

- scale seaborn plots
- set the plot style
- set the figure size
- rotate label text
- set xlim or ylim
- set log scale
- add titles

Some useful `Seaborn` methods:

- plt.xlabel()
- plt.ylabel()
- plt.annotate()
- plt.legend()
- plt.ylim()
- plt.savefig()

`Seaborn` supports various built-in datasets, just like `NumPy` and `Pandas`, including the `Iris` dataset and the `Titanic` dataset, both of which you will see in subsequent sections. As a starting point, the three-line code sample in the next section shows you how to display the rows in the built-in "tips" dataset.

Seaborn Built-in Datasets

Listing F.23 displays the contents of `seaborn_tips.py` that illustrates how to read the `tips` dataset into a data frame and display the first five rows of the dataset.

LISTING F.23: seaborn_tips.py

```
import seaborn as sns
df = sns.load_dataset("tips")
print(df.head())
```

Listing F.23 is very simple: after importing `seaborn`, the variable `df` is initialized with the data in the built-in dataset `tips`, and the `print()` statement displays the first five rows of `df`. Note that the `load_dataset()` API searches for online or built-in datasets. The output from Listing F.23 is here:

```
   total_bill   tip     sex smoker  day    time  size
0       16.99  1.01  Female     No  Sun  Dinner     2
1       10.34  1.66    Male     No  Sun  Dinner     3
2       21.01  3.50    Male     No  Sun  Dinner     3
3       23.68  3.31    Male     No  Sun  Dinner     2
4       24.59  3.61  Female     No  Sun  Dinner     4
```

The Iris Dataset in Seaborn

Listing F.24 displays the contents of `seaborn_iris.py` that illustrates how to plot the `Iris` dataset.

LISTING F.24: seaborn_iris.py

```
import seaborn as sns
import Matplotlib.pyplot as plt

# Load iris data
iris = sns.load_dataset("iris")

# Construct iris plot
sns.swarmplot(x="species", y="petal_length", data=iris)

# Show plot
plt.show()
```

Listing F.24 imports `seaborn` and `Matplotlib.pyplot` and then initializes the variable `iris` with the contents of the built-in `Iris` dataset. Next, the `swamplot()` API displays a graph with the horizontal axis labeled `species`, the vertical axis labeled `petal_length`, and the displayed points are from the `Iris` dataset.

Figure F.20 displays the images in the `Iris` dataset based on the code in Listing F.24.

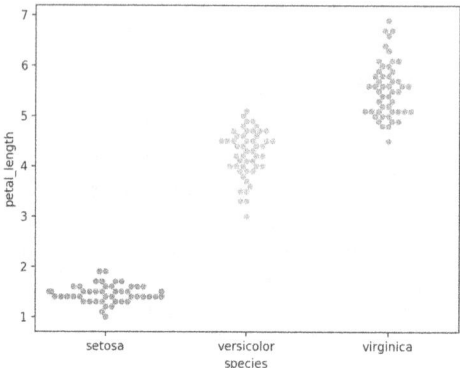

Figure F.20. The Iris Dataset.

The Titanic Dataset in `Seaborn`

Listing F.25 displays the contents of `seaborn_titanic_plot.py` that illustrates how to plot the `Titanic` dataset.

LISTING F.25: seaborn_titanic_plot.py

```
import matplotlib.pyplot as plt
import seaborn as sns

titanic = sns.load_dataset("titanic")
g = sns.factorplot("class", "survived", "sex", data=titanic,
kind="bar", palette="muted", legend=False)

plt.show()
```

Listing F.25 contains the same `import` statements as Listing F.24, and then initializes the variable `titanic` with the contents of the built-in `Titanic` dataset. Next, the `factorplot()` API displays a graph with dataset attributes that are listed in the API invocation.

Figure F.21 displays a plot of the data in the `Titanic` dataset based on the code in Listing F.25.

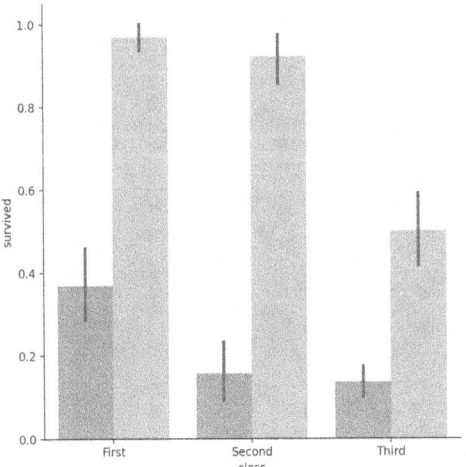

Figure F.21. A Histogram of the Titanic Dataset.

Extracting Data from the Titanic Dataset in Seaborn (1)

Listing F.26 displays the contents of seaborn_titanic.py that illustrates how to extract subsets of data from the Titanic dataset.

LISTING F.26: seaborn_titanic.py

```
import matplotlib.pyplot as plt
import seaborn as sns

titanic = sns.load_dataset("titanic")
print("titanic info:")
titanic.info()

print("first five rows of titanic:")
print(titanic.head())

print("first four ages:")
print(titanic.loc[0:3,'age'])

print("fifth passenger:")
print(titanic.iloc[4])

#print("first five ages:")
#print(titanic['age'].head())

#print("first five ages and gender:")
#print(titanic[['age','sex']].head())
```

```
#print("descending ages:")
#print(titanic.sort_values('age', ascending = False).head())

#print("older than 50:")
#print(titanic[titanic['age'] > 50])

#print("embarked (unique):")
#print(titanic['embarked'].unique())

#print("survivor counts:")
#print(titanic['survived'].value_counts())

#print("counts per class:")
#print(titanic['pclass'].value_counts())

#print("max/min/mean/median ages:")
#print(titanic['age'].max())
#print(titanic['age'].min())
#print(titanic['age'].mean())
#print(titanic['age'].median())
```

Listing F.26 contains the same `import` statements as Listing F.25, and then initializes the variable `titanic` with the contents of the built-in `Titanic` dataset. The next portion of Listing F.26 displays various aspects of the `Titanic` dataset, such as its structure, the first five rows, the first four ages, and the details of the fifth passenger.

As you can see, there is a large block of "commented out" code that you can uncomment in order to see the associated output, such as age, gender, persons over 50, unique rows, and so forth. The output from Listing F.26 is here:

```
titanic info:
<class 'pandas.core.frame.DataFrame'>
RangeIndex: 891 entries, 0 to 890
Data columns (total 15 columns):
survived      891 non-null int64
pclass        891 non-null int64
sex           891 non-null object
age           714 non-null float64
sibsp         891 non-null int64
parch         891 non-null int64
fare          891 non-null float64
embarked      889 non-null object
class         891 non-null category
who           891 non-null object
adult_male    891 non-null bool
deck          203 non-null category
embark_town   889 non-null object
alive         891 non-null object
alone         891 non-null bool
```

```
dtypes: bool(2), category(2), float64(2), int64(4), object(5)
memory usage: 80.6+ KB

first five rows of titanic:
   survived  pclass     sex   age  sibsp  parch     fare embarked  class  \
0         0       3    male  22.0      1      0   7.2500        S  Third
1         1       1  female  38.0      1      0  71.2833        C  First
2         1       3  female  26.0      0      0   7.9250        S  Third
3         1       1  female  35.0      1      0  53.1000        S  First
4         0       3    male  35.0      0      0   8.0500        S  Third

     who  adult_male deck  embark_town alive  alone
0    man        True  NaN  Southampton    no  False
1  woman       False    C    Cherbourg   yes  False
2  woman       False  NaN  Southampton   yes   True
3  woman       False    C  Southampton   yes  False
4    man        True  NaN  Southampton    no   True

first four ages:
0    22.0
1    38.0
2    26.0
3    35.0
Name: age, dtype: float64

fifth passenger:
survived                 0
pclass                   3
sex                   male
age                     35
sibsp                    0
parch                    0
fare                  8.05
embarked                 S
class                Third
who                    man
adult_male            True
deck                   NaN
embark_town    Southampton
alive                   no
alone                 True
Name: 4, dtype: object

counts per class:
3    491
1    216
2    184
Name: pclass, dtype: int64

max/min/mean/median ages:
80.0
0.42
```

```
29.69911764705882
28.0
```

Extracting Data from the Titanic Dataset in Seaborn (2)

Listing F.27 displays the contents of seaborn_titanic2.py that illustrates how to extract subsets of data from the Titanic dataset.

LISTING F.27: seaborn_titanic2.py

```
import matplotlib.pyplot as plt
import seaborn as sns

titanic = sns.load_dataset("titanic")

# Returns a scalar
# titanic.ix[4, 'age']
print("age:",titanic.at[4, 'age'])

# Returns a Series of name 'age', and the age values associated
# to the index labels 4 and 5
# titanic.ix[[4, 5], 'age']
print("series:",titanic.loc[[4, 5], 'age'])

# Returns a Series of name '4', and the age and fare values
# associated to that row.
# titanic.ix[4, ['age', 'fare']]
print("series:",titanic.loc[4, ['age', 'fare']])

# Returns a DataFrame with rows 4 and 5, and columns 'age' and
# 'fare'
# titanic.ix[[4, 5], ['age', 'fare']]
print("dataframe:",titanic.loc[[4, 5], ['age', 'fare']])

query = titanic[
    (titanic.sex == 'female')
    & (titanic['class'].isin(['First', 'Third']))
    & (titanic.age > 30)
    & (titanic.survived == 0)
]
print("query:",query)
```

Listing F.27 contains the same import statements as Listing F.26, and then initializes the variable titanic with the contents of the built-in Titanic dataset. The next code snippet displays the age of the passenger with index 4 in the dataset (which equals 35).

The following code snippet displays the ages of passengers with index values 4 and 5 in the dataset:

```
print("series:",titanic.loc[[4, 5], 'age'])
```

The next snippet displays the age and fare of the passenger with index 4 in the dataset, followed by another code snippet displays the age and fare of the passengers with index 4 and index 5 in the dataset.

The final portion of Listing F.27 is the most interesting part: it defines a variable `query` as shown here:

```
query = titanic[
    (titanic.sex == 'female')
    & (titanic['class'].isin(['First', 'Third']))
    & (titanic.age > 30)
    & (titanic.survived == 0)
]
```

The preceding code block will retrieve the female passengers who are in either first class or third class, and who are also over 30, and they did not survive the accident. The entire output from Listing F.27 is here:

```
age: 35.0

series: 4    35.0
5     NaN
Name: age, dtype: float64

series: age      35
fare      8.05
Name: 4, dtype: object

dataframe:      age    fare
4    35.0    8.0500
5    NaN     8.4583

query:  survived  pclass    sex    age  sibsp  parch     fare embarked  class  \
18             0       3  female  31.0      1      0  18.0000        S  Third
40             0       3  female  40.0      1      0   9.4750        S  Third
132            0       3  female  47.0      1      0  14.5000        S  Third
167            0       3  female  45.0      1      4  27.9000        S  Third
177            0       1  female  50.0      0      0  28.7125        C  First
254            0       3  female  41.0      0      2  20.2125        S  Third
276            0       3  female  45.0      0      0   7.7500        S  Third
362            0       3  female  45.0      0      1  14.4542        C  Third
396            0       3  female  31.0      0      0   7.8542        S  Third
503            0       3  female  37.0      0      0   9.5875        S  Third
610            0       3  female  39.0      1      5  31.2750        S  Third
638            0       3  female  41.0      0      5  39.6875        S  Third
```

657	0	3	female	32.0	1	1	15.5000	Q	Third
678	0	3	female	43.0	1	6	46.9000	S	Third
736	0	3	female	48.0	1	3	34.3750	S	Third
767	0	3	female	30.5	0	0	7.7500	Q	Third
885	0	3	female	39.0	0	5	29.1250	Q	Third

Visualizing a Pandas Dataset in Seaborn

Listing F.28 displays the contents of pandas_seaborn.py that illustrates how to display a Pandas dataset in Seaborn.

LISTING F.28: pandas_seaborn.py

```
import pandas as pd
import random
import matplotlib.pyplot as plt
import seaborn as sns

df = pd.DataFrame()

df['x'] = random.sample(range(1, 100), 25)
df['y'] = random.sample(range(1, 100), 25)

print("top five elements:")
print(df.head())

# display a density plot
#sns.kdeplot(df.y)

# display a density plot
#sns.kdeplot(df.y, df.x)

#sns.distplot(df.x)

# display a histogram
#plt.hist(df.x, alpha=.3)
#sns.rugplot(df.x)

# display a boxplot
#sns.boxplot([df.y, df.x])

# display a violin plot
#sns.violinplot([df.y, df.x])

# display a heatmap
#sns.heatmap([df.y, df.x], annot=True, fmt="d")

# display a cluster map
#sns.clustermap(df)
```

```
# display a scatterplot of the data points
sns.lmplot('x', 'y', data=df, fit_reg=False)
plt.show()
```

Listing F.28 contains several familiar `import` statements, followed by the initialization of the `Pandas` variable `df` as a `Pandas` data frame. The next two code snippets initialize the columns and rows of the data frame and the `print()` statement display the first five rows.

For your convenience, Listing F.28 contains an assortment of "commented out" code snippets that use `Seaborn` in order to render a density plot, a histogram, a boxplot, a violin plot, a heatmap, and a cluster. Uncomment the portions that interest you in order to see the associated plot. The output from Listing F.29 is here:

top five elements:

```
    x   y
0  52  34
1  31  47
2  23  18
3  34  70
4  71   1
```

Figure F.22 displays a plot of the data in the `Titanic` dataset based on the code in Listing F.28.

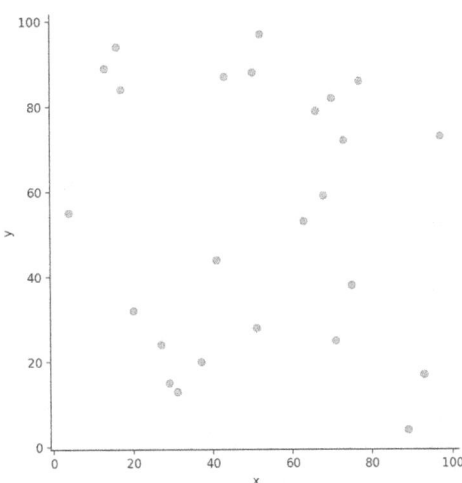

Figure F.22. A Pandas Data Frame Displayed via Seaborn.

Data Visualization in Pandas

Although `Matplotlib` and `Seaborn` are often the "go to" `Python` libraries for data visualization, you can also use `Pandas` for such tasks.

Listing F.29 displays the contents `pandas_viz1.py` that illustrates how to render various types of charts and graphs using `Pandas` and `Matplotlib`.

LISTING F.29: pandas_viz1.py

```
import pandas as pd
import numpy as np
import matplotlib.pyplot as plt

df = pd.DataFrame(np.random.rand(16,3),
columns=['X1','X2','X3'])
print("First 5 rows:")
print(df.head())
print()

print("Diff of first 5 rows:")
print(df.diff().head())
print()

# bar chart:
#ax = df.plot.bar()

# horizontal stacked bar chart:
#ax = df.plot.barh(stacked=True)

# vertical stacked bar chart:
ax = df.plot.bar(stacked=True)

# stacked area graph:
#ax = df.plot.area()

# non-stacked area graph:
#ax = df.plot.area(stacked=False)

#plt.show(ax)
```

Listing F.29 initializes the data frame `df` with a 16×3 matrix of random numbers, followed by the contents of `df`. The bulk of Listing F.29 contains code snippets for generating a bar chart, a horizontal stacked bar chart, a vertical stacked bar chart, a stacked area graph, and a nonstacked area graph. You can uncomment the individual code snippet that displays the graph of your choice with the contents of `df`. Launch the code in Listing F.29 and you will see the following output:

```
First 5 rows:
         X1        X2        X3
0  0.051089  0.357183  0.344414
1  0.800890  0.468372  0.800668
2  0.492981  0.505133  0.228399
3  0.461996  0.977895  0.471315
4  0.033209  0.411852  0.347165

Diff of first 5 rows:
         X1        X2        X3
0       NaN       NaN       NaN
1  0.749801  0.111189  0.456255
2 -0.307909  0.036760 -0.572269
3 -0.030984  0.472762  0.242916
4 -0.428787 -0.566043 -0.124150
```

Summary

This appendix started with some basic features of Matplotlib, along with examples of plotting lines, histograms, and simple trigonometric functions.

You also learned about Sklearn, including examples of working with the Digits and Iris datasets, and also how to process images. In addition, you saw how to perform linear regression with Sklearn.

Then you were introduced to Seaborn, which is an extension of Matplotlib, and saw examples of plotting lines and histograms. You also learned how to plot a Pandas data frame using Seaborn.

INDEX

20Newsgroup dataset, 427–428

A

Abstractive text summarization, 377
Academic community, 111
Activation functions
    Common, 354–357
    Relu and elu, 357–358
Adaptive boosting, 322
Affine transformation, 551
Afro-asiatic, 113
Algorithms
    Toolkits (I), 211–248
    Toolkits (II), 249–282
Analyzing classifiers, 518–519
    Anova, 519
    Lime, 518–519
Andas `mapapply()` method
    Pandas `mapapply()`, 86
Andrei lupas, 497
Anomalies and outliers, 512–513
Appending elements to arrays, 4, 5
Arrays and vector operations, 10
Article den, 119
Ascii letters, 130
Associated, 16
Attention, 460–462

Auto
    Ml, ml-zero, nlp, 326–327
Availability bias, 532
Avere, 121
Avoir, 121

B

Bayesian inference, 562–564
    Terminology, 563
    Theorem, 562–563
Bayesian information criteria (bic), 305
Bert family, 481–483
Bert features, 468
Best-fitting line with `numpy`, 28–29
Bias, 530
Bias-variance trade-off, 530–532
    Bias in data, 531–532
Blending, 323
Boolean operations, 44
Bootstrapping, 323
Brown corpus, 143
Brown university, 143
Byte-pair encoding (BPE), 474

C

C, 271
C++, 271

Calculating
    Mean, 16–18
    Mse manually, 26–28
    Mse successive approximation, 29–31, 32–34
    Standard deviation, 16–18
Calculating gini impurity and entropy values, 534–535
Calculating `tf`, `idf`, and `tf-idf`, 179–183
    Term frequency, 180
Callback function, 641
Canada, 59
Cardinal data, 503
Categorical data, 508
Changes in spelling of words, 125
Chatbots, 410–413
    Abuses, 412
    Logic flow, 411–412
    Open domain, 411
    Types, 411
Classification, 288
Classification algorithms, 287
Classifiers
    Evaluating, 349–350
    Training, 347–349
Cleaning data with regular expressions, 212–216
Clinical abbreviation recognition and disambiguation (CARD), 160
Collaborative filtering
    Algorithm, 385–386
    Item-item, 385–386
    User-user, 385
Collaborative interactive recommenders (CIRS), 389
Common boosting algorithms, 323–324
Comparison of word embeddings, 201–202
Compile time, 577
Complexity of natural languages, 118–123
    Auxiliary verbs, 121–122
    What about verbs?, 120–121
    What are case endings?, 122
    Word order in sentences, 119
Conditional random fields (CRF), 161
Confirmation bias, 532
Context-free grammar (CFG), 271
Context vector, 463

Continuous, 522
Continuous bag of words (CBOW), 191
Continuous data, 504–505
Converting categorical data to numeric data, 49–52
Convolutional neural networks (CNNS), 287, 331
Correlation, 538–540
    Matrix, 540
Cosine similarity, 186
Covariance, 538–539
    Matrix, 538–539
Creating a keras-based model, 630–633
Cross-entropy, 536
Custering, 287

D

Daily to-do, 101
Data and statistics, 499–566, 528–530
    Central limit theorem, 529
    Correlation versus causation, 529
    Statistical inferences, 530
Data frames
    Aggregate operations in pandas, 92–93
    Combining pandas, 58–59
    Data manipulation with pandas, 59–62
    Describing a pandas, 42–44
    Managing columns, 65–70
    Pandas boolean, 44–46
    Transposing a pandas, 45–46
Data normalization techniques, 300–301
Datapoint, 500
Datasets, 500–503
    Data preprocessing, 501–502
    Data types, 502–503
Data visualization, 699–742
Decision tree code samples, 337–341
Decision trees, gini impurity, and entropy, 341–344
Declension, 119
Deep averaging network (DAN), 168
Deep learning method, 159
Deferred execution, 654
Detecting spam, 405
Dimensionality reduction, 296, 545–546
Dimensionality reduction techniques, 546–550

Curse, 547
   Manifolds, 547–548
Dimensionality reduction
   techniques, 547
Discrete data, 504
Discrete random variables, 522
Distance metrics, 552–554
Distributional hypothesis, 185
Document
   Classification, 168
   Similarity, 168–169
Document-feature matrix, 416
Donald rubin, 514
Doubling the elements in a list, 6–7

E

Eager execution, 654
Early stopping, 641
East bay, 116
Eigenvalues, 540
Eigenvectors, 540–542
   Calculating, 540–541
   New matrix, 544–545
Elon musk, 492
English dictionary, 468
English in
   Canada, UK, Australia, and
      United states, 140
English pronouns and prepositions, 141–142
Entropy, 534
Eskimos, 111
"Ess," "zee," and "sh" sounds, 137
Euclidean plane, 20, 23, 24
Example of bow with tf2, 426–427
Explainable boosting machine (EBM), 328
Exponential linear unit (ELU), 358
Exponents, 7
   Arrays, 7
   Lists, 7
Extractive text summarization, 376

F

Factoring the rating matrix R, 383–384
False causality, 532
Feature
   Engineering, 294

Extraction, 296
Selection, 294–295
Feature engineering, 294
Feature engineering, selection, and
   extraction, 293–296
Feature extraction, 296
Feature scaling, 299
Feature selection, 630
Few-shot, 495
Filter out, 63
Foreign service institute (FSI), 125
Four language, 114
Function
   Agg(), 92
   Apply(), 84
   Clean_text(), 215
   Count(), 94
   Dir(), 575
   Group(), 608, 613
   Group(num), 606
   Groups(), 606
   Help(), 575
   Iloc(), 49
   Input(), 594
   Isalpha(), 587
   Main(), 598
   Mapapply(), 86
   Match(), 605, 613
   Math.Sqrt(), 86
   Nunique(), 94
   Raw_input(), 594
   Rjust(), 590
   Softmax, 461
   Str(), 590
   Synsets(), 258
   Tanh(), 355
   To_categorical(), 630
Fundamental concepts in statistics, 523–526
   Chebyshev's inequality, 526
   Mean, 523–524
   Median, 524
   Mode, 524
   Variance and standard deviation, 525

G

Gaussian distribution, 10, 523
Gauss jordan elimination, 541–542

General data protection regulation (GDPR), 327
Generating bert
  Tokens (1), 478–479
  Tokens (2), 479–480
Generative, 411
German, 153
Gini impurity, 533–534, 537
Global matrix factorization (GMF), 200
Google, 467
Google cloud platform (GCP), 689
Google colaboratory, 34–36, 467
  Uploading csv, 35–36
Google colaboratory, 688–689
Google research, 481
Google translate, 126
Groucho marx, 119

H

Handling contracted words, 216–218
Handling stop words, 154–155
Hausdorff metric, 553
Hidden markov models (HMM), 161
Hierarchical cluster analysis (HCA), 289
Holdout method, 347
Html, 35, 107, 501
Html anchor, 231, 232, 233
Html pages, 148
Html string, 214
Html tag, 148, 231
Html tags, 213, 214
Html web page, 106, 107, 231, 232, 233, 261
Html web pages, 211, 234, 237
Huggingface, 467
Hybrid approach, 382
Hybrid languages, 114
Hyperparameter optimization, 325–326
  Bayesian, 326
  Grid search, 325
  Randomized search, 325
Hyperparameters for neural networks, 360–362
  Backward error propagation, 361–362
  Dropout rate, 361
  Learning rate, 361
  Loss function, 360
  Optimizer, 360–361
Hyper plane, 307

I

I18n (internationalization), 502
Identical words, 166
Il faut fatiguer la salade, 116
Indo-european, 114
Information extraction and retrieval, 148–149
Information extraction (IE), 208–209
Inner workings of bert, 469–473
Internet, 112, 518
Introduction
  Keras, 625–650
  Machine learning, 283–328
  Numpy, 1–36
  Pandas, 37–108
  Python, 567–598
  Regular expressions, 599–624
  Tensorflow 2, 651–698
Inverse document frequency (IDF), 181, 182
Invert, 116
Iranian plateau, 114
Iris dataset, 558–560

J

Jaccard similarity, 555
Japanese
  Ambiguity, 128–129
  Expressing negative opinions, 132
  Google translate, 130
  Grammar, 125–133
  Korean, 131
  Mutating consonant spelling, 131
  Nominalization, 129
  Postpositions, 125–128
  Vowel-optional languages and word direction, 131
  Word tokenization, 152
Java, 105, 271
Javascript, 105
Je-ne-sais-quoi, 113

K

Kanji character, 152
Keras
    Cnns, and cifar10, 637–639
    Early stopping (1), 641–642
    Early stopping (2), 642–645
    Linear regression, 633–634
    Metrics, 645–646
    Mlps, mnist, 635–637
    Resizing images, 639–640
    Saving and restoring, 646–648
Keras-based
    Tokenizer, 417–418
    Word embedding, 423–426
Keyword extraction, 162
K-fold cross-validation, 297, 347
Kitab, 131
Kl divergence, 536, 537
Kullback-leibler (KL), 500

L

L10n (localization), 502
Lambda expressions, 694–695
Language models and nlp, 204–205
Languages, 114
    Arabic, 123
    Dialects, 117–118
    English, 114
    Finnish, 123
    French, 114
    Gender, 124
    German, 123
    Greek, 123
    Hindi, 114
    Latin, 123
    Lithuanian, 123
    Mandarin, 114
    Russian, 123
    Slang, 116–117
    Spanish, 114
Languages and regional accents, 115–116
Lasso regression, 299
Latent dirichlet allocation (LDA), 162, 276
Latent dirichlet analysis (LDA), 167
Latent semantic analysis (LSA), 162, 200
Launching python, 570–571

Lemmatization, 157
Lexical ambiguity, 147
Lexical-based methods, 159
Lexrank, 163
Likelihood, 520
Line, 19
Linear algebra, 2
Linear classifier, 333
Linear regression, 287
    Keras, 371–373
    Scipy, 369–370
    Sklearn, 367–369
Linear transformation, 551
Linear versus nonlinear reduction
    techniques, 551
Line segment, 19, 309
Local context window (LCW), 200
Locally linear embedding (LLE), 549
Local sensitivity hashing, 555–556
Local sensitivity hashing (LSH), 555
Logistic regression, 330, 362–364
Long short-term memory (LSTM),
    167, 330
Looking ahead, 496–497
Ludwig wittgenstein, 111

M

M2m model, 142
Machine learning, 142
    Text classification algorithms, 416–417
Machine learning
    Classifiers, 329–374
Major language groups, 113–114
Managing columns, 65
    Appending, 66
    Deleting, 67
    Inserting, 67
    Scaling numeric, 68
    Switching, 65–66
Managing rows in pandas, 70–75
    Finding duplicate rows, 71–74
    Inserting new rows, 74–75
    Selecting a range of rows, 70–71
Mandarin, 121
Manifold learning, 547
Mapping categorical data to numeric values,
    508–510

Matching character classes
    `Findall()` method, 610–612
    Re module, 605
    `Re.Search()` method, 609–610
Matplotlib
    Colored grid, 708–709
    Colored square in an unlabeled grid, 709–710
    Display iq scores, 715–716
    Dotted grid, 706–707
    Grid of points, 705–706
    Histogram, 712
    Horizontal lines, 702–703
    Lines in a grid, 707–708
    Parallel slanted lines, 704–705
    Plot a best-fitting line, 716–717
    Plotting multiple lines, 713–714
    Randomized data points, 710–711
    Set of line segments, 712–713
    Slanted lines, 703–704
    Trigonometric functions, 714–715
Matrix factorization, 199, 383
Mean, 523
    Code sample, 17–18
    Trimmed, 16–17
    Weighted, 16–17
Mean absolute error (MAE), 26, 316
Mean squared error (MSE), 309
Mean squared error (MSE), 2
Median, 524
Meme, 117
Method
    `Agg()`, 92
    `Apply()`, 84
    `Applymap()`, 87
    `Compile()`, 425
    `Describe()`, 43
    `Encode()`, 491
    `Evaluate()`, 425
    `Fit()`, 431
    `Fit_transform()`, 431
    `Groupby()`, 94
    `Linspace()`, 10
    `Mean()`, 10
    `Np.Mean()`, 16
    `Np.Std()`, 10, 16
    `Pandas apply()`, 84, 85
    `Pandas applymap()`, 86
    `Pandas groupby()`, 82
    `Pandas loc()`, 49
    `Pd.Reset()`, 38
    `Pipe()`, 106
    `Predict()`, 431, 632
    `Re.Match()`, 605
    `Replace()`, 52
    `Reshape()`, 10, 15
    `Re.Sub()`, 602
    `Search()`, 609
    `Std()`, 10
    `Summary()`, 378
    `To_csv()`, 96
    `Wikipedia.Page()`, 380
    `Wordshape()`, 420
Metrics in machine learning, 301–305
    Confusion matrix, 302–303
    R-squared and its limitations, 301–302
Microsoft ecosystem, 483
Minimum word count, 193
Miscellaneous topics, 327–328
    Causality, 327
    Explainability, 327
    Interpretability, 328
Missing data
    Missing at random (MAR), 514
    Missing completely at random (MCAR), 514
    Missing not at random (MNAR), 514
Missing data, anomalies, and outliers, 511–515
Ml algorithms
    Trade-offs, 350–352
Mode, 524
Model selection, 296
Moments of a function, 526–528
    Kurtosis, 527–528
    Skewness, 527
Morpheme, 135
Mse formula, 25–26
Multidimensional gini index (MGI), 535
Multiple types of missing values, 77–78
Multiple ways to pronounce consonants, 135–140

Challenging english sounds, 139
Diphthongs and triphthongs in
    English, 138
"Hard" vs "soft" consonant sounds, 136
Letter "j" in various languages, 135–136
Semi-vowels in english, 139
Three consecutive, 138
Multiply lists and arrays, 6

N

Naive bayes (NB), 346
Named entity recognition (NER), 109, 110, 152
Named entity recognition (NER), 242
Natural language generation (NLG), 145, 149
Natural language processing (NLP), 160, 190
Natural language toolkit (NLTK), 208, 249
Natural language understanding (NLU), 145, 149, 209
Never ending language learning (NELL), 209
Next sentence prediction (NSP), 482, 483
NLP
    Concepts (I), 109–164
    Concepts (II), 165–210
NLP and text mining, 208
NLP applications, 375–414
NLP techniques in ML, 149–150
    Training model, 150
NLTK
    Bow, 250–251
    Context-free grammars, 271–273
    Lemmatization, 254–256
    Lxml, and xpath, 261–263
    N-grams, 263–264
    Pos (1), 264–268
    Pos (2), 268–269
    Stemmers, 251–254
    Stop words, 256–257
    Tokenizers, 270–271
Noam chomsky, 111
Nominal data, 503
Nonlinear datasets, 24–25
Nonlinear least squares, 26, 317
Normalization, 300
Numpy and dot products, 11, 12
Numpy and other operations, 14
Numpy and the "norm" of vectors, 13

Numpy methods, 10

O

One-hot encoding, 509
One-hot encoding examples, 222–224
One-shot, 495
Ordinal data, 503
Origin of languages, 110–118
    Fluency, 112–113
Other cloud platforms, 689–690
Other types of regression, 308–309
Outlier detection, 513–514
Out of vocabulary (OOV), 173, 422, 474
Overfitting versus underfitting, 298–300
Overview of word embeddings and
    algorithms, 189–191
    Word embedding algorithms, 190–191
    Word embeddings, 190

P

Pandas
    Alternatives, 40
    Converting strings to dates, 55
    Data cleaning tasks, 39
    Data frames, 39, 46–47
    Data frames and csv files, 62–65
    Data frames and scatterplots, 89–90
    Data frames and simple statistics, 90–92
    Data visualization, 740–741
    Excel spreadsheets, 96
    Handling missing data, 75–80
    Handling outliers, 87–89
    Managing rows, 70–75
    Matching and splitting strings, 53–55
    Merging and splitting columns, 56–58
    Options and settings, 38
    Profiling, 106
    Random numbers, 46–47
    Reading csv files, 48
    Useful one-line commands, 104–105
Pandas data frame with numpy example, 40–42
Parts of speech (POS), 109, 147, 158 258
Peak usage of some languages, 115
Pearson correlation coefficient, 554–555
Perplexity, 533, 537

Phoneme, 134
Phonetic languages, 133–134
Pizza, 137
Pointwise mutual information (PMI), 184
Pos tagging, 158–159
    Techniques, 159
Post positions, 125
Precision, 303
Preparing a dataset and training a model, 292–293
Preparing datasets, 503–511
Prevalence, 304
Principal component analysis (PCA), 542–545
Probabilistic method, 159
Probability, 519–522
    Expected value, 521–522
Probability distribution, 533
Probability distributions, 523
Projection, 551
Protein folding, 496
Pythagorean theorem, 186
Python
    Character classes, 604–605
    Emojis, 596
    Exception handling, 592–593
    Handling user input, 594
    Identifiers, 571–572
    Installation, 569–570
    Metacharacters, 600–603
    Other bases, 579
    Quotation and comments, 573–574
    Simple data types, 577–578
    Slicing and splicing strings, 586–587
    Standard modules, 575
    Tools, 567–569
    Workign with fractions, 581–582
    Working with dates, 591
    Working with numbers, 578–579
    Working with strings, 583–585
    Working with unicode, 582
Python code samples of bow, 219–222
Python library, 148

Q

Quadratic equation, 22
Quadratic scatterplot with numpy and matplotlib, 314–316

R

Random number, 2
Random oversampling, 515
Random resampling, 515
Random undersampling, 515
Random variables, 522–523
Recall, 303
Receiver operating characteristic (ROC), 304
Recommender systems, 381
    Movie, 382–383
Recommender systems and reinforcement learning, 386–389
Recurrent neural networks (RNNS), 330
Referential ambiguity, 147
Regular expressions, 600
    Additional matching function, 612–613
    Additional topics, 623
    Grouping with character classes, 613–614
    Using character classes, 614–615
Regular expressions, 100–103
    Grouping, 622
Reinforcement, 286
Reinforcement learning (RL), 389
Relation extraction, 146
Relation extraction (RE), 208–209
Retrieval-based, 411
Reuters dataset, 455–457
Ridge regression, 299
Roman empire, 115
Root mean squared error (RMSE), 26, 316
Root mean squared (RMS), 317
Rule-based, 411
Rule-based method, 159

S

Sapir-whorf, 111
Scala, 105
Scaling numeric data via
    Normalization, 505–506
    Standardization, 507–508
Scatter plots
    Numpy and matplotlib (1), 311–313
    Numpy and matplotlib (2), 313–314
Seaborn
    Built-in datasets, 731

Extracting data from the titanic dataset, 733–738
Iris dataset, 731–732
Titanic dataset, 732–733
Visualizing a pandas dataset, 738–739
Working, 729–730
Self-attention, 461
Self-learning, 411
Semantic context, 184–185
Semi-supervised, 286
Sensitivity, 303
Sentence encoders, 167
Sentence-order prediction (SOP), 482
Sentence similarity, 167–168
Sentence similarity in bert, 476–478
Sentiment analysis, 145, 163, 390–393
Aspect-based, 392–393
Deep learning, 393
Flair, 403–404
Logistic regression, 405–408
Naïve bayes, 393–397
Nltk and vader, 398–400
Textblob, 400–404
Useful tools, 392
Sigmoid, softmax, and hardmax
Differences, 359–360
Similarities, 358–359
Silver bullet, 296
Simple string matches, 622–623
Singular and plural forms of nouns, 124
Singular value decomposition (SVD), 200, 500, 548–549
Sklearn, 556–562
Digits dataset, 718–721
Faces dataset (optional), 728–729
Introduction, 717–718
Iris dataset, 721–725
Iris dataset (optional), 725–728
Outlier detection, 560–562
Sklearn and word embedding examples, 224–230
Sorting data frames in pandas, 80–82
Spacy
Ner, 242–243
Word vectors, 244–247
Spacy and lemmatization, 241–242
Spacy and stop words, 238–239
Spacy and tokenization, 239–240
Spacy pipelines, 243–244
Specificity, 303
Splitting text strings
`Re.Split()` method, 616
Using digits and delimiters, 617
Stacking ensembles, 320
Standard deviation, 17–18, 88
Standardization, 300
Strong minimalist thesis (SRT), 111
Sukun, 131
Sunk cost, 532
Supervised learning, 285
Support vector machines (SVM), 161, 345
Support vector machines (SVMS), 168, 717
Survivorship bias, 532
Svg, 35
Syntactical ambiguity, 147
Synthetic minority oversampling technique (SMOTE), 512, 517–518
Extensions, 518

T

Tabula rasa, 111
Techniques for text similarity, 169–170
Teenagers, 116
Tensorflow hub (TFH), 168
Term-document matrix, 207, 416
Term frequency (TF), 180
Test-driven development (TDD), 284
Text classification
Decision tree algorithm, 433–437
Kmeans algorithm, 446–449
Knn algorithm, 428–433
Naïve bayes algorithm, 443–446
Random forest algorithm, 437–440
Text encoding techniques, 171–175
Additional encoders, 174–175
Document vectorization, 171–172
Index-based encoding, 174
One-hot encoding (OHE), 172–173
Text normalization and tokenization, 151–154
Tokenization with unix commands, 153–154
Textrank, 163
Text summarization, 163
Text summarization with tf2/keras, 455–457

Textual entailment, 185
Text vectorization, 188–189
Tf2, 652–698
    Architecture: the short version, 654–655
    Arithmetic operations, 671–673
    Based toolkits, 656–657
    Built-in functions, 673–674
    Calculating exponential values, 675–676
    Calculating trigonometric values, 674–675
    Constants, 659–660
    Convert python arrays to tf tensors, 681–682
    Differentiation and tf.Gradienttape, 682–683
    Eager execution, 657
    Encoding, 421–423
    Multiplying two second-order tensors, 680–681
    Python repl, 655–656
    Second-order tensor, 679–680
    Tensors, data types, primitive types, 657
    @Tf.Function, 665–668, 668–669
    Tokenization, 419–421
    Use cases, 654
    Variables, 660–661, 664–665
    Working with generators i, 695–697
    Working with strings, 676–677
    Working with tensors and operations, 677–679
Tf2-keras
    Word encodings, 453–454
    Word tokenization, 451–453
Tf.Rank() api, 661–662
Tf.Shape() api, 662–664
The bow algorithm, 175–176
Tokenization
    Subword, 474–476
Topic modeling, 276–278
Toyota technological institute, 481
Transformer
    Mask filling tasks, 466–467
    Ner tasks, 464–465
    Qna tasks, 465
    Sentiment analysis tasks, 465–466
Transformer architecture, 462–467
Transformers library from huggingface, 463–464

Trax, 687–688
True positive rate (TPR), 304, 350
Types of attention and algorithms, 461–462
Types of ensemble methods, 321–323
    Bagging, 321
    Boosting, 321–322
Types of machine learning algorithms, 286–292
    Machine learning tasks, 290–292

U

Undersampling, 515
Unicorn, 166
Uniform manifold approximation and projection (UMAP), 549
United states, 59
Universal sentence encoder (USE), 199

V

Variance, 530
Variational auto encoders (VAE), 167
Vector space models, 205–208
    Tradeoffs, 207–208
Vector space models (VSMS), 500
Vector spaces, 564–565

W

Web page, 147, 237
Web scraping with pure regular expressions, 234–237
Website, 410, 570, 630, 689
What are activation functions?, 352–354
What are decision trees?, 335–337
    Trade-offs, 336–337
What are ensemble methods?, 319–321
What are n-grams?, 176–179
    Calculating probabilities, 178–179
What are numpy arrays?, 2–3
What are random forests?, 344–345
What are skip-grams?, 195–199
    Architecture, 196–198
    Neural network reduction, 198–199
What are support vector machines?, 345–346
What is a bayesian classifier?, 346–347
What is a bleu score?, 209–210

What is beautifulsoup?, 231–234
What is bert?, 468–469
What is classification?, 330–332
    Binary versus multiclass, 332
    Common classifiers, 331
    Multilabel, 332
What is cosine similarity?, 186–188
What is data visualization?, 700–701
What is gensim?, 273–275
    Gensim and tf-idf example, 274
    Saving a word2vec model in genism, 275
What is gpt-3?, 492–495
What is jax?, 34
What is lemmatization?, 157–158
What is linear regression?, 23–25, 305–308
    Solutions exact values, 307
    Versus curve-fitting, 306–307
What is machine learning?, 284–286
    Learning style of machine learning algorithms, 285–286
What is matplotlib?, 701–702
What is nlp?, 142–144
    Evolution, 143–144
What is nltk?, 249–250
What is numpy?, 2
What is pandas?, 37–40
What is scrapy?, 237
What is spacy?, 238
What is stemming?, 155–157
    Common, 155–156
    Over and under, 157
        Singular versus plural word endings, 155
        Stemmers and word prefixes, 156–157
What is t5?, 467–468
What is text encoding?, 170–171
What is text similarity?, 166–167
What is topic modeling?, 202–204
    Algorithms, 202–203
    Lda, 203–204
What is topic modeling?, 161–162
What is word2vec?, 191–194
    The intuition, 193
    Word2vec architecture, 193–194

What is wordnet?, 258–261
What is word relevance?, 166
Wide-angle view of nlp, 144–148
    Applications and use cases, 145–146
    NLU and NLG, 146–147
    Text classification, 147
Wikipedia, 114, 470
Within-cluster sum of squares (WSS), 447
Word embeddings, 142, 190, 460–461
Wordpiece, 475
Wordpiece, 469
Word sense disambiguation, 149
Word vectorization, 167
Working with
    Currency, 511
    Dates, 510–511
    Gpt-2, 484–491
    Keras namespaces in tf2, 626–627
    Keras.Tf.Datasets namespace, 628
    Other tf.Keras namespaces, 629–630
    Tf.Keras.Activations namespace, 628
    Tf.Keras.Experimental namespace, 629
    Tf.Keras.Layers namespace, 627
Working with covid-19, 408–410
Working with datasets
    Training data versus test data, 297
Working with datasets, 296–297
Working with documents, 168–169
Working with json-based data, 97–99
Working with lines, 18–21
Working with lines in the plane (optional), 309–311
Working with ner, 159–161
    Abbreviations and acronyms, 160–161
    Techniques, 161
Working with pos, 158–159

X

Xxlarge, 52

Z

Zero-shot, 495

www.ingramcontent.com/pod-product-compliance
Lightning Source LLC
Chambersburg PA
CBHW080335240526
45466CB00028B/2247